David Hopkins and Harold Randall

Cambridge International AS and A Level

Accounting

Coursebook

Second edition

CAMBRIDGE
UNIVERSITY PRESS

CAMBRIDGE
UNIVERSITY PRESS

University Printing House, Cambridge CB2 8BS, United Kingdom

One Liberty Plaza, 20th Floor, New York, NY 10006, USA

477 Williamstown Road, Port Melbourne, VIC 3207, Australia

314–321, 3rd Floor, Plot 3, Splendor Forum, Jasola District Centre, New Delhi – 110025, India

79 Anson Road, #06–04/06, Singapore 079906

Cambridge University Press is part of the University of Cambridge.

It furthers the University's mission by disseminating knowledge in the pursuit of education, learning and research at the highest international levels of excellence.

Information on this title: www.cambridge.org/9781316611227

First published 2012
Second edition 2017

20 19 18 17 16 15 14 13 12 11 10 9 8 7 6 5 4 3 2

Printed in Malaysia by Vivar Printing

A catalogue record for this publication is available from the British Library

ISBN 978-1-316-61122-7 Paperback

Additional resources for this publication at www.cambridge.org/9781316611227

Contents

Preface

In 2014, Cambridge International Examinations undertook a complete revision of the AS and A Level accounting syllabus. As a result, it was necessary to re-write the textbook to bring it in line with the changes in the syllabus. What follows is the result of those revisions. The book is still aimed at AS and A Level accounting students studying the Cambridge syllabus, who still face the problems by asking 'How do I do this?' It could also be useful to those students studying other AS and A Level accounting syllabuses.

The textbook covers the entire Cambridge AS and A Level Accounting syllabus. Ideally, students should already have taken O Level or IGCSE Accounting before starting on AS Level or A Level studies. Many do not have such a background, and this text has such students in mind in Part 1. The essentials of double-entry bookkeeping are covered in sufficient detail to equip students to progress to more advanced work. It must be emphasised, however, that thorough mastery of the basics is absolutely necessary if real progress is to be made with the subsequent chapters.

Part 2 covers the financial accounting requirements of the AS and A Level syllabus. Each chapter is devoted to a particular topic on the syllabus. Similarly, Part 3 covers the AS and A Level requirements on a topic-by-topic basis. There is, though, some flexibility in the sequence in which the topics are studied. In whichever order the chapters are studied, it is of paramount importance that the whole of the syllabus is covered.

Throughout each chapter there are Activity exercises to attempt. At the end of the chapter there are further exercises, ranging from multiple-choice questions to practice examination questions. The new syllabus brought with it a change in emphasis in the type of questions set. Not only are students asked how to prepare statements and ledger accounts, but also to explain what is happening and make decisions based on their work. Both of these elements are covered in the practice questions at the end of the relevant chapters.

New topics have been added and old ones deleted. I have also retained and, in some cases expanded, the Hints sections, renamed Top Tip boxes. Despite numerous re-reads and re-working of questions, any mistakes are solely down to me!

The study of accountancy can be extremely rewarding. I have been involved in it now for more years than I care to admit to and am still learning! To all my readers, both old and new, I send my best wishes for success.

David Hopkins

Part I
The accounting system

Chapter 1
Double-entry bookkeeping: cash transactions

Learning objectives

In this chapter you will learn:

- that every transaction has two aspects
- that double-entry bookkeeping records both aspects of a transaction
- what ledger accounts are
- the meanings of the terms 'debit' and 'credit'
- how to record cash transactions in ledger accounts.

1.1 What is double-entry bookkeeping?

It is important for every business to have an **accounting system** in place to record its financial transactions. This usually comprises an organised set of manual or computerised records which classify the transactions, allowing them to be used to make decisions or report the financial performance of the business to others. The accounting system will be based on **double-entry bookkeeping**.

Double-entry bookkeeping is a system of recording transactions that recognises that there are two sides (or aspects) to every transaction. For example, you give your friend $10 in exchange for his watch. This involves you giving him $10 (one aspect) and your friend receiving $10 (the other aspect). Every transaction involves giving and receiving. It is important that you **recognise** and **record** both aspects of every transaction in your bookkeeping. The term double-entry bookkeeping comes from the fact that both aspects are recorded. It is the starting point of your studies as it underpins everything else which follows. It is probably the most important thing to remember: that every transaction is recorded twice in the books of account. The two entries to record the two aspects are made in **ledger** accounts.

1.2 Ledger accounts

Transactions are recorded in **ledger accounts**. An account is a history of all transactions of a similar nature. A ledger is a book that contains the ledger accounts. An account separates what is received from what is given.

Walkthrough

For example, a cash account records cash received and cash paid, as in the following ledger account:

Cash account					
Debit			**Credit**		
		$			$
Mar 1	Cash received from customers	240	Mar 2	Cash paid to suppliers	80
Mar 4	Cash received from customers	118	Mar 3	Wages paid	116

The **left-hand** side of the account is called the **debit side** and is used to record cash received (that is, coming into the account).

The **right-hand** side of the account is the **credit side** and shows cash paid (that is, going out of the account).

- All accounts have a debit side on the left to record what is received, and a credit side on the right to record what is given.
- In practice, the words 'debit' and 'credit' are not shown because bookkeepers do not need to be reminded of them.

TOP TIP

When recording transactions, think very carefully about which account 'gives' and which account 'receives'. Credit the account that 'gives' and debit the account that 'receives'.

KEY TERMS

Accounting system: A system of collecting, storing and processing financial information and accounting data used by managers.

Double-entry bookkeeping: A system of recording accounting transactions that recognises that there are two sides (or aspects) to every transaction.

Ledger: A book containing accounts.

Ledger account: A history of all transactions of a similar nature.

Debit side: Left-hand side of an account.

Credit side: Right-hand side of an account.

1.3 How to record cash transactions

Bookkeeping treats businesses as 'persons' with separate identities from their owners. For example, if Abdul is a trader, all his business transactions are recorded as those of the business and not as Abdul's own transactions.

In the example that follows, some transactions are recorded in ledger accounts. Make sure you understand the bookkeeping entries, and observe the wording carefully. This is important as you must be able to record transactions in ledger accounts correctly.

TOP TIPS

- Remember, all transactions are recorded from the point of view of Abdul's business, not from those of its customers and suppliers.
- Date every entry and enter the name of the other account in which the double entry is completed in the details column.
- Make sure you complete the double entry for every transaction before starting to record the next one.

Walkthrough

Transaction 1 April 1. Abdul starts business as a trader by paying $10 000 into a bank account which he opens for the business. Abdul gives, and the business receives, $10 000. An account for Abdul will be opened (his capital account) and credited with his 'capital'. The business bank account will be debited.

Business bank account

Debit			Credit		
		$			$
Apr 1	Abdul – capital	10 000 [1]			

Abdul – capital account

Debit			Credit		
		$			$
			Apr 1	Bank	10 000 [2]

[1] The business has received $10 000 which has been paid into the business bank account, hence that account has been **debited**.

[2] In this example, Abdul has given the business $10 000, hence his capital account has been **credited**.

KEY TERM

Postings: The process of recording financial transactions in ledger accounts.

Notes:

- Each entry is dated and shows the name of the other account in which the double entry is completed. Make sure you show these details for every entry you make in a ledger account.
- Entries in ledger accounts are known as **postings**, and bookkeepers are said to 'post' transactions to the accounts.

Transaction 2 April 2. Abdul buys a motor vehicle for the business and pays $2 000 from the business bank account. A motor vehicles account must be opened.

Bank account					
Debit			Credit		
		$			$
Apr 1	Abdul – capital	10 000	Apr 2	Motor vehicles	2 000

Motor vehicles account					
Debit			Credit		
		$			$
Apr 2	Bank	2 000			

Transaction 3 April 3. Abdul buys goods which he will resell in the normal course of trade for $3 000 and pays by cheque.

Bank account					
Debit			Credit		
		$			$
Apr 1	Abdul – capital	10 000	Apr 2	Motor vehicles	2 000
			Apr 3	Purchases	3 000

Purchases account					
		$			$
Apr 3	Bank	3 000			

Transaction 4 April 4. Abdul sells a quantity of the goods for $800 and pays the money into the bank.

Bank account					
Debit			Credit		
		$			$
Apr 1	Abdul – capital	10 000	Apr 2	Motor vehicles	2 000
Apr 4	Sales	800	Apr 3	Purchases	3 000

Sales account					
		$			$
			Apr 4	Bank	800

Transaction 5 April 7. A customer returns some goods and receives a refund of $40.

Bank account					
		$			$
Apr 1	Abdul – capital	10 000	Apr 2	Motor vehicles	2 000
Apr 4	Sales	800	Apr 3	Purchases	3 000
			Apr 7	Sales returns	40

Sales returns account					
		$			$
Apr 7	Bank	40			

Note: Goods returned are not debited to sales account, but to sales returns account. This account is also known as goods inwards, or returns inwards, account.

Transaction 6 April 8. Abdul returns some goods costing $100 to a supplier and receives a refund.

Bank account					
		$			$
Apr 1	Abdul – capital	10 000	Apr 2	Motor vehicles	2 000
Apr 4	Sales	800	Apr 3	Purchases	3 000
Apr 8	Purchases returns	100	Apr 7	Sales returns	100

Purchases returns account					
		$			$
			Apr 8	Bank	100

Note: Goods returned to a supplier are credited to purchases returns account. This account is also known as goods outward account or returns outwards.

KEY TERM

Golden rule: For every debit entry in a ledger account there must be an equal credit entry in another ledger account.

TOP TIPS

- Notice how quickly the number of accounts increase as more transactions take place. It may start to look very complicated. Work through things logically and never be afraid to open new accounts.
- Always remember to keep track of the debit and credit postings and include the correct wording and the $ sign.
- The most important thing is to remember the **golden rule**: **for every debit entry in one account there must be an equal credit entry in another account.**

Transaction 7 April 10. Abdul buys another motor vehicle for the business and pays $4 000 by cheque.

Bank account					
		$			$
Apr 1	Abdul – capital	10 000	Apr 2	Motor vehicles	2 000
Apr 4	Sales	800	Apr 3	Purchases	3 000
Apr 8	Purchases returns	100	Apr 7	Sales returns	40
			Apr 10	Motor vehicles	4 000

Motor vehicles account					
		$			$
Apr 2	Bank	2 000			
Apr 10	Bank	4 000			

Note: As explained in Section 1.2, an account is a history of all transactions of a similar nature. Therefore, it is not necessary to open another account for the second motor vehicle. Similarly, all purchases of office equipment are posted to office equipment account, and all purchases of office furniture are posted to office furniture account. You will encounter other examples such as plant and machinery, and fixtures and fittings.

Transaction 8 April 11. Tania lends the business $5000. Abdul pays the money into the business bank account.

Bank account					
		$			$
Apr 1	Abdul – capital	10000	Apr 2	Motor vehicles	2000
Apr 4	Sales	800	Apr 3	Purchases	3000
Apr 8	Purchases returns	100	Apr 7	Sales returns	40
Apr 11	Tania – loan	5000	Apr 10	Motor vehicles	4000

Tania – loan account					
		$			$
			Apr 11	Bank	5000

Transaction 9 April 12. Abdul pays rent on a warehouse by cheque, $1000.

Bank account					
		$			$
Apr 1	Abdul – capital	10000	Apr 2	Motor vehicles	2000
Apr 4	Sales	800	Apr 3	Purchases	3000
Apr 8	Purchases returns	100	Apr 7	Sales returns	40
Apr 11	Tania – loan	5000	Apr 10	Motor vehicles	4000
			Apr 12	Rent payable	1000

Rent payable account					
		$			$
Apr 12	Bank	1000			

Transaction 10 April 14. Abdul sublets part of the warehouse and receives a cheque for $300 for the rent. This is paid into the bank.

Bank account					
		$			$
Apr 1	Abdul – capital	10000	Apr 2	Motor vehicles	2000
Apr 4	Sales	800	Apr 3	Purchases	3000
Apr 8	Purchases returns	100	Apr 7	Sales returns	40
Apr 11	Tania – loan	5000	Apr 10	Motor vehicles	4000
Apr 14	Rent receivable	300	Apr 12	Rent payable	1000

Rent receivable account					
		$			$
			April 14	Bank	300

Note: Rent receivable is not posted to the rent payable account. It is important to keep income and expenditure in separate accounts.

Transaction 11 April 15. Abdul pays wages by cheque, $1 200.

Bank account

		$			$
Apr 1	Abdul – capital	10 000	Apr 2	Motor vehicles	2 000
Apr 4	Sales	800	Apr 3	Purchases	3 000
Apr 8	Purchases returns	100	Apr 7	Sales returns	40
Apr 11	Tania – loan	5 000	Apr 10	Motor vehicles	4 000
Apr 14	Rent receivable	300	Apr 12	Rent payable	1 000
			Apr 15	Wages	1 200

Wages

		$			$
Apr 15	Bank	1 200			

Transaction 12 April 16. Abdul withdraws $600 from the business bank account for personal use.

Bank account

		$			$
Apr 1	Abdul – capital	10 000	Apr 2	Motor vehicles	2 000
Apr 4	Sales	800	Apr 3	Purchases	3 000
Apr 8	Purchases returns	100	Apr 7	Sales returns	40
Apr 11	Tania – loan	5 000	Apr 10	Motor vehicles	4 000
Apr 14	Rent receivable	300	Apr 12	Rent payable	1 000
			Apr 12	Wages	1 200
			Apr 16	Drawings	600

Drawings account

		$			$
Apr 16	Bank	600			

Note: Money drawn out of a business by the owner for personal use is debited to a drawings account, not to the owner's capital account.

Chapter summary

In this chapter you have learnt about the most important aspects of double-entry bookkeeping. You should now understand that every transaction a business makes has two aspects to it and that double-entry bookkeeping records both aspects of the transactions.

You should also know that each aspect of the transaction is recorded in its own ledger account, which has two sides (the left-hand side is the debit side and the right-hand side is the credit side). Finally, you should now have a good understanding of how to use these accounts to record basic cash transactions.

TOP TIP

If you make a mistake in an exercise, study the answers online and make sure you understand what you should have done **and why**.

Practice exercises

1 Complete the entries for the following table. The first item has been done for you.

		Debit account	Credit account
1	Noel pays a cheque into his business bank account as capital	Bank	Noel – capital
2	Purchases some goods for resale and pays by cheque		
3	Sells some goods and banks the takings		
4	Pays rent by cheque		
5	Purchases shop fittings and pays by cheque		
6	Cashes cheque for personal expenses		
7	Pays wages by cheque		
8	Returns goods to supplier and banks refund		
9	Receives rent from tenant and banks cheque		
10	Refunds money to customer by cheque for goods returned		
11	Motor vehicle purchased and paid for by cheque		
12	Pays for petrol for motor vehicle and pays by cheque		

2 Open the necessary ledger accounts and post the following transactions to them. All transactions took place in the bank account.

May 1 Martine started business as a florist by paying $300 into a business bank account.
2 Charline lent the business $1 000.
Martine then had the following transactions:
3 Paid rent, $100.
4 Purchased shop fittings, $400.
Purchased flowers $300, paying by cheque.
5 Received refund of $20 for flowers returned to supplier.
6 Sold some flowers and received $40.
7 Paid wages, $60.
8 Withdrew $100 for personal use.

3 **a** Complete the entries for the following table:

		Debit account	Credit account
July 1	Lee started business by paying $20 000 of his savings into a business bank account		
	He also had $500 in cash which he decided to use to pay cash expenses for the business		
2	Bought some goods for resale for $1 300, paying by cheque		
3	Paid $2 500 by cheque to rent some business premises		
4	Bought some office furniture by cheque for $750		
	Bought office stationery for $120, paying by cash		
6	Sold some goods for $1 700 and paid the money into the bank		
	Sold more goods for $180. He received cash for this sale		
8	Returned some faulty goods valued at $60 to the supplier and received a cheque refund		
9	A customer returned some faulty goods. Lee gave the customer a cash refund of $25		
10	Sold goods for $420. Lee received cash for the goods. He kept $200 as business cash and banked the rest		
11	Lee took cash drawings of $160		

b Now open the necessary ledger accounts to record these transactions.

4 Complete the entries for the following table with information taken from the accounts of a trader:

		Debit account	Credit account
1	Local taxes paid by cheque		
2	Bank pays interest to trader		
3	Other operating expenses paid by cheque		
4	Postage and stationery paid by cheque		
5	Telephone bill paid by cheque		
6	Carriage inwards* paid by cheque		
7	Carriage outwards** paid by cheque		
8	Interest paid by cheque to brother in respect of a loan received from him		
9	Interest paid to bank		

* Carriage inwards is the delivery cost of bringing the goods from the supplier to the business.
** Carriage outwards is the cost of delivering goods to a customer.

5 Open the necessary ledger accounts and post the following transactions to them:

June 1	Farook commenced business by paying $15 000 into his business bank account.
	Amna lent the business $5 000.
	Farook then had the following business transactions:
2	Purchased premises and paid $8 000, paying by cheque.
3	Bought office furniture for $2 000 and paid by cheque.
4	Paid $5 000 by cheque for goods for resale.
5	Sold some goods for $1 500 and banked the proceeds.
6	Paid insurance premium by cheque, $600.
7	Bought motor van and paid $3 000 by cheque.
8	Drew cheque for $50 to pay for petrol for motor van.
9	Bought some goods costing $2 000 for resale and paid by cheque.
10	Sold goods for $2 400 and banked the proceeds.
	Drew cheque for wages, $400.
11	Repaid $1 200 by cheque to customers for goods returned.
12	Received a refund of $900 from suppliers for goods returned.
13	Received a refund of insurance of $100.
	Withdrew $200 from business bank account for personal expenses.
14	Returned some office furniture that was damaged and received a refund of $800.
15	Repaid $1 000 of the loan from Amna.

Exam practice questions

Multiple-choice questions

1 Joel occupies part of Natasha's business premises. Which entries in Natasha's books record the rent Joel pays her by cheque?

	Debit account	Credit account
A	Bank	Rent payable
B	Bank	Rent receivable
C	Rent payable	Bank
D	Rent receivable	Bank

2 Yasmina purchased some office equipment for use in her business. The equipment was faulty and she returned it to the supplier who refunded the cost to Yasmina. Which entries in Yasmina's books record the return of the equipment?

	Debit account	Credit account
A	Bank	Purchases returns
B	Bank	Office equipment
C	Purchases returns	Bank
D	Office equipment	Bank

3 A trader withdraws money from his business bank account for personal expenses. Which entries record this in his books?

	Debit account	Credit account
A	Bank	Capital
B	Bank	Drawings
C	Capital	Bank
D	Drawings	Bank

4 A trader returns goods to the supplier and receives a refund. Which entries record the refund in the trader's books?

	Debit account	Credit account
A	Bank	Purchases
B	Bank	Purchases returns
C	Purchases	Bank
D	Purchases returns	Bank

Total: 4 marks

Chapter 2
Double-entry bookkeeping: credit transactions

Learning objectives

In this chapter you will learn:

- how to record transactions which do not involve immediate cash payments in ledger accounts
- the difference between trade and cash discounts and how to treat them.

KEY TERMS

Credit transaction: A business transaction where no money changes hands at the time of the transaction.

Debtor: A customer (or other party) that owes the business money.

Creditor: Suppliers (or other parties) to whom the business owes money.

2.1 What are credit transactions?

Many transactions take place without any money being paid or received at the time. For example, Lai sells goods to Chin for $500 on 31 May and gives Chin until 30 June to pay. The transaction is **'on credit'** (a **credit transaction**). The sale has taken place on 31 May and must be recorded in the books of account of both Lai and Chin **at that date**. No entries to record payment are made in their books until Chin pays Lai.

2.2 How to record credit transactions

TOP TIP

Remember to record all transactions from the point of view of the business, not from those of its customers and suppliers.

In a seller's books, a sale on credit is credited to sales account and debited to an account opened in the name of the customer. In accounting, someone who owes the business money (in this case, Chin, the customer) is known as a **debtor**. When the customer, or debtor, pays, their account is credited and the bank account debited.

In a customer's books, a purchase on credit is debited to purchases account and credited to an account opened in the name of the supplier. In accounting, someone to whom the business owes money is known as a **creditor**. When the supplier is paid, their account is debited and the bank account credited.

Walkthrough

Lai sells goods to Chin for $500 on 31 May and gives Chin until 30 June to pay.

In Lai's books, credit the sale to sales account and debit it to an account for Chin:

Sales account					
Debit			**Credit**		
		$			$
			May 31	Chin	500

Chin account					
Debit			**Credit**		
		$			$
May 31	Sales	500			

The debit entry in Chin's account shows that he is a **debtor** in Lai's books; that is, Chin owes Lai $500 until he pays for the goods.

In Chin's books, debit the purchase to purchases account and credit it to an account for Lai:

Purchases account					
Debit			**Credit**		
		$			$
May 31	Lai	500			

Lai account					
Debit			Credit		
		$			$
			May 31	Purchases	500

The credit entry in Lai's account shows that he is a **creditor** in Chin's books.

Goods returned

On 4 June, Chin returns some of the goods costing $100 to Lai because they are damaged.

In Lai's books, credit Chin's account and debit sales returns account:

Chin account					
Debit			Credit		
		$			$
May 31	Sales	500	Jun 4	Sales returns	100

Sales returns account					
Debit			Credit		
		$			$
Jun 4	Chin	100			

In Chin's books, debit Lai's account and credit purchases returns account:

Lai account					
Debit			Credit		
		$			$
Jun 4	Purchases returns	100	May 31	Purchases	500

Purchases returns account					
Debit			Credit		
		$			$
			Jun 4	Lai	100

2.3 How to record payments for goods bought or sold on credit

Trade discount

Trade discount is an allowance made by one trader to another. In the above example, the goods which Lai sold to Chin may have been sold normally for $625. Lai knows that Chin, also a trader, must make a profit on the goods when he sells them. He has allowed Chin a trade discount of $125 (20% of $625) so that when Chin sell the goods for $625 he will make a profit of $125.

This type of discount is only given where the buyer and seller are in the same line of business. In this example Lai and Chin will both be in the same line of work. Perhaps Lai may sell spare parts

KEY TERM

Trade discount: A reduction in the selling price of goods made by one trader to another.

for cars to Chin. Chin may use those parts to repair the cars for his customers. Both Lai and Chin are in the same line of work, so Lai offers Chin a trade discount.

It may seem strange that by reducing his selling price, Lai is giving away some of his profit. However, it allows Chin to make some profit. It will also encourage Chin to use Lai as his regular supplier, so Lai's future sales will be increased and his cash flow may also be improved.

TOP TIP

Although the normal price of the goods was $625, the transaction was for $500 only, and only $500 is entered into the books of both Lai and Chin. Trade discount is **never** recorded in ledger accounts.

Cash (or settlement) discount

KEY TERM

Cash (or settlement) discount: An allowance given by a seller to a customer to encourage the customer to pay an invoice before its due date for payment.

Lai has given Chin one month to pay for the goods. To encourage Chin to pay by 30 June, Lai may allow Chin to pay less than the amount due. This allowance is a **cash (or settlement) discount**. (Notice the difference between cash discount and trade discount: trade discount is not dependent on payment being made promptly, or even at all.)

TOP TIP

Cash discounts are **always** recorded in ledger accounts.

Walkthrough

Suppose Lai has allowed Chin a cash discount of 5% provided Chin pays by 30 June, and Chin pays Lai on 28 June. Chin owes Lai $400 ($500 – $100), 5% of $400 = $20. He will, therefore, pay only $380.

In Lai's books, debit the discount to discounts allowed account:

Chin account					
Debit			**Credit**		
		$			$
May 31	Sales	500	Jun 4	Sales returns	100
			Jun 28	Bank	380
			Jun 28	Discounts allowed	20

Bank account					
Debit			**Credit**		
		$			$
Jun 28	Chin	380			

Discounts allowed account					
Debit			**Credit**		
		$			$
Jun 28	Chin	20			

In Chin's books, credit the discount to discounts received account:

Lai account					
Debit			**Credit**		
		$			**$**
Jun 4	Purchases returns	100	May 31	Purchases	500
Jun 28	Bank	380			
Jun 28	Discounts received	20			

Bank account					
Debit			**Credit**		
		$			**$**
			Jun 28	Lai	380

Discounts received account					
Debit			**Credit**		
		$			**$**
			Jun 28	Lai	20

TOP TIPS

- Note carefully whether cash discount is to be deducted from settlements.
- Remember to complete the entries for cash discounts in the correct discount accounts.
- Be accurate in all your calculations.

Walkthrough

The following worked example aims to bring together everything you have learnt in this chapter. It covers how to deal with trade discount and how to record cash (or settlement) discount.

Work through it logically and follow how each transaction is recorded in Andrew's ledger.

Andrew had the following transactions in May:

May 1	Purchased goods on credit from David. The goods cost $1 000 less 10% trade discount.
2	Purchased goods on credit from Rafael for $1 600 less 15% trade discount.
3	Purchased a computer for the office on credit from Bernard for $2 000.
4	Sold goods on credit to Mario for $800.
5	Returned goods which had cost $100 after trade discount to David.
6	Purchased goods on credit from Ludovic for $700 less trade discount at 20%.
7	Sold goods on credit to Ravin for $500.
8	Mario returned goods which had been sold to him for $40.
9	Received cheque from Ravin for amount owing less cash discount of 5%.
10	Paid amount owing to David less cash discount of 5%.
11	Paid amount owing to Rafael less cash discount of 5%. Paid Bernard for computer.
12	Received cheque from Mario for amount owing less 5% cash discount.
	Paid amount owing to Ludovic less 5% cash discount.

If you want to test yourself use the following table to record the names of the accounts in which you feel each transaction should be recorded. Then check the answers online and see if you were correct.

	Details	Name of accounts to debit	Name of accounts to credit
May 1	Purchased goods on credit from David The goods cost $1 000 less 10% trade discount		
2	Purchased goods on credit from Rafael for $1 600 less 15% trade discount		
3	Purchased a computer for the office on credit from Bernard for $2 000		
4	Sold goods on credit to Mario for $800		
5	Returned goods which had cost $100 after trade discount to David		
6	Purchased goods on credit from Ludovic for $700 less trade discount at 20%		
7	Sold goods on credit to Ravin for $500		
8	Mario returned goods which had been sold to him for $40		
9	Received cheque from Ravin for amount owing less cash discount of 5%		
10	Paid amount owing to David less cash discount of 5%		
11	Paid amount owing to Rafael less cash discount of 5%. Paid Bernard for computer		
12	Received cheque from Mario for amount owing less 5% cash discount Paid amount owing to Ludovic less 5% cash discount		

As all the transactions have been carried out by Andrew, they are all recorded in Andrew's books of account. They are recorded as follows:

David account

Debit			Credit		
		$			$
May 5	Purchases returns	100	May 1	Purchases	900
May 10	Bank	760			
May 10	Discounts received	40			

KEY TERM

Discount received: Cash discount received by the purchaser from the seller of goods.

This account records all Andrew's transactions with David: the goods Andrew bought (purchases of $1 000 less a 10% trade discount), the goods he returned (purchases returns), the amount Andrew paid David (bank) and the discount Andrew received from David (**discount received**). Andrew owed David $800 (900 – 100). He received a 5% settlement discount when he paid David (800 × 5% = 40) so he wrote a cheque to David for $760 (800 – 40).

Rafael account					
Debit			Credit		
		$			$
May 11	Bank	1292	May 2	Purchases	1360
May 11	Discounts received	68			

This account records all Andrew's transactions with Rafael: the goods Andrew bought (purchases of $1600 less the trade discount of 15%), the amount Andrew paid Rafael (bank) and the discount Andrew received from Rafael (discount received). The discount Andrew received was 5% of $1360, so Andrew paid Rafael $1292 (1360 – 68).

Bernard account					
Debit			Credit		
		$			$
May 11	Bank	2000	May 3	Office computer	2000

This account records the purchase of the office computer from Bernard, and Andrew paying Bernard for it from his bank account.

Ludovic account					
Debit			Credit		
		$			$
May 12	Bank	532	May 6	Purchases	560
May 12	Discounts received	28			

This account records all Andrew's transactions with Ludovic: the goods he bought (purchases of $700 less a trade discount of 20%), the amount Andrew paid Ludovic (bank) and the discount Andrew received from Ludovic (discount received). Again, the discount received is 5% of $560, so the cheque payment was for $532 (560 – 28).

Mario account					
Debit			Credit		
		$			$
May 4	Sales	800	May 8	Sales returns	40
			May 12	Bank	722
			May 12	Discounts allowed	38

This account records all Andrew's transactions with Mario: the goods he sold to Mario (sales), the goods Mario returned (sales returns), the amount Mario paid Andrew (bank) and the discount Andrew allowed Mario (**discount allowed**). Mario owed Andrew $760 (800 – 40). Andrew allowed him a settlement discount of 5% ($760 × 5%), so Mario sent Andrew a cheque for $722 (760 – 38).

KEY TERM

Discount allowed: Cash discount allowed by the seller to the purchaser of goods.

Ravin account					
Debit			Credit		
		$			$
May 7	Sales	500	May 9	Bank	475
			May 9	Discounts allowed	25

This account records all Andrew's transactions with Ravin: the goods he sold to Ravin (sales), the amount Ravin paid Andrew (bank) and the discount Andrew allowed Ravin (discounts allowed). Ravin owed Andrew $500. Andrew allowed him a settlement discount of 5% ($500 × 5%), so Ravin sent Andrew a cheque for $475 (500 – 25).

Purchases account					
Debit			Credit		
		$			$
May 1	David	900			
May 2	Rafael	1 360			
May 6	Ludovic	560			

This account records all the purchases of goods made by Andrew from his credit suppliers. They are debited to the purchases account and the credit entries are in the individual accounts for each supplier.

Purchases returns account					
Debit			Credit		
		$			$
			May 5	David	100

This account records the return of goods made by Andrew to David.

TOP TIP

Purchases returns always go to a purchases returns account. They are never entered on the credit side of the purchases account.

Sales account					
Debit			Credit		
		$			$
			May 4	Mario	800
			May 7	Ravin	500

This account records all the sales of goods by Andrew to his credit customers. The debit entries are in the individual accounts of those customers.

Sales returns account					
Debit			Credit		
		$			$
May 8	Mario	40			

This account records the return of goods from customers to Andrew. The credit entry will be in the account of the customer.

TOP TIP

Sales returns always go to a sales returns account. They are never entered on the debit side of the sales account.

Discounts allowed account					
Debit			Credit		
		$			$
May 9	Ravin	25			
May 12	Mario	38			

All the discounts which Andrew has allowed his customers are entered in this account. The credit entry will be in the accounts of Ravin and Mario.

Discounts received account					
Debit			Credit		
		$			$
			May 10	David	40
			May 11	Rafael	68
			May 12	Ludovic	28

All the discounts which Andrew received from his suppliers are entered in this account. The debit entry will be in the accounts of David, Rafael and Ludovic.

Office computer account					
Debit			Credit		
		$			$
May 3	Bernard	2000			

This accounts records the purchase by Andrew of the office computer from Bernard. As Andrew intends to use this for the business rather than resell it to a customer, it goes to its own account and not to the purchases account.

Bank account					
Debit			Credit		
		$			$
May 9	Ravin	475	May 10	David	760
May 12	Mario	722	May 11	Rafael	1292
			May 11	Bernard	2000
			May 12	Ludovic	532

This is Andrew's business bank account. On the debit side, all the money received is recorded. All the money Andrew pays out is recorded on the credit side.

This is one account which has entries on both sides.

Calculations

Purchases		Amount before trade discount	Trade discount	Cost to Andrew
		$	$	$
From:	David	1000	(10%) 100	900
	Rafael	1600	(15%) 240	1360
	Ludovic	700	(20%) 140	560

Cash settlements	Amount before cash discount	Cash discount (5%)	Amount paid
	$	$	$
By:			
Ravin	500	25	475
Mario	760	38	722

Chapter summary

In this chapter you have learnt how to record in the ledger transactions which do not involve the immediate payment of cash. You should also now be aware of what is meant by trade discount and cash (or settlement) discount and the difference between the two.

You should now be able to record credit transactions in both the seller's and customer's books of account.

Finally, you should now be familiar with the difference between discounts allowed and discounts received and how to record each in the appropriate account.

Practice exercises

1 Post the following transactions in the books of Geraud:

TOP TIPS

- If it helps, write down the names of the accounts you should debit or credit before you start posting the transactions to them.
- Work out the amounts of trade and cash discounts before you post them to their correct accounts.

June 1	Purchased goods from Khor which cost $3 000 less trade discount of 10%.
5	Sold goods to Lai for $600.
10	Returned goods which had cost Geraud $200 less discount to Khor.
15	Purchased goods from Lim which cost $2 800 before trade discount of 10%.
20	Sold goods to Chin for $1 300.
25	Lai returned goods which had cost him $200 less discount.
30	Geraud paid Khor and Lim the amounts due to them after deducting 5% cash discount.
	Lai and Chin paid Geraud the amounts they owed him after deducting 5% cash discount.

2 Post the following transactions in the books of both Brian and Ken:

		Name of accounts to be debited	Name of accounts to be credited
April 1	Brian sold goods to Ken for $1 500		
2	Ken sold goods to Brian at $500 less trade discount of 20%		
3	Brian sold goods to Ken for $800 less trade discount at 25%		
6	Ken sold goods to Brian at $900 less trade discount of 20%		
10	Ken paid Brian for the goods he bought on 1 April less a cash discount of 3%		
12	Brian paid Ken for the goods he had bought on 2 April less a cash discount of 5%		

3 Fleming had the following transactions:

July 1 Purchased goods from Adams for $5 000 less trade discount of 15%. Adams allowed Fleming 4% cash discount.

4 Purchased goods from Bond for $2 500 less trade discount of 10%. Bond allowed Fleming 4% cash discount.

5 Returned goods which had cost $600 less trade discount to Adams.

7 Purchased goods from Astle for $7 000 less trade discount of 20%. Astle allowed Fleming 5% cash discount.

9 Returned goods which had cost $800 less trade discount to Astle.

10 Purchased goods from Cairns for $4 200 less 10% trade discount. Cairns allowed Fleming 5% cash discount.

14 Fleming settled all accounts owing to his suppliers by cheque, taking advantage of the cash discount in each case.

Post the transactions listed above in Fleming's books in good form.

4 Streak had the following transactions in March:

Mar 1 Sold goods to Blignaut for $2 500 less trade discount of 10%, and allowed him cash discount of 4%.

4 Sold goods to Ebrahim for $4 000 less trade discount of 15%, and allowed him cash discount of 5%.

6 Ebrahim returned goods which had cost him $200 less trade discount.

8 Sold goods to Friend for $3 200 less trade discount of 20%, and allowed him cash discount of 5%.

12 Sold goods to Flowers for $2 000 less trade discount of 10%, and allowed him cash discount of 4%.

14 Flowers returned goods which had cost him $350 less trade discount.

15 Blignaut, Ebrahim, Friend and Flowers settled their accounts by cheque, each taking advantage of the cash discount.

Post the transactions listed above in Streak's books in good form.

Exam practice questions

Multiple-choice questions

1 Davina bought goods on credit from Sharon for $600 less trade discount of $120. Which entries record this transaction in Davina's books?

	Account to be debited	Account to be credited
A	Purchases $480	Sharon $480
B	Purchases $480	Sharon $600
	Discounts allowed $120	
C	Purchases $600	Sharon $600
D	Purchases $600	Sharon $480
	Discounts received $120	

2 Kristal bought goods on credit from Prisca. The goods had a list price of $1 000 but Prisca allowed Kristal trade discount of 10% and cash discount of 4%. What is the least amount that Kristal has to pay Prisca?

A $860 **B** $864 **C** $900 **D** $960

3 Shirley bought goods from Corrine. The goods had a list price of $800. Corrine allowed Shirley trade discount of 20% and cash discount of 5%. In Corrine's books, which entries record the cheque she received from Shirley?

	Account to be debited	Account to be credited
A	Bank $608	Shirley $640
	Discounts allowed $32	
B	Bank $608	Shirley $640
	Discounts received $32	
C	Bank $608	Shirley $760
	Discounts allowed $152	
D	Bank $608	Shirley $760
	Discounts received $152	

Total: 3 marks

Chapter 3
Books of prime entry

Learning objectives

In this chapter you will learn:

- the purpose of books of prime entry
- how to enter transactions in books of prime entry
- how to post transactions from the books of prime entry to ledger accounts.

KEY TERMS

Book of prime entry: A book used to list all transactions of a similar nature before they are posted to the ledger.

Cash book: A book of prime entry for all bank, cash and cash discount transactions.

Invoice: A document that a business issues to its customers, asking the customers to pay for the goods or services that the business has supplied to them.

Credit note: A receipt given to a customer who has returned goods, which can be offset against future purchases.

3.1 What is a book of prime entry?

A **book of prime entry** is used to list all transactions of a similar kind **before** they are posted to ledger accounts. They are sometimes known as books of first (or original) entry, but they will be referred to as books of prime entry in this text. As they list transactions before they are posted to ledger accounts, they are **outside** the double-entry model. **It is important to remember that they are not part of double-entry bookkeeping**. There is, however, one exception to this rule, and that is the **cash book**, as explained later in Section 3.4.

The names of the books of prime entry and their uses are:

Book of prime entry	Use
Sales journal (or sales day book)	To record all sales made **on credit**. The entries are made from copies of **invoices** sent to customers.
Sales returns journal (or returns inwards journal)	To record all goods returned from credit customers. When customers return goods that were bought on credit they are sent **credit notes** showing the amount credited to their account for the returns. The sales returns journal is prepared from the copies of credit notes sent to customers.
Purchases journal (or purchases day book)	To record all purchases made **on credit** of goods bought for resale. These are entered in the purchases journal from suppliers' invoices.
Purchases returns journal (or purchases returns book, or returns outwards journal)	To record all goods returned to suppliers. The purchases returns journal is prepared from credit notes received from suppliers.
Cash book	To record all cash and bank transactions. In this book, any money that is received or paid out in cash is recorded. Any money received or paid out by cheque will also be included. (But see Section 3.4.)
Journal (or general journal)	To record all transactions for which there is no other book of prime entry. These are often of a special nature. For example, to record the owner of the firm introducing their own computer into the business as capital.

3.2 How to write up books of prime entry

Walkthrough

Jayasuriya has sent and received the following invoices and credit notes:

	Invoices sent to customers	Amount of invoice
		$
May 1	Atapattu	2350
May 4	de Silva	1746
May 6	Arnold	520

	Credit notes sent to customers	Amount of credit note
		$
May 3	Atapattu	350
May 5	de Silva	146
May 7	Arnold	60

	Invoices received from suppliers	Amount of invoice
		$
May 2	Vaas	5 000
May 5	Fernando	3 600
May 7	Mubarak	2 200

	Credit notes received from suppliers	Amount of credit note
		$
May 6	Vaas	1 000
May 7	Fernando	600

With the more frequent use of technology in the workplace, an accounting package for a computer will print these journals directly from the invoices and credit notes. However, it is important that you aware of what the computer is doing, so the transactions will be entered manually in the books of prime entry as follows:

Sales journal			Sales returns journal		
		$			$
May 1	Atapattu	2 350	May 3	Atapattu	350
May 4	de Silva	1 746	May 5	de Silva	146
May 6	Arnold	520	May 7	Arnold	60
		4 616			556

Purchases journal			Purchases returns journal		
		$			$
May 2	Vaas	5 000	May 6	Vaas	1 000
May 5	Fernando	3 600	May 7	Fernando	600
May 7	Mubarak	2 200			
		10 800			1 600

TOP TIPS

- Recognise the correct book of prime entry for every transaction.
- Enter invoices and credit notes **net of trade discount** in the books of prime entry. So, for example, Jayasuriya may sell to a customer for $1 000. However, he may allow the customer trade discount of 20%. In the sales journal the invoice will be entered as $800 (1 000 – 20%).
- Similarly, if it is Jayasuriya's policy to offer a cash or settlement discount to his customers, this is **never** recorded in the sales journal.

3.3 How to post from books of prime entry to ledger accounts

Use the information in the books of prime entry in Section 3.2.

Step 1

Post each item in the books of prime entry to the supplier's or customer's account in the ledger following the procedure already learnt in Chapter 2.

Do **not** post the **individual items** to the purchases, purchases returns, sales or sales returns accounts.

Atapattu account

Debit			Credit		
		$			$
May 1	Sales	2350	May 3	Sales returns	350

de Silva account

Debit			Credit		
		$			$
May 4	Sales	1746	May 5	Sales returns	146

Arnold account

Debit			Credit		
		$			$
May 6	Sales	520	May 7	Sales returns	60

Vaas account

Debit			Credit		
		$			$
May 6	Purchases returns	1000	May 2	Purchases	5000

Fernando account

Debit			Credit		
		$			$
May 7	Purchases returns	600	May 5	Purchases	3600

Mubarak account

Debit			Credit		
		$			$
			May 7	Purchases	2200

Step 2

Post the **total** of each book of prime entry to the sales, sales returns, purchases or purchases returns accounts, as appropriate.

Sales account					
Debit			Credit		
		$			$
			May 7	Sales journal total	4 616

Sales returns account					
Debit			Credit		
		$			$
May 7	Sales returns journal total	556			

Purchases account					
Debit			Credit		
		$			$
May 7	Purchases journal total	10 800			

Purchases returns account					
Debit			Credit		
		$			$
			May 7	Purchases returns journal total	1 600

One of the advantages of using books of prime entry is to cut down on the entries in some of the ledger accounts. By posting only the **totals** of the sales, sales returns, purchases and purchases returns journals to the ledger, the number of entries in the sales, sales returns, purchases and purchases returns accounts is reduced.

As all transactions of a certain type are grouped together (sales, purchases, and so on), it makes it easier to track them into their accounts in the ledger. This also works the other way; if there is an error in posting to the ledger account, it is easier to track it back to the appropriate book of prime entry.

3.4 The cash book

A **cash book** is the book of prime entry for all cash and bank transactions. However, as we saw in Chapter 1, we had both a bank account and a cash account in the ledger. When we use a cash book these two accounts no longer appear in the ledger. They are replaced by the cash book. This is why the cash book is the only book of prime entry that is also part of the double-entry model. The cash book has both a debit and credit side, unlike the sales, sales returns, purchases and purchases returns journals, where invoices and credit notes are simply listed and totalled.

Removing the cash and bank account from the ledger is done mainly to divide the work between a number of employees. It is now possible to employ someone specifically to write up the cash book. Another person can then post the transactions recorded in the cash book to the appropriate ledger account. This is known as **internal control**. One person does not have complete control over all the books of account. This will help in preventing fraud. It should also help to locate errors in posting more easily.

The cash book is also used as the book of prime entry for cash discounts. A column is provided on the **debit side** of the bank account to record **discounts allowed**, and a column on the **credit side** to record **discounts received**.

Walkthrough

Cash book							
Debit side				Credit side			
		Discounts (allowed)	Bank			Discounts (received)	Bank
		$	$			$	$
May 7	Attapattu	100	1 900	May 7	Vaas	200	3 800
May 7	de Silva	80	1 520	May 7	Fernando	150	2 850
May 7	Arnold	23	437	May 7	Mubarak	110	2 090
		203				460	

TOP TIP

The words 'allowed' and 'received' are sometimes omitted because bookkeepers know which is which.

3.5 How to enter discounts in the cash book

When a payment is received from a customer who has deducted **cash** discount, enter the amount of the discount in the discounts allowed column, next to the amount received in the bank column.

Enter discounts received from suppliers in the discounts received column, next to the amount paid in the bank column.

Walkthrough

Carrying on with the earlier walkthrough, all payments due from customers and all payments to suppliers in Section 3.2 were settled on 7 May. In each case, cash discount of 5% was allowed or received.

The ledger accounts to record the receipts from the customers and payments to suppliers are shown below. Looking at Atapattu's account before he made the payment to Jayasuriya, he owed a net total of $2 000 (2 350 – 350). Jayasuriya allowed him a 5% cash discount, which meant he only had to pay $1 900 (2 000 – 5%) and was allowed a discount of $100. Both of these are recorded on the **credit** side of Atapattu's account. The same thing is done for each of Jayasuriya's customers.

Atapattu account					
Debit			Credit		
		$			$
May 1	Sales	2 350	May 3	Sales returns	350
			May 7	Bank	1 900
			May 7	Discounts allowed	100

de Silva account					
Debit			**Credit**		
		$			$
May 4	Sales	1746	May 5	Sales returns	146
			May 7	Bank	1520
			May 7	Discounts allowed	80

Arnold account					
Debit			**Credit**		
		$			$
May 6	Sales	520	May 7	Sales returns	60
			May 7	Bank	437
			May 7	Discounts allowed	23

Vaas was a supplier to the business. The amount due to Vaas was $4000 (5000 – 1000). Jayasuriya received a 5% cash discount from Vaas when he paid him. This meant that Jayasuriya wrote a cheque for $3800 and received a discount of $200. Both of these are recorded on the **debit** side of Vaas's account. The same thing is done for each of Jayasuriya's suppliers.

Vaas account					
Debit			**Credit**		
		$			$
May 6	Purchases returns	1000	May 2	Purchases	5000
May 7	Bank	3800			
May 7	Discounts received	200			

Fernando account					
Debit			**Credit**		
		$			$
May 7	Purchases returns	600	May 5	Purchases	3600
May 7	Bank	2850			
May 7	Discounts received	150			

Mubarak account					
Debit			**Credit**		
		$			$
May 7	Bank	2090	May 7	Purchases	2200
May 7	Discounts received	110			

All the transactions from each account relating to the cheques paid and received and discounts allowed and received are recorded in Jayasuriya's cash book, and are shown below.

Notice that the receipts are entered on the debit side, together with the discounts allowed relating to them. Similarly, all the payments are recorded on the credit side, together with the discounts received alongside.

Cash book									
Debit side				**Credit side**					
		Discounts (allowed)	**Bank**			**Discounts (received)**	**Bank**		
		$	$			$	$		
May 7	Attapattu	100	1900	May 7	Vaas	200	3800		
May 7	de Silva	80	1520	May 7	Fernando	150	2850		
May 7	Arnold	23	437	May 7	Mubarak	110	2090		
		203				460			

3.6 How to post discounts from the cash book to the discounts allowed and discounts received accounts

Notice that in Section 3.5 the amount of discounts received from suppliers and discounts allowed to customers have been entered in their respective accounts. Now comes the tricky bit:

the **total** of the discounts allowed column in the cash book is posted to the **debit** of the discounts allowed account. The **total** of the discounts received column is posted to the **credit** of the discounts received account. These postings are shown below.

Discounts allowed account					
Debit			**Credit**		
		$			$
May 7	Cash book total	203			

Discounts received account					
Debit			**Credit**		
		$			$
			May 7	Cash book total	460

This now means that double entry to record discounts allowed and received has been completed in the ledger. The discount columns in the cash book **are not** part of the double-entry model. They simply list the discounts allowed and received.

The double entries are shown below.

For discounts allowed:

- debit the discounts allowed with the total of the discounts allowed column in the cash book
- credit the individual customer's accounts with the discount allowed to them when they made their payment.

For discounts received:

- debit the individual supplier's accounts with the discount they permitted you to take when you paid their account
- credit the discounts received account with the total of the discounts received column in the cash book.

ACTIVITY 1

Murgatroyd had the following transactions, all on credit, in March:

March 1 Purchased goods from Tikolo for $10 000 less trade discount of 20%. Tikolo allowed him 5% cash discount.

4 Sold goods to Snyman for $1 200 less trade discount of 10%. He allowed Snyman 4% cash discount.

6 Purchased goods from Walters for $8 000 less trade discount of 10%. Walters allowed Murgatroyd 5% cash discount.

10 Sold goods to Karg for $2 500 less trade discount of 10%. He allowed Karg 4% cash discount.

11 Snyman returned goods which had cost him $200.

12 Returned goods which had cost $400 to Tikolo.

13 Purchased goods from Burger for $7 000 less trade discount of 25%. Burger allowed him cash discount of 4%.

17 Sold goods to Kotze for $3 000 less trade discount of 10%. He allowed Kotze 5% cash discount.

18 Purchased goods from Tikolo for $6 000 less trade discount of 20%. Tikolo allowed him 5% cash discount.

20 Karg returned goods which had cost him $300.

22 Returned to Burger goods which had cost $1 000.

25 Sold goods to Snyman for $1 800 less trade discount of 10%. Murgatroyd allowed Snyman 5% cash discount.

31 Received cheques from Snyman, Karg and Kotze respectively in full settlement of their accounts, and sent cheques in full settlement of their accounts to Tikolo, Walters and Burger.

Required

Enter the transactions for March in Murgatroyd's books of prime entry and post them in good form to the proper accounts.

Note: The transactions should all be dated. However, for the purpose of this activity, ignore the dates and simply post the transactions to the cash book, the correct journal, and the correct ledger account.

3.7 Three-column cash book

Most businesses receive cash that they do not bank and pay some of their expenses out of the unbanked cash. An account for this cash is kept in the cash book. It is usually found convenient to have columns for cash next to those for the bank account for cash receipts and payments. The account is then a combined bank and cash account.

		Bank and cash			
Discounts (allowed)	Cash account	Bank account	Discounts (received)	Cash account	Bank account
	$	$		$	$

3.8 How to write up a three-column cash book

The cash columns are entered in exactly the same way as the bank columns. Cash received is debited, and cash payments credited, in the cash columns. When cash is banked, the cash column must be credited and the bank column debited with the amount. When cash is drawn from the bank, the bank column must be credited and the cash column must be debited.

This type of posting is known as a **contra entry**. As an account has been debited (bank or cash) and another credited (cash or bank) the double entry has been completed. There is no need to make any other postings in the ledger to record this.

KEY TERM

Contra entry: The completing of the double entry within the bank or cash account.

Walkthrough

The following transactions took place in Cassius's business for the first week of May:

May 1 Received $700 in cash from a customer, Alisha.
3 Paid postages of $40 in cash.
4 Made cash sales of $2 000.
5 Banked $1 500 cash.
7 Paid $70 on other operating items in cash.
8 Withdrew $500 from the bank to pay wages.

Cash book

		Disc	Cash	Bank			Disc	Cash	Bank
		$	$	$			$	$	$
May 1	Alisha		700		May 3	Postages		40	
May 4	Sales		2 000		May 5	Bank ¢		1 500	
May 5	Cash ¢			1 500	May 7	Other operating expenses		70	
May 8	Bank ¢		500		May 8	Cash ¢			500
					May 8	Wages		500	

Note: ¢ is an abbreviation for 'contra', indicating that the double entry is completed on the opposite sides of the bank and cash accounts.

ACTIVITY 2

Enter the following transactions in Joshua's three-column cash book:

March 1 Received takings from cash sales, $1 100.
2 Paid electricity in cash, $130.
3 Received takings from cash sales, $900.
4 Banked cash, $1 700.
5 Paid other operating operating expenses in cash, $25.
6 Drew $800 from bank for the office cash float.
7 Paid for inventory by cash, $750.

3.9 The journal (or general journal)

All transactions should be recorded in one of the books of prime entry before being posted to ledger accounts. The **journal (or general journal)** is the book of prime entry for transactions for which there is no other book of prime entry. Items which will require entries in the journal are:

- corrections of posting errors
- adjustments to accounts (which are dealt with later)
- transfers between accounts
- purchase and sale of items other than inventory-in-trade (machinery, delivery vans, and so on used in the business) on credit
- opening entries in a new set of ledgers (e.g. when there is no more room in the existing ledgers and the balances on the accounts are transferred to new ledgers, or to make the opening entries at the start of a new accounting period).

Each journal entry shows the account to be debited, and the account to be credited. It follows that the debits should always equal the credits. The journal is ruled as follows:

Date	Accounts	Dr	Cr

Note: Dr is short for 'debit' and Cr is short for 'credit'.

Although it contains the words 'debit' and 'credit', the journal is not part of the double-entry model. It is simply a book of instructions, telling the bookkeeper which account in the ledger to debit and which to credit.

KEY TERMS

Journal (or general journal): A book of prime entry for recording transactions and events for which there is no other book of prime entry.

Narrative: Something recorded under a journal entry to explain why the journal entry is to be made.

3.10 How to make journal entries

Always state the account to be debited before the one to be credited. Every entry should have a brief but informative explanation of the reason for the entry; this is called the **narrative**. The journal is an important book as it identifies adjustments to the accounts. Before they are posted the owner of the business should authorise them. Thus, the person preparing the journal will write the narrative to tell the owner why the entry is being made. It is another form of checking which should go on in any good accounting system.

TOP TIPS

- Sometimes you may be told to ignore narratives. If that is the case, don't waste valuable time writing them out. As mentioned, ideally the name of the account to be debited is recorded first. This is normal accounting practice.
- Prepare journal entries only to ledger accounts, **never to other books of prime entry**.

Walkthrough

1 Jonah discovered that he had credited $100 that he had received from A. Burger on 1 April to an account for L. Burger in error. The journal entry to correct the error will be:

Date	Accounts	Dr	Cr
		$	$
April 1	L. Burger	100	
	A. Burger		100

Narrative: Correction of an error. A remittance from A. Burger on this date was posted incorrectly to L. Burger's account.

2 On 4 May Jonah bought office furniture from A. Whale on credit for $400.

Date	Accounts	Dr	Cr
		$	$
May 4	Office furniture	400	
	A. Whale		400

Narrative: Purchase of office furniture from A. Whale. See A. Whale invoice no. 123 dated 4 May.

Note: The narrative gives Jonah the information he needs to enable him to check on the details later if needs be.

3 On 13 May Jonah bought a delivery van from Wheeler for $3 000 and paid by cheque. (The book of prime entry for this cash transaction is the cash book but, by also entering the purchase in the journal, Jonah will be able to see more detail about this important item than if he had entered it in the cash book only.)

Date	Accounts	Dr	Cr
		$	$
May 13	Delivery van account	3 000	
	Bank		3 000

Narrative: Purchase of delivery van, registration no. G1234PYD. See Wheeler's invoice no. 6 789 dated 13 May.

ACTIVITY 3

Prepare journal entries in proper form to correct the following.

Add a suitable narrative with proper detail to every entry in the journal.

Show the debit entry before the credit entry in the journal.

- **a** Credit note no. 964, for $120, received from A & Co., a supplier, has been posted to A. Cotter's account in error.
- **b** Invoice no. 104, for $400, received from Hussain, a supplier, has not been entered in the purchases journal.
- **c** Invoice no. 6 789, for $150, sent to Maya, a customer, has been entered in the sales journal as $105.
- **d** The purchase of a machine for use in the business, and costing $2 300, has been debited to purchases account in error.
- **e** Credit note no. 23, for $68, sent to Hanif, a customer, has been omitted from the sales returns journal.

Chapter summary

You should now be familiar with the books of prime entry. Remember, they are the sales and sales returns journals, purchases and purchases returns journals, three-column cash book and general journal.

You should now be able to enter the transactions in the books of prime entry and should know how to post to the ledger from the books of prime entry.

These techniques will feature again throughout the remainder of the text, particularly the cash book and general journal, so it is important that you are familiar with the uses of each and how they link in with the ledger.

Practice exercises

1 Adeel's transactions for the month of April were as follows:

April 1	Bought goods from Bilal for $3 000 less 20% trade discount. Bilal allowed Adeel 5% cash discount.
2	Sold goods to Imran for $800 less 10% trade discount. He allowed Imran 5% cash discount.
3	Bought goods from Asad for $1 300 less 20% trade discount. Asad allowed Adeel 5% cash discount.
5	Purchased a delivery van on credit from Syed for $6 000. The invoice for the van was no. 324.
8	Returned goods which had cost $100 to Bilal.
10	Sold goods to Raza for $1 100 less 20% trade discount. He allowed Raza 5% cash discount.
13	Imran returned goods which had cost him $60.
15	Purchased goods from Asma for $4 000 less 25% trade discount. Asma allowed Adeel 5% cash discount.
16	Sold goods to Amna for $1 500 less 20% trade discount. He allowed Amna 5% cash discount.
17	Sold goods to Raza for $1 600 less 20% trade discount. He allowed Raza 5% cash discount.
21	Returned goods which had cost him $600 to Asma.
24	Amna returned goods which had cost her $300.
26	Purchased goods from Bilal for $4 000 less 20% trade discount. Bilal allowed Adeel 5% cash discount.
30	Adeel settled all accounts he owed by cheque, and received cheques for all amounts owing by his customers. All discounts were taken.

Required

a Enter all the transactions for April into the books of prime entry.

b Post the books of prime entry to the ledger accounts.

TOP TIPS

- Remember that books of prime entry, **except the cash book**, are not part of the double-entry model.
- Post the periodic totals of the sales journal, sales returns journal, purchases journal and purchases returns journal to the sales, sales returns, purchases and purchases returns accounts respectively.
- Remember that the discount columns in the cash book are memorandum columns only and not part of the double-entry model.
- Prepare cash books in columnar form if possible (see Section 3.8).

2 Prepare journal entries with suitable narratives to record the following:

TOP TIP

Prepare journal entries only to ledger accounts, **never to other books of prime entry**.

a Received from Mumtaz invoice no. 506, dated 3 March for $10 000. This was in respect of the purchase of a machine on credit.

b Invoice no. 495, dated 6 March for $675, for goods sold to Wayne. The invoice has been entered twice in the sales journal.

c Invoice no. 998, dated 7 March for $4 250, in respect of a delivery van purchased on credit from Younas and paid for by cheque.

d Credit note no. 103, dated 10 March for $190, sent to Browne but omitted from the sales returns journal.

e Invoice no. 854, dated 15 March for $1 300, for goods purchased from Sandra. The invoice has been posted to Geeta's account in error.

Exam practice questions

Multiple-choice questions

1 Tania purchased goods for $1 000 less 25% trade discount. She was allowed a cash discount of 10%. Which amount should she enter in her purchases journal?

A $650 **B** $675 **C** $750 **D** $1 000

2 Lara purchased goods costing $1 800 less trade discount of 30%. She was allowed a cash discount of 5%. How much should Lara have to pay for the goods?

A $1 080 **B** $1 197 **C** $1 260 **D** $1 800

3 Cora sent an invoice to Maria for $2 000 less 20% trade discount. Cora has omitted to enter the invoice in her sales journal. What effect will this have on her accounts?

	Maria's account		Sales account	
	Debit	Credit	Debit	Credit
A		understated $1 600	understated $1 600	
B	understated $1 600			understated $1 600
C		understated $2 000	understated $2 000	
D	understated $2 000			understated $2 000

4 Cheung has received a cheque for $1 540 from Raju in full settlement of a debt of $1 700. How should this be recorded in Cheung's books of account?

	Debit		Credit	
		$		$
A	Bank	1 540	Raju	1 540
B	Bank	1 700	Raju	1 700
C	Bank	1 540	Raju	1 700
	Discounts allowed	160		
D	Bank	2 000	Raju	1 540
			Discounts received	160

Total: 4 marks

Chapter 4
Balancing accounts

Learning objectives

In this chapter you will learn:

- how to find and record a balance on a ledger account
- what debit balances and credit balances mean.

4.1 Why accounts need to be balanced

At some point during the trading period all the accounts in existence must be balanced. The cash book is balanced periodically to determine how much money is left in the bank account or how much cash the business has left. Similarly, the ledger accounts are balanced to determine how much the business owes other people, how much it is owed, and how much has been received from, or spent on, the various activities.

4.2 How to balance an account

The procedure of **balancing an account** is quite straightforward:

a Add each side of the account to find which has the lesser total.

b Insert on that side the amount needed to make both sides equal, or, in other words, balance.

c Insert the total on each side of the account and carry the balance down to the other side of the account on the next day.

KEY TERMS

Balancing an account: The process of finding which side of a ledger account is the greater.

Debit balance: The amount by which the debit side of an account is greater than the credit side.

Walkthrough

1 Balancing the bank account

Abdul does not keep a cash book. The following shows how he would balance his bank account at 20 April.

Bank account

Debit			Credit		
		$			$
Apr 1	Abdul – capital	10 000	Apr 2	Motor vehicles	2 000
Apr 4	Sales	800	Apr 13	Purchases	3 000
Apr 8	Purchases returns	100	Apr 7	Sales returns	40
Apr 11	Tania – loan	5 000	Apr 10	Motor vehicles	4 000
Apr 14	Rent receivable	300	Apr 12	Rent payable	1 000
			Apr 15	Wages	1 200
			Apr 16	Drawings	600
			Apr 20	Balance carried down	4 360
		16 200			16 200
Apr 21	Balance brought down	4 360			

The balancing figure was then carried down to the debit side on the next day.

The balancing figure of $4 360 was entered on the credit side to make the total of the credit side agree with the total of the debit side.

The account has been balanced at 20 April.

- The account has a **debit balance** showing how much money is left in the bank account on 20 April. It is a debit balance because the total of the debit side of the account was greater than the total of the credit side before the balancing figure of $4 360 was inserted.
- The totals of each column ($16 200) are placed level with each other although there are more items on the credit side than on the debit side. In bookkeeping nothing is usually written against these figures. They are simply the totals of each column. However, see Walkthrough 4.

2 Balancing a customer's account

Charley is a customer whose account has been balanced and is as follows:

Charley's account					
Debit			**Credit**		
		$			$
Jun 4	Sales	1 040	Jun 6	Sales returns	400
Jun 10	Sales	3 105	Jun 14	Bank	600
Jun 19	Sales	900	Jun 14	Discount	40
			Jun 30	Balance c/d	4 005
		5 045			5 045
Jul 1	Balance b/d	4 005			

Charley's account has a debit balance which shows that he owes the business $4 005; he is a 'debtor' of the business.

This credit entry on 14 June is described simply as 'discount' because it is understood that it is discount allowed.

Note: c/d is short for 'carried down' and b/d is short for 'brought down'. These abbreviations are common in accounting.

TOP TIPS

- The balances carried down on accounts should always be shown as brought down on the accounts on the next day. The dates are important and must be included.
- You should always indicate a balance carried down (c/d) or brought down (b/d). In most cases bal b/d and bal c/d is acceptable. However, do not just write c/d and b/d.

3 Balancing a supplier's account

Sara is a supplier whose account has been balanced and is as follows:

Sara's account					
Debit			**Credit**		
		$			$
May 8	Purchases returns	1 000	May 1	Balance b/d	1 940
May 29	Bank	2 005	May 12	Purchases	7 330
May 29	Discount	125			
May 31	Balance c/d	6 140			
		9 270			9 270
			June 1	Balance b/d	6 140

KEY TERM

Credit balance: The amount by which the credit side of an account is greater than the debit side.

When Sara's account was balanced on the previous day, 30 April, a balance of $1 940 was brought down and appears as an opening credit balance on her account at 1 May.

Sara's account has a **credit balance**. This shows that Sara is owed $6 140; she is a creditor of the business.

Note: If an account has only one entry on each side and they are of equal amount, the account is simply ruled off.

4 Balancing an account with only one entry on each side

Gerald's account					
Debit			**Credit**		
		$			$
Mar 4	Sales	1000	Mar 23	Bank	1000

In this case, as there is only one entry on each side and they are equal, and there is no balance to carry down, it is acceptable to rule off the account in this manner.

5 Balancing an account with an entry on one side only

Paula is a supplier to a business. Her account is balanced below:

Paula's account					
Debit			**Credit**		
		$			$
Mar 31	Balance c/d	1500	Mar 22	Purchases	1500
			April 1	Balance b/d	1500

The account was balanced by entering the balance c/d on the debit side.

The balance was brought down the next day to the credit side.

The only entry made in the account before it was balanced was the purchase of goods for $1 500.

6 Balancing the three-column cash book

In Section 3.7 the entries in the three-column cash book were explained. Balancing the three-column cash book is an important task and is shown below:

Bank and cash									
Debit					**Credit**				
		Disc	Cash	Bank			Disc	Cash	Bank
		$	$	$			$	$	$
May 1	Sales		700		May 3	Other operating exps.		40	
May 4	Sales		2000		May 5	Bank ¢		1500	
May 5	A & Co.	100		2080	May 6	Z & Sons	50		600
May 5	Cash ¢			1500	May 7	Other operating exps.		70	
May 7	P Ltd	80		450	May 8	Q Bros.	40		160
May 8	Bank ¢		500		May 8	Cash ¢			500
					May 8	Wages		500	
					May 8	Balance c/d		1090	2770
		180	3200	4030			90	3200	4030
May 9									
Balances b/d			1090	2770					

TOP TIP

Remember from Section 3.6 that the discount columns are not balanced. The totals are carried to the discounts allowed and discounts received accounts respectively.

4.3 When are accounts balanced?

The cash book will usually be balanced at frequent intervals because it is always important to know how much money is in the bank account. It will be balanced at weekly intervals in small businesses, daily in large ones.

Accounts for customers and suppliers are balanced monthly because of the practice of sending and receiving statements of account. The statements are copies of the accounts of customers in the sellers' books and are sent to customers so that they can reconcile their ledger accounts with those of their suppliers. Any differences can be enquired into and agreement reached between supplier and customer. The statements also remind customers that payment of outstanding balances is due.

The other accounts are usually balanced as and when required; this will always be when a trial balance is being prepared. Trial balances are explained in Chapter 6.

Chapter summary

In this chapter you have learnt how to balance ledger accounts and the three-column cash book. The procedure is not difficult if you follow the steps set out. You'll find it helpful to remember the importance of proper dates and labels when you balance any account.

Practice exercise

1 Al has the following transactions for the first week of March:

		$
March 1	Paid his savings into a business bank account.	10 000
2	Bought goods for resale on credit from Joe.	4 000
	Paid rent of a shop by cheque.	1 000
3	Sold goods to Barney on credit.	2 000
	Made cash sales of goods. The money was used to set up a cash float.	550
5	Returned faulty goods to Joe.	200
7	Paid Joe by cheque for the goods he had bought, after deducting a 5% cash discount.	
7	Paid for postages by cash.	20

a Prepare the necessary ledger accounts and the three-column cash book to record the transactions.

b Balance the accounts at 7 March and bring down the balances.

Chapter 5
The classification of accounts and division of the ledger

Learning objectives

In this chapter you will learn:

- that accounts are classified as either personal or impersonal
- about the division of impersonal accounts into real accounts and nominal accounts
- how a single ledger can be divided into a number of ledgers or books, each containing transactions of a similar nature.

5.1 The classification of accounts

All accounts fall into one of two classes: **personal account** or **impersonal account**. Each of these classes can be further divided into subgroups.

a **Personal accounts** are those for persons (including sole traders, partnerships and companies). The subgroups are as follows:

- **Accounts for trade receivables**. We saw in Section 2.2 that a customer who owes the business money is known as a debtor. Their accounts have **debit** balances. When all the debit balances for all the customers are added together, the total is referred to as trade receivables. They can also be classified as current assets. Other current assets include cash in hand, cash at the bank and inventory, as explained below under impersonal accounts.
- **Accounts for trade payables**. Persons to whom the business owes money are known as creditors. They are usually those who supply goods or services to the business, and their accounts have **credit** balances. Similarly they are collectively known as trade payables. This group also includes loan accounts. Amounts owing to creditors who have to be paid within one year are current liabilities. Amounts owing to creditors who do not have to be paid within one year (e.g. for a long-term loan) are non-current liabilities.
- The owner's **capital and drawings** accounts.

b **Impersonal accounts** are all accounts other than personal accounts. These can be classified as follows:

- **Accounts with debit balances**.

  These can be divided into:

  i **Asset accounts** (**real accounts**) are things that the business owns.

TOP TIP

Sometimes you may be asked to define an **asset**. It is important to say that it is both something **owned** by the business or **owed** to the business. Remember to state both aspects of owned and owing.

Asset accounts may be further subdivided into:

- **Non-current assets**, which are things acquired for use in the business and not for resale. This includes such things as premises, plant and machinery, vehicles, office furniture and equipment. These assets are intended to be used in the business for a number of years. Expenditure on non-current assets is **capital expenditure**.
- **Current assets**, in addition to the trade receivables referred to above, are those that arise in the course of trading, such as inventories of goods bought to resell to customers, fuel for business vehicles, and cash at the bank and in hand.

ii **Nominal accounts**. These can be subdivided into:

- **Expenses accounts**, which are things such as rent payable, wages, salaries, heating and lighting, postage and stationery. This type of expenditure is **revenue expenditure (expense)**, the costs incurred in running the business on a day-to-day basis. These accounts have a debit balance.

KEY TERMS

Personal account: An account relating to a person.

Impersonal account: Any account other than a personal account.

Real account: An account which contains the transactions relating to non-current assets.

Asset: Something which is owned by or owed to a business.

Capital expenditure: Money spent on acquiring non-current assets.

Nominal account: An account used to record the revenue and expenses of a business. It also relates to an account or accounts which record the revenue of the business from sales.

Revenue expenditure (expense): The day-to-day expenditure incurred in the day-to-day running of a business.

- **Revenue accounts** or accounts with credit balances. These accounts record the revenue of the business, such as sales and other income (rent receivable, discounts received and interest receivable).

The distinction between the types of accounts is very important. Care must always be taken to ensure that capital expenditure is not confused with revenue expenditure. The cost of purchasing a motor vehicle is capital expenditure and must be debited to the motor vehicles account. The cost of running the vehicle is revenue expenditure and must be debited to motor vehicles running expenses account.

As a result, you will always find capital expenditure on the statement of financial position of a business (see Chapter 8). Revenue expenditure, on the other hand, is always found in the income statement of a business (see Chapter 7).

ACTIVITY 1

Copy and complete this table, ticking the boxes which correctly describe the given accounts in the books of a bakery.

Account	Personal	Non-current asset	Current asset	Revenue or other income	Expense
Capital					
Sales returns					
Delivery vans					
Purchases					
Rent payable					
Trade receivables					
Inventory					
Discounts allowed					
Drawings					
Bank					
Rent receivable					
Trade payables					
Computer					
Wages					
Discounts received					

5.2 Division of the ledger

Except in very small businesses there are too many accounts to be kept in a single ledger. It is usual to divide the accounts among several ledgers as follows:

- **sales ledger** for the accounts of customers
- **purchase ledger** for the accounts of suppliers

KEY TERMS

Sales ledger: The ledger which contains the individual accounts of all the business's credit customers.

Purchase ledger: The ledger which contains the individual accounts of all the business's credit suppliers.

- general (or nominal) ledger for the impersonal accounts for assets, revenue, other income, and expenses
- private ledger for accounts of a confidential nature, such as the owner's capital and drawings accounts and loan accounts; also the income statements and statements of financial position (see Chapters 7 and 8)
- cash book containing the bank and cash accounts. The business owner might want to keep a private ledger as they would not want their employees to know how much the business had borrowed, or how much profit the business makes and how much the owner has taken from the business as their private drawings
- petty cash book containing the records of amounts paid from petty cash for minor items such as tea, postage, window cleaning and perhaps stationery.

The division of the ledger as above is essential in a business which employs several bookkeepers; the work may be divided between them so that they do not all need to be working on the same ledger at the same time. It makes sense to group items of a similar nature – for example, sales are all together in one ledger, the sales ledger. This allows staff to be trained in different aspects of the business. Perhaps most importantly, it helps to detect and prevent errors occurring in the books of account. It may also help to detect and prevent fraud by the accounts staff. This is known as **internal control**.

Chapter summary

In this chapter you have learnt how the different classifications of ledger accounts work, including:

- personal/impersonal accounts
- real/nominal accounts.

You should also now have an understanding of the way the ledger can be divided into several ledgers, each containing transactions of a similar nature. You should know about the following ledgers in particular:

- sales ledger
- purchase ledger
- general or nominal ledger
- private ledger.

Practice exercises

1 Complete the following table to indicate whether or not each statement is true or false:

Statement	True or false
The purchase of a motor car is revenue expenditure	
The payment of wages to employees is revenue expenditure	
The accounts for customers are kept in the sales ledger	
Repairs to the office windows is an example of capital expenditure	
The purchase of office stationery is revenue expenditure	
The sales account is a nominal account	
The fixtures and fittings account is a real account	
Suppliers' accounts are kept in the nominal ledger	
The day-to-day costs of running the business are an example of revenue expenditure	

2 Complete the following sentences by inserting the correct word from the following list:

non-current revenue capital nominal real petty cash book

a The sales account records the _______ of the business and is an example of a _______ account.

b The purchase of a new machine is an example of _______ expenditure and the account is an example of a _______ account.

c Small items of expenditure are recorded in the _______.

d A _______ asset is bought to keep in the business for a long period of time.

Chapter 6
The trial balance

Learning objectives

In this chapter you will learn:

- the purpose of trial balances
- how to prepare a trial balance
- the limitations of trial balances
- six types of error which do not affect the agreement of the two sides of a trial balance.

6.1 What is a trial balance?

A **trial balance** is a list of the balances on each account extracted from the ledgers at a particular date. Its purpose is to check that the total of the debit balances equals the total of the credit balances. The principle of double entry determines that the two totals should agree. If the totals do not agree there must be an error somewhere in the bookkeeping. It depends on the size of the business how often a trial balance is prepared. For a sole trader it is probably only done once a year at the year-end. For a large company it would be usual to prepare a trial balance every month in order to prepare monthly management accounts. Of course, if the accounts are kept using a computerised accounting system, it is possible to prepare a trial balance at any time simply by using the function in the accounting package.

KEY TERM

Trial balance: A list of the balances on each account extracted from the ledgers at a particular date. Its purpose is to check that the total of the debit balances equals the total of the credit balances.

6.2 How to prepare a trial balance

a First balance all the ledger accounts including the cash book (see Chapter 4).

b Then list the accounts with the debit balances and those with credit balances in separate columns.

c The total of the debit balances should equal the total of the credit balances. If the totals are equal, the trial balance agrees.

Walkthrough

Zabine has balanced each of the accounts in her ledger, together with the cash book at 31 March 2016. She has then prepared a trial balance by listing each account and the balance on it at that date as follows:

Trial balance extracted from the books of Zabine at 31 March 2016

Account	Debit balances	Credit balances
	$	$
Premises	70 000	
Machinery	10 000	
Office furniture	5 000	
Sales		100 000
Sales returns	700	
Purchases	6 900	
Purchases returns		1 000
Trade receivables*	1 100	
Trade payables**		1 575
Rent payable	1 600	
Wages and salaries	4 080	
Heating and lighting	960	
Other operating expenses	1 430	
Cash	500	
Bank	12 600	
Loan from Ludmilla		2 000
Capital – Zabine		13 000
Drawings	2 705	
	117 575	117 575

* The balances on the accounts in the sales ledger are listed and totalled separately; the total is entered in the trial balance as trade receivables (see Section 5.1).

** The balances on the accounts in the purchase ledger are listed and totalled separately; the total is entered in the trial balance as trade payables (see Section 5.1).

The total of the debit balances and credit balances agree at $117 575. The trial balance balances. This means that for every debit entry made in the ledger, an equal and opposite credit entry has been made in another account. This goes a long way to confirming the accuracy of the bookkeeping.

ACTIVITY 1

Prepare a trial balance from the following balances that have been extracted from the books of a grocer at 31 December.

Account	
	$
Premises	50 000
Motor vans	8 000
Office furniture	2 000
Computer	3 000
Sales	60 000
Sales returns	700
Purchases	4 000
Purchases returns	500
Motor vehicle running expenses	4 200
Wages	1 800
Rent	2 000
Bank	1 650 (debit)
Capital	20 000
Drawings	3 150

6.3 Limitations of a trial balance

If a trial balance does not agree, there must be a mistake somewhere in the bookkeeping. Unfortunately, even if a trial balance agrees, it does not mean that there are no errors. It only proves that for every debit entry an equal credit entry has been made. However, it does not prove that those entries have been made in the correct accounts! There are six types of error that do not affect the agreement of the trial balance. They are as follows:

a **Errors of omission** A transaction omitted completely from the books results in there being neither a debit nor credit entry for the transaction. This could happen if a transaction is not entered in a book of prime entry.

b **Errors of commission** A transaction is posted to the wrong account, but the account is of the same class as the account to which the posting should have been made. Example: the payment of a telephone bill is posted in error to heating and lighting account. Telephone account and heating and lighting account are both expense accounts.

- **c** **Errors of principle** A transaction is posted to a wrong account which is not of the same type as the correct account. Example: revenue expenditure treated as capital expenditure. For instance, payment for petrol for a vehicle has been debited to motor vehicles account (a non-current asset account) instead of to motor vehicles running expenses account (an expense account).
- **d** **Errors of original entry** A wrong amount is entered in a book of prime entry for a transaction. Example: a sales invoice for $200 is entered in the sales journal as $20.
- **e** **Complete reversal of entries** An account which should have been debited has been credited, and the account which should have been credited has been debited. Example: a payment received from Hussain is debited to Hussain's account and credited to bank account.
- **f** **Compensating errors** Two or more errors cancel each other out. Example: an invoice for $1100 in the sales journal is posted to the customer's account as $1 000. At the same time, the sales journal total is understated by $100. The debit balance on the customer's account and the credit balance on sales account will both be understated by $100.

It is really important to consider these types of error. Just because the trial balance has balanced doesn't mean that everything in the ledger is correct. For example, if the purchase of a motor vehicle is entered in the motor expenses account then the profit for the year will be understated. Similarly, if the accountant does not send out cheques to suppliers at the year-end but keeps them in the safe, the balance on the bank account will be wrong. This may have been done to make it seem that the bank account is more healthy than it really is. Even worse, not recording some invoices from suppliers would boost the profit, but is fraud.

ACTIVITY 2

State which type of error each of the following represents:

- **a** Payment of rent has been debited to the bank account and credited to the rent payable account.
- **b** The purchase of a computer has been debited to the office expenses account.
- **c** A supplier's invoice has been omitted from the purchases journal.
- **d** The total of wages account has been overstated by $1 000, and rent received of $1 000 has been posted twice to the rent received account.
- **e** Discount allowed to Amna has been credited to Asma's account.
- **f** A purchase of goods for $960 has been entered in the purchases journal as $690.

TOP TIP

Learn the six types of error which do not affect the trial balance. You must be able to give examples of them.

6.4 What to do if the trial balance fails to agree

Look for the cause of a difference on a trial balance by carrying out the following simple checks before spending a lot of time checking all your postings:

- check the additions of the trial balance
- if the difference is divisible by 2, look for a balance equal to half the difference which may have been entered on the wrong side

- if the difference is divisible by 9, two figures may have been transposed in a balance (e.g. $269 may have been copied as $296)
- if you still haven't found the cause of the imbalance then go back to the start and check the balances on each of the accounts and that you have transferred them correctly to the trial balance.

Chapter summary

In this chapter the nature and purpose of a trial balance has been considered. The process of how to prepare a trial balance has been set out. We have also seen the types of errors which won't stop the trial balance balancing. Finally, we looked at what to do if the trial balance fails to agree.

TOP TIP

The trial balance is an important part of bookkeeping. It is always done and has to be balanced **before** the preparation of financial statements takes place.

Practice exercises

1 The following balances at 31 December 2015 have been extracted from Hassan's books.

	$
Sales	160 000
Sales returns	2 600
Purchases	84 000
Purchases returns	3 400
Wages	26 000
Heating and lighting	3 160
Rent payable	5 000
Rent receivable	1 000
Advertising	2 900
Postage and telephone	2 740
Discounts allowed	6 100
Discounts received	5 900
Plant and machinery	50 000
Delivery van	9 000
Bank	2 300
Trade receivables	7 400
Trade payables	3 700
Drawings	8 800
Capital	?

Prepare a trial balance at 31 December 2015 from the balances extracted from Hassan's books and calculate the balance on his capital account.

2 An inexperienced bookkeeper has extracted a trial balance at 31 December 2015 from Andrea's books. It contains some errors and does not balance.

Trial balance at 31 December 2015		
	$	$
Premises	70 000	
Plant and machinery	30 000	
Office equipment	5 000	
Wages	7 600	
Rent payable		4 000
Heating and lighting	1 500	
Other operating expenses	1 720	
Sales		133 000
Purchases	57 000	
Discounts allowed		2 450
Discounts received	1 070	
Bank	2 910	
Trade receivables	14 000	
Trade payables		10 140
Purchases returns	2 400	
Sales returns		3 150
Rent receivable	1 200	
Capital		80 000
Drawings		28 480
	194 400	261 220

Re-write the trial balance and correct the errors so that it balances.

TOP TIP

If you are not sure if the account should have a debit or credit balance, check back to Section 5.1.

Exam practice questions

Multiple-choice questions

1 Which of the following accounts normally has a credit balance?

A discounts allowed

B discounts received

C purchases

D sales returns

2 After which error will a trial balance still balance?

A an invoice for $400 in the sales journal not posted to the customer's account in the sales ledger

B a purchase of goods from Ratna for $1 000 credited to Ravin's account in the purchase ledger

C payment of $60 to Josan entered correctly in the bank account and credited to Josan's account

D rent payment of $660 entered correctly in the cash book but posted to rent payable account as $600

3 A business has paid rent of $800. The payment has been entered in the books as follows:

Account debited	Account credited
Bank $800	Rent $800

Which type of error is this?

A commission

B compensating

C complete reversal

D principle

4 Discounts allowed of $160 for one month have been posted to the credit of the discounts received account. What effect has this had on the trial balance?

A $160 too much credit

B $160 too little debit

C $160 too little debit and $160 too much credit

D $320 too much credit

Total: 4 marks

Part II
Financial accounting

Chapter 7
Income statements for sole traders

Learning objectives

In this chapter you will learn:

- how to prepare income statements for sole traders for the purpose of the inventory account
- how to prepare the inventory account
- how to treat goods taken by a business owner for their own use
- how to deal with carriage inwards and carriage outwards when preparing an income statement.

7.1 What is an income statement?

Most people carry on business in order to make a living. They depend upon the profit of the business for their income to enable them to buy food, clothes and other necessities. They compare revenue earned by the business with its expenses. If the revenue exceeds expenses the business has made a profit. On the other hand, if the expenses exceed the revenue the business has made a loss. Profit or loss is found by the preparation of an income statement covering a period of time, usually one complete year. Until now, double-entry bookkeeping may have seemed a tiresome and largely pointless exercise of recording transactions and opening accounts with no end product in sight, but it is the only system that enables the income statements to be prepared.

Set out below is an example of the structure of an income statement for a **sole trader**, someone who is the only owner of the business. They may have staff working for them but they are solely responsible for debts of the business and, of course, benefit as the only one entitled to the profit. At this stage the income statement is fairly basic. A full income statement would include other items of income and expenditure which have not yet been covered in the book.

KEY TERM

Sole trader: The owner of a business who runs the business on their own.

A. Trader
Income statement for the year ended 31 December 2015

	$	$	$
Revenue			102 000
Less: sales returns			(2 000)
			100 000
Less: cost of sales			
Opening inventory		5 000	
Purchases	48 000		
Less: purchase returns	(1 500)		
	46 500		
Less: goods for own use (drawings)	(900)		
Add: carriage inwards	2 300	47 900	
		52 900	
Less: closing inventory		(6 000)	
Cost of sales			46 900
Gross profit			53 100
Add: other income			
Discount received			300
Rent or interest received			2 400
			55 800
Less: expenses			
Wages and salaries		(3 000)	
Rent and rates		(8 000)	
Telephone		(2 600)	
Insurance		(1 400)	
Heat and light		(3 100)	
Selling expenses		(850)	
Loan interest paid		(1 050)	
Total expenses			(20 000)
Profit for the year			35 800

KEY TERMS

Cost of sales: The net cost of the goods sold to customers.

Profit for the year: The profit calculated by adding other income to the gross profit and deducting the business expenses. Sometimes called 'the bottom line'.

Notes:

- The heading is important, particularly the fact that it is the income statement **for the year (or × months) ended……..** The statement covers a period of time so it is necessary to state the period covered.
- Carriage inwards is taken as part of the **cost of sales**, not an expense (see Section 7.4).
- You should add any other operating income received to the gross profit. Never treat it as a negative expense.
- The **profit for the year** figure is important. You will need to use it again when you prepare the next document, the statement of financial position.
- If the business is a service business – one which doesn't buy and sell goods (e.g. an accountant)–then there will be no cost of sales. You will only need to show the income, which will be the fees received less the expenses to leave the profit for the year.

7.2 How to prepare an income statement for a sole trader

Step 1 Prepare the trial balance

All ledger accounts must be balanced and a trial balance prepared at the date to which the income statement is to be prepared.

Walkthrough

Andrew commenced business on 1 January 2015. The following trial balance has been extracted at 31 December 2015 from his books of account.

Andrew
Trial balance at 31 December 2015

Account	Debit	Credit
	$	$
Sales		126 000
Sales returns	2 000	
Purchases	55 200	
Purchases returns		2 200
Discounts received		2 340
Discounts allowed	3 260	
Wages	28 000	
Rent	16 000	
Heating and lighting	3 400	
Postage and stationery	1 070	
Motor van expenses	9 830	
Interest on loan	800	
Other operating expenses	920	
Premises	40 000	
Motor vans	18 000	
Office furniture	5 000	
Trade receivables	7 400	
Trade payables		3 420
Bank	2 160	
Loan from Marie (repayable in 2020)		10 000
Andrew – capital		60 000
Drawings	10 920	
	203 960	203 960

TOP TIP

It is important to note that the income statement is part of the double-entry model.

Step 2 Transfer the balances on the nominal (revenue, income and expense) accounts.

These are **transferred** to the trading section of the income statement by debiting or crediting the nominal accounts and posting the opposite entries in the income statement. All the nominal accounts are then closed for the current accounting period. In this sense, transferring the balance does not mean money physically being transferred. It is simply the accounting term to complete the double entry for a transaction.

Walkthrough

For example, Andrew's sales account is shown below:

Sales account					
	$				$
		2015			
		31 December	Sales for the year (This would be the total from the sales journal)		126 000

Andrew's accountant would now prepare a journal entry to close the sales account and transfer the figure to the income statement.

Date	Details	Dr	Cr
		$	$
Dec 31	Sales account	126 000	
	Income statement		126 000

Transfer of sales for the year to the income statement.

Step 3 Prepare the trading section of the income statement

The trading section of the **income statement** calculates the profit on the activity of buying and selling goods. The balances on the sales, sales returns, purchases and purchases returns accounts are **transferred** to the income statement by journal entry.

KEY TERM

Income statement: An account prepared periodically to find the profit or loss made by a business.

Walkthrough

Set out below is the complete journal entry to transfer these items from their ledger accounts to the income statement. (Narratives have been omitted.)

Account	Debit	Credit
	$	$
Sales	126 000	
Income statement		126 000
Income statement	2 000	
Sales returns		2 000
Income statement	55 200	
Purchases		55 200
Purchases returns	2 200	
Income statement		2 200

When asked to close, say, the sales account at the end of a trading period, ensure that in the ledger account you show the correct wording. For example, the sales account in the walkthrough above is closed as follows:

Walkthrough

Sales account					
2015		**$**	**2015**		**$**
31 December	Income statement	126 000	31 December	Sales journal	126 000
		126 000			126 000

These journal entries produce a trading section of the income statement as follows:

Andrew Trading section of the income statement for the year ended 31 December 2015			
Debit		**Credit**	
	$		$
Sales returns	2 000	Sales	126 000
Purchases	55 200	Purchases returns	2 200

Notice that, as mentioned earlier, the income statement is part of the double-entry system. Thus it is set out as an account with a debit and credit side. The posting of each item to the appropriate side comes from the journal entry in Step 2.

TOP TIPS

- Give all income statements proper headings.
- Include in the heading the name of the trader or business.
- State the period covered by the account.

The trading section of the income statement is improved if sales returns are deducted from sales to show the revenue actually earned (called **revenue** or **turnover**). Similarly, it is better to deduct purchases returns from purchases. By doing this similar items are grouped together. On the debit side is everything relating to purchases and on the credit side everything relating to sales. This is shown below.

KEY TERMS

Revenue/ turnover: The sales of goods or services made by a business.

Inventory: The unsold goods of a trading business at a point in time.

Walkthrough

Andrew

Trading section of the income statement for the year ended 31 December 2015

Debit		**Credit**	
	$		**$**
Purchases	55 200	Sales	126 000
Less: purchases returns	2 200	Less: sales returns	2 000
	53 000*		124 000

*$53 000 is the cost of the goods which were available for selling.

ACTIVITY 1

Liz commenced business on 1 April 2015 and has taken the following account balances from her books of account at 31 March 2016:

	$
Sales	150 000
Purchases	68 000
Sales returns	4 200
Purchases returns	1 700

Prepare the trading section of Liz's income statement for the year ended 31 March 2016.

Step 4 Make an adjustment in respect of closing inventory

Walkthrough

It is unlikely that Andrew has sold all his goods by 31 December, therefore some remains to be sold next year. These goods represent Andrew's closing **inventory**. Andrew has valued the closing inventory at $5 000. This should be the cost price of the goods when Andrew bought them. This value must be deducted from the cost of the goods that were available for selling in the trading section of the income statement to arrive at the cost of the goods sold. The double entry for this requires a journal entry to open an inventory account.

Date	**Details**		
		$	**$**
Dec 31	Inventory	5 000	
	Income statement		5 000

Transfer the closing inventory at 31 December 2015 to income statement.

Note: This journal entry now requires an inventory account to be opened. The debit to the inventory account creates a new asset and a new account that is not in the trial balance. This is shown below.

Inventory account					
2015		**$**	**2015**		**$**
Dec 31	Income statement	5000	Dec 31	Balance c/d	5000
2016					
Jan 1	Balance b/d	5000			

Notice that at the end of the year the balance on the account is carried down to the start of the new financial year.

The closing inventory is credited to the trading section of the income statement. In strict double entry it should be credited in the income statement as in the following example:

Andrew
Trading section of the income statement for the year ended 31 December 2015

Debit		**Credit**	
	$		**$**
Purchases	55200	Sales	126000
Less: purchases returns	(2200)	Less: sales returns	(2000)
	53000		124000
		Closing inventory	5000
			129000

However, the inventory represents unsold purchases. To keep it with the purchases it is moved over to the debit side of the income statement.

This is done by **deducting** it on the debit side from net purchases. The trading section of the income statement now shows the cost of the goods which have been sold. The debit side of the account is therefore headed with the words 'cost of sales' (in this case $48000).

Walkthrough

The following income statement shows how the closing inventory should be recorded:

Andrew
Trading section of the income statement for the year ended 31 December 2015

Debit		**Credit**	
	$		**$**
Cost of sales		Sales	126000
Purchases	55200	Less: sales returns	(2000)
Less: purchases returns	(2200)		124000
	53000		
Less: closing inventory	(5000)		
Cost of sales*	48000		
Gross profit**	76000		
	124000		124000

*Cost of sales: the net cost of the goods which were sold. It is calculated in this case by:

(purchases – purchases returns) – closing inventory

The balance on the trading section of the income statement is **gross profit, or the profit made on buying and selling goods before any other expenses are taken into account.

As it is a ledger account, the trading section of the income statement is balanced in exactly the same way as any other account (see Section 4.2). In this case the credit side totals $124 000. The cost of sales figure is $48 000, so the balancing figure (the gross profit) is $76 000. This is the figure which makes both sides of the account add to $124 000.

KEY TERM

Gross profit: The profit calculated by deducting the cost of sales from the net sales in the income statement.

TOP TIP

Always include the words 'cost of sales' and 'gross profit' in full.

ACTIVITY 2

Rodney started in business on 1 October 2014. He has taken the following balances from his books of account at 30 September 2015:

	$
Revenue	140 000
Purchases	84 000
Sales returns	1 200
Purchases returns	1 400

At 30 September 2015, Rodney had unsold goods valued at $4 900.

Prepare the trading section of Rodney's income statement for the year ended 30 September 2015.

Step 5 Prepare the rest of the income statement

By preparing the rest of the income statement, it is now possible to calculate the profit for the year. To do this, the remainder of the income statement follows the trading section without a break, starting with the gross profit, to which is added other income, if any. Next, the overhead expenses included in the trial balance are deducted. (The balances on these ledger accounts are transferred to the income statement by journal entries in the same way as before.) The income statement is now completed as follows:

Walkthrough

Andrew

Income statement for the year ended 31 December 2015

	$		$
Cost of sales		Sales	126 000
Purchases	55 200	Less: sales returns	(2 000)
Less: purchases returns	(2 200)		124 000
	53 000		

Income statement for the year ended 31 December 2015			
	$		$
Less: closing inventory	(5 000)		
Cost of sales	48 000		
Gross profit	76 000		
	124 000		124 000
Less: overhead expenses			
Wages	(28 000)	Gross profit brought down	76 000
Rent	(16 000)	Discounts received	2 340
Heating and lighting	(3 400)		78 340
Postage and stationery	(1 070)		
Motor van expenses	(9 830)		
Discounts allowed	(3 260)		
Other operating expenses	(920)		
Interest on loan	(800)		
Total overhead expenses	(63 280)		
Profit for the year*	15 060		
	78 340		78 340

*The profit for the year ($15 060) is the difference between the gross profit ($76 000) plus any other income ($2 340), minus the total of all the overheads ($63 280).

TOP TIP

Make sure you copy accurately all the nominal accounts included in the trial balance into your income statement.

Income statements like this have debit and credit sides like ledger accounts and are described as being in **horizontal** form. In other words, the debits and credits are next to each other as in other ledger accounts.

Many people reading these accounts are not accountants; they know nothing about debits and credits and find the accounts difficult to understand. It is now normal to prepare these accounts in **vertical** form, which is easier for non-accountants to understand. This means that the information in the income statement is listed down the page.

Andrew's income statement in vertical form is shown below.

Andrew Income statement for the year ended 31 December 2015		
	$	$
Sales		126 000
Less: sales returns		(2 000)
Revenue		124 000
Less: cost of sales		
Purchases	55 200	
Less: purchases returns	(2 200)	
	53 000	
Less: inventory at 31 December	(5 000)	
Cost of sales		(48 000)
Gross profit		76 000
Add: discount received		2 340
		78 340
Less: expenses		
Wages	(28 000)	
Rent	(16 000)	
Heading and lighting	(3 400)	
Postage and stationery	(1 070)	
Motor van expenses	(9 830)	
Discounts allowed	(3 260)	
Other operating expenses	(920)	
Loan interest	(800)	(63 280)
Profit for the year		15 060

Set out below are some key points to remember about the income statement:

- Give the income statement a proper heading including the name of the business.
- The income statement is known as a period statement because it covers a period of time; it must be described as 'for the year ended' (or other period). Always state the date in full with the day, month and year.
- It is part of the double-entry model and the balances on the accounts are transferred to it by journal entry.
- 'Sales less sales returns' is the revenue or turnover of the business (in this case $124 000).
- The words 'cost of sales' are important and should always be shown.

- A trader may take some items which were purchased to resell from the business for personal use. The goods taken should be deducted from purchases at cost price and added to the trader's drawings. This, again must be done by a journal entry, as shown below:

Account	Debit	Credit
	$	$
Drawings	500	
Purchases		500

Transfer of goods valued at $500 taken for his own use by Andrew.

- The words 'gross profit' are important and must be shown. The gross profit is the profit earned on selling goods before any other expenses are taken into account.
- Trading sections of the income statement should only be prepared for traders – that is, people who trade in (buy and sell) goods. People who sell their services, such as accountants, lawyers, dentists and gardeners, only require income statements.
- Any other income should always be added to the gross profit figure.
- There is no particular order in which overheads should be shown in the income statement of a sole trader, but it is often best to place the larger amounts before the smaller.
- It is also a good plan to group together similar kinds of expenses – for example, property expenses (rent, heating and lighting, and insurance). Profit for the year is the trader's income after all expenses have been taken into account.
- A loss for the year arises if the expenses exceed the gross profit.

TOP TIP

Accounts are often prepared in vertical form, since it makes them easier to read. You should study the vertical form carefully until you are quite familiar with it.

ACTIVITY 3

Sofia began trading on 1 January 2015. The following trial balance as at 31 December 2015 has been extracted from her books.

Trial balance as at 31 December 2015

Account	$	$
Sales		200 000
Sales returns	6 300	
Purchases	86 500	
Purchases returns		5 790
Rent received		3 000
Discounts received		3 210
Discounts allowed	5 110	

Trial balance as at 31 December 2015		
Wages	61 050	
Rent paid	12 000	
Electricity	5 416	
Insurance	2 290	
Motor van expenses	11 400	
Other operating expenses	3 760	
Loan interest	1 000	
Land and buildings	84 000	
Plant and machinery	22 000	
Motor van	19 000	
Trade receivables	12 425	
Trade payables		4 220
Bank	5 065	
Loan (repayable in 2022)		20 000
Drawings	25 904	
Capital at 1 January 2015		127 000
	363 220	363 220

Sofia had unsold inventory of goods of $10 000 at 31 December 2015.

Prepare Sofia's income statement for the year ended 31 December 2015. (Save your answer; it will be required again in Chapter 8.)

7.3 Opening inventory

One year's closing inventory is the next year's opening inventory and it must be included in the cost of sales for that year. The debit balance on the inventory account is transferred by journal entry to the trading section of the income statement.

Shown below is the journal entry and the inventory account.

Walkthrough

When Andrew (see Section 7.2) prepares the trading section of his income statement for the year ended 31 December 2016, the opening inventory will be transferred from the inventory account to the trading section of the income statement:

Journal			
2016		**$**	**$**
Dec 31	Income statement	5 000	
	Inventory		5 000

Inventory account					
2016		**$**	**2016**		**$**
Dec 31	Income statement	5000	Dec 31	Balance c/d	5000
2017			**2017**		
Jan 1	Balance b/d	5000	Dec 31	Income statement	5000

In the year ended 31 December 2016, Andrew's sales totalled $150000 and his purchases were $62000. Inventory at 31 December 2016 was valued at $8000.

Andrew's trading section of the income statement will be as follows:

Andrew
Income statement for the year ended 31 December 2016

	$	**$**
Revenue		150000
Less: cost of sales		
Opening inventory	5000	
Purchases	62000	
	67000	
Less: closing inventory	(8000)	(59000)
Gross profit		91000

Note: In almost every case, inventory shown in a trial balance is opening inventory. The exception occurs when the trial balance has been extracted from the books **after** a trading section of the income statement has been prepared, in which case the trial balance will not include sales, sales returns, purchases or purchases returns accounts.

ACTIVITY 4

The following financial information is available for Khor at 31 December 2015:

	$
Sales	48000
Sales returns	1600
Purchases	21000
Purchases returns	900
Inventory at 1 January 2015	4000
Inventory at 31 December 2015	7500

Prepare Khor's trading section of the income statement for the year ended 31 December 2015.

ACTIVITY 5

The following trial balance has been extracted from the books of Lamar, a sole trader, at 31 March 2016:

	$	$
Premises	60 000	
Plant and machinery	12 000	
Sales		104 000
Sales returns	3 700	
Purchases	59 000	
Purchases returns		2 550
Inventory at 1 April 2015	6 000	
Wages	13 000	
Rent payable	2 000	
Rent receivable		1 800
Heating and lighting	2 700	
Repairs to machinery	4 100	
Interest on loan	750	
Discounts allowed	1 030	
Discounts received		770
Trade receivables	1 624	
Trade payables		1 880
Bank	5 000	
Drawings	10 096	
Long-term loan		15 000
Capital		55 000
	181 000	181 000

Inventory at 31 March 2016 was $10 000.

Prepare Lamar's income statement for the year ended 31 March 2016. (Save your answer; it will be required again in Chapter 8.)

7.4 Carriage inwards and carriage outwards

When goods are purchased, the supplier may make an additional charge to cover the cost of delivery. This charge is **carriage inwards** and adds to the cost of the goods. Carriage inwards is added to the cost of purchases in the trading section of the income statement.

The cost of delivering goods to a customer is **carriage outwards** and is debited in the income statement as an overhead. Carriage inwards and carriage outwards are both expense items but it is important to treat them correctly in income statements.

The treatment of carriage inwards and carriage outwards is illustrated below.

KEY TERMS

Carriage inwards: The additional delivery cost paid by a business in excess of the purchase price of the goods purchased for resale. It is added to the cost of goods by the supplier.

Carriage outwards: The additional cost charged by the seller to deliver goods sold.

Walkthrough

A. Trader

Income statement for the year ended 31 December 2015

	$	$	$
Sales		93 000	
Less: sales returns		(2 700)	90 300
Less: cost of sales			
Inventory at 1 January 2015		3 000	
Purchases	45 200		
Less: purchases returns	(3 400)		
	41 800		
Carriage inwards	4 000	45 800	
		48 800	
Less: inventory at 31 December 2015		(7 000)	(41 800)
Gross profit			48 500
Less: overheads			
Wages		(12 000)	
Rent		(5 600)	
Carriage outwards		(2 220)	
Other operating expenses		(1 760)	(21 580)
Profit for the year			26 920

TOP TIP

Double-check the treatment of carriage inwards and carriage outwards.

ACTIVITY 6

Sara's trial balance at 31 March 2016 was as follows:

Trial balance at 31 March 2016		
Account	**$**	**$**
Sales		40 000
Opening inventory	5 000	
Purchases	20 500	
Wages	6 000	
Rent	10 000	
Electricity	2 600	
Carriage inwards	1 320	
Carriage outwards	1 080	
Other operating expenses	1 250	
Plant and machinery	8 000	
Office equipment	1 000	
Trade receivables	1 900	
Trade payables		800
Bank	820	
Drawings	6 330	
Capital		25 000
	65 800	65 800

Inventory at 31 March 2016 was $3 000.

Prepare Sara's income statement for the year ended 31 March 2016.

7.5 Wages treated as cost of sales

Goods purchased may not be in a suitable condition for selling to customers. Further work may be required on them before they are sold. The wages paid to employees for performing this work should be debited as part of cost of sales in the trading section of the income statement.

Walkthrough

The following balances are extracted from a trial balance at 30 April 2016:

	$	$
Revenue		80 000
Inventory at 1 May 2015	5 000	
Purchases	35 000	
Wages	16 000	

Inventory at 30 April 2016 was $6 000, and 25% of the wages were paid to staff who prepared the goods for sale to customers.

Trading section of the income statement for the year ended 30 April 2016		
	$	$
Revenue		80 000
Cost of sales		
Inventory at 1 May 2015	5 000	
Purchases	35 000	
	40 000	
Less: inventory at 30 April 2016	(6 000)	
	34 000	
Wages (25% of $16 000)	4 000	(38 000)
Gross profit		42 000

You will be told if any of the amounts paid for wages should be entered in the trading section of the income statement. If no instructions are given then always show wages as an expense in the income statement.

TOP TIPS

- Copy the vertical layouts of the accounts given in the examples in this chapter as far as possible.
- Deduct goods taken by the trader for personal use from purchases and add to drawings at cost price.
- Include **carriage inwards** as an addition to purchases in the trading section of the income statement, but **carriage outwards** as an overhead in the income statement.
- Do not prepare journal entries for the income statements unless you are specifically asked to do so. They have been shown in this chapter simply to help you understand how balances are transferred from ledger accounts to the income statements.

Chapter summary

In this chapter you have encountered quite a few complicated topics. You should now fully appreciate the reason why it is important to prepare ledger accounts accurately and why it is crucial to ensure the trial balance is always prepared. In particular, you should now know how to:

- prepare an income statement for a sole trader
- deal with opening and closing inventory when preparing an income statement for a sole trader
- calculate the gross profit for the business (including the treatment of goods taken by a business owner for their own use)
- deal with carriage inwards and carriage outwards when preparing an income statement
- calculate the profit for the year for a business.

Practice exercises

1 The following trial balance has been extracted from Hadlee's books at 31 December 2015:

	$	$
Plant and machinery	25 000	
Office furniture	6 000	
Inventory at 1 January 2015	11 000	
Trade receivables	4 740	
Trade payables		1 976
Bank	3 327	
Loan (repayable in 2020)		5 000
Sales		72 800
Purchases	28 540	
Sales returns	1 600	
Purchases returns		2 144
Wages	3 100	
Rent	4 000	
Heating and lighting	5 120	
Advertising	2 400	
Other operating expenses	2 010	
Loan interest	250	
Drawings	4 833	
Capital		20 000
	101 920	101 920

Inventory at 31 December 2015 cost $9 000.

Required

Prepare Hadlee's income statement for the year ended 31 December 2015. (Keep your answer; it will be needed again in Chapter 8.)

2 The trial balance extracted from Tikolo's books at 31 March 2016 is as follows:

Tikolo Trial balance at 31 March 2016		
	Debit	**Credit**
	$	**$**
Sales		204 000
Sales returns	3 600	
Purchases	120 000	
Purchases returns		4 440
Inventory at 1 April 2015	18 000	
Carriage inwards	5 000	
Carriage outwards	3 724	
Discounts received		3 160
Discounts allowed	5 020	
Wages	36 800	

	Debit	Credit
	$	$
Rent	8000	
Heating and lighting	6450	
Other operating expenses	1143	
Fixtures and fittings	9000	
Office furniture	2000	
Trade receivables	1970	
Trade payables		2130
Bank	2496	
Drawings	20527	
Capital		30000
	243730	243730

During the year, Tikolo had taken goods costing $2000 for his own use. This had not been recorded in the books. Inventory at 31 March 2016 cost $20000.

Required

Prepare Tikolo's income statement for the year ended 31 March 2016. (Keep your answer; it will be needed again in Chapter 8.)

Exam practice questions

Multiple-choice questions

1 Which of the following does not appear in an income statement?

A motor vehicles
B carriage outwards
C discounts allowed
D discounts received

2 The following information has been extracted from the trial balance of a business:

	$
Sales	100000
Purchases	60000
Wages	21000

Closing inventory was $3000 more than opening inventory. One-third of the wages was charged to cost of sales in the trading section of the income statement. What was the gross profit?

A $30000
B $33000
C $36000
D $37000

3 The carriage inwards of a business amounted to $6 000, and the carriage outwards was $7 000. The carriage outwards was charged in the trading section of the income statement in error, and the carriage inwards was debited in the income statement. What has been the effect of these errors?

	Gross profit	Profit for the year
A	understated by $1 000	understated by $1 000
B	overstated by $1 000	overstated by $1 000
C	understated by $1 000	not affected
D	overstated by $1 000	not affected

4 Discounts received amount to $10 500 and discounts allowed to $13 000. The discounts received have been debited, and the discounts allowed have been credited in the income statement. What has been the effect of these errors on profit for the year?

A understated by $2 500
B overstated by $2 500
C understated by $5 000
D overstated by $5 000

5 Carriage inwards in a trial balance is $2 300. It has been entered in the trading section of the income statement as $3 200. In addition, motor expenses of $600 has been posted to the motor vans account. What effect has this had on the income statement?

	Gross profit	Profit for the year
A	understated by $900	understated by $300
B	overstated by $900	overstated by $300
C	understated by $900	overstated by $1 500
D	overstated by $900	understated by $1 500

Total: 5 marks

Chapter 8
Statements of financial position for sole traders

Learning objectives

In this chapter you will learn:

- what a statement of financial position is
- how to close the capital account for a sole trader
- why statements of financial position are prepared
- how to prepare a statement of financial position for a sole trader.

8.1 What is a statement of financial position?

A **statement of financial position** is a list of the assets and liabilities of a business at a particular date. A trader needs to know if his business will continue to provide an income for the business owner and will continue to trade for the foreseeable future. A statement of financial position can provide a good indication of the answer to this question.

Unlike an income statement, a statement of financial position is **not** part of the double-entry model. After the nominal account balances have been transferred to the income statement, the only balances left in the ledger are those for assets and liabilities. The statement of financial position is a list of these balances.

Although a statement of financial position is not an account, the income statement and statement of financial position are known collectively as the **financial statements** of a business. This may also include the statement of cash flow (see Chapter 23). You will find both terms used throughout the book.

8.2 How to prepare a statement of financial position

Before setting out how to prepare a statement of financial position for a sole trader there are some terms which need to be revised. These were covered in Section 5.1, so it may help you to look back at that section as a form of revision.

a **Non-current assets** – these are items which are purchased to use in the business for a long period of time. Certainly longer than the 12-month trading period. They include such things as land and buildings, plant and machinery, motor vehicles and office equipment.

b **Current assets** – these are things which arise in the normal course of business. They include inventory, trade receivables, and cash and bank balances which are usually added together and called 'cash and cash equivalents'.

c **Current liabilities** – included here are the trade payables and, if the bank is overdrawn, the bank overdraft.

d **Non-current liabilities** – these are items which the business has to pay at a date more than 12 months after the end of the trading period.

e **Capital** – this is the owner's interest in the business.

In Section 7.2 the income statement was prepared from the trial balance of Andrew at 31 December 2015. When the income statement had been completed, the revenue and expense accounts were closed by journal entry and their balances transferred to the income statement. This now leaves the following accounts from the trial balance:

Walkthrough

Account	Debit	Credit
	$	$
Premises	40 000	
Motor vans	18 000	
Office furniture	5 000	
Trade receivables	7 400	

KEY TERMS

Statement of financial position: A list of the assets, liabilities, capital and reserves of a business at a particular point in time.

Non-current asset: Items bought by a business which are not for resale. Examples are land and buildings, plant and machinery or motor vehicles.

Current asset: Cash and other assets, typically inventory and trade receivables, that are expected to give rise to cash in the course of trading within 12 months.

Current liability: Those items which the business is due to pay less than 12 months after the date of the statement of financial position.

Non-current liability: An amount owed by a business which is repayable more than 12 months after the date of the statement of financial position.

KEY TERMS

Capital: Initially the amount of money invested in the business by the owner. After the business has been trading for a period, it is adjusted by the profit for the year made by the business less any drawings made by the owner. It is the net amount which the business owes to the owner.

Drawings: The money (or goods) taken from the business by the owner.

Account	Debit	Credit
	$	$
Trade payables		3 420
Bank	2 160	
Loan from Marie (repayable in 2020)		10 000
Andrew – capital		60 000
Drawings	10 920	

There is also the balance of profit for the year from the income statement. This was $15 060. In addition there is closing inventory of $5 000.

Before preparing the statement of financial position for Andrew, it is first necessary to complete Andrew's capital account. This is done by transferring the profit for the year and Andrew's **drawings** into the capital account.

Walkthrough

Andrew – capital account

2015		**$**	**2015**		**$**
Dec 31	Drawings	10 920	Jan 1	Capital introduced	60 000
	Balance carried down	64 140	Dec 31	Income statement	15 060
		75 060			75 060
			2016		
			Jan 1	Balance brought down	64 140

The drawings account is now closed. Notice that as Andrew made a profit for the year, it is credited to his capital account. If he had made a loss for the year this would be debited to his capital account.

It is now possible to prepare Andrew's statement of financial position at 31 December 2015.

Walkthrough

Illustration 1

Andrew
Statement of financial position at 31 December 2015

	Debit	Credit
	$	$
Non-current assets		
Premises		40 000
Motor vans		18 000
Office furniture		5 000
		63 000

	Debit	Credit
	$	$
Current assets		
Inventory	5 000	
Trade receivables	7 400	
Cash and cash equivalents	2 160	
	14 560	
Less: current liabilities		
Trade payables	(3 420)	11 140
		74 140
Less: non-current liabilities		
Loan from Marie		(10 000)
		64 140
Represented by:		
Capital at 1 January 2015		60 000
Add: profit for the year		15 060
		75 060
Deduct: drawings		(10 920)
Capital at 31 December 2015		64 140

As the statement of financial position is not part of the double-entry model, it is possible to set it out in other ways. The other most common approach is as follows:

Illustration 2

Andrew Statement of financial position at 31 December 2015	
	$
Non-current assets	
Premises	40 000
Motor vans	18 000
Office furniture	5 000
	63 000
Current assets	
Inventory	5 000
Trade receivables	7 400
Cash and cash equivalents	2 160
	14 560
Total assets	77 560
Capital and liabilities	
Capital at 1 January 2015	60 000
Add: profit for the year	15 060
	75 060

Andrew Statement of financial position at 31 December 2015	
	$
Deduct: drawings	(10 920)
Capital at 31 December 2015	64 140
Non-current liabilities	
Loan from Marie	10 000
Current liabilities	
Trade payables	3 420
Total liabilities	77 560

Notice that in both cases the capital account is shown in full rather than simply giving the closing balance figure. Good presentation of statements of financial position is key, so it is important to learn the format. You must show that you know under which headings items should be shown, so look at what is included as non-current assets, current assets, current liabilities, non-current liabilities and capital.

A statement of financial position is a 'position' statement showing the position of a business **at a particular moment in time**. It is not a period statement like an income statement. The date at which the statement of financial position is prepared must be included in the heading. Thus the correct heading is:

Name of the business (in this case Andrew)

Statement of financial position **at** 31 December 2015.

TOP TIP

Give every statement of financial position a proper heading which should include the name of the business and the date.

Notes:

- **Non-current assets** These are grouped together and totalled. The assets which are likely to have the longest useful life are placed first.
- **Current assets** These are grouped next and totalled. The order in the statement of financial position is:
  - **i** closing inventory
  - **ii** trade receivables
  - **iii** cash and cash equivalents. This is the total of a debit balance on the bank account and cash (if any).

  The order is sometimes referred to as the **order of liquidity** and the current assets are the most liquid assets of the business. A **liquid asset** is one which is in the form of cash (cash in hand) or nearly so (cash at bank). Inventory is not a liquid asset because it has not been sold and no money has been, or will be, received for it until it is sold. Trade receivables should soon become a liquid asset when they pay the business.

- **Capital** The capital shown in the trial balance is the balance on the capital account brought forward from the previous year. Added to this is the profit for the year shown by the income statement (a loss for the year must be deducted). Profit increases capital and losses reduce capital. The owner's drawings are then deducted. This gives the closing balance on the capital account which will be carried forward as the opening capital next year.
- **Non-current liabilities** These are liabilities, or debts which are not due to be settled within one year of the date of the statement of financial position.
- **Current liabilities** These are liabilities or debts which are due to be settled within one year of the date of the statement of financial position. In illustration 1 they are deducted from the total of current assets to give the **working capital**. In this example, the working capital is \$11 140. This figure is also known as the **net current assets**. If the current liabilities are greater than the current assets then the figure is known as **net current liabilities**.

TOP TIP

Try to remember the order of liquidity. However, it is more important that you know what should be in current assets than the order in which they should be listed.

Working capital is a very important item. The liquid current assets should exceed the current liabilities and show that the business resources adequately cover the payments it must make to its creditors. If the current assets are insufficient to meet the current liabilities, the trader may be forced to sell non-current assets to pay his creditors and that could be the beginning of the end of the business.

KEY TERM

Accounting equation: Assets – liabilities = capital.

The total of the non-current and current assets \$(63 000 + 14 560 = 77 560), less the total of the current and non-current liabilities \$(3 420 + 10 000 = 13 420), equals the closing balance on the capital account, \$64 140. This is always true, and the formula 'assets – liabilities = capital' is known as the **accounting equation** or **statement of financial position equation**. If the total of the non-current and current assets is greater than the total of the non-current and current liabilities, this is known as the **net assets** of the business.

All that now remains to complete the accounts for the year is to close all the accounts (other than the capital account) whose balances appear in the statement of financial position. The balances on each of those accounts is transferred to the start of the new financial year in a manner similar to the way in which the capital account was closed.

The premises account is shown by way of an example. How to balance an account was covered in Chapter 4. It may be useful to refer back to that chapter to see how accounts are closed and the balances brought forward to the start of the new accounting period.

Walkthrough

Premises account

2015		**\$**	**2015**		**\$**
Jan 1	Balance b/d	40 000	Dec 31	Balance c/d	40 000
2016					
Jan 1	Balance b/d	40 000			

As there is only one entry in the account it is quite acceptable to rule it off in the way shown above.

Chapter summary

In this chapter you have learnt what a statement of financial position is, why they are prepared, and how to prepare a statement of financial position for a sole trader.

TOP TIP

The source of information for the preparation of a statement of financial position is the trial balance (with the exception of the closing inventory). Pay particular attention to the headings and format of the statement.

You should now understand the way in which the owner's capital account is closed and how to carry down the balance to the next account period. Similarly, you should also be able to follow the same process for the remaining ledger accounts.

Practice exercises

1 Prepare a statement of financial position at 31 December 2015 for Sofia from the trial balance given in Activity 3 of Chapter 7.

2 Prepare a statement of financial position at 31 March 2016 for Lamar from the trial balance given in Activity 5 of Chapter 7.

3 Prepare the statement of financial position at 31 December 2015 for Hadlee from the trial balance given in Practice exercise 1 in Chapter 7.

4 Prepare the statement of financial position at 31 March 2016 for Tikolo from the trial balance given in Practice exercise 2 in Chapter 7.

TOP TIP

Prepare statements of financial position as shown in this chapter, with headings for non-current assets, current assets, current liabilities and non-current liabilities. Show the total of each group.

Exam practice questions

Multiple-choice questions

1 The purchase of an office computer has been debited to office expenses instead of to office equipment. What row will show the effect this will have on the statement of financial position?

	Non-current assets	Profit for the year	Capital
A	no effect	understated	no effect
B	no effect	understated	understated
C	understated	no effect	understated
D	understated	understated	no effect

2 The owner of a business has taken goods for her own use but no entry has been made in the books to record this. What row will show the effect of this on the statement of financial position?

	Inventory	Capital
A	no effect	no effect
B	no effect	overstated
C	overstated	no effect
D	overstated	overstated

3 The following information has been extracted from a statement of financial position at 31 December 2015.

	$
Non-current assets	310 000
Working capital	30 000
Long-term loan	20 000
Profit for the year	35 000
Drawings	25 000

What was the balance on the capital account at 31 December 2015?

A $300 000
B $320 000
C $340 000
D $350 000

4 Which of the following statements is **not** correct?

A assets = liabilities + capital
B capital = assets – liabilities
C capital – liabilities = assets
D liabilities = assets – capital

Total: 4 marks

Chapter 9
Accounting principles or concepts

Learning objectives

In this chapter you will learn:

- why it is necessary to have generally accepted rules for accounting
- the most important rules and what they aim to achieve.

9.1 Accounting principles or concepts

Accounting principles are basic rules that are applied in recording transactions and preparing financial statements. They are also known as concepts. These rules are necessary to ensure that accounting records provide reliable information. All businesses should apply the rules in their financial statements. The most important of these rules are now described, and should be learnt, understood and applied when preparing financial statements.

KEY TERMS

Accounting principles: Basic rules that are applied in recording transactions and preparing financial statements. They are also known as concepts.

Duality: This recognises that there are two aspects for each transaction – represented by debit and credit entries in accounts.

9.2 Duality

This is the first concept you came across at the start of the book. The concept of **duality** recognises that there are two aspects for each transaction – represented by debit and credit entries in accounts. The concept is the basis of the accounting equation which was covered in Section 8.2:

assets – liabilities = capital

The equation is also expressed in its other form: assets = capital + liabilities. As we saw, statements of financial position are prepared in this form.

The accounting equation is a very useful tool for solving some accounting problems.

9.3 Business entity

Every business is regarded as having an existence separate from that of its owner. This is recognised when an owner's capital is debited in the business bank account and credited to the owner's capital account. The credit in the capital account shows that the owner is a creditor of the business, which owes him the money. This can only be the case if the business is regarded as being separate from the owner as no one can owe himself money. When the owner withdraws money from the business, the amount is debited to his drawings account. The business accounts do not show if he or she spends the money on food, clothes or holidays because these are not business transactions.

It is essential that this happens. If the owner charged the cost of their summer holiday to the business as an expense then:

- the expenses in the income statement will be overstated
- the business accounts will not show the true profit made by the business
- the business owner is committing fraud
- if someone calculates the performance of the business by, say, comparing the profit for the year as a percentage of the business sales, then what they have calculated will be meaningless; it will not indicate if the business performance has improved year on year
- it will be impossible to determine the true financial status of the business.

(It is important to remember that this is only an accounting concept. Anyone who has a grievance against a business may legally sue a sole trader or a partner in a firm. The business is not a separate entity for that purpose.)

9.4 Money measurement

Only transactions that can be expressed in monetary terms are recorded in ledger accounts. Goods, non-current assets, trade receivables and expenses may be recorded in ledger accounts because they have resulted from transactions that can be expressed in monetary terms.

Although there are obvious advantages in being able to record things in monetary terms, it has disadvantages. Things which cannot be expressed in monetary terms, such as the skills of workers or their satisfaction with their working conditions, are not recorded in the accounts. Some people think it would be useful if these and some other 'non-monetary' items could be included in financial statements.

KEY TERMS

Historic cost: Transactions are recorded at their cost to the business.

Realisation: Revenue is recognised or accounted for by the seller when it is earned whether cash has been received from the transaction or not.

Goods on sale or return: This is not a principle or concept but a very important point in relation to ownership of goods relating to a transaction. When a trader sends goods on sale or return to a customer, no sale takes place until the customer informs the seller that he has decided to buy them.

9.5 Historic cost

Transactions are recorded at their cost to the business. Cost cannot be disputed as invoices or other documentary evidence may be produced to support it. Recording transactions in this way is said to be objective because it is based on fact and not on opinion.

The opposite of objectivity is subjectivity, which is based upon personal opinion. For example, somebody may give his friend a watch that cost $50. The friend may already have a good watch or perhaps several watches. He would not have paid $50 for another. He would probably value the gift at less than $50. On the other hand, if the friend had great need of a watch, he might value the watch at much more than $50. Values based on personal opinions are said to be subjective and are not reliable bases on which to record transactions.

While the principle of recording transactions at their **historic cost** has obvious advantages, it has two disadvantages:

- It ignores the changing value of money. An item that was purchased five years ago for $100 might have been sold then for $200 making a profit of $100. If inflation since then has been 25%, today's selling price would be $250 giving an apparent profit of $150. A more realistic calculation of the profit would be to express the original cost at today's prices, $125, giving a profit of $125, which would be enough to buy no more than $100 would have bought five years ago! Historic cost may produce misleading results unless its limitations are understood.
- Like the concept of money measurement, historic cost does not allow things that cannot be expressed in monetary terms to be recorded in accounting.

9.6 Realisation

When accountants speak of **realisation**, they mean that something becomes an actual fact, or that something has been converted into money. For example, if a man goes into a shop and says that he will return tomorrow and buy a pair of shoes, there is no sale yet; but if the man returns the next day and buys the shoes, the sale has become a fact. By selling the shoes, the shopkeeper has converted goods into money. The sale has been **realised**. Transactions are realised when cash or a debtor replaces goods or services. This principle is important as it prevents revenue from being credited in the accounts before it has been earned.

Goods on sale or return

When a trader sends **goods on sale or return** to a customer, no sale takes place until the customer informs the seller that he has decided to buy them. The customer has the right to return the goods to the trader. For example, Maria runs a small shop by the sea. One of the things she sells is postcards. Roberto supplies the postcards to Maria on a sale or return basis. Each month, Roberto visits Maria's shop and checks the inventory of postcards from his records and calculates how many cards Maria has sold. He then invoices Maria's business for the cards she has sold and replaces them with new items. The goods remain the property of Roberto until the sale actually takes place. Goods held by Maria on sale or return must **never** be treated as Maria's inventory when her financial statements are being prepared. If they are then Maria's inventory in her financial statements will be incorrect. Her profit for the year will be overstated and her inventory figure in the statement of financial position will also be overstated. Wrong treatment such as this must be reversed.

Similarly, in Roberto's accounts, he must not treat the postcards in Maria's shop as sales. Until Maria actually sells them he can't invoice her for them. In Roberto's finacial statements the items in Maria's shop are included in his closing inventory at cost. If Roberto does treat them as goods sold rather than inventory, then his profit for the year will be overstated and his inventory in his statement of financial position will be understated.

Walkthrough

George has sent goods on sale or return to Helen for $500 and treated the transaction as a sale. Helen has not yet accepted the goods. The goods cost George $350. The following balances have been extracted from George's trial balance: sales $30 000; trade receivables $1 000. Inventory on hand has been valued at $900. The following adjustments must be made for the financial statements.

Sales		Trade receivables		Inventory	
	$		$		$
Per trial balance	30 000	Per trial balance	1 000	As given	900
Less:	(500)	Less:	(500)	Add:	350
Trading section of the income statement	29 500	Statement of financial position	500	Statement of financial position	1 250

9.7 Consistency

Transactions of a similar nature should be recorded in the same way (that is, consistently) in the same accounting period and in all future accounting periods. For example, the cost of redecorating premises should always be debited to an expense account for the redecoration of premises and charged to the income statement. It would not be correct the next time that the offices are redecorated to debit the cost to the premises (non-current assets) account.

Consistency in the treatment of transactions is important to ensure that the profits or losses of different periods, and statements of financial position, may be compared meaningfully.

> **KEY TERM**
>
> **Consistency:** Transactions of a similar nature should be recorded in the same way (that is, consistently) in the same accounting period and in all future accounting periods.

9.8 Materiality

Sometimes a business may depart from the generally accepted principles for recording some transactions. They may do this when the amounts involved are not considered **material** (or significant) in relation to the amounts of the other items in their income statements and statements of financial position.

A company may prepare its statement of financial position showing all amounts rounded to the nearest $000 or even $m. It would treat the purchase of any asset not exceeding, say, $1 000 as revenue expenditure instead of adding it to its non-current assets, as it would not make any noticeable difference to the figure of non-current assets in the statement of financial position. It would not be considered a material item.

On the other hand, the same amount of expenditure in a small business may be very significant and would need to be treated as capital expenditure in order not to distort profit and the assets in the statement of financial position.

An amount may be considered material in the accounts if its inclusion in, or omission from, the income statement or statement of financial position would affect the way people would read and interpret those financial statements. However, as different organisations have different rules on what is regarded as material, it is a subjective concept. For example, Andy, who is a window cleaner, buys new ladders costing $400. He may well treat these as a non-current asset and show them on his statement of financial position. On the other hand, a large company will probably regard the purchase of the ladders as an expense and include it in the income statement.

9.9 Matching

If the financial statements of a business are to give reliable information, the revenue and other income must be no more and no less than the business has earned in the period covered by the income statement. The expenses in the income statement should fairly represent the expenses incurred in earning that revenue. The difference between an income statement prepared on a cash basis and one prepared on a matching basis will be apparent from the following example.

Walkthrough

A business occupies premises at an annual rental of $2 000. In one year it has paid $2 500 because it has paid one quarter's rent in advance. It has also used $2 100 worth of electricity but it has paid only $1 200 because it has not paid the latest bill for $900. Its gross profit for the year is $10 000.

Income statements prepared on (a) a 'cash basis', that is, on the actual payments made, and (b) on a matching basis, would look as follows:

	Cash basis		Matching basis	
	$	$	$	$
Gross profit		10 000		10 000
Less: rent	(2 500)		(2 000)	
Electricity	(1 200)	(3 700)	(2 100)	(4 100)
Profit of the year		6 300		5 900

The matching basis is the correct one as it records the actual costs incurred in the period for rent and electricity.

Income statements should be prepared on the **matching** basis so that expenses are matched to the revenue earned; that is, expenses should be shown in the income statement as they have been **incurred** rather than as they have been paid.

KEY TERM

Prudence: This principle is sometimes known as the concept of conservation. The correct procedure is that profits should not be overstated and losses should be provided for as soon as they are recognised.

9.10 Prudence

The **prudence** concept is intended to prevent profit from being overstated. If profit is overstated, a trader may believe that his income is more than it really is, and he may withdraw too much money from the business. That would lead to the capital invested in the business being depleted. If it happens too often the business will collapse because there will not be enough money to pay creditors or to renew assets when they are worn out. The principle is sometimes known as the **concept of conservation**. It is safer for profit to be understated rather than overstated.

The correct procedure is:

- profits should not be overstated
- losses should be provided for as soon as they are recognised.

TOP TIP

Students often make the mistake of saying that the prudence concept means that profits must be understated. That is not so; the concept is meant to ensure that profits are realistic without being overstated.

9.11 Going concern

A business is a **going concern** if there is no intention to discontinue it in the foreseeable future. If it is short of working capital and the owner is unable to put more money into it, or to find somebody who will be prepared to lend it money, it may be unable to pay its creditors and be forced to close.

Unless stated to the contrary, it is assumed that the accounts of a business are prepared on a going concern basis. If the business is not a going concern, the assets should be valued in the statement of financial position at the amounts they could be expected to fetch in an enforced sale, which could be much less than their real worth. Statements of financial position should always show a realistic situation, bearing in mind the weakness of the business. This will be considered again in Chapters 11 and 24.

9.12 Substance over form

These words are used to describe the accounting treatment of something that does not reflect the legal position.

For example, a machine bought on hire purchase remains the property of the seller until the final instalment has been paid. If the purchaser fails to pay the instalments as they become due, the seller may reclaim the machine. That is the legal position, or the 'form'.

However, the machine is being used in the purchaser's business in the same way as the other machines that have not been bought on hire purchase. From an accounting point of view and for all practical purposes, the machine is no different from the other machines; that is the 'substance' of the matter.

The practical view (the substance) is preferred to the legal view (the form) in the accounting treatment. This is known as **substance over form**.

Walkthrough

Antonio bought a machine on hire purchase on 1 January 2015. The cash price of the machine was \$50 000. Antonio paid \$10 000 on 1 January 2015. The balance was to be settled by four payments of \$10 100 (including interest of \$100) on 1 April 2015, 1 July 2015, 1 October 2015 and 1 January 2016. The following entries should appear in Antonio's financial statements at 31 December 2015:

Income statement: interest on hire purchase \$400

Statement of financial position: non-current assets \$50 000 (the cash price although only \$40 000 has been paid)

current liabilities \$10 000 (the final instalment) not paid until 1 January 2016.

KEY TERMS

Going concern: When there is no intention to discontinue a business in the foreseeable future. Unless stated to the contrary, it is assumed that the accounts of a business are prepared on a going concern basis.

Substance over form: When deciding how or whether a transaction is recorded, this principle or concept states that the economic substance of the transaction must be recorded in the financial statements rather than its legal form. This is done to present a true and fair view of the affairs of the business.

Chapter summary

In this chapter you have learnt why it is important to have generally accepted rules for accounting, and the most important accounting principles and concepts and what they aim to achieve. Simply put, these are the rules that are applied when recording transactions and financial statements, and include:

- duality
- business entity
- money measurement
- historic cost
- realisation
- consistency
- materiality
- matching
- prudence
- going concern
- substance over form.

Exam practice questions

Multiple-choice questions

1 A trader who sells food does not include food that is past its sell-by date in his inventory in the statement of financial position. Which concept has he applied in valuing his inventory?

A matching
B prudence
C realisation
D going concern

2 A business is about to be closed down as it has insufficient funds to pay its trade payables. The owner places a very low value on his inventory in the statement of financial position. Which concept is being applied?

A going concern
B materiality
C money measurement
D prudence

3 The owner of a business paid her private telephone bill from the business bank account. The amount was debited to her drawings account. Which concept was applied?

A business entity
B matching
C prudence
D realisation

4 A trader has included rent which is due but not paid in his income statement. Which accounting concept has been applied?

A historic cost
B matching
C money measurement
D prudence

5 The balances in a sales ledger total $16 000. A customer who owes $800 is known to be in financial difficulty. The figure of trade receivables shown in the statement of financial position is $15 200. Which concept has been applied?

A matching
B prudence
C realisation
D substance over form

6 A trader sends goods on sale or return to a customer. When the trader prepares her statement of financial position at 31 March 2016, the customer has still not indicated that she has accepted the goods. Which concept should the trader apply when she prepares her accounts at 31 March 2016?

A consistency
B matching
C prudence
D realisation

Total: 6 marks

Chapter 10
Accruals and prepayments (the matching concept)

Learning objectives

In this chapter you will learn:

- the practical application of the matching principle
- how to record accruals and prepayments in ledger accounts
- how to adjust trial balances for accruals and prepayments
- the effect of accruals and prepayments on the expenses and income recorded in the income statement
- how to show accruals and prepayments in the statement of financial position
- how to account for inventories of consumables in both the ledger and statement of financial position.

10.1 What are accruals and prepayments?

Accruals are expenses that have been incurred but not paid for. For example, an unpaid electricity bill is an accrued expense; the electricity has been consumed (the cost has been incurred), but not paid for.

Prepayments are payments made in advance of the benefits to be derived from them. Rent is an example because it usually has to be paid in advance.

KEY TERMS

Accrual: An expense which is due within the accounting period but which has not yet been paid. When preparing the statement of financial position these are collectively known as other payables.

Prepayment: Payments made by a business in advance of the benefits to be derived from them. When preparing the statement of financial position these are collectively known as other receivables.

10.2 How to treat an accrued expense in an account

An accrued expense is an amount that is owed to somebody; that somebody is a creditor. The creditor must be represented in the expense account by a credit balance carried down on the account.

Walkthrough

The accounting year of a business ended on 31 December 2015. In the 11 months ended 30 November 2015, bank payments for electricity amounted to $900. At 31 December 2015 there was an unpaid electricity bill for $130. That amount is carried down on the account as a credit balance. The electricity account is prepared as follows:

Electricity account

2015		$	2015		$
Jan–Nov	Bank [1]	900	Dec 31	Income statement	1 030
Dec 31	Electricity owing c/d	130			
		1 030			1 030
			2016		
			Jan 1	Balance b/d [2]	130

[1] Only $900 has been paid. However, the income statement will be debited with $1 030, the full cost of electricity for the year.

[2] The balance b/d will be shown in the statement of financial position under current liabilities as an 'accrued expense', as an 'expense creditor' or 'other payables' to distinguish it from trade payables.

10.3 How to treat a prepaid expense in an account

The person to whom a payment has been made in advance is a **debtor** of the business (someone who owes the business money). The debtor is represented on the expense account by a debit balance carried down.

Walkthrough

Yousif occupies premises at a rental of $2 000 per annum, the rent being payable in advance on 1 January, 1 April, 1 July and 1 October. In 2015, Yousif paid the rent on each of those dates, but on 31 December he paid the rent due on 1 January 2016.

At 31 December, the landlord is a debtor for the amount of the prepayment. At 31 December, he owes Yousif the rent for those months which Yousif has paid in advance.

Rent payable account					
2015		**$**	**2015**		**$**
Jan 1	Bank [1]	500	Dec 31	Income statement	2 000
Apr 1	Bank [1]	500			
Jul 1	Bank [1]	500	Dec 31	Rent paid in advance c/d [2]	500
Oct 1	Bank [1]	500			
Dec 31	Bank [1]	500			
		2 500			2 500
2016					
Jan 1	Balance b/d [2]	500			

[1] Payments during the year amount to $2 500, but the income statement has been debited with the rent for one year only.

[2] The debtor (the landlord) is represented by the debit balance on the account.

The debit balance will be included in the statement of financial position under current assets as a prepayment or 'other receivables' to distinguish it from trade receivables.

ACTIVITY 1

During the year ended 31 December 2015, Alexander had paid $1 450 for telephone calls by cheque. At 31 December 2015, he owed $360 for calls. He had also paid $2 000 for the rental of the telephone line by cheque. This covered the period from 1 January 2015 to 31 March 2016.

a Prepare Alexander's telephone account for the year ended 31 December 2015.

b State the total telephone expense for Alexander for the year ended 31 December 2015.

c State how the balances carried down on the account are treated in the statement of financial position at 31 December 2015.

10.4 How to record inventory of stores on expense accounts

Some expense accounts represent inventories of consumable stores. Examples are stationery, heating fuel and fuel for motor vehicles. Inventories of consumable stores may be unused at the year-end. According to the matching concept, these inventories should not be charged against the profit for the year; they are an asset and not an expense at the year-end. Carry them down as a debit balance on the account. This may result in an expense account having debit and credit balances at the year-end.

In the statement of financial position, the inventories of unused consumable stores will appear under current assets. They should be shown under their own headings of, say, inventory of unused stationery. They should never be included with the closing trading inventory in the income statement, or inventory of goods for resale in the statement of financial position.

Walkthrough

In the year ended 31 December 2015, Prospero had paid $1 200 for stationery. At 31 December 2015, he owed $270 for stationery and had an inventory of unused stationery which had cost $400.

Stationery account

2015		**$**	**2015**		**$**
Jan 1			Dec 31	Income statement	1 070
Dec 31	Bank	1 200			
Dec 31	Amount owing c/d [1]	270	Dec 31	Inventory c/d [2]	400
		1 470			1 470
2016			**2016**		
Jan 1	Inventory b/d [2]	400	Jan 1	Balance b/d [1]	270

[1] The amount owing at 31 December 2015 is carried down to 1 January 2016.

[2] The inventory of unused stationery is carried down in the same way.

In the statement of financial position at 31 December 2015, the inventory of unused stationery, $400, will be shown under current assets as inventory of stationery. The amount owing of $270 will be shown as 'other payables' under current liabilities.

10.5 How to adjust income for accruals and prepayments

Some income accounts, such as rents or interest receivable, may need to be adjusted for income received in advance or in arrears. Income received in advance of its due date indicates the existence of a creditor (trade or other payable) and requires a credit balance equal to the prepayment to be carried down on the account. Income accrued at the date it is due indicates the existence of a debtor (trade or other receivable) and a debit balance equal to the amount should be carried down on the account.

Walkthrough

In the year ended 31 January 2016, Smriti had received $500 for rent from a tenant and $160 for interest on a loan. At that date, the rent prepaid amounted to $100, and $40 interest was due from the borrower. The entries in the rent receivable and interest receivable accounts at 31 January 2016 are as follows:

Rent receivable account

2016		**$**	**2016**		**$**
Jan 31	Income statement	400	Jan 31	Bank	500
Jan 31	Rent prepaid c/d	100			
		500			500
			Feb 1	Balance b/d	100

Interest receivable account

2016		$	2016		$
Jan 31	Income statement	200	Jan 31	Bank	160
			Jan 31	Interest accrued c/d	40
		200			200
Feb 1	Balance b/d	40			

ACTIVITY 2

In the year ended 31 December 2015, Alex made the following payments: rent $1 000; electricity $630; stationery $420. In addition he had received $300 rent from a tenant.

At 31 December 2015, Alex had prepaid rent of $200. Accrued expenses were electricity $180 and stationery $130. The inventory of stationery was $140. The tenant owed rent of $100.

Required

Show how the accounts concerned will appear in Alex's books of account after the adjustments for accruals and prepayments have been made. Show clearly the amounts to be transferred to the income statement.

10.6 How to adjust a trial balance for accruals and prepayments

You will often come across trial balances that have to be adjusted for accruals and prepayments. A reliable technique to deal with this situation is important for success. The workings should be shown. Two methods are suggested here. You should try both methods, decide which one you prefer and stick to it.

Walkthrough

Extract from a trial balance

The following is an extract from a trial balance at 31 December 2015:

	$	$
Rent payable	2 400	
Heating and lighting	1 860	
Stationery	1 100	
Interest receivable		600
Rent receivable		1 200

The following amounts were owing at 31 December 2015: heating and lighting $290; stationery $100. Rent receivable of $200 had been received in advance.

At 31 December 2015, rent payable of $400 had been paid in advance; interest receivable of $120 was due but had not been received.

There was an unused inventory of stationery, $230, at 31 December 2015.

Method 1 Adjust the items in the trial balance in the question. Make lists of the debtors (trade receivables) and creditors (trade payables) you create. Insert inventory of stationery in the trial balance. (The adjustments are shown in *italics*.)

Show your workings with your answer.

			Other receivables	Other payables
	$	$	$	$
Rent payable	2400 – *400*		*400*	
Heating and lighting	1860 + *290*			290
Stationery	1100 + *100* – *230*			100
Inventory of stationery shown under current assets	*230*			
Interest receivable		600 + *120*	*120*	
Rent receivable		1200 – *200*		*200*
			520	*590*

The total of $520 will be shown in the statement of financial position as other receivables in current assets. The total of $590 will be shown as other payables under current liabilities.

Method 2 Delete the items on the trial balance after cross-referencing them to calculations shown as workings with your answer (Inc. st. – income statement).

W1 Rent payable	$	**W2 Heat and light**	$	**W3 Stationery**	$
Per trial balance	2400	Per trial balance	1860	Per trial balance	1100
Less: prepaid	(400)*	Add: owing	290**	Add: owing	100**
Inc. st.	2000	Inc. st.	2150	Less: inventory	(230)
				Inc. st.	970

W4 Interest receivable	$	**W5 Rent receivable**	$
Per trial balance	600	Per trial balance	1200
Add: due	120*	Less: prepaid	(200)**
Inc. st.	720	Inc. st.	1000

- Items marked * will be listed as debit balances and shown as other receivables under current assets as in method 1.
- Items marked ** will be listed as credit balances and shown as other payables under current liabilities as in method 1.

ACTIVITY 3

Devram extracted a trial balance at 31 December 2015 from his books after he had prepared the trading account section of his income statement for the year ended on that date. It was as follows:

	$	$
Non-current assets	40000	
Inventory at 31 December 2015	7000	
Trade receivables	1600	

Trade payables		1 400
Bank	2 524	
Long-term loan		10 000
Gross profit		30 000
Rent	2 600	
Electricity	926	
Stationery	405	
Motor expenses	725	
Interest on loan	500	
Drawings	5 120	
Capital		20 000
	61 400	61 400

Additional information

1 At 31 December 2015, rent had been prepaid in the sum of $300.

2 The following amounts were owing at 31 December 2015: electricity $242; stationery $84; motor expenses $160.

3 The long-term loan was made to the business on 1 January 2015. Interest at the rate of 10% per annum is payable on the loan.

4 The inventory of unused stationery on hand at 31 December 2015 was valued at cost: $100.

Required

a Prepare Devrams's income statement for the year ended 31 December 2015.

b Prepare the statement of financial position at 31 December 2015.

Note: Inventory shown in the trial balance is the closing inventory.

This is quite a complicated topic and one which can sometimes cause problems for students.

Whichever method you use:

- Read questions carefully before starting to answer them. Note any adjustments required for accruals and prepayments.
- Calculate adjustments carefully and **show your workings**.
- Take care to complete the double entry for each adjustment you make to the trial balance.
- As you make each adjustment, tick the item. Before starting to copy out the answer, check that all adjustments have been ticked.
- The following table summarises the treatment of accruals and prepayments:

Item	Treatment in income statement	Treatment in statement of financial position
Accrued expense	Add to expense amount in the trial balance It has the effect of increasing the total expense	Show as other payable under current liabilities

Item	Treatment in income statement	Treatment in statement of financial position
Prepaid expense	Deduct from expense amount in the trial balance It has the effect of reducing the total expense	Show as other receivable under current assets
Accrued income This might be, say, where you are owed rent by someone who rents your premises from you but hasn't paid at the year-end	Add to the income amount in the trial balance	Show as other receivable under current assets
Prepaid income Perhaps a tenant has paid you in advance at the end of the year	Deduct from the income amount in the trial balance	Show as other payable under current liabilities

Chapter summary

In this chapter you have learnt about the accounting treatment of accruals (amounts owing but unpaid at the end of a trading period), prepayments (amounts paid in advance at the end of an accounting period), and inventories of stores such as stationery.

You should be familiar with one of the two methods for adjusting a trial balance to ensure the correct amounts are shown in the income statement and statement of financial position.

TOP TIP

When focusing on this topic, you may be asked to prepare the ledger account for an item of expenditure or income, as was demonstrated in Section 10.2. However, when you are asked to prepare financial statements for any type of organisation, be it a sole trader from incomplete records (see Chapter 16), or a partnership (see Chapters 17 and 18), or limited companies (see Chapters 21 and 22), there will be adjustments to make for accruals and prepayments. Thus it is essential that you have a sound knowledge of how to deal with them in the financial statements. The practice exercises below (Antonia and Desmond) will give you a chance to practise and test your knowledge.

Practice exercises

1 Antonia's trial balance at 31 December 2015 was as follows:

	$	$
Sales		120 000
Purchases	62 400	
Sales returns	7 300	
Purchases returns		4 190
Wages	17 310	
Rent	3 200	

(cont.)

	$	$
Heating and lighting	2 772	
Motor expenses	1 284	
Interest on loan	500	
Inventory	5 660	
Trade receivables	12 440	
Trade payables		6 167
Bank	5 055	
Loan		10 000
Premises	24 000	
Motor vehicles	7 400	
Drawings	7 036	
Capital		16 000
	156 357	156 357

Additional information

1 Inventory at 31 December 2015 was valued at $8 000.

2 The loan was received on 1 April 2015 and is repayable in 2018. Interest is charged at 10% per annum.

3 Expenses owing at 31 December 2015 were as follows:

	$
Wages	558
Heating and lighting	328

4 Rent in the sum of $800 was prepaid at 31 December 2015.

Required

a State **two** accounting concepts a business applies when preparing an income statement and statement of financial position.

b Prepare the income statement for the year ended 31 December 2015.

c Prepare the statement of financial position at 31 December 2015.

d Explain how Antonia should show the loan received on 1 April in her statement of financial position at 31 December 2015.

2 Desmond's trial balance at 31 March 2016 was as follows:

	$	$
Plant and machinery	36 000	
Motor vehicles	17 000	
Inventory	9 000	
Trade receivables	7 060	
Bank	5 400	
Trade payables		3 950
Capital		70 000
Drawings	22 088	
Sales		219 740

	$	$
Purchases	100 100	
Sales returns	17 420	
Purchases returns		8 777
Wages	67 000	
Rent payable	8 000	
Rent receivable		2 600
Interest receivable		840
Discounts allowed	2 826	
Discounts received		1 040
Carriage inwards	5 170	
Carriage outwards	7 920	
Stationery and other sundry expenses	1 963	
	306 947	306 947

Additional information

1 Inventory at 31 March 2016 was valued at $11 000.

2 Expenses owing at 31 March 2016 were: rent payable $2 000; carriage inwards $330; carriage outwards $280.

3 Other operating expenses of $200 had been paid in advance; interest receivable of $160 had accrued.

4 At 31 March 2016, rent receivable of $200 had been received in advance.

5 At 31 March 2016 there was unused inventory of stationery valued at $120.

Required

a Prepare Desmond's income statement for the year ended 31 March 2016.

b Prepare the statement of financial position at 31 March 2016.

c Explain the difference between carriage inwards and carriage outwards.

3 Joe runs a shop. At 1 January 2015, he had prepaid rent of $2 000 brought forwards, and accrued electricity of $150 brought forward. During the year ended 31 December 2015, Joe made the following cheque payments:

1 Rent – four payments of $2 500 each. These covered the period from 1 April 2015 to 31 March 2016.

2 Electricity – three payments totalling $1 800. On 3 February 2016, Joe received an electricity invoice for $480. This covered the period from 1 November 2015 to 31 January 2016.

Required

a Explain why a business must take into account accrued and prepaid expenses when preparing its annual financial statements.

b Prepare the following accounts for the year ended 31 December 2015 and bring down the balances in each case:

i Rent

ii Electricity

Exam practice questions

Multiple-choice questions

1 A trader prepares his accounts annually to 30 April. He pays annual rent of $12 000 and makes the payments quarterly in advance on 1 January, 1 April, 1 July and 1 October. Which amount should be included in his accounts for the year ended 30 April 2016?

A $1 000 accrual
B $1 000 prepayment
C $2 000 accrual
D $2 000 prepayment

2 A trader commenced business on 1 February 2015. He paid rent on his premises as follows:

Date	Period covered	Amount
1 Feb 2015	1 Feb to 31 Mar	$1 200
1 Apr 2015	1 Apr to 30 Jun	$1 800
1 Jul 2015	1 Jul to 31 Sept	$1 800
1 Oct 2015	1 Oct to 31 Dec	$2 100
1 Jan 2016	1 Jan to 31 Mar	$2 100

Which amount for rent should be shown in the income statement for the year ended 31 January 2016?

A $6 900 **B** $7 600
C $7 800 **D** $9 000

3 A business has an accounting year that ends on 30 September. Its insurance payments are made in advance on 1 July each year. Payments have been made in the past three years as follows:

	$
Year 1	1 800
Year 2	2 000
Year 3	2 400

How much will be debited in the income statement for insurance in year 3?

A $2 000
B $2 100
C $2 300
D $2 400

4 The accounts of a business have been prepared, but no adjustments have been made for accrued expenses at the end of the year. What effect will these omissions have on the accounts?

	Profit for the year	Current assets	Current liabilities
A	overstated	no effect	understated
B	understated	no effect	overstated
C	overstated	understated	no effect
D	understated	overstated	no effect

Total: 4 marks

Chapter 11
Provisions for the depreciation of non-current assets

Learning objectives

In this chapter you will learn:

- what depreciation is and why it must be provided for in accounts
- how to calculate it by the straight-line and reducing-balance methods
- how to calculate depreciation using the revaluation method
- how to account for the disposal of non-current assets
- the accounting concepts which apply to depreciation.

Until the machinery is sold, the balance on this account will be transferred to the next year. Set out below is the provision for depreciation of machinery account:

Provision for depreciation of machinery account

		$			$
Year 1	Balance c/d	3 000	Year 1	Income statement	3 000 [1]
Year 2	Balance c/d	6 000 [2]	Year 2	Balance b/d	3 000
				Income statement	3 000 [1]
		6 000			6 000
Year 3	Balance c/d	9 000 [2]	Year 3	Balance b/d	6 000
				Income statement	3 000 [1]
		9 000			9 000
Year 4	Balance c/d	12 000 [2]	Year 4	Balance b/d	9 000
				Income statement	3 000 [1]
		12 000			12 000
Year 5	Balance c/d	15 000 [2]	Year 5	Balance b/d	12 000
				Income statement	3 000 [1]
		15 000			15 000

[2] The balance is then carried down to the next year.

[1] Each year this account is credited with the annual charge for depreciation ($3 000).

There are some key points here which need to be understood and remembered:

- The non-current asset account continues to show the machine at cost each year of its life. Non-current asset accounts sometimes include the words '**at cost**' in their titles to emphasise this point.
- The balance on the provision for depreciation of machinery account increases or accumulates each year.
- A **provision** in accounting is an amount set aside for a particular purpose.
- A separate provision for depreciation account must be opened for each **class** of non-current asset, such as plant and machinery, motor vehicles and so on.

In the statement of financial position, the balance on the provision for depreciation account is deducted from the cost of the non-current asset as shown below:

Non-current assets

Machinery	Cost	Accumulated depreciation	Net book value
	$	$	$
Year 1: Machinery	20 000	(3 000)	17 000
Year 2: Machinery	20 000	(6 000)	14 000
Year 3: Machinery	20 000	(9 000)	11 000
Year 4: Machinery	20 000	(12 000)	8 000
Year 5: Machinery	20 000	(15 000)	5 000

KEY TERM

Net book value / written-down value: The cost of a non-current asset minus the accumulated depreciation.

The balance remaining after depreciation has been deducted from cost is known as the **net book value** (NBV), or **written-down value** (WDV), of the asset. It is the amount of the cost of the asset which has not yet been charged as an expense against profit in the income statement.

The net book values of assets at which the assets are 'carried' in the statement of financial position are known as **carrying amounts**.

When preparing a statement of financial position, the following three headings should be shown, as in the example above:

- non-current assets at cost
- accumulated depreciation
- net book value.

ACTIVITY 1

A motor vehicle cost $18 000. It is expected to have a useful life of seven years and to be sold for $4 000 at the end of that time.

a Prepare the provision for depreciation of motor vehicles account for each year.

b Prepare a statement of financial position extract to show the cost, accumulated depreciation and net book value of the motor vehicles at the end of each year.

KEY TERMS

Carrying amount: The net book value of the non-current asset. It is calculated by deducting the accumulated depreciation from the cost of the non-current asset.

Reducing-balance depreciation: Depreciation is calculated as a fixed percentage of the written-down (or net book) value of the asset each year.

11.5 Reducing-balance depreciation

With **reducing-balance depreciation**, depreciation is calculated as a fixed percentage of the written-down value of the asset each year.

Walkthrough

A machine cost $20 000. It is expected to have a useful life of five years. Depreciation is to be calculated at the rate of 25% per annum on the reducing balance.

Calculation	
	$
Cost	20 000
Year 1 (25% × 20 000)	(5 000)*
	15 000
Year 1 (25% × 15 000)	(3 750)*
	11 250
Year 1 (25% × 11 250)	(2 813)*
	8 437
Year 1 (25% × 8 437)	(2 109)*
	6 328
Year 1 (25% × 6 328)	(1 582)*
	4 746

* Notice that the charge for depreciation using this method **reduces** each year.

The bookkeeping entries for the reducing-balance method are similar to those for the straight-line method; only the amounts differ.

The provision for depreciation of machinery account is shown below:

Provision for depreciation of machinery account

		$			$
Year 1	Balance c/d	5 000	Year 1	Income statement	5 000
Year 2	Balance c/d	8 750	Year 2	Balance b/d	5 000
				Income statement	3 750
		8 750			8 750
Year 3	Balance c/d	11 563	Year 3	Balance b/d	8 750
				Income statement	2 813
		11 563			11 563
Year 4	Balance c/d	13 672	Year 4	Balance b/d	11 563
				Income statement	2 109
		13 672			13 672
Year 5	Balance c/d	15 254	Year 5	Balance b/d	13 672
				Income statement	1 582
		15 254			15 254

The asset is shown in the statement of financial position in exactly the same way under this method as the straight-line method. Only the values for accumulated depreciation and net book value will change. This is shown below:

Extract for the statement of financial position at the end of each year

Non-current assets

Machinery	Cost	Accumulated depreciation	Net book value
	$	$	$
Year 1: Machinery	20 000	(5 000)	15 000
Year 2: Machinery	20 000	(8 750)	11 250
Year 3: Machinery	20 000	(11 563)	8 437
Year 4: Machinery	20 000	(13 672)	6 328
Year 5: Machinery	20 000	(15 254)	4 746

ACTIVITY 2

A machine costing $40 000, and with an expected useful life of five years, is to be depreciated by the reducing-balance method. The annual rate of depreciation is 30%.

a Prepare the provision for depreciation of machinery account for years 1 to 5.

b Prepare a statement of financial position extract to show the cost, depreciation and net book value of the machinery at the end of each of the five years.

TOP TIP

Always calculate depreciation to the nearest $.

11.6 Comparing the two methods

Both methods are designed to achieve the same thing: to distribute the cost of the non-current asset over its useful working life and to match the depreciation charge with the revenue earned in the accounting period.

In year 1, whichever method is used, if the same percentage rate is used in both cases the charge for depreciation will be the same. However, quite often the percentage used for the reducing-balance method is much higher than that used for the straight-line method. As a result, in the early years of an asset's life, the annual charge for depreciation for the reducing-balance method is higher than for the straight-line method. The higher rate is charged to reflect the fact that some assets (such as computer equipment) depreciate by a large amount in the early years of their life. Some specialist machines too may depreciate more in their early life. This is illustrated below.

Walkthrough

A machine cost $50 000. It is expected to have a useful life of ten years at the end of which time it will have no residual value. The annual depreciation for each year is compared in the following table:

	Annual charge for depreciation	
Year	**Straight line (10%)**	**Reducing balance (40%)**
	$	**$**
1	5 000	20 000
2	5 000	12 000
3	5 000	7 200
4	5 000	4 320
5	5 000	2 592
6	5 000	1 555
7	5 000	933
8	5 000	560
9	5 000	336
10	5 000	202
Total depreciation	50 000	49 698

A much higher rate of depreciation has had to be used for the reducing-balance method, and the annual depreciation for the first three years is very much higher than under the straight-line method. In fact, using the reducing-balance method, 50% of cost is provided for within the first 18 months, but the machine has not been completely depreciated at the end of ten years – there is still a residual balance of $302.

In this example, the net book value of the asset is reduced to zero if straight-line depreciation is used. The cost of $50 000 has been fully depreciated over the ten years. However, it will never be written down to zero with the reducing-balance method unless a small residual value is deliberately transferred to the income statement.

Provision for depreciation of an asset should cease to be made once it has been completely written off. Assets that have been completely written off in the books may still be of use to the business, but no further depreciation will be provided for them.

11.7 Choice of depreciation method

Providing for depreciation is an application of the matching principle, and the method chosen for any particular type of asset should depend upon the contribution the asset makes towards earning revenue. Some general principles may be explained as follows:

- The **straight-line method** should be used for assets that are expected to earn revenue **evenly** over their useful working lives, or whose value will decline gradually over their useful lives. This method is used for office furniture. It is also generally used where the pattern of an asset's earning power is uncertain. It should always be used to amortise (write off the cost of) assets with fixed lives, such as leases.
- The **reducing-balance method** should be used when it is considered that an asset's earning power will diminish as the asset gets older. This method is also used when the asset loses more of its value in the early years of its life (e.g. a car or delivery vehicle).

A common excuse for using the reducing-balance method rather than the straight-line method is that the reducing charges for depreciation compensate for increases in the cost of maintaining and repairing assets as they get older. It is highly improbable that the two costs will balance each other out. The proper way of dealing with this situation would be to depreciate the asset on the straight-line method and to create a provision for repairs and maintenance by equal transfers annually from the income statement. The costs of repairs are debited to this provision as and when they arise.

Whichever method is used it must **not** be thought that charging depreciation is setting aside a fund of money to replace the asset when it comes to the end of its useful life. It is quite common for a business to use an asset well beyond the period in which it has been depreciated and has a zero net book value.

11.8 Which assets should be depreciated?

All assets that have finite useful lives should be depreciated. Therefore depreciation should be provided on all assets except freehold **land**, which does not have a finite useful life. Freehold **buildings** will eventually need to be replaced and should be depreciated. In this sense 'freehold' means that the business has complete ownership of the land or buildings and, subject to any government regulations, can decide freely how these assets are used. This differs from leasehold land or buildings where the landlord owns the land or buildings and may restrict what it is used for.

Land that is used in an extractive industry, such as quarries and mines, will lose value as the mineral or resource is extracted and should be depreciated. Quite often the charge for depreciation in this case is linked to how much tonnage of material is extracted. For example, Digitup Mining purchases a sand quarry for $1 00 000. It estimates that there is a total of 2 50 000 tonnes of sand in the quarry. The rate at which it will charge depreciation is $0.40 (1 00 000/2 50 000) for every tonne of sand extracted from the quarry.

11.9 More important points about depreciation

Provision for depreciation in the year of acquisition of an asset

Businesses vary in the way they depreciate non-current assets in the year in which they are acquired.

The two possibilities are:

- A full year's depreciation is taken in the year of acquisition, but none in the year of disposal.
- Depreciation is calculated from the date of acquisition; in the year of disposal, depreciation is calculated from the commencement of the year to the date of disposal, that is, only a proportion of the annual depreciation will be provided. This is sometimes referred to as a 'month-by-month basis'.

TOP TIP

In general, if you are given the dates of acquisition and disposal, calculate depreciation on a monthly basis for the years of acquisition and disposal. Otherwise, calculate depreciation for a full year in the year of acquisition, but not for the year of disposal.

Consistency

The chosen method of depreciating an asset should be used consistently to ensure that the profits or losses of different periods of account can be compared on a like-for-like basis.

A change in the method of calculating depreciation should only be made if it will result in the financial results and position of the business being stated more fairly. A change should never be made in order to manipulate profit.

Exceptional depreciation

Sometimes an event may occur that causes the amount that may be recovered on the disposal of a non-current asset to fall below its net book value (carrying amount). In this case the asset is said to be **impaired**. When this happens, the asset should immediately be written down to the amount which could be received if it was sold. This is known as its **recoverable amount.** The loss should be charged as an expense in the income statement. This is covered in more detail in Chapter 22.

The remaining useful life of the asset should now be reviewed, in order to calculate the depreciation to be charged for the remainder of the asset's useful life. This is calculated by dividing the new carrying amount by the number of years of useful life remaining.

Walkthrough

A machine was purchased in 2010 at a cost of $30 000. It had an estimated useful life of ten years and a residual value of $2 000. Straight-line depreciation of $2 800 was provided each year until 31 December 2014, when the machine had a written-down value of $16 000. At 31 December 2015, it was then found that the recoverable amount of the machine was only $9 000 and that it had only three years useful life left and no residual value.

In the year ended 31 December 2015, the income statement should be debited with $7 000 (16 000 – 9 000), and the annual depreciation for the next three years should be $9 000 ÷ 3 = $3 000.

11.10 How to account for the disposals of non-current assets

When a non-current asset is sold, the difference between its net book value and the proceeds of sale represents a profit or loss on disposal. This is transferred to the income statement. The profit or loss is calculated in a **disposal** account. The bookkeeping entries are as follows:

Step 1

Debit the disposal account and **credit** the non-current asset account, with the original cost of the asset. This will remove the cost of the asset sold from the ledger.

Step 2

Debit the provision for depreciation account and **credit** the disposal account, with the depreciation provided to date on the asset. This will remove from the ledger the accumulated depreciation charged on the asset from the time it was bought to the time it was sold.

Step 3

Debit the bank account and **credit** the disposal account, with the proceeds (if any) of the disposal.

A debit balance remaining on the disposal account is a loss on disposal. A credit balance is a profit on disposal. The balance is transferred to the income statement.

Walkthrough

At 1 December 2015, a machine which had cost $20 000 was sold for $500. A total of $18 000 had been provided for depreciation on the machine. The bookkeeping is as follows:

Machinery at cost account

2015		**$**	**2015**		**$**
Jan 1	Balance b/d	20 000	Dec 1	Machinery disposal	20 000

Provision for depreciation of machinery account

2015		**$**	**2015**		**$**
Dec 1	Machinery disposal	18 000	Jan 1	Balance b/d	18 000

Machinery disposal account

2015		**$**	**2015**		**$**
Dec 1	Machinery at cost	20 000 [1]	Dec 1	Provision for depreciation	18 000 [2]
				Bank	500 [3]
			31	Income statement (loss on disposal)	1 500 [4]
		20 000			20 000

Notes:

- The cost of the machine [1] exceeds the accumulated depreciation [2] + the sale proceeds [3]; there is a loss on disposal [4].
- The debit entry in the income statement is really an adjustment to previous years' depreciation charges, which have proved to be insufficient. This should be listed with the expenses in the income statement.
- Had the accumulated depreciation and sale proceeds been greater than the cost, the disposal account would have had a credit balance. This would mean a profit on disposal. This should be transferred to the income statement and labelled 'profit on disposal'. It should be added to the gross profit, before the deduction of any expenses.

Part exchange

A new asset may be acquired in part exchange for one that is being disposed of. The part exchange value of the asset being disposed of is debited to the non-current asset account and credited to the disposal account as the proceeds of disposal.

Walkthrough

On 5 March 2016, a motor vehicle X100 was purchased for $15 000. The cost was settled by a payment of $13 000 and the part exchange of motor vehicle Z23 for the balance.

Motor vehicle Z23 cost $11 000 and had a net book value of $800 at 5 March 2016.

The business year-end is 31 March 2016. No depreciation is charged on the new vehicle for the year ended 31 March 2016.

Motor vehicles at cost account

2016		**$**	**2016**		**$**
Jan 1	Balance b/d (Z23)	11 000	Mar 5	Motor vehicles disposal a/c	11 000
			31	Balance c/d	15 000
Mar 5	Bank (X100)	13 000			
	Motor vehicles disposal a/c	2 000			
		26 000			26 000
Apr 1	Balance b/d	15 000			

Provision for the depreciation of motor vehicles account

2016		**$**	**2016**		**$**
Mar 5	Disposal a/c	10 200	Jan 1	Balance b/d	10 200

Motor vehicles disposal account

2016		**$**	**2016**		**$**
Mar 5	Motor vehicles at cost (Z23)	11 000	Mar 5	Provision for depreciation of motor vehicles (Z23)*	10 200
31	Income statement (profit on disposal)	1 200**		Motor vehicles at cost	2 000
		12 200			12 200

*No depreciation has been charged in the year of disposal.

**The profit of $1 200 is credited in the income statement and is, in effect, an adjustment for over-depreciation of the motor vehicle in previous years.

ACTIVITY 3

The following balances have been extracted from Yuki's books at 31 December 2015. Machinery at cost $18 000; provision for depreciation of machinery $9 600.

Yuki's transactions in 2016 included the following:

May 7 Sold machine No. 1 for $1 500. This machine cost $6 000 when purchased in 2012.

June 3 Purchased machine No. 3 which was priced at $10 000. Yuki paid $7 000 and gave machine No. 2 in part exchange. Machine No. 2 cost $12 000 when purchased in 2010.

Yuki depreciates his machinery using the straight-line method at the rate of 10% per annum. He provides for a full year's depreciation in the year of purchase, but none in the year of disposal.

Required

Prepare the following accounts to show the transactions on 7 May and 3 June:

a machinery at cost

b provision for depreciation of machinery

c machinery disposal

11.11 How to adjust a trial balance for depreciation

You may be asked to adjust the trial balance to provide for a further year's depreciation of the non-current assets. The amount that has to be debited in the income statement should be inserted in the debit column of the trial balance and added to the credit side.

Walkthrough

The following extract is taken from a trial balance:

	$	$
Leasehold premises	30 000	
Provision for depreciation of leasehold premises		6 000
Plant and machinery	40 000	
Provision for depreciation of plant and machinery		23 120

Additional information

1 Leasehold premises are to be amortised over the term of the lease of ten years on the straight-line basis.

2 Plant and machinery are to be depreciated at the rate of 25% per annum by the reducing-balance method. The trial balance should be adjusted as follows (adjustments shown in *italics*).

	$	$
Leasehold premises	30 000	
Provision for depreciation of leasehold premises	*3 000*	6 000 + *3 000*
Plant and machinery	40 000	
Provision for depreciation of plant and machinery	*4 220**	23 120 + *4 220*

* 25% of (40 000 – 23 120).

The result of this will be to charge the depreciation on the premises ($3 000) and the depreciation on the plant and machinery ($4 220) as expenses in the income statement.

The accumulated depreciation figures of $9 000 ($6 000 + $3 000) for premises and $27 340 ($23 120 + $4 220) for plant and machinery will be shown in the statement of financial position. They will be deducted from the cost of their respective assets to show the net book value.

11.12 The revaluation method of depreciation

With some items which are treated as non-current assets it is sometimes difficult to keep track of them. A good example would be loose tools in a manufacturing business. The individual tools may not cost enough to treat them as separate assets. Each tool may have a different useful life. However, their total value may be quite large. In this case the **revaluation method of depreciation** may be used to find out how much to charge as an expense to the income statement. It is calculated by opening valuation + purchases made during the period – closing valuation = depreciation charge for the period.

KEY TERM

Revaluation method of depreciation: Used to calculate the cost of consumption in the accounting period of small non-current assets such as power tools.

Walkthrough

Josephine runs a small manufacturing business. At 1 January 2015, she valued her loose tools at $5 000. During the year ended 31 December 2015, Josephine bought more tools at a total cost of $400. At 31 December she valued the total loose tools at $4 800.

Required

Calculate how much Josephine should charge for depreciation of loose tools in her income statement for the year ended 31 December 2015.

	$
Cost at 1 Jan 2015	5 000
Add: additions during the year	400
	5 400
Less: valuation at 31 Dec 2015	(4 800)
Charge to income statement	600

In this case the sum of $600 will be charged as an expense in the income statement. The total valuation of $4 800 will appear in Josephine's statement of financial position at 31 December 2015. Where this is shown will vary from business to business. However, the most usual place to record the value is as a current asset. It is often labelled as 'inventory of loose tools' and shown underneath the usual trading inventory in a similar manner to, say, inventories of stationery (see Section 10.4).

11.13 Provisions for depreciation and the accounting concepts

Provisions for depreciation are made to comply with the following concepts:

- **Matching** The cost of using non-current assets to earn revenue should be matched in the income statement to the revenue earned.
- **Prudence** If the cost of using non-current assets was not included in the income statement, profit would be overstated.

Whichever method of depreciation is chosen for a non-current asset, it should be used consistently and not changed unless there is a very good reason to do so.

Chapter summary

In this chapter you have learnt about the topic of depreciation of non-current assets. You have learnt the two most common methods of charging depreciation: straight-line and reducing-balance. You have also learnt how to record depreciation in both the ledger accounts and financial statements, and how to charge depreciation using the revaluation method. Finally, you should now be familiar with the accounting concepts which apply to depreciation.

TOP TIP

Depreciation is an important topic. How to record it must be understood and you may be asked to explain what depreciation is or what causes it. It's also not sufficient just to know one method of calculating depreciation, as you may be asked to explain one or both of the most common methods of depreciation used. When focusing on depreciation always read questions carefully to make sure you understand which method of depreciation you should use and always show all workings.

Practice exercises

1 The following trial balance was extracted from the books of Piccolo at 31 May 2016:

	$	$
Freehold land and buildings at cost	100 000	
Provision for depreciation of freehold buildings		40 000
Plant and machinery at cost	76 000	
Provision for depreciation of plant and machinery		32 000
Trade receivables	14 000	
Trade payables		6 300
Bank	5 500	
Sales		300 000
Purchases	190 000	
Inventory	30 000	
Wages	56 000	
Heating and lighting	17 600	
Repairs to plant and machinery	5 100	
Advertising	7 000	
Drawings	27 100	
Capital		150 000
	528 300	528 300

(cont.)

Additional information

1 Inventory at 31 May 2016: $42 000.

2 Freehold land and buildings at cost is made up as follows: land $20 000; buildings $80 000.

3 Freehold buildings are depreciated at 4% per annum on the straight-line basis.

4 Plant and machinery are depreciated at 25% per annum on the reducing-balance basis.

5 At 31 May 2016, $1 800 was owing for heating and lighting. $6 000 of the cost of advertising related to the year beginning 1 June 2015.

6 In the year ended 31 May 2016, Piccolo had taken inventory costing $4 000 for his personal use. No entry had been made in the books for this.

Required

a Explain the difference between the straight-line method of depreciation and the reducing-balance method of depreciation.

b Prepare Piccolo's income statement for the year ended 31 May 2016. Prepare the statement of financial position at 31 May 2016.

Additional information

Piccolo is considering changing the method of depreciation he currently used for plant and machinery to the straight-line method.

Required

c Advise Piccolo whether or not he should change his method of depreciation for plant and machinery. Justify your answer by discussing any relevant accounting concept.

2 Wilhelmina is a trader whose financial year ends on 31 March. Her trial balance at 31 March 2016 was as follows:

	$	$
Leasehold property at cost	45 000	
Provision for depreciation of leasehold property		13 500
Plant and machinery at cost	21 000	
Provision for depreciation of plant and machinery		9 200
Office equipment at cost	7 000	
Provision for depreciation of office equipment		2 400
Trade receivables	1 526	
Trade payables		973
Inventory	13 000	
Bank	1 964	
Wages	13 017	
Electricity	1 012	
Repairs to machinery	643	
Other operating expenses	1 234	
Interest on loan	1 000	
Sales		80 600
Sales returns	1 590	

	$	$
Purchases	50914	
Purchases returns		825
Long-term loan		20000
Drawings	18598	
Capital		50000
	177498	177498

Additional information

1 Inventory at 31 March 2016 cost $16000.

2 The loan was received in 2013 and is repayable in 2020. Interest on the loan is at the rate of 10% per annum.

3 Plant and machinery at cost include $6000 for a machine bought on hire purchase on 1 January 2016. The cash price of the machine is $30000. The balance is payable in four quarterly instalments of $6200, including interest, on 1 April 2016, 1 July 2016, 1 October 2016 and 1 January 2017.

4 The leasehold property was acquired on 1 October 2014 for a period of 15 years. It is being amortised on the straight-line basis.

5 Plant and machinery are depreciated on the reducing-balance method using the annual rate of 25%.

6 Office equipment is depreciated at 15% per annum on the straight-line basis.

7 At 31 March 2016, $300 was owing for electricity, and other operating expenses of $180 had been prepaid.

Required

a Prepare Wilhelmina's income statement for the year ended 31 March 2016.

b Prepare the statement of financial position at 31 March 2016.

Exam practice questions

Multiple-choice questions

1 Why is depreciation on non-current assets charged in the accounts of a business?

- **A** to ensure that assets are replaced when they are worn out
- **B** to make sure that cash is available to replace assets when they are worn out
- **C** to show what assets are worth in the statement of financial position
- **D** to spread the cost of assets over their useful lives

2 A business purchased a crane for $40000 on 1 January 2013. The crane was depreciated at the rate of 30% per annum using the reducing-balance method. The crane was sold on 31 December 2015 for $7750. A full year's depreciation was charged in the year of disposal. What was the profit or loss on disposal?

- **A** $3750 loss
- **B** $3750 profit
- **C** $5970 loss
- **D** $5970 profit

3 The following information relates to the non-current assets of a business:

	$
Cost at 1 April 2015	32 000
Accumulated depreciation at 1 April 2015	13 600
Non-current assets purchased in year ended 31 March 2016	7 000
Depreciation charged for the year ended 31 March 2016	4 200

Depreciation is calculated on the reducing-balance basis at the rate of 30%. What was the net book value of the assets that were disposed of in the year ended 31 March 2016?

A $11 400
B $16 800
C $18 400
D $25 400

4 The following information is extracted from the books of a business:

	At 31 Dec 2014	At 31 Dec 2015
	$	$
Non-current assets (at cost)	230 000	275 000
Less: accumulated depreciation	85 000	98 000

Further information for the year ended 31 December 2015 is as follows:

	$
Depreciation charged in the income statement	25 000
Additions to non-current assets (at cost)	60 000
Loss on sale of non-current assets	1 000

How much was received from the sales of non-current assets?

A $2 000 **B** $3 000 **C** $4 000 **D** $5 000

Total: 4 marks

Structured question

1 Carley is a sole trader. At 31 May 2015 her statement of financial position included the following:

Extract from Carley's statement of financial position	
	$
Non-current assets:	
Motor vehicles	
Cost	28000
Accumulated depreciation	12000
Office equipment	
Cost	20000
Accumulated depreciation	8000

During the year ended 31 May 2016, the following took place:

1 A motor vehicle was sold for $3000. The vehicle had cost $8000. There was a loss on disposal of $1000.

2 On 1 December 2015, a new vehicle was bought for $12000.

3 On 1 March 2016, a new item of office equipment was bought for $2000.

Carley's depreciation policy is as follows:

i Motor vehicles are depreciated at 25% per annum using the reducing-balance method. A full year's depreciation is charged in the year of acquisition. No depreciation is charged in the year of disposal.

ii Office equipment is depreciated at 10% per annum using the straight-line method. Depreciation is charged on a month-by-month basis.

Required

a Explain, using examples, why a business uses different methods of depreciation for different types of non-current assets. **[4 marks]**

b Prepare the asset disposal account for the year ended 31 May 2016. **[3 marks]**

c Calculate the following balances to include in Carley's statement of financial position at 31 May 2016:

i motor vehicles at cost
ii motor vehicles accumulated depreciation
iii office equipment at cost
iv office equipment accumulated depreciation **[8 marks]**

Total: 15

Chapter 12
Irrecoverable and doubtful debts

Learning objectives

In this chapter you will learn:

- the difference between an irrecoverable debt and a doubtful debt
- how to account for irrecoverable debts and irrecoverable debts recovered
- how to provide for doubtful debts.

KEY TERM

Irrecoverable debt: A debt due from a customer which it is expected will never be paid by them.

12.1 Irrecoverable debts

When somebody owes money but is unable to pay, the debt is an irrecoverable one. As soon as debts are known to be irrecoverable, they should be cleared from the sales ledger by transferring them, by journal entry, to an **irrecoverable debts** account.

Walkthrough

Akram is owed $1 200 by Samuel and $850 by Asha. Both of these customers became bankrupt on 1 November 2015 and are unable to pay their debts. Akram writes the debts off as irrecoverable.

Journal entries

	Account	Dr	Cr
2015		**$**	**$**
Nov 1	Irrecoverable debts account	1 200	
	Samuel		1 200
Samuel has become bankrupt and unable to pay amount due.			
Nov 1	Irrecoverable debts account	850	
	Asha		850
Asha has become bankrupt and unable to pay amount due.			

Sales ledger accounts:

Samuel account

2015		**$**	**2015**		**$**
Nov 1	Balance b/d	1 200	Nov 1	Irrecoverable debts	1 200

Asha account

2015		**$**	**2015**		**$**
Nov 1	Balance b/d	850	Nov 1	Irrecoverable debts	850

General ledger
Irrecoverable debts account

2015		**$**	**$**
Nov 1	Samuel	1 200	
	Asha	850	

When Akram prepares his annual accounts at, say, 31 December 2015, he will transfer the balance on the irrecoverable debts account to the income statement as an expense. This too is usually done by means of a journal entry:

Date	Details	Dr	Cr
		$	$
Dec 31	Income statement	2 050	
	Irrecoverable debts		2 050
Irrecoverable debts for the year written off.			

The irrecoverable debts account is then closed:

General ledger Irrecoverable debts account					
2015		**$**	**2015**		**$**
Nov 1	Samuel	1 200	Dec 31	Income statement	2 050
	Asha	850			
		2 050			2 050

12.2 Irrecoverable debts recovered

A debt that has been written off as irrecoverable may be recovered at a later date if the customer becomes able to pay. The debt must be recorded once more on the sales ledger account by a journal entry. The customer's account will be debited and an irrecoverable debts recovered account credited with the amount recovered. The amount received from the customer may then be credited to his account and debited in the cash book.

Walkthrough

On 6 January 2016, Asha had sufficient funds to enable her to pay Akram and sent him a cheque for $850. The journal entry was as follows:

	Account	Dr	Cr
2016		**$**	**$**
Jan 6	Asha	850	
	Irrecoverable debts recovered		850

An amount of $850 is received from Asha. This debt was previously written off as irrecoverable on 1 November 2015.

On 8 January 2016, Akram received a cheque for $300, being a part payment of 25% of Samuel's debt. The journal entry was as follows:

	Account	Dr	Cr
2016		**$**	**$**
Jan 8	Samuel	300	
	Irrecoverable debts recovered		300

$300 was received in respect of 25% of Samuel's debt of $1 200, which was written off as an irrecoverable debt on 1 November 2015.

Sales ledger accounts:

Samuel account					
2015		**$**	**2015**		**$**
Nov 1	Balance b/d	1200	Nov 1	Irrecoverable debts	1200
2016			**2016**		
Jan 8	Irrecoverable debts recovered	300	Jan 8	Bank	300

Asha account					
2015		**$**	**2015**		**$**
Nov 1	Balance b/d	850	Nov 1	Irrecoverable debts	850
2016			**2016**		
Jan 6	Irrecoverable debts recovered	850	Jan 6	Bank	850

General ledger accounts:

Irrecoverable debts recovered account					
2016		**$**	**2016**		**$**
			Jan 6	Asha	850
			Jan 8	Samuel	300

The balance on irrecoverable debts recovered account will be credited to the income statement again by way of a journal entry. It should be shown under gross profit as part of other income and should be added to the gross profit.

TOP TIP

Never show the amount recovered as a negative expense.

Sometimes, only the difference between the balances on the irrecoverable debts account and the irrecoverable debts recovered account will be included in the income statement. If the net difference is an expense then it is included in the income statement with the other expenses. If the net difference is a credit then it will be added to the gross profit as other income.

12.3 Provisions for doubtful debts

A debt may not actually have become irrecoverable, but there may be doubt as to whether it will be paid; it may turn out eventually to be irrecoverable. It would be misleading to include that debt as an asset in the statement of financial position pretending that the amount is not in doubt.

On the other hand, since it has not yet become irrecoverable, it would be wrong to write it off as an expense in the income statement. It is what is called a **doubtful debt**. A provision is made to cover that and other doubtful debts.

KEY TERM

Doubtful debt: A debt due from a customer where it is uncertain whether or not it will be repaid by them.

12.4 How to create and maintain a provision for doubtful debts

When the provision is first created, debit the income statement and credit a provision for doubtful debts account with the full amount of the provision.

In the years that follow, the entries in the accounts will only be for increases or decreases in the amounts required for the provision:

- Debit the income statement and credit the provision for doubtful debts with any **increases** in the provision.
- Debit the provision for doubtful debts and credit the income statement with any **decreases** in the provision.

The provision for doubtful debts is deducted from trade receivables in the statement of financial position.

Walkthrough

The following information is extracted from Jonah's accounts:

At 31 December	Total of all receivables	Doubtful debts
	$	$
2013	12 000	900
2014	14 000	1 100
2015	10 000	800

Jonah had not previously made a provision for doubtful debts. His year-end is 31 December. The following entries will be made in his accounts:

Income statement (extracts) for the year ended 31 December		
	Debit	**Credit**
	$	$
2013 Provision for doubtful debts	900	
2014 Provision for doubtful debts	200	
2015 Provision for doubtful debts		300

In 2013 and 2014, the amounts of $900 and $200 will appear in the expenses section of the income statement. In 2015, the amount of $300 will be added to the gross profit as other income.

TOP TIP

In the income statement, never show a decrease in the provision for doubtful debts as a negative expense, always add it to the gross profit.

Provision for doubtful debts account
(3 years ended 31 December 2013/2014/2015)

2013		**$**	**2013**		**$**
Dec 31	Balance c/d	900	Dec 31	Income statement	900
2014			**2014**		
Dec 31	Balance c/d	1 100	Jan 1	Balance b/d	900
			Dec 31	Income statement	200
		1 100			1 100
2015			**2015**		
Dec 31	Income statement	300	Jan 1	Balance b/d	1 100
	Balance c/d	800			
		1 100			1 100
			2016		
			Jan 1	Balance b/d	800

Jonah's statement of financial position at 31 December (extracts)

2013	**$**	**$**
Trade receivables	12 000	
Less: provision for doubtful debts	(900)	11 100
2014		
Trade receivables	14 000	
Less: provision for doubtful debts	(1 100)	12 900
2015		
Trade receivables	10 000	
Less: provision for doubtful debts	(800)	9 200

12.5 How to calculate the amount of a provision for doubtful debts

The calculation of a provision for doubtful debts depends upon the type of provision required. There are three kinds of provision:

- specific
- general
- specific and general.

Specific Certain debts are selected from the sales ledger as doubtful. The provision will be equal to the total of those debts. The amount of the provision is based on specific knowledge the business owner has of the particular customer's financial position.

General The provision is calculated as a percentage of the total trade receivables. The average percentage of debts by amount that prove to be irrecoverable is usually taken for this purpose.

Specific and general The provision is made up of the debts that are thought to be doubtful plus a percentage of the remainder.

Walkthrough

Job maintains a specific and general provision for doubtful debts. The general provision is based on 4% of trade receivables after deducting doubtful debts.

At 31 December	Total receivables	Doubtful debts	Provision		Total
			Specific	General	
	(a)	(b)		(c)	
	$	$	$	$	$
2012	31 000	4 500	4 500	1 060	5 560
2013	37 000	5 000	5 000	1 280	6 280
2014	34 200	3 700	3 700	1 220	4 920
2015	35 640	4 090	4 090	1 262	5 352

TOP TIPS

- Specific provisions must always be deducted from trade receivables first, before the general provision is calculated. In the above example:

  [column (a) – column (b)] × 4% = column (c)
- Never refer to a provision for irrecoverable debts. Irrecoverable debts are never provided for; they should always be written off as soon as they become irrecoverable.

ACTIVITY 1

Saul maintains a provision for doubtful debts in his books. It is made up of a specific provision for doubtful debts and a general provision equal to 5% of the remainder. The following information is extracted from Saul's books:

At 31 March	Total trade receivables	Doubtful debts (included in total trade receivables)
	$	$
2012	27 000	4 000
2013	33 900	6 400
2014	30 000	7 500
2015	28 000	3 000
2016	36 700	8 300

Required

a Calculate the total provision for doubtful debts for each of the above years.

b Prepare the provision for doubtful debts account for each of the years. (Assume that Saul had not made a provision for doubtful debts before 31 March 2012.)

12.6 How to adjust a trial balance for irrecoverable and doubtful debts

The adjustments to a trial balance for irrecoverable and doubtful debts are demonstrated in the following example.

Walkthrough

A trial balance includes:

Trade receivables of $40 650 (including $400 which are irrecoverable debts) and a provision for doubtful debts of $1 900.

A provision of 8% is to be made for doubtful debts. (The adjustments are shown in *italics*.)

Trial balance		
	Debit	**Credit**
	$	**$**
Trade receivables	40 650 – *400*	
Irrecoverable debts	*400*	
Provision for doubtful debts	*1 320*	1 900 + *1 320*

Step 1

Deduct the irrecoverable debts, $400, from trade receivables. Insert 'Irrecoverable debts 400' as a new debit balance; this will be debited in the income statement.

Step 2

Calculate the new provision for doubtful debts and deduct the provision brought forward: $(40 650 – 400) × 8% – $1 900 = $1 320. Add the result to both sides of the trial balance.

12.7 Provisions for doubtful debts and the concepts

A provision for doubtful debts complies with the following accounting concepts:

- **Prudence** Amounts expected to be received from trade receivables should not be overstated in the statement of financial position. The income statement should provide for the loss of revenue and not overstate profit.
- **Matching** The possible loss of revenue should be provided for in the period in which the revenue was earned, not in a later period when the debt becomes irrecoverable.

TOP TIPS

- Read questions carefully and make sure you know exactly what you are required to do.
- Debit an increase, but credit a decrease, in a provision to the income statement.
- Be sure to complete the double entry for each adjustment.
- Show your workings with your answer.
- Tick the adjustments, as this will ensure you do not overlook them.
- Deduct the new balance on the provision for doubtful debts account from the trade receivables in the statement of financial position.

Chapter summary

In this chapter you have learnt about irrecoverable and doubtful debts, and should be familiar with the difference between them. You should now be able to prepare journal and ledger entries to record writing off an irrecoverable debt.

You should also now be able to prepare the journal and ledger entries to show the payment if a customer repays in full, or in part, a debt which was previously written off as irrecoverable.

Finally, you should now be able to calculate the provision for doubtful debts and record it both in the ledger and the financial statements.

TOP TIP

Irrecoverable and doubtful debts are topics that you may be asked about, either on their own or as part of a major question when preparing the financial statements for a sole trader, partnership or limited company.

Practice exercises

1 David's trial balance at 31 March 2016 was as follows:

David **Trial balance at 31 March 2016**		
	Debit	**Credit**
Sales		210 000
Sales returns	9 240	
Purchases	84 000	
Purchases returns		5 112
Wages	37 000	
Rent	7 600	
Electricity	1 027	
Telephone	900	
Postage and stationery	359	
Carriage inwards	1 840	
Carriage outwards	1 220	
Discounts allowed	6 015	
Discounts received		2 480
Leasehold premises at cost	70 000	
Provision for depreciation of leasehold premises		5 000
Delivery vans at cost	18 000	

(cont.)

	Debit	Credit
Provision for depreciation of delivery vans		3600
Office furniture at cost	3000	
Provision for depreciation of office furniture		1500
Inventory	4000	
Bank	1245	
Trade receivables	19800	
Provision for doubtful debts		800
Trade payables		7200
Drawings	20446	
Capital		50000
	285692	285692

Additional information

1 Inventory at 31 March 2016 was value at cost, $5000.

2 Sales include goods sent on sale or return to a customer who has not yet indicated acceptance of the goods. The goods cost $3000 and the customer has been invoiced for $4000.

3 Trade receivables included debts totalling $1700 which were known to be irrecoverable.

4 The provision for doubtful debts is to be adjusted to include a specific provision of $3100 and a general provision of 5%.

5 The following expenses are to be accrued: wages $400, electricity $360 and telephone $100.

6 Rent of $1600 has been prepaid.

7 Depreciation is to be provided on the following bases: leasehold premises at 5% straight line; delivery vans at 25% reducing-balance; office furniture at 10% straight line.

Required

a Prepare David's income statement for the year ended 31 March 2016.

b Prepare the statement of financial position at 31 March 2016.

2 Saul is a trader and his trial balance at 31 May 2016 was as follows:

Saul Trial balance at 31 May 2016		
	Debit	**Credit**
Account	**$**	**$**
Freehold property at cost	180000	
Provision for depreciation of freehold property		45000
Plant and machinery at cost	97000	
Provision for depreciation of plant and machinery		53000
Motor vehicles at cost	41000	
Provision for depreciation of motor vehicles		27000
Trade receivables	34600	
Provision for doubtful debts		1200
Trade payables		5720

Account	Debit $	Credit $
Bank	11 374	
Sales		700 000
Sales returns	6 670	
Purchase	410 890	
Purchases returns		3 112
Wages	137 652	
Rent payable	10 000	
Rent receivable		1 020
Heating and lighting	4 720	
Telephone and postage	3 217	
Stationery	6 195	
Repairs to machinery	17 600	
Discounts allowed	3 220	
Discounts received		2 942
Carriage inwards	4 240	
Carriage outwards	1 819	
Inventory	40 000	
Drawings	28 797	
Capital		200 000
	1 038 994	1 038 994

Additional information

1 Inventory at 31 May 2016 cost $58 000.

2 Depreciation is to be calculated as follows:
- freehold property at 4% per annum, straight line
- plant and machinery at 15% per annum, straight line
- motor vehicles at 30% per annum on the reducing-balance.

3 Included in trade receivables is an irrecoverable debt of $1 800. The provision for doubtful debts is to be 5% of trade receivables.

4 At 31 May 2016, heat and light of $400 was owing. An amount of $220 for stationery was also owing. The inventory of unused stationery at 31 May 2016 had cost $450.

5 At 31 May 2016, there was an amount of $2 000 in respect of rent paid in advance. Rent receivable was owing in the sum of $280.

6 During the year, Saul had taken goods for his own use. The goods had cost $2 400. No entries for this had been made in the books.

Required

a Prepare Saul's income statement for the year ended 31 May 2016.

b Prepare the statement of financial position at 31 May 2016.

Exam practice questions

Multiple-choice questions

1 Kapil has decided to maintain a provision for doubtful debts. Which of the following concepts should he apply in his accounts?

- **i** going concern
- **ii** matching
- **iii** prudence
- **iv** realisation

A i and iii **B** i and iv **C** ii and iii **D** ii and iv

2 The following information is available about a business:

	$
Provision for doubtful debts at 1 April 2015	1100
Trade receivables at 31 March 2016	24800
Irrecoverable debt included in trade receivables at 31 March 2016	600
Charge to income statement for irrecoverable and doubtful debts including irrecoverable debt of $600	1194

Which percentage was used to calculate the provision for doubtful debts at 31 March 2016?

A 6.8 **B** 7 **C** 9.25 **D** 9.5

3 At 31 December 2014, a business had a provision for doubtful debts of $1200. At 31 December 2015, the provision was adjusted to $900. How did this affect the financial statements?

	Profit for the year	Net trade receivables
A	decrease by $300	decrease by $300
B	decrease by $300	increase by $300
C	increase by $300	decrease by $300
D	increase by $300	increase by $300

4 Before any end-of-year adjustments had been made, the trial balance of a business at 31 May 2016 included the following:

	Debit	Credit
	$	$
Trade receivables	13400	
Provision for doubtful debts		500

At 31 May 2016, it was found that trade receivables included an irrecoverable debt of $650. It was decided to adjust the provision for doubtful debts to 4% of trade receivables. A debt of $420, which had been written off as irrecoverable in January 2015, was recovered in January 2016. What was the effect of these events on the income statement for the year ended 31 May 2016?

A Expense $384 **B** Expense $410 **C** Income $430 **D** Income $456

Total: 4 marks

Chapter 13
Bank reconciliation statements

Learning objectives

In this chapter you will learn:

- what a bank reconciliation statement is
- how to ensure that the bank balance in the cash book equals the correct balance of cash at bank
- how to adjust a trial balance after the cash book has been reconciled to the bank statement.

KEY TERMS

Bank reconciliation statement: A statement prepared periodically to ensure that the bank account in the business cash book matches the business bank account shown on the bank statement.

Timing difference: The delay between items recorded in the cash book and their appearance on the bank statement.

13.1 What is a bank reconciliation statement?

A **bank reconciliation statement** shows the correct balance on a bank account. It is carried out to ensure that the only difference between the balance on the bank column of the cash book and balance on the bank statement is due to the reasons below and not an error in either. The balance on the bank account in a cash book may not agree with the balance on the bank statement at any particular date. This may be because of:

- **timing differences** (the delay between items being entered in the cash book and their entry on the bank statement)
- items on the bank statement that have not been entered in the cash book (e.g. bank charges and interest, direct debits and other items).

A bank statement is a copy of a customer's account in the books of a bank. Consequently items debited in the customer's own cash book appear as credits in the bank statement, and items credited in the cash book are debited in the bank statement. A debit balance in the cash book will appear as a credit balance in the bank statement. If a bank account is overdrawn, the customer owes the bank money. The bank is now a creditor represented by a credit balance in the cash book; the customer is the bank's debtor and is shown as a debit balance on the bank statement.

When the balances in the cash book and bank statement do not agree, the correct balance must be found by preparing a bank reconciliation statement.

13.2 How to prepare a bank reconciliation statement

Follow these **three** steps:

- **Step 1 Compare the entries in the cash book with the bank statements.** Tick items that appear in both the cash book **and** the bank statement. Be sure to tick them in both places.
- **Step 2 Enter in the cash book any items that remain unticked in the bank statement.** Then tick those in both places. Then calculate the new cash book balance.
- **Step 3 Prepare the reconciliation statement.** Begin with the final balance shown on the bank statement and adjust it for any items that remain unticked in the cash book. The result should equal the balance in the cash book.

The cash book balance will now be the correct balance of cash at bank. This figure can then be used to record the bank figure in the statement of financial position. If the final balance in the cash book is a debit then it will appear under current assets, together with the cash in hand. This is headed 'cash and cash equivalents'. If the final balance in the cash book is a credit, it will appear under current liabilities as 'bank overdraft'.

TOP TIPS

- Remember the three steps required to reconcile a bank account.
- Note carefully if the balances given for the cash book or bank statement are overdrafts.

Walkthrough

Step 1

After Step 1 has been completed, A. J. Belstrode's cash book and bank statement appear as follows at 31 March 2016. (Note the items which have been ticked.)

Cash book
Bank account

	Details			Cheque number	Details	
2016		$				$
Mar 1	Balance brought forward	1 250	Mar 8	001022	Electricity	300✓
			10	001023	Wages	600✓
7	Cash banked	700✓	11	001024	Rent	400✓
12	P. Romano	200✓	14	001025	T. Martinez	920✓
15	Cash banked	600✓	15	001026	Wages	440✓
20	T. McNichol	430✓	28	001027	A. Danshov	120
31	T. Matkin	594	29	001028	F. Goswami	96
			31	001029	H. Wenger	300
			31		Balance c/d	598
		3 774				3 774
April 1	Balance b/d	598				

Bank statement
The Reddypay Bank

Account: A. J. Belstrode

		Money out	Money in	
		$	$	$
March 1	Balance brought forward			1 250 Cr
7	Paid in		700 ✓	1 950 Cr
10	Paid by cheque 1023	600 ✓		1 350 Cr
11	Paid by cheque 1022	300 ✓		1 050 Cr
12	Paid in		200 ✓	1 250 Cr
14	Direct debit: I. Mallapati	227		1 023 Cr
15	Paid in		600 ✓	1 623 Cr
	Paid by cheque 1026	440 ✓		1 183 Cr
16	Paid by cheque 1024	400 ✓		783 Cr
	Paid by cheque 1025	920 ✓		137 Dr
20	Paid in		430 ✓	293 Cr
25	Bank Giro credit – bank interest received		200	493 Cr
31	Bank charges	112		381 Cr

Step 2

The unticked items in the bank statement are entered in the cash book and ticked.

Cash book
Bank account

2016		$	**2015**		$
Apr 1	Balance b/d	598	Mar 14	D/d I. Mallapati	227✓
Mar 25	Bank interest received	200✓	Mar 31	Bank charges	112✓
			Mar 31	Balance c/d	459
		798			798
April 1	Balance b/d	459			

TOP TIP

Start with the balance brought down in the cash book. Do not re-write the whole cash book to enter the new items.

Step 3

A bank reconciliation statement is prepared commencing with the bank statement balance which is adjusted for the items remaining unticked in the cash book.

Bank reconciliation statement at 31 March 2016			
		$	$
Balance per bank statement			381
Add: item not credited in bank statement			594
			975
Deduct cheques not presented	001 027	(120)	
	001 028	(96)	
	001 029	(300)	(516)
Balance per cash book			459

The correct bank balance, $459, has been calculated and, if a statement of financial position at 31 March 2016 is prepared, $459 will be the amount included in it as the bank balance.

It is possible to start the reconciliation statement with the balance from the cash book. The final figure will be the balance on the bank statement.

Using the figures above, this would be:

Bank reconciliation statement at 31 March 2016			
		$	$
Balance per the cash book			459
Add: **unpresented cheques**	001 027	120	
	001 028	96	
	001 029	300	516
			975
Less: item not credited on bank statement			(594)
Balance per the bank statement			381

KEY TERM

Unpresented cheques: Cheque payments recorded in the cash book but not yet appearing on the bank statement.

Notice that if you start with the revised cash book balance then the items are adjusted the opposite way round than starting with the bank statement balance.

Walkthrough

At 30 June 2016, Eliza's bank statement shows a balance at bank of $1 000. When Eliza checks her cash book she finds the following:

- A payment of $200 into the bank on 30 June does not appear in the bank statement.
- Cheques totalling $325 sent to customers on 29 June do not appear in the bank statement.
- The bank statement shows that Eliza's account has been debited with bank charges of $40. These have not been recorded in the cash book.

Required

a Prepare Eliza's bank reconciliation at 30 June 2016.

b Calculate Eliza's cash book balance at 30 June 2016, before it was corrected.

Answer

a	**Bank reconciliation statement at 30 June 2016**	
		$
	Balance per bank statement	1 000
	Add: amount paid in not credited	200
		1 200
	Deduct cheques not presented	(325)
	Balance at 30 June 2016	875
b	**Cash book balance before correction**	
	Correct balance at bank at 30 June 2016	875
	Add: bank charges not debited in cash book	40
	Cash book balance before it was corrected	915

13.3 Uses of bank reconciliation statement

The process of preparing a bank reconciliation statement is an important part of the accounting system. If the reconciliation is prepared by somebody other than the cashier, the risk of fraud or embezzlement of funds is reduced. This division of duties is called **internal check**. This method of internal check is something which external auditors rely on to help them verify the accuracy of the financial data.

There are a number of uses of a bank reconciliation statement, for example:

- They reveal the correct amount of the cash at bank. Without a reconciliation, the cash book and bank statement balances may be misleading.
- They ensure that the correct bank balance is shown in the statement of financial position.
- They are an important system of control:
  - o unintended overdrawing on the bank account can be avoided
  - o a surplus of cash at bank can be highlighted and invested to earn interest
  - o if reconciliations are prepared regularly, errors are discovered early.

ACTIVITY 1

The balance on a bank statement at 31 January 2016 was $1 220 credit. The following items had been entered in the cash book in January but did not appear on the bank statements:

1 amount paid into the bank $300

2 cheques sent to customers $1 045.

Required

Calculate the cash book balance at 31 January 2016.

ACTIVITY 2

The bank balance in a cash book at 31 July 2016 was $310 (debit). The following items did not appear in the bank statement at that date:

1 cheques totalling $1 340 which had been paid into the bank on 31 July 2016
2 cheques sent to customers in July, totalling $490.

Required

Calculate the bank statement balance at 31 July 2016.

ACTIVITY 3

At 31 March 2016, a cash book showed a balance of $80 at bank. On the same date the bank statement balance was $650 (credit). When the cash book was compared with the bank statement the following were found:

1 a cheque sent to a supplier for $1 000 had not been presented for payment
2 a cheque for $220 paid into the bank had not been credited on the bank statement
3 bank charges of $210 were omitted from the cash book.

Required

a Calculate the corrected cash book balance at 31 March 2016.
b Prepare a bank reconciliation statement at 31 March 2016.

ACTIVITY 4

The following balances were extracted from the trial balance of a business at 31 December 2015:

	$	$
Trade receivables	1 055	
Trade payables		976
Rent	800	
Bank	1 245	

When the bank statement for December was received it was discovered that the following items had not been entered in the cash book:

	$
Payment to a supplier by direct debt	360
Amount received from a customer by bank transfer	420
Rent paid by standing order	200
Customer's cheque returned, dishonoured	323

Required

Prepare the adjusted trial balance to include the items omitted from the cash book.

TOP TIPS

- Complete the double entry for all items entered in the cash book. Amend the other balances in the trial balance.
- Show bank overdrafts as current liabilities in statements of financial position, never as current assets.

Chapter summary

In this chapter you learnt about the reasons why a bank reconciliation is prepared. You should now be familiar with the three steps in preparing a bank reconciliation statement (as set out in Section 13.2), including:

- how to ensure that the bank balance in the cash book equals the correct balance of cash at bank
- how to adjust a trial balance after the cash book has been reconciled to the bank statement.

TOP TIP

At this level, you will probably find that a bank reconciliation statement is a small part of a major question. For example, when preparing the financial statements for a business you may be told that the accountant has discovered that some bankings or cheque payments have not been recorded in the books of account. In this case, it will be necessary to adjust the bank balance (cash and cash equivalents figure) in the trial balance. It is important, therefore, that you are aware of how to make the necessary adjustments using the techniques in this chapter.

Practice exercise

1 The following balances have been extracted from a trial balance at 30 June 2016:

	$	$
Trade receivables	400	
Trade payables		380
Rent receivable		750
Bank charges	100	
Bank	990	

After the preparation of the trial balance, a bank statement was received and revealed that the following had not been entered in the cash book:

	$
Bank interest receivable credited to account	10
Bank charges	130
Standing order payment to supplier	298
Amount received from customer by direct debit	78
Rent received by bank transfer	150

Required

Prepare an amended trial balance extract at 30 June 2016 to take account of the amounts not entered in the cash book.

Exam practice questions

Multiple-choice questions

1 At 30 April 2016, the balance in Jenny's cash book was $1 740. At the same date, the balance on her bank statement was $2 240. Comparison of the cash book and bank statement showed the following:

i bank interest, $200, credited to Jenny in the bank statement, had not been entered in the cash book

ii cheques totalling $300 sent to suppliers in April had not been entered in the bank statement.

Which amount should be shown in the statement of financial position at 30 April 2016?

A $1 640
B $1 740
C $1 940
D $2 240

2 A cash book balance at 31 October 2015 was $1 600. When the bank statement was received the following were discovered:

i a cheque for $425 sent to a supplier had been entered in the cash book as $452

ii a cheque for $375 sent to a supplier had not been presented for payment

iii a cheque for $400 paid into the bank had not been credited in the bank statement.

What was the balance on the bank statement at 31 October 2015?

A $1 548
B $1 575
C $1 602
D $1 652

3 Yolande's bank statement showed a credit balance of $2 170 at 31 May 2016. An examination of the statement showed the following:

i a direct debit for $300 had been debited twice in the bank statement

ii a cheque for $1 015 sent to a supplier had not been presented for payment

iii a cheque for $600 paid into the bank had not been credited in the bank statement.

What was the cash book balance at 31 May 2016?

A $1 455

B $2 055

C $2 285

D $2 885

4 A bank statement at 31 January 2016 showed a balance of $1 000 Dr. The following did not appear on the statement:

i cheques not presented for payment, $230

ii a cheque for $400 banked on 31 January 2016

iii bank charges of $200 had not been entered in the cash book.

What was the original balance in the cash book at 31 January 2016, before it was amended?

A $630 Cr

B $630 Dr

C $970 Cr

D $970 Dr

5 A bank statement showed an overdraft of $360 at 31 July 2016. The following discoveries were made:

i cheques totalling $2 100 banked in July had not been credited in the bank statement

ii cheques drawn for $875 in the cash book in July had not been entered on the bank statement.

What was the balance in the cash book at 31 July 2016?

A $865 Cr

B $865 Dr

C $1 585 Cr

D $1 585 Dr

Total: 5 marks

Chapter 14
Control accounts

Learning objectives

In this chapter you will learn:

- what sales and purchase ledger control accounts are and how to prepare them
- how to reconcile the control accounts with the sales and purchase ledgers
- how to calculate revised profit for the year per draft accounts, after the control and ledger accounts have been reconciled
- how to revise the current assets and current liabilities in a draft statement of financial position.

14.1 What is a control account?

A **control account** contains the totals of all postings made to the accounts in a particular ledger.

Control accounts are usually maintained for the sales and purchase ledgers. The totals are the periodic totals of the books of prime entry from which postings are made to the ledger.

The balance on a control account should equal the total of the balances in the ledger it controls. The entries in the control accounts are the totals of the books of prime entry. As a result they are also known as total accounts. Control (or total) accounts are always kept in the nominal (or general) ledger.

Just as a trial balance acts as a check on the arithmetical accuracy of **all** the ledgers, a control account checks the arithmetical accuracy of a single ledger. A difference between a control account balance and the total of the balances in the ledger it controls, helps to show where a cause of a difference on a trial balance may be found. Any difference between the control account and the total of the balances in the ledger must be found without delay. The sales ledger control account is also known as the trade receivables control account, and the purchase ledger control account is also known as the trade payables control account.

The following examples show how postings are made from the books of prime entry to the ledgers and the control accounts, and how the balances on the control accounts should equal the totals of the balances on the accounts in the ledgers.

KEY TERM

Control account: Contains the totals of all postings made to the accounts in a particular ledger.

14.2 The purchase ledger and its control account

Books of prime entry

Purchases journal

	$
Alan	100
Peter	50
Xanthe	240
	390

Purchases returns journal

	$
Peter	8
Xanthe	10
	18

Cash book

	$		$
		Alan	80
		Peter	40
		Xanthe	200
			320

Purchase ledger
Alan account

	$		$
Cash book	80	Purchases	100
Balance c/d	20*		
	100		100
		Balance b/d	20

Purchase ledger
Peter account

	$		$
Purchases returns	8	Purchases	50
Cash book	40		
Balance c/d	2*		
	50		50
		Balance b/d	2

Purchase ledger
Xanthe account

	$		$
Purchases returns	10	Purchases	240
Cash book	200		
Balance c/d	30*		
	240		240
		Balance b/d	30

General ledger
Purchase ledger control account

	$		$
Purchase returns journal	18	Purchase journal	390
Cash book	320		
Balance c/d	52*		
	390		390
		Balance b/d	52

*Balancing figure

This is equal to the total of the balances on the individual suppliers' accounts:

	$
Alan	20
Peter	2
Xanthe	30
	52

As the two totals agree the purchase ledger reconciles with the purchase ledger control account.

14.3 How to prepare a purchase ledger control account

Enter items in the control account as follows:

Debit side	Credit side
Total of purchase ledger debit balances (if any) brought forward from the previous period	Balance on the account brought forward from the previous period
Total of goods returned to suppliers (from purchases returns journal)	Total of purchases on credit (from purchases journal)
Total of cash paid to suppliers (from cash book)	Refunds from suppliers (from cash book)
Cash discounts received (from discount column in cash book)	Interest charged by suppliers on overdue invoices (from purchases journal)
Purchase ledger balances set against balance in sales ledger (from journal)	Total of debit balances (if any) at end of period in purchase ledger, carried forward
Balance carried forward (to agree with total of credit balances in purchases ledger)	

TOP TIP

Always bring down the balance(s) on the control account to the start of the next accounting period. Remember to change the date. You must be able to show that you can complete the account by bringing down the balances.

Debit balances in the purchase ledger must **never** be netted against (deducted from) the credit balances. If you have to enter the balances in the statement of financial position, the credit balances are entered under current liabilities and shown as trade payables. Any debit balances brought down must always be shown under current assets as trade receivables.

TOP TIP

Warning: only **credit** purchases are entered in the purchase ledger control account. Do not enter cash purchases in it.

14.4 The sales ledger and its control account

Books of prime entry

Sales journal

	$
Bali	300
Carla	520
Paula	140
	960

Sales returns journal

	$
Bali	50
Paula	10
	60

Cash book

	$		$
		Bali	180
		Carla	480
		Paula	100
			760

Sales ledger
Bali account

	$		$
Sales	300	Sales returns	50
		Cash book	180
		Balance c/d	70*
	300		300
Balance b/d	70		

Sales ledger
Carla account

	$		$
Sales	520	Cash book	480
		Balance c/d	40*
	520		520
Balance b/d	40		

Purchase ledger
Paula account

	$		$
Sales	140	Sales returns	10
		Cash book	100
		Balance c/d	30*
	140		140
Balance b/d	30		

Nominal (general) ledger
Sales ledger control account

	$		$
Sales journal	960	Sales returns journal	60
		Cash book	760
		Balance c/d	140*
	960		960
Balance b/d	140		

* Balancing figure

This equals the total of the balances on the individual customers' accounts:

	$
Bali	70
Carla	40
Paula	30
	140

As the two totals agree, the sales ledger reconciles with the sales ledger control account.

14.5 How to prepare a sales ledger control account

Enter items in the control account as follows:

Debit side	Credit side
Balance brought forward from previous period	Total of sales ledger credit balances (if any) brought forward from previous period
Credit sales for period (total sales journal)	Sales returns for the period (total of sales returns journal)
Refunds to credit customers (from cash book)	Cash received from credit customers (from cash book)
Dishonoured cheques (from cash book)	Cash discounts allowed (discounts columns in cash book)
Interest charged to customers on overdue accounts (sales journal or cash book)	Irrecoverable debts written off (journal) Cash from irrecoverable debts recovered, previously written off (cash book)
Irrecoverable debts previously written off, now recovered (journal)	Sales ledger balances set against balances in purchase ledger (journal)
Total of credit balances (if any) in sales ledger at end of period carried forward	Balance carried forward to agree with total of debit balances in sales ledger

TOP TIP

Always bring down the balance(s) on the control account to the start of the next accounting period. Remember to change the date. You must show that you can complete the account by bringing down the balances.

TOP TIP

Warning: Only **credit** sales should be entered in the sales ledger control account. Never enter the following in a sales ledger control account:

- cash sales
- provisions for doubtful debts.

It is unusual for a credit balance to occur on a customer's account and on the sales ledger control account. However, from time to time it does happen for the following reasons:

- The customer may have overpaid their sales invoice.
- The customer may pay in advance, or may pay a deposit before the delivery of the goods, and thus before the sales invoice has been raised.
- The customer may have paid the invoice in full, but returned some or all of the goods. The seller has raised a credit note and posted it to the customer's account and also to the sales ledger control account.

By the same token, if these actions are reversed between buyer and seller, a debit balance can occur on the supplier's account in the purchase ledger and also in the purchase ledger control account.

14.6 Control accounts and the double-entry model

Control accounts duplicate the information contained in the purchase and sales (personal) ledgers. Control accounts **and** personal ledgers cannot both be part of the double-entry model. It is usual to treat the control accounts as part of the double entry and to regard the personal ledgers as memorandum records containing the details which support the control accounts. This means that all customer and supplier accounts are kept together in one place, making them easier to refer to. By doing this, the work can be shared between a number of staff. It also means that, like a bank reconciliation, a system of internal checks is in place, something which external auditors rely on.

Walkthrough

In this example, the information from the books of Useful Controls Limited has been used to prepare a purchase ledger control and a sales ledger control for the month of June 2016.

At 1 June 2016		
		$
Purchase ledger balances brought forward	Debit	900
	Credit	16 340
Sales ledger balances brought forward	Debit	30 580
	Credit	620
Month to 30 June 2016		
		$
Purchases journal total		65 000
Purchases returns journal total		3 150

At 1 June 2016

	$
Sales journal total	96 400
Sales returns journal total	1 980
Cash book:	
Payments to suppliers	59 540
Cheques received from customers (see note below)	103 900
Discounts received	2 670
Discounts allowed	4 520
Dishonoured cheques	3 300
Journal:	
Irrecoverable debts written off	1 220
Sales ledger balances set against purchase ledger balances	4 800

At 30 June 2016

	$
Debit balances on purchase ledger accounts	600
Credit balances on sales ledger accounts	325

Note: The cash received from customers includes $800 relating to an irrecoverable debt previously written off.

Purchase ledger control account

2016		$	2016		$
June 1	Balance b/d	900	June 1	Balance b/d	16 340
30	Purchases returns journal	3 150	30	Purchases journal	65 000
	Cash book	59 540	30	Balance c/d	600
	Discounts received	2 670			
	Sales ledger – contra	4 800			
	Balance c/d (balancing figure)	10 880			
		81 940			81 940
July 1	Balance b/d	600	July 1	Balance b/d	10 880

Sales ledger control account

2016		$	2016		$
June 1	Balance b/d	30 580	June 1	Balance b/d	620
30	Sales journal	96 400	30	Sales returns journal	1 980
	Irrecoverable debt recovered	800		Cash book	103 900
				Discounts allowed	4 520
	Bank – dishonoured cheques	3 300		Irrecoverable debts written off	1 220
	Balance c/d	325		Purchase ledger – contra	4 800
			30	Balance c/d (balancing figure)	14 365
		131 405			131 405
July 1	Balance b/d	14 365	July 1	Balance b/d	325

ACTIVITY 1

The following information has been obtained from the books of Byit Limited:

		$
At 1 March 2016 purchase ledger balances brought forward	(credit)	10 000
	(debit)	16
In the month to 31 March 2016		
Total of invoices received from suppliers		33 700
Goods returned to suppliers		824
Cheques sent to suppliers		27 500
Discounts received		1 300
At 31 March 2016 debit balances in purchase ledger		156
Credit balances in purchase ledger		?

Required

Prepare the purchase ledger control account for the month of March 2016.

ACTIVITY 2

Information extracted from the books of Soldit Limited is as follows:

		$
At 1 May 2016 sales ledger balances brought forward	(debit)	27 640
	(credit)	545
In the month to 31 May 2016		
Total of invoices sent to customers		109 650
Goods returned by customers		2 220
Cheques received from customers		98 770
Discounts allowed		3 150
Cheque received in respect of irrecoverable debt previously written off (not included above)		490
Sales ledger balance set against balance in purchase ledger		2 624
At 31 May 2016 credit balances in sales ledger		800
Debit balance carried down		?

Required

Prepare the sales ledger control account for the month of May 2016.

14.7 Uses and limitations of control accounts

As their name implies, control accounts are an important system of control on the reliability of ledger accounts. Their advantages include:

- They warn of possible errors in the ledgers they control if the totals of the balances in those ledgers do not agree with the balances on the control accounts.
- They **may** identify the ledger or ledgers in which errors have been made when there is a difference on a trial balance.

- They provide totals of trade receivables and trade payables quickly when a trial balance is being prepared.
- If a business employs several accounting staff, the control accounts should be maintained by somebody who is not involved in maintaining the sales or purchase ledgers. This increases the likelihood of errors being discovered and reduces the risk of individuals acting dishonestly. This division of duties is called internal check. For this reason control accounts are kept in the general ledger and not in the sales and purchase ledgers.
- The business accounts may not be maintained using a full double-entry system (see Chapter 16). The preparation of sales and purchases ledger control accounts are an important part of preparing the financial statements of a business in this case.

However, there are some limitations in using them:

- Control accounts may themselves contain errors (see items a and b in Section 14.8).
- Control accounts do not guarantee the accuracy of individual ledger accounts, which may contain compensating errors (e.g. items posted to wrong accounts).
- It may add to the business costs as even though a computerised accounting system will prepare them automatically, someone with specialist accounting knowledge is required to verify their accuracy.

Overall, the advantages of using them outweigh the disadvantages and they are an important aspect of accounts preparation.

14.8 How to reconcile control accounts with ledgers

When there is a difference between the balance on a control account and the total of the balances in the ledger it controls, the cause or causes must be found and the necessary corrections made. This is known as reconciling the control accounts.

It is helpful to remember the following:

a If a transaction is omitted from a book of prime entry, it will be omitted from the personal account in the sales or purchase ledger **and** from the control account. Both records will be wrong and the control account will not reveal the error. (Error of omission.)

b If a transaction is entered incorrectly in a book of prime entry, the error will be repeated in the personal account in the sales or purchase ledger **and** in the control account. Both records will be wrong and the control account will not reveal the error. (Error of original entry.)

c If an item is copied incorrectly from a book of prime entry to a personal account in the sales or purchase ledger, the control account will **not** be affected, and it will reveal that an error has been made.

d If a total in a book of prime entry is incorrect, the control account will be incorrect **but** the sales or purchase ledgers will not be affected. The control account will reveal that an error has been made.

Walkthrough

In this example, the information from Duprey's books will be used to:

a calculate the revised sales ledger balances at 31 December 2015

b calculate the revised purchase ledger balances at 31 December 2015

c prepare the amended sales ledger and purchase ledger control accounts

d prepare a statement of the revised profit for the year ended 31 December 2015

e prepare an extract from the statement of financial position at 31 December 2015 to show the trade payables and trades receivables.

You can practise this yourself in the activities that follow.

		$
Total of sales ledger balances	debit	17 640
	credit	110
Balance on sales ledger control account	debit	18 710
Total of purchase ledger balances	credit	6 120
	debit	80
Balance on purchase ledger control account	credit	6 330

The following errors have been discovered:

1 A sales invoice for $100 has been omitted from the sales journal.

2 A credit balance of $35 in the sales ledger has been extracted as a debit balance in the list of sales ledger balances.

3 The sales journal total for December has been overstated by $1 000.

4 A balance of $250 on a customer's account in the sales ledger has been set against the amount owing to him in the purchase ledger, but no entries have been made for this in the sales and purchase ledger control accounts.

5 A supplier's invoice for $940 has been entered in the purchases journal as $490.

6 An item of $340 in the purchases returns journal has been credited in the supplier's account in the purchase ledger. There was a credit balance of $800 on the supplier's account at 31 December.

7 Discounts received in December amounting to $360 have been credited to the purchase ledger control account.

Additional information

Duprey's draft accounts for the year ended 31 December 2015 show a profit for the year of $36 000. He makes a provision for doubtful debts of 6%.

Required

a Calculate the following at 31 December 2015:

i the revised sales ledger balances

ii the revised purchase ledger balances.

b Prepare the amended sales ledger and purchase ledger control accounts.

c Prepare a statement of the revised profit for the year ended 31 December 2015.

d Prepare an extract from the statement of financial position at 31 December 2015 to show the trade receivables and trade payables.

Answer

a i Revised sales ledger balances:

	Debit	Credit
	$	$
Before adjustment	17 640	110
Invoice omitted from sales journal	100	
Credit balance listed as a debit	(35)	35
Revised balances	17 705	145

a ii Revised purchase ledger balances:

	Debit	Credit
	$	$
Before adjustment	80	6 120
Error in purchases journal $(940 – 490)		450
Adjustment of return credited to supplier $(340 × 2)*		(680)
Revised balances	80	5 890

* An adjustment for an item placed on the wrong side of an account must be twice the amount of the item.

b

Amended sales ledger control account

2015		$	2015		$
Dec 31	Balance brought forward	18 710	Dec 31	Correction of sales journal total	1 000
	Invoice omitted from sales journal	100		Contra to purchase ledger	250
	Balance c/d	145		Balance c/d	17 705
		18 955			18 955
2016			**2016**		
Jan 1	Balance b/d	17 705	Jan 1	Balance b/d	145

Amended purchase ledger control account

2015		$	2015		$
Dec 31	Contra to sales ledger ¢	250	Dec 31	Balance brought forward	6 330
	Correction of discounts $(360 × 2)	720		Error in purchase journal	450
				Balance c/d	80
	Balance c/d	5 890			
		6 860			6 860
2016			**2016**		
Jan 1	Balance b/d	80	Jan 1	Balance b/d	5 890

c Revised profit for the year ended 31 December 2015:

	Decrease	Increase	
	$	$	$
Profit per draft accounts			36 000
Sales invoice omitted from sales journal		100	
Overcast of sales journal	1 000		
Purchase invoice understated	450		
Increase in provision for doubtful debts 6% of $(17 705 – 17 640)	4		
	1 454	100	(1 354)
Revised profit for the year			34 646

d Statement of financial position extracts at 31 December 2015:

	$	$
Trade receivables		
Sales ledger	17 705	
Deduct provision for doubtful debts	(1 062)	
	16 643	
Purchase ledger (debit balances)	80	16 723
Trade payables		
Purchase ledger	5 890	
Sales ledger (credit balances)	145	6 035

Notes:

- Trade receivables should never be deducted from trade payables, or trade payables from trade receivables, in a statement of financial position.
- Do not provide for doubtful debts on debit balances in the purchase ledger.

ACTIVITY 3

The following information has been extracted from the books of Rorre Limited at 31 December 2015:

	$	
Total of purchase ledger balances	64	debit
	7 217	credit
Total of sales ledger balances	23 425	debit
	390	credit
Purchase ledger control account	7 847	credit
Sales ledger control account	22 909	debit

Draft accounts show a profit of $31 000 for the year ended 31 December 2015. The following errors have been discovered:

1. An invoice for $100 has been entered twice in the purchases journal.
2. A total of $84 has been omitted from both the discounts received account and the purchase ledger control account.
3. A debit balance of $50 has been entered in the list of purchase ledger balances as a credit balance.
4. An amount of $710 owing to Trazom, a supplier, has been offset against their account in the sales ledger, but no entry has been made in the control accounts.
5. An invoice in the sales journal for $326 has been entered in the sales ledger as $362.
6. The sales journal total for December has been understated by $800.

Required

a Prepare a statement to show the corrected purchase and sales ledger balances.

b Prepare corrected purchase and sales ledger control accounts.

c Calculate the amended profit for the year ended 31 December 2015.

d Prepare a statement of financial position extract at 31 December 2015 to show the trade receivables and trade payables.

When preparing control accounts there are a number of key points you need to remember:

- Give the control accounts their correct title and head the money columns with $ signs.
- Check carefully that the entries are on the correct sides of the accounts.
- Enter the dates for the entries, distinguishing between the start and end of the period.
- Make sure that you enter the total of any credit balances in the sales ledger into the sales ledger control account, and the total of any debit balances in the purchase ledger into the purchase ledger control account.
- Calculate the other closing balances if necessary.
- Bring down the closing balances on the first day of the next period.
- Assume that control accounts, when they are kept, are part of the double entry and that the personal ledgers contain memorandum accounts, unless indicated otherwise. If control accounts are not maintained, the double entry is completed in the personal ledger accounts.
- Enter irrecoverable debts recovered on the debit side of the sales ledger control account as well as showing the cash received for them on the credit side.
- Enter 'contra' items (balances in the sales ledger set off against balances in the purchase ledger) in **both** control accounts. The entries will always be credited in the sales ledger control account and debited in the purchase ledger control account.

Chapter summary

In this chapter you learnt the preparation, purpose and uses of the sales and purchase ledger control accounts. You should now be familiar with how to prepare both accounts, and how to reconcile the control accounts with the sales and purchase ledgers. You should also have a good understanding of how to calculate revised profit for the year per draft accounts after the control and ledger accounts have been reconciled, and how to revise the current assets and current liabilities in a draft statement of financial position.

TOP TIP

The preparation of control accounts will be an important part of Chapter 16. When focusing on this topic you may be asked a specific question on preparing a control account. However, you may also be asked to reconcile the control accounts with their individual ledgers. You may be asked to calculate the effect on profit for the year of any errors discovered when reconciling the control accounts with the individual ledgers. It is important, therefore, that you practise the exercises to ensure that all these aspects are thoroughly understood.

Practice exercises

1 The following information was taken from Peter's books:

2016		
		$
March 1	Sales ledger control account balance	55 650 debit
	Purchase ledger control account balance	34 020 credit
31	Sales for March	47 700
	Purchases for March	21 840
	Cheques received from credit customers	36 900
	Payments to trade payables	24 300
	Customers' cheques returned unpaid	1 920
	Irrecoverable debts written off	2 250
	Discounts received	600
	Discounts allowed	930
	Returns inwards	580
	Returns outwards	330
	Credit balance in purchase ledger offset with sales ledger	810

Required

Prepare the sales ledger control account and the purchase ledger control account for the month of March 2016.

2 At 31 December 2015, the balance on Sellit's sales ledger control account was $17 584 (debit). It did not agree with the total of balances extracted from the sales ledger. The following errors have been found:

1 The total of the discounts allowed column in the cash book has been overstated by $210.

2 A receipt of $900 from P. Ford, a customer, has been treated as a refund from B. Ford, a supplier.

3 An invoice for $1 200 sent to P. Williams, a customer, has been entered in the sales journal as $1 020.

4 The total of the sales journal for December has been understated by $600.

5 Goods with a selling price of $578 were sent to Will Dither, a customer, in December, and he has been invoiced for that amount. It has now been discovered that the goods were sent on sale or return and the customer has not yet indicated whether he will purchase the goods.

6 An invoice for $3 160 sent to W. Yeo, a customer, has been entered correctly in the sales journal but has been entered in the customer's account as $3 610.

Required

a Prepare the sales ledger control account showing clearly the amendments to the original balance.

b Calculate the total of the balances extracted from the sales ledger before the errors listed above had been corrected.

c Prepare the journal entries to correct the sales ledger accounts. Narratives are required.

3 At 31 May 2016, the debit balance on Julie's sales ledger control account was $18 640. This balance did not agree with the total of balances extracted from the sales ledger. The following errors have now been found:

1 Cash received from trade receivables entered in the control account included $400 in respect of a debt which had previously been written off. This fact had not been recognised in the control account.

2 A debit balance of $325 in the sales ledger had been set off against an account in the purchase ledger. This transfer had been debited in the sales ledger control account and credited in the purchase ledger control account.

3 Cash sales of $1 760 had been recorded in the cash book as cash received from trade receivables.

4 Cash received from K. Bali, $244, had been entered in the account of B. Kali in the sales ledger.

5 Credit balances in the sales ledger totalled $436.

Required

a State **two** reasons why there may a credit balance on a customer's account in the sales ledger.

b Prepare the corrected sales ledger control account at 31 May 2016.

Exam practice questions

Multiple-choice questions

1 The debit balance on a sales ledger control account at 30 September is $104 000. The following errors have been discovered:

	$
Total of sales journal overstated	1 300
Discounts allowed omitted from sales ledger control account	870
Irrecoverable debts written off not recorded in sales ledger control account	240
Increase in provision for doubtful debts	600

What is the total of the balances in the sales ledger?

A $100 990
B $101 590
C $102 070
D $103 330

2 The credit balance on a purchases ledger control account at 31 October is $28 000. The following errors have been found:

	$
Amount transferred from Calif's account in the sales ledger to his account in the purchase ledger not recorded in the control accounts	1 400

	$
A debit balance in the purchase ledger at 31 October not carried down in the purchase ledger control account	300
A refund to a cash customer debited in purchase ledger control account	150

What is the total of the credit balances in the purchase ledger?

A $26 450

B $26 750

C $27 050

D $28 950

3 A purchase ledger control account has been reconciled with the purchase ledger balances as shown:

	$
Balance per control account	76 000
Total of purchases journal for one month not posted to general ledger	4 000
Cash paid to trade payables not posted to purchase ledger	5 000
Total of balances in purchase ledger	85 000

Which figure for trade payables should be shown in the statement of financial position?

A $75 000

B $77 000

C $80 000

D $85 000

Total: 3 marks

Structured questions

1 Haeun Joo is a sole trader who maintains full accounting records. The following information was extracted from his books of account for the year ended 30 April 2016:

	$
Purchase ledger balances at 1 May 2015	64 680
Credit purchases	1 236 210
Credit purchases returns	18 600
Cheques paid to trade payables	1 118 970
Cash purchases	13 410
Discount received on credit purchases	47 100
Credit balances offset with sales ledger accounts	7 815

Required

a State **two** advantages to a business of maintaining sales and purchases ledger control accounts. **[2 marks]**

b Prepare the purchase ledger control account for the year ended 30 April 2016. **[4 marks]**

Additional information

The total of the balances extracted from Haeun Joo's purchase ledger at 30 April 2016 amounted to $101 490. This did not agree with the closing balance in the control account. The following errors were then discovered:

1. The total discount received had been overstated by $1 500.
2. A purchase invoice for $3 060 had been completely omitted from the books.
3. A credit balance in the purchase ledger account had been understated by $150.
4. A credit balance of $1 275 in the purchase ledger had been set off against a contra entry in the sales ledger, but no entry had been made in either control account.
5. A payment of $2 175 had been debited to the creditor's account but was omitted from the bank account.
6. A credit balance of $4 815 had been omitted from the list of trade payables.

Required

c Prepare an amended purchase ledger control account for the year ended 30 April 2016. **[4 marks]**

d Complete the following table to reconcile the amended balance on the purchase ledger control account with the list of balances extracted from the purchase ledger at 30 April 2016.

	Add	Minus	Balance
	$	$	$
Total of purchase ledger balances at 30 April 2016			101 490
Amended balance on purchase ledger control account at 30 April 2016			

[5 marks]

[Total: 15]

2 State **three** reasons for keeping control accounts.

3 The following information was extracted from the books of Dinh Truong for the year ended 30 April 2016:

	$
Purchase ledger balance at 1 May 2015	43 120
Credit purchases for the year	824 140
Credit purchases returns	12 400
Cheques paid to trade payables	745 980

	$
Cash purchases	8940
Discount received on credit purchases	31400
Credit balances offset against sales ledger accounts	5210

Required

a Explain why balances in the purchase ledger are offset against balances in the sales ledger. **[3 marks]**

b Prepare the purchase ledger control account for the year ended 30 April 2016. **[4 marks]**

Additional information

The total of the balances in Dinh Truong's purchase ledger did not agree with the closing balance in the purchase ledger control account. The following errors have been discovered:

1 Discounts received had been overstated by $1000.

2 A credit purchases invoice for $2040 had been completely omitted from the books.

3 A purchases ledger account had been understated by $100.

4 A credit balance of $850 in the purchases ledger had been set off against a contra entry in the sales ledger, but no entry had been made in either control account.

5 A payment of $1450 had been debited to the creditor's account but was omitted from the bank account.

6 A credit balance of $3210 had been omitted from the list of trade payables.

Required

c Prepare an amended purchase ledger control account for the year ended 30 April 2016. **[4 marks]**

d Prepare a statement to show the changes to be made in the purchase ledger to reconcile it with the new control account balance. **[4 marks]**

Total: 15

Chapter 15
Suspense accounts

Learning objectives

In this chapter you will learn:

- the purpose of suspense accounts and how to prepare them
- how to prepare journal entries to correct errors
- how to revise the profit for the year per draft accounts after errors have been corrected
- how to revise the working capital in a draft statement of financial position.

15.1 What is a suspense account?

Suspense accounts are sometimes used when transactions are recorded in the books before any decision has been made about their proper accounting treatment. For example, an invoice may contain a mixture of capital and revenue expenditure. The expenditure may be recorded in a suspense account until it is decided how much is capital expenditure and how much is revenue.

However, this chapter is only concerned with suspense accounts that are opened when the causes of differences on trial balances cannot immediately be found and corrected.

KEY TERM

Suspense account: An account opened to record a difference between the debit and credit totals of the trial balance.

15.2 When a suspense account should be opened

A suspense account should be opened only when attempts to find the cause of a difference on a trial balance have been unsuccessful. The following checks should be carried out before opening a suspense account:

a Check the additions of the trial balance.

b If the difference is divisible by 2, look for a balance of half the difference which may be on the wrong side of the trial balance. (Example: a difference of $1 084 may be caused by 'discounts allowed $542' being entered on the credit side of the trial balance.)

c If the difference is divisible by 9, look for a balance where digits may have been reversed. (Example: a difference of $18 may be caused by $542 entered in trial balance as $524.)

d Check the totals of sales ledger balances and purchase ledger balances against the control accounts, if these have been prepared.

e Check the extraction of balances from the ledgers.

If the cause of the difference has still not been found, and an income statement and a statement of financial position are required urgently, a suspense account may be opened.

15.3 How to open a suspense account

A suspense account is opened in the general ledger with a balance on whichever side of the account will make the trial balance agree when the balance is inserted in it. For example, if the total of the credit side of a trial balance is $100 less than the total of the debit side, the suspense account will be opened with a credit balance of $100. When the suspense account balance is inserted in the trial balance, the latter will balance. A statement of financial position may then be prepared.

15.4 When a suspense account has been opened

The cause or causes of the difference on the trial balance must be investigated at the earliest opportunity and the errors corrected.

In real life, if there is still a small balance on a suspense account after all reasonable attempts have been made to find the difference, a business may decide that the amount involved is not material. It will save further time and expense in searching for errors by writing the balance off to the income statement. However, there may be a danger that a small difference hides large errors which do not quite cancel each other out.

The types of error which will require a suspense account to be opened will include:

- When only half of the transaction has been posted. For example, the payment of wages has been entered as a credit in the bank account, but no other entry has been made on the debit side of an account.

- When both entries have been made on the same side of two separate accounts. For example, when the payment of wages has been credited to both the bank account and the wages account.
- When the entries have been made on the correct side of the account, but the figures differ. For example, the payment of wages has been correctly entered in the bank account as a credit of $230. However, the debit in the wages account is $320.

There are other instances, as you will see in some of the exercises.

15.5 How to correct errors

The correction of errors will require journal entries which will be posted to the suspense (and other) accounts **unless** they are errors that do **not** affect the trial balance, which are as follows:

- errors of omission
- errors of commission
- errors of principle
- errors of original entry
- errors caused by the complete reversal of entries
- compensating errors.

(These types of errors have been explained more fully in Section 6.3.)

To decide how to correct an error, ask the following three questions:

a How has the transaction been recorded?

b How should the transaction have been recorded?

c What adjustments are required to correct the error?

Remember the following:

- An item on the wrong side of an account must be corrected by an adjustment equal to twice the amount of the original error (once to cancel the error and once to place the item on the correct side of the account).
- Some errors do not affect the double entry; an example would be a balance on a sales ledger account copied incorrectly onto a summary of balances for inclusion in the trial balance. The summary of balances should be amended and a one-sided entry in the journal prepared to correct the suspense account. Such errors are not required to be corrected by debit and credit entries.

Walkthrough

Kadriye extracted a trial balance from her ledgers on 31 December 2015. The trial balance totals were $23 884 (debit) and $24 856 (credit). She placed the difference in a suspense account so that she could prepare a draft income statement for the year ended 31 December 2015, and a statement of financial position at that date.

Kadriye then found the following errors:

1 The debit side of the telephone account had been overstated by $200.

2 An invoice sent to Singh for $240 had been completely omitted from the books.

3 A cheque for $124 received from X and Co. had been posted to the debit of their account.

4 The purchase of some office equipment for $1 180 had been debited to office expenses account.

5 Discounts received, $90, had been posted to the purchase ledger but not to the discounts received account.

6 Rent paid, $800, had been credited to the rent receivable account.

7 A refund of an insurance premium, $60, had been recorded in the cash book but no other entry had been made.

8 A purchase of office stationery, $220, had been debited to purchases account in error.

9 A credit balance of $30 in the purchase ledger had been omitted from the list of balances extracted from the ledger. The total of the list had been included in the trial balance. Kadriye does not keep control accounts in the nominal ledger.

10 Goods returned to Speedsel had been credited to Speedsel's account and debited to purchases returns account. The goods had cost $400.

Kadriye prepared the following journal entries to correct errors 1 to 10 (narratives have been included):

TOP TIP

Always check if narratives are required when preparing journal entries. Do not waste valuable time writing narratives if these are **not** required. When writing the narrative it is always a good idea to include the word 'corrected', 'correction' or 'correcting'.

Journal entries to correct the errors			
		$	$
1	*Note: The debit side of the telephone account is overstated by $200. Reduce this by crediting the account and debiting the suspense account with $200.*		
	Suspense account	200	
	Telephone account		200
	Correction of the overcast of $200 of the telephone account.		
2	*Note: This transaction has been omitted from the books entirely. It has not affected the trial balance and the suspense account is not involved. (Error of omission.)*		
	Singh	240	
	Sales		240
	Recording invoice for $240 sent to Singh but omitted from books.		
3	*Note: $124 has been posted to the wrong side of X and Co.'s account. This is corrected by crediting their account with double that amount.*		
	Suspense account	248	
	X and Co. account		248
	Correction of $124 received from X and Co., debited to their account in error.		
4	*Note: This is an error of principle; do not adjust through the suspense account.*		
	Office equipment (asset) account	1 180	
	Office expenses account		1 180
	Purchase of office equipment treated as revenue expense in error.		

Journal entries to correct the errors		$	$
5	*Note: This is not an error of complete omission; correct through the suspense account.*		
	Suspense account	90	
	Discounts received account		90
	Discounts received, $90, omitted from discounts received account.		
6	*Note: Rent receivable account must be debited to cancel error; rent payable must be debited to record payment correctly. Note separate debit entries must be made.*		
	Rent receivable account	800	
	Rent payable account	800	
	Suspense account		1600
	Correction of rent paid incorrectly treated as rent received.		
7	*Note: This refund has not been completely omitted from the books. Adjust through the suspense account.*		
	Suspense account	60	
	Insurance account		60
	Refund of insurance premium omitted from the insurance account.		
8	*Note: This is an error of commission. Do not adjust through the suspense account.*		
	Office stationery account	220	
	Purchases account		220
	Purchase of office stationery treated as inventory for resale in error.		
9	*Note: This is not a double entry error but it has affected the trial balance. The list of balances must be corrected and a one-sided entry in the suspense account is required. This is quite a tricky problem and requires some further explanation. When the list of balances was extracted from the purchase ledger, one of the balances amounting to $30 was not included in the list. This incorrect total was used in the trial balance, so the trial balance would not balance by $30 as a result. In order to correct the error, $30 must be debited in the suspense account. The total of the purchase ledger balances in the trial balance must also be increased by $30. However, no entry needs to be made on the credit side of any of the balances in the purchase ledger as they have been correctly added to arrive at their individual totals.*		
	Suspense account	30	
10	*Note: This is a complete reversal of entries. The correcting entry is twice the original amount and the suspense account is not involved.*		
	Speedsel		800
	Purchases returns account		800
	Goods returned to Speedsel, $400, credited to their account and debited to purchases returns account in error.		

Having completed the journal entries, it is now possible to prepare the suspense account. This is shown below.

Suspense account

	$		$
Difference on trial balance [1]	972	Rent receivable	800*
Telephone	200	Rent payable	800*
X and Co.	248		
Discounts received	90		
Insurance	60		
Correction of trade payables	30		
	1600		1600

[1] The suspense account is opened with the difference on the trial balance and then posted from the journal entries.

*These two entries should be shown separately as the double entry is completed in different accounts.

Kadriye opened the suspense account as she failed to agree the totals on her trial balance when she prepared it. One of the advantages of doing this is that it enabled her to provide draft financial statements quickly. She could then go back and find the differences, which she has done.

Her draft income statement showed a profit for the year ended 31 December 2015 of $8400 and the statement of financial position at that date showed working capital (current assets less current liabilities) of $1250.

Kadriye is now able to:

- calculate the revised profit for the year ended 31 December 2015
- calculate the revised working capital at 31 December 2015.

This is done below.

Calculation of corrected profit for the year ended 31 December 2015

		Decrease	Increase	
		$	$	$
Profit per draft income statement				8400
Error 1	Decrease in telephone expense		200	
Error 2	Increase in sales		240	
Error 3	No effect on profit			
Error 4	Decrease in office expenses		1180	
Error 5	Increase in discounts received		90	
Error 6	Reduction in rent receivable	800		
	Increase in rent payable	800		
Error 7	Reduction in insurance premium		60	
Error 8	No effect on profit for the year			
Error 9	No effect on profit for the year			
Error 10	Increase in purchases returns		800	
		1600	2570	
			(1600)	970
Revised profit for the year				9370

TOP TIP

Set the calculation out as shown above. Untidy, 'straggly' calculations are not easy to follow.

Debit entries to nominal accounts in the journal decrease profit, and credit entries to nominal accounts increase profit.

Calculation of working capital at 31 December 2015

		Decrease	Increase	
		Dr	Cr	
		$	$	$
Working capital per draft statement of financial position				1250
Error 1	Singh invoice omitted	240		
Error 3	X and Co. $124 cheque misposted		248	
Error 9	Credit balance omitted		30	
Error 10	Goods returned to Speedsel	800		
		1040	278	
		(278)		762
Revised working capital				2012

This is a comprehensive example of what types of errors can cause a difference on the trial balance. Work through it a few times if necessary to make sure you are happy with the journal entries. Also look at which errors affect the profit, and whether or not they increase or decrease it. Likewise, work through which adjustments will have an effect on the statement of financial position.

The layout of the answer given above is a good one and should be followed whenever possible. Adjust working capital by journal postings to personal accounts and by personal accounts omitted from the trial balance.

TOP TIP

Never make a journal entry to, say, trade payables or non-current assets. These are headings in the statement of financial position. Always make your journal entry with a posting to a ledger account, such as sales or rent receivable, as in this example.

ACTIVITY 1

Lee's trial balance at 30 June 2016 fails to agree and he places the difference in a suspense account. Lee then discovers the following errors:

1. The total of the sales journal for one month was $5430. This had been posted to the sales account as $5340.
2. An invoice for $150 for the purchase of goods for resale from Bilder had been entirely omitted from the books.

3 A cheque for $75 from Doyle, a customer, had been credited to his account as $57.
4 A debt of $50 in the sales ledger had been written off as irrecoverable but no entry had been made in the irrecoverable debts account.
5 An improvement to a machine at a cost of $400 had been debited to machinery repairs account. (Lee depreciates machinery by the straight-line method over ten years; a full year's depreciation is calculated for the year of purchase.)

Required

a Prepare the suspense account in Lee's ledger, showing clearly the difference on the trial balance at 30 June as the first entry, and the entries required to adjust the errors.

b Prepare journal entries for errors 2 and 5. (Narratives are **not** required.)

Additional information

Lee's draft income statement for the year ended 30 June 2016 showed a profit for the year of $3 775.

Required

c Calculate the corrected profit for the year ended 30 June 2016.

ACTIVITY 2

When Jayesh extracted a trial balance from his books at 31 December 2015, he found that it did not balance. He entered the difference in a suspense account and then prepared a draft income statement which showed a draft profit for the year of $2 500. Jayesh later found the following errors:

1 The balance of opening inventory, $8 500, had been entered in the trial balance as $5 800.
2 The inventory at 31 December 2015 had been understated by $2 000.
3 Repairs to a machine, $3 500, had been posted to machinery at cost account as $5 300.
4 An invoice in the sum of $800 for the sale of goods to Bane had been posted to Bane's account but had not been entered in the sales account.
5 A credit balance of $63 in the sales ledger had been extracted as a debit balance. Jayesh does not maintain control accounts.

Required

a Prepare the journal entries to correct the errors. (Narratives are **not** required.)

b Prepare the suspense account showing the trial balance difference and the correcting entries.

Additional information

Jayesh's draft statement of financial position at 31 December 2015 showed working capital of $3 200.

Required

c Calculate Jayesh's corrected working capital at 31 December 2015.

This is a difficult topic and one which causes problems for many learners. Set out below are a number of key points to help you with your understanding of this topic:

- Remember the six types of error that do not affect the trial balance. These are not corrected through the suspense account.
- Prepare correcting journal entries in proper form. (Revise Section 3.10.) Note whether narratives are required.
- The first entry in a suspense account is the difference on the trial balance. Enter it on the same side of the account as it will be entered in the trial balance.
- Post the suspense account from journal entries. If these have not been required it may be helpful to prepare them in rough.
- The suspense account should never have a balance on it when you have posted the journal entries to it.
- Calculate revised profit or loss from the nominal account entries in the journal.
- Calculate revised working capital from the journal entries affecting current assets and current liabilities.
- Do not make journal entries to other books of prime entry. Postings from the journal should always be to named accounts in the ledgers.

Chapter summary

In this chapter you have considered the correction of errors. Some of the errors affect the suspense account (the purpose and preparation of which you have learnt about in this chapter), and others don't. You also learnt about some of these errors in Chapter 6 (the trial balance), so it might also be worth checking back to that chapter as well if you are at all unsure of this topic. All require correction by use of journal entries, which you have learnt about in this chapter, and you should know which of those errors do and do not affect the suspense account. You should also be able to correct errors by journal entry and show the impact of their correction on the profit for the year. Finally, you should be able to show how the correction of the errors affects sections of the statement of financial position.

TOP TIPS

- The whole of this chapter covers an area which students have difficulty with. The most common error is to complete the journal entries the wrong way round. For example, debiting the account which should be credited and vice versa. Another common error is to reverse the entries in the suspense account when it is prepared.
- The type of questions you have encountered in this chapter form a wider test of your understanding of the double-entry method, so it pays to ensure you have a strong understanding of all aspects covered.

Practice exercises

1 Bastien does not maintain control accounts. His trial balance does not balance and he has opened a suspense account. The following errors have now been discovered:

1 Discount received from Veeraj, amounting to $70, has been included in the discount column of the cash book but has not been posted to Veeraj's account.

2 Goods have been sold on credit to Bernard for $1 400 less 25% trade discount. Correct entries have been made in the sales journal but $1 000 has been posted to Bernard's ledger account.

3 A cheque for $400 received from Rodney has been debited in the cash book and also debited in Rodney's ledger account.

4 A motor vehicle costing $12 000 has been bought on credit from Nedof Motors. The purchases account has been debited and Nedof Motor's account credited.

5 $60 spent by Bastien on his personal expenses has been posted to the other operating expenses account.

Required

Prepare the entries in Bastien's journal, with suitable narratives, to correct the above errors.

2 Boulder's trial balance at 31 March did not balance and the difference was entered in a suspense account. Boulder does not maintain control accounts. The following information was later discovered:

1 A receipt of $313 from Head, a customer, has been entered correctly in the cash book but has been debited to Head's account in the sales ledger as $331.

2 Goods sold to Joey for $100 have been returned by him and entered correctly in the sales returns account. No entry has been made for the return in Joey's account in the sales ledger.

3 The purchase of a second-hand motor vehicle costing $3 000 has been debited to the motor vehicle expenses account.

4 The total of the discount allowed column in the cash book has been overcast by $300.

5 A dishonest employee has stolen $700 from the business and the cash will not be recovered. No entry to record the theft has been made in the accounts.

Required

a Prepare journal entries to correct errors 1 to 5. Narratives are required.

b Prepare a suspense account commencing with the trial balance difference.

Additional information

The working capital shown in the statement of financial position at 31 March, before the errors were corrected, was $2 400.

Required

c Calculate the working capital after the errors have been corrected.

3 Amber's trial balance at 31 December failed to agree and the difference was entered in a suspense account. The total of the purchase ledger balances had been entered as creditors in the trial balance, but it did not agree with the credit balance of $5 419 on the purchase ledger control account. The following errors were found:

1 No entry had been made in the books to record a refund by cheque of $90 from Victor, a supplier.

2 A cheque for $420 sent to Shah, a supplier, had been entered correctly in the cash book but debited to general expenses account as $240.

3 Goods returned, $900, by Amil, a customer, had been credited in Amil's account and debited in the purchases account.

4 Goods which cost $350 had been returned to Hussein, a supplier. No entry had been made in the books for this.

5 The discounts received column in the cash book had been undercast by $600.

Required

a Prepare journal entries to correct errors 1 to 5. Narratives are not required.

b Prepare the suspense account commencing with the difference on the trial balance.

4 Logan has prepared the following trial balance at 31 March 2016:

Logan
Trial balance at 31 March 2016

Account	**$**	**$**
Sales		131 940
Purchases	33 000	
Sales returns	260	
Purchase returns		315
Opening inventory	6 900	
Trade receivables control	14 125	
Trade payables control		16 070
Discounts allowed	700	
Discounts received		614
Wages and salaries	20 600	
Advertising	1 000	
General expenses	2 340	
Bank	13 710	
Premises	70 000	
Motor vehicles	5 000	
Equipment	3 500	
Capital		25 000
Drawings	3 000	
Suspense		196
	174 135	174 135

Logan is unable to find the difference on the trial balance and has entered the difference in the suspense account. The following errors have been made in the accounts:

1 Discounts allowed of $55 have been posted to the credit of discounts received.

2 Purchase returns of $108 have been posted to the debit of sales returns.

3 A cheque for $400 from a customer has been dishonoured, but no record has been made of this in the accounts. There is no reason to believe that payment will not be made in April 2016.

4 Equipment bought during the year for $4 400 has been debited to purchases account.

5 During the year, Logan had taken goods for resale which cost $800 for his own personal use.

6 $90 of the general expenses related to an amount paid out of the business bank account for one of Logan's private expenses. In his attempt to correct the accounts, Logan made another debit entry of $90 in the general expenses account, with no other entry being made.

Required

a Prepare journal entries to correct errors 1 to 6. Narratives are not required.

b Prepare the suspense account to show the correcting entries.

c Prepare a corrected trial balance at 31 March 2016.

Additional information

The profit for the year per the draft accounts, prepared before the above errors were corrected, was $68 069.

Required

d Prepare a statement of corrected profit for the year showing the effect of each error on the profit for the year per the draft accounts.

Exam practice questions

Multiple-choice questions

(In each of the following cases, a trial balance has failed to agree and the difference has been entered in a suspense account.)

1 A credit balance in the sum of $93 has been omitted from the list of balances extracted from the sales ledger. What is the effect on the trial balance?

A the credit side is understated by $93
B the credit side is overstated by $93
C the debit side is understated by $93
D the debit side is overstated by $93

2 A credit note for $46 sent to A. Moses has been debited to A. Mason's account in the sales ledger. Both A. Moses and A. Mason had large debit balances. What effect will this have on the trial balance?

	Debit total	Credit total
A	none	none
B	$46 overstated	$46 understated
C	none	$92 understated
D	$92 overstated	none

3 The total of the sales journal for one month is $9 160. It has been entered in the sales account as $9 610. Which entries are required to correct the error?

	Debit		Credit	
A	Sales account	$450	Sales journal	$450
B	Sales journal	$450	Sales account	$450
C	Sales account	$450	Suspense account	$450
D	Suspense account	$450	Sales account	$450

4 An invoice for repairs to machinery, $500, has been entered in the machinery at cost account. Which entries are required to correct the error?

	Debit		Credit	
A	Machinery at cost account	$500	Repairs to machinery account	$500
B	Repairs to machinery account	$500	Machinery at cost account	$500
C	Repairs to machinery account	$500	Suspense account	$500
D	Suspense account	$500	Machinery at cost account	$500

5 Which of the following will cause a difference on a trial balance?

A an invoice omitted from the sales journal
B an invoice for $415 entered in the sales journal as $451
C an invoice for $600 entered in the sales journal not included in the monthly total
D a credit note entered in the sales journal

6 After which error will a trial balance still balance?

A wages paid, $1 500, was entered correctly in the bank account but debited to the wages account as $2 500
B rent receivable of $200 was debited to the rent payable account
C goods returned to supplier, $150, were entered in purchases returns journal as $105
D the sales journal was undercast by $200

7 A trial balance failed to agree and a suspense account was opened. It was then found that rent received of $500 had been debited to the rent payable account. Which entries are required to correct this error?

	Rent received account		Rent payable account		Suspense account	
		$		$		$
A	credit	500	credit	500	debit	1000
B	credit	500	debit	500	no entry	
C	debit	500	credit	500	debit	1000
D	debit	500	credit	500	no entry	

Total: 7 marks

Chapter 16
Incomplete records

Learning objectives

In this chapter you will learn:

- how to calculate profit or loss from statements of affairs
- how to value inventory when preparing the income statement and statement of financial position
- an introduction to International Accounting Standard 2 (IAS 2)
- how to prepare income statements and statements of financial position from incomplete records
- the relationship between mark-up and margin
- how to calculate the cost of inventory lost by fire or theft
- the advantages and disadvantages of using a double-entry bookkeeping system.

16.1 Introduction

This chapter and the following chapters on financial accounting, up to and including Chapter 27, will start to consolidate all the knowledge of financial accounting you have gained so far. Thus many of the topics covered such as accruals, depreciation and irrecoverable and doubtful debts will come into questions and illustrations in this and the next few chapters. Before starting on this chapter therefore, it may be worthwhile looking back at the earlier chapters to make sure that you are familiar with the topics and techniques explained.

KEY TERMS

Incomplete records: Any method of recording transactions that is not based on the double-entry model.

Single-entry bookkeeping: Only one aspect of each transaction is recorded.

Statement of affairs: A list of the business assets and liabilities at a point in time, usually prepared to calculate the capital of the business at that point in time.

16.2 What are incomplete records?

The term **incomplete records** describes any method of recording transactions that is not based on the double-entry model. Often, only a cash book, or only records of trade receivables and trade payables, are kept by many small business owners, who lack the knowledge of double-entry bookkeeping. This means that only one aspect of each transaction is recorded. This is **single-entry bookkeeping**. Incomplete records also describe situations where the only records kept may be invoices for purchases, copies of sales invoices, cheque counterfoils and bank statements. In all these cases, income statements and statements of financial position cannot be prepared in the normal way. At the end of the financial year it is not unusual for the owners of small businesses to present their accountant with a variety of paperwork. It is then up to the accountant to prepare the financial statements for the business owner.

16.3 How to calculate profit or loss from the statement of financial position

When records of transactions are insufficient to enable an income statement to be prepared, the profit or loss for the year of a business for a given period may be calculated if the assets and liabilities of the business, at both the start and end of the period, are known. The method is based upon two principles:

a the accounting equation:

assets – liabilities = capital

b profit increases capital; losses reduce capital.

The difference between the opening and closing capitals, after making adjustments for new capital introduced and the owner's drawings in the period, will reveal the profit or loss. Capital is calculated by listing the assets and liabilities in a **statement of affairs**. This is similar to a statement of financial position. However, in the statement of affairs the assets and liabilities are only listed. Headings such as non-current assets or current liabilities are not included.

Walkthrough

Fatima is a hair stylist who has been in business for some time. She has never kept records of her takings and payments. However, she wishes to know how much profit or loss she has made in the year ended 31 December 2015. In order to do this she has prepared the following list of her assets and liabilities at the start and end of her financial year. They were as follows:

	1 January 2015	31 December 2015
	$	$
Equipment	800	1 000
Inventory of hair styling sundries	70	45
Amounts owing from clients	50	70
Rent paid in advance	100	120
Balance at bank	150	160
Creditors for supplies	25	30
Electricity owing	40	50

Fatima has drawn $100 per week from the business for personal expenses.

In order to calculate her profit for the year ended 31 December 2015, Fatima calculated her net assets at the start of the year (1 January 2015) and the end of the year (31 December 2015). In effect this is a calculation of her capital at those dates.

Statements of affairs at	1 January 2015		31 December 2015	
	$	$	$	$
Equipment		800		1000
Inventory of hair styling sundries		70		45
Amounts owing from clients		50		70
Rent paid in advance		100		120
Balance at bank		150		160
		1 170		1 395
Less:				
Trade payables	(25)		(30)	
Electricity owing	(40)	(65)	(50)	(80)
Net assets (= capital)		1 105		1 315

The difference between her two net asset figures is a measure of how much her business grew during the year as a result of the profit made:

net assets at 31 December 2015 – net assets at 1 January 2015 = $210 (1 315 – 1 105).

So was Fatima's profit for the year $210?

No, because she took drawings during the year which, had she not done so, would have remained in her bank account. This would have had the effect of increasing her net assets at 31 December 2015 to $6 515 (1 315 + 5 200). Her profit for the year was therefore $5 410 (6 515 – 1 105) or:

	$
Net assets at 31 December 2015	1 315
Add: drawings in year to 31 December 2015 (52 × $100)	5 200
	6 515
Deduct capital at beginning of year	(1 105)*
Profit for the year ended 31 December 2015	5 410

*From above.

In effect, Fatima has written down her capital account in exactly the same way as we saw in Chapter 8:

Fatima
Capital account

2015			**2015**		
		$			**$**
Dec 31	Drawings	5200	Jan 1	Balance	1105
	Balance c/d	1315	Dec 31	Profit for the year (balancing figure)	5410
		6515			6515
			2016		
			Jan 1	Balance b/d	1315

The balancing figure in the account above is the profit for the year.

TOP TIP

When an asset is valued at more or less than cost, it should be included in a statement of affairs at valuation.

ACTIVITY 1

Liam has run a business repairing motor vehicles for some years but has not kept proper accounting records. However, the following information is available:

	At 1 January 2015	**At 31 December 2015**
	$	**$**
Premises at cost	4000	4000
Motor van at cost	5000	5000
Motor car at cost		3000
Plant and equipment	1100	1300
Inventory of parts	400	200
Trade receivables for work done	700	800
Balance at bank	1300	900
Owing to suppliers for parts	170	340

The premises were bought some years ago and were valued at $9000 at 31 December 2015.

At the same date, the motor van was valued at $4000. The motor car was Liam's own car, which he brought into the business during the year at its original cost. Liam's weekly drawings were $120.

Required

Calculate Liam's profit or loss for the year ended 31 December 2015.

16.4 How to prepare an income statement and a statement of financial position from incomplete records

Most businesses keep some records of receipts and payments. The records may consist of bank paying-in book counterfoils, chequebook counterfoils and bank statements, in addition to suppliers' invoices and copies of sales invoices. From these records it may be possible to prepare an income statement and a statement of financial position. The steps are as follows:

Step 1 Prepare an opening statement of affairs for this business. This statement of financial position will allow the opening capital to be calculated.

Step 2 Prepare a receipts and payment account. This is similar to preparing a bank account and a cash account for the business. You may need this to calculate the closing bank/cash balances for the closing statement of financial position.

Step 3 Prepare control accounts for trade receivables and trade payables, if necessary, to calculate sales and purchases. These will usually be the amounts required to make the control accounts balance.

Step 4 Adjust the receipts and payments for accruals and prepayments at the beginning and end of the period.

Step 5 Calculate provisions for doubtful debts, depreciation and any other matters not mentioned above.

Step 6 Prepare the income statement and statement of financial position from the information now available.

Walkthrough

Aasim is a sole trader who runs a small shop. The only financial records that he kept for his business are bank paying-in book counterfoils, chequebook counterfoils and records of trade receivables and trade payables. He has asked his brother, Salim, who is an accountant, to help him prepare his income statement and statement of financial position for the year ended 31 December 2015. From his financial records, Aasim has made notes summarising his transactions with the bank in the year ended 31 December 2015 as follows:

Note 1

Bankings – takings paid into the bank: $8 000.

Payments – cheque payments:

- to suppliers $2 430
- rent $600
- electricity $320
- postage and stationery $80
- purchase of shop fittings $480
- personal expenses $2 700.

Aasim banked all his takings after paying the following in cash:

- trade payables $400
- other operating expenses $115.

Next, he prepared a summary of assets and liabilities at 1 January 2015.

Note 2

Aasim estimated his assets and liabilities at 1 January 2015 to be:

- shop fittings $1 600
- inventory $1 960
- trade receivables $240
- rent prepaid $80
- bank balance $1 500
- cash in hand $50
- trade payables for goods $420
- electricity owing $130.

He then prepared a summary of his assets and liabilities at 31 December 2015.

Note 3

At 31 December 2015, Aasim listed his assets and liabilities as follows:

- shop fittings $1 800
- inventory $1 520
- trade receivables $380
- rent prepaid $50
- bank balance $2 640 debit
- cash in hand $50
- suppliers trade payables $390
- electricity owing $225.

Aasim now wishes to prepare his income statement for the year ended 31 December 2015 and his statement of financial position at that date. To do that he will apply the six steps.

TOP TIP

With questions like this it is very much a case of looking through the question to find the relevant information.

Step 1 Opening statement of affairs at 1 January 2015

The information for this is all in note 2 above.

Statements of affairs at 1 January 2015		
	$	$
Shop fittings		1 600
Inventory		1 960
Trade receivables		240
Rent prepaid		80
Bank		1 500
Cash in hand		50
		5 430

Statements of affairs at 1 January 2015		
	$	$
Less liabilities:		
Trade payables	(420)	
Electricity owing (other payables)	(130)	(550)
Capital at 1 January		4880

TOP TIP

Make sure that you show assets and liabilities the correct way. It is quite a common mistake for students to mix up the amounts owing and prepaid, putting them the wrong way round.

Step 2 Receipts and payments account

The next step is for Aasim to prepare his receipts and payment account (or his bank account).

Most of the information for this is contained in notes 1, 2 and 3 above. However, Aasim needs to remember that his opening cash and bank balances are in his opening statement of affairs in step 1. This is done in exactly the same way as the cash book was written up in Chapter 3.

The receipts and payments account includes only those amounts actually received and spent. It is a cash book summary with columns for cash and bank.

Aasim
Receipts and payments account

		Cash	Bank		Cash	Bank
		$	$		$	$
Jan 1	Balance b/f	50	1500	Trade payables	400	2430
	Takings (8000 + 400 + 115)	8515		Rent		600
	Cash ¢		8000	Electricity		320
				Postage and stationery		80
				Shop fittings		480
				Other operating expenses	115	
				Drawings (2700 + 250) [1]		2950
				Bank ¢	8000	
				Balance c/d	50	2640
		8565	9500		8565	9500
2016						
Jan 1	Balance b/d	50	2640			

[1] $250 is money not accounted for and is treated as Aasim's drawings. It is the balancing figure which makes the bank balance $2640 at 31 December 2015.

Step 3 Preparation of the trade receivables and trade payables control accounts

Before he can prepare the income statement, Aasim needs to know what his total sales and purchases were for the year. To do this he will prepare trade receivables and trade payables control accounts. These are done in the same way as the control accounts were prepared in Chapter 14.

Trade receivables control account

		$			$
Jan 1	Balance b/f	240*	Dec 31	Takings [1]	8515
Dec 31	Sales [3]	8655		Balance c/f	380
		8895			8895

Trade payables control account

		$			$
Dec 31	Bank and cash [2]	2830	Jan 1	Balance b/f	420*
	Balance c/f	390	Dec 31	Purchases [3]	2800
		3220			3220

[1] From receipts and payments account.

[2] From receipts and payments account.

[3] Balancing figures.

* The opening balances are from Aasim's statement of affairs at 1 January 2015.

Step 4 Adjust for prepayment and accruals

Notes 2 and 3 above contained information relating to how much Aasim's accruals (expenses owing) and prepayments (expenses paid in advance) were at the start and end of the year. By using this information and the amounts paid from the receipts and payments account, Aasim can work out the true value of those expenses for the year. He will do this in a similar way to that demonstrated in Chapter 10.

	$		$
Rent paid	600	Electricity paid	320
Add: prepaid at 1 Jan	80	Less: owing at 1 Jan	(130)
Deduct prepaid at 31 Dec	(50)	Add: owing at 31 Dec	225
Rent payable for the year	630	Electricity payable for the year	415

Step 5 Calculate depreciation of shop fittings

The final thing Aasim has to do before he can prepare his income statement for the year and his statement of financial position at the end of the year, is work out any depreciation of his non-current assets.

There is no indication of which method of depreciation Aasim uses. In this case, an opening and closing valuation for each class of assets, in this case shop fittings, is given in notes 2 and 3 above.

Aasim will calculate the depreciation using the revaluation method described in Section 11.12. This is done below.

	$
Shop fittings at valuation at 1 Jan	1600
Add: fittings purchased in year	480
	2080
Shop fittings at valuation at 31 Dec	(1800)
Depreciation for the year	280

Aasim now has all the necessary information to prepare his financial statements. This is done in step 6.

Step 6 Prepare financial statements

Aasim Income statement for the year ended 31 December 2015		
	$	$
Revenue		8655
Less: cost of sales		
Inventory at 1 January	1960	
Purchases	2800	
	4760	
Less: inventory at 31 December	(1520)	(3240)
Gross profit		5415
Less:		
Rent	(630)	
Electricity	(415)	
Postage and stationery	(80)	
Other operating expenses	(115)	
Depreciation of shop fittings	(280)	(1520)
Profit for the year		3895

Where did the information come from?

- The revenue and purchases figures were calculated in step 3.
- The opening and closing inventory figures were in notes 2 and 3.
- The postage and stationery and other operating expenses figures came from the receipts and payments account in step 2.
- After adjusting for accruals and prepayments, the rent paid and electricity figures came from step 4.
- The depreciation figure came from step 5.

Finally, Aasim can complete his statement of financial position at 31 December 2015.

Aasim Statement of financial position at 31 December 2015		
	$	$
Non-current assets		
Shop fittings (from note 3)		1800
Current assets		
Inventory (from note 3)		1520
Trade receivables (from note 3)		380
Other receivables [1]		50
Cash and cash equivalents [2]		2690
		4640
Total assets		6440
Capital and liabilities		
Capital at 1 January (from step 1)		4880

[1] The figure for **other receivables** ($50) is the prepaid rent from step 4

[2] The figure for **cash and cash equivalents** ($2690) is the total of the balance at the bank $2640 + the cash on hand $50 from step 2.

Aasim Statement of financial position at 31 December 2015		
	$	$
Add: profit for the year		3 895
		8 775
Less: drawings (from step 2)		(2 950)
		5 825
Current liabilities		
Trade payables (from note 3)		390
Other payables [3]		225
		615
Total liabilities		6 440

[3] The figure for **other payables** ($390) is the amount owing for electricity at the end of the year from step 4.

TOP TIP

This may seem like a complicated process. Take a few minutes to work back through it, making sure you know where all the information comes from and how it is used.

16.5 The importance of valuing inventory in accordance with recognised accounting principles

The value placed upon inventory is of great importance in ensuring the financial statements accurately present the profit earned by the business and its assets and liabilities.

In Chapter 7, opening and closing inventories were included in the income statement to calculate the cost of sales and gross profit. In Chapter 8, closing inventory was included in the statement of financial position as the first item of current assets.

There are three possible ways in which inventory may be valued. They are:

- at its cost price
- at its selling price
- at what it is considered to be worth.

The third way, at what it is considered to be worth, should be ruled out immediately. 'Worth' is a very subjective term. It can mean different things to different people and even different things to the same person at different times and in different circumstances. This aspect has already been discussed in Section 9.5.

Selling price is also an unsatisfactory way of valuing inventory, as the following example shows.

Walkthrough

Hakim makes up his accounts to 31 December each year and values his closing inventory at selling price. He purchased goods for $800 on 30 November 2015. He sold the goods on 30 January 2016 for $1 000.

If these were Hakim's only transactions, the trading section of his income statement for the years ended 31 December 2015 and 2016 would be as follows:

Year ended 31 December 2015			Year ended 31 December 2016		
	$	$		$	$
Revenue		0	Revenue		1 000
Cost of sales:			Cost of sales:		
Opening inventory	0		Opening inventory	1 000	
Purchases	800		Purchases	0	
	800			1 000	
Less: closing inventory	(1 000)	(200)		0	(1 000)
Profit for the year		200	Profit for the year		0

Hakim is making a profit of $200 for the year ended 31 December 2015, although he had not sold the goods. For the year ended 31 December 2016, he is not making any profit in the year when he sold them.

Valuing the inventory at selling price goes against three important accounting principles:

- realisation – profit was shown as realised in the year ended 31 December 2015 even though no sale had taken place
- matching – the profit has not been matched to the time the sale took place
- prudence – the profit was overstated in 2015; it was not even certain then that the goods could be sold at a profit.

It is an important principle that inventory should never be valued at more than cost. Valuing inventory at historic cost observes the principles of realisation, matching and prudence.

Another important principle is that the method used to value inventory should be used consistently from one accounting period to the next.

16.6 Valuation of inventory at the lower of cost and net realisable value

Having stated the principle that inventory should be valued at cost price (how much it was originally bought for), there is another complication which may arise. Suppose the inventory is not worth the price it was bought for? How is it valued in this case?

It may be that it is not worth how much it was bought for because it has become obsolete. Perhaps fashions have changed and no one will buy the goods. Or perhaps it is damaged and requires work to be done to it to bring it to a condition where it can be sold.

The principle of inventory valuation is set out in International Accounting Standard 2 (IAS 2). International Accounting Standards are generally accepted standards used when preparing and presenting financial statements. They set out the way in which items should be treated in the financial statements. Some of the principles of inventory valuation set out in IAS 2 will be considered here. It will also be reviewed again in Chapter 22. We have also seen that whichever method is chosen can affect the gross profit which the company makes and, as a result, the profit for the year. Incorrectly valuing inventory, either by mistake or deliberately, will result in the income statement showing the wrong gross profit and profit for the year. In the statement of financial position the inventory will be wrong, which means the current assets will also be incorrect. Anyone using the financial statements to assess the performance of the business, such as a bank manager who is asked to give a loan to the business, will be misled and may make a wrong decision. Thus the value placed on inventory is an extremely important aspect when preparing the financial statements of a business.

The standard states that **inventories should be valued at the lower of cost and net realisable value**. Cost has already been considered. What is meant by 'net realisable value'? This is the price that may be expected to be received from the sale of the goods, less the cost of putting them into a saleable condition. The costs involve include the costs of completing the goods if they are manufactured, plus the marketing, selling and distribution costs.

TOP TIP

Notice the exact wording. It is the lower of cost **and** net realisable value, **not** the lower of cost **or** net realisable value.

The term net realisable value can be compared to the selling price of the product. So if the expected selling price (realisable value) is **lower** than the cost price, then inventory should be valued at selling price (realisable value).

Walkthrough

Christine runs a shop selling clothes. When reviewing her inventory at the end of the year she discovers some unsold dresses which she bought over a year ago and are now out of fashion.

When she bought the dresses they cost a total of $350 and were marked to be sold for $500. However, as they are now out of fashion Christine thinks she will only be able to sell them for $200.

When preparing her financial statements, Christine should value this item of inventory at $200, its net realisable value. This is lower than cost and is all Christine expects to receive for the goods when they are eventually sold.

Inventory is **never** valued at selling price when the selling price is greater than the cost. By using the lowest price possible to value inventory, it means that inventory valuation follows the **prudence** concept.

Inventories which are similar in nature and use to the company will use the same valuation method. Only where inventories are different in nature or use can a different valuation method be used.

Once a suitable method of valuation has been adopted by a company then it should continue to use that method unless there are good reasons why a change should be made. This is in line with the **consistency** concept.

Walkthrough

1 Goods were bought at a cost of $1 300. They have become damaged and will cost $400 to be put into a saleable condition. They can then be sold for $1 900. Net realisable value is $(1 900 – 400) = $1 500. As this is more than cost, the goods should be valued for inventory purposes at cost ($1 300).

2 Details as above but, after repair, the goods can be sold for only $1 500. The net realisable value is $(1 500 – 400) = $1 100. This is less than cost and is the value to be placed upon the goods for inventory purposes.

Individual items, or groups of items, of inventory should be considered separately when deciding whether they should be valued at cost or net realisable value. This is to ensure that losses on individual items or groups of items are not 'hidden'.

3 A company sells six different grades of compact discs for computers. The following are the cost to the company and the net realisable values (NRVs) of the inventories of the six grades of discs:

	Cost	**NRV**	**Value to be used for inventory valuation**
	$	**$**	**$**
Grade 1	2 000	2 400	2 000
Grade 2	4 500	3 800	3 800
Grade 3	3 000	3 100	3 000
Grade 4	5 750	5 000	5 000
Grade 5	1 250	2 000	1 250
Grade 6	2 500	2 200	2 200
	19 000	18 500	17 250

If the inventory was valued as a whole, without taking the individual items into consideration, it would be valued at NRV ($18 500), as this is less than cost. However, the items where NRV is more than cost are hiding the losses made on grades 2, 4 and 6. The items must be valued separately at $17 250 as this recognises the losses.

16.7 Margin and mark-up

It may be necessary to calculate margin and mark-up to solve some incomplete record problems.

Margin is gross profit expressed as a percentage or fraction of selling price. This is shown by the following calculation.

KEY TERM

Margin: The gross profit expressed as a percentage or fraction of selling price.

Walkthrough

	$
Cost price of goods	100
Profit	25
Selling price	125

The margin is:

profit/selling price × 100

$$= \frac{25}{125} \times 100$$

$$= 20\% = \frac{1}{5}$$

Mark-up is gross profit expressed as a percentage or fraction of cost of sales. This is shown below.

In the above example, mark-up is profit/cost price. This is:

$$\frac{25}{100} \times 100 = 25\% \text{ or } \frac{1}{4}$$

There is a close relationship between margin and mark-up. In the above examples:

margin $\frac{1}{5}$ or $\left(\frac{1}{4+1}\right)$; mark-up $\frac{1}{4}$ or $\left(\frac{1}{5-1}\right)$.

From this, a general rule will be observed:

When margin is $\frac{a}{b}$, mark-up is $\frac{a}{b-a}$ and, when mark-up is $\frac{a}{b}$, margin is $\frac{a}{b+a}$.

If margin is $\frac{1}{3}$, mark-up is $= \frac{1}{3-1} = \frac{1}{2}$; if mark-up is $\frac{1}{6}$, margin is $= \frac{1}{6+1} = \frac{1}{7}$.

If margin is $\frac{2}{5}$, mark-up is $\frac{2}{5-2} = \frac{2}{3}$; if mark-up is $\frac{2}{5}$, margin is $\frac{2}{5+2} = \frac{2}{7}$.

All of this is quite mathematical, so the following table summarises all this information.

Mark-up	Margin
$\frac{1}{2}$	$\frac{1}{3}$
$\frac{1}{3}$	$\frac{1}{4}$
$\frac{1}{4}$	$\frac{1}{5}$
$\frac{1}{5}$	$\frac{1}{6}$
$\frac{1}{6}$	$\frac{1}{7}$
$\frac{2}{3}$	$\frac{2}{5}$
$\frac{2}{5}$	$\frac{2}{7}$

Conversion of percentage to fractions Accountants often have to convert fractions to percentages and vice versa. To do this, enter the **rate** percentage as the numerator of the fraction, and 100 as the denominator, and reduce to a common fraction, for example:

$$25\% = \frac{25}{100} = \frac{1}{4}$$

Conversion of fraction to a percentage Multiply the numerator of the fraction by 100, cancel top and bottom of the fraction and add 'per cent' or % sign, for example:

$$\frac{2}{5} = \frac{200}{5} = 40\%$$

KEY TERM

Mark-up: The gross profit expressed as a percentage or fraction of cost of sales.

TOP TIP

The most useful examples to remember are:

$12.5\% = \frac{1}{8}$ $20\% = \frac{1}{5}$ $25\% = \frac{1}{4}$ $33.3\% = \frac{1}{3}$ $40\% = \frac{2}{5}$

$50\% = \frac{1}{2}$ $66.7\% = \frac{2}{3}$ $75\% = \frac{3}{4}$ $80\% = \frac{4}{5}$

Again, the following table should help with the arithmetic for this.

Fraction	Equivalent percentage
1	100%
$\frac{9}{10}$	90%
$\frac{4}{5}$	80%
$\frac{3}{4}$	75%
$\frac{3}{5}$	60%
$\frac{1}{2}$	50%
$\frac{2}{5}$	40%
$\frac{1}{3}$	33.3%
$\frac{1}{4}$	25%
$\frac{1}{5}$	20%
$\frac{1}{6}$	16.7%
$\frac{1}{10}$	10%

Walkthrough

1 Yanni does not keep proper accounting records. He has been asked by his accountant what he thinks his sales were for a month. Yanni knows that his cost of sales for the month were \$30 000. He always expects to earn a gross margin of 25%.

It is possible for Yanni to calculate his sales as follows:

- Cost of sales: \$30 000
- Gross margin is 25%.

From the information above we know that 25% is the same as $\frac{1}{4}$ when expressed as a fraction.

We also know that when the gross margin is $\frac{1}{4}$ the mark-up is $\frac{1}{3}$.

This means that Yanni will mark up his cost of sales by $\frac{1}{3}$.

Yanni's mark-up is therefore $\frac{1}{3} \times \$30\,000 = \$10\,000$.

Yanni's sales for the month were therefore cost of sales (\$30 000) + mark-up (\$10 000) = \$40 000.

2 Salim's sales for the month were \$ 7 000. His mark-up is 40%.

Salim wishes to know his gross profit for the month.

In this case we know that 40% is equal to $\frac{2}{5}$ when expressed as a fraction.

This means that Salim's gross margin is $\frac{2}{7}\left(\frac{2}{5+2}\right)$.

Therefore Salim's gross profit = $\frac{2}{7} \times \$7\,000 = \$2\,000$.

3 Maheen provides the following information for the year ended 31 December 2015.

	\$
Inventory at 1 January 2015	9 000
Inventory at 31 December 2015	11 000
Sales in the year ended 31 December 2015	84 000

Maheen sells her goods at a mark-up of 33.3%.

Prepare the trading section of Maheen's income statement for the year ended 31 December 2015 in as much detail as possible, clearly showing the sales, cost of sales and gross profit for the year.

This a typical example of problem that is solved by working backwards.

The first thing to calculate is Maheen's gross margin.

We know her mark-up is 33.3%, or $\frac{1}{3}$ when expressed as a fraction.

Thus her gross margin will be $\frac{1}{4}$.

This means that her gross profit will be $\$84\,000 \times \frac{1}{4} = \$21\,000$.

With this and the information given at the start, it is now possible to prepare the trading section of Maheen's income statement. This is shown below.

Maheen trading section of the income statement for the year ended 31 December 2015

		\$	\$
	Sales (given)		84 000
	Less: Inventory at 1 January (given)	9 000	
Step 4	Purchases (balancing figure 3)	65 000	
Step 3	(Balancing figure 2)	74 000	
	Inventory at 31 December (given)	(11 000)	
Step 2	Cost of sales (balancing figure 1)		(63 000)
Step 1	Gross profit $\frac{1}{4} \times \$84\,000$		21 000

ACTIVITY 2

Ammar provides the following information for the year ended 30 June 2016:

	$
Opening inventory	4 000
Closing inventory	7 000
Cost of sales	28 000

Ammar's margin on all sales is 20%.

Prepare the trading section of Ammar's income statement for the year ended 30 June 2016 in as much detail as possible, clearly showing the sales, cost of sales and gross profit for the year.

16.8 Inventory lost in fire or by theft

The methods used for preparing accounts from incomplete records are also used to calculate the value of inventory lost in a fire or by theft when detailed inventory records have not been kept, or have been destroyed by fire.

Solve this problem by preparing a 'pro forma' trading section of the income statement. (It is described as 'pro forma' because it is not prepared by transferring balances from the ledger accounts, but is prepared in the form of a trading statement from the information available.)

Walkthrough

Shahmir's warehouse was burgled on 10 April 2016. The thieves stole most of the goods but left goods which cost $1 250.

Shahmir has been asked by his insurance company to provide a statement showing the value of the goods stolen.

Shahmir asks his accountant to calculate the value of goods stolen and supplies the following information:

Extracts from Shahmir's statement of financial position at 31 December 2015	
	$
Inventory	30 000
Trade receivables	40 000
Trade payables	20 000
Extracts from cash book, 31 December 2015 to 10 April 2016	
	$
Receipts from customers	176 000
Payments to suppliers	120 000
Other information:	
Trade receivables at 10 April 2016	24 000
Trade payables at 10 April 2016	26 000

Shahmir sells all his goods at a mark-up of 25%.

The accountant first worked out Shahmir's sales for the period by preparing a trade receivables control account.

Trade receivables control account

		$			$
1 January	Trade receivables	40 000	10 April	Cash	176 000
10 April	Sales (balancing figure)	160 000		Trade receivables	24 000
		200 000			200 000

Shahmir uses a mark-up of 25%. This means that his gross margin is 20%, so the accountant calculated Shahmir's gross profit for the period to be $32 000 ($160 000 × 20%).

The accountant then calculated Shahmir's purchases for the period by preparing a trade payables control account.

Trade payables control account

		$			$
10 April	Cash	120 000	1 January	Trade payables	20 000
	Trade payables	26 000	10 April	Purchases (balancing figure)	126 000
		146 000			146 000

All the information was then available to prepare the pro forma trading section of the income statement for the period 1 January to 10 April 2016. This is shown below.

Shahmir pro forma trading section of the income statement for the period 1 January to 10 April 2016

	$	$
Sales (from the trade receivables control account)		160 000
Cost of sales:		
Inventory at 1 January 2016	30 000	
Purchases (from the trade payables control account)	126 000	
	156 000	
Inventory at 10 April 2016 (balancing figure)	(28 000)	
Gross profit (mark-up is 25% so margin is 20%; $160 000 × 20%)		(128 000)
		32 000

The final stage was to calculate the cost of goods stolen:

Cost of goods stolen: $(28 000 – 1 250) = $26 750

ACTIVITY 3

Neha's warehouse was damaged by fire on 5 November 2015 and most of the goods were destroyed. The goods that were salvaged were valued at $12 000. Her insurance company has asked her to calculate the cost of goods damaged by the fire.

Neha has provided the following information for her accountant to enable the cost of the goods lost to be calculated:

Extracts from statement of financial position at 30 June 2015	
	$
Inventory	47 000
Trade receivables	16 000
Trade payables	23 000

Further information for the period 30 June 2015 to 5 November 2015	
	$
Receipts from credit customers	122 000
Cash sales	17 000
Payments to credit suppliers	138 000
At 5 November:	
Trade receivables	37 000
Trade payables	28 000

Neha's mark-up on goods sold is $33\frac{1}{3}$%.

Calculate the cost of the inventory lost in Neha's fire.

16.9 The advantages and disadvantages of keeping full accounting records

The owners of most small businesses are so busy managing their day-to-day affairs that they don't have enough time to prepare a full set of accounting records with journals, cash books and ledgers. They will often provide their accountant with as much (or as little!) information as they can and expect the accountant to prepare the income statement and statement of financial position for them using the techniques covered in this chapter. However, keeping full accounting records has a number of advantages and disadvantages for the business owner.

Advantages of keeping full accounting records

- It allows the financial statements of the business (income statement and statement of financial position) to be prepared quickly and soon after the year-end.
- It allows for income statements and statements of financial position to be prepared more often than once a year, which can help the manager run their business more efficiently.
- It helps guard against errors and possible fraud by employees. If financial statements are prepared regularly, inventory losses or cash losses can be picked up earlier and corrective action taken.
- The accuracy of the records kept can be improved.
- There may be a legal requirement to keep certain records. For example, payroll records for employees where regular payments of deductions made from their wages and salary have to be paid over to the government.

Disadvantages of keeping full accounting records

- The most obvious one is the time it takes to set them up and maintain them. It is perhaps easier now that there are a number of computerised accounting packages designed to help small business owners. The benefits of computerised accounting are covered in Chapter 26.

- The second major disadvantage is cost. The purchase of a computer package can be expensive. The business owner will have to go on a training course.
- Quite often business owners lack the expert knowledge of how to prepare double-entry accounts. This means they will have to employ a specialist who is familiar with it. This too adds to the costs of the business.

At the end of the day the business owner will have to make a judgement call as to how far they go in keeping financial records for their business. It will depend on three factors:

a The accounting knowledge and skill of the business owner. Most sole traders lack detailed accounting knowledge and are happy to employ an accountant to do it for them.

b The time available to the business owner to write up full double-entry accounting records.

c The cost of employing a member of staff to prepare their accounting records.

Most business owners are quite happy to keep a cash book showing receipts and payments for the business. Often this is analysed to show the income received and payments made under their own headings. So for income, often the trader will distinguish between money received from cash and credit sales. Expenditure would be broken down into, say, goods for resale, wages, telephone, heat and light and so on. They should also keep detailed records of the customers who owe them money and suppliers they owe. Both of the last items affect the cash the business receives and pays. To most small business owners cash flow is critical to their survival.

Key points to remember

This is an important chapter with a number of things you need to try to remember:

- A question that gives only assets and liabilities requires the preparation of statements of affairs to find the profit or loss of the business. The 'requirement' usually begins with 'calculate'.
- If required to prepare an income statement and statement of financial position, prepare them in as much detail as possible.
- Be careful to distinguish between 'mark-up' and 'margin'. Review this section so you are happy you know how to convert mark-up to margin, and vice versa, and use it appropriately.
- Include all your workings with your answer.
- Tick each item as you deal with it; check that everything has been ticked before writing your answer to ensure you have not missed anything.
- Incomplete records questions focus on a whole range of accounting knowledge and skills. Some students fear this topic unnecessarily. Keep calm and follow the steps taught in this chapter carefully. If your statement of financial position does not balance first time, don't panic.

Chapter summary

In this chapter you have learnt how to prepare income statements and statements of financial position from incomplete records. When records of transactions are insufficient to enable an income statement to be prepared, profit or loss may sometimes be calculated from statements of affairs, which you should now have an understanding of from this chapter. To solve incomplete record problems, it is often necessary to calculate margin and mark-up, which were covered in Section 16.7.

This chapter also covered inventory, and you should now know how to value inventory when preparing the income statement and statement of financial position, and how to calculate the cost of inventory lost by fire or theft. You should also have a basic understanding of IAS 2 (the principle of inventory valuation), which will be looked at in more detail in Chapter 22.

Finally, you should now be able to explain the advantages and disadvantages of keeping full accounting records.

TOP TIP

The preparation of accounts from incomplete records tests every aspect which has been covered in the book so far. It is, therefore, extremely important that you are fully familiar with the contents of the chapter. Work carefully through the chapter activities and the ones which follow. They will provide good practice for this tricky topic.

Practice exercises

1 Seng commenced business on 1 January 2015, when he paid $40 000 into the bank together with $20 000 which he had received as a loan from his brother. At 31 December 2015, Seng's assets and liabilities were as follows:

	$
Shop premises	20 000
Motor van	8 000
Shop fittings	3 000
Inventory	4 000
Trade receivables	1 000
Bank balance	5 000
Trade payables	6 000
Loan from brother	16 000

Seng's drawings were $100 per week.

Required

a Prepare Seng's statements of affairs at:

i 1 January 2015

ii 31 December 2015.

b Calculate Seng's profit or loss for the year ended 31 December 2015.

2 Miriam does not keep proper books of account for her business but she has provided the following details of her assets and liabilities:

	At 1 July 2015	At 30 June 2016
	$	$
Land and buildings at cost	60 000	60 000
Fixtures and fittings	10 000	12 000
Office machinery	8 000	7 000
Inventory	17 000	21 000
Trade receivables	4 000	5 000
Rent prepaid	1 000	600
Bank balance	14 000	16 000
Trade payables	3 000	1 600
Wages owing	2 000	1 000

Additional information

1 Land and buildings have been revalued at $90 000 at 30 June 2016.

2 Office machinery at 30 June 2016 included a computer costing $1 400, which Miriam had paid for from her personal bank account.

3 Miriam had withdrawn $200 per week from the business in cash, and a total of $2 000 of goods for her own use during the year to 30 June 2016.

Required

Calculate Miriam's profit or loss for the year ended 30 June 2016.

3 Kim, who does not keep proper records for her business, supplies the following information:

	At 1 July 2015	At 30 June 2016
	$	$
Inventory of goods	16 000	11 000
Trade payables for goods	3 600	5 200

In the year ended 30 June 2016, Kim paid suppliers $54 000. Kim sells her goods at a gross margin of 40%.

On 17 January 2016, Kim's premises were flooded and inventory that cost $5 000 was damaged and could only be sold at half cost price. In the year ended 30 June 2016, Kim took goods which cost $1 300 for her personal use.

Required

Prepare a statement for the year ended 30 June 2016, clearly showing Kim's revenue, cost of sales and gross profit for the year.

4 Cornelius commenced business on 1 April 2014. He has not kept complete records of his transactions but he supplies the following information:

	At 1 April 2014	At 31 March 2015	At 31 March 2016
	$	$	$
Balance at bank	30 000	116 000	111 110
Equipment	15 000	28 000	45 900
Inventory of goods at cost	37 500	52 000	74 250
Long-term loan from father	20 000	20 000	20 000
Premises		80 000	80 000
Trade receivables		22 400	34 200
Trade payables		56 000	67 410
Other operating expenses in arrears		2 280	875
Other operating expenses in advance		700	4 050

Additional information

1 Cornelius made payments of $371 340 to suppliers in the year ended 31 March 2016.

2 Complete records of takings are not available but goods are sold at a mark-up of 30%.

3 Takings were banked after deduction of the following:
- From 1 April 2014 to 31 March 2015, Cornelius drew $400 per week from takings for his personal expenses. From 1 April 2015, the weekly amounts drawn were increased to $500.
- On 1 July 2015, Cornelius paid $5 000 out of takings to pay for a family holiday.
- Cornelius has taken various other amounts from takings for personal expenses, but he has not kept a record of these.

4 Cornelius purchased the business premises on 1 October 2014. He paid $40 000 for these from his own private bank account. The balance was obtained as a bank loan on which interest is payable at 15% per annum on 31 December each year.

5 Cornelius's father has agreed that his loan to the business will be free of interest for the first year. After that, interest will be at the rate of 8% per annum, payable annually on 31 March.

6 Cornelius purchased additional equipment costing $24 000 in the year ended 31 March 2016.

7 Other operating expenses paid in the year ended 31 March 2016 amounted to $27 000.

Required

a Calculate Cornelius's profit or loss for the year ended 31 March 2015.

b Prepare, in as much detail as possible, an income statement for Cornelius for the year ended 31 March 2016.

c Prepare a statement of financial position as at 31 March 2016.

Exam practice questions

Multiple-choice questions

1 Jennifer commenced business with $10 000 that she had received as a gift from her aunt, and $8000 that she had received as a loan from her father. She used some of this money to purchase a machine for $15 000. She obtained a mortgage for $20 000 to purchase a workshop. How much was Jennifer's capital?

A $3000 **B** $10 000
C $18 000 **D** $38 000

2 At 1 January 2015, Robert's business assets were valued at $36 000 and his liabilities amounted to $2 000. At 31 December 2015, Robert's assets amounted to $57 000 and included his private car, which he had brought into the business on 1 November 2015 when it was valued at $9 000. His trade payables at 31 December 2015 totalled $17 000 and his drawings during the year were $19 000. What was Robert's profit for the year ended 31 December 2015?

A $6 000 **B** $16 000
C $24 000 **D** $33 000

3 At 1 April 2015, Tamsin's business assets were: motor van valued at $5000 (cost $8000), tools $1 600, inventory $700, trade receivables $168, cash $400. Her trade payables totalled $1 120. At 31 March 2016, her assets were: workshop which had cost $20 000 and on which a mortgage of $16 000 was still outstanding, motor van $4 000, tools $1 900, inventory $1 000, trade receivables $240 (of which $70 were known to be irrecoverable), cash $500. Her trade payables amounted to $800. During the year Tamsin's drawings amounted to $5 200. What was Tamsin's profit for the year ended 31 March 2016?

A $6 222 **B** $6 292
C $9 222 **D** $9 292

4 At 1 March 2015, Nadiya's trade receivables amounted to $12 100. In the year ended 28 February 2016, she received $63 500 from trade receivables and allowed them cash discounts of $3 426. At 28 February 2016, her trade receivables totalled $14 625. How much were Nadiya's sales for the year ended 28 February 2016?

A $62 599 **B** $64 401
C $66 025 **D** $69 451

5 At 1 October 2015, Maria's trade receivables amounted to $7 440. Of this amount, $384 is known to be irrecoverable. In the year to 30 September 2016, she received $61 080 from trade receivables. Her trade receivables at 30 September 2016 were $8 163. How much were Maria's sales for the year ended 30 September 2016?

A $60 741 **B** $61 419
C $61 803 **D** $62 187

6 All of Makin's inventory was stolen when his business was burgled on 4 March 2016. His inventory at 31 December 2015 was $23 000. From 1 January to 4 March 2016, sales totalled $42 000 and purchases were $38 000. Makin's mark-up on goods is 33.3% to arrive at the selling price.

What was the cost of the inventory that was stolen?

A $28 000 **B** $29 500
C $33 000 **D** $40 000

7 How should inventory be valued in a statement of financial position?

A at the lower of net realisable value and selling price
B at the lower of replacement cost and net realisable value
C at lower of cost and replacement cost
D at lower of cost and net realisable value

8 A business has an item of inventory which had cost $2 500 to buy. It has been damaged and $150 has to be spent on it to bring it to a saleable condition. It can then be sold for $1600. At what cost should it be valued for inventory purposes?

A $2 500 **B** $2 350
C $1 750 **D** $1 450

9 The inventory of a business at 31 December had been valued at a cost of $6 200. It was then discovered that it included some items which had cost $420. They could now only be sold for $360. To buy them again would cost $450. What should the value of inventory be at 31 December?

A $6 260 **B** $6 140
C $5 840 **D** $5 780

10 Included in the inventory of a business are three items. Details of them are:

Item	Cost	Net realisable value	Replacement cost
	$	$	$
1	3 000	2 300	3 100
2	4 500	5 000	4 000
3	2 500	1 200	2 000

What is the total value of the three items for inventory purposes?

A $10 000 **B** $9 100
C $8 500 **D** $8 000

Total: 10 marks

Structured questions

1 Ahmed carries on business as a general trader. He has not kept proper accounting records. Ahmed's assets and liabilities at October 2015 were as follows:

	$
Premises	60 000
Motor van	8 000
Inventory	6 250
Trade receivables	3 200
Rent paid in advance	400
Balance at bank	9 450 debit
Cash in hand	50
Trade payables	1 800
Electricity owing	600
Interest on loan owing	150
10% loan from brother	2 000

Required

a State **three** benefits to Ahmed of maintaining proper books of account. **[3 marks]**

b Calculate Ahmed's opening capital at 1 October 2015. **[5 marks]**

Additional information

Ahmed has also provided the following summary of his bank and cash accounts for the year ended 30 September 2016:

Ahmed Bank account summary for the year ended 30 September 2016			
Receipts		**Payments**	
	$		**$**
Receipts from trade receivables	29 400	Payments to credit suppliers	23 000
Cash banked from cash sales	17 000	Electricity	2 200
		Rent	4 000
		Motor van expenses	1 800
		Interest on loan	200
		Wages	7 400
		Telephone and stationery	1 650
		Purchase of fixtures and fittings	3 000
		Drawings	11 800

Ahmed Cash account summary for the year ended 30 September 2016			
Receipts		**Payments**	
	$		**$**
Cash sales	21 750	Goods for resale	3 140
		Stationery	300
		Motor van expenses	600
		Other operating expenses	400

Additional information

1 Ahmed states that he has taken private drawings out of the cash takings, but cannot remember how much is involved.

2 The balance of cash in hand is to be maintained at $50.

Required

c Calculate the amount of cash drawings Ahmed made for the year ended 30 September 2016. **[4 marks]**

Additional information

The following information is also available at 30 September 2016:

1 Trade receivables were $1 600.

2 Irrecoverable debts written off during the year were $250.

3 Trade payables for supplies were $1 300.

4 Discounts received from suppliers in the year were $420.

5 At 30 September 2016, electricity owing was $320 and rent of $450 had been prepaid.

6 Closing inventory was valued at cost $8 000.

7 At 30 September 2016, the motor van was valued at $6 000.

8 Fixtures and fittings are to be depreciated using the reducing-balance method at 25% per annum. A full year's depreciation is to be taken in the year ended 30 September 2016.

9 Ahmed does not provide for depreciation on the premises.

Required

d Prepare Ahmed's income statement for the year ended 30 September 2016. **[15 marks]**

e Advise Ahmed whether or not he should start to make a charge in his annual accounts for depreciation of the premises. **[3 marks]**

Total: 30

2 Nadia was ill when her inventory should have been counted on 31 December 2015. The inventory count did not take place until 8 January 2016.

At that date the inventory was valued at $62 040. The following was then discovered:

1 The inventory had been valued at selling price instead of at cost. The gross margin on all goods sold is 20%.

2 Goods had been sent to a customer on 15 December 2015 on a sale or return basis. The customer had not yet accepted the goods. The customer had been sent an invoice for $2 000. This had been treated as a sale by Nadia.

3 The following transactions had taken place between 1 January and 8 January 2016, but had not been taken into account in the inventory taking:

- goods costing $4 400 had been received from suppliers
- sales of goods for $12 000 (not including goods sent on sale or return).

Required

a Explain the difference between margin and mark-up. **[4 marks]**

b Calculate the value at cost of Nadia's inventory at 31 December 2015. **[7 marks]**

Additional information

1 At 1 January 2015, Nadia's inventory was valued at cost, $65 000.

2 For the year ended 31 December 2015, Nadia had calculated her sales to be $225 000. She also had sales returns of $3 200.

Required

c Calculate to the nearest dollar the value of Nadia's purchases for the year ended 31 December 2015. **[4 marks]**

Total: 15

3 Korn, a retailer, does not keep proper books of account but he has provided the following information about his business:

	Balances at 30 April 2015	30 April 2016
	$	$
Land and buildings at cost	60 000	70 000
Fixtures and fittings at valuation	8 000	10 000
Motor vehicles	10 000	8 000
Trade payables	7 500	6 900
Trade receivables	20 400	32 000
Rent owing	800	1 000
Wages and salaries owing	800	600
Inventory	22 400	21 923
Bank	39 000	To be calculated

Korn's bank account transactions for the year ended 30 April 2016 were as follows:

Korn
Summary bank account for the year ended 30 April 2016

Receipts		Payments	
	$		$
Trade receivables	170 430	Trade payables	227 668
Cash sales	103 000	Wages	17 200
Sales of non-current assets [see note 4 below]	2 400	Rent	8 000
		Electricity	9 670
		General expenses	5 150
		Purchases of non-current assets (see note 4 below)	27 000

Additional information

Korn banks his receipts from cash sales after taking $300 each week as drawings.

Required

a Calculate the following for Korn for the year ended 30 April 2015:

i credit sales **[2 marks]**

ii total sales **[2 marks]**

iii total purchases. **[2 marks]**

Additional information

1 During the year ended 30 April 2016, Korn had taken goods costing $1 350 for his own use.

2 Korn normally valued his inventory at cost but on the advice of a friend he decided to value his inventory at 30 April 2016 at selling price. His normal mark-up on inventory was 30%.

3 Korn had borrowed $30 000 from his brother on a long-term basis on 1 May 2015. He had not recorded this transaction. Interest on the loan at 10% per annum is payable on 1 May each year.

4 During the financial year ended 30 April 2016, the following transactions had taken place in respect of Korn's non-current assets:

	$
Purchases	
Freehold land and buildings	10 000
Motor vehicles	10 000
Fixtures and fittings	7 000
Sales	
Motor vehicles	2 000 (net book value at 30 April 2015 $3 500)
Fixtures and fittings	400 (net book value at 30 April 2015 $800)

Required

b Prepare Korn's income statement for the year ended 30 April 2016. **[14 marks]**

c Prepare the statement of financial position at 30 April 2016. **[6 marks]**

d Advise Korn whether or not he should value his inventory at selling price. Justify your answer, and refer to any relevant accounting principle. **[4 marks]**

Total: 30

Chapter 17
Partnership accounts

Learning objectives

In this chapter you will learn:

- what a partnership is
- how profits are shared when there is a partnership agreement
- how to apply the Partnership Act 1890 when there is no partnership agreement
- how to prepare partnership capital and current accounts
- how to prepare the partnership appropriation account
- how to prepare the income statement and statement of financial position for a partnership
- the advantages and disadvantages of partnerships.

KEY TERMS

Capital account: An account to record the sum of money which a partner introduces into the partnership. It is only adjusted for any further capital introduced, any capital withdrawn, any share of goodwill or any profit on the revaluation of partnership assets.

Current account: An account which records a partner's share of profits and any drawings made by them.

in the account. Capital withdrawn is debited in the account. There are other items of a special nature which are entered in the **capital account**, such as goodwill and profit on revaluation of assets. These are dealt with fully in Chapter 18.

The current account

The **current account** is used to complete the double entry from the partnership appropriation account for the partner's share of profits, losses, interest on salary or drawings and salary. It is also credited with interest on a partner's loan to the firm, if any, from the income statement. At the end of the year, the balance on a partner's drawings account is transferred to the debit side of his current account.

Drawings account

Just as for a sole trader, this account records any drawings made by the partner during the year. However, unlike a sole trader, the balance on it is transferred to the debit side of his current account.

TOP TIP

If partners do not maintain current accounts, the double entry for interest, their salaries and shares of profit must be completed in their capital accounts. However, it is likely that partners will have both capital and current accounts. Familiarise yourself with the information each contains.

Walkthrough

(No partnership agreement is in existence regarding interest, partners' salaries or sharing of profits/losses.)

Andreas and Tygo began to trade as partners on 1 January 2015. Andreas introduced $60 000 into the business as capital, and Tygo contributed $40 000.

On 1 July 2015, Tygo lent $10 000 to the business. The partners have asked their accountant to prepare the following accounts for the partnership:

a the income statement and appropriation account for the partnership for the year ended 31 December 2015

b the partners' current accounts at 31 December 2015

c the statement of financial position for the partnership at 31 December 2015.

In order to do this they have provided their accountant with the following partnership trial balance at 31 December 2015:

	$	$
Revenue		300 000
Purchases	120 000	
Staff wages	42 000	
Rent	10 000	
Electricity	7 000	
Other operating expenses	5 400	
Premises at cost	60 000	
Fixtures and fittings at cost	28 000	

	$	$
Trade receivables	5460	
Trade payables		2860
Bank balance	94000	
Capital accounts:		
Andreas		60000
Tygo		40000
Drawings:		
Andreas	24000	
Tygo	17000	
Loan from Tygo		10000
	412860	412860

In addition, at 31 December 2015 the following information was also available for the accountant:

1 Inventory at 31 December 2015 was valued at cost, $18000.

2 Depreciation is to be provided as follows:

  i premises 5% per annum on cost

  ii fixtures and fittings 12.5% per annum on cost.

3 The partners had not made any agreement regarding interest on capital and drawings, salaries or sharing of profits and losses.

Required

a Prepare the income statement and appropriation account for the year ended 31 December 2015.

b Prepare the partners' current accounts at 31 December 2015.

c Prepare the statement of financial position at 31 December 2015.

Answer

a The income statement and appropriation account for Andreas and Tygo for the year ended 31 December 2015 is shown below. Note that the income statement is prepared in exactly the same way as it would be for a sole trader.

	$	$	$
Revenue			300000
Less: cost of sales			
Purchases		120000	
Less: inventory at 31 December 2015		(18000)	(102000)
Gross profit			198000
Staff wages		(42000)	
Rent		(10000)	
Electricity		(7000)	
Other operating expenses		(5400)	

	$	$	$
Depreciation:			
Premises	(3 000)		
Fixtures and fittings	(3 500)	(6 500)	
Interest on loan (six months at 5% p.a.) [1]		(250)	(71 150)
Profit for the year [2]			126 850
Shares of profit [3]			
Andreas $\left(\frac{1}{2}\right)$		63 425	
Tygo $\left(\frac{1}{2}\right)$		63 425	126 850

[1] The interest on Tygo's loan is charged as an expense in the income statement, before splitting the profit for the year between the partners. It is, however, entered in Tygo's current account as Tygo is entitled to withdraw it from the business. As no partnership agreement exists, the rate of interest on the loan is 5%.

[2] The appropriation account begins at the point where the profit for the year of $126 850 is shown.

[3] As there is no partnership agreement, the residual profit of $126 850 is split equally between the partners.

b Before preparing the statement of financial position for the partnership at 31 December 2015, the accountant first had to complete the partners' current accounts. These are shown below.

Partners' current accounts

		Andreas	Tygo			Andreas	Tygo
2015				**2015**			
		$	$			$	$
Dec 31	Drawings	24 000	17 000	Dec 31	Interest on loan [1]	–	250
	Balances c/d	39 425	46 675		Share of profit	63 425	63 425
		63 425	63 675			63 425	63 675
				2016			
				Jan 1	Balance b/d	39 425	46 675

[1] The interest on the loan is credited to Tygo's current account.

TOP TIP

Showing the partners' current accounts side by side like this is known as showing them in **columnar form**. Questions may ask for the partners' current accounts (and sometimes their capital accounts) in this format. Showing accounts in columnar form is a good way to show them and saves time having to write everything out twice.

c Finally, using the remaining balances in the trial balance and the current accounts, the accountant completed the statement of financial position for the partnership. This is what it looked like:

Andreas and Tygo Statement of financial position at 31 December 2015			
	Cost	**Accumulated depreciation**	**Net book value**
	$	**$**	**$**
Non-current assets:			
Premises	60 000	(3 000)	57 000
Fixtures and fittings	28 000	(3 500)	24 500
	88 000	(6 500)	81 500
Current assets:			
Inventory			18 000
Trade receivables			5 460
Cash and cash equivalents			94 000
			117 460
Total assets:			198 960
Capital and liabilities			
Capital accounts:			60 000
Andreas			40 000
Tygo			100 000
Current accounts:			39 425
Andreas			46 675
Tygo			86 100
Total capital and current accounts			186 100
Non-current liability: loan from Tygo			10 000
Current liabilities: trade payables			2 860
Total capital and liabilities			198 960

How would this have been different if the partners had a partnership agreement in place?

This can be shown by using the same trial balance, but assuming the partners had a partnership agreement in place.

The partnership agreement includes the following terms:

- Interest on capitals and annual drawings: 5% per annum.
- Partnership salaries (per annum): Andreas $20 000; Tygo $10 000.
- The balance of profits and losses is to be shared as follows: Andreas $\left(\frac{2}{3}\right)$; Tygo $\left(\frac{1}{3}\right)$.
- Tygo is to be credited with interest on his loan to the partnership at a rate of 8% per annum.

The income statement would have been identical except for the change in the rate of interest paid on Tygo's loan. This was 5% but is now 8%.

Andreas and Tygo
Income statement and appropriation account for the year ended 31 December 2015

	$	$	$
Revenue			300 000
Less: cost of sales			
Purchases		120 000	
Less: inventory at 31 December 2015		(18 000)	(102 000)
Gross profit			198 000
Staff wages		(42 000)	
Rent		(10 000)	
Electricity		(7 000)	
Other operating expenses		(5 400)	
Depreciation:			
Premises	(3 000)		
Fixtures and fittings	(3 500)	(6 500)	
Interest on loan (six months)		(400)	(71 300)
Profit for the year			126 700
Add: interest on drawings:*			
Andreas		1 200	
Tygo		850	2 050
			128 750
Less: interest on capital:*			
Andreas (5% × $60 000)		(3 000)	
Tygo (5% × $40 000)		(2 000)	(5 000)
Partners' salaries:*			
Andreas		(20 000)	
Tygo		(10 000)	(30 000)
			93 750
Shares of profit:			
Andreas $\left(\frac{2}{3}\right)$		62 500	
Tygo $\left(\frac{1}{3}\right)$		31 250	93 750

* Adjustments are made for interest on drawings, interest on capital and partners' salaries **before** the remaining profit for the year is split in the profit-sharing ratios. This is an important point. The profit for the year is **never** split until these adjustments have been made.

The partners' current accounts now look like this:

Partners' current accounts

		Andreas	Tygo			Andreas	Tygo
2015				**2015**			
		$	$			$	$
Dec 31	Drawings	24 000	17 000	Dec 31	Interest on capital	3 000	2 000
	Interest on drawings	1 200	850		Interest on loan	–	400
					Salary	20 000	10 000
	Balanced c/d	60 300	25 800		Share of profit	62 500	31 250
		85 500	43 650			85 500	43 650
				2016			
				Jan 1	Balance b/d	60 300	25 800

Note: The statement of financial position will be the same as in the previous Walkthrough, except for the different balance on the partners' current accounts: Andreas $60 300 and Tygo $25 800.

ACTIVITY 1

(No partnership agreement.)

Tee and Shirt are trading in partnership. Their trial balance at 31 March 2016 is as follows:

	$	$
Capital accounts at 1 April 2015:		
Tee		100 000
Shirt		50 000
Current accounts at 1 April 2015:		
Tee		5 000
Shirt		10 000
Drawing accounts:		
Tee	29 000	
Shirt	31 000	
Revenue		215 000
Purchases	84 000	
Inventory at 1 April 2015	16 000	
Selling expenses	30 000	
Administration expenses	42 000	
Fixtures and fittings at cost	48 000	
Provision for depreciation of fixtures and fittings		8 000

	$	$
Office equipment at cost	27 000	
Provision for depreciation of office equipment		5 000
Trade receivables	24 000	
Trade payables		11 000
Bank balance	85 000	
Loan from Shirt		12 000
	416 000	416 000

Additional information

1 Inventory at 31 March 2016 was valued at cost, $20 000.
2 Selling expenses prepaid at 31 March 2016: $6 000.
3 Administration expenses accrued at 31 March 2016: $4 000.
4 Depreciation is to be provided as follows: on fixtures and fittings 10% of cost; on office equipment 20% of cost.
5 Shirt made the loan to the business on 1 April 2015.
6 The partners had not made any agreement regarding interest, salaries or profit-sharing.

Required

a Prepare the partnership income statement and appropriation account for the year ended 31 March 2016.
b Prepare the partners' current accounts at 31 March 2016 in columnar form.
c Prepare the partnership statement of financial position at 31 March 2016.

ACTIVITY 2

(Partnership agreement in place.)

The facts are as in Activity 1, but Tee and Shirt have a partnership agreement which includes the following terms:

1 Shirt is to be credited with interest on his loan to the partnership at the rate of 10% per annum.
2 The partners are allowed interest at 10% per annum on capitals and are charged interest at 10% per annum on drawings.
3 Shirt is entitled to a salary of $4 000 per annum.
4 The balance of profit/loss is to be shared as follows:

Tee $\frac{3}{5}$ Shirt $\frac{2}{5}$

Required

a Prepare the partnership income statement and appropriation account for the year ended 31 March 2016.
b Prepare the partners' current accounts at 31 March 2016 in columnar form.
c Prepare the partnership statement of financial position at 31 March 2016.

17.4 Advantages and disadvantages of partnerships

Whether of not people should go into partnership with one another really depends on the circumstances. However, set out below are the advantages and disadvantages of doing so.

Advantages

- The capital invested by partners is often more than can be raised by a sole trader.
- A greater fund of knowledge, experience and expertise in running a business is available to a partnership.
- A partnership may be able to offer a greater range of services to its customers (or clients).
- The business does not have to close down, or be run by inexperienced staff, in the absence of one of the partners; the other partner(s) will provide cover.
- Losses are shared by all partners.

Disadvantages

- A partner doesn't have the same freedom to act independently as a sole trader has.
- A partner may be frustrated by the other partner(s) in their plans for the direction and development of the business.
- Profits have to be shared by all partners.
- A partner may be legally liable for acts of the other partner(s).

TOP TIP

Set out below are the key learning points from this chapter.

- Learn the provisions of the Partnership Act 1890 as they affect partners' rights to salaries, interest and sharing of profits and losses.
- Read each question carefully to see if you have to apply the terms of a partnership agreement or the provisions of the Partnership Act 1890.
- Debit interest on a partner's loan to the firm in the income statement and credit it to the partner's current account.
- Complete the double entries from the appropriation account to the partners' current accounts.
- Transfer the end-of-year balances on the partners' drawings accounts to their current accounts.
- If partners do not maintain current accounts, the entries to current accounts referred to above must be made in their capital accounts instead.
- Tick every item as you give effect to it. Check that all items are ticked before copying out your answer.

Chapter summary

In his chapter you have learnt about partnerships. They are a different form of business organisation to a sole trader. There are special rules regarding the way in which the profit (or loss) of a partnership is shared between the partners, and you should now be familiar with the rules of how the profit (or loss) is divided in circumstances where there is a partnership agreement and where there is no partnership agreement.

As a result there is a need to introduce additional accounts. These are:

- partners' capital accounts
- partners' current accounts
- a partnership appropriation account.

You should now be familiar with how these accounts are completed. You should also be familiar with how the capital and current accounts are shown in the statement of financial position. More broadly, you'll also need to be able to discuss the advantages and disadvantages of partnerships.

Practice exercises

1 The following trial balance has been extracted from the books of Bell and Binn at 30 April 2016:

Bell and Binn
Trial balance at 30 April 2016

	$	$
Revenue		425000
Purchases	200000	
Inventory at 1 May 2015	30000	
Wages	98000	
Rent	25000	
Heating and lighting	16000	
Office expenses	12600	
Vehicle expenses	5510	
Advertising	3500	
Irrecoverable debts written off	416	
Plant and machinery at cost	125000	
Provision for depreciation of plant and machinery		36000

	$	$
Motor vehicles at cost	41 000	
Provision for depreciation of motor vehicles		22 000
Trade receivables and payables	45 750	18 000
Provision for doubtful debts		1 000
Bank balance	15 724	
Loan from Bell		60 000
Capital accounts:		
Bell		50 000
Binn		40 000
Current accounts:		
Bell		7 000
Binn		3 000
Drawing accounts:		
Bell	30 000	
Binn	13 500	
	662 000	662 000

Additional information

1 Inventory at 30 April 2016 is valued at cost, $27 000.

2 Bell is to be credited with interest on the loan at a rate of 10% per annum.

3 The bank reconciliation shows that bank interest of $314 and bank charges of $860 have been debited in the bank statements. These amounts have not been entered in the cash book.

4 At 30 April 2016, rent of $1 500 and advertising of $2 000 have been paid in advance.

5 Depreciation is to be provided as follows:
 i plant and machinery: 10% per annum on cost
 ii motor vehicles: 20% per annum on their written-down values.

6 The partners are to be charged interest on drawings and allowed interest on capitals at a rate of 10% per annum.

7 Partnership salaries are to be allowed as follows: Bell $10 000 per annum; Binn $8 000 per annum.

8 The balance of profits and losses is to be shared as follows: Bell $\frac{3}{5}$; Binn $\frac{2}{5}$.

Required

a Prepare the partnership income statement and appropriation account for the year ended 30 April 2016.

b Prepare the partners' current accounts for the year ended 30 April 2016.

c Prepare the statement of financial position at 30 April 2016.

2 Miller has been a second-hand car dealer for some years. His income statement for the year ended 31 December 2015 was as follows:

Miller Income statement for the year ended 31 December 2015		
	$	$
Revenue		160 000
Less: cost of sales		(95 000)
Gross profit		65 000
Wages	(31 000)	
Rent	(7 000)	
Heating and lighting	(4 000)	
Advertising	(1 000)	
Other operating expenses	(2 400)	(45 400)
Profit for the year		19 600

Miller's profits for the previous two years were as follows:

	$
Year ended: 31 December 2013	30 000
31 December 2014	24 000

Miller's friend, Meredith, has also been trading for some years, repairing and servicing motor vehicles. Meredith's profits for the past three years have been as follows:

	$
Year ended: 31 December 2013	11 600
31 December 2014	14 500
31 December 2015	18 000

Meredith has suggested to Miller that the two businesses should be combined and that she and Miller should become partners.

Miller estimates that combining the businesses will immediately improve his profit for the year by 10% and that the improvement will be maintained in future years. Meredith estimates that her profit for the year will be increased by 20% and that this increase will also be maintained in the future.

The proposed partnership agreement would provide as follows:

- capitals: Miller $20 000; Meredith $30 000
- interest on capitals to be allowed at 10% per annum
- the balance of profits and losses to be shared equally.

Required

a Prepare a **forecast** appropriation account of the partnership for the year ending 31 December 2016, assuming the partnership is formed on 1 January 2016.

b State, with reasons, whether Miller should agree to Meredith becoming a partner in the combined businesses.

Exam practice questions

Multiple-choice questions

1 Left and Right are partners, sharing profits and losses in the ratio of 2 : 1. They are allowed interest at 10% per annum on capitals and loans to the partnership. Other information is as follows:

	Left	Right
	$	$
Capitals	20000	8000
Loan to firm	3000	–

The partnership has made a profit for the year of $40000. How much is Left's total share of the profit for the year?

A $24800 **B** $25100 **C** $26800 **D** $27100

2 Ethel and David are in partnership. Ethel has lent the partnership $10000 on which she is entitled to interest at 10%. She is also entitled to a salary of $12000 per annum. Profits and losses are shared equally. The partnership has made a profit for the year of $25000. How much is Ethel's total share of the profit for the year?

A $500 **B** $5500 **C** $6000 **D** $6500

3 Samir and Antonia are partners sharing profits and losses equally. Samir has lent the partnership $8000 on which he is entitled to interest at 10% per annum. The partners are entitled to annual salaries as follows: Samir $6000; Antonia $4000. The partnership has made a profit for the year of $17000. How much is Samir's total share of the profit for the year?

A $3500 **B** $3900 **C** $8500 **D** $9300

Total: 3 marks

Structured question

Up and Down have prepared their draft statement of financial position as at 30 June 2016 as follows:

	$
Non-current assets:	
Fixtures and fittings at cost	45000
Less: depreciation to date	(34500)
	10500
Current assets:	
Inventory	28500
Trade receivables	24000
Bank	9000
	61500
Total assets:	72000
Capital and liabilities	
Capital accounts:	
Up	22000
Down	14000
	36000

	$
Current accounts:	
Up	7 500
Down	1 500
	45 000
Non-current liability:	
Up – long-term loan	15 000
Current liabilities:	
Trade payables	12 000
Total capital and liabilities	72 000

It has now been discovered that the following errors and omissions have been made.

1 Some fixtures and fittings were sold for $3 500 in January 2016. These items had cost $15 000 and their net book value at 30 June 2015 was $4 500. The sale proceeds were credited to the fixtures and fittings at cost account. No further entries had been made in the books for this sale.

2 The partnership provides for depreciation using the straight-line method at 10% per annum on the balance on the fixtures and fittings account at the end of each financial year.

3 Interest at the rate of 10% per annum is to be provided on the long-term loan from Up for the year ended 30 June 2016.

4 The accounts for the year ended 30 June 2016 included certain items of inventory at 30 June 2016 in the sum of $20 000. The correct value of this inventory should have been $30 000. The partners have agreed that this error should be corrected in the partnership accounts.

5 The partners have decided that a provision for doubtful debts equal to 4% of the trade receivables should be provided in the accounts.

6 An adjustment should be made for the prepaid rent at 30 June 2016 in the sum of $750.

7 During the year ended 30 June 2016, Down had taken goods costing $1 075 for his personal use. No entry for this has been made in the books of account.

8 In addition to the interest allowed on Up's loan, the partners are allowed interest at 10% per annum on their capital account balances.

9 The balance of profits and losses are divided between Up and Down in the ratio of 3 : 2.

Required

a State **two** advantages and **two** disadvantages of a partnership. **[4 marks]**

b Explain why the partners maintain separate capital and current accounts. **[4 marks]**

c Prepare the corrected statement of financial position as at 30 June 2016 for the partnership. **[14 marks]**

d Prepare the revised current accounts for Up and Down at 30 June 2016. **[4 marks]**

Additional information

Up has asked Down to introduce more cash into the business so that the balances on their capital accounts are equal. Down has advised that he does not have any spare cash available.

Required

e Discuss the ways in which Down could increase the balance on his capital account without paying more cash into the business. **[4 marks]**

Total: 30

Chapter 18
Partnership changes

Learning objectives

In this chapter you will learn:

- how to prepare partnership accounts when a partner joins or leaves the firm
- how to account for the revaluation of assets when there is partnership change
- how to account for partnership goodwill
- how to account for the dissolution of a partnership.

Total assets	15
	105
Capital and liabilities	
Capital accounts:	
Abdul	40
Bashir	40
	80
Current accounts:	
Abdul	11
Bashir	10
	21
Current liabilities:	
Trade payables	4
Total capital and liabilities	105

They decide to revalue their assets to bring them in line with their latest values. The revised values are:

- property $90 000
- plant and machinery $24 000
- inventory $6 000 and trade receivables $5 000.

In order to do this they will prepare a revaluation account. This is shown below.

Revaluation account

	$000		$000
Property (old value)	60	Property (new value)	90
Plant and machinery (old value)	30	Plant and machinery (new value)	24
Inventory (old value)	7	Inventory (new value)	6
Trade receivables (old value)	6	Trade receivables (new value)	5
Profit on revaluation – Abdul	11		
Profit on revaluation – Bashir	11		
	125		125

The profit on revaluation is now credited to each partner's capital account as follows:

Capital accounts

	$000	$000		$000	$000
	Abdul	**Bashir**		**Abdul**	**Bashir**
Balance c/f	51	51	Opening balances	40	40
			Profit on revaluation	11	11
	51	51		51	51

TOP TIP

The question may give dates of the revaluation. These should be inserted in the capital accounts.

Finally, it is necessary for the partners to prepare a revised statement of financial position to reflect the change in values of the assets and liabilities. This is shown below.

Statement of financial position at 31 October 2016 following revaluation	
	$000
Non-current assets:	
Property	90
Plant and machinery	24
	114
Current assets:	
Inventory	6
Trade receivables	5
Bank account	2
	13
Total assets	127
Capital and liabilities:	
Capital accounts:	
Abdul	51
Bashir	51
	102
Current accounts:	
Abdul	11
Bashir	10
	21
Current liabilities:	
Trade payables	4
Total capital and liabilities	127

Notice that the balance at the bank has remained unchanged. If the partners had drawn the profit on revaluation from the business, it would have resulted in an overdraft.

TOP TIP

When answering questions on this, you may find that the bank account is labelled cash and cash equivalents.

ACTIVITY 1

Ann and John are in partnership, sharing the profits and losses in the ratio of 2 : 1. Their summarised statement of financial position at 31 October 2016 is as follows:

	$000
Non-current assets:	
Property	120
Plant and machinery	60
	180
Current assets:	
Inventory	20
Trade receivables	30
Bank account	1
	51
Total assets	231
Capital and liabilities	
Capital accounts:	
Ann	120
John	60
	180
Current accounts:	
Ann	17
John	10
	27
Current liabilities:	
Trade payables	24
Total liabilities	24
Total capital and liabilities	231

They decide to revalue their assets to bring them in line with their latest values. The revised values are:

- property $150 000
- plant and machinery $51 000
- inventory $17 000 and trade receivables $28 000
- trade payables $22 000.

Required

a Prepare the revaluation account to reflect the changes in value of the assets.

b Prepare the partners' capital accounts after the changes have taken place.

c Prepare a revised statement of financial position after the revaluation has taken place.

In some cases, the partners may decide to change their profit-sharing ratios part of the way through the trading year. At that time they may also revalue the partnership assets. As we have seen, any increase or decrease is adjusted through a revaluation account with any profit or loss transferred to the partners' capital accounts. If the changes take place part way through the year the profit or loss on revaluation must be shared in the **old** profit-sharing ratios because any gain or loss in values has occurred before the ratios were changed.

Walkthrough

Grace and Grant are in partnership, sharing profits and losses in the ratio of 2 : 1. On 1 July 2016, they agree to change the profit-sharing ratio so that they will share profits and losses equally in future. The partnership statement of financial position at 30 June 2016 was as follows:

	$
Non-current assets at net book values:	
Freehold premises	60 000
Plant and machinery	35 000
Motor vehicles	23 000
	118 000
Current assets:	
Inventory	29 000
Trade receivables	13 000
Cash and cash equivalents	8 000
	50 000
Total assets	168 000
Capital and liabilities	
Capital accounts:	
Grace	90 000
Grant	71 000
	161 000
Trade payables	7 000
	168 000

After discussion, the partners agree that the assets shall be revalued at 30 June 2016 as follows:

	$
Freehold premises	100 000
Plant and machinery	30 000
Motor vehicles	20 000
Inventory	25 000
Trade receivables	12 000

This is being done to bring the values of the non-current assets in line with current market prices. The partners have also identified that only $12 000 can be collected from trade receivables, as a result of one customer becoming bankrupt.

They have asked their accountant to make the necessary entries to record the changes. He first starts by preparing a journal entry to show the ledger entries to reflect the changes.

Journal entries show the adjustments required in the ledger (shown in *italics*):

Journal		
Name of account	**Dr**	**Cr**
	$	**$**
Freehold premises	40000	
Plant and machinery		5000
Motor vehicles		3000
Inventory		4000
Trade receivables control [1]		1000
Revaluation account		27000
Revaluation of assets at 30 June 2016		
Revaluation account	27000	
Capital accounts:		
Grace		18000
Grant		9000
Profit on revaluation of assets credited to the partners' capital accounts in their former profit-sharing ratios: Grace 2, Grant 1 .		

Note: All these entries will be made in the respective ledger accounts.

[1] It will also be necessary to adjust the individual account of the customer in the sales ledger by crediting them with $1000. This is not shown in the journal entry.

TOP TIP

In this example, only the increase or decrease has been recorded. Either use the full values of the old and new assets or the differences in the values. However, choose one approach and stick with it. The author's personal preference is to use the full values as there is less chance of a mistake.

Finally, the accountant prepared a revised statement of financial position after the changes had been made in the ledger:

Grace and Grant Statement of financial position at 30 June 2016	
	$
Non-current assets at net book values:	
Freehold premises (60000 + 40000)	100000
Plant and machinery (35000 – 5000)	30000
Motor vehicles (23000 – 3000)	20000
	150000

Statement of financial position at 30 June 2016

	$
Current assets:	
Inventory (29 000 – 4 000)	25 000
Trade receivables (13 000 – 1 000)	12 000
Cash and cash equivalents	8 000
	45 000
Total assets	195 000
Capital and liabilities	
Capital accounts:	
Grace (90 000 + 18 000)	108 000
Grant (71 000 + 9 000)	80 000
	188 000
Current liabilities:	
Trade payables	7 000
Total capital and liabilities	195 000

ACTIVITY 2

Tom and Tilly shared profits and losses equally until 1 September 2016, when they agreed that Tilly would be entitled to a salary of $10 000 per annum from that date. Profits and losses would continue to be shared equally.

The partnership statement of financial position at 1 September 2016 was as follows:

	$
Non-current assets at net book values:	
Freehold premises	40 000
Fixtures and fittings	18 000
Office equipment	7 000
	65 000
Current assets:	
Inventory	17 000
Trade receivables	4 000
Cash and cash equivalents	6 000
	27 000
Total assets	92 000
Capital and liabilities	
Capital accounts:	
Tom	48 000
Tilly	41 000
	89 000

Current liabilities:	
Trade payables	3000
Total liabilities	92000

The partners agreed that the assets should be revalued at 1 September 2016 as follows:

	$
Freehold premises	65000
Fixtures and fittings	15000
Office equipment	5000
Inventory	14000
Trade receivables	3000

Prepare journal entries to give effect to the revaluation of the partnership assets at 1 September 2016. (Note: you can either prepare the journal entries using the full values of the assets or the increase or decrease in the values.)

a Prepare the revaluation account.

b Prepare the partnership statement of financial position as at 1 September 2016 to include the effects of revaluation of the assets.

c Discuss why the partners revalued the assets, stating whether or not they were right to do so.

18.4 How to account for goodwill

Goodwill is the amount by which the value of a business as a going concern exceeds the value its net assets would realise (be sold for) if they were sold separately. It is an **intangible** asset; that is, it cannot be touched or felt, unlike buildings, plant and machinery and other 'tangible' assets which can be touched and felt.

There are two types of goodwill to consider:

- **Purchased goodwill** This arises when one business buys another. If the purchaser pays more for the business than the net book value of the net assets it buys, then the difference is goodwill. The **International Accounting Standards** allow this type of goodwill to be shown as an intangible non-current asset in the statement of financial position. If goodwill clearly has a fixed useful life it is depreciated each year until it is written off. If not, the asset is tested for impairment annually. This is dealt with more fully in Chapter 22.
- **Inherent goodwill** This has not been paid for and so does not have an objective value. It is someone's best estimate or guess of the value of the business's goodwill. This is immediately written off in the accounts when a change in the partnership occurs and will be dealt with in Section 18.5.

Goodwill is always accounted for:

- when the existing partners agree to change the profit-sharing ratio
- when an existing partner retires from the partnership
- when a new partner is admitted into the partnership.

You may need to combine some of the aspects covered. For example, if the assets are revalued at the time a new partner is admitted into the partnership, or an existing partner retires:

- Always prepare the revaluation account first and calculate the profit or loss on revaluation. Credit (or debit if it is a loss) the existing partners' capital accounts with it.
- Then adjust the partners' capital accounts for the goodwill.
- **Never** bring goodwill into the revaluation account.
- **Never** adjust for goodwill in the current account of a partner.

Walkthrough

Will and Wendy are partners who have shared profits and losses in the ratio of 2 : 1 respectively. On 1 January 2016, they agree to share profits and losses equally in future. At that date the partnership assets and liabilities are recorded in the books at the following valuations:

	$
Premises	100 000
Fixtures and fittings	48 000
Motor vehicles	35 000
Inventory	12 000
Trade receivables	6 000
	201 000
Less: trade payables	(3 250)
Net assets	197 750

Will and Wendy have recently been informed that they can expect to receive $230 000 for their business if they decide to sell it. They have agreed to record goodwill in the partnership books as from 1 January 2016, and to value the business at $230 000 for the purpose of valuing goodwill.

The first thing to do is calculate the value of goodwill. In this case, goodwill is valued at $(230 000 – 197 750) = $32 250.

Their accountant has prepared the following journal entry to record the goodwill:

	Dr	Cr
	$	$
Goodwill account	32 250	
Capital accounts:		
Will		21 500 [1]
Wendy		10 750 [1]

[1] Goodwill recorded at valuation and credited to partners in their **old profit-sharing ratios**.

Now that a journal entry has been made which includes goodwill, it is necessary for an account for goodwill to be opened in the partnership books. The journal entry will result in a debit of $32 250 being posted to the goodwill account. The value of goodwill should be depreciated and eventually written off. As the value of $230 000 is only an estimate, then it should be written off in a short space of time, probably no more than three years.

It is also inherent goodwill and, strictly speaking, should be written off immediately. However, this has not been done in order to illustrate the bookkeeping entries required to initially record goodwill.

ACTIVITY 3

Vera and Ken are partners who have shared profits and losses equally. On 1 July 2016, they decide to change the profit-sharing ratio to: Vera 3/5, Ken 2/5. The partnership assets and liabilities at book values at 1 July 2016 are as follows:

	$
Premises	140 000
Fixtures and fittings	65 000
Motor vehicles	35 000
Office equipment	15 000
Inventory	6 500
Trade receivables	11 800
Cash and cash equivalents	3 620
Trade payables	5 830

The partners have been informed that the value of the business as a going concern is $300 000 and have decided to value goodwill based on this figure.

a Calculate the value of goodwill.

b Calculate the amounts to be credited to the partners' capital accounts for goodwill.

18.5 How to account for goodwill when no goodwill account is opened

Partners often do not wish to record goodwill in their books for two reasons:

a The value placed on goodwill is usually very difficult to justify, being a matter of opinion; it may not even exist.

b If goodwill is shown in a statement of financial position at, say, $20 000, it would be very difficult to persuade a prospective purchaser of the business to pay more, even if the value had increased since goodwill was first introduced into the books.

When there is a partnership change, say a change in the profit-sharing ratios or the admission of a new partner or retirement of an existing partner, and the partners decide not to open a goodwill account, the procedure is as follows:

Step 1 Credit the partners' capital accounts with their share of goodwill **in their old profit-sharing ratio**.

Step 2 Debit the partners' capital accounts with their share of the goodwill **in their new profit-sharing ratio**.

Steps 1 and 2 can be combined in a single operation, as shown in the following example.

Walkthrough

Noat and Koyn have shared profits and losses in the ratio of 2 : 1 respectively, but have now agreed they will share profits and losses equally in future.

Goodwill is valued at $30 000, and the partners' capital accounts will be adjusted as follows:

	Column A	Column B	Column C combining steps 1 and 2
	Goodwill shared in **old** profit-sharing ratio (credit capital accounts)	Goodwill shared in **new** profit-sharing ratio (debit capital accounts)	Net adjustment to capital accounts (column A – column B)
	$	$	$
Noat	20 000	15 000	5 000 Credit
Koyn	10 000	15 000	5 000 Debit
	30 000	30 000	

The capital account of a partner who loses a share of goodwill is credited with the amount of the loss. The capital account of a partner who gains a share of goodwill is debited with the amount of the gain.

It would also be possible to show the entries in full. Suppose the balance on each partner's capital account before the adjustment was

Noat $50 000
Koyn $25 000

then their capital accounts would appear as follows:

Capital accounts					
	Noat	Koyn		Noat	Koyn
	$	$		$	$
Goodwill (new profit-sharing ratios)	15 000	15 000	Opening balances goodwill (old profit-sharing ratios) b/d	50 000	25 000
Balance c/d	55 000	20 000		20 000	10 000
	70 000	35 000		70 000	35 000
			Balances b/d	55 000	20 000

Thus, a partner who loses a share of goodwill (Noat) is compensated by a partner who gains a share (Koyn).

In the example, Koyn has 'purchased' his increased share of goodwill from Noat. A goodwill account has not been opened.

Additional information for the year ended 31 December 2016 is as follows:

	$
Sales (spread evenly throughout the year)	200 000
Cost of sales	87 500
Rent	25 000
Wages	35 000
General expenses	15 000

e Of the general expenses, $5 000 was incurred in the six months to 30 June 2016.

f New's car is to be depreciated over four years on the straight-line basis and is assumed to have no value at the end of that time.

g All sales produce a uniform rate of gross margin.

You may be asked to prepare the income statement and appropriation accounts for the year ended 31 December 2016.

This must be tackled in three stages.

Stage 1

The gross profit is 'earned at a uniform rate'. This means that as a result of the change during the year, the gross profit covers the whole year. Therefore, the first thing to do is calculate the gross profit for the year. This is shown below:

Trading section of the income statement to calculate the gross profit for the year ended 31 December 2016

	$
Sales	200 000
Less: cost of sales	(87 500)
Gross profit carried down	112 500

Stage 2

The gross profit covers the whole year. This must now be split between the two trading periods, before and after the revision, to change to the terms of the partnership.

This is done as follows:

Old and New
Income statement and appropriation account for the year ended 31 December 2016

	Six months to 30 June 2016		Six months to 31 December 2016		Year to 31 December 2016	
	$	$	$	$	$	$
Gross profit brought down		56 250		56 250		112 500
Rent	(12 500)		(12 500)		(25 000)	
Wages	(17 500)		(17 500)		(35 000)	
General expenses	(5 000)		(10 000)		(15 000)	
Interest on loan	–		(250)		(250)	
Depreciation – car	–		(1 500)		(1 500)	
		(35 000)		(41 750)		(76 750)
Profit for the period		21 250		14 500		35 750

Stage 3

The profit for the year is now split between the partners using their old and new terms of agreement, as follows:

Less:						
Salary:						
Old		(5 000)		–	5 000	
New		–		2 500	2 500	(7 500)
		16 250		12 000		28 250
Share of profit:						
Old	8 125		7 200		15 325	
New	8 125		4 800		12 925	
		16 250		12 000		28 250

Finally, the partners' current accounts can be prepared as follows:

Partners' current accounts

		Old	New			Old	New
2016		**$**	**$**	**2016**		**$**	**$**
Dec 31	Bal c/d	28 075	20 425	Jan 1	Bal b/d	7 500	5 000
				Dec 31	Salary	5 000	2 500
					Loan interest	250	
					Share of profit	15 325	12 925
		28 075	20 425			28 075	20 425
				2017			
				Jan 1	Bal b/d	28 075	20 425

ACTIVITY 5

Hook, Line and Sinker have shared profits and losses in the ratio 3 : 2 : 1 for a number of years. On 1 July 2016, the partners agreed that, from that date:

- Hook will be entitled to a salary of $6 000 per annum
- profits and losses will be shared equally.

Information extracted from their books for the year ended 31 December 2016 was as follows:

	$
Sales	129 500
Cost of sales	66 500
Wages	14 000
General expenses	5 250
Depreciation of non-current assets	1 750

Additional information

1. Two-thirds of the general expenses were incurred in the six months ended 31 December 2016.
2. On 1 April 2016, Hook made a loan of $8 000 to the partnership. Interest on the loan is at a rate of 10% per annum.
3. Sales have accrued evenly throughout the year and all sales have earned a uniform rate of gross profit.

Required

Prepare the income statement for the year ended 31 December 2016 in columnar form to show the appropriation of profit before and after the change.

18.7 How to account for the introduction of a new, or the retirement of an existing, partner

When a partner leaves a firm, or a new partner joins, it marks the end of one partnership and the beginning of a new one. As in the case of a simple change in profit-sharing ratios, a change in partners may occur at any time in a firm's financial year, and no entries may be made in the books to record the change until the end of the year.

The procedures are similar to those already described in Section 18.2. Account must be taken of:

- asset revaluation
- goodwill
- changes in the profit/loss-sharing ratios.

If a partnership change occurs on the first day of a firm's financial year, the procedure is very straightforward. There is no reason why partners should join on the first day of a firm's financial year, or why one should leave on the last day of the financial year. In practice, changes usually occur during a financial year and the accounting records are continued without interruption; financial statements are not produced until the end of the year.

Admission of a new partner

Walkthrough

Grey and Green have shared profits and losses in the ratio of 3:2. On 1 October 2016, they decided to admit Blue as a partner. No entries to record Blue's admittance as a partner were made in the books before the end of the financial year on 31 December 2016.

1 Information extracted from the books for the year ended 31 December 2016 included the following:

	$	
Revenue	400 000	
Cost of sales	240 000	
Wages	40 000	
Rent	8 000	
General expenses	9 600	
Depreciation of non-current assets:		
1 January to 30 September 2016	6 000	
1 October to 31 December 2016	4 350	(based on asset revaluation as shown below)

2 At 31 December 2015, the balances on Grey and Green's capital and current accounts were as follows:

	Capital accounts	Current accounts
	$	$
Grey	50 000	2 000
Green	30 000	3 000

3 On 1 October 2016, the partnership assets were revalued as follows:

	$	
Freehold premises	50 000	increase
Other non-current assets	14 000	decrease
Current assets	3 000	decrease

4 The partners agreed the value of goodwill at 1 October 2016 at $40 000 and decided that no goodwill account should be opened in the books.

5 On 1 October 2016, Blue paid $20 000 into the firm's bank account as capital. On the same day, Grey lent the partnership $20 000. He is entitled to interest at a rate of 10% per annum on the loan.

6 The balances on the partners' drawings accounts at 31 December 2016 were as follows:

	$
Grey	23 000
Green	17 000
Blue	3 000

7 The new partnership agreement provided for the following as from 1 October 2016:

i Interest was allowed on the balances on capital accounts at 31 December each year at a rate of 5% per annum.

ii Green was entitled to a salary of $12 000 per annum.

iii The balance of profits and losses were to be shared: Grey 2; Green 2; Blue 1.

Required

a Prepare the capital accounts of Grey, Green and Blue at 31 December 2016.

b Prepare the partnership income statement and appropriation account for the year ended 31 December 2016.

c Prepare the partners' current accounts at 31 December 2016.

Step 1

1 Calculate the profit or loss on revaluation of non-current assets from 3, above.

2 Calculate the adjustments required for goodwill on the admission of Blue as a partner.

Both of these are then entered in the partners' capital accounts as follows:

1 There is a profit of $33 000 $(50 000 – 14 000 – 3 000) on the revaluation of the non-current assets.

2 The net adjustments required for goodwill are calculated below:

Working: Goodwill	Before 1 Oct 2016	After 1 Oct 2016	Capital accounts
	$	$	$
Grey	24 000	16 000	8 000 credit
Green	16 000	16 000	no change
Blue	–	8 000	8 000 debit

Step 2

The partners' capital accounts can now be prepared:

Partners' capital accounts

			Grey	Green	Blue				Grey	Green	Blue
2016						**2016**					
			$	$	$				$	$	$
Oct 1	Goodwill				8000	Jan 1	Balance	b/d	50000	30000	–
Dec 31	Balance	c/d	77800	43200	12000	Oct 1	Bank		–	–	20000
							Profit on revaluation		19800	13200	–
							Goodwill		8000		
			77800	43200	20000				77800	43200	20000
						2017					
						Jan 1	Balance	b/d	77800	43200	12000

There is an alternative presentation. From the workings, the full amount of the goodwill could have been credited to Grey ($24000) and Green ($16000). In other words, credit the old partners in the old profit-sharing ratio.

The second entry could be to debit each partner: Grey ($16000), Green ($16000) and Blue ($8000). In other words debit the new partners in the new profit-sharing ratio.

Again, either is acceptable, though the way set out here is generally less likely to result in an error.

TOP TIP

Pay particular attention to the way goodwill is adjusted in the accounts. As with revaluation, choose the way you are most comfortable with, but never mix the two approaches.

Step 3

Prepare the income and appropriation accounts for the two periods before and after the admission of Blue as a partner.

Grey, Green and Blue
Income statement and appropriation accounts for the year ended 31 December 2016

	$
Turnover	400000
Less: cost of sales	240000
Gross profit carried down	160000

	Nine months to 30 June 2016		Three months to 31 December 2016		Year to 31 December 2016	
	$	$	$	$	$	$
Gross profit brought down		120000		40000		160000
Wages	(30000)		(10000)		(40000)	
Rent	(6000)		(2000)		(8000)	
General expenses	(7200)		(2400)		(9600)	
Interest on loan	–		(500)		(500)	

	Nine months to 30 June 2016		Three months to 31 December 2016		Year to 31 December 2016	
	$	$	$	$	$	$
Depreciation	(6000)	(49200)	(4350)	(19250)	(10350)	(68450)
Profit for periods		70800		20750		91550
Interest on capital: [1]						
Grey	–		(973)			
Green	–		(540)			
Blue	–		(150)			
			(1663)			
Salary:	–		(3000)			
Green	–			(4663)		(4663)
Profit shares:		70800		16087		86887
Grey	42480		6435		48915	
Green	28320		6435		34755	
Blue	–		3217		3217	
		70800		16087		86887

[1] The interest on capital is only payable for three months, in other words, from the date it was set up by the partnership agreement.

Step 4

Finally, prepare the partners' current accounts at 31 December 2016.

Partners' current accounts

		Grey	Green	Blue				Grey	Green	Blue
2016		$	$	$	**2016**			$	$	$
Dec 31	Drawings	23000	17000	3000	Jan 1	Balance b/d		2000	3000	–
Dec 31	Balance c/d	29388	24295	367	Dec 31	Loan interest		500	–	–
						Interest on capital		973	540	150
						Salary		–	3000	–
						Profit		48915	34755	3217
		52388	41295	3367				52388	41295	3367
					2017					
					Jan 1	Balance	b/d	29388	24295	367

ACTIVITY 6

Hardeep and Nasma have been partners for some years, making up their accounts annually to 31 December. The partnership agreement contained the following provisions:

1. Interest was allowed on capitals at 10% annum.
2. Nasma was entitled to a salary of $15000 per annum.
3. Profits and losses were to be shared: Hardeep 2/3; Nasma 1/3.

At 31 December 2015, the partners' capital and current account balances were as follows:

	Capital accounts	Current accounts
	$	$
Hardeep	100 000	16 000
Nasma	60 000	12 000

On 1 September 2016, Hardeep and Nasma admitted their manager, Arfan, as a partner. Arfan had been receiving a salary of $24 000.

The revised partnership agreement provided as follows:

1 Partner's salary: Nasma $18 000 per annum.
2 Interest on capitals at 10% per annum.
3 Profits and losses shared: Hardeep 2/5, Nasma 2/5, Arfan 1/5.

The partnership's non-current assets at cost at 31 December 2015 were as follows:

	At cost	Depreciation to date	Net book value
	$	$	$
Freehold premises	180 000	(45 000)	135 000
Plant and machinery	90 000	(60 000)	30 000
Motor cars	30 000	(25 000)	5 000
Office equipment	21 000	(14 000)	7 000

No additions to, or disposals of, non-current assets had taken place between 31 December 2015 and 31 August 2016.

The assets were revalued at 1 September as follows:

	$
Freehold premises	210 000
Plant and machinery	27 000
Motor cars	5 000
Office equipment	6 000

1 Depreciation of non-current assets is calculated on cost and is provided as follows: freehold premises 4% per annum; plant and machinery 20% per annum; motor cars 25% per annum; office equipment 10% per annum.
2 Goodwill was valued at $60 000, but no goodwill account was to be opened in the books.
3 On 1 September 2016, Arfan paid $50 000 into the firm's bank account as capital, and also brought his private car, valued at $7 000, into the business. On the same day, Hardeep transferred $20 000 from his capital account to a loan account on which interest is to be paid at a rate of 12% per annum.
4 The following information is available from the partnership books for the year ended 31 December 2016:

	$
Turnover	600 000
Cost of sales	330 000
Wages and salaries	106 000

	$
Rent	42000
Heating and lighting	6000
Other operating expenses	12000

Note: Sales were spread evenly throughout the year and earned a uniform rate of gross profit. Drawings in the year ended 31 December 2016 were: Hardeep $30000; Nasma $40000; Arfan $4000.

Required

a Prepare an income statement and appropriation account for the year ended 31 December 2016.

b Prepare the partners' capital and current accounts for the year ended 31 December 2016.

The retirement of a partner

The following will illustrate the situation when one of the partners retires from the partnership.

Walkthrough

Norman, Jack and David have traded in partnership for some years. Norman decided to retire on 30 September 2016, but no accounts were prepared for the partnership until the end of the financial year on 31 December 2016.

The following balances have been extracted from the trial balance at 31 December 2016:

	$	$
Sales		720000
Purchases	400000	
Inventory at 1 January 2016	20000	
Wages	100000	
Rent	26000	
Heating and lighting	21000	
Other operating expenses	12000	

Additional information

1 Inventory at 31 December 2016 cost $24000.

2 At 31 December 2016, rent of $2000 had been prepaid and $1200 had accrued for heating and lighting.

3 Non-current assets at 1 January 2016 at cost were as follows:

	$
Plant and machinery	80000
Office equipment	10000

Additional machinery was purchased on 1 October 2016 for $12000.

4 Depreciation of non-current assets is to be provided at 10% per annum on cost.

5 Goodwill was valued at $45000, but no goodwill was to be recorded in the books.

6 The partners' capital and current account balances at 1 January 2016 were as follows:

	Capital accounts	Current accounts
	$	$
Norman	50 000	8 000 (Cr)
Jack	40 000	9 000 (Cr)
David	20 000	3 000 (Cr)

7 The partners' drawings were as follows:

	$
Norman (up to 30 September 2016)	30 000
Up to 31 December 2016	
Jack	50 000
David	32 000

8 Norman left $60 000 of his capital in the business as a loan with interest at 10% per annum. The interest was payable on 30 June and 31 December each year.

9 The partnership agreement up to 30 September 2016 allowed for the following:

- interest on capitals: 8% per annum (based on balances on capital accounts at 1 January 2016)
- salary: David $6 000 per annum
- profits and losses to be shared: Norman ½, Jack ⅓, David ⅙.

The agreement was amended on 1 October 2016 as follows:

- interest on capitals: 10% per annum (based on balances on capital accounts at 1 October 2016)
- salary: David $10 000 per annum
- profits and losses to be shared Jack ⅗, David ⅖.

10 The assets were not revalued at 30 September 2016.

11 It is assumed that gross profit has been earned evenly throughout the year.

The starting point with this is to prepare the partners' capital accounts. It is necessary to start here because in the appropriation account, each partner receives interest on capital. Without knowing the capital account balances it will not be possible to calculate the interest on capital.

The data above is quite extensive, so to complete the capital accounts it is necessary to sift through it and find:

i the opening capital balances
ii the valuation and treatment of goodwill
iii details of how Norman's capital account will be closed when he leaves the partnership.

Required

a Prepare the partnership's income statement and appropriation accounts for the year ended 31 December 2016.

b Prepare the partners' current accounts for the year ended 31 December 2016.

c Prepare the partners' capital accounts.

Finally, it is now possible to prepare the partners' current and capital accounts. These are shown below.

It is possible to complete the income statement for the two periods. This is done in the same way as the previous examples and is shown below.

Norman, Jack and David
Income statement and appropriation accounts for the year ended 31 December 2016

	$	$
Sales		720 000
Less: cost of sales		
Inventory at 1 Jan 2016	(20 000)	
Purchases	(400 000)	
	(420 000)	
Less: inventory at 31 Dec 2016	(24 000)	(396 000)
Gross profit		324 000

	Nine months to 30 Sep 2016		Three months to 31 Dec 2016		Total	
	$	$	$	$	$	$
Gross profit		243 000		81 000		324 000
Wages	(75 000)		(25 000)		(100 000)	
Rent (26 000 – 2 000)	(18 000)		(6 000)		(24 000)	
Heating and lighting (21 000 + 1 200)	(16 650)		(5 550)		(22 200)	
Other operating expenses	(9 000)		(3 000)		(12 000)	
Depreciation:						
Plant and machinery	(6 000)		(2 300)		(8 300)	
Office equipment	(750)		(250)		(1 000)	
Interest on loan	–	(125 400)	(1 500)	(43 600)	(1 500)	(169 000)
Profit		117 600		37 400		155 000
Interest on capital:						
Norman	(3 000) [1]		–		(3 000)	
Jack	(2 400) [1]		(700) [2]	–	(3 100)	
David	(1 200) [1]		(238) [2]		(1 438)	
	(6 600)		(938)		(7 538)	
Salary:						
David	(4 500)	(11 100)	(2 500)	(3 438)	(7 000)	(14 538)
		106 500		33 962		140 462
Shares of profit:						
Norman	53 250		–		53 250	
Jack	35 500		20 377		55 877	
David	17 750	106 500	13 585	33 962	31 335	140 462

[1] Interest on capital is calculated at 8% on the opening capital balances (Norman $50 000, Jack $40 000 and David $20 000) for nine months.

[2] Interest on capital is calculated at 10% on the capital balances of Jack ($28 000) and David ($9 500) for three months. These are the new balances after Norman has retired from the partnership.

The partners' current accounts can be completed as set out below:

Partners' current accounts

		Norman	Jack	David			Norman	Jack	David
2016		$	$	$	**2016**		$	$	$
Sep 30	Drawings	30000			Jan 1	Balance b/d	8000	9000	3000
	Capital a/c	34250 [1]			Sep 30	Int. on capital	3000		
						Profit	53250		
Dec 31	Drawings		50000	32000	Dec 31	Int. on capital		3100	1438
	Balance c/d		17977	10773		Salary			7000
						Profit		55877	31335
		64250	67977	42773			64250	67977	42773
					2017				
					Jan 1	Balance b/d		17977	10773

[1] The final balance on Norman's current account is now transferred to his capital account.

Partners' capital accounts

		Norman	Jack	David			Norman	Jack	David
2016		$	$	$	**2016**		$	$	
Sep 30	Goodwill		27000	18000	Jan 1	Balance b/d	50000	40000	20000
	Loan a/c	60000 [1]			Sep 30	Goodwill	22500	15000	7500
	Bank	46750				Current a/c	34250 [2]		
Dec 31	Balance c/d		28000	9500					
		106750	55000	27500			106750	55000	27500
					2017				
					Jan 1	Balance b/d		28000	9500

[1] Note 8 in the data states that Norman left $60000 of his capital account as a loan to the business. This is debited in his capital account and will be credited to a loan account.

[2] When a partner retires, the final balance on that partner's current account is transferred to the capital account. This keeps everything together in one account. However, until the income statement and appropriation account have been completed and the amounts due to Norman transferred to his current account, it is not possible to transfer the final balance to his capital account. (See above.)

ACTIVITY 7

Wilfrid, Hide and Wyte were partners sharing profits and losses in the ratio of 3 : 2 : 1 after charging interest on capitals at 10% per annum. Their capital and current account balances at 1 July 2015 were as follows:

	Capital accounts	Current accounts
	$	$
Wilfrid	80000	12000
Hide	50000	3000
Wyte	30000	4000

Wilfrid decided to retire on 31 December 2015. He left $75 000 of the balance on his capital account as a loan to the firm, with interest at 10% per annum. The balance on his capital account was paid to him by cheque.

At 31 December 2015:

- Goodwill was valued at $60 000 but goodwill was not to be shown in the books.
- It was also agreed that the partnership assets should be revalued at $21 000 less than their current book values.

Additional information

1 Hide and Wyte continued in partnership from 1 January 2016, with interest allowed on capitals at 10% per annum and with profits and losses being shared equally.

2 The partners' drawings in the year ended 30 June 2016 were as follows:

	$
Wilfrid (6 months to 31 December 2015)	23 000
Hide (12 months to 30 June 2016)	28 000
Wyte (12 months to 30 June 2016)	18 000

3

	$	
Gross profit for the year ended 30 June 2016	187 000	(assumed to have been earned evenly throughout the year)
Expenditure for the year ended 30 June 2016:		
Wages	91 000	
Rent paid	14 000	
Electricity paid	7 000	
Other operating expenses	9 000	

4 At 30 June 2016, rent of $2 000 had been paid in advance, and electricity in the amount of $1 400 had accrued.

Required

a Prepare the partnership income statement and appropriation account for the year ended 30 June 2016.

b Prepare the capital and current accounts of the partnership for the year ended 30 June 2016.

TOP TIP

In this case, work through the revaluation account, transferring any profit or loss on revaluation to the old partners in their old profit-sharing ratios. Then introduce the new partner and adjust the capital accounts for goodwill in line with this section.

18.8 How to account for the dissolution of a partnership

There may come a time in the life of any business when the owner or owners no longer wish to run the firm any more. When this decision is made, one of two things can happen. All the business assets and liabilities can be sold to a new business. This situation is known as the realisation of a partnership. The partnership is purchased by another business and all the assets and liabilities are transferred to the new business. In addition, some assets may be taken over by one or more

KEY TERMS

Dissolution of a partnership: The process by which all the assets of the partnership are sold, and liabilities paid, when the partnership ceases trading.

Realisation account: An account prepared when a partnership is ceasing to trade, to record the book value of the assets and liabilities and how much is received for them if sold, or paid out in respect of liabilities. The result will be a profit or loss on realisation.

of the partners, or perhaps the liabilities are paid before the sale of the business is completed. This topic is dealt with in Chapter 24.

Alternatively, the assets may be sold to several people, and the money received used to pay off the liabilities, such as trade payables. The owner or owners then retire and the balance on the business bank account is transferred to them. In this case the partnership is **dissolved** (there is a **dissolution of a partnership**).

When the business is sold, the accounting treatment is to open an account called a **realisation account**:

Step 1 All the assets to be sold are debited to the realisation account at their book values.

Step 2 All the liabilities to be paid are credited to the realisation account at their book values.

Step 3 Any money received is credited to the realisation account. The opposite entry is a debit to the bank account.

Step 4 Any money paid is debited to the realisation account. The opposite entry is a credit to the bank account.

Step 5 In some cases, a partner may take over an asset, such as a car, at an agreed valuation. Credit this to the realisation account and debit the partner's capital account.

Step 6 Any expenses arising from the dissolution are also debited to the realisation account. This would include such things as legal or accountancy fees.

Once these entries have been made, the balance on the realisation account is now (hopefully) a profit on dissolution. In the case of a partnership, this profit is split between the partners in their **profit-sharing ratios** and credited to their capital accounts. If it results in a loss on dissolution, then this loss is debited to their capital accounts in their **profit-sharing ratios.**

Step 7 The balances on the partners' current accounts are transferred to their capital accounts. Finally, their capital accounts are then closed by debiting them with the money from the business bank account.

In some cases, the result may be that the final balance on a partner's capital account is a debit. In this case, that partner will need to pay money into the partnership. In that case, debit the bank account and credit the partner's capital account with the amount paid.

TOP TIP

Make sure that the partners' capital accounts are closed by a transfer to or from the bank account. Most questions will instruct you to do this. If they don't, then always close the account. The question may be exploring your knowledge of the final entries to close the books.

The closing, or dissolving of, a partnership business will now be illustrated below.

Walkthrough

Colin and Jessica are in business, sharing the profits and losses equally. Their summarised statement of financial position at 31 December 2016 is as follows:

Colin and Jessica's Statement of financial position at 31 December 2016	
	$000
Non-current assets:	
Property	40
Motor vehicles	20

Statement of financial position at 31 December 2016	
	$000
	60
Current assets:	
Inventory	16
Trade receivables	14
Bank account	1
	31
Total assets	91
Capital and liabilities	
Capital accounts:	
Colin	30
Jessica	30
	60
Current accounts:	
Colin	10
Jessica	8
	18
Current liabilities:	
Trade payables	13
Total liabilities	13
Total capital and liabilities	91

The partners are unable to work together any more and decide to dissolve the business.

- The property is sold for $70 000.
- Colin agrees to take one of the vehicles at a value of $5 000. The remaining vehicles are sold for $12 000.
- The inventory is sold for $13 000 and the partners collect $11 000 from the trade receivables.
- They pay their trade suppliers $12 000.
- The expenses of dissolving the partnership amount to $2 000.

The first thing to do is prepare the realisation account. This is shown below.

Realisation account			
	$000		$000
Property (book value)	40	Bank – sale of property	70
Motor vehicles (book value)	20	Colin's capital account –	
Inventory (book value)	16	value of car taken	5
Trade receivables (book value)	14	Bank – sale of vehicles	12
Bank – payments to trade payables	12	Bank – sale of inventory	13
		Bank – from trade receivables	11
Bank – expenses of sale	2	Trade payables (book value)	13
Profit on dissolution:			
Colin	10		
Jessica	10		
	124		124

Capital accounts					
	Colin	Jessica		Colin	Jessica
	$000	$000		$000	$000
Vehicle taken	5	–	Opening balances	30	30
Bank	45	48	Current accounts	10	8
			Profit on realisation	10	10
	50	48		50	48

The bank account can now be completed to show the complete closure of the partnership:

Bank account			
	$000		$000
Opening balance	1	Trade payables	12
Sale of property	70	Expenses of sale	2
Sale of vehicles	12	Colin – capital account	45
Sale of inventory	13	Jessica – capital account	48
From trade receivables	11		
	107		107

A partnership will be dissolved when the partners can no longer agree with each other. Strictly speaking, it should also be dissolved when one of the partners dies or decides to retire. However, if there are two partners left after this event and they agree to continue, then the adjustments will be reflected as has been shown throughout this chapter.

ACTIVITY 8

Raul and Samir are in business, sharing the profits and losses in the ratio of 3:2. Their summarised statement of financial position at 31 August 2016 is as follows:

	$000
Non-current assets:	
Property	80
Motor vehicles	20
	100
Current assets:	
Inventory	19
Trade receivables	16
	35
Total assets	135
Capital and liabilities:	
Capital accounts:	
Raul	60
Samir	55
	115

	$000
Current accounts:	
Raul	10
Samir	(4)
	6
Trade payables	10
Bank overdraft	4
	14
Total liabilities	135

The partners decide to dissolve the business.

1 The property is sold for $106 000.
2 Samir agrees to take one of the vehicles at a value of $7 000. The remaining vehicles are sold for $9 000.
3 The inventory is sold for $18 000 and the partners collect $13 000 from the trade receivables.
4 They pay their trade suppliers the full amount owed.
5 The expenses of realising the partnership amount to $3 000.

Required

a Prepare the partnership realisation account.
b Prepare the partners' capital accounts.
c Prepare the partnership bank account, showing the closing entries to close the account.

This chapter is quite involved and there are a number of key points which you need to be familiar with. These are set out below:

- Read questions involving partnership changes very carefully two or three times before starting to answer them. Highlight or underline important information and instructions. Tick every item as you give effect to it in your answer.
- Treat partnership changes as the ending of one partnership and the commencement of a new one.
- A partnership change requires separate income statements to be prepared for the old and new firms. It will normally be assumed that revenue has been earned evenly over the whole period before and after the change. Apportion expenses in the income statement on a time basis unless any expense has to be apportioned on some other basis. Perform your arithmetical calculations carefully and show your workings.
- Adjust for accrued and prepaid expenses before apportioning them.
- Partners' salaries, interest on drawings and capital will be stated on an annual basis. These must be apportioned on a time basis.
- Check very carefully to see whether or not a goodwill account is to be opened when there is a partnership change.
- If a goodwill account is not to be opened, goodwill is credited to the partners' capital accounts before the change in their old profit-sharing ratio, and debited after the change to the partners' capital accounts in their new profit-sharing ratio.

- When assets are revalued on a partnership change, they are retained in the books of the new partnership at their new values.
- The balance on an outgoing partner's current and drawings accounts must be transferred to his capital account. Make sure you treat the final balance on his capital account exactly as required.
- If partners do not maintain current accounts in their books, the entries that would normally be posted to the current accounts must be posted to the capital accounts.
- Before beginning to copy out your answer, make sure that you have ticked every piece of information and every instruction.

Chapter summary

In this chapter you have learnt the accounting treatment for changes in a partnership. Some of the topics covered are quite complicated. Specifically, you have learnt how to prepare partnership accounts when a partner joins or leaves the firm, and the steps involved in revaluing assets following a partnership change (this is covered in Section 18.3). The concept of goodwill has been introduced in previous chapters, however in this chapter you have learnt how to account for goodwill in a partnership. For partnerships, remember that you'll need to think about purchased and inherent goodwill when preparing the accounts. Finally, you should now know how to account for the dissolution of a partnership in cases where a new partner joins or where an existing partner retires.

TOP TIP

Work through the illustrations and make sure you are fully familiar with how each aspect of a change in a partnership is dealt with. Pay particular attention to the key study points and apply them. Finally, work through the questions below and check your answers.

Practice exercises

1 Ali and Siri are in partnership, sharing the profits and losses equally. Their statement of financial position at 31 October 2016 is as follows:

Statement of financial position at 31 October 2016	
	$000
Non-current assets:	
Property	40
Motor vehicles	20
	60

Statement of financial position at 31 October 2016	
Current assets:	
Inventory	12
Trade receivables	10
	22
Total assets	82
Capital and liabilities:	
Capital accounts:	
Ali	36
Siri	36
	72
Current liabilities:	
Trade payables	8
Bank overdraft	2
	10
Total capital and liabilities	82

The partners did not operate current accounts.

Additional information

1 On 1 November 2016 they admit Fiona as a partner, taking an equal share of the profits.

2 Fiona will pay $30 000 into the bank as her capital.

3 The goodwill is valued at $24 000. No goodwill account is to appear in the books.

4 Ali and Siri also revalue the assets at the same date. The property is revalued at $60 000 and the inventory revalued at $10 000.

Required

a Explain why it is necessary to revalue the assets of a partnership when a new partner is admitted. **[3 marks]**

b Prepare the following:

i revaluation account **[3 marks]**

ii partners' capital accounts after the revaluation of assets and introduction of Fiona as a partner have taken place. **[6 marks]**

c Explain your treatment of goodwill in the partners' capital accounts on the admission of Fiona as a partner. **[3 marks]**

Total: 15

2 Wilson, Keppel and Betty were in partnership and shared profits and losses equally. On 1 May 2015, their capital accounts showed the following balances:

	$
Wilson	40 000
Keppel	30 000
Betty	15 000

3 L and M are in partnership, sharing profits and losses in the ratio of 3:2. They admit N as a partner on 1 January. On the same date, the partnership net assets are revalued and show a loss on revaluation of $40 000. The new profit/loss-sharing ratio is: L 2/5, M 2/5, N 1/5. How will the revaluation of the net assets be recorded in the partners' capital accounts?

	Capital accounts		
	L	**M**	**N**
	$	**$**	**$**
A	Credit 16 000	Credit 16 000	Credit 8 000
B	Debit 16 000	Debit 16 000	–
C	Credit 24 000	Credit 16 000	Debit 8 000
D	Debit 24 000	Debit 16 000	–

4 P, Q and R were partners, sharing profits and losses equally. P retired and Q and R continued in partnership, sharing profits and losses equally. Goodwill was valued at $60 000 but was not shown in the books. Which entries will record the adjustments for P's retirement in the books?

	Capital accounts		
	P	**Q**	**R**
	$	**$**	**$**
A	–	Credit 10 000	Credit 10 000
B	Credit 20 000	Debit 10 000	Debit 10 000
C	Debit 20 000	Credit 10 000	Credit 10 000
D	–	Debit 30 000	Credit 30 000

5 S and T are partners, sharing profits and losses in the ratio of 1:2. They admit V as a partner and revise the profit-sharing ratio to: S 2/5, T 2/5, V 1/5. Goodwill is valued at $60 000 but no goodwill is to be recorded in the books. Which entries will be made in the partners' capital accounts?

	Capital accounts		
	S	**T**	**V**
	$	**$**	**$**
A	Debit 4 000	Credit 16 000	Debit 12 000
B	Credit 24 000	Credit 24 000	Debit 48 000
C	Credit 4 000	Debit 16 000	Credit 12 000
D	Debit 24 000	Debit 24 000	Credit 48 000

Total: 5 marks

Chapter 19
An introduction to the accounts of limited companies

Learning objectives

In this chapter you will learn:

- what limited companies are and how they differ from partnerships
- the UK Companies Act 2006 and some of the legal requirements for companies
- the format of financial statements: income statement and statement of financial position in line with IAS 1
- types of share capital and reserves
- the accounting entries for the issue of shares
- the effect of the issue of shares on the statement of financial position of a limited company
- which profits are distributable in cash as dividends and how the dividends are calculated
- what debentures are and how they differ from shares
- the difference between a bonus issue and a rights issue of shares
- how to record a rights issue and bonus issue in the statement of financial position.

> **KEY TERM**
>
> **Limited company:** A separate legal entity whose existence is separate from its owners; the liabilities of the members are limited to the amounts paid (or to be paid) on shares issued to them.

19.1 What is a limited company?

A **limited company** differs from other organisations because it is a **separate legal entity**; its existence is separate from that of its shareholders (the people who own it). It is important to distinguish this from the **accounting concept of entity**, which, as explained in Section 9.3, applies to every business for the purposes of bookkeeping and accounting, stating that the owner and the business are two separate entities. However, the concept of **legal entity** applies only to limited companies. For example, if Mr Banik, a sole trader, is a butcher, a customer who wishes to sue him for food poisoning will be able to sue him as a person; the **entity concept** will not protect Mr Banik from a legal action. If, though, Mr Banik has formed his business into a limited company, M. Banik Limited, the concept of **separate legal entity** applies and the customer must sue the company and not Mr Banik because the goods were purchased from the company and not from Mr Banik!

19.2 The growth of limited companies

The concept of limited liability goes back to the 16th century but it became important in the 18th century because of the Industrial Revolution. Before that, people earned their living by farming, or from cottage industries that did not require large sums of capital. With the invention of machinery powered by steam engines, increased productivity led to manufacturing being concentrated in factories. Larger amounts of capital were needed to construct the factories and equip them with machinery. This capital could be raised by inviting people to buy shares (or invest) in the business without taking part in its management. These investors were the **shareholders**, or members, of the companies. By the middle of the 19th century, limited companies had become very important as business organisations.

Limited companies are sometimes known as **limited liability companies** because the liability of their shareholders is limited to the amounts they have paid, or have agreed to pay, for their shares. For example, a shareholder owning 100 shares of $1 each cannot be compelled to pay more than the $100 he has already paid for his shares if the company cannot pay its creditors, people such as trade suppliers or banks; the creditors may be the losers.

This is not necessarily the case with sole traders or partnerships. If they are unable to pay their business creditors with their business assets, then the creditors can try to get them to pay their business debts with their personal assets. This may result in a sole trader or partner losing some, or all, of their personal possessions such as their house or car. (It is possible to have limited partnerships in which the liability of some, but not all, of the partners for the firm's debts is limited. Limited partnerships are outside the scope of this book.)

19.3 Partnerships and limited companies compared

	Partnerships	Limited companies
Number of partners	Not less than 2.	n/a
Number of shareholders	Not more than 20 (except in certain professional firms such as accountants, lawyers, etc.).	For a public limited company there is no maximum. For a private limited company there is often a restriction on the number of shareholders. This is set out in the Articles of Association (see next section).

	Partnerships	Limited companies
Liability of sole traders, partners/ shareholders	Unlimited. The private assets of partners or the sole trader may be seized to pay the firm's creditors (except in the case of limited partners in a limited partnership).	Shareholders' liability is limited to the amount they have paid, or agreed to pay, on their shares.
Capital	Determined by the partnership agreement, or the amount of money a sole trader is able to invest from their own savings.	The potential share capital available to a public limited company is unlimited. The share capital for a private limited company will depend on how much money the shareholders have or choose to invest in the business.
Management	All partners (except those with limited liability) may manage the firm's affairs.	Shareholders are not entitled to manage the affairs. This must be left to the directors. (The directors act because they have been appointed directors, not because they are shareholders.) Quite often though a shareholder is a director. This is the case mostly with private limited companies. In such cases the shareholder/director will take part in the day-to-day management of the company. It is also quite common for directors of public limited companies to receive shares as part of their remuneration. It must be noted that although they are both shareholders and directors, their roles are quite separate in law.
Taxation	The businesses of the sole traders or partners are not liable to pay tax on their profits. The liability to pay tax on their shares of profit rests with the sole trader or partners individually.	Companies are liable to pay tax on their profits. The tax payable is treated as an appropriation of profit.
Distribution of profit	The sole trader owns all the profit. Partners share profits and losses in line with the partnership agreement.	Profits are distributed as dividends. Undistributed profits are retained in the company.

TOP TIP

Profit is not the same thing as cash. A common mistake is to think it is cash and is available to be spent. This will be covered in Chapter 23.

KEY TERMS

Private limited company: A company that is not authorised to issue shares to the public. The shares of such a company are generally owned by a small number of shareholders, say a family, and can only be transferred to existing shareholders.

Public limited company (plc): A company that is authorised to issue shares to the public. Usually those shares are freely traded on a recognised stock exchange.

19.4 The UK Companies Act 2006

Two characteristics of limited companies have already been identified:

a Creditors risk not being paid if a company has insufficient funds, that is, the company is insolvent (unable to pay its debts).

b Shareholders are not entitled to help manage a company simply because they own shares in it; they rely on directors to manage the company for them (but note the points above about shareholders in **private limited companies** and director's remuneration).

Since limited companies first came into existence in the United Kingdom, there has been a series of Companies Acts. This type of legislation has been replicated all over the world, such that most countries now have their own Companies Acts. Take a few minutes to look up online if your country has its own company legislation.

This chapter though, will concentrate on company legislation established in the UK. The UK Companies Act 2006, is designed to protect the interests of creditors and shareholders, including those who might in future become creditors or shareholders. Some of the provisions of the Companies Act 2006 are discussed below.

Formation

A company is formed when certain documents are registered by people, known as its 'founders', with the Registrar of Companies, and various fees and duties are paid to the Registrar.

Memorandum and articles of association

These are two of the documents which must be filed with the Registrar of Companies.

The **Articles of Association** is the main constitutional document of a company that defines the existence of the company and regulates the structure and control of the company and its members. It contains such things as:

- liability of members
- directors' powers and responsibilities
- appointment and removal of directors
- issue and transfer of shares
- dividends and other distributions to members
- members' decision making and attendance at general meetings.

The **Memorandum of Association** forms part of the articles and defines the relationship of the company to the rest of the world. It contains information about:

- the name of the company, which must end with the words **public limited company (plc)** if it is a public company, or **Limited** or **Ltd** if it is a private company (the difference between the two types of company will be explained later)
- a statement that the liability of the company is limited.

Public and private companies

Companies register as either public companies or private companies:

- **Public companies** may offer their shares to the public and may arrange for the shares to be bought and sold on the stock exchange.
- **Private companies** are not allowed to offer their shares to the public and shares cannot, therefore, be bought and sold on the stock exchange.

The distinction between public and private companies applies in the United Kingdom, but may not apply in all other countries. To cater for this situation, companies will be described as 'Limited' or 'Ltd' in this text, but will be assumed to be public companies unless they are specifically stated to be private companies, or the context implies that they are private.

TOP TIP

This distinction becomes important when the International Accounting Standards are required. Compliance with IAS is permitted in UK legislation for private companies. If they wanted to, partnerships and sole traders could apply them too. IAS require some additional information from public companies but on general matters the same level of detail is required of both private and public companies.

19.5 The Companies Act and share capital

In the past, a company used to have to state its authorised **share capital** (that is, the maximum amount of share capital that the company is authorised by its constitutional documents to issue to shareholders). However, under the Companies Act 2006 there is no longer any requirement for a company to have an authorised share capital. Instead, the Companies Act 2006 introduced the requirement to submit a statement of capital and initial shareholdings when registering a company, which shows the company's share capital at the point of registration. It needs to contain:

- the total number of shares of the company to be taken on formation
- the nominal value of those **shares**
- the total number of shares of each class
- the nominal value of shares of each class
- the amount to be paid up and the amount to be unpaid on each share.

Issued capital

This is the nominal value of the shares issued by the company.

Public limited companies must have a minimum issued capital of £50 000 or the prescribed euro equivalent.

A private limited company must have a share capital of £50 000 or less (there is no minimum).

- A company may:
  - issue bonus shares
  - increase its share capital by the issue of new shares and if members have passed an ordinary resolution or a resolution requiring a higher majority
  - consolidate its shares into shares of a larger amount than its existing shares (e.g. if it has a share capital of 10 000 ordinary shares of $1, it can convert them into (say) 2 000 shares of $5 or 1 000 shares of $10)
  - divide its shares into shares of a lower denomination (e.g. convert its ordinary share capital of 10 000 ordinary shares of $1 into 20 000 shares of $0.50 or 40 000 shares of $0.25)
  - convert its paid-up shares into inventory (inventory may be described as 'bundles of shares'; the advantage of inventory is that it may be bought and sold in fractional amounts, e.g. $35.50 or $41.80; if the shares had not been converted into inventory they could only be bought in multiples of $1)

KEY TERMS

Share capital: The capital raised by a business by the issue of shares (usually) for cash, but may also be for consideration for other than cash, such as non-current or current assets.

Share: The smallest division of the total share capital of the company which can be issued in order to raise funds for the company.

- re-convert inventory back into shares of any nominal value (e.g. shares of $1 may be converted into inventory then, later, re-converted back into shares of, say, $0.25, $0.50, $5, $10 or any other amount)
- reduce its capital by redeeming or purchasing its shares, provided it complies with strict conditions laid down under the Companies Act (this is not covered in this book, as it is not a requirement of the syllabus).

19.6 Share capital

After the legal requirements of completing the memorandum and articles of association have been completed, it is then possible for the company to raise capital by issuing shares. There are some new terms which you need to be familiar with in this respect:

a **Issued capital** is the total of the shares which have been issued to the shareholders.

b **Called-up capital** is money required to be paid by shareholders immediately. A newly formed company may not require all the money due from shareholders immediately. If it has to have a factory built and then equip it with machinery, the money could lie idle in the company's bank account until those items have to be paid for. It may require the shareholders to pay only part of the amount due on their shares until further sums are required, when it will call on (ask) the shareholders to make further payments.

c **Uncalled** capital is any amount of the share capital not yet called up (asked for) by the company.

d **Paid-up capital** is the money received from shareholders on the called-up capital. Some shareholders may be late in paying their calls, or may fail to pay them at all.

e **Calls in advance** is money received from shareholders who have paid calls before they are due.

f **Calls in arrear** is money due from shareholders who are late in paying their calls.

g **Forfeited shares** are shares which shareholders have forfeited because they have failed to pay their calls. The shares may be re-issued to other shareholders.

Walkthrough

Startup Limited has invited members of the public to buy ordinary shares of $1 each. The price of $1 per share is known as the **nominal**, **par** or **face value** of the share. The terms of the issue are:

1. 1 May: an amount of $0.50 per share is to be paid when someone applies for the shares.
2. 1 June: those people who have been successful in their application will have to pay a further $0.25 per share.
3. 1 July: the balance of $0.25 per share must be paid.

Sally applied for 1 000 shares on 1 May. She had to send the company a cheque for $500 with her application form.

She was advised by the company that her application was successful. On 1 June she paid the company $250. This would be known as the first call.

Finally, on 1 July, she paid a further $250. This is the second call. Sally received a share certificate for 1 000 shares which is her proof of ownership.

Had Sally failed to pay either of the calls on 1 June or 1 July, then she would have forfeited her right to the shares. The company would have cancelled her application. They would probably have kept any money she had paid.

Sometimes, more people apply to buy the shares than the company has made available for sale. For example, if Startup Limited had offered a total 50 000 ordinary shares for sale, perhaps people applied to buy 60 000 of them. In this case the shares are **over-subscribed**. The company would have received $30 000 with the application forms (60 000 shares × $0.50). The directors would decide who would be allowed to buy the 50 000 shares. The people who had been unsuccessful would have received their money back.

19.7 Classes of shares

There are a number of different types of share a company may issue. Shares may be **preference shares** or **ordinary shares**.

> **KEY TERMS**
>
> **Preference share:** A share which does not give the owner any ownership rights in the company. The holder will receive (usually) dividends at a fixed rate, payable before (in preference to) dividends to the ordinary shareholder.
>
> **Ordinary share:** A share which represents equity ownership in a limited company. It entitles the holder to vote in matters put before them by the directors. It also entitles the holder to a dividend at a varying amount, as determined by the directors and depending on the profits made by the company and supposing all other liabilities can be satisfied.

Preference shares

Preference shares are so called because they entitle holders of them to certain rights which ordinary shareholders do not enjoy. These shareholders are entitled to receive dividends at a fixed rate out of profits before the ordinary shareholders become entitled to dividends. The rate of the dividend is expressed as a percentage of the nominal value (see Section 19.6 above and Section 19.8 below). When a company is **wound up** (ceases to exist), preference shareholders are entitled to have their capital repaid before any repayment is made to the ordinary shareholders. If there are insufficient funds after the preference shareholders have been repaid, the ordinary shareholders will lose some, if not all, of their money.

Non-cumulative preference shares

This class of preference share is not entitled to have any arrears of dividend carried forward to future years if the profit of any year is insufficient to pay the dividend in full.

Cumulative preference shares

This class of preference share is entitled to have arrears of dividend carried forward to future years when sufficient profits may become available to pay the arrears.

The following example shows the effect of fluctuating profits on non-cumulative preference shares and ordinary shareholders, and also shows the difference between cumulative and non-cumulative preference shares.

Walkthrough

Upandown Limited was formed with a share capital of 10 000 8% non-cumulative preference shares of $1 each, and 20 000 ordinary shares of $1 each. The profits available for dividend were as follows: 2011 $1 200; 2012 $900; 2013 $600; 2014 $1 000; 2015 $700; 2016 $1 300.

The dividends paid to the preference shareholders, and the balances of profit available to pay dividends to the ordinary shareholders, were as follows:

	2011	2012	2013	2014	2015	2016
	$	$	$	$	$	$
Profit for the year	1 200	900	600	1 000	700	1 300
Preference dividend paid	(800)	(800)	(600)	(800)	(700)	(800)
Profit left for ordinary shareholders	400	100	nil	200	nil	500
Maximum ordinary dividend payable	2%	0.5%	0%	1%	0%	2.5%

If the preference shares in Upandown Limited had been cumulative preference shares, the position would have been as follows:

	2011	2012	2013	2014	2015	2016
	$	$	$	$	$	$
Profit for the year	1200	900	600	1000	700	1300
Preference dividend for year	(800)	(800)	(600)	(800)	(700)	(800)
Arrears of dividend brought forward				(200)		(100)
Profit left for ordinary shareholders	400	100	nil	nil	nil	400
Maximum ordinary dividend payable	2%	0.5%	0%	0%	0%	2%

Notice that in this case it is the ordinary shareholders who will suffer. In some years they will not receive any dividend at all!

ACTIVITY 1

Badry Limited's share capital consists of 60 000 10% preference shares of $1, and 100 000 ordinary shares of $1. Profits for six years were as follows: 2011 $10 000; 2012 $5 000; 2013 $7 000; 2014 $4 000; 2015 $7 000; 2016 $12 000.

Prepare tables showing the dividends payable to the preference shareholders and ordinary shareholders if the preference shares are:

a non-cumulative

b cumulative.

TOP TIP

It should indicate in the question if the preference shares are cumulative or otherwise.

Preference shares may also be **redeemable** or **non-redeemable**. If they are redeemable this means that the company can approach the preference shareholders and buy back the shares from them. If preference shares are redeemable then they will appear under non-current liabilities in the statement of financial position. If, on the other hand, they are non-redeemable, in other words the company will not buy them back in the future, then they appear in the equity section of the statement, together with the ordinary shares, reserves and retained earnings. The dividends payable on non-redeemable preference shares will be disclosed in the statement of changes in equity (see Section 19.11), as will their nominal value.

Participating preference shares

These shares entitle the holders to be paid a dividend at an agreed rate. However, if profits for the year are very good, the company may pay them an additional amount of dividend.

Ordinary shares

The people who own ordinary shares are the owners of the company. They are the people who are entitled to attend the **annual general meeting (AGM)** and vote on the propositions put forward by the directors.

The ordinary share capital is known as the **equity** of a company. The profit that remains after any dividend has been paid on preference shares belongs to the ordinary shareholders, and the ordinary dividend will be paid out of that. The ordinary shareholders are, therefore, the risk takers, as if the profit for the year is low, or there is a loss, they may not receive any dividends at all. All the reserves (including retained profit, or retained earnings) also belong to the ordinary shareholders. When a company is wound up, after all creditors (including the **debenture** holders) and the preference shareholders have been paid, the assets remaining belong to the ordinary shareholders, and the proceeds from the sale of the assets will be paid to them. The shareholders may receive more than their original investment in the company, but may receive less than they paid for their shares. It all depends upon the circumstances in which the company is wound up.

19.8 Shares issued at a premium

Shares have a **nominal (or par) value**. For example, shares of $1 have a nominal value of $1, and shares of $0.50 have a nominal value of $0.50. The directors of a company may issue shares at a price exceeding their nominal value if they believe that the issue will attract a lot of subscribers, or the shares are already being bought and sold on the stock exchange at a price higher than the nominal value. When shares are issued at a price above their nominal value, they are said to be **issued at a premium**. If shares with a nominal value of $1 are issued at, say, $1.25, the **share premium** on each share is $0.25. The premium on each share must be credited to a special account called the share premium account. Only the nominal value of $1 may be credited to the share capital account. The balances on the share capital account and the share premium account are shown separately in the statement of financial position.

Walkthrough

The directors of The Very Good Company Limited issued 60 000 ordinary shares of $1 at $1.30 per share. All the shares were subscribed for and issued. The recording of the issue of shares will be made firstly by journal entry. The journal entry to record the issue of the shares is shown below:

	$	$
Bank	78 000	
Ordinary share capital		60 000
Share premium account		18 000
Issue of 60 000 ordinary shares of $1 at $1.30 per share		

The ledger entries to record the issue of shares are quite straightforward. They are:

- debit the bank account with the cash received by the company for the issue
- credit each share capital account with the **nominal** value of the shares of the particular class issued
- credit the share premium account with the **premium** received on the issue of the shares.

KEY TERMS

Annual general meeting (AGM): A meeting held after the end of the financial year. All ordinary shareholders are entitled to attend. At the meeting, the proposals made by the directors are voted on by the ordinary shareholders.

Debenture: A loan of a fixed amount given to a company. The loan is repayable at a fixed date in the future and carries interest at a fixed rate.

Nominal (or par) value: The face value of a share.

Share premium: The excess over the nominal or par value of a share when it is issued.

Walkthrough

On 1 January DJ Limited issued the following shares:

- 100 000 ordinary shares of $1 each at $1.20
- 50 000 6% preference shares of $1 each at par.

All the shares were fully subscribed and the company received the money on that date.

The ledger accounts to record the issue will be:

Bank account (extract)

Debit			Credit		
		$			$
1 Jan	Ordinary share capital	100 000			
	Share premium	20 000			
	6% preference share capital	50 000			

Ordinary share capital account

Debit			Credit		
		$			$
			1 Jan	Bank	100 000

Share premium account

Debit			Credit		
		$			$
			1 Jan	Bank	20 000

6% preference share capital account

Debit			Credit		
		$			$
			1 Jan	Bank	50 000

Note: The term 'fully subscribed' means that all the money was received for the shares. A bank account extract has been shown to illustrate the recording of the money received into the bank. In practice there would be a lot more items recorded in the bank account.

ACTIVITY 2

On 1 June, the directors of Premium Shares Limited offered 100 000 ordinary shares of $1 each at $1.20 per share. All the shares were subscribed and paid for on that date.

a Prepare journal entries to record the issue of the ordinary shares.

b Prepare the ledger accounts, including the cash book, to record the issue of ordinary shares.

ACTIVITY 3

On 1 August Doingwell Limited offered 150 000 ordinary shares of $1 each for sale at $2.00. The terms of the issue were:

1 August: $1.00 payable per share. This amount included the full share premium.

1 October: the balance of $1.00 per share was payable.

The issue was over-subscribed and on 1 August the company received applications for 220 000 shares:

1 September: the company refunded the money to the unsuccessful applicants.

1 October: the company received the balance due from successful applicants.

Required

a Prepare journal entries to record the issue of the ordinary shares, including the refund to unsuccessful applicants.

b Prepare the ledger accounts, including the cash book, to record all the transactions relating to the issue of the ordinary shares.

19.9 Reserves

There are two classes of reserves: **revenue reserves** and **capital reserves**. The differences between them are important.

Revenue reserves

Revenue reserves are created by transferring an amount from the profit for the year. The transfer is shown in the statement of changes in equity (see Section 19.11). Revenue reserves may be created for specific purposes (replacement of non-current assets, or planned expansion of the business), or generally (general reserve), to strengthen the financial position of the company. The creation of revenue reserves reduces the amount of profit available to pay dividends. If the reserves are later considered by the directors to be excessive and no longer required, they may be credited back to retained earnings and become available for the payment of dividend. Again, this adjustment is made in the statement of changes in equity.

Retained earnings shown in the statement of financial position is one of the revenue reserves. Another would be a general reserve.

Capital reserves

Capital reserves are **not normally** created by transferring profit from the income statement. They represent gains that arise from particular circumstances and usually represent gains which have not yet been realised. Capital reserves are part of the capital structure of a company; they should **never** be credited back to the income statement and can never be used to pay cash dividends to shareholders.

The most common capital reserves, and ones with which you should become familiar, are given below.

Share premium account

This has already been explained in Section 19.8. The Companies Act 2006 permits the share premium account to be used for certain specific purposes only:

- to pay up unissued shares to existing ordinary shareholders as fully paid-up bonus shares
- to write off the expenses arising on a new issue of shares at a premium
- to write off any commission paid on a new issue of shares at a premium.

(Some of these topics are covered later in the book, and it will be seen that there are certain important restrictions on the use of the share premium account to provide for the premium payable on the redemption of shares.)

KEY TERMS

Revenue reserves: The profits made by a company which have not been distributed to shareholders.

Capital reserves: Gains which (usually) arise from non-trading activities, such as the revaluation of a company's non-current assets.

Capital redemption reserve

This reserve must be created when a company redeems, or buys back, any of its shares from existing shareholders, otherwise than out of the proceeds of a new issue of shares. It is created by transferring amounts from retained earnings and can be used to issue bonus shares to existing shareholders. The bookkeeping entries for the redemption of shares are not covered in this book as they are not on the syllabus.

Revaluation reserve

A company may revalue its non-current assets and any gain on the revaluation must be credited to a revaluation reserve; it is an unrealised profit and must not be credited to the income statement.

The revaluation reserve may be used to issue shares to existing shareholders of the company as bonus shares.

Walkthrough

An extract from Premises Limited's books of account shows the following:

	$
Freehold buildings: cost	60 000
Provision for depreciation	(18 000)
Net book value	42 000

The buildings have been professionally revalued at $100 000 and the directors have decided to revalue the buildings in the books. The entries in the books are shown by the following journal entry:

Journal		
Name of account		
	$	$
Freehold buildings at cost	40 000	
Provision for depreciation of freehold buildings	18 000	
Freehold buildings revaluation reserve		58 000

Note: The buildings are being increased from a net book value of $42 000 to $100 000, an increase of $58 000. The amount already provided for depreciation must be transferred to the revaluation reserve.

As a result of the journal entry, the freehold buildings at cost account will now become freehold buildings at valuation account with a debit balance of $100 000. The balance on the provision for depreciation of freehold buildings will be zero. If it is decided to depreciate the buildings in future then the annual charge will be based on the revalued amount of $100 000.

ACTIVITY 4

Freehold premises are shown in the statement of financial position of a company as follows: cost $60 000, net book value $42 000. It has been decided to revalue the premises in the books of the company at $80 000.

Prepare the journal entry for the revaluation of the premises in the company's books.

19.10 Income statement for a limited company

The way the financial statements of limited companies are prepared is set out in International Accounting Standard 1 (IAS 1). The statement allows income and expenses of a company to be presented in one of two ways:

a in a single statement of profit or loss and other comprehensive income covering the accounting period

b in two separate statements:

  i a separate statement of profit or loss

  ii a statement of other comprehensive income.

IAS 1 permits alternative titles to be used, but for the remainder of the textbook an **income statement** will be used.

A gain on the revaluation of a non-current asset (as in Section 19.9) is an example of an item that is presented in the statement of other comprehensive income.

The format of the income statement is extremely important and should be learnt.

Walkthrough

Exhibit Co. Limited income statement for the year ended ....*		
	This year*	**Last year***
	$000	**$000**
Revenue [1]	100 000	80 000
Cost of sales [2]	(60 000)	(45 000)
Gross profit	40 000	35 000
Distribution costs [3]	(8 000)	(7 000)
Administrative expenses [4]	(11 000)	(10 000)
Profit/(loss) from operations [5]	21 000	18 000
Other income [6]	2 000	1 500
Other expenses [7]	(1 000)	(500)
Finance costs [8]	(3 000)	(2 000)
Profit/(loss) before tax	19 000	17 000
Tax [9]	(5 000)	(4 000)
Profit/(loss) for the year [10]	14 000	13 000

* In practice, dates would be included. This is an example of the expenses being classified by function – distribution, administrative and so on.

[1] Revenue is the income generated by the company from its trading activities. In other words, its sales for the year.

[2] Cost of sales. The detail does not have to be shown here, but show as a working: opening inventory + purchases – closing inventory.

TOP TIP

If you are provided with the information to calculate the cost of sales, you may want to show it as part of the income statement or as separate workings. If you do it as workings, indicate where it can be found. This will be useful if there is an error in calculation.

[3] Distribution costs include expenses such as salespeople's salaries or expenses, warehousing costs, carriage outwards, depreciation of warehouses or delivery vans, or any other expenses associated with the transfer of goods from the company to its customers.

[4] Administrative expenses would include office salaries or costs, selling costs not treated as part of the distribution expenses, general depreciation of cars or office equipment. It may also include discounts allowed, provision for doubtful debts and irrecoverable debts.

[5] Profit from operations is the profit earned by the company in its day-to-day trading activities. Other sources of income and expenditure, which are not part of its normal trading activities, are shown below this.

[6] Other income would include such things as profit on disposal of non-current assets, or rental income, where renting property or equipment is not the main object of the company.

[7] Other expenses would include items not included under either 3 or 4 above. It may include, say, loss on disposal of non-current assets.

[8] Finance costs would include bank overdraft or loan interest, debenture interest or interest on loans from other companies. It also includes dividends paid on redeemable preference shares. These type of shares are regarded as a long-term loan of the business. There may also be finance income. This could be, say, bank interest received.

[9] The tax is payable on the profits the company earns. It may be given either as a figure, or perhaps you will be told the percentage rate to charge it at. If this is the case, the figure will be calculated on the profit before tax.

[10] Profit/(loss) for the year. The ordinary shareholders are the owners of the company. All the profit earned by the company belongs to them. In some companies this figure is called 'profit or loss attributable to equity holders'. Either term is acceptable.

It is likely that you will be given figures for the total distribution and administrative expenses. You may also be asked to make adjustments for accruals and prepayments of certain individual expenses. You may be told whether they are administrative or distribution expenses, but you may have to make a judgement. As in all cases, show all the workings.

Remember also that the layout above is for accounts which will be published by the company and available for the general public to look at. It is likely that the company will produce internal accounts which are much more detailed than the statement shown above. It may, for instance, list each individual expense rather than group them under two or three headings. This is to allow managers to look in more detail at the performance of the company. It is possible that you may have to list all the expenses rather than classify them by function. If this is the case, then a format similar to the one below will be acceptable.

Walkthrough

Exhibit Co. Limited
Income statement for the year ended .... *

	$000	$000
Revenue		100 000
Opening inventories	20 000	
Purchases	55 000	
	75 000	
Closing inventories	(15 000)	
Cost of sales		(60 000)
Gross profit		40 000
Rental income		2 000
		42 000
Overheads:		
Office salaries	(4 100)	
Selling expenses	(4 000)	
Delivery costs	(800)	
Salespeople's salaries	(4 300)	
Provision for irrecoverable debts	(900)	
Loss on sale of non-current assets	(1 000)	
Depreciation:		
Delivery vehicles	(2 900)	
Office equipment	(2 000)	
		(20 000)
Profit from operations		22 000
Finance costs (bank interest)		(3 000)
Profit before tax		19 000
Tax		(5 000)
Profit for the year		14 000

* In practice, dates would be included.

In this illustration only one year is shown. Dates should also be included in the heading. Notice also that for management purposes the items do not have to be shown in the same places as for the published accounts; for example, the loss on disposal of non-current assets which is listed with all the other expenses.

19.11 Dividing up the profit for the year

Having generated a profit for the year and paid tax on it, what does the company do with it? Unlike a sole trader where all the profit belongs to the owner, a limited company can have a large number of owners in the form of shareholders. They will be rewarded for their investment by the company paying them a dividend. It would be unwise for a company to pay out all its profit to the shareholders. Indeed, most companies, after paying some of the profit as dividend, keep the balance as retained earnings. This is added to the retained earnings from previous years and shown as a separate figure on the statement of financial position.

KEY TERM

Statement of changes in equity: A statement prepared to show the changes in a company's share capital, reserves and retained earnings over a reporting period.

In other instances, after paying the dividend the company may transfer part of the remaining profit to a reserve, which was discussed earlier.

What is important to note is that profit and reserves are not cash funds, as the next chapter will illustrate. They are represented by assets shown in the statement of financial position.

In IAS 1, the splitting of the profits is shown in a statement known as a **statement of changes in equity**. This is shown below.

Walkthrough

Exhibit Co. Limited

Statement of changes in equity for the year ended ....*

Retained earnings	This year*	Last year*
	$000	$000
Balance at start of year	43000	34000
Profit for the year [1]	14000	13000
Transfers for other reserves	–	–
	57000	47000
Dividends paid	(5000)	(4000)
Transfers to other reserves	–	–
Balance at end of year	52000	43000

[1] This is the final profit figure from the income statement.

* Note also that no dates are included. This would not be the case in practice where the actual date of the year end and previous year, say 31 December, would be stated.

An alternative and more detailed presentation is shown below:

Statement of changes in equity for the year ended ....*

	Share capital and reserves	Retained earnings	Revaluation reserve	
	$000	$000	$000	$000
Balance at start of year	50000	43000	–	93000
Total profit for the year		14000		14000
Dividends paid		(5000)		(5000)
Balance at the end of the year	50000	52000	–	102000

* Note also that no dates are included. This would not be the case in practice where the actual date of the year end and previous year, say 31 December, would be stated.

TOP TIP

Notice that the total at the bottom right-hand corner ($102000) is the same if the bottom line is added across and the end (total) column is added down. This is always a good check.

IAS 1 also requires a statement showing details of dividends paid during the year. An example of this is shown below. The important thing to note here is that only dividends **paid** during the year are included in the statement. This means that the statement of changes in equity could include the payment of the final dividend in respect of the previous year. It doesn't matter to which year the dividend relates. Provided money has left the business as payment of dividend to the shareholders, it is always recorded in the statement of changes in equity.

Proposed dividends are usually voted on by the shareholders at the annual general meeting and approved by them at that time. The annual general meeting takes place after the end of the final year and the preparation of the accounts for that year. There is always the possibility that the shareholders may not vote to approve the dividend payment. Thus, they are never recorded in the financial statements for the year recently ended. This results in them being paid some months after the end of the financial year, often well into the next financial year.

Thus, proposed dividends are **never** shown in the financial statements. They are referred to by way of a note to the published accounts, as set out in the example below:

Walkthrough

Dividends for the year ended ....*
(Note for the published accounts)

	This year*	Last year*
	$000	$000
Amounts recognised as distributions to equity holders during the year:		
Final dividend for last year of $0.075 per share	3000	2200
Interim dividend for this year of $0.050 per share	2000	1800
	5000	4000
Proposed final dividend for this year of $0.095 per share	3800	3000

* Note also that no dates are included. This would not be the case in practice where the actual date of the year end and previous year, say 31 December 2016, would be stated.

The statement of changes in equity can be expanded further to include transfers to and from reserves, and the issue of shares.

Walkthrough

Using the information from above:

- During the year, Exhibit Co. Limited issued 10 000 ordinary shares of $1 each at $1.20.
- At the end of the year, the directors transferred $6 000 to the general reserve.

As a result of these actions the statement of changes in equity would appear as shown below:

Statement of changes in equity for the year ended........*

	Ordinary share capital	Share premium	General reserve	Retained earnings	Total equity
	$000	$000	$000	$000	$000
Balance at start of year	40 000	2000	8000	43 000	93 000
Profit for the year				14 000	14 000
Dividends paid				(5 000)	(5 000)
Issue of ordinary shares	10 000	2000			12 000
Transfer to general reserve			6 000	(6 000)	
Balance at end of year	50 000	4 000	14 000	46 000	114 000

* Note also that no dates are included. This would not be the case in practice where the actual date of the year end and previous year, say 31 December 2016, would be stated.

TOP TIPS

- Note the columns in which the figures are recorded and whether or not they are added or subtracted. A common mistake is not to include anything in the total column. Check whether or not you have been asked for total columns. If not, then they can be ignored.
- Another common error is to put figures in every row. For example, entering the $14 000 profit for the year under share capital, share premium, general reserve, retained earnings and the total column. This is wrong. Again, note the total at the bottom right-hand column ($114 000) is the same whether added across or down. You'll gain credit for this cross addition, even if the figures are incorrect.

IAS 1 allows for alternative ways of setting out the statement of changes in equity. One such alternative is to prepare a **statement of recognised income and expenses**. This is much less detailed, as it includes such things as the profit for the year and gains on revaluation of non-current assets. It does not include dividends paid or issue of shares. You should be aware of its existence and what it does and does not include.

TOP TIP

The statement of changes in equity set out above is an important part of the financial statements. Learn the layout and how to adjust the figures as a result of the changes.

19.12 Statement of financial position for a limited company

IAS 1 specifies the minimum information which must be shown in the statement of financial position for a limited company.

Walkthrough

Statement of financial position as at ......*

	This year*	Last year*
	$000	$000
Assets		
Non-current assets: [1]		
Tangible		
Property, plant and equipment	98 000	90 100
Intangible		
Goodwill	7 700	8 000
	105 700	98 100
Current assets: [2]		
Inventories	1 000	800

	This year*	Last year*
	$000	$000
Trade receivables and other	5000	4000
Cash and cash equivalents	500	300
	6500	5100
Total assets: [3]	112200	103200
Equity and liabilities		
Share capital and reserves [4]		
Share capital	40000	40000
Share premium	2000	2000
General reserve	8000	8000
Retained earnings	52000	43000
	102000	93000
Non-current liabilities: [5]		
Bank loan	5500	5200
Current liabilities: [6]		
Trade and other payables	1200	1000
Tax liabilities	3500	4000
	4700	5000
Total equity and liabilities [7]	112200	103200

* Note that no dates are included. This would not be the case in practice where the actual date of the year end and previous year, say 31 December 2016, would be stated.

[1] Non-current assets includes both tangible assets such as plant and machinery, motor vehicles and office equipment, as well as intangible assets such as goodwill. In this case, goodwill should only be shown if it is purchased goodwill; in other words, included in the purchase price of another business acquired by the company. Other intangible assets could include the cost of developing the company's products and acquiring patents and trade marks. Notice that only the net book value of the non-current assets is shown. Most companies provide a series of notes to accompany the financial statements. These would have the detailed breakdown of the cost of the assets, any additions or disposals made during the year and the depreciation charge for the year (see Chapter 22).

[2] Current assets includes inventories, trade receivables and bank balances identified as cash and cash equivalents. The figure for inventories would include raw materials, work in progress and finished goods in the case of a manufacturing company. In the case of receivables, show the trade receivables as one figure, being the amount receivable from customers, and other receivables (such as prepayments) as a separate figure. Cash and cash equivalents include short-term deposits as well as bank current accounts.

[3] Total assets is simply the sum of non-current and current assets.

[4] The capital of the company is analysed, showing the separate classes of paid-up capital, share premium and reserves. Notice that the figure for retained earnings is the closing figure from the statement of changes in equity. Unless this is calculated, the statement of financial position will not balance.

[5] Non-current liabilities are amounts which fall due for payment more than 12 months after the end of the financial year. This would cover such items as long-term loans which the company owes. It would also include debentures and redeemable preference shares.

Although not shown here, it is also possible for a company to have non-current receivables. This may be something such as a debt which is due to be received more than 12 months after the date of the statement. Such items would be shown as a separate heading in the statement.

[6] Current liabilities would include trade payables (amounts due to suppliers) and other payables such as accruals. It would also include other short-term borrowings such as a bank loan and the current portion of long-term borrowings, such as that part of a long-term loan which is repayable within 12 months from the date of the statement of financial position.

[7] Total liabilities is the sum of the equity, non-current and current liabilities.

The format for the statement of financial position is one which is widely used in practice. IAS 1 allows other layouts. However, the layout here will be used for the rest of the book.

19.13 Calculation of the value of ordinary shares

The value of shares depends upon many factors. Shares are no different from other commodities, the prices of which depend upon supply and demand. The past performance and, more importantly, the future prospects of the company and economic, political and sociological factors at home and abroad may all influence the demand, and the price which has to be paid, for shares on the stock exchange. The aspect of share prices is outside the scope of this book.

The net asset value of ordinary shares, however, may be of some importance. It is based on the fact that all the reserves of a company belong to the ordinary shareholders.

Walkthrough

The following is the summarised statement of financial position of Appoggiatura Limited.

	$000
Total assets less current liabilities	1 400
Non-current liabilities: 10% debentures 2 020	(300)
	1 100
Equity	
1 000 000 ordinary shares of $0.50 each	500
Share premium	180
Capital redemption reserve	100
General reserve	200
Retained earnings	120
	1 100

The net asset value of **one** ordinary share is calculated as follows:

The total of the ordinary share capital and reserves = $1 100 000.

The net asset value of one ordinary share is:

$$\frac{\$1\,100\,000}{1\,000\,000} = \$1.10$$

ACTIVITY 5

The following is an extract from the statement of financial position of Gracenote Limited:

	$
Share capital and reserves	
200 000 ordinary shares of $1	200 000
Long-term loan	150 000
Share premium account	50 000
General reserve	100 000
Retained earnings	(40 000)
	460 000

Calculate the net asset value of 100 ordinary shares.

19.14 Liabilities, provisions and reserves

The differences between liabilities, provisions and reserves, including how they are created, are important and are summarised here.

Liabilities are amounts owing by a company to trade or other creditors when the amounts can be determined with substantial accuracy. They are created in the books by carrying down credit balances on personal or expense accounts (see Chapter 10).

Provisions are created to provide for liabilities that are known to exist but of which the amounts cannot be determined with substantial accuracy (e.g. doubtful debt provisions). Provisions are created by debiting the amounts to the income statement and crediting them to provision accounts. Awkwardly, accountants also use the word 'provision' when making reductions in the values of assets. This alternative meaning is seen when provisions are made for the depreciation of non-current assets (see Chapter 11) and unrealised profit on inventory of manufactured goods (see Chapter 20).

Reserves are any other amounts that are set aside and not included in the definition of provisions above. They may be created by debiting the appropriation section of a company's income statement and crediting reserve accounts. They may also be created by revaluing non-current assets.

19.15 Distributable profits and dividends

Distributable profit

The distributable profits of a company consist of:

- its accumulated realised profits which have not already been distributed or used for any other purpose **less**
- its accumulated realised losses which have not previously been written off.

For our purposes, distributable profits are the profits for the year plus any retained earnings brought forward from last year. Once the directors have decided how much, if any, of this should be transferred to reserves, the balance can be used to pay dividends to the shareholders.

Dividends

Dividends are the means by which shareholders share in the profits of a company. Directors may not pay dividends to shareholders except out of distributable profits as defined above.

Interim dividends may be paid to shareholders during a company's financial year provided the directors are satisfied that profits for the purpose have been earned and the cash resources of the company are sufficient to pay the dividend.

A final dividend is paid after the end of the financial year. However, the directors may only recommend the amount of dividend to be paid. Before it can be paid, the shareholders must approve payment by passing a resolution at the company's annual general meeting.

Interim dividends paid during the year are shown in the statement of changes in equity. Final dividends approved after the end of the financial year appear as a note to the accounts.

Dividends are usually declared as so many cents per share or as a percentage of the nominal value of the shares. This is shown below.

KEY TERMS

Interim dividend: A dividend paid to existing shareholders during the year provided the directors are satisfied that sufficient profits have been earned and the cash is available to pay the dividend.

Final dividend: The dividend the directors recommend should be paid to shareholders after the end of the year. The directors can only propose the dividend. It must be approved by the shareholders at the annual general meeting.

Walkthrough

A company has issued 100 000 ordinary shares of $1 per share.

a The directors have recommended a dividend of $0.07 per share. In this case the company will pay a total dividend of 100 000 × $0.07 = $7 000.

b The directors have recommended a dividend of 5%. In this case the company will pay a total dividend of 5% of $100 000 = $5 000 (or $0.05 per share).

Dividend policy

Before paying or recommending dividends, directors of a company must consider the following important matters:

- whether sufficient distributable profits are available
- whether the company's funds will be sufficient to pay the dividend; a cash forecast is needed
- whether there is any need to transfer profits into revenue reserves to strengthen the business
- whether there is a proper balance between dividend growth and capital growth; unless dividends and share values increase, shareholders' wealth is diminished by inflation in the economy (undistributed profit increases the company's reserves and the statement of financial position value of the ordinary shares)
- a generous dividend policy may increase the value of shares on the stock exchange, and a 'mean' policy will have the opposite effect.

19.16 Debentures

A debenture is a document given by a company to someone who has lent it money. It states the amount of loan, the annual amount of interest payable, and the dates on which interest is to be paid. It also includes the date on which the loan is to be repaid by the company. Usually, repayment is spread over a period, and the dates of commencement and end of the period are included in the description of the debenture.

Debentures are usually secured on all or some of the company's assets. If the company gets into financial difficulties, the assets on which the debentures are secured will be sold and the proceeds used to repay the loans to the debenture holders. This gives the debenture holders an advantage over other creditors of the company.

The difference between shares and debentures

Shares	Debentures
Shareholders are members of the company.	Debenture holders are not members of the company. They are creditors of the company as, at some point in the future, the company will have to repay the debenture to the person, bank or company who lent it.
Share capital is shown in the statement of financial position under equity.	Debentures are shown in the statement of financial position as non-current liabilities unless they are due for redemption within one year, when they must be shown as current liabilities.
Shareholders are the last people to be repaid when a company is wound up.	Debenture holders are entitled to be repaid before shareholders when a company is wound up.

Shares	Debentures
Dividends may only be paid if distributable profits are available.	Interest on debentures must be paid even if the company has not made a profit.
Dividends are an appropriation of profit.	Debenture holders receive interest. This is an expense which is shown under finance costs in the income statement.

Walkthrough

The trial balance of Rawson Limited at 30 April 2016 is as follows:

	$	$
Revenue		756 000
Purchases	446 000	
Inventory at 1 May 2015	32 000	
Sales staff salaries and commission	83 000	
Administration salaries	57 000	
Carriage outwards	24 000	
General expenses	45 000	
Interest on debentures	5 000	
Goodwill at cost	100 000	
Freehold premises at cost	240 000	
Provision for depreciation of freehold premises		71 000
Delivery vans at cost	75 000	
Provision for depreciation of delivery vans		30 000
Office machinery at cost	35 000	
Provision for depreciation of office machinery		10 000
Trade receivables	60 000	
Trade payables		42 000
Cash and cash equivalent	66 000	
180 000 ordinary shares of $1 each		180 000
10% debentures 2023/2025		100 000
Share premium account		30 000
General reserve		40 000
Retained profit at 1 May 2015		13 900
Interim dividends paid:		
Ordinary	4 900	
	1 272 900	1 272 900

Additional information

1 Inventory at 30 April 2016: $54 000.

2 Depreciation for the year ended 30 April 2016 is to be provided as follows:

- freehold warehouse $4 000
- freehold offices $12 000
- delivery vehicles: 20% on cost
- office machinery: 20% on cost.

3 Debenture interest is payable half-yearly on 1 May and 1 November.
4 Provision is to be made for taxation on the year's profits in the sum of $25 000.
5 A transfer of $20 000 is to be made to general reserve.
6 The directors have recommended a final dividend on the ordinary shares of $0.05 per share.

Required

a Prepare Rawson Limited's income statement for the year ended 30 April 2016 in as much detail as possible.

b Prepare Rawson Limited's income statement for the year ended 30 April 2016, in line with IAS 1, classifying the expenses by function.

c Prepare Rawson Limited's statement of changes in equity for the year ended 30 April 2016.

d Prepare Rawson Limited's statement of financial position at 30 April 2016 in line with IAS 1.

Answer

a Below is Rawson Limited's income statement for the year ended 30 April 2016, set out in as much detail as possible:

Rawson Limited
Income statement for the year ended 30 April 2016

	$	$	$
Revenue			756 000
Cost of sales:			
Inventory at 1 May 2015		32 000	
Purchases		446 000	
		478 000	
Inventory at 30 April 2016		(54 000)	(424 000)
Gross profit			332 000
Selling and distribution:			
Sales staff salaries and commissions	(83 000)		
Carriage out	(24 000)		
Depreciation:			
Warehouse	(4 000)		
Delivery vehicles	(15 000)	(126 000)	
Administration:			
Administrative salaries	(57 000)		
General expenses	(45 000)		
Depreciation:			
Office premises	(12 000)		
Office machinery	(7 000)	(121 000)	(247 000)
Profit from operations			85 000
Debenture interest ($5 000 + $5 000)			(10 000)
Profit before tax			75 000
Tax			(25 000)
Profit for the year			50 000

b Set out below is Rawson Limited's income statement for the year ended 30 April 2016 (in line with IAS 1).

Rawson Limited
Income statement for the year ended 30 April 2016

	$
Revenue	756 000
Cost of sales	(424 000)
Gross profit	332 000
Distribution costs	(126 000)
Administrative expenses	(121 000)
Other expenses	–
Profit from operations	85 000
Finance costs	(10 000)
Profit before tax	75 000
Tax	(25 000)
Profit for the year	50 000

c The statement of changes in equity for Rawson Limited for the year ended 30 April 2016 would look like this:

Rawson Limited
Statement of changes in equity for the year ended 30 April 2016

	Share capital	Share premium	General reserve	Retained earnings	Total equity
	$	$	$	$	$
Balance at start of year	180 000	30 000	40 000	13 900	263 900
Profit for the year				50 000	50 000
Dividends paid				(4 900)	(4 900)
Transfer to general reserve			20 000	(20 000)	
Balance at end of year	180 000	30 000	60 000	39 000	309 000

d Finally, set out below is Rawson Limited's statement of financial position at 30 April 2016 (in line with IAS 1).

Rawson Limited
Statement of financial position at 30 April 2016

	$
Assets	
Non-current assets:	
Intangible – goodwill	100 000
Tangible – property, plant and equipment	201 000
	301 000
Current assets:	
Inventories	54 000
Trade receivables	60 000

Statement of financial position at 30 April 2016	
	$
Cash and cash equivalents	66 000
	180 000
Total assets	481 000
Equity and liabilities:	
Share capital and reserves	
Share capital [1]	180 000
Share premium	30 000
Reserves	60 000
Retained earnings	39 000
	309 000
Non-current liabilities:	
Debentures	100 000
Current liabilities:	
Trade payables	42 000
Other payables [2]	5 000
Current tax payable	25 000
	72 000
Total equity and liabilities	481 000

[1] 180 000 ordinary shares of $1 each.

[2] Debenture interest due, but not yet paid.

ACTIVITY 6

Michel Pillay Limited's trial balance at 30 April 2016 was as follows:

	$000	$000
Revenue		300
Inventory at 1 May 2015	20	
Purchases	113	
Sales office salaries	57	
Selling expenses	39	
General office wages	32	
Other general expenses	35	
Warehouse machinery at cost	70	
Provision for depreciation of warehouse machinery		30
Office machinery at cost	42	
Provision for depreciation of office machinery		20
Trade receivables	38	
Balance at bank	28	
Trade payables		11
10% debentures 2023/25		5
60 000 ordinary shares of $1		60

	$000	$000
Share premium account		15
General reserve		25
Retained earnings		8
	474	474

Additional information

1 Inventory at 30 April 2016 was valued at $31 000.

2 Depreciation for the year is to be provided as follows:
- warehouse machinery $8 000
- office machinery $10 000.

3 $10 000 is to be transferred to the general reserve.

Required

a Prepare Michel Pillay Limited's income statement for the year ended 30 April 2016 in as much detail as possible.

b Prepare Michel Pillay Limited's statement of changes in equity for the year ended 30 April 2016.

c Prepare Michel Pillay Limited's statement of financial position at 30 April 2016 in as much detail as possible.

19.17 Bonus shares

The Companies Act gives companies the power to use their reserves to issue shares to the ordinary shareholders as fully paid-up shares. This is known as a **bonus share issue** because the shareholders do not have to pay for them; they own all the reserves anyway and are not being given anything they do not already own!

The main reason why companies issue bonus shares is because the issued share capital does not adequately represent the long-term capital of the company. They can also be issued to shareholders in place of cash dividends when the company may need to preserve cash for future expansion. They can also be seen as a reward to shareholders for their continuing investment in the company.

KEY TERM

Bonus share issue: An issue of free shares to existing shareholders from the accumulated reserves of the company. The issue is usually in proportion to the existing ordinary shares (e.g. one bonus share for every four held).

Walkthrough

Consider the following summarised statement of financial position of Island Limited.

	$000
Non-current assets	1 000
Net current assets	500
	1 500
Equity	
Ordinary shares of $1	700
Share premium	200
General reserve	400
Retained earnings	200
	1 500

The directors could, theoretically, distribute the revenue reserves of $600 000 (general reserve + retained earnings) as a cash dividend to the shareholders. The problem with this suggestion is that the non-current assets are long-term assets which should be financed by long-term capital, but they exceed the share capital of the company by $300 000. In order to make the long-term capital of the company adequately support the long-term assets, the directors may transfer $300 000 of the reserves to the share capital account, making the balance on that account $1 000 000, equal to the non-current assets. The directors could use any of the reserves for the purpose, but will no doubt prefer to use the share premium account, $200 000, and $100 000 of the general reserve. This would leave the revenue reserves almost intact and these may be used for other purposes, including the payment of cash dividends. The reserves have been left in the most **flexible** form (see Section 19.19 below).

Revised statement of financial position after the capitalisation of the share premium account

	$000
Non-current assets	1 000
Net current assets	500
	1 500
Equity	
Ordinary shares of $1	1 000
General reserve	300
Retained earnings	200
	1 500

The balance on the share capital account has increased by $300 000, but the shareholders have share certificates for 700 000 shares. They must be issued with certificates for another 300 000 bonus shares on the basis of three shares for every seven shares they already hold.

Another reason for capitalising reserves is concerned with the payment of dividends to the ordinary shareholders. If the directors were to recommend paying the whole of the retained profit of $200 000 as a dividend on a share capital of $700 000, the shareholders would receive a dividend of more than 28%. This could cause problems with:

a the workforce, who may have had little or no increase in their wages

b the company's customers, who think that the company should reduce its prices rather than pay excessive dividends to the shareholders

c the cash reserves of the company.

In fact, the dividend does not represent 28% of the amount the shareholders have invested in the company; their investment includes the share capital and all the reserves and amounts to $1 500 000. The true return to the shareholders is therefore 13% on the amount invested. If the bonus shares were issued, a dividend payment of $200 000 would look a little more reasonable (20% on the issued capital).

ACTIVITY 7

The following is the summarised statement of financial position of Good Offers Limited:

	$000
Non-current assets	1 400
Net current assets	350
	1 750

	$000
Equity	
Ordinary shares of $1	800
Share premium	200
Revaluation reserve	600
General reserve	100
Retained earnings	50
	1750

The directors have decided to make a bonus issue of three new shares for every four already held. They wish to leave the reserves in the most flexible form.

Redraft Good Offers Limited's statement of financial position to show how it will appear following the bonus issue.

TOP TIP

Remember, if the ordinary shares have a nominal value of, say $0.50 each, and the total share capital is, say, $100 000 ordinary shares, then a total of 200 000 shares will be issued. This is important if a bonus issue of one ordinary share for every ten held is made; it means that 20 000 shares will be issued.

19.18 Rights issues

When a company needs to raise more capital, it may do so by issuing more shares. An invitation to the general public to subscribe for shares is an expensive process because the company must issue a prospectus which gives the past history of the company, its present situation and much other information in great detail. Preparation of a prospectus is very time consuming, requiring perhaps hundreds of labour hours. In addition, the company must employ lawyers, accountants and auditors to advise and check on the preparation of the prospectus.

If a company restricts the invitation to subscribe for shares to existing shareholders, the requirements are less stringent and less costly. In any case, if the company is a private company, it is not permitted to invite the general public to subscribe for shares; it must restrict the invitation to its existing shareholders. Such an issue of shares is known as a **rights issue of shares** because the right to apply for the shares is restricted to existing shareholders.

KEY TERM

Rights issue of shares: An issue of shares made for cash. The shares are offered first to existing shareholders, usually in proportion to the shares held by them.

A rights issue entitles existing shareholders to apply for a specified number of shares, depending on how many they already hold. For example, they may apply for one share (or any other number of shares) for every share they already hold. The offer price will be below the price at which shares are currently changing hands on the stock exchange, or their current valuation in the case of private companies.

Shareholders who do not wish to exercise their rights may sell the rights to some other person who might be willing to buy them, if the cost of the rights plus the share offer price is less than the price at which the shares are already being traded. For example, a rights issue may be offered at $1.20 per share. The current price at which shares are changing hands may be $1.60. If the rights can be bought for less than $0.40, the person buying the rights will be able to acquire the new shares at a price below that at which they are being traded.

The accounting entries for a rights issue are no different from those for an ordinary issue of shares. In any case, students are not required to know the bookkeeping entries for share issues, but it is important to note the differences between rights issues and bonus issues.

Rights and bonus issues compared	
Rights issue	**Bonus issue**
Subscribers pay for shares.	Shareholders do not pay for shares.
The company's net assets are increased by the cash received.	The net assets of the company are unchanged.
Shareholders do not have to exercise their right to subscribe for the new shares.	All the ordinary shareholders will receive their bonus shares.
Shareholders may sell their rights if they do not wish to exercise them.	Shareholders may sell their bonus shares if they do not wish to keep them.

19.19 How to record issues of bonus shares and rights issues

Walkthrough

Handout Limited's statement of financial position at 1 April 2016 is summarised as follows:

	$000
Net assets	1 600
Equity	
Share capital and reserves	
Ordinary shares of $1	1 000
Share premium	400
Retained earnings	200
	1 600

On 1 April 2016, the directors made a bonus issue of shares on the basis of one new share for every two already held, leaving the reserves in the most flexible form.

Required

Redraft Handout Limited's statement of financial position at 1 April 2016, after the issue of the bonus shares.

Answer

A journal entry would have been made to record this transaction. This is shown below.

Date	Account name	Dr	Cr
2016		**$**	**$**
Apr 1	Share premium	400 000	
	Retained earnings	100 000	
	Ordinary share capital		500 000
	Entry to record the issue of bonus shares to existing shareholders		

After the entries in the ledger accounts have been made, the redrafted statement of financial position at 1 April 2016 for Handout Limited would look like this:

	$000
Net assets	1600
Equity	
Share capital and reserves	
Ordinary shares of $1	1500
Retained earnings	100
	1600

TOP TIP

As the bonus shares are free to existing shareholders, there is no entry in the bank as no cash is received by the company.

In the example above, it was decided to issue the bonus shares in such as way as to keep its reserves in their most flexible form, but what does this mean? The most flexible reserve the company has is its retained earnings. It is flexible because the directors of the company can use this reserve to do with as they choose. It can be used to issue bonus shares, it could be used to pay a special dividend to shareholders, part or all of it could be converted into a specific reserve, say to replace non-current assets.

The next most flexible reserve is the general reserve, which can be used to issue bonus shares or pay dividends.

The least flexible reserves are the capital reserves, such as the share premium, the revaluation reserve and capital redemption reserve. Their use is restricted.

If the directors wish to keep the reserves of the company in their most flexible form they will take as much of the bonus issue of shares from the **least** flexible reserves first. Thus, in this example, the largest amount of the bonus issue has been taken from the share premium account as this is less flexible than the retained earnings.

You may see questions worded like the example below.

Walkthrough

Following the bonus issue, Handout Limited made a rights issue on 7 April 2016 of 150 000 ordinary shares of $1 at a price of $1.50. All the shares were subscribed (paid for) by the shareholders.

Re-draft Handout Limited's statement of financial position at 7 April 2016, after the completion of the rights issue.

	$000
Net assets	1825
Equity	
Share capital and reserves	
Ordinary shares of $1	1650
Share premium	75
Retained earnings	100
	1825

In this case money is received by the company. This means that in the ledgers: the bank account will be debited with $225 000, ordinary share capital account will be credited with $150 000 and the share premium account will be credited with $75 000.

ACTIVITY 8

The summarised statement of financial position of Bonarite Limited at 30 June 2016 was as follows:

	$000
Net assets	2000
Equity	
Share capital and reserves	
Ordinary shares of $1	1000
Share premium	500
Revaluation reserve	300
General reserve	120
Retained earnings	80
	2000

On 1 July 2016, before any other transactions had taken place, the company made a bonus issue of shares on the basis of four new shares for every five already held. The directors wished to leave the reserves in the most flexible form.

a Prepare the journal entry to record the issue of bonus shares.

b Show how Bonarite Limited's statement of financial position will appear at 1 July 2016 immediately after the issue of the bonus shares.

Additional information

Following the issue of the bonus shares, the company made a rights issue of one new share for every three shares already held. The shares were offered at $1.25 per share and all the shares were taken up.

c Prepare the journal entry to record the rights issue of ordinary shares.

d Show how Bonarite Limited's statement of financial position will appear immediately after the rights issue has been completed.

19.20 Redemption of debentures

As we have seen, a debenture is a loan to the company. It is repaid (or redeemed) either at the amount of the loan (par) or at a premium. Costs and losses on settling a liability are passed through the income statement.

Walkthrough

Happy Limited has a 6% debenture of $50 000. It redeems this at:

a par

b a premium of 20%.

The journal entries in each case are as follows (narratives are included).

(a)	Dr	Cr
	$000	$000
6% debentures	50	
Bank		50
Amount paid to debenture holders on redemption.		
(b)	**Dr**	**Cr**
	$000	$000
6% debentures	50	
Finance costs share premium (or retained earnings)	10	
Bank		60
Amount paid to debenture holders on redemption including a premium of 20%.		

19.21 Other sources of finance for a limited company

There are a number of other sources of finance available to limited companies (and other businesses) apart from the issue of shares. These include the sources discussed below.

Bank loans

Bank loans are available to a company provided it can satisfy the bank that the funds are required for a sound purpose, such as capital investment or expansion, and that the company will be able to pay the interest on the due dates, and repay the loan in due course. The loan may be for a short term, such as three months, or for a longer term of a number of years depending on the purpose for which it is required. A bank will usually be unwilling to lend to a company that has got into difficulties through bad management. Loans will usually be secured on the assets of the company. The rate of interest charged may be fixed or variable. The interest is charged on the full amount of the loan whether it is used or not.

Bank overdrafts

Bank overdrafts are temporary facilities that allow companies to become overdrawn on their bank accounts. Interest is calculated on the overnight amount of the overdraft so that interest is only paid by a company on the amount of the facility it uses day by day. Banks may cancel overdraft facilities at any time without notice, exposing the borrower to the risk of financial embarrassment.

Hire purchase

Hire purchase enables a purchaser to have the beneficial use of an asset while the ownership of the asset remains with the hire purchase company. At the end of the hire purchase agreement, the purchaser may become the owner of the asset on payment of a (usually) nominal sum. Under the principle of substance over form, the purchaser shows the asset as a non-current asset in the statement of financial position at its normal cash price, and shows the outstanding liability to the hire purchase company as a creditor.

Leasing

Leasing allows a company leasing an asset (the lessee) to use the asset while the ownership of the asset remains with the company from which it is leased (the lessor). The asset will never become the property of the lessee and the rental is shown in the lessee's income statement as an expense.

Trade payables

Some of a company's finance is provided by its trade and expense creditors. This is a short-term form of finance. However, a company that abuses this source of finance risks losing the goodwill of its suppliers and sacrificing advantageous credit terms. The creditors may insist that future dealings are on a cash basis, or may even withdraw supplies or services altogether.

Limited companies will use a mix of all the forms of financing covered in this chapter. The main principles that should decide how a company is financed are briefly explained below.

Long-term capital

Long-term requirements should be financed by long-term sources. Financing the acquisition of non-current assets (e.g. by short-term loans) runs the very great risk that the loans will have to be repaid before the assets in question have generated sufficient funds for the repayment. The non-current assets of a company should be adequately covered by share capital and reserves, and possibly by long-dated debentures.

An acquisition of a non-current asset may be financed by a bank loan for an agreed term, to allow the asset to generate the funds for repayment by the time the term has expired. Alternatively the funds may be raised by an issue of debentures which will be repayable when the asset has started to earn revenue. This enables the shareholders to enjoy all the benefits accruing from the asset without having to share them with the provider of the capital used to purchase the asset.

Working capital

A positive current ratio (greater than 1 : 1) shows that the current assets are not wholly financed by the current liabilities (short-term trade payables). The possibility that inventory turnover may be low (slow-moving goods), and that customers may take a long time to pay, means that some of the current liabilities could be funded by non-current finance. For example, the company may take a loan to pay its creditors or use it to buy inventory.

The easiest way to show how a business finances itself is with the following diagram (no figures are included):

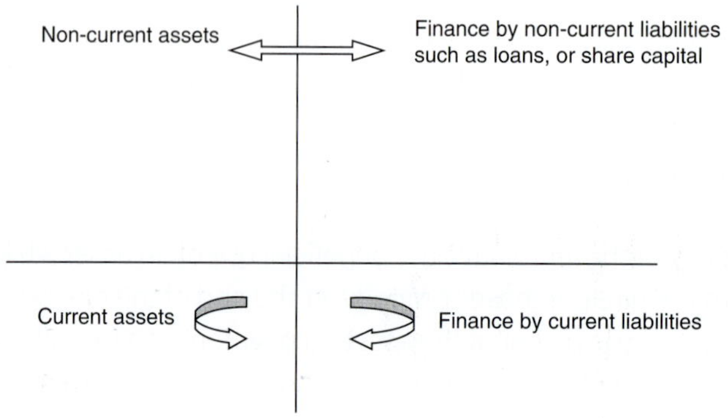

This shows that long-term assets **must** be paid for by long-term finance such as share capital, loans or debentures. The working capital of current assets and current liabilities are self financing. Under no circumstances should the arrows change. For example, long-term finance must never be used to buy inventory or pay creditors.

Chapter summary

In this chapter you have learnt the basics of limited company accounts, including what limited companies are and how they compare to partnerships. Limited companies are very important business organisations, and you have learnt about some of the legal requirements governing the practice of limited companies, including Companies Act 2006.

There are a number of different types of share a limited company may issue, and in this chapter you have learnt about the main types of share capital and reserves, the accounting entries for the issue of shares, the effect of issuing shares on the statement of financial position of a limited company, and how shares differ from debentures. You should also know the difference between a bonus issue and a rights issue of shares, and how to record these in the statement of financial position.

IAS 1 sets out the rules for preparing financial statements for limited companies, which you should now be able to do if you have followed the steps set out in Section 19.10. You should also know how to divide up the profit for the year for a limited company. With limited companies, unlike with sole traders, there is the shareholder to consider, and you should now have developed an understanding of which profits are distributable in cash as dividends, and how the dividends are calculated.

TOP TIP

Take a few minutes to look back through the chapter and familiarise yourself with the terms, many of which will be new to you. Study the layout of the various statements and be able to set out your answers in a similar way. Attempt the practice exercises and check your answers, making sure you understand why and where you may have gone wrong, and remember to show your workings.

4 The following are extracts from a company's statement of financial position.

	$000
Share capital and reserves	
1 200 000 ordinary shares of $0.50	600
Long-term loan	100
Share premium	200
General reserve	80
Retained earnings	20
	1 000

What is the net asset value of each ordinary share?

A $0.75 **B** $1.50
C $0.83 **D** $1.67

5 The following are extracts from a company's statement of financial position.

Non-current assets:
Freehold premises at cost $400 000
Provision for depreciation of freehold premises $160 000

Equity	$
Ordinary shares of $1	500 000
Long-term loan	100 000
Share premium	80 000
Retained earnings	40 000
	720 000

It has been decided to revalue the freehold premises to $500 000. What will be the statement of financial position value of the ordinary shares after the revaluation?

A $1.44 **B** $1.64 **C** $1.76 **D** $1.96

6 Ali holds 500 ordinary shares of $0.50 in Riski Limited. He has paid in full the amount of $0.35 called up on each share. The company is unable to pay its creditors. What is the maximum amount that Ali can now be required to pay on his shares?

A $75 **B** $250 **C** $325 **D** $500

7 Which of the following will not be shown as equity in the statement of financial position?

A debentures **B** retained earnings
C revaluation reserve **D** share premium

8 Which is the safest form of investment in a limited company?

A long-term debentures **B** ordinary shares
C preference shares **D** short-term debentures

9 A shareholder sold 1 000 ordinary shares of $1 for $1 500. What effect will this have on the share capital of the company?

A it will decrease by $1 000
B it will decrease by $1 500
C it will increase by $1 500
D it will remain unchanged

10 A company has issued 300 000 ordinary shares of $0.50 each. It makes a bonus issue of two shares for every three already held. It follows that with a rights issue of one share for every two already held at $0.75 per share. The rights issue was fully taken up. What was the increase in the share capital account as a result of the bonus and rights issues?

A $150 000 **B** $175 000 **C** $225 000 **D** $275 000

11 A company redeems its debentures at a premium. How may the company treat the premium on the redemption?

A debit share premium account
B debit ordinary share capital account
C debit preference share capital account
D debit an expense in the income statement

12 A company, which has already issued ordinary shares of $1 each, issues 200 000 bonus shares and follows this with a rights issue of 100 000 ordinary shares at $1.50 per share. What is the increase in the share capital and reserves of the company after these transactions?

A $100 000 **B** $150 000 **C** $300 000 **D** $350 000

13 Which reserves are the most flexible for a company?

i general reserve
ii revenue reserve
iii revaluation reserve
iv share premium

A i and ii **B** i and iii **C** ii and iii **D** iii and iv

14 The opening and closing balances of a company's statement of changes in equity were:

	Ordinary share capital	Share premium	General reserve	Retained earnings
	$000	$000	$000	$000
Opening balances	400	60	40	30
Closing balances	500	80	100	70

What was the profit for the year?

A $40 000 **B** $60 000 **C** $100 000 **D** $120 000

Structured questions

1 At 1 April 2015, Morecap Limited had the following share capital and reserves:

	$000
Ordinary shares of $1 each	400
Share premium	40
Retained earnings	55

On 1 April 2015 it invites applications from the public for an issue of 100 000 ordinary shares to be issued at $1.50 each. The terms of the issue are as follows:

- 1 May 2015: a payment of $1.00 per share to include the full share premium
- 1 July 2015: a payment of $0.25 per share
- 1 August 2015: a final payment of $0.25 per share.

Additional information

1 On 1 May 2015, applications were received for 120 000 shares.

2 On 1 June 2015, unsuccessful applicants were refunded in full the money they had paid.

3 On 1 July 2015, the successful applicants paid the next instalment due.

4 On 1 August 2015, the successful applicants paid the final amount due.

Required

a Prepare the relevant ledger accounts (including an extract from the bank account) to record these transactions. **[7 marks]**

b Explain the difference between an ordinary share and a debenture. **[3 marks]**

Additional information

The company's year end is 31 March 2016. During the year ended 31 March 2016, the following took place:

- On 1 January 2016, the company paid an interim dividend of $0.10 on all ordinary shares issued at that date.
- Profit for the year ended 31 March 2016 was $180 000.

Required

c Prepare the statement of changes in equity for the year ended 31 March 2016. **[5 marks]**

Total: 15

2 Pecnut Limited's trial balance at 31 March 2016 was as follows:

	$000	$000
Issued share capital: ordinary shares of $1 each		600
General reserve		120
10% debentures 2021/23		360
Freehold buildings at cost	1 500	
Provision for depreciation of freehold buildings		180
Motor vehicles at cost	246	
Provision for depreciation of motor vehicles		162
Trade receivables	96	
Bank balance		51
Inventory at 1 April 2015	85	
Trade payables		60
Retained earnings		69
Revenue		2 683
Purchases	1 152	
Distribution expenses	540	
Administrative expenses	648	
Debenture interest	18	
	4 285	4 285

Additional information

1 Inventory at 31 March 2016: $105 000.

2 The freehold buildings are to be revalued to $2 000 000 at 31 March 2016.

3 The motor vehicles are to be depreciated at the rate of 25% per annum using the reducing-balance method. The charge is to be included in distribution expenses.

4 $10 000 is to be transferred to general reserve.

5 The directors have recommended a final dividend of $0.25 per share.

Required

a Prepare Pecnut Limited's income statement for the year ended 31 March 2016. **[5 marks]**

b Prepare Pecnut Limited's statement of changes in equity for the year ended 31 March 2016. **[6 marks]**

Additional information

Companies should prepare their annual accounts on the basis that they are going concerns.

Required

c Explain what this means and how their annual accounts will be affected if this is not the case.

[4 marks]

Total: 15

3 The trial balance of Square Limited at 30 June 2016 is as follows:

	$000	$000
Freehold premises at cost	1 000	
Provision for depreciation of freehold premises		60
Delivery vehicles at cost	80	
Provision for depreciation of delivery vehicles		28
Office machinery at cost	70	
Provision for depreciation of office machinery		21
Trade receivables	82	
Trade payables		33
Balance at bank	67	
12% debentures 2025/27		100
900 000 ordinary shares of $1		900
General reserve		50
Retained earnings		7
Revenue		1 000
Inventory at 30 June 2015	46	
Purchases	630	
Sales staff salaries	79	
Administration wages	36	
Delivery vehicle expenses	38	

	$000	$000
Advertising	34	
Office expenses	24	
Debenture interest paid	6	
Interim ordinary dividends paid	7	
	2 199	2 199

Additional information

1 Inventory at 30 June 2016 was valued at $38 000.

2 Account is to be taken of the following.
- accrued expenses at 30 June 2016: delivery vehicle expenses $2 000; office expenses $3 000
- advertising include $6 000 paid for services to be received after the year end.

3 Freehold premises were revalued to $1 200 000 at 30 June 2016. No adjustment for this has been made.

4 Depreciation is to be provided as follows for the year ended 30 June 2016:
- delivery vehicles 25% per annum using the reducing balance
- office machinery 10% on cost.

5 Debenture interest is payable half-yearly on 1 July and 1 January.

6 Tax on the profit for the year is estimated to be $16 000.

7 $50 000 is to be transferred to the general reserve.

8 The directors have recommended a final dividend of 3% on the ordinary shares.

Required

a Prepare Square Limited's income statement for the year ended 30 June 2016 in as much detail as possible. **[11 marks]**

b Prepare Square Limited's statement of changes in equity for the year ended 30 June 2016. **[5 marks]**

c Prepare Square Limited's statement of financial position for the year ended 30 June 2016 in as much detail as possible. **[7 marks]**

Additional information

The directors are considering expansion plans for the business. This will involve obtaining additional capital. They are considering two options:

i issuing an additional 100 000 ordinary shares of $1 each at a premium of $0.50

ii issuing a further debenture of $150 000.

Required

d State **two** uses of the share premium account. **[2 marks]**

e Advise the directors which option they should chose to finance the proposed expansion. Justify your answer. **[5 marks]**

Total: 30

Chapter 20
Manufacturing accounts

Learning objectives

In this chapter you will learn:

- how to prepare a manufacturing account
- how to calculate manufacturing profit in the income statement
- how to provide for unrealised profit inventories of finished goods.

KEY TERMS

Factory profit: The amount added to the factory cost of production to arrive at the transfer price.

Work in progress: Inventory of partly finished goods in the factory at any point in time.

Prime cost / direct cost: The total of direct materials, direct labour and direct expenses.

20.1 What is a manufacturing account?

Manufacturing accounts are prepared by manufacturing companies to show the cost of producing goods.

The manufacturing accounts are prepared before the income statements. The cost of goods manufactured is transferred to the trading section of the income statement and replaces the figure for purchases which would be found if the business is buying and selling wholly completed goods.

Trading companies purchase finished goods, but a manufacturing company's purchases consist of materials it uses in its manufacturing process. A large part of a manufacturing company's wages will most probably be paid to employees engaged on making goods, and some of the overheads will relate to the manufacturing process. A manufacturing account groups all the manufacturing expenses together as factory expenses. If the goods are produced more cheaply than they can be purchased from an outside supplier, the factory may be considered to have made a profit and will be credited with **factory profit**.

Manufacturing companies' inventories include raw materials, **work in progress** and finished goods. Any factory profit included in the inventory of finished goods must be excluded from the value of inventory shown in the statement of financial position.

20.2 How to prepare a manufacturing account

Select from the trial balance those expenses that relate to the company's manufacturing operation. The expenses are either direct (e.g. the cost of materials from which the goods are made and the wages of the workers who actually make the goods) or indirect (all other manufacturing expenses).

A manufacturing account is prepared in four stages.

Stage 1

The calculation of the **prime cost** – this comprises the **direct costs** associated with the manufacturing process: direct or raw materials. It is calculated as:

	$000	$000
Opening inventory of raw material		40
Add: purchases of raw materials [1]	200	
Less: purchase returns of raw materials	(10)	
	190	
Add: carriage inwards on raw materials [2]	15	
		205
		245
Less: closing inventory of raw materials		(35)
Cost of raw materials consumed [3]		210
Direct labour		140
Direct expenses		12
Prime cost [3]		362

[1] You may have to add or deduct accruals or prepayments in respect of raw materials purchases when calculating the purchase cost.

[2] Note that it is only carriage inwards that is included here.

[3] Always insert the labels of 'cost of raw materials consumed' and 'prime cost'.

The whole process is similar to calculating the cost of sales for a non-manufacturing business, covered in Chapter 7. The only differences here are:

- we refer to the purchases of raw materials, not just purchases
- direct labour is included in the calculation
- the final total ($362 000) is known as the prime cost, not the cost of sales.

Stage 2

Calculation of the **factory overheads / indirect costs** – this can include a number of items such as depreciation of factory machinery, indirect wages, indirect materials, factory rent and so on. Anything to do with the running of the factory is included here. List all the factory overheads individually.

> **KEY TERM**
>
> **Factory overheads / indirect costs:** Costs incurred from the running of the factory. This would include such things as indirect factory wages and depreciation of factory machinery.

> **TOP TIP**
>
> You will probably be told a total, say, rent figure for the business and be given the proportion of it which is for the factory and the proportion for the offices. You will need to split the figure accordingly. Only the proportion belonging to the factory should be included in the manufacturing account.

Walkthrough

In a trial balance for a manufacturing business the figure of $5 000 for rent is included.

In the notes two statements appear:

a At the end of the year rent of $1 000 is owing.

b The amount of rent due to the factory is 60%. The balance is for the offices.

The factory accountant has been asked to calculate the amount of rent for the factory to be included in the manufacturing account. She makes the following calculation:

	$
Total from the trial balance	5 000
Add: amount owing	1 000
Total charge for rent for the period	6 000

Amount to include in the manufacturing account = $6 000 × 60% = $3 600.

This means that $2 400 must be included for office rent in the income statement.

> **TOP TIP**
>
> Remember to make a note somewhere to include the sum of $2 400 in the income statement.

Stage 3

An adjustment for work in progress.

Stage 4

The calculation of any factory profit.

Walkthrough

The accountant of Sample Limited has been asked to prepare a manufacturing account for the year ended 31 December 2016. He has produced the following:

Sample Limited
Manufacturing account for the year ended 31 December 2016

	$000	$000
Direct costs:		
Direct materials [1]		200
Direct labour [2]		380
Other direct expenses [3]		60
Prime cost [4]		640
Factory overheads:		
Indirect materials [5]	95	
Indirect labour [6]	120	
Other overheads [7]	330	545
		1 185
Work in progress at 1 January 2016 [8]	78	
Work in progress at 31 December 2016 [9]	(53)	25
Factory cost of finished goods (or cost of production) [10]		1 210
Factory profit [11]		242
Cost of goods transferred to trading section of the income statement [12]		1 452

[1] **Direct materials:** materials from which goods are made. The cost includes carriage inwards on raw materials.

[2] **Direct labour:** the wages of the workers who actually make the goods.

[3] **Direct expenses:** royalties, licence fees, and so on, which have to be paid to other persons for the right to produce their products or to use their processes. The payment is often a fixed sum for every unit of goods produced.

[4] Prime cost/direct cost**:** the total of the direct costs. This description **must** always be shown.

[5] **Indirect materials:** all materials purchased for the factory but which do not form part of the goods being produced (e.g. cleaning materials or lubricating oil for the machinery).

[6] **Indirect labour:** the wages of all factory workers who do not actually make the goods (e.g. factory managers, supervisors, stores staff, cleaners, etc).

[7] **Other overheads:** overheads relating exclusively to the factory and production (e.g. factory rent, heating and lighting, depreciation of the factory building and machinery, etc).

[8] **Work in progress:** goods in the process of being made at the end of the previous year but which were not finished are brought into the current year as an input to this year's production.

[9] Goods that are not completely finished at the end of the current year must be deducted from the year's costs in order to arrive at the cost of finished goods.

[11] **Factory profit**: the percentage to be **added** to **cost of production** as profit. The amount is decided by management and will always be given in questions if necessary. It is debited in the manufacturing account and credited in the income statement (see below).

[10] **Factory cost of finished goods**: either these words or the alternative, **cost of production**, should be shown at this point in the account.

[12] The total of the manufacturing account is debited in the trading section of the income statement under the heading 'cost of sales'.

Walkthrough

The following balances have been extracted from Make It Limited's trial balance at 31 December 2016 by the accountant:

	Debit $000	Credit $000
Inventories at 1 January 2016:		
Direct materials	10	
Work in progress	38	
Finished goods at cost	40	
Purchases (direct materials)	140	
Carriage inwards	24	
Direct labour	222	
Direct expenses	46	
Indirect materials	45	
Indirect labour	72	
Rent:		
Factory	100	
Offices	90	
Heating, lighting and power:		
Factory	45	
Offices	35	
Revenue		1300
Administration salaries and wages	173	

Further information

1 Inventory at 31 December 2016 was as follows:

	$000
Direct materials	18
Work in progress	20
Finished goods	69

2 Depreciation is to be provided on non-current assets as follows:

	$000
Factory building	20
Factory machinery	36
Office equipment	24

3 Factory profit is to be calculated at 15% on cost of production.

Prepare the manufacturing account and income statement for the year ended 31 December 2016.

Answer:

Make It Limited
Manufacturing account and income statement for the year ended 31 December 2016

	$000	$000
Direct materials inventory at 1 January 2016		10
Add: purchases	140	
Add: carriage inwards	24	
	164	
Less: inventory at 31 December 2016	(18)	146
Direct labour		222
Direct expenses		46
Prime cost		424
Indirect materials	45	
Indirect labour	72	
Rent of factory	100	
Heating, lighting and power	45	
Depreciation:		
Factory	20	
Machinery	36	318
		742
Work in progress 1 January 2016	38	
Work in progress 31 December 2016	(20)	18
Factory cost of finished goods		760
Factory profit (15%)		114
Transferred to income statement		874
Revenue		1 300
Sales		
Cost of sales		
Inventory of finished goods at 1 January 2016	40	
Transferred from factory – factory cost of production	874	
	914	
Inventory of finished goods at 31 December 2016	(69)	(845)
Gross profit		455
Wages and salaries	(173)	
Rent of offices	(90)	
Heating and lighting	(35)	
Depreciation of office equipment	(24)	(322)
Profit on trading [1]		133
Add: factory profit [2]	114	
Less: unrealised profit on closing inventory of finished goods [3]	(9)	105
Profit for the year		238

[1] Profit on trading is the profit that has been made from the trading activity and does not include factory profit.

[3] See Section 20.3.

[2] Factory profit is added to the profit on trading to show Make It Limited's total profit.

TOP TIP

The income statement follows on from the manufacturing account without a break. It is included in the heading to the manufacturing account.

20.3 Unrealised profit included in the inventories of finished goods

The figure of closing inventory in Make It Limited's income statement includes factory profit. This profit will not be realised, or earned, by the company until the goods are sold. It must therefore be excluded to arrive at the actual or realised factory profit. (The concept of realisation must be applied.)

Make It Limited's unrealised profit is calculated as follows. The inventory of finished goods at 31 December 2016 is $69 000. This is 115% of the cost of manufacture, as the profit of 15% has been added to the cost of goods (100%). The unrealised profit is therefore:

$$\$69\,000 \times \frac{15}{115} = \$9\,000$$

This means that the income statement includes $9 000 of profit which will not be earned until the goods have been sold. It must, therefore be shown as an expense in the income statement.

The double entry for unrealised profit, $9 000, is:

- debit the income statement
- credit to a provision for unrealised profit account.

In future years, it will be necessary only to **adjust** the provision for unrealised profit for increases or decreases in the closing inventories of finished goods. For example, if Make It Limited's finished goods inventory one year later, at 31 December 2017, is, say $92 000, the provision required for unrealised profit will be:

$$\$92\,000 \times \frac{15}{115} = \$12\,000$$

Only the increase of $3 000 ($12 000 – $9 000) in the provision will be debited in the income statement and credited to the provision for unrealised profit.

The provision for unrealised profit account is as follows:

Provision for unrealised profit account

2017		**$**	**2017**		**$**
Dec 31	Balance c/d $(92\,000 \times \frac{15}{115})$	12 000	Jan 1	Balance b/f	9 000
			Dec 31	Income statement	3 000
		12 000			12 000
			2018		
			Jan 1	Balance b/d	12 000

To summarise, an increase in the provision for unrealised profit would be recorded as follows:

- **debit** income statement
- **credit** provision for unrealised profit

with the amount of the increase.

If there had been a decrease in the provision, this would be recorded as follows:

- **debit** provision for unrealised profit
- **credit** income statement

with the amount of the decrease.

(The accounting for a provision for unrealised profit is similar to that of a provision for doubtful debts in Chapter 12.)

20.4 Manufacturing statement of financial position

For a manufacturing business, the statement of financial position includes three inventories:

- raw materials
- work in progress
- finished goods at cost.

Walkthrough

This can be shown by looking at the inventory to include in the current assets of Make It Limited's statement of financial position at 31 December 2016. The inventories will appear as follows:

	$000	$000
Current assets		
Inventory:		
Materials		18
Work in progress		20
Finished goods	69	
Less: unrealised profit	(9)	[1] 60
		98

[1] Notice that the finished goods inventory is shown at cost by deducting the unrealised profit.

ACTIVITY 1

The Fabric Company carries on a manufacturing business. Information extracted from its trial balance at 31 March 2016 is as follows:

	Debit	Credit
	$000	$000
Revenue		700
Inventory at 1 April 2015:		
Raw materials	10	
Work in progress	12	
Finished goods	24	
Purchase of raw materials	130	
Carriage inwards	14	
Direct labour	170	
Other direct expenses	16	
Factory overheads	128	
Office overheads	96	

The following further information is given:

	$000
Inventory at 31 March 2016:	
Raw materials	20
Work in progress	22
Finished goods	36
Depreciation charges for the year:	
Factory	12
Office	3

Completed production is transferred to the warehouse at a mark-up on factory cost of 20%.

Prepare a manufacturing account and income statement for the year ended 31 March 2016.

ACTIVITY 2

The following balances have been extracted from the books of a glue-making company at 30 April 2016:

	$
Revenue	800 000
Purchase of raw materials	132 000
Direct labour	146 250
Indirect labour	19 500
Rent	45 000
Heating and lighting	42 300
Insurance	3 150
Office salaries	51 450
Carriage inwards	11 505
Carriage outwards	2 520
Advertising	7 000
Motor van expenses	6 000
Inventories at 1 May 2015:	
Raw materials	11 250
Work in progress	18 000
Finished goods	27 000

Additional information

1 Inventories at 30 April 2016:

	$
Raw materials	13 125
Work in progress	15 750
Finished goods	24 000

2 The following expenses must be accrued at 30 April 2016.

	$
Rent	3750
Heating and lighting	2700

3 The following expenses have been prepaid at 30 April 2016.

	$
Insurance	900
Advertising	3500

4 Expenses are to be apportioned as follows:
Rent: factory 75%; office 25%
Heating and lighting: factory 2/3, office 1/3
Insurance: factory 9/10, office 1/10
Motor costs: factory 50%.

5 Provision for depreciation is to be made as follows:

	$
Factory building	3000
Factory machinery	10000
Office machinery and equipment	4000
Motor vans	8000

6 Completed production is transferred to the warehouse at a mark-up on factory cost of 20%.
Prepare a manufacturing account and income statement for the year ended 30 April 2016
(Make all calculations to the nearest $.)

TOP TIP

You will need to decide which of the values for inventory of finished goods are at cost, and which are at factory cost, and thus include an element of factory profit.

Remember to adjust for accruals and prepayments, where necessary, **before** apportioning overhead expenses between the manufacturing account and the income statement.

Take care to calculate the provision for unrealised profit, based on closing inventory, correctly. The fraction to be used is:

$$\frac{\text{percentage of mark-up}}{100 + \text{percentage of mark-up}}$$

See Section 20.3. The entry in the income statement for unrealised profit is the increase or decrease in the amount of the provision brought forward from the previous year. Ensure that the closing inventory of finished goods is shown in the statement of financial position at cost, by deducting the balance on the provision for unrealised profit account.

Chapter summary

In this chapter you have learnt about the preparation of the financial statements for a manufacturing business, including how to calculate manufacturing profit in the income statement, and how to provide for unrealised profit included in inventories of finished goods. You should now know the reasons why financial statements for a manufacturing business differ from a non-manufacturing company, including:

- a manufacturing account is prepared before the income statement
- there are three different classes of inventory: raw materials, work in progress and finished goods
- there may be a profit charged when goods are transferred from the factory to finished goods inventory
- there is a need to ensure that the finished goods inventory is included in the statement of financial position at cost by deducting any unrealised profit included in it.

TOP TIP

You will have noticed that quite a few new terms have also been introduced in this chapter, such as cost of raw materials consumed, prime cost and factory cost of production. Make sure that you include these labels. Take time to review the calculation of the provision for unrealised profit and how it is adjusted in the income statement.

Practice exercises

1 The following balances have been extracted from the books of a television manufacturing company at 30 April 2016:

	$
Premises at cost	250 000
Plant and machinery (net book value)	70 000
Motor vehicles at cost	40 000
Inventories at 1 May 2015:	
Raw materials	42 000
Work in progress	50 000
Finished goods at transfer price	48 000
Factory labour (direct)	280 000
Royalty expenses (direct)	40 000
Indirect wages	12 000
Indirect labour	8 000
Selling expenses	42 000

Administrative expenses	62 000
Revenue	1 240 000
Purchases of raw materials	390 000
Carriage inwards	26 000

Additional information

1 Inventories at 30 April 2016:

	$
Raw materials	36 000
Work in progress	46 000
Finished goods at transfer price	62 400

2 Finished goods are transferred to the income statement at factory cost plus a mark-up of 20%.

3 Depreciation is to be provided as follows:

- premises 5% per annum on cost
- plant and machinery 20% per annum on the written-down value
- motor vehicles 20% per annum on cost.

4 Depreciation charges are to be apportioned as followed:

Premises:	
Factory	50%
Administration	50%
Plant and machinery:	
Factory	80%
Administration	20%
Motor vehicles:	
Factory	90%
Administration	10%

Required

a Prepare the manufacturing account for the year ended 30 April 2016. **[8 marks]**

b Prepare the income statement for the year ended 30 April 2016. **[7 marks]**

c Explain how finished goods should be shown in the statement of financial position at 30 April 2016. Make reference to any relevant accounting concepts. **[3 marks]**

d Discuss whether or not the television manufacturing company should continue to transfer goods from the factory at a mark-up. **[7 marks]**

Total: 25

2 The following balances have been extracted from Yendor's books at 31 March 2016:

	$000	$000
Inventories at 1 April 2015:		
Raw materials	450	
Work in progress	375	
Finished goods at transfer price	390	

Factory wages		
Direct	900	
Indirect	90	
Purchases of raw materials		
Direct materials	2250	
Indirect materials	45	
Carriage inwards	162	
Other factory overheads	245	
Revenue		6075
Office salaries	391	
Other administration expenses	675	
Provision for unrealised profit		65
Freehold premises at cost	1000	
Provision for depreciation of freehold premises		160
Manufacturing plant and machinery at cost	600	
Provision for depreciation of manufacturing plant and machinery at 31 March 2015		350
Office equipment at cost	300	
Provision for depreciation of office equipment at 31 March 2015		100

Additional information

1 Inventories at 31 March 2016 were as follows (in $000s):
- raw materials $440
- work in progress $562
- finished goods at transfer price $594.

2 Finished goods are transferred from the factory to the warehouse at a mark-up of 20%.

3 The factory occupies 75% of the freehold premises and the administrative offices occupy the remainder.

4 Depreciation should be provided as follows:
- freehold premises 4% per annum on cost
- plant and machinery 30% per annum on net book value
- office equipment 15% per annum on net book value.

Required

a Prepare Yendor's manufacturing account for the year ended 31 March 2016. **[8 marks]**

b Prepare Yendor's income statement for the year ended 31 March 2016. **[7 marks]**

c Prepare the provision for unrealised profit account for the year ended 31 March 2016. **[3 marks]**

d Prepare an extract from Yendor's statement of financial position at 31 March 2016 to show how the inventory is recorded. **[2 marks]**

Additional information

Yendor does not understand why it is necessary to prepare both a manufacturing account and an income statement.

e Discuss whether or not Yendor should continue to prepare a manufacturing account in the future. **[5 marks]**

Total: 25

Exam practice questions

Multiple-choice questions

1 Goods are transferred from the manufacturing account to the income statement at factory cost of production plus a mark-up of 20%. The transfer prices of the closing inventories of finished goods were as follows:

Year 1	$39 600
Year 2	$42 000
Year 3	$45 600

What was the provision for unrealised profit charged against the profit for year 3?

A $400
B $600
C $720
D $1 200

2 Goods are transferred from the factory to the warehouse at a mark-up of 33%. At 1 April 2015, the balance on the provision for unrealised profit was $17 000. At 31 March 2016, the closing inventory of finished goods was $60 000. What was the effect on profit of the entry in the provision for unrealised profit on 31 March 2016?

A decrease of $2 000
B decrease of $3 000
C increase of $2 000
D increase of $3 000

3 The following items appear in the accounts of a manufacturing company:

i carriage inwards
ii carriage outwards
iii depreciation of warehouse machinery
iv provision for unrealised profit

Which items will be included in the manufacturing account?

A i and ii
B i and iii
C ii and iii
D ii and iv

4 A manufacturing company adds a factory profit of 25% to its cost of production. The following information is available:

	$
Inventory of finished goods at 1 April 2015 (per statement of financial position at that date)	30 000
Cost of goods produced (per manufacturing account for the year ended 31 March 2016)	300 000
Closing inventory of finished goods (per income statement for the year end 31 March 2016)	60 000

How much will be credited as factory profit in the income statement for the year ended 31 March 2016?

A $67 500
B $69 000
C $70 500
D $71 500

Total: 4 marks

Structured question

1 The following balances have been extracted from the books of Spinners & Co. at 31 December 2015:

	$
Inventories at 1 January 2015:	
Raw materials	8 000
Work in progress	12 000
Factory expenses	
Direct labour	40 000
Indirect labour	28 000
Licence fees paid	16 000
Heating and lighting	5 000
General factory expenses	14 000
Insurance of plant and machinery	6 000
Purchases of raw materials	140 000
Plant and machinery at cost	70 000

Additional information

1 Inventories at 31 December 2015:

	$
Raw materials	10 000
Work in progress	9 700

2 Expenses owing at 31 December 2015:

	$
Direct labour	600
Indirect labour	400
General expenses	300

3 Expenses prepaid at 31 December 2015:

	$
Insurance	400
Heating and lighting	180

4 Plant and machinery are to be depreciated at the rate of 10% on cost.

5 A factory profit of 10% is added to the factory cost of goods produced.

Required

Prepare the manufacturing account for the year ended 31 December 2015. **[8 marks]**

Chapter 21
Not-for-profit organisations (clubs and societies)

Learning objectives

In this chapter you will learn:

- new terms used for not-for-profit organisations
- the preparation of ledger accounts for subscriptions, life membership and entry fees
- new forms of financial statements for not-for-profit organisations
- how to apply the techniques used for incomplete records to prepare accounts for not-for-profit organisations.

KEY TERMS

Income and expenditure account: The account prepared to determine if the non-profit-making organisation has made a surplus or deficit. The equivalent of the income statement.

Surplus of income over expenditure: The equivalent of the profit for the year. The opposite would be a deficit of income over expenditure.

Accumulated fund: The equivalent of the capital for a profit-making organisation.

Receipts and payments account: The bank account of the non-profit-making organisation.

Subscriptions: The amount paid by members to be part of the club or society. It is the main source of income for non-profit-making concerns and is the equivalent of sales for a profit-making organisation.

21.1 What are not-for-profit organisations?

Not-for-profit organisations exist to provide facilities for their members. Examples include: sports and social clubs, dramatic societies and music clubs. Making a profit is not their main purpose, although many carry on fund-raising activities to provide more or better facilities for the members. The organisation is 'owned' by all of its members and not by just one person or partnership. Records of money received and spent are usually kept by a club member who is often not a trained bookkeeper or accountant. Usually no other records are kept. There is, therefore, a great similarity between the work covered in this chapter and that in Chapter 16, dealing with the preparation of accounts from incomplete records. Not-for-profit organisations are a different type of enterprise from trading organisations. As a result, they have their own terms for some of the items you will come across (see Section 21.2).

21.2 Special features of the accounts of not-for-profit organisations

There are a number of new terms which you will need to know when preparing financial statements for a not-for-profit organisation. These are set out below, together with the corresponding term for a profit-making organisation, such as a shop or manufacturing business:

- An **income and expenditure account** takes the place of the income statement.
- The words **surplus of income over expenditure** are used in place of 'profit for the year'.
- The words **excess of expenditure over income** are used in place of 'loss for the year'.
- The term **accumulated fund** is used in place of 'capital account', or simply 'capital'.
- A **receipts and payments account** takes the place of a bank account.
- **Subscriptions** take the place of sales as the main source of income in the income and expenditure account. Other types of club income may come from dances or the sale of tickets for a particular activity.

Items are grouped together, or matched in the income and expenditure account, so that it is possible to see whether a particular activity, say a dance, has made a surplus or deficit.

A trading account is only prepared for an activity that is in the nature of trading and is carried on to increase the club's funds (e.g. a cafe). Any profit or loss calculated will be transferred to the income and expenditure account. If it is a profit, it will be added to the income. If it is a loss, it will be added to the expenditure. A loss should never be shown as a negative under the income column of the income and expenditure account.

TOP TIP

Knowledge of these terms is important and should be used correctly. For example, when preparing an income and expenditure account, label the final figure as 'surplus of income over expenditure', not 'profit for the year'.

21.3 The treatment of income

The income of a club (which is the term that will be used in the rest of this chapter to cover all not-for-profit organisations) should be treated in the club's accounts as set out below.

Subscriptions

The amount credited to the income and expenditure account should equal the annual subscription per member, multiplied by the number of members. It may be helpful to prepare a subscriptions account as workings to decide how much should be credited to the income and expenditure account.

Subscriptions in arrears and **subscriptions in advance** should **normally** be treated as accruals and prepayments. However, each club has its own policy for treating subscriptions in arrears or in advance. The two possible policies are as follows:

- **Cash basis** The amount actually received in the year is credited to the income and expenditure account. This may include subscriptions for a previous year or paid in advance for the next year.
- **Matching basis** All subscriptions due for the year, including those not yet received, are credited to the income and expenditure account. It will usually be the club's policy to write off, as irrecoverable debts, subscriptions that are not received in the year after they were due.

Walkthrough

The Rowing Club is a not-for-profit organisation. It has 100 members who each pay an annual subscription of $20. At 31 December 2015, the club had received subscriptions from 95 members for the year. In addition, two members had paid their subscriptions for the following year.

The subscriptions account for the year ended 31 December 2015 is shown below.

Subscriptions account

2015			**2015**		
		$			$
Dec 31	Income and expenditure account [1]	2000	Dec 31	Receipts and payments account [2]	1940
	Balance c/d [4]	40		Balance c/d [3]	100
		2040			2040
2016			**2016**		
Jan 1	Balance b/d	100	Jan 1	Balance b/d	40

[1] The club expected to receive annual subscriptions from all its members. They have therefore transferred the total due for the year (100 members × $20 each) to the income and expenditure account for the year.

[4] This is the total amount received from members who have paid in advance. The balance is carried down to the start of 2016. When preparing the statement of financial position at 31 December 2015, the figure will appear under current liabilities as 'subscriptions in advance'. They are creditors of the club at that date.

[3] This is the total amount due from members who have yet to pay for 2015. These are subscriptions in arrears. The balance is carried down to open the account for 2016. When preparing the statement of financial position at 31 December 2015, the figure will appear under current assets as 'subscriptions in arrears', or 'subscriptions owing'. They are debtors of the club at that date.

[2] During the year, the club treasurer will have banked the subscriptions received for the 95 members who paid for the year ($1900), plus the money from the two members who paid in advance for 2016 ($40).

TOP TIP

Preparing a subscriptions account is a good way to tackle a question on not-for-profit organisations. Notice the terms used in the account and make sure you use them properly. For example, you should label the debit entry 'income and expenditure account' rather than 'income statement'. Likewise the credit entry should really be labelled 'receipts and payments account', not bank account.

ACTIVITY 1

A golf club has 200 members. The annual subscription is $450. At the start of the year, three members had paid in advance and four members owed their subscriptions from last year.

During the year the treasurer banked $88 650 for subscriptions received from members. This included one member who had paid in advance for the next year.

Required

a Prepare the subscriptions account for the year.

b State what the balance on the account represents.

TOP TIP

Notice that the preparation of the subscriptions account is used to ask students to identify missing items. This is similar to incomplete records, where control accounts were prepared for trade receivables and trade payables to find missing sales and purchases figures.

A subscriptions account can be prepared to find different things:

- the amount of subscriptions for the year to transfer to the income and expenditure account
- the subscriptions paid in advance
- the subscriptions owing at the end of the year.

Life subscriptions and entry fees

a Life subscriptions are received as lump sums but should not be credited in full to the income and expenditure account when received. The club should have a policy of spreading this income over a period of, say, five years. The amounts received should be credited to a separate **life membership** account and credited to the income and expenditure account in equal annual instalments over a period determined by the club committee. Any balance on the account at the end of the year will be carried forward to the next year.

b Entry fees are also lump sum payments to the club, but are paid by new members when they join the club. In some cases they may be credited to the income and expenditure account in full in the year a member joins. In other cases they are treated in the same way as life subscriptions; entered in an entry fees account and credited to the income and expenditure account in equal instalments over a period of time.

KEY TERM

Life membership: The amount paid by a member of a club which entitles them to be members of the club for their lifetime.

Walkthrough

A cycle club asks all new members to pay an entry fee of $500, in addition to their first year's subscription. It is the club's policy to write down the entry fee over five years.

During 2015, three new members joined, each paying the entry fee.

The entry fees account is shown below:

Entry fees account

2015		**$**	**2015**		**$**
Dec 31	Income and expenditure account ($1 500 ÷ 5) [1]	300	Dec 31	Receipts and payment account (3 × $500)	1 500
	Balance c/d [2]	1 200			
		1 500			1 500
2016					
Jan 1	Balance b/d				1 200

[2] The balance carried down of $1 200 will be included under the accumulated fund (see Section 21.2).

[1] In the income and expenditure account, $300 will be included under income.

ACTIVITY 2

During 2016, there were two new members who joined the cycle club. Each paid the $500 entry fee.

Required

Prepare the entry fees account for 2016.

Donations

Donations refers to money given to the club by members in addition to their annual subscription or entry fee. It may also include legacies, an amount left to the club when a member dies. Often they are made for particular purposes (e.g. towards the cost of a new pavilion or a piece of equipment). Such donations should be credited to an account opened for the purpose. Expenditure on the project relating to the donation or legacy can be debited to the account.

Money received for special purposes should also be placed in a separate bank account to ensure that it is not spent on other things.

At the end of the year, the balance on the donations or legacy account is listed under the accumulated fund in the statement of financial position. The balance on the bank account may appear under current assets as a separate item. Some clubs also list it as a non-current asset in the statement of financial position.

KEY TERM

Donations: Money given freely to an organisation. Sometimes donors may stipulate the use of the money (e.g. to purchase new catering equipment or to purchase trophies as prizes).

Other club activities

The club may undertake other activities which are incidental to its main purpose. They raise money to supplement income from subscriptions. If they involve some sort of trading, a trading account should be prepared for them as part of the annual accounts, and the profit or loss from trading should be transferred to the income and expenditure account. In this respect it is perfectly acceptable to refer to the money made (or lost) on running the activity as a profit or loss.

Non-trading activities, such as socials, outings and dinner-dances, may be dealt with in the income and expenditure account with the income and costs being grouped together, or matched as follows:

Extract from income section of the income and expenditure account		
	$	$
Annual dinner-dance		
Sale of tickets		600
Less:		
Hire of band	(100)	
Catering	(240)	(340)
Net receipts/net surplus on dinner-dance		260

If the net effect of the activity had resulted in a deficit, then the items would have been netted off in the expenditure section of the income and expenditure account.

TOP TIP

It is important to always net-off income and expenditure on specific activities as shown above, either as net income or net expenditure.

21.4 How to prepare club accounts

The preparation of club accounts follow the same procedures as those used for businesses whose records are incomplete (see Chapter 16) together with the principles explained in Sections 21.2 and 21.3.

Walkthrough

Often the amount of information given in questions such as this looks terrifying but don't let that worry you. Keep calm. Read the question carefully two or three times, making sure you understand it, and underline important points. Decide what workings are required and which must be shown in your answer. Then proceed as set out below.

The Star Sports Club provides recreational activities, refreshments and social events for its members. It also sells sports equipment to its members at reduced prices.

Its assets and liabilities at 1 January 2016 were as follows:

	$
Non-current assets	
Pavilion	120 000
Club sports equipment	40 000
Motor roller	2 000
Current assets	
Inventory of equipment for sale to members	4 000
Annual subscriptions owing	1 200
Bank balance	6 730

Current liabilities	
Trade payables for equipment for sale to members	1 300
Annual subscriptions received in advance	800
Life subscriptions fund	1 750

Step 1

Prepare a statement of affairs at 1 January 2016. This is done to find the opening accumulated fund of the club. This is identical to the procedure for preparing accounts from incomplete records.

The assets of the club are added up and the liabilities of the club deducted from the total assets. The answer will be the accumulated fund of the club at the start of its financial year. This is shown below.

Statement of affairs at 1 January 2016		
	$	$
Non-current assets:		
Pavilion		120 000
Club sports equipment		40 000
Motor roller		2 000
Current assets:		
Inventory of equipment for sale to members		4 000
Annual subscriptions owing		1 200
Bank balance		6 730
Total assets		173 930
Current liabilities:		
Trade payables for equipment for sale to members	(1 300)	
Annual subscriptions received in advance	(800)	
Life subscription fund	(1 750)	(3 850)
Accumulated fund at 1 January 2016		170 080

Additional information

During the year ended 31 December 2016, the club's cash receipts and payments were as follows:

	$
Receipts:	
Annual subscriptions	18 000
Proceeds from sale of equipment	12 000
Sale of tickets for dinner-dance	4 400
Snack bar takings	2 660
Life member subscriptions	400
Payments:	
Caretaker's wages	8 000
Repairs to club equipment	1 700
Purchase of sports club equipment	2 000
Equipment for sale to members	4 000
Heating and lighting	1 800

Dinner-dance expenses:	
Hire of band	200
Catering	1 000
Food for snack bar	1 400
Secretary's expenses	840

Step 2

Prepare a receipts and payment account. This will summarise all the transactions affecting the income and expenditure account and statement of financial position and calculate the bank balance at 31 December 2016.

Receipts and payments account for the year ended 31 December 2016

2016		**$**	**2016**		**$**
Jan 1	Balance b/f	6 730	Dec 31	Caretaker's wages	8 000
Dec 31	Annual subscriptions	18 000		Repairs: club equipment	1 700
	Sales of equipment	12 000		Purchase: club equipment	2 000
	Sales of tickets for dinner-dance	4 400		Purchase of equipment for resale	4 000
	Takings – refreshments	2 660		Heating and lighting	1 800
	Life membership subscriptions	400		Dinner-dance—hire of band	200
				Catering	1 000
				Food for snack bar	1 400
				Secretary's expenses	840
				Balance c/f	23 250
		44 190			44 190
2017					
Jan 1	Balance b/f	23 250			

Additional information

At 31 December 2016:

1. Annual subscriptions in arrears were $1 400; annual subscriptions received in advance were $900.
2. Inventory of equipment for sale to members: $2 000.
3. Trade payables for equipment for sale to members: $900.
4. A member donated $5 000 to a fund to encourage young people to train for sport. This donation was invested immediately in five-year savings bonds.
5. The club transfers life subscriptions to the income and expenditure account in equal instalments over five years.
6. Depreciation is to be provided on non-current assets by the reducing-balance method as follows:
   - pavilion 6%
   - sports equipment 20%
   - motor roller 20%.

Step 3

Prepare workings to adjust for accruals, prepayments, depreciation and any other items. Show these workings with your answer.

You may show your workings as ledger (T) accounts or as calculations. Decide which method is best for you and practise it in all your exercises. Both methods will be shown here.

		T-accounts			Calculations	
		$		$		$
1	**Purchase of equipment for resale**					
	Cash paid	4 000	Trade payables b/f	1 300	Cash paid	4 000
	Trade payables c/f	900	I & E a/c	3 600	Less: Trade payables b/f	(1 300)
		4 900		4 900		2 700
						900
						3 600
		$		$		$
2	**Annual subscriptions**					
	Owing at 1 Jan	1 200	Prepaid at 1 Jan	800		
	Prepaid at 31 Dec	900	Cash	18 000	Received in year	18 000
	I & E a/c	18 100	Owing at 31 Dec	1 400	Less: owing 1 Jan	(1 200)
		20 200		20 200	Prepaid 31 Dec	(900)
						15 900
					Add: prepaid 1 Jan	800
					Owing 31 Dec	1 400
					I & E a/c	18 100
		$		$		$
3	**Life subscriptions**					
	I & E a/c 1/5 × 2 150	430	b/f	1 750	Balance b/f	1 750
	c/f	1 720	Cash received	400	Cash received	400
		2 150		2 150		2 150
					I & E a/c (1/5)	430
		$		$		$
4	**Club sports equipment**					
	b/f	40 000	I & E a/c (20%) [1]	8 400	Balance b/f	40 000
	Cash	2 000	c/d	33 600	Cash	2 000
		42 000		42 000		42 000
					I & E a/c (20%)	(8 400)
					Net book value	33 600

[1] I & E a/c is the notation for income and expenditure account.

The club sells equipment to its members. This is a trading activity, so a trading account should be prepared even though one is not asked for in the question. This is shown below.

Step 4

Preparation of club trading account to find the profit or loss on its trading activity.

Star Sports Club Trading account for sales of equipment		
	$	$
Sales		12 000
Less: cost of sales		
Inventory at 1 January 2016	4 000	
Purchases *	3 600	
	7 600	
Less: inventory at 31 December 2016	(2 000)	(5 600)
Profit transferred to income and expenditure account		6 400

* The figure for purchases comes from T-account 1 in step 3.

Step 5

The next thing is to complete the income and expenditure account for the club for the year ended 31 December 2016. This is done below.

Star Sports Club Income and expenditure account for the year ended 31 December 2016			
	$	$	$
Annual subscriptions (working 2)			18 100
Life subscriptions (working 3)			430
Profit on sale of equipment			6 400
Dinner-dance*			
Sale of tickets		4 400	
Less: hire of band	(200)		
Catering	(1 000)	(1 200)	3 200
Snack bar*			
Takings		2 660	
Less: cost of food		(1 400)	1 260
			29 390
Less: expenses			
Caretaker's wages		(8 000)	
Repairs to club equipment		(1 700)	
Heating and lighting		(1 800)	
Secretary's expenses		(840)	
Depreciation:			
Pavilion (6% of $120 000)		(7 200)	
Equipment (working 4)		(8 400)	
Motor roller (20% of $2 000)		(400)	(28 340)
Surplus of income over expenditure			1 050

*Expenses of dinner-dance and snack bar are grouped with the income from those activities to help members see how those activities have contributed to the club's funds.

Step 6

Finally, the statement of financial position of the club at 31 December 2016 is completed below.

Star Sports Club Statement of financial position at 31 December 2016	
	$
Non-current tangible assets at net book value	
Pavilion	112 800
Club equipment	33 600
Motor roller	1 600
	148 000
Non-current financial asset savings bond (see note 4 in Additional Information) [1]	5 000
Current assets	
Inventory of equipment for sale to members	2 000
Subscriptions owing	1 400
Bank	23 250
	26 650
Total assets	179 650
Accumulated fund and liabilities	
Accumulated fund at 1 January 2016 (from step 1)	170 080
Add: surplus of income over expenditure (from step 5)	1 050
Accumulated fund at 31 December 2016	171 130
Non-current liability Training donation [1]	5 000
Life subscriptions	1 720
Current liabilities	6 720
Trade payables	900
Subscriptions prepaid	900
	1 800
Total accumulated fund and liabilities	179 650

[1] The savings bond has been treated as a non-current asset and the training donation has been treated as a non-current liability. The interest the bond will pay will be credited to income and expenditure account in future years. Any money spent on encouraging young people to train for sport will be matched against it.

TOP TIP

Notice that some of the terms used for trading organisations are not included here. For example, trade receivables and payables and cash and cash equivalents. These financial statements are prepared for the benefit of the members, so often different terms are used. Read the question and use the terms given in the question.

ACTIVITY 3

A drama club has 120 members. The annual subscription is $20 per member. Subscriptions not paid in one year are written off if not paid by the end of the next year.

The club presents two plays a year, each play being performed over ten days. The club hires a local hall for the performance and the dress rehearsals, which take place over three days before the presentation of each play. The club donates half of its net surpluses to the Actors Benevolent Fund.

The receipts and payments of the club in the year ended 31 December 2016 were as follows:

Receipts		Payments	
	$		$
Sales of tickets	20 000	Hire of hall	2 600
Sales of programmes	3 000	Printing of posters, tickets and programmes	180
Sales of refreshments	3 500	Hire of costumes	4 700
Subscriptions for the year ended 31 December 2016	2 000	Cost of refreshments	2 200
Subscriptions for the year ended 31 December 2015	280	Payments for copyrights	1 400
Subscription for the year ending 31 December 2017	360		

At 31 December 2015, members' subscriptions of $280 were owing.

Required

a Prepare the drama club's subscription account for the year ended 31 December 2016.

b Prepare the drama club's income and expenditure account for the year ended 31 December 2016.

c Prepare a statement of financial position extract at 31 December 2016 to show the items for subscriptions.

ACTIVITY 4

The Hutt River Dining Club is funded partly by the members' annual subscriptions ($20 per member), partly by restaurant takings, and partly from profits from the sale of books on dieting, healthy eating and cooking.

At 31 December 2015, the club's statement of financial position showed the following:

	$	$
Catering equipment at cost	11 000	
Depreciation of catering equipment	3 000	8 000
Inventory of food		200
Inventory of books		1 100
Subscriptions owing		180
Cash at bank		1 520
Amount owing for supplies of food		40
Subscriptions in advance		60

Receipts and payments for the year ended 31 December 2016 were as follows:

Receipts	$	Payments	$
Annual subscriptions	5 000	Restaurant staff wages	39 000
Restaurant takings	73 760	Cost of food	24 980
Sales of books	12 150	Purchase of books	4 840
		New catering equipment	3 750
		Heating and lighting	8 390
		Other operating expenses	2 270

Additional information

1 Subscriptions owing at 31 December 2016: $40.

2 Subscriptions paid in advance at 31 December 2016: $140.

3 Inventories at 31 December 2016: food $270; books $965.

4 Trade payables at 31 December 2016: for food $360; for books $200.

5 Annual depreciation of catering equipment is 10% on cost.

Required

a Calculate the accumulated fund at 1 January 2016.

b Prepare a receipts and payments account for the year ended 31 December 2016.

c Prepare the members subscriptions account for the year ended 31 December 2016.

d Prepare a trading account for the year ended 31 December 2016 for the sale of books.

e Prepare a restaurant account for the year ended 31 December 2016.

f Prepare The Hutt River Dining Club's income and expenditure account for the year ended 31 December 2016.

g Prepare the statement of financial position as at 31 December 2016.

Chapter summary

The preparation of accounts for not-for-profit organisations can prove tricky for students. However, having followed the steps set out in the chapter, you should now know how to prepare a subscriptions account. Setting out all workings should make the questions on this topic less daunting.

Having first learnt about the special features of the accounts of not-for-profit organisations, you then learnt how to prepare the accounts. In particular, you should now know how to prepare the ledger accounts for subscriptions, life membership and entry fees. In Chapter 16 you learnt the techniques for preparing accounts where there are incomplete records. In this chapter you have learnt how to apply these techniques to the accounts of not-for-profit organisations.

TOP TIP

Practise the exercises in the chapter and those that follow. Make sure you are familiar with the terms used when preparing financial statements for not-for-profit organisations. Pay particular attention to the treatment of subscriptions in arrears and in advance. Also look closely at the treatment for donations and life memberships, as these often appear in questions on this topic.

Practice exercises

1 The International Athletics Club's receipts and payments account for the year ended 31 May 2016 is as follows:

Receipts		Payments	
	$		$
Balance at bank 1 June 2015	4 650	Refreshment supplies bought	2 654
Subscriptions received	7 970	Wages	4 000
		Rent of rooms	540
Sales of tickets for dance	1 897	Purchase of new equipment	1 778
Snack bar takings	4 112	Teams' travelling expenses	995
Sale of old equipment	94	Balance at bank at 31 May 2016	8 846
Donation	90		
	18 813		18 813

Additional information

1 Snack bar inventories were valued at $150 at 1 June 2015, and at $180 at 31 May 2016.

2 Trade payables for snack bar inventories were: at 1 June 2015 $15; at 31 May 2016 $40.

3 At 1 June 2015, subscriptions owing were $330, of which $310 was paid in the year to 31 May 2016. It is the club's policy to write off subscriptions if they have not been received by the end of the year following their due date. Subscriptions owing at 31 May 2016 were $275.

4 Of the wages paid, $900 was paid to staff serving refreshments.

5 On 1 June 2015, the club's equipment was valued at $4 700. The equipment sold during the year had a book value of $70 at the date of sale. At 31 May 2016, the equipment was valued at $6 000.

Required

a State **two** differences between the financial statements prepared by a not-for-profit organisation and a trading business. **[2 marks]**

b Prepare the club's subscription account for the year ended 31 May 2016. **[4 marks]**

c Prepare the refreshments trading account for the year ended 31 May 2016. **[6 marks]**

d Prepare the income and expenditure account for the year ended 31 May 2016. **[8 marks]**

Additional information

The club management are considering introducing a life membership scheme.

Required

e Advise the club management whether or not they should introduce such a scheme. Justify your answer. **[5 marks]**

Total: 25

2 The Cooking Club's bank current account for the year ended 30 September 2016 was as follows:

	$		$
Balance at 1 October 2015	8 400	Purchases for shop	3 745
Subscriptions received	6 435	Shop wages	4 000
Donations	600	General expenses	1 500
Cash taken at door	3 500	Cost of annual dance	1 490
Grant from local council	6 000	Transfer to deposit account	16 000
Annual dance receipts	1 400	New equipment	2 000
		Rent	8 000
Shop takings	7 168		
Balance at 30 Sept 2016	3 232		
	36 735		36 735

Additional information

1 At 31 March 2016, members' subscriptions owing amounted to $2 000; members' subscriptions in advance for next year were $3 400.

2 The club's depreciation policy is as follows:
- freehold premises, boatyard and launch facilities, and boats and yachts: 5% per annum on net book value
- fixtures and fittings, and yacht maintenance shop: 10% per annum on net book value.

3 Trade payables at 31 March 2016 were as follows:

	$
Repairs and maintenance of yachts	1 350
Refreshments	970
Wages:	
Training-school staff	700
Snack bar staff	400

4 Snack bar inventory at 31 March 2016 was valued at $1 600.

Required

a Prepare the sailing club's income and expenditure account for the year ended 31 March 2016 in good format. A trading account should be prepared for the snack bar. **[12 marks]**

b Prepare the club's statement of financial position as at 31 March 2016. **[8 marks]**

Chapter 22
Published company accounts

Learning objectives

In this chapter you will learn:

- the financial statements and reports that must be published and sent to shareholders
- reporting standards relating to the income statement
- reporting standards relating to the statement of financial position
- the role of the shareholders of a limited company
- the role of the directors of a limited company
- the contents of directors' reports
- the role of the auditors of a limited company
- the importance and contents of the auditor's reports.

22.1 Introduction to published company accounts

There are three important groups of people who are very involved in ensuring that the business operates smoothly, ethically and legally, and that the accounts which are published are accurate. They are:

- shareholders
- directors
- auditors.

Each has a vital role to play which will be considered in this chapter. The following are rules for public limited companies (PLCs) and there are many simplifications and also many exemptions that are available to small companies and to private companies.

Shareholders

The shareholders do not usually manage the company on a day-to-day basis, unless they are also directors. They do though have **two** important duties to perform:

- They appoint the members of the board of directors. Each year the company must hold an annual general meeting (AGM). At this meeting the ordinary shareholders, who are the owners of the company, will vote on a number of items put forward by the directors. One of these will be to elect the members of the board of directors.
- They vote at the AGM on key issues which ensure the effective governance of the company by the directors. By voting on these issues they are giving clear and detailed instructions to the board of directors as to how the company should be managed, and what is expected of them as directors. The directors act as stewards of the shareholders' investment in the company, and as such, are in a position of trust. Apart from voting on the appointment of directors at the AGM, the shareholders are also asked to vote on other issues such as:
  - the appointment of the company's auditors
  - to approve the dividends proposed by the directors
  - to approve charitable donations by the company.

Under company law, the shareholders can also request the directors to convene a special meeting if something is happening of which they disapprove. For example, if they feel that the directors are acting unethically or if they wish to ask the director who is taking this action to resign.

The directors can also convene a special meeting of the shareholders if they have an important decision to make, such as the closure of factory in an area of high unemployment. At this meeting the directors will ask the ordinary shareholders to vote on their proposal.

Directors

The directors act as **stewards** of the shareholders' investments in the company; they are in a position of trust. The directors account to the shareholders regularly for their stewardship of the company. The documents which are required to be prepared and published annually are:

- income statement
- statement of financial position
- statement of cash flows
- directors' report
- auditor's report.

These documents must be sent to shareholders in advance of every annual general meeting. They must also be sent to debenture holders and every person who is entitled to receive notice of general meetings. The directors must file an annual return, which includes the annual accounts, with the Registrar of Companies, and the returns may be inspected by any member of the public. Apart from shareholders and debenture holders, other persons who may be interested in a company's accounts are:

- trade and other creditors
- providers of long-term finance, such as banks and finance houses
- trade unions, representing the company's workforce
- financial analysts employed by the financial press
- fund managers managing client's investments
- the stock exchanges.

22.2 The financial statements

The overall objectives of a set of financial statements is that they provide a **true and fair view** of the profit or loss of the company for the year, and that the statement of financial position likewise gives a true and fair view of the state of affairs of the company at the end of the financial year. The word **true** may be explained in simple terms as meaning that, if financial statements indicate that a transaction has taken place, then it has actually taken place. If a statement of financial position records the existence of an asset, then the company has that asset. The word **fair** implies that transactions, or assets, are shown in accordance with accepted accounting rules of cost or valuation.

Window dressing describes attempts by directors of a company to make a statement of financial position to show the financial position of the company to be better than it really is. For example, the directors may cause cheques to be drawn and entered in the books of account on the last day of the financial year, but not send the cheques to the creditors until the next financial year. This would have the effect of artificially reducing a company's liabilities in the statement of financial position, but it would not give a true and fair view because the creditors had not, in fact, been paid. An attempt to inflate the retained profit figure in the statement of financial position by including unrealised profits in the income statement would not give a true and fair view. Only profits which have been realised at the statement of financial position date should be included in the income statement.

The accounting principle of **substance over form** (see Section 9.12) is one accounting principle intended to give a true and fair view. The Companies Act sets out rules for the presentation of company accounts. If accounts prepared in accordance with those rules do not provide sufficient information to meet the requirement to present a true and fair view:

- any necessary information must be provided in the financial statements, or in notes to the accounts
- if necessary, because of special circumstances, the directors shall depart from the normal rules in order to present a true and fair view and state why they have departed from the normal rules.

22.3 Generally accepted accounting principles (GAAP)

Accounting standards ensure compliance with the true and fair view concept. All companies are required to comply with accounting standards, or to publish reasons for departing from them.

Company auditors are required to ensure that company accounts are prepared in accordance with the standards and to report any significant departure from the standards to the shareholders. The standards help to increase uniformity in the presentation of company accounts and to reduce the subjective element in the disclosure of information.

TOP TIP

Students are not required to know the historical background to the origin of the accounting standards. It is very important, however, for students to learn the requirements of the standards referred to in this chapter.

KEY TERM

International Accounting Standards (IASs): Standards created by the International Accounting Standards Board stating how particular types of transactions or other events should be reflected in the financial statements of a business entity. Most commonly adopted by companies listed on a stock exchange.

International accounting standards have been developed in the form of **International Accounting Standards (IASs)** and **International Financial Reporting Standards (IFRSs)** since 2005, with the aim of harmonising, or standardising, financial reporting. Private UK companies are permitted to choose between international and UK standards. Companies listed on a stock exchange are required to adopt international standards, and many large or multinational private companies adopt them voluntarily.

The Cambridge International Examinations syllabus identifies a number of international accounting standards, the contents of which students need to be aware of. The following table identifies these. Some have already been covered in other chapters. The remaining ones, and some aspects of the others not previously mentioned, will be covered here.

IAS	Topic	Covered in
1	Presentation of financial statements	Chapter 19
2	Inventories	Chapters 16, 22 and 28
7	Statement of cash flows	Chapter 23
8	Accounting policies	Chapter 22
10	Events after the statement of financial position date	Chapter 22
16	Property, plant and equipment	Chapter 22
33	Earnings per share	Chapter 22
36	Impairment of assets	Chapter 22
37	Provisions, contingent liabilities and contingent assets	Chapter 22
38	Intangible assets	Chapter 22

As we saw in Chapter 19, company law in the United Kingdom also plays an important part in the way financial accounts are presented. In particular, it makes it a requirement for companies to state that their accounts have been prepared in accordance with applicable accounting standards. If this has not been the case then details must be given as to why not.

22.4 Accounting concepts

Although not an accounting standard, a **conceptual framework** has been developed by the body which sets the International Accounting Standards. This sets out the principles which underlie the preparation and presentation of financial statements. The framework identifies the main users of financial statements as set out below.

The framework surrounding IAS identifies the typical user groups of accounting statements. The table below identifies these user groups (stakeholders) and gives likely reasons (by no means exhaustive) for them referring to financial statements.

Main users	Reasons for use
Investors	To assess past performance as a basis for future investment
Employees	To assess performance as a basis of future wage and salary negotiations
	To assess performance as a basis for continuity of employment and job security
Lenders	To assess performance in relation to the security of their loan to the company
Suppliers	To assess performance in relation to them receiving payment of their liability
Customers	To assess performance in relation to the likelihood of continuity of trading
Government	To assess performance in relation to compliance with regulations and assessment of taxation liabilities
Public	To assess performance in relation to ethical trading

Chapter 9 set out a number of accounting concepts which are important when preparing the financial statements of any business. However, these are perhaps more important in the context of limited company accounts. When preparing financial statements, it is assumed that they are prepared on a matching basis and that the business is a going concern:

- **Matching** (see Section 9.9). Companies must compile their financial statements (except statements of cash flows) on a matching basis. This means that transactions are recorded in the accounting period in which they occur and to which they relate, not when cash is received or paid. A good example here is a sale made on credit. The sale is recorded in the month it takes place. The cash may be received for it some months afterwards, perhaps even in another accounting year.
- **Going concern** (see Section 9.11). Financial statements are prepared on the basis and assumption that the business will continue trading for the foreseeable future. There is no intention that the business is to cease trading. If that were the case, then the directors would have to prepare the financial statements on a different basis.

There are a number of other accounting concepts which should also be considered when preparing the financial statements. These have also been discussed elsewhere in the text. They are:

- business entity (see Section 9.3)
- materiality (see Section 9.8)
- consistency (see Section 9.7)
- prudence (see Section 9.10)
- money measurement (see Section 9.4).

All of these are designed to ensure that the information provided in the financial statements is useful to users with four objectives in mind:

- **Relevance** Information should have the ability to influence the economic decisions of the users of the statements, and be provided in time to influence those decisions.

- **Reliability** Information is reliable if it faithfully represents the facts and is free from bias and material error. It must be complete 'within the bounds of materiality' and prudently prepared.
- **Comparability** It should be possible to compare information with similar information about the company in a previous period (trend analysis – see Chapter 27) and with similar information about other companies (inter-firm comparison – see Chapter 27).
- **Understandability** Information should be able to be understood by users who have a reasonable knowledge of business and accounting, and who are willing to study the information reasonably diligently.

22.5 IAS 2 Inventories

This statement deals with the valuation of inventory which is entered in the income statement and statement of financial position. The term inventory refers to the unsold goods which the business holds. Companies have inventories in a variety of forms:

- raw materials for use in a subsequent manufacturing process
- work in progress, partly manufactured goods
- finished goods, completed goods ready for sale to customer
- finished goods which the business has bought for resale to customers.

The principle of inventory valuation set out in IAS 2 is:

Inventories should be valued at the lower of cost and net realisable value.

TOP TIP

This was also covered in Chapter 16 when the preparation of accounts from incomplete records was discussed.

Notice the exact wording. It is the lower of cost **and** net realisable value, **not** the lower of cost **or** net realisable value.

Walkthrough

Henri has ten items of inventory which he bought for \$6 each. They are normally sold for \$8 each. However, they have been damaged and can now only be sold for \$4 each.

Before they can be sold, Henri will have to spend \$1 per item on new labels and packaging.

There are three possible options to calculate the value of this inventory to include in the financial statements:

a cost, \$6 each

b estimated current selling price, \$4 each

c estimated selling price of \$4 each, less the cost of getting the items into a saleable condition \$1 each = \$3 each.

In this case the net realisable value is $3 each, the cost of $1 per item is deducted from the estimated selling price in line with the IAS. So that is their value for the purpose of the financial statements:

Income statement and statement of financial position $30 (10 items × $3 each).

Note that inventory is never valued at selling price when the selling price is greater than the cost.

ACTIVITY 1

The ABC Stationery Company bought 20 boxes of photocopier paper at $5 per box. Following a flood in their stockroom five of the boxes were damaged. They were offered for sale at $3 per box. All were unsold at the end of the company's financial year.

Required

Calculate the value of the items for inclusion in the financial statements.

The situation when a company holds a number of different lines of inventory

It is rare for a limited company to hold just one particular line of inventory. For example, a clothing store may hold both men's and women's clothes. For men it may hold shirts and trousers. These would be regarded as individual product lines. In this case, inventory value should also be considered on a line-by-line basis.

Walkthrough

Fabulous Fashions Limited holds three different product lines. Details of the inventory for each product line at the year end are as follows:

	Cost	Net realisable value
	$	$
New dresses	1 000	1 800
Children's clothing	2 000	2 600
Bargain fashions	1 200	900

The value of inventory to include in the statement of financial position will be:

	$
New dresses	1 000
Children's clothes	2 000
Bargain fashions	900
Total inventory value	3 900

Notice the valuation of the bargain fashions. This is the lowest of the three choices. This means that inventory valuation follows the **prudence** concept.

Inventory valuation methods where items are bought and used on a regular basis

Certain businesses, particularly manufacturing businesses, may hold a number of different items which are used in making the product. The cost of these items may vary, both over time and depending on which firm the business buys the items from. This causes a number of problems with the valuation of such inventory.

IAS 2 allows **two** different methods to be used for valuing this type of inventory:

1. First in, first out (FIFO). This assumes that the first items to be bought will be the first to be used, although this may not be the physical distribution of the goods. Thus, remaining inventory valuation will always be the value of the most recently purchased items.
2. Average cost (AVCO). Under this method, a new average value (usually the weighted average using the number of items bought) is calculated each time a new delivery of inventory is acquired.

This is covered in detail in Section 28.5, to which reference should also be made.

Valuation of inventory at the lower of cost and net realisable value

The principle of inventory valuation is set out in IAS 2. So far, we have seen that inventory can be valued using one of two different methods, FIFO or AVCO. These are the only two methods of inventory valuation which IAS 2 allows to be used. We have also seen that whichever method is chosen can affect the gross profit which the company makes.

We also saw that the standard states that **inventories should be valued at the lower of cost and net realisable value**. This is the price that may be expected to be received from the sale of the goods, less the cost of putting them into a saleable condition. The costs include the costs of completing the goods if they are manufactured, plus the marketing, selling and distribution costs.

The term net realisable value can be compared to the selling price of the product. If the expected selling price is **lower** than the cost price, then inventory should be valued at its selling price.

Inventory is never valued at selling price when the selling price is greater than the cost. By using the lowest price possible to value it, this means that inventory valuation follows the **prudence** concept.

Similarly, inventories which are similar in nature and use to the company will use the same valuation method. Only where inventories are different in nature or use can a different valuation method be used.

Once a suitable method of valuation has been adopted by a company, then it should continue to use that method unless there are good reasons why a change should be made. This is in line with the **consistency** concept.

Walkthrough

Goods were bought at a cost of $1 300. They have become damaged and will cost $400 to be put into a saleable condition. They can then be sold for $1 900. Net realisable value is $(1 900 – 400) = $1 500. As this is more than cost, the goods should be valued inventory at cost ($1 300).

Walkthrough

Details as in the previous walkthrough example but, after repair, the goods can be sold for only \$1 500. The net realisable value is \$(1 500 – 400) = \$1 100. This is less than cost and is the value to be placed upon the goods.

Valuing work in progress and finished goods

IAS 2 requires that the valuation of work in progress and finished goods includes not only their raw or direct materials content, but also includes an element for direct labour, direct expenses and production overheads.

The cost of these two items, therefore, consists of:

- direct materials
- direct labour
- direct expenses
- production overheads; these are costs to bring the product to its present location and condition
- other overheads which may be applicable to bring the product to its present location and condition.

The cost of these two items excludes:

- abnormal waste in the production process
- storage costs
- selling costs
- administration costs not related to production.

Walkthrough

The XYZ Manufacturing Company makes wooden doors for the building trade. For the period under review it manufactured and sold 10 000 doors. At the end of the trading period there were 1 000 completed doors ready for despatch to customers, and 200 doors which were half completed as regards direct materials, direct labour and production overheads.

Cost for the period under review were:

	\$
Direct materials used	20 000
Direct labour	5 000
Production overheads	8 300
Non-production overheads	10 000
Total costs for the period	43 300

Set out below is the calculation of the value of work in progress and finished goods at the end of the year:

Total units sold	10 000
Finished goods units	1 000
Half completed units (200 × 0.5)	100
Production for the period	11 100
Attributable costs	$33 300
Cost per unit	33 300 / 11 100 = $3

Value of work in progress:

200 × 0.5 × $3 = $300

Value of finished goods:

1 000 × 3 = $3 000

Note: Non-production overheads are **excluded** from the calculations.

The value of finished goods will be compared with their net realisable value when preparing the annual accounts. Whichever is the lower will be used.

TOP TIP

Under IAS 2, non-production overheads are not included in the inventory valuation.

ACTIVITY 2

Weaver Limited produces window frames. For month 1 the following costs were incurred:

	$
Direct materials	8 840
Direct labour	6 630
Factory overheads	4 420
Selling and distribution costs	11 050

There was no opening inventory.

- During the month the company produced and sold 2 000 fully completed units.
- At the end of the month 200 finished units were ready for sale.
- There were also a further 20 part-finished units. These were 50% complete in respect of direct materials, labour and factory overheads.

The finished goods could be sold for $20 each.

Required

a Calculate the cost per unit of production.

b Calculate the value of work in progress and finished goods to be included in the financial statements.

Replacement cost

Replacement cost is the price that will have to be paid to replace goods used or sold. The replacement cost may be the latest price of the good, or an estimate of what the price will be at some future date.

Replacement cost is **not** acceptable as a basis for valuing inventory under IAS 2. However, replacement cost may be used to estimate the cost of a particular job when quoting for an order. Using a price based on historic cost may lead to an underestimate of the price for the job and a lower profit. Replacement cost is usually more realistic for this purpose. Replacement cost should also be used when preparing budgets (see Chapter 34).

The standard does **not** allow for inventory to be valued using the last in, first out (LIFO) method. Similarly, inventories which are similar in nature and use to the company will use the same valuation method. Only where inventories are different in nature or use can a different valuation method be used.

Once a suitable method of valuation has been adopted by a company then it should continue to use that method unless there are good reasons why a change should be made. This is in line with the **consistency** concept.

22.6 IAS 8 Accounting policies, changes in accounting estimates and errors

This statement deals with the treatment of changes in accounting estimates, changes in accounting policies and errors in the financial statements.

Accounting policies

These are the principles, bases, conventions, rules and practices applied by a business when preparing and presenting its financial statements. These policies are selected by the directors of the business. In selecting them, they must make sure that where an accounting policy is given in an accounting standard, then the policy they select must comply with the standard.

Where there is no accounting policy provided to give guidance then the directors must use their judgement to give information that is relevant and reliable. The directors must refer to any other standards or interpretations or to other standard-setting bodies to assist them. However, they must ensure that their subsequent interpretation or recommended method of treatment for the transaction does not result in conflict with international standards or interpretations.

Examples of accounting policies can include the method of valuing inventory or the method(s) used to depreciate non-current assets.

Accounting principles

These are covered in the statement, although no formal definition is given for them, they are regarded as the broad concepts that apply to almost all financial statements. These would include such things as going concern, materiality, prudence and consistency, mentioned earlier (see Chapter 9).

Accounting bases

These are the methods developed for applying the accounting principles to financial statements. They are intended to reduce subjectivity by identifying and applying acceptable methods. The general rule is that once an entity adopts an accounting policy then it must be applied consistently for similar transactions. Changes in accounting policies can only occur if the change is required by a standard or interpretation, or if the change results in the financial statements providing more reliable and relevant information.

Once any changes are adopted then they must be applied retrospectively to financial statements. This means that the previous figure for equity and other figures in the income statement and statement of financial position must be altered, subject to the practicalities of calculating the relevant amounts.

Examples here are the method and rate used by a company to depreciate its non-current assets. Another would be the way in which it values inventory; for example, if the value includes material and labour costs or a proportion of factory overheads. Alternatively whether FIFO or AVCO is used.

Dealing with errors

If an error in the financial statements is discovered, then the business must correct material errors from prior periods in the next set of financial statements. Comparative amounts from previous periods must be restated, subject to the practicalities of calculating the relevant amounts.

In this instance, errors are omissions from, or misstatements in, the business financial statements covering one or more prior periods. They could be something as simple as a mathematical mistake made when preparing the accounts. They may also include the failure by directors to use reliable information which was available when the financial statements were prepared.

TOP TIP

Say the directors are considering changing the way in which depreciation is calculated or inventory valued in order to increase the profit for the year. It is important to remember that they should not make any changes, as to do so would mean this IAS not being followed.

22.7 IAS 10 Events after the statement of financial position date

These are events, either favourable or unfavourable, which occur between the statement of financial position date and the date on which the financial statements are authorised for. Such items may occur as a result of information which becomes available after the end of the year, and therefore need to be disclosed in the accounts. If they occur then amounts included in the financial statements must be adjusted; they may indicate that the going concern is not appropriate to the financial statements.

The key is the point in time at which changes to the financial statements can be made. Once the financial statements have been approved for issue by the board of directors, they cannot be altered. For example, the accounts are prepared up to 31 December. They are approved for issue by the board of directors on 30 April in the following year. Between these two dates, changes resulting from events after 31 December can be disclosed in the accounts. After 30 April, nothing can be changed until the next annual accounts are prepared.

The statement distinguishes between two types of events, adjusting events and non-adjusting events.

Adjusting events

If, at the date of the statement of financial position, evidence of conditions existed that would **materially** affect the financial statements, then the financial statements should be changed to reflect these conditions.

Examples of adjusting events could include:

- the settlement, after the date of the statement of financial position, of a court case which confirms that an obligation existed at the date of the statement of financial position
- the purchase price or proceeds from the sale of a non-current asset bought or sold before the year end, but not known about at the date of the statement of financial position
- inventories where the net realisable value falls below the cost price
- assets where a valuation shows that impairment is required
- trade receivables where a customer has become insolvent
- the discovery of fraud or errors which show the financial statements to be incorrect.

Non-adjusting events

No adjustment is made to the financial statements for such events. If material, they are disclosed by way of notes to the financial statements.

Examples of non-adjusting events include:

- major purchase of assets
- losses of production capacity caused by fire, floods or strike action by employees
- announcement or commencement of a major reconstruction of the business
- the company entering into significant commitments or contingent liabilities
- commencing litigation based on events arising after the date of the statement of financial position
- major share transactions, such as the issue of new shares and debentures or capital reductions or reconstructions.

There are three situations in addition to the above which require consideration:

a Dividends declared or proposed after the date of the statement of financial position are no longer recognised as a current liability in the financial statements. They are non-adjusting events and are now to be shown by way of a note to the accounts.

b If, after the date of the statement of financial position, the directors determine that the business intends to cease trading and that there is no alternative to this course of action, then the financial statements cannot be prepared on a going concern basis.

c A business must disclose the date when the financial statements were authorised for issue and who gave that authorisation. If anyone had the power to amend the financial statements after their authorisation then this fact must also be disclosed.

TOP TIP

You may be asked about events occurring after the date of the statement of financial position and for re-drafted financial statements to take account of any changes required as a result of these. Learn the items in the list and apply them accordingly.

22.8 IAS 16 Property, plant and equipment

This statement deals with the accounting treatment of the non-current assets of property, plant and equipment. The issues covered by the statement are:

- the recognition of the assets; when the item is recorded in the accounts
- the determination of their carrying amounts; what value is placed on it in the financial statements
- their depreciation charges
- their impairment losses; what happens when the value of the asset is below than that shown in the accounts.

Property, plant and equipment are tangible assets held for use in the production or supply of goods and services, for rental to others and for administrative purposes. They are expected to be used by the business for a period of more than one year.

For example, a company may buy some plant and machinery at a cost of $15 000. It expects the plant to be used for 10 years and at the end of that time to be sold for $1 000. The depreciable amount will be $14 000. Assuming the company uses the straight-line method of depreciation (see Section 11.4), then each year $1 400 will be recorded as an expense in the income statement. This example allows reference to be made to the definitions included in the standard. They are:

- **Depreciation** This is the allocation of the cost of an asset over its useful life. This will be the $1 400 written off each year.
- **Depreciable amount** This is the cost or valuation of the asset, less any residual amount. This will be the figure of $14 000 ($15 000 – $1 000).
- **Useful life** This is usually the length of time for which an asset is expected to be used. This will be the period of 10 years for which the company intends to hold and use the plant. There is an alternative. If the asset is depreciated on the basis of the number of units it produces then the estimated output of the item over its useful life can be used.
- **Residual value** The net amount the business expects to obtain for an asset at the end of its useful life, after deducting the expected costs of disposal. This will be the figure of $1 000, which the company hopes to sell the asset for at the end of its useful life.

The standard also uses some other terms which you need to be aware of:

- **Fair value** This is the amount for which an asset could be exchanged between knowledgeable, willing parties in an arm's-length transaction. If, for example, after five years the company decided to sell the plant, it may offer it to a buyer at $5 000. This would be regarded as a fair value for the item being sold.
- **Carrying amount** This is the amount at which an asset is recognised in the statement of financial position, after deducting any accumulated depreciation and impairment loss. This is, in effect, the net book value of the asset shown in the statement of financial position.

At what point does an entity recognise the asset? Or put more simply, at what point is the asset to be recorded in the financial statements? This must be done when it is probable that the business will be able to use it to generate revenue and a cost can be assigned to it. If an item of property, plant and equipment qualifies for recognition as an asset by meeting these criteria, then it is brought into the accounts and initially valued at cost.

Additional costs associated with the asset

The statement recognises that in addition to the initial purchase price of the asset, other amounts may also be spent on it. The statement provides the following guidelines to assist with the treatment of such expenditure:

a Day-to-day costs of servicing or repairing the asset should be charged as expenditure in the income statement.

b Where parts require replacement at regular intervals, say the seats in an aeroplane, then these costs can be added to the cost of the asset in the statement of financial position and depreciated accordingly.

c Where the asset requires regular inspections in order for the asset to continue operating, then the costs of such inspections can also be added to the cost of the asset in the statement of financial position and depreciated accordingly.

When the asset is purchased, apart from its original cost, a business may also pay other costs as part of the purchase price. The standard provides information as to what can be included as part of the cost in the statement of financial position:

- any import duties; taxes directly attributable to bring the asset to its present location and condition
- the costs of site preparation
- initial delivery and handling costs
- installation and assembly costs
- cost of testing the asset
- professional fees; say architects or legal fees.

Valuation of the asset

Once the asset is acquired, the business must adopt one of two models for its valuation:

a Cost less accumulated depreciation.

b Revaluation – the asset is included (carried) at a revalued amount. Revaluations are to be made regularly by suitably qualified people to ensure that the carrying amount does not differ significantly from the fair value of the asset at the date of the statement of financial position. Revaluations should be undertaken by the business with sufficient regularity to ensure that the carrying amount is up to date (e.g. every three to five years), unless assets are bought and sold frequently. If an asset is revalued then every asset in that **class** must be revalued. Thus, if one parcel of land and buildings is revalued then all land and buildings must be revalued. Any surplus on revaluation is reported in the statement of comprehensive income and transferred to the equity section of the statement of financial position as a revaluation reserve; this may not be used to pay dividends to the shareholders. Any loss on revaluation is recognised as an expense in the income statement, unless the revaluation reserve has surplus from the same asset.

Depreciation

The expected life and residual value of the asset are to be reviewed at least annually. If there is a difference from previous estimates this must be recognised as a change in an estimate under IAS 8 (accounting policies, changes in accounting estimates and errors). Depreciation must also continue to be charged even if the fair value of an asset exceeds its carrying amount. However, depreciation need not be charged when the residual value is greater than the carrying amount. Depreciation is to be included as an expense in the income statement.

The business must choose a method of depreciation which reflects the pattern of its usage over its useful economic life. Ideally, once the method has been decided this should not be changed. It is possible though to review the method, and if a change in the pattern of usage of the asset has occurred, then the method of depreciation should be changed to reflect this. Such a change would come under IAS 8.

Disclosure in the financial statements

For each class of property, plant and equipment, the financial statements must show:

- the basis for determining the carrying amount
- the depreciation method used
- the useful life or depreciation rate
- the gross carrying amount at the beginning and end of the accounting period
- the accumulated depreciation and impairment losses at the beginning and end of the accounting period
- additions during the period
- disposals during the period
- depreciation and impairments for the period.

These are likely to be shown by way of a non-current asset schedule and included as a note to the accounts. An example of this is shown below.

Non-current assets	Premises	Plant and machinery	Motor vehicles	Total
Cost	**$000**	**$000**	**$000**	**$000**
Cost at start of year*	800	400	230	1430
Revaluation	200			200
Additions during the year	–	246	170	416
Disposals during the year	–	(80)	(96)	(176)
Cost at end of year	1000	566	304	1870
Depreciation				
Balance at start of year*	400	256	164	820
Revaluation	(400)	–	–	(400)
Charge during year	–	115	70	185
Disposals	–	(70)	(80)	(150)
	–	(301)	(154)	(455)
Net book value at end of year*	1000	265	150	1415
Net book value at start of year**	400	144	66	610

* Dates at the start and end of the year would be provided in practice.
** This is the value at the end of the previous year.
Note: A revaluation reserve of $600 000 $(200 000 + 400 000) will have been created at the end of the year and recorded in the equity section of the statement of financial position. The final figures for net book value will be recorded in the statement of financial position.

ACTIVITY 3

Approval Limited provides the following balances of its non-current assets at the start of its financial year:

	Cost	Accumulated depreciation
	$000	**$000**
Freehold land and buildings	1000	40
Plant and equipment	600	250
Motor vehicles	870	660

During the year the following took place:

1 Land which had cost $800 000 was revalued at $1 200 000. The remaining balance at the start of the year represented buildings.
2 New plant costing $320 000 was purchased.
3 Old plant costing $60 000 was sold for $6 000. This resulted in a loss on disposal of $4 000.
4 An old motor vehicle, which had cost $24 000 and had been depreciated by $22 000, was sold.
5 A new motor vehicle costing $32 000 was purchased.

The company's depreciation policy is:

- buildings at 2% per annum using the straight-line method
- plant and machinery at 20% on the cost of the assets at the end of the year
- motor vehicles at 25% on the net book value at the end of the year, **before** charging the depreciation.

Required

Prepare the non-current assets schedule to include as a note to accounts at the end of the year.

22.9 IAS 18 Revenue

This statement is no longer in the syllabus. However, for the purpose of clarifying what is meant by the term revenue in an income statement, it is included here.

Revenue is defined in the statement as 'the gross inflow of economic benefits arising from the ordinary activities of an entity.' This means sales, either of goods or services. It also includes income from interest, say bank interest, dividends received and royalties received and gains from non-revenue activities, such as the proceeds from the disposal of non-current assets.

It does not include money collected by a business on behalf of another party, say where the business acts as an agent. However, any commission earned for collecting money as an agent is included as revenue.

When a transaction takes place, the amount of revenue is usually decided by the agreement between the buyer and the seller. The amount of revenue measured will take into account any trade discounts, which will not be included as part of the revenue.

The sale of goods is to be accounted for when **all** of the following criteria have been met:

a The seller of the goods has transferred to the buyer the significant rewards of ownership. This is usually when the legal title to the goods transfer, or possession of the goods passes from seller to buyer. This covers goods sold on a sale or return basis, where the title has not passed from seller to buyer.

b The seller retains no continual managerial involvement in, and no effective control over, the goods. The amount of revenue can be reliably measured.

c It is probable that the economic benefits will now flow to the seller.

d The costs incurred, or to be incurred, in respect of the transaction can be reliably measured.

When the income is interest, the amount to be recognised is calculated using a time basis (**matching** concept). If the income is dividends, these are brought into the income statement when the shareholder's right to receive payment is established. Dividends received are brought into the accounts when the shareholder's right to receive payment is established.

22.10 IAS 23 Borrowing costs

This statement is no longer in the syllabus. However, to illustrate what is meant by borrowing costs and how they fit in with the finance costs shown in the income statement, it is included here.

This covers such items in the accounts as interest on bank overdrafts and how they should be recognised in the income statement of the period for which they are incurred.

A borrowing cost is interest and other costs incurred by a business in connection with borrowing funds. This covers such things as bank loans or overdraft interest. The statement provides that borrowing costs are to be recognised as an expense in the income statement in the period in which they are incurred.

An alternative to this is when the borrowing relates to the acquisition, construction or production of a qualifying asset. In this instance the borrowing costs can be capitalised as part of the cost of the asset. For example, if an asset is being constructed, and is financed by use of borrowed funds, then any interest payable on the borrowings can also be capitalised. Suppose a company borrows $10 000 to construct a new building. Whilst the building is being constructed, any interest payable on the $10 000 can be capitalised as part of the cost of the building. Once the building is completed, then any further interest payable on the $10 000 is entered in the income statement under finance costs.

If any of the funds borrowed are temporarily invested in the short term and generate interest, then this interest must be offset against the borrowing costs capitalised.

22.11 IAS 33 Earnings per share (EPS)

This statement is no longer in the syllabus. However, the calculation of the earnings per share appears in the list of ratios to be examined, hence its inclusion here.

This is a ratio widely used by investors and analysts to measure the performance of a business and will be considered again in Chapter 28. The earnings of a company are the profits (or losses) for the year that are attributable to the equity holders of the business. In other words, the profit for the year from the income statement, less any dividends payable on **non-redeemable** preference shares.

IAS 33 sets out a basic method of calculating earnings per share, which is:

$$\frac{\text{profit for the year} - \text{non-redeemable preference share dividend}}{\text{number of issued ordinary shares}}$$

As the non-redeemable preference shares are regarded as part of the equity, any dividend payable on them will be adjusted in the statement of changes in equity.

Walkthrough

For the year ended 31 December the income statement of a company shows the following:

	$000
Profit from operations before tax	1 500
Tax	(500)
Profit for the year	1 000

At the start of the year the company had 2 million ordinary shares of $1 each.

The earnings per share are:

Profit for the year attributable to equity holders:

$$\frac{\$1\,000\,000}{2\,000\,000} = \$0.50 \text{ per share}$$

ACTIVITY 4

Using the facts in the example above, but assuming the company also had $400 000 of 10% non-redeemable preference shares, calculate the earnings per share.

In published accounts, earnings per share are always shown in the income statement for both the current year and the previous year. They are always expressed in cents per share.

Dividends on non-redeemable preference shares should be deducted from the profit attributable to equity holders **before** calculating the earnings per ordinary share.

22.12 IAS 36 Impairment of assets

The purpose of this standard is to ensure that assets are shown in the statement of financial position at no more than their value or recoverable amount. The term **recoverable amount** means the value that the business can recoup by one means or another from an asset; the formal definition is given below. If the recoverable amount is less than the amount of the asset shown in the accounts (its **carrying amount**, in effect its net book value), then the carrying amount must be reduced. This is an **impairment loss** and must be recognised as an expense in the income statement.

The standard applies to most non-current assets such as land and buildings, plant and machinery, motor vehicles and so on. It also applies to intangible assets such as goodwill and investments. It does not apply to inventories, which are the subject of their own standard, IAS 2.

Some of the terms in this standard have already been covered in Section 22.8 on IAS 16. However, there are some other terms used in this standard which require explanation:

- **Amortisation** This usually refers to the write-down of an intangible asset, such as goodwill.
- **Impairment loss** The amount by which the carrying amount of an asset exceeds its recoverable amount.
- **Fair value less costs to sell** The amount obtainable from the sale of an asset in an arm's-length transaction between knowledgeable, willing parties, less the costs of the disposal.
- **Recoverable amount** In respect of the asset, 'the higher of its fair value less costs to sell and its value in use'.
- **Value in use** The present value of the future cash flows obtainable as a result of an asset's continued use, including cash from its ultimate disposal.
- **Useful life** This can be either the period of time which an asset is expected to be used by the business, or the number of units of output expected to be obtained from the asset.

The impairment review

Businesses are expected to undertake an impairment review of their assets when there is an indication that the assets may be impaired (e.g. because there is a reduced demand for the product made by a particular machine or factory). In other words, assess whether or not the asset's net book value in the financial statement is a fair representation of its true value to the business. The impairment review involves comparing the asset's carrying amount with the recoverable amount. It is carried out in three stages, as follows:

Stage 1 Calculate the asset's carrying amount – its net book value.

Stage 2 Compare this with the asset's recoverable amount. The recoverable amount will be the **higher** of:

a the asset's fair value less costs to sell

b the asset's value in use. This is the present value of future cash flows to the business generated as a result of using the asset.

Stage 3 Compare all the values calculated. If **either** (a) or (b) is **higher** than the asset's carrying amount, then there is no need to reduce the carrying value of the asset. However, if both are lower than the carrying value of the asset then the carrying value must be reduced.

Walkthrough

A company is reviewing its assets at the end of its financial year. It identifies that:

a the net book value of an asset is $30 000 (cost minus accumulated depreciation)

b the company could sell the asset for $25 000 but would have to pay costs when selling of $2 000.

The company estimates the future net cash flows of the asset as:

Year	Future net cash flows from the asset	Discount factors at 10%	Present values of future net cash flows
	$		$
1	15 000	0.909	13 635
2	18 000	0.826	14 868
3	30 000	0.751	22 530
4	20 000	0.682	13 640

Total present value of future net cash flows =

$(13 635 + 14 868 + 22 530 + 13 640) = $64 673

The impairment review will be carried out by comparing $30 000 (the carrying cost) with the higher of $23 000 $(25 000 – 2 000) (the asset's fair value) and $64 673 (the asset's value in use).

As the carrying value is lower than the highest of the other two amounts ($64 673), then it will still be shown in the statement of financial position at $30 000.

If the carrying value is greater than the recoverable amount, then the asset is impaired. It must be written down to its recoverable amount in the statement of financial position. The amount of the impairment is recognised as an expense in the income statement as additional depreciation, or under its own heading of impairment loss.

Walkthrough

A business has three items of plant and machinery in its non-current assets in use at its year end. Details of their carrying values and recoverable amounts are set out below:

Asset	Carrying amount	Fair value less costs to sell	Value in use
	$	$	$
1	30 000	10 000	50 000
2	15 000	12 000	14 000
3	20 000	15 000	9 000

In the statement of financial position they should be shown at the following values:

Asset	Value in statement of financial position	Reason
	$	
1	30 000	The carrying amount is less than the recoverable amount; its value in use
2	14 000	The carrying amount is greater than the recoverable amount, the higher of which is its value in use
3	15 000	The carrying amount is greater than the recoverable amount, the higher of which is its fair value less costs to sell

The difference between the carrying value and the value to include the assets in the statement of financial position will be written off in the income statement. Their revised values will be included in the statement of financial position.

TOP TIP

Learn the way in which the carrying value is compared with the greater of the future net cash flows from the asset (often called the asset's value in use), and the fair value less costs to sell. You may also be asked to write about what you have done.

22.13 IAS 37 Provisions, contingent assets and contingent liabilities

These items represent uncertainties at the time the financial statements are prepared. They need to be fully accounted for on a consistent basis so that readers and users of the accounts can have a better understanding of their effect on the accounts.

A **provision** can be defined as a liability of uncertain amount or timing. An example here would be provision for the cost of repairing goods that it has sold with long term warranties, and where it knows from experience that at least some will break down. Provisions are only shown in the accounts when there are valid grounds for them. They should never be used as a way of window dressing the figures. If it is likely that a firm will have to make a payment for something and the amount it will have to pay can be reasonably estimated, then it can reasonably bring a provision into the accounts.

On the other hand, a **liability** is a present obligation a business has as a result of past events, where its settlement amount is known and is expected to result in a payment being made. For example, a business has a liability to pay its suppliers for goods and services they have provided. There is also another class of liability known as a **contingent liability**. This is a possible liability to the business which arises from some past event. However, it may result in the business having to pay for it only when a decision is made which is outside the company's control. For example, someone may be suing the company for faulty goods supplied. There is a possibility that the company will have to pay damages to the other party. However, that decision will be made by the courts. This decision and the amount of the payment is outside the company's control.

A contingent liability is not recognised in the accounts, but is disclosed by way of a note to them. This will describe the nature of the contingent liability, an estimate of how much it is likely to cost and an indication of the uncertainties relating to the amount or timing of any outflow of funds.

There is also **a contingent asset** which may affect a company. This is a possible asset arising from past events which will materialise when something happens which is not entirely within the company's control.

A contingent asset should **never be recognised in the accounts**, as to do so may be to bring in revenue that may never be realised. However, when the profit is almost certain to arise it is no longer a contingent asset and it should then be recognised in the accounts.

In other words the accounts will include an amount which will be received.

The IAS uses three words when it talks about provisions, contingent assets and contingent liabilities. They are:

- Probable – more than a 50% chance that the event will occur.
- Possible – less than 50% chance that the event will occur.
- Remote – little or no chance of the event occurring.

The following provides guidance of how items falling within these headings should be treated:

a **Provisions more that 50% likely to happen (probable)** In this case the amount should be entered in the financial statements. There must also be a note to the accounts giving details of these figures.

b **Contingent liabilities less than 50% likely to happen (possible)** In this case no amount is included in the financial statements, but a note to the accounts is given about the contingent liability.

c **Contingent liabilities which are remote, in other words most unlikely to happen** In this case no figures are shown in the accounts, neither is any note to the accounts included.

d **Contingent assets with more than a 50% chance of occurring (probable)** In this case no amount is included in the accounts. However, a note to the accounts is provided about the contingent asset.

e **Contingent assets with less than a 50% chance of occurring (Both possible and remote)** In both cases no amount is included in the accounts, neither is a note to the accounts included.

TOP TIP

Make sure you remember the 50% rule.

22.14 IAS 38 Intangible assets

An intangible asset is an identifiable non-monetary asset without physical substance. The best example of an intangible asset is goodwill. However patents and trade marks are also regarded as intangible assets. In other words, it is something which has value but, unlike, say, plant and machinery, cannot be touched.

In terms of the definition given above, in order for it to be identifiable, the asset must be capable of being sold separately from other parts of the business. Thus, for instance, a customer list could be an intangible asset as it can be sold separately by the entity. In an instance such as this, the entity has control of the asset and its use. The asset will also bring future economic benefits to the organisation.

Intangible assets can come from two sources. Firstly, they may be purchased. For instance a business may buy the patents of a particular product from another entity. Alternatively, when a business buys another at a figure in excess of the net book value of the assets taken over, then it purchases goodwill.

Alternatively, they are generated internally within the business. For instance, the goodwill which is valued when a partner leaves a partnership or a new partner is introduced. In both cases the goodwill has been internally generated by the efforts of the existing partners.

The general rule is that only purchased intangible assets are recognised in the accounts. The intangible asset is shown at cost less any accumulated amortisation (depreciation) and impairment losses. An intangible asset of a type that is freely traded at a public market price may also be shown at a revalued amount, being its fair value (see IAS 36, Impairment of assets), less any amortisation or impairment losses. In this case any loss in value is shown as an expense in the income statement. Any surplus is credited to a revaluation reserve on the statement of financial position.

In every case the business must identify the useful life of the intangible asset. In the case of those intangible assets having a finite life, they should be amortised using the straight-line method. In this case the residual value should be assumed as zero and the amount of the amortisation should be charged as an expense in the income statement. The amortisation period should be reviewed at least annually, and any changes to the amounts charged made in line with such a review.

Where the asset is deemed to have an indefinite life, then it will not be amortised. Instead, accounting standards require that it will undergo an annual impairment review. Part of the review must also consider whether or not an indefinite life is still valid in respect of the asset. Any loss in value arising from such a review is charged as an expense in the income statement. Thus an asset with an indefinite life will be written down, if at all, by one or a series of irregular impairment charges, whereas an asset with a definite life is written off in predictable instalments.

The standard also provides guidance to businesses which undertake research and development. In doing so, it provides definitions of each.

Research is theoretical work undertaken to gain new knowledge. This may or may not have some commercial benefit in the future. In this case, expenditure on research is to be written off as an expense in the income statement. Any non-current assets which are purchased as a result of the research can be capitalised and written off over their expected useful lives.

Development is moving on a stage. It is, perhaps, using research to develop a product which the business can use to generate sales at some point in the future. A good example here is the automotive industry, where the research into green technology may result in the development of an emission-free car.

In this case, development expenditure can be written off as an expense in the income statement in the period in which it is incurred. Alternatively, the expenditure can be recognised as an intangible asset in the statement of financial position of the business.

22.15 The role of the directors

As we saw in Section 22.1, the directors are the stewards of the shareholders. This means that they are appointed to manage the company on behalf of the owners, its ordinary shareholders. As there is most likely to be more than one director, collectively they are known as the **board of directors**. Their main role, having been appointed by the shareholders, is to manage the business on a day-to-day basis. They are directly accountable to the shareholders for their actions. As we have seen, each year the company will hold an annual general meeting (AGM) at which the directors must provide a report to the shareholders on the performance of the company, its future plans and strategies and recommend any dividends. Directors are usually only appointed for a set period of time as set out in the articles of association. If that period of time has expired, then at the AGM they must also offer themselves for re-election by the shareholders. If the shareholders vote not to re-elect a director then he or she must step down and can no longer take part in managing the company.

Overall, the key role of the board of directors is to ensure the prosperity of the company by directing the company's affairs and, at the same time, meeting the interests of the shareholders and other stakeholders, ensuring that they always act in a responsible and ethical manner.

Directors' report and strategic report

The directors of the company are required by the Companies Act to prepare a report for each financial year. The purpose of the report is to supplement the information given by the financial statements. The directors of a company qualifying as large or medium-sized must now prepare a strategic report, as well as a directors' report, within their annual report.

The **directors' report** contains the following information:

- The names of the directors, together with their responsibilities, interests and shareholdings in the company. The shareholders are entitled to know who have been stewards of their interests during the year.
- Proposed dividends payable by the company. These will be voted on for recommendation by the shareholders at the company's annual general meeting.
- Political donations made by the company. Shareholders may not want their money to be used for political purposes.
- Company policy on the employment of disabled people. Legislation dictates that companies must not discriminate against employees on grounds of any disability.
- A report on the annual quantity of greenhouse gas emissions from activities for which the company is responsible.
- A statement confirming that all relevant audit information has been provided to the company's auditor and an auditor's independence statement.
- Details of any post year-end important events affecting the company or group.
- Likely future developments in the business, research and development.
- Information on acquisition of own shares.
- Voting rights along with details of the annual general meeting.
- What action the company has taken on employee involvement in the running of the business, and consultation which has taken place between management and workers on the management and running of the business.

The strategic report contains the following information:

- a fair review of the company's business
- a description of the principal risks and uncertainties facing the company
- analysis using financial key performance indicators

KEY TERM

Directors' report: A report prepared by the directors of a plc at the end of the financial year. The Companies Act specifies which items must be included in such a report.

- additional explanations of amounts included in the company's annual accounts

In addition for plcs:

- the main trends and factors likely to affect future performance
- the company's strategy and business model
- information about environmental matters, employees and social, community and human rights issues
- information about gender diversity of the directors, the senior managers and the employees of the company.

Companies that qualify for the small companies' exemptions are not required to prepare a strategic report.

Companies with fewer than 250 staff members are not required to give the employee information set out above.

22.16 Auditors and the audit report

In connection with a limited company there are two types of auditor:

- **Internal auditor** The internal auditor is an employee of the company, appointed by the directors. Their main role is to help 'add value' to the company and help the organisation achieve its strategic objectives. They are thus part of the day-to-day management team of the business. Their key roles are therefore:
  - **a** evaluate and assess the control systems in place within the company
  - **b** evaluate information security and risk within the company
  - **c** consider and test the anti-fraud measures in place in the company
  - **d** overall, help to ensure that the company meets its strategic and ethical objectives.

- **External auditor** The external auditor is not an employee of the company. They are independent, usually large, firms of accountants. They are appointed by the shareholders to ensure that the financial statements prepared by the directors are a **true and fair view** of the state of financial affairs of the company. The auditors examine the financial records and systems in an honest and forthright manner and prepare an audit report. The **auditor's report** is presented to the shareholders at the annual general meeting. The shareholders are unable to inspect the company's books of account, indeed they may well lack the technical knowledge to do so. However, they are, along with the debenture holders, entitled to receive copies of the annual accounts. It is important that shareholders and debenture holders can be sure that the directors can be trusted to conduct the company's business well and that the financial statements and directors' report are reliable.

  The shareholders appoint auditors to report at each annual general meeting whether:
  - **a** proper books of account have been kept
  - **b** the annual financial statements are in agreement with the books of account
  - **c** in the auditor's opinion, the statement of financial position gives a true and fair view of the position of the company at the end of the financial year, and the income statement gives a true and fair view of the profit or loss for the period covered by the account
  - **d** the accounts have been prepared in accordance with the Companies Act and all current, relevant accounting standards.

KEY TERM

Auditor's report: A report prepared by the auditors of a limited company. It provides a statement to the shareholders as to whether or not the annual financial statements provide a true and fair view of the company's activities.

If auditors are of the opinion that the continuance of a company is dependent on a bank loan or overdraft, they have a duty to mention that fact in their report, as it is relevant to the **going concern concept**.

The auditor's responsibility extends to reporting on the directors' and any strategic report and stating whether the statements in it are consistent with the financial statements. They must also report whether, in their opinion, the report contains misleading statements.

Auditors must be qualified accountants and independent of the company's directors and their associates. They report to the shareholders and not to the directors; as a result, auditors enjoy protection from wrongful dismissal from office by the directors.

The structure of the auditor's report

There is a set format for the auditor's report. It will usually begin with:

> 'We have audited the accompanying financial statements of XYZ Limited for the year ended...'

(Here, the financial statements includes not only the income statement and statement of financial position, but also statement of cash flow and any schedules, say of non-current assets. The audit will have meant that they will have examined such things as the ledgers and bank reconciliation. They will have looked at vehicle log books and title deeds to property, and physically inspected the assets concerned. All the time the auditor is trying to ensure the accuracy and validity of figures set out in the financial statements.)

The report will then go on to set out management's responsibility for the preparation of accurate financial statements. The principle here is that the financial statements have been, and have to be, prepared by the directors. It is not the auditors who prepare the financial statements.

In the next section, the report will set out the responsibility of the directors and auditors in connection with the financial statements. These include:

a that the audit has been conducted in accordance with the Standards of Auditing issued by their professional body in their country – the International Standards on Auditing, for example

b that the directors are fully aware of their responsibility to prepare accurate financial statements

c that they, as auditors, have taken all the necessary steps to obtain enough information to express their opinion

d that they have also taken into account the relevant IAS and Companies Act provisions as part of their audit.

The final stage is for the report then to give an opinion on the financial statements. This will usually be written as:

> 'In our opinion, the financial statements give a true and fair view of (the name of the company) affairs at (the date of the end of the financial year, effectively the date of the statement of financial position) and of the profit and cash flows for the 52 weeks ended on that date…'
>
> '…that they have been properly prepared in accordance with the requirements of the Companies Act 2006 and IAS…'
>
> '…that the information given in the directors' report is consistent with the data contained in the financial statements.'

This is known as an **unqualified** report. In other words the auditors are happy that everything to do with the financial statements and the directors' report is fine.

If, during the course of their audit they found anything which they feel was in doubt or inaccurate they can issue a **qualified** audit report. In this case, at the end, a statement will be inserted which draws the attention of the shareholders to this fact. For example:

> 'During the course of our audit we discovered that the method of valuing inventory changed from last year, but no mention of this has been made in the directors' report. We believe that this has a material effect on the profit stated.'

This type of qualified audit report is unusual, as the auditors will have raised the matter with the directors and asked them to make the necessary changes. It is usually only if the directors have refused to amend the financial statements in accordance with the auditor's request that the audit report is qualified.

TOP TIP

Practise answering discursive-type questions based on published accounts. Answers should be clear, concise and relevant.

Chapter summary

Having worked through this chapter, you should now have developed an understanding of the way in which International Accounting Standards should be applied when preparing the published accounts of limited companies. You should also be familiar with some of the specific standards relevant to this topic.

You should have an understanding of the role of the directors and auditors of a limited company, as well as the structure and contents of the audit report.

In particular, you should have an understanding of:

- the financial statements and reports that must be published and sent to shareholders
- reporting standards relating to income statements
- reporting standards relating to statement of financial position
- the role of shareholders, directors, and auditors in a limited company
- the contents of directors' and auditor's reports
- why auditor's reports are important.

Practice exercises

1 X Limited was formed on 1 January 2015. The directors understand that at the end of the financial year they are obliged to prepare financial statements which give a true and fair view of the company's financial statements in accordance with International Accounting Standards.

Required

a Explain what is meant by a true and fair view of the financial statements of a limited company. **[2 marks]**

Additional information

The directors have prepared the following draft statement of financial position at 31 December 2015, and presented it to the company's auditors:

X Limited
Draft statement of financial position at 31 December 2015

	$000
Non-current assets	
Tangible	1810
Intangible – goodwill	250
	2060
Current assets	
Inventory	105
Trade receivables	96
Total current assets	201
Total assets	2261
Equity and liabilities	
Share capital and reserves	
Share capital	1000
Revaluation reserve	300
General reserve	130
Retained earnings	342
Total equity	1772
Non-current liabilities	
Debentures 2022/24	360
Current liabilities	
Trade payables	50
Other payables:	
Debenture interest	18
Proposed dividend	10
Bank overdraft	51
Total current liabilities	129
Total equity and liabilities	2261

During the course of their audit, the auditors have discovered the following:

1 The tangible non-current assets includes land which had cost $500 000. This had been revalued by the son of one of the directors who is training to be an architect. He estimated the increase in value to be $50 000. This increase has been included in the revaluation reserve. Included in the remaining non-current assets are some buildings which cost $40 000. These have not been depreciated as the directors consider they have not lost value during the year.

2 The value of goodwill has been estimated by the directors based on the high profits earned during the first year of trading.

3 Included in inventories are some items which were purchased for $6 000. They can now only be sold for $4 000.

4 Included in trade receivables is a customer who owes $18 000. He originally owed $24 000 for the goods which he purchased in June 2015, but was unable to pay. He is now paying back the debt at $2 000 a month, but has not paid the last three instalments.

5 The company is being sued by a customer for faulty goods which had been sold to them. The company's solicitors estimate that the company has a 35% chance of losing the case. If it were to lose, the amount the company would be liable to pay would be $8 000.

Required

b Prepare a revised statement of financial position at 31 December 2015, taking into consideration the information in items 1–5 and any other relevant matters. **[7 marks]**

c Explain the adjustments you have made in respect of these items, making reference to any relevant accounting standard. **[7 marks]**

d Prepare any notes which you feel should be included with the accounts when they are presented to the shareholders at the annual general meeting. **[4 marks]**

Additional information

After discussion, the directors have told the auditors that they do not accept their proposal to adjust the accounts. They have stated that the accounts they have prepared will be used to obtain additional funding from the bank for expansion. If they are adjusted they may fail to obtain this.

Required

e Advise the auditors whether or not they should present a qualified audit report at the annual general meeting. Justify your answer.

[5 marks]

Total 25 marks

2 Y Limited has been trading for a number of years. The directors are preparing their annual financial statements for the year ended 31 March 2016 for presentation to the auditors. The following information is available:

Non-current assets at 1 April 2015:

	Cost	Accumulated depreciation
	$000	$000
Freehold land and buildings	650	60
Office equipment	300	150
Motor vehicles	360	200

During the year the following took place:

1 Land which had cost $250 000 was revalued at $450 000. It had been depreciated by $10 000. The remaining balances at the start of the year represented buildings.

2 Included in office equipment was the company's computer system, which they had used for a number of years. This had cost $120 000 and had been depreciated by $65 000. An impairment review had revealed the computer system's fair value was $5 000 and its value in use was $50 000.

3 Old office equipment which had cost $20 000 had been sold for $2 000. This resulted in a loss on disposal of $3 000.

4 A new motor vehicle costing $32 000 had been purchased.

The company's depreciation policy is:

- land is no longer depreciated following the revaluation
- buildings at 4% per annum using the straight-line method
- office equipment at 20% on the net book value at the end of the year, **before** charging the depreciation
- motor vehicles at 25% on the cost at the end of the year.

Required

a Prepare the non-current assets schedule to include as a note to accounts at the end of the year. **[11 marks]**

Additional information

1 The following balances are available at 31 March 2016:

	$000
Ordinary share capital of $1 each	900
Share premium	200
Retained earnings at 1 April 2015	225
Draft profit for the year before depreciation	175

2 During the year the directors made a bonus issue of one ordinary share for every three held. The directors wished to keep the reserves in their most flexible form.

3 Inventories which had cost $17 000 could now only be sold for $12 000.

4 The draft profit for the year ended 31 March 2016 was arrived at after charging:

	$000
Final dividend for the year ended 31 March 2015	60
Interim dividend for the current financial year	35
Proposed final dividend for the current financial year	40

Required

b Prepare the statement of changes in equity for the year ended 31 March 2016. (A total column is not required.) **[5 marks]**

c Explain the difference between the role of the auditors and the role of the directors with respect to the financial statements of a limited company. **[4 marks]**

Additional information

The directors believe that it is the responsibility of the auditors to prepare the financial statements for the business. 'After all', said one of the directors, 'why are we paying them all this money?'

Required

d Advise the directors whether or not it is their responsibility to prepare the financial statements for the business. Justify your answer by discussing the roles of the directors and the auditors in this respect.

[5 marks]

Total: 25

Exam practice questions

Multiple-choice questions

1 How should inventory be valued in a statement of financial position?

A at the lower of net realisable value and selling price
B at the lower of replacement cost and net realisable value
C at lower of cost and replacement cost
D at lower of cost and net realisable value

2 A company bought and sold goods as follows:

	Bought		Sold
	Units	Unit price ($)	Units
March 1	20	2.00	
3	10	2.50	
4			12
5	20	3.00	
6			16

What is the value of the inventory at 6 March based on FIFO?

A $44 **B** $45
C $65 **D** $66

3 A company had the following inventory transactions in June:

June 1 Purchased 50 units at $3 per unit
14 Purchased 100 units at $4.50 per unit
23 Sold 70 units
30 Purchased 62 units at $5 per unit

What is the value of inventory at 30 June based on AVCO?

A $4.292 **B** $4.437
C $4.50 **D** $5.00

4 At the end of its financial year, a company provides the following information in respect of its inventory:

Item	Cost price	Net realisable value	Selling price (when new)
	$	$	$
New dresses	1000	1500	2000
Children's clothes	2000	3000	3000
Bargain fashions	1200	900	2000

What is the total inventory value to be included in the financial statements?

A $3900 **B** $4200
C $4700 **D** $5400

5 On which amount are earnings per share calculated?

A profit after interest, tax and preference dividend
B profit after interest, tax, preference dividend and transfer to general reserve of a publicly traded (listed) PLC
C profit before interest, tax and preference dividend
D profit before interest, tax, preference dividend and transfer to general reserve

6 A company is undertaking a review of its non-current assets as it includes them at revalued amounts in its statement of financial position. It discovers that some items of plant and machinery should be shown at a value below their carrying amount. Others are valued above their carrying amount. Which of the following statements is true about the actions it should take as a result of this?

A it must revalue all its non-current assets

B it must revalue all its non-current assets in that class

C it only needs to revalue those items which are above their carrying amount

D it only needs to revalue those items which are below their carrying amount

7 A business carries out an impairment review of its assets. The following information is discovered about an item:

	$
Cost when purchased	20 000
Carrying amount	12 000
Recoverable amount	14 000
Value in use	10 000

What figure should it be shown as in the statement of financial position?

A $10 000 **B** $12 000

C $14 000 **D** $20 000

8 Which of the following is a non-adjusting event?

A a non-current asset which is the subject of an impairment review loss

B a major customer becoming insolvent three weeks after the end of the financial year

C a discovery that the value of items of inventory have fallen below their cost

D the purchase of a new machine costing $500 000 made one month after the end of the financial year

9 A company is being sued by a customer for defective goods sold to them. The company's solicitors have advised that there is a 75% chance they will lose the case and have to pay the customer compensation of $50 000. How should this be recorded in the annual accounts?

A no reference to it is included

B a note only is included

C a note and a provision of $37 500 is included

D a note and a provision of $50 000 is included

Total: 10 marks

Additional questions

10 Explain the difference between a shareholder and a director, and the roles and responsibilities of each in respect of managing a limited company. **[6 marks]**

11 Explain the difference between an internal and external auditor and the roles and responsibilities of each. **[6 marks]**

Chapter 23
Statements of cash flows

Learning objectives

In this chapter you will learn:

- what a statement of cash flows is and why it is an important addition to the annual financial statements of a business
- how and why companies are required to include a statement of cash flows in their annual accounts
- how to prepare a statement of cash flows in line with IAS 7
- how to prepare a statement of financial position with the aid of a statement of cash flows
- how to prepare a statement of cash flows for sole traders and partnerships
- the advantages and disadvantage of statements of cash flows.

23.1 What is a statement of cash flows?

A statement of cash flows is one that lists the cash flows of a business over a period of time, usually the same period as that covered by the income statement.

A cash flow is any increase or decrease in **cash** in a business. Cash includes cash in hand and deposits repayable on demand, less overdrafts that are repayable on demand. For our purpose, **deposits** and **overdrafts** will generally be balances at, and overdrafts with, banks. The words on **demand** mean either immediately (e.g. current accounts) or within 24 hours of giving notice of repayment.

> **KEY TERM**
>
> **Cash:** Includes cash in hand and bank deposits repayable on demand, less any overdrafts repayable on demand. 'On demand' is generally taken to mean within 24 hours.

23.2 Why statements of cash flows are important

While it is necessary to know how much profit a business has made, profit is not cash in the bank. The business does not pay its suppliers from the balance on the retained earnings account. Suppliers are paid from the money the business has in its bank account. No business has ever been forced to close down by its suppliers or trade payables because it made an operating loss. But a business can be forced to close down because it has insufficient money in its bank account to pay its debts when they fall due. This is known as being insolvent. The amount by which the ready money in a business exceeds its immediate liabilities is its **liquidity**. There is a big difference between profit and liquidity. A business may make a large profit but finish up with less money in its bank account at the end of its year than it started with!

Over a period of time a business needs to generate **cash inflows** that at least match its **cash outflows**.

Cash **inflows** include:

- money received from the issue of shares or capital put into the business by the owners
- loans received from banks or other lenders
- money received from the sale of surplus non-current assets
- payments from its customers; its trade receivables for goods sold to them
- interest received on deposits with banks and other companies.

Cash **outflows** include:

- payments to suppliers; its trade payables or other creditors (as already mentioned) and the running costs of carrying on the business (e.g. wages)
- renewal of, and additions to, non-current assets
- interest on loans and debentures
- payment of tax on profits (companies)
- payment of drawings for a sole trader or partnership
- costs involved in the growth of the business (expansion and development)
- dividends payable to shareholders, or drawings of sole traders and partners
- repayment of loans or redemption of shares by the company.

23.3 Statements of cash flows and limited companies

The International Accounting Standard which covers the structure and layout of the statement of cash flows for a limited company is IAS 7. This requires that limited companies produce a statement of cash flows as part of the annual financial statements.

The statement provides guidelines for the format of statements of cash flows. The statement is divided into four categories:

a **Operating activities** – the main revenue generating activities of the business, together with the payment of interest and tax.

> **KEY TERM**
>
> **Operating activities:** The main revenue-generating activities of the company.

If the trade receivables have increased over the two accounting periods, then money has not been collected from them. Thus, the difference between the two figures is deducted from profit from operations. If, on the other hand they have gone down, then this is a positive adjustment for the business.

If the trade payables have decreased over the two accounting periods, then money has been spent paying them. In this case the difference between the two figures is deducted from profit from operations. If, on the other hand, they have increased, then this is a positive adjustment for the business.

d **Interest paid, which also has to be deducted**

e **Taxes paid on income (usually corporation tax).** Taking all these items into account, when preparing the statement of cash flows for a business, the section on cash flows from operating activities will look like this.

	$
Profit from operations	120 000
Adjustments for:	
Depreciation	30 000
Loss on disposal of non-current assets	2 000

Walkthrough

Carrying on with the example earlier, the following has also been discovered:

	Closing	Opening
	$	$
Inventory	6 000	5 000
Trade receivables	8 000	10 500
Trade payables	4 200	5 100

During the year the company received bank interest of $800 and paid corporation tax of $12 600.

The cash flow from operating activities will be:

	$
Profit from operations	120 000
Adjustments for:	
Depreciation	30 000
Loss on disposal of non-current assets [1]	2 000
Increase in inventory [1]	(1 000)
Decrease in trade receivables	2 500
Decrease in trade payables	(900)
Bank interest received	800
Tax paid	(12 600)
Net cash from operating activities	140 800

[1] Items which increase the cash received are shown as positives, whilst those as decreases are shown in brackets as cash outflows.

TOP TIP

Work on making sure that you know which direction the adjustments above should be. The most common error is to treat them the wrong way round.

ACTIVITY 1

Everyday Limited made a profit from operations for the year of $175 000. The following information is also available:

1. Included in the expenses was depreciation of $42 100, and a profit of $2 300 on the disposal of a non-current asset.
2. During the year, inventory decreased by $5 800, trade receivables increased by $2 600 and trade payables increased by $3 400.
3. During the year the company paid $27 500 in corporation tax.

Required

Prepare a statement to show the cash flow from operating activities for the year.

Investing activities

This is calculated by including:

- inflows from: proceeds from sale of non-current assets, both tangible and intangible, together with other long-term non-current assets
- outflows from: cash used to purchase non-current assets, both tangible and intangible, together with other long-term non-current assets
- interest received
- dividends received.

Financing activities

This is calculated by including:

- inflows from:
  - cash received from the issue of share capital
  - raising or increasing loans
- outflows from:
  - repayment of share capital
  - repayment of loans and finance lease liabilities
- dividends paid.

Reconciliation of cash and cash equivalents:

- net increase/(decrease) in cash and cash equivalents for the year
- cash and cash equivalents at the beginning of the year
- cash and cash equivalents at the end of the year.

Set out below is a full statement of cash flows for a limited company, taking all the above into account.

Walkthrough

Exhibit Co Limited
Statement of cash flows for the year ended ......*

	$	$
Cash flows from operating activities:		
Profit from operations (before tax and interest)		50 000
Adjustments for:		
Depreciation charge for the year		12 000
Increase in inventories		(3 000)
Decrease in trade receivables		2 000
Increase in trade payables		4 000
Cash (used in)/from operations		65 000
Interest paid (during the year)		(5 000)
Tax paid (during the year)		(8 000)
Net cash (used in)/from operating activities		52 000
Cash flows from investing activities:		
Purchase of non-current assets	(20 000)	
Proceeds from the sale of non-current assets	1 000	
Interest received	2 000	
Dividends received	500	
Net cash (used in)/from investing activities		(16 500)
Cash flows from financing activities:		
Proceeds from issue of share capital (this would include both the share and share premium amounts)	80 000	
Repayment of long-term borrowings	(30 000)	
Dividends paid	(4 000)	
Net cash (used in)/from financing activities		46 000
Net increase/(decrease) in cash and cash equivalents		81 500
Cash and cash equivalents at the beginning of the year		10 000
Cash and cash equivalents at the end of the year		91 500

*No dates are included. This would not be the case in practice, where the actual date of the year end, say 31 December, would be stated. Comparative figures for the previous year would also be shown alongside.

IAS 7 allows some flexibility in the way some information can be shown. For example, cash flows from interest and dividends received and paid can be shown as above or in the first section relating to cash flows from operating activities.

TOP TIP

Practise the layout as much as you can. Also take care to include items in the correct section and make sure they are fully labelled.

23.4 How to prepare a statement of cash flows from statements of financial position and an income statement

Statements of cash flows are prepared by comparing the amounts for items in the latest statement of financial position with the amounts for the same items in the previous year's statement of financial position. Some additional calculations for non-current asset details will be required. The following example, with explanatory notes, demonstrates the procedure.

Walkthrough

Accounting Limited's statements of financial position at 30 June 2015 and 2016, and an extract from its income statement for the year ended 30 June 2016, are shown below.

Accounting Limited
Statements of financial position

	At 30 June 2015 [1]			At 30 June 2016		
	Cost	Acc dep'n	NBV [2]	Cost or valuation	Acc dep'n	NBV [2]
	$000	$000	$000	$000	$000	$000
Non-current assets						
Freehold property	900	300	600	1000	–	1000
Plant and machinery	700	300	400	800	400	400
Motor vehicles	450	180	270	500	200	300
	2050	780	1270	2300	600	1700
Current assets						
Inventories			200			300
Trade receivables			260			215
Short-term investments			500			800
Cash and cash equivalents			98			200
			1058			1515
Total assets			2328			3215
Equity and liabilities						
Share capital and reserves						
Ordinary shares of $1 each			600			1200
Share premium			350			200
Freehold property revaluation reserve			–			400
General reserve			700			800
Retained earnings			102			166
			1752			2766

[1] For illustration purposes here, the earlier year is shown first. In practice, you may find that the most recent year appears first. Make sure to read the dates.

[2] NBV: net book value

	At 30 June 2015			At 30 June 2016		
	$000	$000	$000	$000	$000	$000
Non-current liabilities						
10% debentures 2022/2024			150			200
Current liabilities						
Trade payables			336			163
Taxation			90			86
			426			249
Total equity and liabilities			2 328			3 215

Note: For illustration purposes a full breakdown of the non-current assets has been given.

Accounting Limited
Income statement (extract) for the year ended 30 June 2016

	$000
Profit from operations	420
Finance costs (debenture interest)	(20)
Profit before tax	400
Tax	(80)
Profit for the year	320

Note: During the year the company paid dividends of $156 000. This would be included in the statement of changes in equity, not shown here.

Additional information

1 During the year ended 30 June 2016, the following transactions took place:

i Plant and machinery which had cost $105 000, and on which depreciation of $85 000 had been provided, was sold for $24 000.

ii Motor vehicles which had cost $60 000, and which had a net book value of $15 000 at the date of sale, were sold for $28 000.

iii A bonus issue of shares was made on the basis of one bonus share for every two ordinary shares already held. This was done by using part of the balance on the share premium account.

iv Following the bonus issue in (iii), the company issued a further 300 000 ordinary shares at $1.50 per share.

v $50 000 of 10% debentures 2022/2024 were issued on 1 July 2015.

vi The directors transferred $100 000 to the general reserve from the profit for the year.

2 There had been no additions to freehold property in the year to 30 June 2016.

The company accountant has been asked to prepare a statement of cash flows for the year ended 30 June 2016.

The statements he prepared are set out below.

Step 1 Prepare workings

The following information will be required but will probably not be given in a question:

- non-current assets: cash paid for new assets or received from the sale of old assets, amounts provided for depreciation in the income statement, profits and losses on the disposal of non-current assets
- dividends, interest and taxation paid.

This information is best discovered by preparing rough T-accounts as workings and calculating the missing information as balancing figures.

Plant and machinery (P & M) a/c				Prov'n for dep'n P & M a/c				Disposal of P & M a/c			
Bal b/f	700	Disposal	105			Bal b/f	300			Dep'n	85
				Disposal	85			Cost	105	Cash	24
Additions (bal. fig.)	205	Bal c/f	800	Bal c/f	400	Charge for year (bal. fig.)	185	Profit	4		
	905		905		485		485		109		109

Motor vehicles (MV) a/c				Prov'n for dep'n MV a/c				Disposal of MV a/c			
Bal b/f	450	Disposal	60	Disposal	45	Bal b/f	180	Cost	60	Dep'n	45
Additions (bal. fig.)	110	Bal c/f	500	Bal c/f	200	Charge for year (bal. fig.)	65	Profit	13	Cash	28
	560		560		245		245		73		73

The creation of the freehold property revaluation reserve shows that the increase in the freehold property was entirely due to revaluation, and no cash flow was involved.

Taxation			
Paid (bal. fig.)	84	Bal b/f	90
Bal c/f	86	Inc. st.	80
	170		170

Once all the workings have been done the statement can now be prepared.

Step 2 Prepare a statement of cash flows for the year ended 30 June 2016

Part 1 Net cash flows from operating activities. This is no different to the process described in Section 23.3. Start with the profit from operations before tax and interest. Then adjust for:

- **Non-cash items in the income statement.** That is those items which do not involve the movement of any cash, such as depreciation and profits or losses on the disposal of non-current assets. These figures will come from the earlier workings.
- **Increases or decreases in inventories, trade receivables and trade payables.** This is done by comparing the figures for each on the two statements of financial position. Remember that if the inventory has increased between the two years, then the company must have spent cash acquiring the extra inventory. This means that it will have a negative effect on the cash flow of the business and will appear in brackets in the statement. Likewise, if trade receivables have increased between the two years, this means that the company has not received cash in from its customers. This too will have a negative effect on the cash flow of the company and will appear in brackets in the statement. If, on the other hand, the trade payables have increased between the years, then the company will have saved its cash by not paying its suppliers. In this case the change will not appear in brackets in the statement, as the cash

flow will have benefited from this action. If these situations are reversed then treat them the opposite way round in the statement.

- **Interest payments made during the year.** Take care as it may be that a loan was taken out part way through the year. Alternatively, perhaps not all the interest will have been paid during the year. Check the closing statement of financial position to see if there is any accrual in the current liabilities.
- **Tax paid during the year.** This will come from the workings above.

Cash flow from operating activities	
	$000
Profit from operations (before tax and interest)	420
Adjustments for:	
Depreciation charge for the year (185 + 65)	250
Profit on disposal of non-current assets (4 + 13)	(17)
Increase in inventories (200 – 300)	(100)
Decrease in trade receivables (260 – 215)	45
Decrease in trade payables (336 – 163)	(173)
Cash (used in)/from operations	425
Interest paid (during the year)	(20)
Tax paid (during the year) from workings	(84)
Net cash (used in)/from operating activities	321

TOP TIPS

- Familiarise yourself with the workings to this example. Check where all the figures came from and how they were calculated.
- All non-cash items in the income statement must be adjusted in the reconciliation of operating profit to net cash flow from operating activities.
- Make sure you understand the effect of changes in inventory, trade receivables and trade payables on cash flow.

Part 2 Identify the items which form the cash flows from investing activities: purchase and sale of non-current assets, interest and dividends received.

Cash flows from investing activities	
	$000
Purchase of non-current assets (205 + 110)	(315)
Proceeds from the sale of non-current assets	52
Interest received	nil
Short-term investment	(300)
Net cash (used in)/from investing activities	(563)

Part 3 Identify the cash flows from financing activities: receipts from the issue of shares, cash spent on repayment of loans and dividends paid.

Net cash flows from financing activities:	
Proceeds from issue of share capital	450
Issue of debentures	50
Dividends paid	(156)
Net cash (used in)/from financing activities	344

Part 4 Reconcile the opening and closing cash and cash equivalents with the net cash flow for the year.

Net increase/(decrease) in cash and cash equivalents: ($321 – 563 + 344)	102
Cash and cash equivalents at the beginning of the year	98
Cash and cash equivalents at the end of the year	200

Now put the whole thing together as one complete statement:

Accounting Limited
Statement of cash flows for the year ended 30 June 2016

	$000	$000
Cash flow from operating activities		
Profit from operations (before tax and interest)		420
Adjustments for:		
Depreciation charge for the year (185 + 65)		250
Profit on disposal of non-current assets		(17)
Increase in inventories (200 – 300)		(100)
Decrease in trade receivables (260 – 215)		45
Decrease in trade payables (336 – 163)		(173)
Cash (used in)/from operations		425
Interest paid (during the year)		(20)
Tax paid (during the year) from workings		(84)
Net cash (used in)/from operating activities		321
Cash flows from investing activities:		
Purchase of non-current assets (205 + 110)	(315)	
Proceeds from the sale of non-current assets	52	
Interest received	nil	
Short-term investment	(300)	
Net cash (used in)/from investing activities		(563)
Cash flows from financing activities:		
Proceeds from issue of share capital	450	
Issue of debentures	50	
Dividends paid	(156)	
Net cash (used in)/from financing activities		344
Net increase/(decrease) in cash and cash equivalents		102
Cash and cash equivalents at the beginning of the year		98
Cash and cash equivalents at the end of the year		200

Note: The reconciliation of the figure for retained earnings at 30 June 2016 is:

	$000
Balance at 30 June 2015	102
Add: profit for the year	320
	422
Less: dividends paid in the year	(156)
Transfer to general reserve	(100)
Balance at 30 June 2016	166

TOP TIPS

- Learn the format of the statement and which items go under which headings. Don't worry when you get to the end if it doesn't balance. Insert the figures for cash and cash equivalents at the start and end of the period.
- Prepare the statement of cash flows in outline, leaving plenty of space between the headings for details to be inserted. Start by filling in the easy items such as payments made to purchase non-current assets, proceeds of disposal, issues and redemptions of shares and debentures, movements in inventory, trade receivables and trade payables, etc. Then proceed to the items requiring more detailed calculations.

ACTIVITY 2

Exchange Limited's statements of financial position at 31 December 2015 and 2016, and an extract from its income statement for the year ended 31 December 2016, were as follows:

	Statement of financial position as at 31 December 2015			Statement of financial position as at 31 December 2016		
	$000	$000	$000	$000	$000	$000
Non-current assets	Cost	Dep'n	NBV	Cost	Dep'n	NBV
Freehold property	400	–	400	364	–	364
Plant and machinery	80	35	45	150	39	111
Motor vehicles	120	90	30	160	95	65
	600	125	475	674	134	540
Current assets						
Inventory			100			85
Trade receivables			40			52
Cash and cash equivalents			55			36
			195			173

	Statement of financial position as at 31 December 2015			Statement of financial position as at 31 December 2016		
	$000	$000	$000	$000	$000	$000
Total assets			670			713
Equity and liabilities						
Capital and reserves						
Ordinary shares of $1			250			300
Share premium			20			25
General reserve			100			100
Retained earnings			101			102
			471			527
Non-current liabilities						
10% debentures 2022/2025			100			70
Current liabilities						
Trade payables			60			73
Taxation			39			43
			99			116
Total equity and liabilities			670			713

Income statement (extract) for the year ended 31 December 2016	
	$000
Profit from operation	94
Interest paid	(7)
	87
Tax	(40)
Profit attributable to equity holders	47

Note: During the year the company paid dividends of $46 000.

Additional information

During the year ended 31 December 2016, the following transactions took place:

1 Freehold buildings which had cost $36 000 were sold for $50 000. The premises had not been depreciated.
2 Plant and machinery which had cost $20 000, and on which depreciation of $16 000 had been provided, was sold for $1 000. New plant and machinery had been purchased.
3 Motor vehicles which had cost $30 000, and which had a net book value of $5 000 at the date of sale, were sold for $4 000. New motor vehicles had been purchased.
4 50 000 ordinary shares of $1 each were issued at a premium of $0.10 per share on 1 July 2016.
5 $30 000 of 10% debentures 2017/2018 were redeemed at par on 1 January 2016.

Required

Prepare a statement of cash flows for the year ended 31 December 2016.

	Cost	Dep'n	NBV
	$000	$000	$000
Trade receivables (77 + 18)			95
Cash and cash equivalents			264
			359
Total assets			1 663
Equity and liabilities			
Share capital (830 + 150)			980
Share premium (110 + 50)			160
General reserve (100 + 100)			200
Retained earnings			105
			1 445
Non-current liability			
10% debentures 2021/2023 (200 – 50)			150
Current liabilities			
Trade payables (44 – 6)			38
Tax			30
			68
Total equity and liabilities			1 663
Calculation of the figure for retained earnings			
Retained earnings at start of year			92
Profit for the year			169
			261
Transfer to reserves			(100)
Dividends paid			(56)
Retained earnings at 31 October 2016			105

Workings

Plant and machinery at cost				Dep'n plant and machinery				Disposal			
B/f	750	Disposal	96	Disposal	60	b/f	220	Cost	96	Dep'n (bal. fig.)	60
Cash	130	c/d (bal. fig.)	784	c/d (bal. fig.)	210	Inc. st.	50	Profit	14	Cash	50
	880		880		270		270		110		110

ACTIVITY 3

Indus Limited's statement of financial position at 31 July 2015 was as follows:

	At cost	Dep'n	Net book value
	$000	$000	$000
Non-current assets			
Freehold premises	300	130	170
Plant and machinery	125	75	50
	425	205	220
Current assets			
Inventory			36
Trade receivables			79
Cash and cash equivalents			42
			157
Total assets			377
Equity and liabilities			
Ordinary shares of $1			150
Share premium			20
General reserve			40
Retained earnings			56
			266
Non-current liabilities			
10% debenture 2023/2024			50
Current liabilities			
Trade payables			43
Tax			18
			61
Total equity and liabilities			377

An extract from Indus Limited's income statement for the year ended 31 July 2016 and the statements of cash flows for that year are as follows:

Extract from Indus Limited's income statement for the year ended 31 July 2016	
	$000
Profit from operations	69
Finance costs	(5)
Profit before tax	64
Tax	(25)
Profit for the year attributable to equity holders	39

Note: The directors decided to transfer $30 000 to the general reserve.

Jaydee
Reconciliation of profit from operations to net cash flow from operating activities for the year ended 31 October 2016

	$
Profit for the year (profit from operations)	21 000
Adjustments for:	
Depreciation charge for the year	4 500
Loss on sale on non-current assets	500
Increase in inventories	(2 000)
Increase in trade receivables	(3 000)
Decrease in trade payables	(2 500)
Cash (used in)/from operations	18 500
Interest paid (during the year)	(1 000)
Net cash (used in)/from operating activities	17 500

Note the differences here. As Jaydee is a sole trader, it is perfectly acceptable to prepare a reconciliation statement of profit from operations (trading) to net cash flow from operations. The opening position is simply referred to as profit for the year. As Jaydee is a sole trader, all the profit belongs to him. There is also no adjustment for tax, as Jaydee will pay this personally. If he pays it from the business it will be included as part of his drawings figure.

The calculation of loss on the sale of the plant and machinery and the purchase of new machinery is as follows:

Plant and machinery at cost account

	$		$
Opening balance	25 000	Closing balance	35 000
Bank – purchases	13 000	Asset disposal	3 000
	38 000		38 000

Plant and machinery accumulated depreciation account

	$		$
Asset disposal account	2 500	Opening balance	12 000
Closing balance	14 000	Charge for the year	4 500
	16 500		16 500

Asset disposal account

	$		$
Cost of plant scrapped	3 000	Depreciation	2 500
		Loss on disposal	500
	3 000		3 000

It is now possible to prepare a statement of cash flows for Jaydee for the year ended 31 December 2016. This is set out below.

Jaydee
Statement of cash flows for the year ended 31 December 2016

	$	$
Net cash (used in)/from operating activities		17 500
Cash flows from investing activities:		
Purchase of non-current assets (plant)	(13 000)	
Net cash (used in)/from investing activities		(13 000)
Cash flows from financing activities:		
Repayment of loan	(2 000)	
Drawings	(4 000)	
Net cash (used in)/from financing activities		(6 000)
Net increase/(decrease) in cash and cash equivalents		(1 500)
Cash and cash equivalents at the beginning of the year		500
Cash and cash equivalents at the end of the year		(1 000)

Again, notice the differences from the statement for a limited company. As Jaydee is a sole trader, then no dividends are paid. Instead, he will take drawings from the business.

It is now possible to advise Jaydee why he has a bank overdraft at the end of the year, even though he has made a profit. It is because:

- he has purchased new plant and machinery
- he has repaid part of his loan
- he has increased his inventory, allowed his trade payables to increase and reduced his trade receivables
- all of these have led to cash leaving the business and resulted in the bank becoming overdrawn at 31 December 2016, despite Jaydee making a profit for the year.

ACTIVITY 4

Janine, a sole trader, presents you with the following financial information in respect of her financial accounts for the year ended 31 October 2016 and 2015:

Statement of financial position

	At 31 Oct 2015			At 31 Oct 2016		
Assets		**$000**			**$000**	
Non-current assets	Cost	Dep'n	NBV	Cost	Dep'n	NBV
Freehold land			30			60
Plant and machinery at cost	39	21	18	55	25	30
	39	21	48	55	25	90
Current assets						
Inventories			11			16
Trade receivables			15			12
Cash and cash equivalents			3			–
			29			28
Total assets			77			118

	At 31 Oct 2015	At 31 Oct 2016
Equity and liabilities		
Capital	52	61
Capital introduced	–	10
	52	71
Profit for the year	20	50
Drawings	(9)	(21)
	61	100
Non-current liabilities		
Long-term loan	–	8
Current liabilities		
Trade payables	16	8
Bank overdraft	–	2
	16	10
	77	118

Income statement (extract) for the year ended 31 October 2016	
	$000
Profit	25
Depreciation of plant and machinery	(5)
Profit on disposal of plant	1
Profit on revaluation of land	30
Interest paid	(1)
Profit for the year	50

Janine tells you that during the year she scrapped some plant which had cost $6 000. She cannot understand why she has an overdraft at 31 October 2016, despite making a profit for the year, and asks for your help to explain the situation.

Required

Prepare a statement of cash flows for Janine for the year ended 31 October 2016. Identify why she has made a profit for the year, yet her bank account is overdrawn.

23.7 Advantages of producing a statement of cash flows

The statement of cash flows is an extremely useful addition to the annual accounts. The advantages to a business producing one are:

- It shows the movement of cash for the year. It also shows the business's ability to generate cash from its trading activities. The ability to generate cash is vital to the future survival of the business.

- Cash flow is easier for a non-accounting person to understand. We all look closely at our cash and bank position! This means it is easier to understand than an income statement and statement of financial position, which rely on technical knowledge and are prepared using accounting conventions which do not apply to cash. Suppliers are more interested in a business's ability to pay them than how much profit it makes. Remember, cash and profit are different things.
- It provides useful information as a backup to the income statement and statement of financial position.

The only real disadvantage of producing a statement is that it ignores the matching concept. This means that the cash coming in or going out may relate to a previous accounting period. However, the advantages of producing a statement of cash flows are far more beneficial to the business. It allows another element to assess the overall performance of the firm.

TOP TIP

Be prepared to draft a statement of cash flows for a sole trader or a partnership.

Chapter summary

In this chapter you have learnt what a statement of cash flows is and why it's important that businesses include this in their annual financial statements. Similarly, you should also know how to prepare a statement of cash flows for both sole traders and partnerships, in line with International Accounting Standard 7.

TOP TIP

Get as much practice as you can at preparing statements of cash flows.

Practice exercises

1 DH plc supplies you with the following information in respect of its annual financial statements for the year ended 31 December 2016:

	$000
Profit from operations	1 998
Interest paid	168
Tax provision	700
Dividends paid during the year	150
Dividends proposed at end of year	180

Statements of financial position at 31 December		
	2016	**2015**
	$000	**$000**
Non-current assets at cost	10 000	9 000
Accumulated depreciation	(1 800)	(1 500)
	8 200	7 500
Current assets		
Inventory	85	70
Trade receivables	250	270
Cash and cash equivalents	50	40
	385	380
Total assets	8 585	7 880
Equity and liabilities		
Capital and reserves		
Ordinary shares of $1 each	3 800	2 600
Share premium	190	–
Retained earnings	3 500	2 520
	7 490	5 120
Non-current liabilities		
Bank loan	700	2 400
Current liabilities		
Trade payables	105	80
Tax	290	280
	395	360
Total liabilities	8 585	7 880

Additional information

During the year the company sold a non-current asset for $10 000 cash. The asset had been depreciated by $20 000 and there was a loss on disposal of $4 000.

Required

a Explain the difference between a statement of cash flows and a cash budget. **[4 marks]**

b Calculate the following for the year ended 31 December 2016:

- **i** the cost of non-current assets purchased during the year **[3 marks]**
- **ii** the charge for depreciation for the year. **[3 marks]**

c Prepare the statement to show the net cash from operating activities as it would appear in the statement of cash flows at 31 December 2016. **[8 marks]**

d Explain the difference between cash and profit. **[3 marks]**

e Explain why there is such a small change in the bank balance even though the company has made a large profit. **[4 marks]**

Total: 25

2 Woodpecker Limited provides the following financial information:

	31 December 2016	31 December 2015
	$000	$000
Non-current assets at net book value	337	310
Current assets	68	72
Current liabilities	36	54
Non-current liabilities		
– 5% debenture	40	–

Statement of changes in equity for the year ended 31 December 2016:

	Ordinary share capital	Share premium	Retained earnings	Total
	$000	$000	$000	$000
At 31 December 2015	140		188	328
Share issue	100	20		120
Loss for the year			(119)	(119)
At 31 December 2016	240	20	69	329

Additional information

1 At 31 December 2015, the non-current assets had a cost of $500 000.

2 During the year, an asset which had cost $35 000, and had been depreciated by $32 000, had been scrapped.

3 During the year, non-current assets costing $85 000 had been purchased. The company's depreciation policy is to depreciate its non-current assets at 10% on the cost at the year-end.

4 The debenture was issued on 1 July 2016. Half year's interest had been paid.

5 Bank balance at 31 December 2015 was $6 000 debit. At 31 December 2016, it was $3 000 credit.

Required

a State **two** advantages and **two** disadvantages of a statement of cash flows. **[4 marks]**

b Prepare Woodpecker's statement of cash flows for the year ended 31 December 2016, in line with IAS 7. **[12 marks]**

c Comment on the performance of the company for the year ended 31 December 2016 on the basis of the statement of cash flows you have prepared and other relevant information. **[4 marks]**

Additional information

The company is looking to expand its operations. In order to do so it is considering either issuing 150 000 ordinary shares of $1 each at a premium of $0.20, or issuing a further 5% debenture for $200 000.

Required

d Advise the directors which option they should choose. Justify your answer. **[5 marks]**

Total: 25

Exam practice questions

Multiple-choice questions

1 An examination of a company's accounts at the end of the year revealed the following:

	$
Cash from operations	50 000
Increase in trade payables	3 000
Decrease in trade receivables	4 000
Increase in inventories	2 000
Depreciation charge for the year	14 000

What was the profit from operations before interest and tax for the year?

A $31 000 **B** $41 000
C $69 000 **D** $73 000

2 The following information has been extracted from the books of a limited company:

	At 31 Dec 2016	At 31 Dec 2015
	$000	$000
Profit from operations	94	
Loss on disposal of non-current assets	3	
Inventories	35	41
Trade receivables	47	49
Trade payables	16	20

What was the cash from operating activities for the year?

A $93 000 **B** $97 000
C $101 000 **D** $115 000

3 The following relates to the plant and machinery for a limited company:

	At 31 Dec 2016	At 31 Dec 2015
	$	$
Cost	80 000	50 000
Depreciation	(30 000)	(28 000)

During the year plant costing $10 000 was sold at a loss of $2 000. What figure will appear as purchase of non-current assets in the statement of cash flows for the year?

A $20 000 **B** $30 000
C $38 000 **D** $40 000

4 The following figures have been extracted from the books of a limited company:

	At 31 Dec 2016	At 31 Dec 2015
	$000	$000
Ordinary share capital	200	150
Share premium	30	10
Debenture 2023/2024	50	20
Dividends paid during the year	12	8

What is the cash from financial activities for the year?

A $28 000 **B** $32 000

C $88 000 **D** $92 000

5 The following relates to the motor vehicles for a limited company:

	At 31 Dec 2016	At 31 Dec 2015
	$	$
Cost	75 000	40 000
Depreciation	(35 000)	(25 000)

During the year a car costing $8 000 was sold for $3 000. This resulted in a loss of $1 000. What figure will appear as depreciation in the statement of cash flows for the year?

A $6 000 **B** $10 000

C $14 000 **D** $18 000

6 A company purchased a motor vehicle for $25 000. Settlement was made by a payment of $22 000 and the part exchange of one of the company's own vehicles for $3 000. The vehicle given in part exchange had a written down value of $7 000, but had a resale value of $2 000. Which amount should be shown in the statement of cash flows for the acquisition of the vehicle?

A $22 000 **B** $24 000

C $25 000 **D** $29 000

Total: 6 marks

Structured question

1 The following is Winston plc's statement of financial position at 31 October 2016.

Statement of financial position at 31 October 2016			
	Cost	Acc dep'n	NBV
	$000	$000	$000
Non-current assets			
Freehold premises	850	90	760
Plant and machinery	1 197	469	728
	2 047	559	1 488
Current assets			
Inventory			191
Trade receivables			82
Cash and cash equivalents			25
			298
Total assets			1 786
Equity and liabilities			
Capital and reserves			
Ordinary shares of $1 each			950
Share premium			150

	Cost	Acc dep'n	NBV
	$000	$000	$000
General reserve			100
Retained earnings			173
			1373
Non-current liability			
10% Debentures 2021/23			300
Current liabilities			
Trade payables			73
Tax			40
			113
Total equity and liabilities			1786

The company's accountant has prepared a budgeted statement of cash flows for the year ended 31 October 2017:

Statement of cash flows for the year ended 31 October 2017		
	$000	$000
Cash flows from operating activities		
Profit from operations (before tax and interest)		243
Adjustments for:		
Depreciation charge for the year:		
Plant and machinery		200
Profit on sale of plant		(20)
Decrease in inventories		76
Increase in trade receivables		(15)
Decrease in trade payables		(26)
Interest paid (during the year)		(20)
Tax paid		(40)
Net cash (used in)/from operating activities		398
Cash flows from investing activities:		
Purchase of non-current assets (plant)	(293)	
Proceeds from the sale of plant	41	
Net cash (used in)/ from investing activities		(252)
Cash flows from financing activities:		
Proceeds from issue of 150 000 shares of $1 each	210	
Repayment of debentures	(100)	
Dividends paid	(30)	
Net cash (used in)/from financing activities		80
Net increase/(decrease) in cash and cash equivalents		226
Cash and cash equivalents at the beginning of the year		25
Cash and cash equivalents at the end of the year		251

Additional information

1 The plant sold during the year had cost $110 000 when purchased.

2 The directors intended to transfer $80 000 to the general reserves at 31 October 2017.

3 The directors intended to revalue the freehold premises to $1 000 000 during the year.

The company accountant also provided the following extract from the company's budgeted income statement for the year ended 31 October 2017:

	$000
Profit from operations	243
Debenture interest	(20)
Profit before tax	223
Tax	(60)
	163

Required

a Prepare Winston plc's budgeted statement of financial position at 31 October 2017. **[12 marks]**

b Prepare Winston plc's budgeted statement of changes in equity for the year ended 31 October 2017. **[6 marks]**

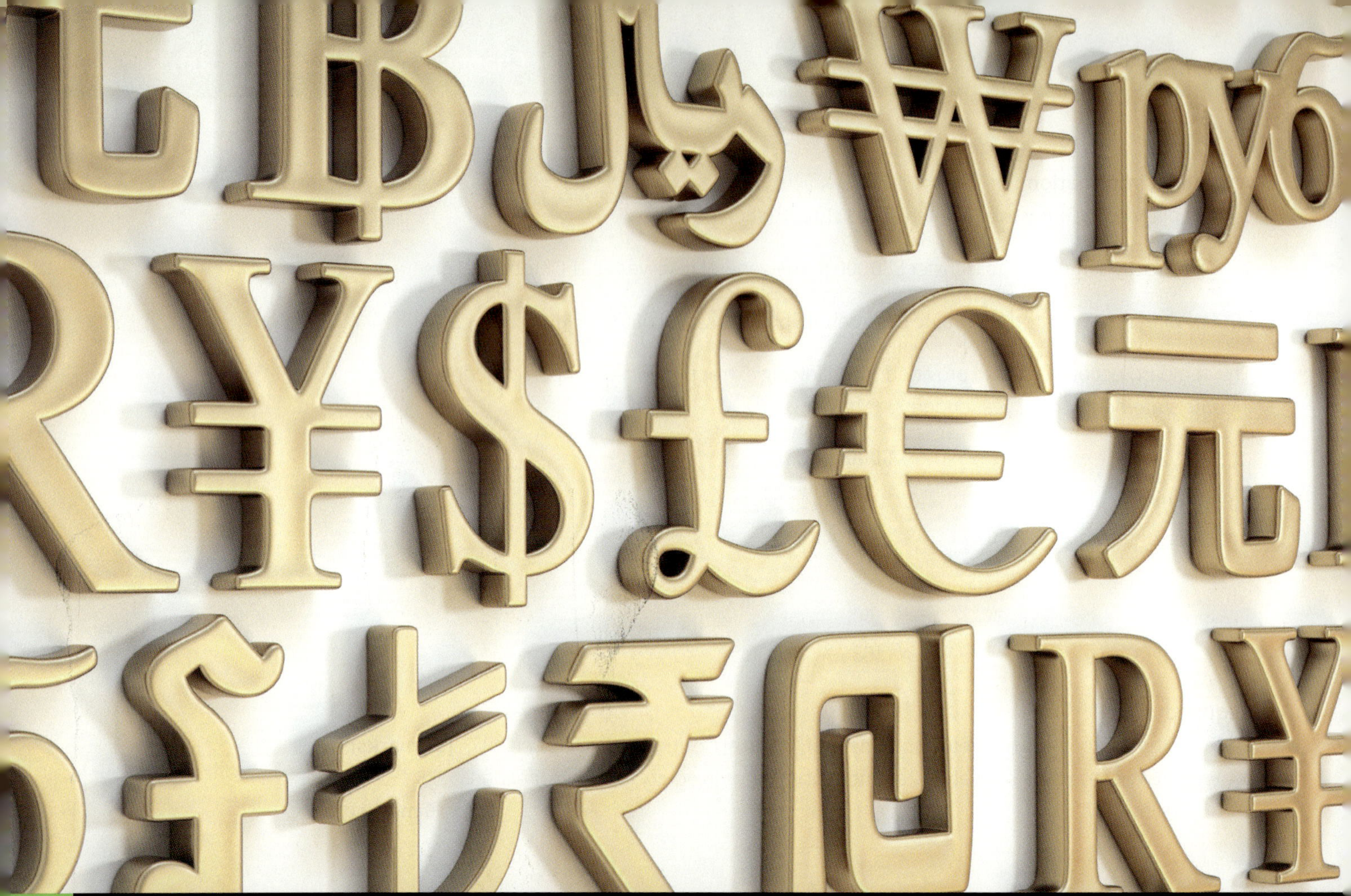

Chapter 24
Business purchase and merger

Learning objectives

In this chapter you will learn:

- the difference between the purchase of a business by another and the merger of two businesses
- the difference between the purchase of a business and the purchase of the assets of a business
- goodwill arising on the purchase of a business
- how to prepare a journal entry to record the purchase of a business in the books of the purchasing company
- the preparation of a statement of financial position following the purchase of a business
- how to calculate the return on an investment in a new business.

24.1 The difference between the purchase of a business by another business and the merger of two businesses

This chapter will look at two aspects of business growth. The first is the **merger** of two existing businesses to form a single, larger business. The second is the purchase of an existing business by another business. This will result in the closure of the business being purchased and the expansion of the business which buys it.

There are three possible situations you could be faced with:

- the merger of two sole traders to form a partnership
- the purchase of the business of a sole trader by a limited company
- the purchase of a partnership by a limited company.

The first thing to consider is the merger of two existing businesses to form a single business. This can be either two sole traders who join together (merge their businesses) to form a partnership, or it may be a sole trader and a business merging to form a single business.

KEY TERM

Merger: Where two or more independent businesses combine their assets and form a completely new business.

Walkthrough

Anna and Sumitra each run their own businesses as sole traders. Their summarised statements of financial position at 31 December 2015 are as follows:

	Anna	Sumitra
	$	$
Non-current assets	50 000	45 000
Current assets		
Inventory and trade receivables	15 000	8 000
Cash and cash equivalents	3 000	1 000
	18 000	9 000
Total assets	68 000	54 000
Capital and liabilities		
Capital accounts	62 000	50 000
Current liabilities		
Trade payables	6 000	4 000
Total capital and liabilities	68 000	54 000

They have been friends for a number of years and feel that if they combined their businesses to form a partnership they would make more profit in total.

On 1 January 2016, they decide to go ahead and create a partnership. It will be called AnSu. They agree to transfer all assets and liabilities of their old businesses at the following values:

	Anna	Sumitra
	$	$
Non-current assets	60 000	52 000
Inventory and trade receivables	12 000	6 000
Cash and cash equivalents	3 000	1 000
Trade payables	(6 000)	(4 000)
Net assets transferred to new partnership at agreed values	69 000	55 000

They have employed Anna's brother, an accountant, to close the accounts of their old business and set up the new partnership.

Her brother has prepared the following statement of financial position at 1 January 2016 to record the opening balances of the new partnership. This is shown below.

AnSu
Statement of financial position at 1 January 2016

	$
Non-current assets ($60 000 + 52 000)	112 000
Current assets	
Inventory and trade receivables ($12 000 + 6 000)	18 000
Cash and cash equivalents ($3 000 + 1 000)	4 000
	22 000
Total assets	134 000
Capital and liabilities	
Capital accounts	
Anna [1]	69 000
Sumitra [1]	55 000
	124 000
Current liabilities	
Trade payables ($6 000 + 4 000)	10 000
Total capital and liabilities	134 000

[1] The balancing figure for each partner is the net value of the assets and liabilities transferred to the new partnership. The values used will be the values agreed between the partners, **not** the values from their final statements of financial position at 31 December 2015.

Anna's brother has simply added together the agreed values of the assets and liabilities transferred to the new partnership. Anna and Sumitra's individual balances no longer exist. A partnership agreement should be drawn up for the new business. It may be that Anna asks Sumitra to put more capital into the partnership so that the balance on their capital accounts are equal. Alternatively, the partnership agreement may include provision for interest on capital to be paid for each partner from the profit made to compensate Anna, who has the higher capital (see Chapter 17).

Sometimes one or both of the partners may also add a value for goodwill on to the assets and liabilities they introduce into the new partnership. This is inherent goodwill and should be written off as soon as possible. The procedure to do this is identical to that discussed in Chapter 18: the capital account of each partner is credited with the value of goodwill they introduce into the new business; it is then debited with the goodwill written off in the profit-sharing ratios.

Walkthrough

Bert and Mary have been in business for many years as sole traders. On 1 May 2016, they agree to merge their two businesses to form a partnership. The following information relates to the merger:

Bert will introduce net assets at a value of $400 000. In addition he values the goodwill of his business at $60 000.

Mary will introduce net assets at a value of $500 000. She values the goodwill of her business at $30 000.

They both agree to share future profits and losses equally. They also agree that no goodwill should remain in the books of account.

The opening balance on their capital accounts at 1 May 2016 will be:

	Bert	Mary	Total
	$	$	$
Net assets at valuation	400 000	500 000	900 000
Goodwill at valuation [1]	60 000	30 000	90 000
	460 000	530 000	990 000
Goodwill written off [2]	(45 000)	(45 000)	(90 000)
Opening capital account balances [3]	415 000	485 000	900 000

[1] The goodwill is added to the value of the net assets introduced at the valuation of each party.

[2] It is then written off in the agreed profit-sharing ratio, in this case equally.

[3] This leaves the final opening balance for each partner to bring into the new partnership.

The situation will be slightly different if a sole trader merges their business with a partnership. This will result in a new partnership with a change in the profit-sharing ratios. The partners may also take the opportunity to revalue some of their assets and liabilities, including goodwill. This will be done to reward them for their efforts in building up their existing business. This was also considered in Chapter 18.

Walkthrough

Don and Tom have been in business for a number of years sharing profits and losses equally. Their summarised statement of financial position at 31 March 2016 is as follows:

	$000
Non-current assets	100
Current assets	50
Total assets	150
Capital accounts	
Don	55
Tom	55
	110
Current accounts	
Don	10
Tom	12
	22
Current liabilities	18
Total capital and liabilities	150

On 1 April 2016, they agree to admit Don's brother, Ron as a partner. Ron has been in business as a sole trader for some time. He agrees to introduce the following assets into the partnership:

	$000
Motor vehicle	14
Inventory	6
Cash	23

Don and Tom take the opportunity to revalue their non-current assets upwards to $122 000. They also value goodwill at $40 000. No goodwill account is to remain in the books of account.

A partnership agreement is drawn up which includes the profit-sharing ratio of Don 2, Tom 2 and Ron 1 respectively.

Don and Tom have asked their accountant to prepare the statement of financial position at 1 April 2016 to show the start of the new partnership.

Before he can do this the accountant must adjust Don and Tom's capital accounts in respect of the revalued assets and goodwill. These are shown below.

Don and Tom
Capital accounts

2016		Don	Tom	2016		Don	Tom
		$000	$000			$000	$000
April 1	Goodwill	16	16	April 1	Balances	55	55
	Opening balance for new partnership	70	70		Profit on revaluation ($122 000 – 100 000) ÷ 2	11	11
					Goodwill ($40 000 ÷ 2)	20	20
		86	86			86	86

Next, Ron's capital account is prepared:

Ron
Capital account

2016		$000	2016		$000
April 1	Goodwill	8	April 1	Motor vehicle	14
	Opening balance for new partnership	35		Inventory	6
				Cash [1]	23
		43			43

[1] In this case the amount of cash which Ron introduced has been given. Sometimes you may be asked to calculate the figure.

It is now possible for the accountant to prepare the following opening statement of financial position for the new partnership:

	$000
Non-current assets $(100 000 + 22 000 + 14 000) [1]	136
Current assets $(50 000 + 6 000 + 23 000) [1]	79
Total assets	215
Capital accounts	
Don	70
Tom	70
Ron	35
	175
Current accounts	
Don	10
Tom	12
Ron [2]	0
	22
Current liabilities	18
Total capital and liabilities	215

[1] The non-current and current assets have been increased, not only by the amount which Ron introduced, but also by the profit on revaluation.

[2] At the start of the new partnership, Ron will have a zero balance on his current account as the business has yet to earn any profit.

ACTIVITY 1

Nitin and Maria are in partnership, sharing profits and losses in the ratio of 2:1 respectively. Their summarised statement of financial position at 31 May 2016 is as follows:

	$000
Non-current assets	220
Current assets	80
Total assets	300
Capital accounts	
Nitin	120
Maria	120
	240
Current accounts	
Nitin	16
Maria	(4)
	12
Current liabilities	48
Total capital and liabilities	300

They agree to admit Sam as a partner with effect from 1 June 2016. The new profit-sharing ratios will be equal.

The following matters should be taken into account:

1 Nitin and Maria will revalue their non-current assets upwards by $24 000.

2 Goodwill is valued at $45 000. No goodwill account is to remain in the books of account.

3 Sam will introduce non-current assets valued at $98 000 and inventory valued at $12 000.

Required

a Prepare Nitin and Maria's capital accounts at 1 June 2016 to show their opening balances in the new partnership.

b Prepare Sam's capital account at 1 June 2016.

c Prepare the opening statement of position for the new partnership immediately after the admission of Sam.

24.2 What is the difference between the purchase of a business and the purchase of the assets of a business?

It is important to distinguish between a company buying the assets of another business, and the purchase by the company of that other business. Some students get confused between the two different kinds of purchase. A company may buy the assets of another business which may then cease to trade. Indeed, it may only buy some of the assets of a business and the seller may still continue to trade. That is very different from a company buying another business. In this case, the company takes over the assets **and** liabilities of that business, together with its customers, and carries on the trade of the business taken over. The distinction is important. The purchase only of assets does not involve any payment for goodwill; the purchase of an entire business usually does involve payment for goodwill.

When a limited company purchases another business it will usually pay for it partly by cash and partly by shares. The shares may be issued at a premium. However, the sellers of the business would not pay for the shares given to them.

Sometimes a sole trader or a partnership may decide to convert their business into a limited company. This is done by forming a new company which purchases the business.

Walkthrough

Aiisha has traded for some years as a sole trader. On 1 October 2016, she decided to form a limited company to take over her business. She will hold ordinary shares of $1 in the company as her capital.

Aiisha's summarised statement of financial position at 1 October 2016 was as follows:

	$
Non-current assets	20 000
Net current assets	14 000
	34 000
Capital account	34 000

The summarised statement of financial position of the new company will appear as follows:

Aiisha Limited	
	$
Non-current assets	20 000
Net current assets	14 000
	34 000
Share capital	
Ordinary shares of $1	34 000

In this case, Aiisha has transferred all the assets and liabilities of her 'old' business to a new limited company. In return, she has received ordinary shares to the value of her old capital. These replace her old capital account. The shares could have been issued at any value. In this case they were ordinary shares of $1 each. They could have been ordinary shares of $2 each, in which case Aiisha would now own 17 000 ordinary shares. In terms of running the business nothing has changed. Aiisha is the only shareholder and may choose to be the only director. She can continue to operate her business as before, taking all the decisions herself. Her one real advantage is that she now has limited liability, which she didn't have as a sole trader.

24.3 Goodwill

As we have seen, goodwill was considered in Sections 18.4 and 18.5, and again in the examples above. It is now necessary to consider it again in the situation where a business purchases the business of a sole trader.

Unlike Aiisha, who continues to run the business, quite often the existing business owner (or owners in the case of a partnership) will sell their business to a limited company and retire. In some cases the old owner or owners may become managers in the new business.

When the company purchases the business, it will usually buy the assets less the liabilities at an agreed valuation. In addition, it usually pays for the advantage of acquiring an established trade. The company does not have to build up a new business from nothing; the business has been built up by the previous owner, who will normally expect to be rewarded for their efforts. Often the total purchase price paid by the limited company will be in excess of the net book value of the assets acquired by them. In this case, **goodwill** arises.

Goodwill is the amount paid for the acquisition of a business in excess of the fair value of its separable net assets. The term 'separable net assets' is used to describe the sale of individual assets and using the money to settle the liabilities of the business.

It is important to distinguish between **purchased goodwill** and **inherent goodwill**. Purchased goodwill has been paid for. Inherent goodwill has not been paid for and will arise, for instance, if a trader decides that he wants to show the goodwill of his business in his statement of financial position; he debits a goodwill account in his books and credits his capital account with any amount that he wishes to show as goodwill. **International Accounting Standard 38** sets out how goodwill should be treated in the books. This was discussed in Section 18.4, when it was seen that only purchased goodwill is shown in the statement of financial position. Inherent goodwill is never shown in the financial statements.

If the amount paid for a business is less than the fair value of its separable net assets, the difference is called **negative goodwill**. This is known as a bargain purchase and the profit is recognised immediately in the income statement of the company buying the business.

KEY TERMS

Purchased goodwill: Goodwill which has been paid for by the purchasing business.

Inherent goodwill: Goodwill which has not been paid for. It has been built up within the business by the owners. The amount is subjective.

TOP TIPS

- Goodwill is the difference between the values of the net assets acquired and the purchase price paid.
- Only purchased goodwill is shown in the books of account of the company buying the business.

24.4 Purchase of a sole trader by a limited company

The second situation you need to know about is when a sole trader sells his business to a limited company.

Before any entries for the purchase of a business are made in a company's ledger accounts, the transaction must be recorded in the company's journal. The entries should include the bank and cash accounts, if these are taken over. However, the bank and cash balances of the business being acquired are **not** usually taken over unless a sole trader or a partnership converts their business into a limited company, such as in the case of Aiisha, or Anna and Sumitra.

TOP TIP

Only take into account the assets and liabilities being bought by the limited company when calculating the value of purchased goodwill.

Walkthrough

Mekong Limited purchased the business of Achara, a sole trader, on 1 October 2016. Achara's statement of financial position at that date was:

	$	$
Non-current assets		
Land and buildings		60 000
Plant and machinery		35 000
Motor vehicles		21 000
		116 000
Current assets		
Inventory	7 000	
Trade receivables	4 000	
Cash and cash equivalents	5 000	
	16 000	
Total assets	132 000	
Capital and liabilities		
Capital account		130 000
Current liabilities		
Trade payables		2 000
Total capital and liabilities		132 000

The net assets were taken over at the following values:

	$
Land and buildings	80 000
Plant and machinery	28 000
Motor vehicles	16 000
Inventory	5 000
Trade receivables	3 000
Trade payables	(2 000)
	130 000

The total of the **agreed** value of the assets purchased by Mekong Limited amounts to $130 000. Mekong Limited did not take over Achara's cash and cash equivalents, so these are **not** entered in the journal.

Mekong Limited paid Achara $150 000, made up as follows: cash $20 000 and 100 000 ordinary shares of $1 each.

The accountant of Mekong Limited prepared the following journal entry to record the purchase of Achara's business.

	Dr	Cr
	$	$
Land and buildings	80 000	
Plant and machinery	28 000	
Motor vehicles	16 000	
Inventory	5 000	
Trade receivables	3 000	
Goodwill [1]	20 000	
Trade payables		2 000
Cash and cash equivalents		20 000
Ordinary share capital		100 000
Share premium account [2]		30 000
	152 000	152 000

[1] Goodwill = purchase consideration ($150 000) less value of net assets acquired ($130 000).

[2] The shares were valued at $(150 000 – 20 000) = $130 000. $30 000 is the share premium.

Narrative: The purchase of the business of Achara on 1 October 2016 for the sum of $150 000 is payable as follows: cash $20 000 and by the issue of 100 000 ordinary shares of $1 at $1.30 per share.

Mekong Limited's statement of financial position at 1 October 2016 before it acquired the business of Achara was as follows:

Mekong Limited
Statement of financial position at 1 October 2016

	$000
Non-current assets	
Land and buildings	200
Plant and machinery	75
Motor vehicles	40
	315
Current assets	
Inventory	21
Trade receivables	16
Cash and cash equivalents	32
	69
Total assets	384
Equity and liabilities	
Equity	
Ordinary share capital	
	300
Retained earnings	77
	377
Current liabilities	
Trade payables	7
Total capital and liabilities	384

Once the assets and liabilities of Achara were purchased by Mekong Limited, it was necessary for the accountant to prepare a statement of financial position immediately after the business of Achara had been acquired.

In order to do this, the accountant added the journal entries to Mekong Limited's assets, liabilities, share capital and reserves. (Workings are shown in parentheses.)

	$000
Non-current assets	
Tangible	
Land and buildings $(200 000 + 80 000)	280
Plant and machinery $(75 000 + 28 000)	103
Motor vehicles $(40 000 + 16 000)	56
	439
Intangible	
Goodwill	20
	459
Current assets	
Inventory ($21 000 + 5 000)	26
Trade receivables ($16 000 + 3 000)	19

	$000
Cash and cash equivalents ($32 000 – 20 000)	12
	57
Total assets	516
Equity and liabilities	
Equity	
Ordinary share capital ($300 000 + 100 000)	400
Share premium	30
Retained earnings	77
	507
Current liabilities	
Trade payables ($7 000 + 2 000)	9
Total capital and liabilities	516

TOP TIPS

- If you are required to prepare journal entries in a company's books to record the purchase of a business, do **not** show the entries in the books of the business being taken over.
- Make sure you prepare the journal entries in good form.
- Show all workings when preparing the company's statement of financial position after the new business has been acquired.

ACTIVITY 2

Hamil Limited purchased the business of Abdul, a sole trader, on 30 June 2016. The statements of financial position of both businesses at that date were as follows:

	Abdul	Hamil Limited
	$	$
Non-current assets		
Freehold property	40 000	100 000
Plant and machinery	15 000	60 000
Office equipment	–	14 000
Office furniture	7 000	–
	62 000	174 000
Current assets		
Inventory	4 000	10 000
Trade receivables	6 000	7 000
Cash and cash equivalents	1 000	25 000
	11 000	42 000
Total assets	73 000	216 000
Capital and liabilities		
Capital account	70 000	

	Abdul	Hamil Limited
	$	$
Current liabilities		
Trade payables	3000	
Total capital and liabilities	73000	
Equity and liabilities		
Ordinary shares of $1		150000
Share premium		20000
Retained earnings		40000
		210000
Current liabilities		
Trade payables		6000
Total capital and liabilities		216000

It was agreed that Abdul's assets should be valued as follows:

	$
Freehold property	70000
Plant and machinery	12000
Office furniture	4000
Inventory	2500
Trade receivables	5500

Hamil Limited did not acquire Abdul's bank account. The consideration for the sale was $120000. This was satisfied by the payment to Abdul of $20000 in cash, and the issue to him of 80000 ordinary shares in Hamil Limited.

Required

a Prepare the journal entries in Hamil Limited's books to record the purchase of Abdul's business.

b Prepare Hamil Limited's statement of financial position immediately after the acquisition of Abdul's business.

24.5 Purchase of a partnership business by a limited company

This is the third situation you must know about. The purchase of a partnership business by a company follows a similar procedure to that for the purchase of a sole trader's business. When one of the partners has made a loan to the firm, and the company takes the loan over, it is usual for the company to issue a debenture to the partner concerned. If the rate of interest on the debenture is different from the rate previously received by the partner on the loan, the amount of the debenture will usually ensure that the partner continues to receive the same amount of interest each year as previously. To calculate the amount of the debenture, find the capital sum, which, at the new rate, will produce the same amount of interest. Multiply the amount of the loan by the rate paid by the partnership and divide by the rate of interest on the debenture, as shown in the following example.

Walkthrough

Partner's loan to partnership: \$100 000 at 8% interest per annum. Annual interest = \$8 000.

A 10% debenture producing annual interest of \$8 000 will be $\$100\,000 \times \frac{8}{10} = \$80\,000$.

If the rate of interest on the debenture is 5%, the amount of debenture is:

$\$100\,000 \times \frac{8}{5} = \$160\,000$. (Interest on \$160 000 at 5% per annum = \$8 000.)

TOP TIP

When a debenture is issued to a partner, and the partner is to receive the same amount of annual interest as he/she received before the sale of the firm, check that you have calculated the amount of the debenture correctly.

ACTIVITY 3

Carol has lent \$60 000 at 5% interest per annum to the firm in which she is a partner. A company has offered to buy the partnership business. Part of the purchase price consists of a debenture to be issued to Carol to ensure that she continues to receive the same amount of interest annually as she had been receiving from the partnership.

Required

a Calculate the amount of the debenture to be issued to Carol if the debenture carries interest at 8% per annum.

b Calculate the amount of the debenture if it carries interest at 4% per annum.

ACTIVITY 4

Christofere and Sarah are partners in a business and their statement of financial position at 31 December 2016 is as follows:

	$
Non-current assets	
Land and buildings	50 000
Fixtures and fittings	18 000
Office machinery	12 000
	80 000
Current assets	
Inventory	17 000
Trade receivables	8 000
Cash and cash equivalents	4 000
	29 000

	$
Total assets	109 000
Capital and liabilities	
Capital accounts	
Christofere	50 000
Sarah	35 000
	85 000
Non-current liability	
Loan from Christofere at 10% per annum	12 000
Current liabilities	
Trade payables	12 000
Total capital and liabilities	109 000

The partners have accepted an offer from Digger Limited to purchase the business for $118 000. Digger Limited will take over all the assets and liabilities of the partnership, except the bank account. The partnership assets are to be valued as follows:

	$
Land and buildings	60 000
Fixtures and fittings	14 000
Office machinery	10 000
Inventory	15 000
Trade receivables	6 000

Digger Limited will settle the purchase price as follows:

1. a payment of cash, $28 000
2. an 8% debenture issued to Christofere to ensure that she continues to receive the same amount of interest annually as she has received from the partnership
3. the balance to be settled by an issue of ordinary shares of $1 in Digger Limited at $1.25 per share.

Digger Limited's statement of financial position at 31 December 2016 is as follows:

	$
Non-current assets	
Land and buildings	90 000
Fixtures and fittings	30 000
Office machinery	15 000
	135 000
Current assets	
Inventory	20 000
Trade receivables	5 000
Cash and cash equivalents	60 000
	85 000
Total assets	220 000

	$
Equity and liabilities	
Ordinary shares of $1 each	200 000
Retained earnings	4 000
	204 000
Current liabilities	
Trade payables	16 000
Total equity and liabilities	220 000

Required

Prepare Digger Limited's statement of financial position immediately after the company has acquired the partnership business.

You may be required to show the entries showing the closure of the partnership books. In this case, all the closing entries are shown in a realisation account. The procedure is exactly the same as the dissolution of a partnership in Section 18.8.

Walkthrough

Alan and Brian are in business, sharing the profits and losses equally. Their summarised statement of financial position at 31 July 2016 is as follows:

	$000
Non-current assets	80
Current assets (including the bank balance of $6 000)	40
Total assets	120
Capital and liabilities	
Capital accounts	
Alan	45
Brian	45
	90
Current liabilities	30
Total capital and liabilities	120

They accept an offer from Scott Limited to purchase their business. The company will take over all the assets and liabilities of the partnership, with the exception of the bank account. Scott Limited will pay the partners $50 000 in cash and 100 000 ordinary shares of $1 each.

The first thing which needs to be prepared is a realisation account in the books of the partnership. This is shown below.

Realisation account

	$000		$000
Non-current assets	80	Current liabilities	30
Current assets $(40 000 – 6 000) [1]	34	Bank – cash paid	50
		Ordinary shares	100
Profit on realisation:			
Alan	33		
Brian	33		
	180		180

[1] The bank account has been deducted as this is not bought by Scott Limited.

In order to close the books of the partnership, it is necessary to complete the partner's capital account and then the partnership bank account. These are shown below.

Capital accounts

	Alan	Brian		Alan	Brian
	$000	$000		$000	$000
Bank	28	28	Opening balances	45	45
Ordinary shares	50	50	Profit on realisation	33	33
	78	78		78	78

Partnership bank account

	$000		$000
Opening balance	6	Alan	28
From Scott Limited	50	Brian	28
	56		56

Notice that even though the business is sold at a figure higher than the net book value of the assets taken over, it is treated as a profit on realisation and not goodwill in the partnership books. In this case, the shares are divided between the partners in the profit-sharing ratios. This may not always be the case.

You may also need to include partners' current accounts. The balances on these accounts should be transferred to the respective partner's capital account. There may also be an asset taken over by a partner on the closure of the business, say a car at a valuation. In this case, credit the realisation account, and debit the partner's capital account, with the value of the asset taken over.

Walkthrough

Lee and Mick are in business, sharing the profits and losses equally. Their statement of financial position at 31 October 2016 is as follows:

	$000
Non-current assets	
Property	50
Plant and machinery	20
Motor vehicle	3
	73
Current assets	
Inventory	8
Trade receivables	12
	20
Total assets	93
Capital and liabilities	
Capital accounts	
Lee	30
Mick	30
	60
Current accounts	
Lee	8
Mick	6
	14
Non-current liabilities	
Loan	11
Current liabilities	
Trade payables	6
Bank overdraft	2
	8
Total capital and liabilities	93

The partners accept an offer from Tay Limited for their business. The terms of the sale are as follows:

1. Mick will take over the motor vehicle at its book value.
2. Tay Limited will take over all the remaining assets and liabilities of the business with the **exception** of the bank overdraft and loan.
3. The purchase of the business will be satisfied by:
   - the issue to each partner of 50 000 ordinary shares of $1 each issued at a premium of $0.20
   - Tay Limited will pay $20 000 in cash into the partnership bank account.

The first thing to do is prepare the realisation account in the partnership books. This is shown below.

Lee and Mick
Realisation account

	$000		$000
Property	50	Trade payables	6
Plant and machinery	20	Bank – cash paid	20
Inventory	8	Ordinary shares	120
Motor vehicle	3	Capital a/c Mick – motor vehicle taken over [1]	3
Trade receivables	12		
Profit on realisation			
Lee	28		
Mick	28		
	149		149

[1] The motor vehicle taken over by Mick is credited in the realisation account at the agreed value.

Sometimes there are expenses to pay in connection with the realisation of the partnership. These should be debited to the realisation account and credited to the partnership bank account.

It is now possible to prepare the partners' capital accounts as follows:

Lee and Mick
Capital accounts

	Lee	Mick		Lee	Mick
	$000	$000		$000	$000
Motor vehicle taken over [1]		3	Opening balances	30	30
Ordinary shares [3]	60	60	Current accounts [2]	8	6
Bank – amounts due to each partner [4]	6	1	Profit on realisation	28	28
	66	64		66	64

[1] This is the double entry for the motor vehicle taken over by Mick.

[4] Finally, the capital accounts of each partner are closed by the payment of cash from the business bank account. Notice that because Mick has taken the motor car, the amount of cash due to him will be reduced. If, as a result of all the transactions, any partner is left with a debit balance on their capital account, then they must pay cash into the partnership bank account to cover this. The entries for this are:

- debit partnership bank account
- credit the partner's capital account.

[3] The $1 ordinary shares are issued equally to each partner at a premium of $0.20. Thus, their total value will be $60 000 for each partner ($50 000 × $1.20).

[2] The current account balances of the partners are transferred to their respective capital accounts. If one of the partners had a debit balance on his current account then it would be debited to his capital account. As a result of this transfer the current accounts of the partners are now closed.

The bank account is now completed to show the closure of the partnership business. This is shown below.

Lee and Mick
Bank account

	$000		$000
From Tay Limited [2]	20	Opening balance	2
		Loan [1]	11
		Lee	6
		Mick	1
	20		20

[2] This is the balance of the purchase price paid by Tay Limited. It will be paid into the partnership bank account and used to pay any outstanding expenses, such as the loan or expenses of realisation, and finally, each partner.

[1] As the loan was not taken over by Tay Limited, the partners had to pay it from the partnership bank account.

When all the transactions are completed there should be no balances left on the partners' capital accounts or the partnership bank account.

24.6 Return on investment

It is important that a company purchasing another business succeeds in making the new business as profitable as its existing business. Profitability is measured by expressing profit as a percentage of capital invested. If a company has purchased a business for $100 000 and the business has made a profit of $12 000 in the first year, the profitability is 12%. This is the **return on capital invested**. If it is equal to, or more than, the return on capital the company was earning on its existing business, the investment may be considered to have been worthwhile. If it is less, overall profitability of the business will be **diluted** (or decreased). However, it is better to measure the profitability over a number of years to get a reliable picture.

The new business may have been merged with the existing business so closely that separate results for the new business are not available. In such a case, the incremental (that is, the additional) profit is measured against the additional capital invested in the business.

Walkthrough

X Limited had a capital of $300 000. Its average annual profit was $54 000. Its return on capital was:

$$\frac{\$54\,000}{\$300\,000} \times 100 = 18\%$$

X Limited purchased another business on 1 January 2016 for $100 000, which was settled by the issue to the vendor (the person selling the business) of shares in X Limited.

X Limited's profit for the year ended 31 December 2016 was $84 000. The profitability of X Limited has increased by 3% to 21%:

$$\frac{\$84\,000}{\$400\,000} \times 100 = 21\%$$

A more reliable picture is obtained if the additional profit of $30 000 is calculated as a percentage of the price paid for the new business:

$$\frac{\$30\,000}{\$100\,000} \times 100 = 30\%$$

Thus, X Limited has benefited from the purchase of the new business.

Chapter summary

In this chapter you have developed an understanding of the entries required when the business of either a sole trader or partnership is sold to a limited company. In particular, you should understand the difference between the merger of two businesses and the purchase of a business by a limited company. You should also understand the difference between the purchase of a business and the purchase of a business's assets. You should also be familiar with how to prepare the accounts for a business purchase, including:

- how to prepare a journal entry to record the purchase of a business in the books of the purchasing company
- the preparation of a statement of financial position following the purchase of a business
- goodwill arising on the purchase of a business.

Finally, you should also know how to calculate the return on an investment in a new business.

TOP TIPS

- If it is a merger of two businesses, add the values of the assets and liabilities together after adjusting for any changes such as revaluation of asset values or goodwill.
- If it is a situation of a business being sold to a limited company, make sure you can prepare all the accounts necessary to close the books of account of the seller(s). Also make sure that you can prepare the opening statement of financial position of the new business after the acquisition has taken place, taking into account goodwill on purchase.

Practice exercises

1 The following is the statement of financial position at 30 April 2016 of Eric and Tia, who have been in partnership for a number of years:

	$
Non-current assets	
Land and buildings	878 000
Plant and machinery	100 000
	978 000
Current assets	
Inventory	40 000
Trade receivables	76 000
Cash and cash equivalents	80 000
	196 000
Total assets	1 174 000
Capital and liabilities	
Partners' capitals	1 045 000
Non-current liability	
8% loan from Eric	100 000
Current liabilities: trade payables	29 000
Total capital and liabilities	1 174 000

Additional information

On 30 April 2016, Istaimy plc acquired the business of Eric and Tia. The following matters were taken into consideration when deciding on the price Istaimy plc would pay for the business:

1 No depreciation had been provided on freehold buildings. It was agreed that a provision of $128 000 should have been made.

2 A customer owing $5 000 at 30 April 2016 has since become bankrupt. The partners have been advised that they will receive $0.20 for every $1 the customer owes.

3 Inventory has been valued at cost. Investigation shows that if inventory had been valued at net realisable value, it would have been valued at $28 000. If a separate valuation at the lower of cost and net realisable value had been applied to each item of inventory, it would have been valued at $30 000.

4 The purchase consideration was as follows:
- The long-term loan was satisfied by the issue of a 10% debenture. The amount of the debenture would ensure that Eric received the same amount of interest as he did on his loan to the partnership.
- The issue of 700 000 ordinary shares of $1 each in Istaimy plc. The shares were issued at a premium of $0.20.
- The balance of the purchase price was paid in cash by Istaimy plc.

Required

a Prepare the journal entry to record the purchase of the partnership business in the books of Istaimy plc. Your answer should include cash transactions. **[12 marks]**

b Advise the partners whether or not they were correct in their decision to sell their business to Istaimy plc. Justify your decision by discussing the advantages and disadvantage of the sale. **[5 marks]**

2 On 1 April 2016, Joel Limited acquired the partnership business of Kay and Ola. The partnership statement of financial position at 31 March 2016 was as follows:

	$000
Non-current assets	
Land and buildings	150
Plant and machinery	280
	430
Current assets	
Inventory	150
Trade receivables	141
Cash and cash equivalents	69
	360
Total assets	790
Capital and liabilities	
Capital accounts	
Kay	300
Ola	260
	560
Non-current liability	
Loan from Kay at $12\frac{1}{2}$% per annum	100
Current liabilities	
Trade payables	130
Total capital and liabilities	790

Additional information

1 The assets (including the bank account) and current liabilities were taken over at the following valuations:

	$000
Land and buildings	220
Plant and machinery	170
Inventory	128
Trade receivables	105
Trade payables	138

2 Kay received a 10% debenture from Joel Limited at a value to ensure that she continued to receive the same amount of interest annually as she had received as a partner.

3 The allocation of 300 000 shares in Joel Limited to Kay and Ola at $1.50 per share.

4 Any balance remaining to the partners was paid in cash by Joel Limited. Joel Limited's statement of financial position at 31 March 2016 was as follows:

	$000
Non-current assets	
Land and buildings	1425
Plant and machinery	803
	2228
Current assets	
Inventory	381
Trade receivables	519
Cash and cash equivalents	420
	1320
Total assets	3548
Equity and liabilities	
Ordinary shares of $1 each	1350
Retained earnings	1248
	2598
Non-current liability	
8% debentures (2025/27)	450
Current liabilities	
Trade payables	500
Total equity and liabilities	3548

Required

a Prepare Joel Limited's statement of financial position as it appeared immediately after it had acquired the partnership of Kay and Ola. **[15 marks]**

Additional information

Joel Limited has been earning a regular return of 25% on its capital.

Required

b Calculate the additional amount of profit Joel Limited must make to earn a 25% return on the amount paid to buy the business. **[10 marks]**

Exam practice questions

Multiple-choice questions

1 The following is information about the assets and liabilities of a business:

	Book value	Market value
	$	$
Non-current assets	90 000	101 000
Current assets	32 000	29 000
	122 000	
Current liabilities	(14 000)	14 000
	108 000	

Goodwill is valued at $50 000. What should be paid for the net assets of the business?

A $116 000 **B** $119 000

C $166 000 **D** $169 000

2 A company paid $1.8 million to acquire the business of a sole trader. The sole trader's assets and liabilities were valued as follows:

Non-current assets	700 000
Current assets	300 000
Current liabilities	50 000
Non-current liability	100 000

How much was paid for goodwill?

A $650 000 **B** $750 000

C $850 000 **D** $950 000

3 The statement of financial position of a sole trader is as follows:

	$
Non-current assets	
Goodwill	30 000
Plant and machinery	100 000
Net current assets	50 000
	180 000

A company purchased the business, paying for the plant and machinery and the net current assets, at the valuations shown above. The company settled the purchase price by issuing 200 000 ordinary shares of $1 at $1.50 per share. How much did the company pay for goodwill?

A $30 000 **B** $50 000

C $120 000 **D** $150 000

Total: 3 marks

Structured questions

1 Ann, Bridget and Chris are in partnership, sharing the profits and losses in the ratio of 2 : 2 : 1. At 31 December, their statement of financial position is as follows:

Ann, Bridget and Chris Statement of financial position at 31 December	
	$000
Non-current assets	
Property	100
Motor vehicles	20
	120
Current assets	
Inventory	15
Trade receivables	12
Cash and cash equivalents	3
	30
Total assets	150

Statement of financial position at 31 December	
	$000
Capital accounts:	
Ann	35
Bridget	30
Chris	20
	85
Current accounts:	
Ann	10
Bridget	8
Chris	(3)
	15
Non-current liabilities:	
Loan from Ann	30
Current liabilities:	
Trade payables	20
Total capital and liabilities	150

The partners agree to sell their business to Janty Limited. The terms of the sale are as follows:

1 Ann will take over a motor vehicle at a book value of $4 000 as part of her settlement.

2 Janty Limited will take over all the remaining assets and liabilities of the partnership, with the exception of the bank account.

3 Janty Limited values the partnership at $152 000.

4 Ann is entitled to interest on her loan at 8% per annum. She will receive a 10% debenture from Janty limited which will give her the same level of income as she received on the loan. This debenture will be repayable in 2025.

5 The remaining consideration was made up of:
   - 80 000 ordinary shares of $1 each issued at $1.25 each. These are split between the partners in their profit-sharing ratios
   - the balance of the consideration was paid in cash.

6 Expenses of the realisation amounted to $1 000.

Required

a Explain the difference between the purchase of a business and the purchase of business assets. **[3 marks]**

b Prepare the following accounts to close the partnership business:

  i the partnership realisation account **[10 marks]**

  ii the partners' capital accounts. **[7 marks]**

Additional information

Since the sale of the partnership, Ann has seen a business which she would like to buy, but requires capital of $150 000 to purchase it. She has no spare cash and, following the sale of the business, Janty Limited has not paid any dividends on the shares issued to the partners, but they have paid Ann the interest on her debenture. She has approached the directors of Janty Limited about them buying back her shares and repaying the debenture early.

The directors have said that they will pay her $0.75 for each ordinary share and 75% of the value of the debenture.

Her only other option is to take a bank loan for the full amount of the business she wants to buy. If she takes it, she will also have to take an overdraft of a further $20 000 as working capital. Interest on the loan is payable at 5% per annum for 20 years and on the overdraft at 7% per annum.

She estimates that if she buys the business, in the first three years her expected profit before bank interest will be $15 000 in year 1, $20 000 in year 2 and $35 000 in year 3.

Required

c Advise Ann whether or not she should accept the offer from Janty Limited to buy her shares and repay the debenture. Justify your answer. **[5 marks]**

Total: 25

2 Brian and Maye have been trading successfully for many years as sole traders. On 1 April 2015, they agree to merge their businesses to form a partnership.

Required

a Explain the difference between a merger and the sale of a business. **[4 marks]**

Additional information

1 At 1 April 2016, their summarised statements of financial position are as follows:

	Brian	**Maye**
	$000	**$000**
Non-current assets	120	180
Current assets:		
Inventory	30	25
Trade receivables	60	40
Cash and cash equivalents	2	1
	92	66
Total assets	212	246
Capital and liabilities:		
Capital account	195	217
Current liabilities	17	29
Total capital and liabilities	212	246

The terms of the merger are as follows:

2 Assets and liabilities are valued as follows:

	Brian	Maye
	$000	$000
Non-current assets	130	190
Inventory	25	24
Trade receivables	55	39

3 Brian values the goodwill of his business at $30 000. Maye values the goodwill of her business at $20 000. They agree that no goodwill account will remain in the books of account of the new partnership.

4 Future partnership profits and losses will be shared equally.

Required

b Calculate the opening balance on each partner's capital account at 1 April 2015. **[7 marks]**

c Prepare the opening statement of financial position of the partnership at 1 April 2015. **[5 marks]**

Additional information

1 In addition to the profit-sharing ratio, the partners have also agreed the following:

- interest on capital at 5% per annum
- annual salaries: Brian $6 000, Maye $4 000.

2 At 31 March 2016, the partnership made a profit for the year of $27 000.

Required

d Prepare the appropriation account for the partnership for the year ended 31 March 2016. **[4 marks]**

Additional information

Before forming the partnership, Brian was making an average profit for the year of $10 000. Maye was making an average profit for the year of $20 000.

Required

e Advise the partners whether or not they were right to form the partnership. Justify your answer. **[5 marks]**

Total: 25

Chapter 25
Consignment and joint venture accounts

Learning objectives

By the end of this chapter you will learn:

- what consignment accounting is
- how to prepare the ledger accounts for consignment transactions
- how to value the closing inventory for consignment transactions
- how to record the consignment account details in the income statement of the consignor
- the advantages and disadvantages of setting up a consignment venture
- what a joint venture is
- how to prepare ledger accounts for joint ventures
- how to calculate the profit or loss for a joint venture
- the advantages and disadvantages of joint ventures.

25.1 Introduction

This chapter will concentrate on two topics: the preparation of accounts relating to consignments and the preparation of accounts dealing with joint ventures. In some ways they are similar types of business ventures. Both involve a trading relationship between two parties for a specific purpose and a specified time period. However, the accounting treatment is different for both. There are a number of terms with which you need to become familiar. These are emboldened, so take some time to jot them down to remember them when you come across them. The first topic considered is that of consignment accounting.

25.2 Consignment accounts

The nature of a **consignment** is for someone, say, in one country, to act as a selling agent for the goods of someone else in another country. For example, Patel runs a clothing business in India, making high-quality shirts and dresses. He sends some goods to Christchurch Traders in New Zealand, who sell the goods on his behalf in their country. Christchurch Traders will take a commission for the goods they sell and send the balance of the funds back to Patel in India, after deducting any expenses paid by them.

The person sending the goods in this case (Patel) is known as the **consignor**. The business receiving the goods (Christchurch Traders) is known as the **consignee**. The consignee is only acting as the agent of the consignor. This means that the ownership of the goods remains with Patel. Quite often the parties agree between themselves that any expenses incurred by the consignee will be reimbursed by the consignor. There is extensive legislation surrounding the relationship between the two parties.

> **KEY TERMS**
>
> **Consignor:** The party which transfers goods for sale to the consignee.
>
> **Consignee:** The party which receives goods for sale.

25.3 Recording the transactions in the books of account of the consignor

As a consignment transaction involves two parties, it will be necessary to consider how it is recorded in the books of account of both the consignor and consignee. The first aspect will be to look at how a consignment transaction is recorded in the books of account of the consignor – the person who sends the goods to another party who will sell them on behalf of the consignor.

Walkthrough

Patel, who is based in India, enters into a consignment arrangement with Christchurch Traders based in New Zealand. Patel agreed to send a consignment of dresses to the owner of Christchurch Traders.

The following transactions took place between them in month 1:

1. Patel sent goods which cost $10 000 to Christchurch Traders.
2. Patel paid shipping costs of $1 000.
3. Christchurch Traders advised Patel that they had paid landing fees of $2 000. Patel agreed that he would pay for these.
4. At the end of the month, Christchurch Traders advised Patel that they had sold goods at a total cost of $15 000. They were entitled to a 10% commission on the sales made.
5. Patel received a schedule from Christchurch Traders of inventory unsold at the end of the month. Patel calculated the cost and added a portion of the shipping costs, to give a total cost of inventory on hand of $4 500.
6. Christchurch Traders sent $11 000 by bank transfer to Patel.

In order to record these transactions, the following three accounts need to be opened in Patel's books of account:

1 Consignment account with [...the name of the consignee...], in this case Christchurch Traders. In this account the costs of the consignment are debited and the sales value credited. This is shown below.

Consignment with Christchurch Traders account

	$		$
Month 1			
Goods sent to consignee	10000	Christchurch Traders – sales	15000
Bank – shipping costs paid [3]	1000	Balance [1] c/d	4500
Christchurch Traders – expenses	2000		
Christchurch Traders – commission	1500		
Income statement – profit [2]	5000		
	19500		19500
Month 2			
Balance b/d	4500		

[3] The shipping costs paid by Patel are included in this account.

[2] The figure for the profit ($5000) is the balancing figure on the account. This would be transferred to the income statement.

[1] The balance on the consignment with Christchurch Traders account is the value of inventory unsold at the end of month 1. It must always be valued at the lower of cost or net realisable value. In this case, cost means the cost of purchase or manufacture, plus any expenses incurred by the seller ($1000) in getting the goods to the premises of the consignee. This would be shown in the current assets of Patel's statement of financial position.

2 Consignee's account, in this case Christchurch Traders. This account is, in effect, a trade receivable's account (Christchurch Traders) in the books of Patel and is shown below.

Christchurch Traders account

	$		$
Month 1			
Consignment account – sales [1]	15000	Expenses paid [2]	2000
		Commission [2]	1500
		Bank [3]	11000
		Balance c/d [4]	500
	15000		15000
Month 2			
Balance b/d	500		

[1] The account is debited with the sales made by Christchurch Traders at the selling price of the goods.

[3] The money sent by Christchurch Traders is credited to the account. The debit will be in Patel's bank account.

[2] Any expenses paid by Christchurch Traders are credited to the account.

[4] The balance on Christchurch Traders account is the balance to date. There will be other entries in the account during month 2 as more sales are made and more cash is sent over to Patel. This balance would also appear in the current assets section of Patel's statement of financial position.

3 Goods sent on consignment account. The final account the accountant has to prepare is a goods sent on consignment account. This is shown below.

Goods sent on consignment account			
Month 1		**Month 1**	
	$		**$**
Income statement [2]	10 000	Consignment with Christchurch Traders a/c [1]	10 000

[2] The goods sent on consignment account is closed by transferring the balance to Patel's income statement. This will match the cost of goods manufactured at cost, or the purchase price of goods sent out on consignment.

[1] The account is credited with the cost of the goods sent to Christchurch Traders. The debit entry is in the first account: consignment with Christchurch Traders account.

If any goods are returned by the consignee (Christchurch Traders) as unsold, then Patel will send them a credit note for their value. This is posted by debiting the goods sent on consignment account and crediting the consignment with Christchurch Traders account.

25.4 Recording the transactions in Patel's income statement

At the end of the trading period, the transactions of the joint venture, together with Patel's own transactions, will be recorded in his income statement.

Walkthrough

Assume that at the start of month 1, Patel had no opening inventory of goods. During month 1, Patel purchased goods to the value of $55 000. Of these, $10 000 represents the value of goods sent on consignment to Christchurch Traders.

All the remaining purchases were sold in month 1 by Patel for $80 000, leaving no closing inventory.

When the accountant prepares Patel's income statement it will show the following:

Patel Income statement for month 1		
	$	**$**
Sales of own goods		80 000
Profit on consignment with Christchurch Traders [1]		5 000
		85 000
Less: cost of sales		
Purchases	55 000	
Less: goods sent on consignment to Christchurch Traders [2]	(10 000)	(45 000)
Gross profit for the month		40 000

[2] The cost of the goods sent to Christchurch Traders is **deducted** from the total purchases made by Patel.

[1] The profit on the consignment of $5 000, recorded in the consignment with Christchurch Traders account, is entered. It has been added to the sales of his own goods made by Patel.

Presenting the income statement in this way will mean that Patel may lose track of the gross profit made on his own sales. In order to overcome this, set out below is an alternative presentation.

Patel Income statement for month 1		
	$	$
Sales of own goods		80 000
Less: cost of sales		
Purchases	55 000	
Less: goods sent on consignment to Christchurch Traders	(10 000)	(45 000)
Gross profit for month on own sales		35 000
Add: profit on consignment with Christchurch Traders		5 000
Gross profit for the month		40 000

Note: Using either approach, the shipping costs ($1 000) of the consignment paid by Patel are not included in the income statement. They were included in the consignment with Christchurch Traders's account and, as a result, have been accounted for when calculating the profit to date on consignment when calculating the profit of $5 000.

Either way is acceptable. However, doing it this way allows Patel to check his gross margin.

Finally, when the accountant prepares the statement of financial position at the end of month 1 for Patel, included in the current assets will be two balances. One being the balance on the consignment with Christchurch Traders account of $4 500, the other being the balance of $500 in Christchurch Traders account. These are shown in the extract from the statement of financial position below.

Patel Extract from statement of financial position at end of month 1	
	$
Current assets	
Inventory with consignee	4 500
Trade receivables	
Due from Christchurch Traders	500

ACTIVITY 1

At the start of month 2, Bertie had an inventory of goods of $8 000.

During month 2:

- Bertie purchased more goods costing $24 600.
- Bertie sent goods to Calum on consignment, invoicing him for their cost of $16 000.

The following information is available at the end of month 2:

1 Calum advised Bertie that he had paid $450 shipping costs for the goods sent on consignment. Bertie agreed to reimburse Calum for this.

2 Calum advised that he had sold some of the goods for $25 000, and had unsold inventory valued at cost of $3 200.

Required

Prepare the following in Bertie's ledger for month 2:

- consignment with Calum account
- Calum's account
- goods sent on consignment account.

25.5 Recording the transactions in the books of the consignee

The situation to record the transactions in the books of the consignee is much simpler. There is no need for Christchurch Traders to record the inventory, as it does not belong to them. All they need to do is to maintain an account for Patel. All the double entries can be made from that account.

Patel account

Month 1	$	Month 1	$
Bank – expenses paid	2 000	Customers' account / sales ledger control	15 000
Income statement – commission	1 500		
Bank	11 000		
Balance c/d [1]	500		
	15 000		15 000
Month 2			
		Balance b/d	500

[1] Notice that the balance on this account is equal and opposite to the balance on Christchurch Traders account in the books of Patel. This will appear as a current liability in the statement of financial position in the books of Christchurch Traders.

ACTIVITY 2

The following transactions took place between Nettie in England, and Alfonso in Spain during month 1:

1. Nettie sent goods which cost $15 000 to Alfonso.
2. Nettie paid shipping costs of $1 800.
3. Alfonso advised Nettie that they had paid landing fees of $1 200. Nettie agreed that she would pay for these.
4. At the end of the month Alfonso advised Nettie that he had sold goods at a total cost of $16 000. He was entitled to a 10% commission on the sales made.
5. Nettie was advised by Alfonso that there was $3 000 of inventory unsold at the end of the month.
6. Alfonso sent $10 000 by bank transfer to Nettie.

Required

a. Prepare the relevant ledger accounts in the books of Nettie to record these transactions for month 1. Bring down the balances at the end of the month.
b. Prepare Nettie's account in the books of Alfonso for month 1. Bring down the balance on the account.

25.6 Goods sent to consignee at more than cost

There may be a situation where the consignor invoices goods to the consignee at a price higher than the cost of the goods. This is similar to a manufacturing business transferring goods from the manufacturing account to the trading section of the income statement at a factory profit. As with a manufacturing business, it is necessary to value closing inventory of unsold goods at cost. Thus, any unrealised profit must be excluded from the closing inventory in the books of account of the consignor. This is illustrated below.

Walkthrough

Chas, in England, sent a consignment of goods to Abdul, in Pakistan, in month 3. The goods cost $8 000, but were invoiced to Abdul at cost plus 25%.

At the end of month 3, Abdul advised Chas that goods at an invoice value of $2 500 remained unsold.

During the month, Abdul had sold goods and invoiced customers for $16 000. Abdul was entitled to 10% commission on the goods sold. He had sent Chas $12 000 by bank transfer. No costs were involved in any of the transactions.

Prepare the relevant ledger accounts in the books of account of Chas to record the transactions for month 3. Bring down the balances on the accounts.

Consignment with Abdul account

Month 3		**Month 3**	
	$		**$**
Goods sent to Abdul [1]	10 000	Abdul – sales	16 000
Abdul – commission	1 600	Goods sent on consignment	2 000
Income statement – profit	8 900	Balance c/d	2 500
	20 500		20 500
Month 4			
Balance b/d	2 500		

[1] The goods will be invoiced to Abdul at cost plus 25% ($8 000 + 25% = $10 000).

Abdul account

Month 3		**Month 3**	
	$		**$**
Consignment account – sales	16 000	Commission	1 600
		Bank	12 000
		Balance c/d	2 400
	16 000		16 000
Month 4			
Balance b/d	2 400		

Inventory reserve account

Month 3	$	Month 3	$
Balance c/d	500	Goods sent on consignment a/c [1]	500
		Month 4	
		Balance b/d	500

[1] At the end of month 3, Abdul has informed Chas that he has unsold goods valued at $2 500. As far as Abdul knows, this is the cost price of the goods. However, they include the profit of 25% which Chas added to them when he invoiced Abdul. The profit included in those goods has to be removed as it has not yet been earned.

The calculation is:

$2 500 ÷ 5 = $500 unrealised profit included in the inventory held by Abdul.

Goods sent on consignment account

Month 3	$	Month 3	$
Income statement	7 500		
Consignment with Abdul [1]	2 000		
Inventory reserve	500	Consignment with Abdul	10 000
	10 000		10 000

[1] The profit added to the cost of the goods transferred has been reversed by debiting the goods sent on consignment account, and crediting the consignment with Abdul account.

The profit included in the closing inventory has been adjusted by the creation of an inventory reserve account. The balance on this account will be offset against the balance brought down on the consignment with Abdul account:

	$
Balance b/d on consignment with Abdul account	2 500
Less: unrealised profit	500
Balance shown in statement of financial position at the end of month 3	2 000

This will mean that the inventory shown in Chas's statement of financial position will be at cost, again in line with the prudence concept.

TOP TIPS

- Work carefully through the data given.
- Make sure you are familiar with which transactions are recorded in the books of which party.
- Be prepared to write a discursive answer about the results you have calculated or the way the consignment should be developed in the future.

ii The joint venture account. This is, in effect, an account which records the profit or loss on the joint venture. It is debited with all the expenses of the venture and credited with the revenue from the venture. The balance will be the profit or loss on the joint venture.

Joint venture account

	$		$
Joint venture bank account	90 000	Joint venture bank account	150 000
Zohir – expenses paid	4 000		
Kagendo – expenses paid	5 000		
Zohir – share of profit on venture [1]	25 500		
Kagendo – share of profit on venture [1]	25 500		
	150 000		150 000

[1] The joint venture account records the profit in this case (or the loss) on the venture.

iii Separate accounts for each party to the joint venture

Zohir account

	$		$
Joint venture bank account [4]	79 500	Joint venture bank account [1]	50 000
		Joint venture account [2]	4 000
		Joint venture account – profit [3]	25 500
	79 500		79 500

Kagendo account

	$		$
Joint venture bank account [4]	80 500	Joint venture bank account [1]	50 000
		Joint venture account [2]	5 000
		Joint venture account – profit [3]	25 500
	80 500		80 500

[4] Finally, the accounts are closed by transferring the balance due to Zohir from the joint venture bank account.

[2] These are the double entries for the expenses in respect of the venture paid by Zohir and Kagendo.

[3] The profit due to each party is transferred from the joint venture account.

[1] This is the capital introduced by each party.

The balance represents the amount of capital introduced into the venture by Zohir and Kagendo plus their share of the profit, less any expenses paid by them. So for Zohir, this will be:

$$\$(50\,000 + 4\,000 + 25\,500) = \$79\,500.$$

As the venture is completely separate from their own business, neither party has any need to pay money they receive from it into their business bank account. However, if they had drawn money from their business bank account to fund the venture, they may want, or need, to have to repay their business. They are also both personally liable for any tax due on their share of profit from the venture.

Situation 2 Each party to the joint venture keeps a record of only the transactions they pay in respect of the venture

In this case, the party to the venture creates accounts within their own ledgers to record transactions made by them in connection with the joint venture. They may also keep a memorandum account of all the transactions made by both parties to account for the profit or loss made.

Walkthrough

Nawaz and Jamil each run their own building company. They form a joint venture to build and sell houses. They agree that the profit or loss on the joint venture will be shared equally. Each partner will only keep the records relating to their own transactions in connection with the joint venture. Nawaz makes the following transactions in this respect:

1. uses some of his own materials to build some of the properties; these cost $80 000.
2. pays legal costs in connection with selling the properties of $5 000
3. sells some of the completed houses for $128 000
4. is advised by Jamil that he has paid total expenses of $98 000 in connection with the joint venture and made sales of $140 000.

Nawaz's accountant prepares the following accounts in the books of Nawaz:

i A joint venture account to record the transactions made by Nawaz. This is shown below.

Joint venture account

	$		$
Purchases account [1]	80 000	Bank – sales made	128 000
Bank account – expenses [1]	5 000		
Income statement – share of profit	42 500		
Bank – Jamil, final settlement	500		
	128 000		128 000

[1] In this case the joint venture account shows only the double entry for transactions made by Nawaz.

ii A memorandum joint venture account to calculate the total profit or loss on the venture and record Nawaz's share in his books of account. The fact that this is a 'memorandum' account means that it is not part of the double-entry system for Nawaz. It is an income statement for the venture.

Memorandum joint venture account

	$		$
Expenses paid by Nawaz	85 000	Sales by Nawaz	128 000
Expenses paid by Jamil	98 000	Sales by Jamil	140 000
Share of profit – Nawaz	42 500		
Share of profit – Jamil	42 500		
	268 000		268 000

Notice that in this case, Nawaz has had to pay money to Jamil. Looking at the memorandum joint venture account, Nawaz seemingly makes a profit on the venture of $43 000 ($128 000 – $85 000). Jamil seemingly makes a profit of $42 000 ($140 000 – $98 000). However, as they agree to share profits equally, both only receive $42 500. Nawaz has to pay the $500 to Jamil as a result of this.

Situation 3 Each party to the joint venture keeps a record of all the transactions

In this case, each party records all the transactions of the joint venture, whoever pays them.

Walkthrough

Using the information from the walkthrough above, if Nawaz had kept full records of all the transactions in respect of the joint venture, the following accounts would appear in his ledger:

1 A joint venture account. This account is also effectively an income statement for the joint venture. It is almost identical to the memorandum joint venture account in situation 2, except the expenses are shown in more detail. It is shown below.

Joint venture account

	$		$
Purchases account	80 000	Bank – sales by Nawaz	128 000
Bank account – expenses paid by Nawaz	5 000	Jamil – sales made by Jamil	140 000
Jamil account – expenses paid by Jamil	98 000		
Income statement – share of profit – Nawaz [1]	42 500		
Jamil – share of profit	42 500		
	268 000		268 000

[1] This is Nawaz's share of the profit on the joint venture and will be transferred to his income statement for the year. It will probably be shown after his profit for the year in his income statement. This way, it will allow Nawaz to see that his regular business is operating efficiently.

2 An account for Jamil as set out below. This account completes the double entry for the transactions made by Jamil and is posted to the joint venture account in situation 1 above.

Jamil account

	$		$
Joint venture account – sales	140 000	Joint venture account – expenses paid	98 000
Bank – balance due to close venture	500	Joint venture – share of profit	42 500
	140 500		140 500

Note: In the books of Jamil, the joint venture account would be identical. However, Jamil would maintain an account for Nawaz. This is shown below.

Nawaz account

	$		$
Joint venture account – sales	128 000	Joint venture account – expenses paid	85 000
		Joint venture – share of profit	42 500
		Bank – balance due to close venture	500
	128 000		128 000

TOP TIPS

- Work carefully through the data given.
- Make sure you are familiar with which transactions are recorded in the books of which party.
- Be prepared to write a discursive answer about the results you have calculated or whether or not the parties should enter into another joint venture in the future.
- Compare the structure of a joint venture with a partnership and be prepared to compare each and make recommendations as to which is the best option.

25.9 The advantages and disadvantages of joint ventures

In many ways the advantages and disadvantages of joint ventures are similar to those of consignments.

Advantages:

- They allow both parties access to a wider market.
- Once the venture is completed there is no need for either party to become involved with the other again.
- There are no legal formalities necessary, other than drawing up a joint venture agreement, between the two parties. This will cover such things as who has what responsibilities, and how profits and losses will be shared.
- Allows parties to the venture to specialise in what they do best.

Disadvantages:

- One party may feel they are doing all the work, yet not receiving what they think is a fair share of the profits.
- It is likely that both parties to the venture will also be running their own businesses. Thus, there may be conflict over whether their own business or the joint venture takes priority.
- There has to be complete trust between both parties to the joint venture. Without that there is potential for fraud or even for the venture to fail if one party decided to leave it.

Like a consignment arrangement, there is no reason for either party to enter into a joint venture unless they want to. Also like a consignment arrangement, it is important that proper records are kept to ensure there should be no disputes, and a formal contract between both parties.

Chapter summary

In this chapter you have learnt the basics of consignment and joint venture accounts, including how to prepare the accounts, to calculate profit and loss, and the advantages and disadvantages of each type of account. In addition, you should also know:

- how to value the closing inventory for a consignment transaction
- how to record the consignment account details in the income statement of the consignor.

Practice exercise

1 Marty and Jerry both run successful building businesses. They agree to form a joint venture to build six new properties. Details of the joint venture are as follows:

- i Both parties will only keep records of their own transactions with regard to the joint venture.
- ii Marty purchases materials valued at \$32 600 which he uses to build the houses. He also pays legal fees of \$4 100.
- iii Jerry purchases materials for the joint venture valued at \$30 000.
- iv Marty sells three houses for \$40 000 each. Jerry sells the remaining three properties for \$42 000 each.
- v The joint venture is then completed and Marty and Jerry agree that any profit on the joint venture will be shared equally.

Required

- a Prepare the joint venture account in Marty's books of account.
- b Prepare the joint venture memorandum account in the books of account of Marty to calculate the profit or loss on the venture.
- c Calculate how much money should be paid by one party to the other at the end of the joint venture.

Additional information

Following the success of the joint venture, Marty and Jerry are considering forming a partnership to buy land and build more houses. This will be in addition to running their own existing businesses.

Required

- d Advise Marty whether or not he should enter into a partnership with Jerry by discussing the advantages and disadvantages of doing so.

Structured questions

1 Krystal has a manufacturing business in New Zealand making high quality ladies' fashions. She wants to expand her market into China and appoints Chen as her agent in Beijing. On 1 March, Krystal made shipments of goods to Chen which were valued at $29 700. At 31 March, the following additional information is available:

March 1	Krystal paid shipping fees of $4 900 and export charges of $3 300 on the goods sent to Chen.
5	Chen paid landing fees of $4 400.
31	Chen had sent $8 000 to Krystal by bank transfer.

Additional information

1 Krystal agreed that Chen should receive a 10% commission on all goods sold in China.

2 Krystal's income statement at 31 March showed a consignment profit of $6 500. Her statement of financial position at that date included consignment inventory of $3 800.

Required

a Prepare the following for the month of March in the books of Krystal:

i consignment with Chen account **[8 marks]**

ii Chen account. **[4 marks]**

b Prepare Krystal's account in the books of Chen for the month of March. **[4 marks]**

Additional information

Krystal is considering two options:

- entering into a partnership with Chen to help her trade in China
- forming a limited company, with Chen and her as the shareholders, to trade in China.

Required

c Advise Krystal whether or not she should choose either option, or stay in a consignment arrangement. Justify your answer by discussing the advantages and disadvantages of the plans she is considering. **[9 marks]**

Total: 25

2 Alan started a business in England on 1 April 2015, selling bicycles. During the first year of trading, Alan bought 2 500 bicycles at $100 each. He shipped 1 000 of these to his agent Zac in Botswana. He also sold 1 300 of the bicycles in England. The following information is available:

	$
Freight charges paid by Alan	7 200
Landing dues paid by Zac	3 800
Cash remitted by Zac to Alan	85 000

Alan agrees to pay Zac commission on the bicycles he sells. This will be paid at a rate of 10%.

Alan's income statement for the year ended 31 March 2016 included the following item:

	$
Consignment profit	9 600

Alan's statement of financial position at 31 March 2016 included the following item:

	$
Inventory of bicycles – Botswana	9900

Required

a Prepare the consignment account with Zac in the books of Alan for the year ended 31 March 2016. **[7 marks]**

b Prepare Zac's account in the books of Alan for the year ended 31 March 2016. **[5 marks]**

c Calculate the number of unsold bicycles which Zac still has at 31 March 2016. **[4 marks]**

d Explain the principle which you have used to value the unsold bicycles. Make reference to any relevant accounting concept or standard. **[4 marks]**

Additional information

Alan is unsure whether or not to continue with the consignment arrangement. He feels that he is paying Zac too much commission. He is considering entering into a joint venture with Zac for all future trade in Botswana.

Required

e Advise Alan which course of action he should take. Justify your answer. **[5 marks]**

Total: 25

3 Bob and Sue both run successful businesses selling motor cars. On 1 August, they enter into a joint venture to sell a new model. The following information is available for the month of August:

August	**1**	Sue bought 10 new vehicles at a cost of $100 000. They have agreed that each will have five of the new cars at their respective showrooms.
	2	Bob paid Sue $50 000 as his contribution to the cost of purchasing the new cars.
	5	Bob paid Sue a further $8 000 towards the cost of licences and insurance for the new vehicles.
	6	Bob received his five new vehicles.
	31	Bob advised Sue that he has sold all his five cars for $80 000 and banked the money in his own bank account.
	31	Sue advised Bob that she has sold all her cars to a single customer for $70 000, having given the customer a discount for buying all the vehicles. They agreed to share this discount equally.

Each agreed to record their own transactions in their own books of account, and that profits on the venture would be shared equally.

Required

a Explain two other ways the transactions for the joint venture could be recorded rather than each party recording their own transactions. **[4 marks]**

b Prepare the following accounts in the books of Bob:

i joint venture **[4 marks]**

ii joint venture memorandum account. **[6 marks]**

Additional information

In September, Bob learnt that Sue had only sold four of the new vehicles in August. She had sold the fifth vehicle privately for $20 000. He also found out that he should only have paid $6 000 towards the cost of licences and insurance for the new cars.

Required

c Advise Bob what course of action he should take when he learns about this information. Justify your answer with suitable calculations showing how much he has lost as a result of Sue's actions. **[5 marks]**

Additional information

Some months later, Sue approached Bob and asked him if he would like to form a partnership to operate both garages. She produced accounts signed by her accountant, who was also her brother, showing a profit for the year considerably greater than Bob was making from his garage.

Required

d Explain the difference between a joint venture and a partnership. **[3 marks]**

e Advise Bob whether or not he should go into partnership with Sue. Justify your answer. **[3 marks]**

Total: 25

Chapter 26
Computerised accounting systems

Learning objectives

By the end of this chapter you will be able to:

- understand the need for a business to introduce a computerised accounting system
- discuss the advantages and disadvantages of introducing a computerised accounting system into a business
- understand how a business can transfer its accounting data onto a computerised accounting system
- understand and discuss the ways in which the integrity of the accounting data can be ensured during and after the transfer to a computerised accounting system.

26.1 The need for a business to computerise its accounting data

Up to now we have considered the ways in which books of account are kept by someone manually writing up the journals and ledgers. However, for a number of years now many businesses have either used ready-made computer accounting packages or employed someone to write the necessary computer programs to enable them to process the firm's accounting data using a computer. With the improvement in computer technology, this process will only gather pace, such that within a few years, it is unlikely that any business will use handwritten books of account. Such a change can bring many benefits to an organisation. It can also cause some problems and perhaps leave the business owner in a dangerous situation in terms of being open to fraud or cyber attack.

Students may not need to be familiar with specific computer packages or how to use them, but you should be able to discuss the process of transferring manual records to the computer and the benefits this brings. Most computerised accounting packages operate in the same way and produce the same information, so no specific package will be mentioned. The basic package can be amended very easily for use by any type of business, from sole trader, partnership and limited company, to not-for-profit organisations.

TOP TIP

Be prepared to answer discursive questions on the advantages and disadvantages of computerising an accounting system.

26.2 The process of transferring a manual accounting system to a computerised accounting system

There are two possible situations which a business may encounter when considering computerising their accounts:

a When setting up a business. In this case, the owner(s) may not even consider a manual bookkeeping system but buy a **computerised accounting system** from the start. They will have various options open to them, such as buying a full computerised accounting system or package. This will provide them with all the journals and ledgers of a manual accounting system but operated on a computer.

b Transferring an existing manual bookkeeping system to a computerised accounting system. The best way to illustrate this is by the following walkthrough.

KEY TERM

Computerised accounting system: A set of programs which allow the accounts to be prepared using a computer. An alternative to manual bookkeeping.

Walkthrough

To illustrate the process of computerising a manual accounting system, the business of Karly and Viji will be used. The business is run by two partners, Karly and Viji. They have been in partnership for a number of years, buying and selling garden furniture and equipment. Their business operates from a single store. They buy goods on credit and sell to customers on both a cash and credit basis. Their accounting year-end is 31 December.

At the present time they employ a bookkeeper who maintains a manual accounting system. The books of account which are kept comprise:

- sales and purchase journals
- sales and purchase returns journals

- cash book
- petty cash book
- general journal
- nominal ledger.

At the end of each financial year, the bookkeeper prepares a trial balance. This is then given to an accountant together with all the journals and ledgers. The accountant prepares the firm's income statement and statement of financial position, charging the business for the service he or she provides.

For some time both partners have been complaining that they spend more time chasing invoices and outstanding customer debts, and worrying if all the sales have been invoiced, than running their business. They have to wait for several months after the end of the year until the external accountant has prepared their financial statements in order to assess how well their business has performed. Even then, the reports the accountant provides do not give them enough information to help them develop their business.

The bookkeeper is due to retire at the end of the current financial year. Karly's son Dilip has just completed a business degree and has offered to help the partners transfer their existing financial records to a new computerised accounting package. Dilip has prepared a step-by-step guide on how to do this.

Step 1 Decide which package to choose

The partners could ask someone to write programs specifically for their business. However, as it is a normal trading business, they can buy a computerised accounting package from an IT dealer or via the internet.

ACTIVITY 1

Identify the advantages and disadvantages of the following ways to obtain a computerised accounting package:

a from an IT provider that runs a business in your local town

b buying it via the internet

c asking someone who is computer literate to write a computerised accounting package for the business.

Step 2 Set up the chart of accounts

Karly and Viji have decided to buy an accounting system from a local IT specialist in their town. The next thing they need to decide is which packages they will buy. After discussing things with Dilip, they have decided to buy a system which gives them computerised access to all their existing manual ledgers and journals. They could have opted to buy only a nominal ledger package and keep the cash book, petty cash book and journals manually.

ACTIVITY 2

Discuss whether Karly and Viji were correct to buy all the available packages for their computerised accounting system, or whether they should have still kept some of their ledgers and journals on a manual basis.

The package they buy will have a chart of (ledger) accounts. This will be set out in a particular format. Usually with the non-current assets listed first, then the current assets, current liabilities, non-current liabilities, capital, income (sales) and expenses. Each account name will have a numerical code assigned to it. For example:

1001 Freehold land and buildings at cost
1002 Freehold land and buildings accumulated depreciation
1200 Bank current account
3000 Capital
4000 Sales 1
5000 Purchases 1
7000 Wages

The number of ledger accounts the package contains will be more than the business requires. For example, there are often three different sales and purchases accounts. This will allow a business owner to identify different types of items bought and sold. For instance the partners could keep separate sales and purchases accounts for tables, chairs, sun loungers and so on. Whilst the situation here involves a partnership, the chart of accounts can be amended for use by a limited company or sole trader.

ACTIVITY 3

Identify how many categories of sales and purchases Karly and Viji should use for their business.

The accounts will also need to have their title changed to make the system personal to the business. For instance, in those listed above, the partners may decide to change account 4000 to Sales – garden furniture. Sensibly they should use the 5000 code to match the sales code and call it 5000 – Purchases – garden furniture.

Once again, having discussed this with Dilip, they have changed the ledger account descriptions to fit their business. This is the correct way to do things. The owner of any business should always make the computerised accounting system fit and match the business. Never change the business to fit the system.

Step 3 Decide on the date to transfer the balances from the manual system to the computer

The most sensible time will be at the end of their financial year. When the bookkeeper has taken the trial balance there will be a complete list of accounts the business uses. The balance on each of the accounts will also be available. At the present time, all their books of account and the trial balance are passed to their accountant. He then prepares the income statement and statement of financial position for the partners. As we have seen, the income statement is a 'history book' of what has taken place over the trading year. There is nothing to be done to the figures. Once agreed they can't be changed.

The most important document to use when setting up the computer accounting system will be the statement of financial position. This document will contain all the opening balances for the start of the new financial year. It is these balances which will be used for the next step of the process.

Step 4 Reconcile the accounts which are entered in the statement of financial position

This is a sort of internal audit function. It is one of the most important parts of the process, as the more accurate the data which is entered into the new system, the easier it will be to check the report data the accounting system produces. The balances on the non-current assets will be taken from the trial balance. In this case, the cost of the non-current asset and the accumulated depreciation relating to it will be entered into the relevant computer ledger account.

However, the most important thing is to carry out the following reconciliations:

- the sales ledger control account with the total of the individual balances on the credit customers' accounts
- the purchase ledger control account with the total of the individual credit supplier's accounts.

A detailed analysis of the individual balances on the customers' and suppliers' accounts must be prepared. For example, for each customer set out the date, invoice number, credit note number and amount included in the total balance on their account. These will be entered into the computerised sales and purchase ledger. They will provide an aged receivables and payables analysis to help the partners manage the business more efficiently.

The partners have identified that at the end of the year their major credit customer, Carla, owed them $6020. When they investigated this they found the figure was made up of three invoices, one for $2520 dated 20 December, one for $2940 dated November and a final one for $560 from October.

They had issued a credit note in November for damaged goods on the October invoice, but the customer has claimed that other items should also be credited as they too were damaged.

ACTIVITY 4

a Draft a worksheet with suitable headings which could be used to post these to an account set up on the computer for Carla.

b Explain the immediate benefit they have obtained from this process.

Once they have all this information it is possible to set up an account for each customer. The partners need to remember that these will be the opening balances at the start of the new accounting year. Setting the correct start date is vital for accurate information. Most computer packages will total the postings and transfer this total to the sales and purchases ledger control accounts as the opening balances on the system.

In addition to reconciling all the customers and supplier accounts the following also needs to be done:

- Complete a bank reconciliation.
- Reconcile the petty cash balance in the ledger with the amount of physical cash.
- The partners may want to record all their separate product lines. Thus a reconciliation of all the inventory, both quantity and value, should be done.
- Reconcile the balances on any non-current liabilities such as long-term loans.

At this stage as much preparatory work as possible should be done.

ACTIVITY 5

a Explain the purpose of the partners reconciling the bank balance, petty cash figure and long term loan figures at this time.

b Apart from inventory identify four other account balances the partners need to confirm at this stage.

The final things which the partners need to take into account at this stage are the opening accruals and prepayments. At the moment you will be familiar with carrying down accrued and prepaid expenses and income on the individual ledger accounts, such as rent paid or receivable.

Most computer packages will have an account called accruals and one called prepayments. For example, at the end of 31 December 2015, the partners told their accountant that there was an unpaid telephone invoice of $200. During the year they had paid $1 400 from the bank for telephone expenses.

Up to now you would record this in the telephone ledger account as follows:

Karly and Viji
Telephone account

Date	Details		Date	Details	
2015		$	2015		$
Dec 31	Bank	1 400	Dec 31	Income statement	1 600
31	Balance c/d [1]	200			
		1 600	2016		1 600
			Jan 1	Balance b/d [1]	200

[1] The accrued expense is carried down to the start of the new year. This increase in the expense in the income statement will be shown as an other payable on the statement of financial position.

However, the accrual would be treated as follows when using a computerised accounting system:

Karly and Viji
Telephone account

Date	Details		Date	Details	
2015		$	2015		$
Dec 31	Bank	1 400	Dec 31	Income statement	1 600
31	Accruals [1]	200			
		1 600	2016		1 600
			Jan 1	Accruals [3]	200

Karly and Viji
Accruals account

Date	Details		Date	Details	
2015		$	2015		$
Dec 31	Balance c/d [2]	200	Dec 31	Accruals [1]	200
2016		200	2016		200
Jan 1	Telephone [3]	200	Jan 1	Balance b/d [2]	200

[1] The debit balance on the telephone account for the accrued telephone expense of $200 is credited to an accruals account at the end of the financial year (31 December).

[2] The balance on the accruals account is carried down at 31 December in the accruals account. This will appear on the statement of financial position at 31 December as an other payable.

[3] At the start of the new year (1 January) there is a debit entry of $200 in the accruals account. This is matched by the credit in the telephone account. At that date this will clear the balance on the accruals account. The telephone account at that date will have a credit balance, leaving it exactly the same as under the first method.

- **Space can be saved**. There will be no need to keep ledgers and books of prime entry. However, it is important that a sensible filing system is set up for the reports taken from the computer.
- From the point of view of the owners, there is a lot more information about the performance of the business which can be obtained by the **increased number of reports on the performance of the business that the system can generate**. We have already mentioned reports showing how long individual customers' debts have been outstanding (aged receivables report). A similar report can be provided in respect of credit suppliers. The owners can produce reports which will tell them which products are selling most quickly or generating the most profit per unit. Budget reports can be produced, as can cash flow forecasts, all of which will allow the owners to focus on the efficient performance of the business.
- **The year end information can be processed more quickly** and passed to the external accountant to prepare the financial statements. One advantage which is sometimes quoted is that the computer will save the costs of an external accountant, who may reduce their charge to the client. In practice this may well not be the case.
- Computerised accounting **improves the accuracy of the financial records**. This may be true in a well-structured and efficiently run system. However, if the system is not properly monitored and regular reconciliations made, this may not be the case. The accuracy of the data entered into the computer must also be checked. It is easy to enter an invoice for $800 as $8 000. The computer does not know that mistake has been made.

26.4 The disadvantages of a computerised accounting system

With the advantages also come the disadvantages:

- **The initial cost of the system**, plus the cost of regular updates and upgrades, say when tax rates change for wages and salaries. Although a basic system may seem relatively cheap if other packages are also purchased, such as wages and inventory control, the costs can soon mount up. There may also be a need to employ an IT specialist to set up the system at the start. In our case the partners were lucky. Dilip was already qualified to undertake the work.
- We saw earlier that one of the first decisions to make was **which system to choose**. The system also needs to be properly maintained.
- **Staff training**. There will be a need to train Karly and Viji on how to operate the system. It is also essential to ensure that their bookkeeper is also trained properly. This should prevent errors in posting. It might also mean that the partners pay an annual fee to the company who installed the system to help with any problems as and when they occur.
- **Guarding against the system crashing**. There will be a need to take regular backups of the data and the system. Ideally a backup should be taken at the end of each day and stored away from the business premises. Some firms operate a system of using three backups, rotating the discs every three days. This is sometimes called the grandfather, father, son system. It should ensure that at the very worst, only the last three days' work needs to be re-input if the whole system crashes.
- **Internal threats to the data**.
  - Karly and Viji will have information in the system that they do not want their clerk to see, perhaps their drawings or shares of profit. To overcome this it is necessary to set up levels of access to the system and password protect the private areas. For example, the clerk may be stopped by the system from accessing the partners' private accounts.

  - As the computer can save time in processing data, it may be possible for one person to process all the data. This can lead to potential fraud if the clerk is unscrupulous. The partners should set up their own monitoring checks on the work of the clerk, perhaps making it a rule that any journal entries must be countersigned by a partner, or two partners have to sign cheques to suppliers.
  - The system can produce poor, wrong and misleading information very quickly. It is vital that regular reconciliations are undertaken and that the data entered is verified at the time of input.
- **External threats to the data**. It is essential that a good anti-virus system is installed and that the computer system generally is as well protected from cyber attack as possible.
- **Information overload**. The system can generate more reports than are needed by the partners. It is important that the partners decide what information and reports they want on a regular basis to help them manage the business.

At first glance it may appear that there are more disadvantages than advantages. However, if the system is properly set up, run and managed, the partners will have more information at their fingertips to enable them to run the business more efficiently and profitably.

TOP TIP

Follow the process outlined for transferring an existing manual accounting system to a computer.

Chapter summary

In this chapter you have learnt the advantages and disadvantages of introducing a computerised accounting system into a business, and why many businesses feel there is a need for this. You should also understand some of the practical challenges for businesses that are associated with transferring accounting data onto a computerised accounting system, including how this happens and the ways in which the integrity of the accounting data can be ensured during and after transfer to a computerised system.

Practice exercises

1 Explain the process of transferring a manual accounting system to a computerised accounting system.

2 State **three** advantages and **three** disadvantages of computerising a manual accounting system.

3 Discuss ways in which the integrity of the accounting data can be ensured during the transfer to a computerised accounting system.

4 John is a sole trader who uses a computerised accounting system. His year end is 31 May. During the year ended 31 May 2016, he paid shop rental of $42 000 from the bank. This included a prepaid amount of $6 000.

Required

a Prepare the rental account for the year ended 31 May 2016.

b Prepare the prepayments account at 31 May 2016. (Note: you can use either T-accounts or the running balance method).

c Explain how the balance brought down on the prepayment account is treated at 1 June 2016.

Chapter 27
Analysis and communication of accounting information

Learning objectives

In this chapter you will learn:

- the limitations of financial statements
- how to analyse and interpret financial statements
- how to calculate ratios from the financial statements of a business
- how to use ratios to analyse the performance of a business
- how to explain (and how not to explain) ratios.

27.1 The limitations of financial statements for shareholders and other interested parties

The purpose of financial statements, such as the income statement and statement of financial position, is to present information in a meaningful way. That is why items in financial statements are placed in groups of similar items: non-current assets, current assets, current liabilities, and so on. It also explains why you should compile financial statements with every item in its correct place.

Accounting standards are intended to ensure that items included in financial statements and described in similar terms are calculated, as far as possible, on the same bases. Companies Acts and accounting standards require companies to add numerous notes to their financial statements to throw more light on the items in the accounts.

To be useful, information must be clear, complete, reliable and timely. In spite of the efforts of numerous accounting standards to ensure some sort of uniformity in the preparation of financial statements, the published accounts of limited companies have a number of limitations as communicators of information:

- They are not clear to people who have an inadequate knowledge of accounting and finance.
- The information they give is not complete. Legislation and accounting standards recognise that companies are entitled to keep certain information confidential because publication would give competitors an unfair advantage.
- The comparability of financial statements is only relative because companies are permitted to exercise a fair degree of subjectivity in selecting their accounting policies. Depreciation, provisions for doubtful debts, inventory valuation and treatment of goodwill are examples of areas where there can be some variability in the application of judgements and the making of estimates.
- Companies are allowed to depart from accounting standards if such departure is justified by the nature of their business and will improve the quality of the information provided by the accounting statements.
- By their very nature, published accounts are of historic interest. They may not be published for many months after the end of the financial year they cover. In the meantime, many circumstances may have changed: the economy may have improved or worsened; the political scene may have altered; new technologies may have been developed; fashions may have changed. A company's performance may have improved or worsened between the date of the statement of financial position and its publication.

The directors' report may help to overcome some of the limitations of the financial statements, but not completely.

Only people with some knowledge of accounting are able to make much sense of the mass of figures in a company's financial statements. Even accountants need to interpret the figures before they are able to understand their significance. As a useful tool for interpreting accounts, accountants calculate ratios that relate certain items in the accounts to other items where there should be some sort of sensible relationship.

The users of financial statements were covered in Chapter 22. However, it is important that you know the internal and external users of the financial statements and the reasons why they review them.

Internal users

User	Reasons for reviewing the financial statements
Owner of the business In the case of a sole trader or partner, these are the people directly involved in the day-to-day running and management of the business.	**1** To assess the overall performance of the business. **2** To identify problem areas, such as poor gross margin or changes in the gross or net margin. **3** To identify areas where corrective action can be taken to improve future performance.
Existing shareholders These are the owners of limited companies, although as we have seen, they may not take any part in the day-to-day management of the company.	**1** To assess the overall performance of the business. **2** To consider the security of their investment. **3** To look at the return they receive both in terms of dividend paid and capital growth of their shares They can then compare this performance with other investment opportunities.
Managers and directors	Often the salary or bonus paid to these employees is based on the performance of the business in certain key areas. Thus they will be interested in the key performance ratios which measure their salary or bonus.
Workers	They too will be interested in the performance to see if future pay or salary increases will be made.

External users

User	Reasons for reviewing the financial statements
Banks	**1** They will be interested to assess whether a loan or overdraft should be granted to the business. **2** If one already exists, then they will be interested to see if the business can maintain the repayments.
Future shareholders	A different group from existing shareholders, they will be comparing the returns from several businesses to decide which to invest in.
Investors This group is different from a bank as it may be, say, an individual who has been asked by the owner to invest funds in the business.	To determine the return they will receive and the security of any investment.
Suppliers to the business This group is most likely the trade suppliers who come under the heading of trade payables.	**1** Their interest will be to decide whether or not to supply a business. **2** Alternatively, if they do supply it, to check that they will be paid on a regular basis.
Customers of the business	They will be assessing the performance to see if the business will be able to supply them in the future.

User	Reasons for reviewing the financial statements
Government	**1** To determine the level of tax which will be charged on the profits of the business. **2** To decide whether or not to give a grant to the business.
Local community	Many of the local community may be customers of the business, or may be seeking employment with it. Thus, they will be interested in seeing if the business will continue to operate in the future.
Trade unions	Their members will be employed by the business. Thus, they will look at profitability to see about future pay increases.
General community	They will be interested in whether or not the business is operating ethically towards its workers, customers and the environment.

27.2 A pyramid of ratios

The ratios that accountants use may be represented as a pyramid, which classifies the ratios into useful types and shows how they relate to one another.

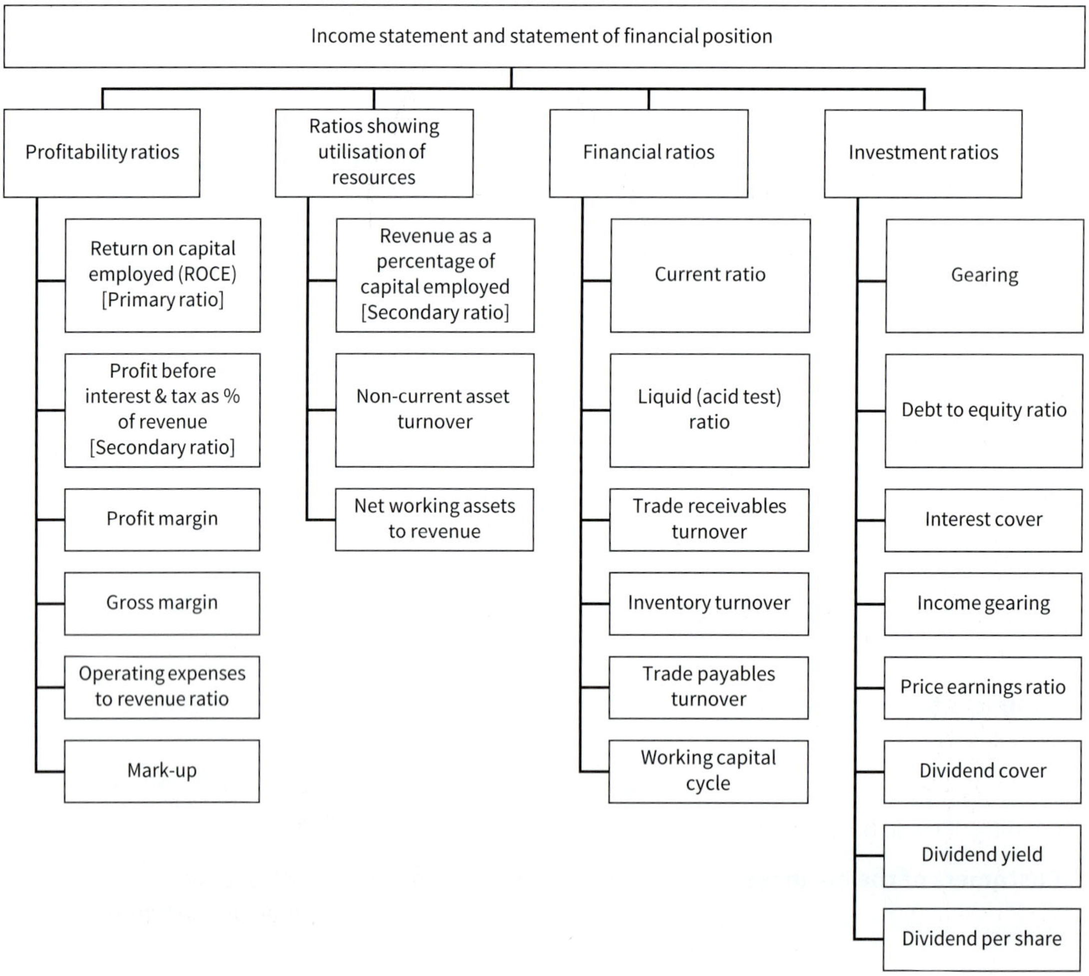

27.3 How to calculate and analyse ratios

All the ratios shown in the pyramid are explained in Sections 27.4 to 27.7.

Lladnar Limited
Income statement for the years ended 31 December

	2016		2015	
	$000	**$000**	**$000**	**$000**
Revenue		1 600		1 200
Cost of sales				
Opening inventory	54		42	
Purchases	1 166		800	
	1 220		842	
Less: closing inventory	(100)	(1 120)	(54)	(788)
Gross profit		480		412
Distribution costs		(184)		(160)
Administrative expenses		(80)		(70)
Profit from operations		216		182
Finance costs		(15)		(10)
Profit for the year		201		172

Lladnar Limited
Statement of changes in equity for the years ended 31 December

	2016	2015
	$000	**$000**
Retained earnings at 1 January	118	11
Profit for the year	201	172
Transfer to general reserve	(60)	(40)
Dividends paid	(30)	(25)
Balance at 31 December	229	118

Lladnar Limited
Statements of financial position at 31 December

	2016	2015
Assets		
Non-current assets	924	670
Current assets		
Inventory	100	54
Trade receivables	200	115
Cash and cash equivalents	29	100
	329	269
Total assets	1 253	939

Statements of financial position at 31 December		
	2016	**2015**
Equity and liabilities		
Share capital and reserves		
Ordinary shares	400	400
General reserve	280	220
Retained earnings	229	118
	909	738
Non-current liabilities		
10% debenture 2023/2025	150	100
Current liabilities		
Trade payables	194	101
Total equity and liabilities	1 253	939

Most ratios are appropriate for both limited companies and other businesses.

The ratios explained and analysed in this chapter are calculated to three decimal places but rounded to two decimal places.

TOP TIP

Read the question to see how many decimal places are required and ensure you make your calculations to the correct number.

27.4 Profitability ratios

KEY TERM

Profitability ratios: A group of ratios which will help to assess the profitability over a period of time.

The primary ratio: return on capital employed (ROCE)

The test of a good investment is its profitability, that is, the reward it yields on the amount invested in it. (Profit and profitability should not be confused. Profit is expressed as an amount of money: $172 000 for 2015 and $201 000 for 2016 in Lladnar Limited's case; profitability is a ratio that relates profit to the amount invested.) The **first (or primary) profitability ratio** for investors in a business is the **return on capital employed**. It relates profit, before interest and tax (profit from operations), to the capital employed in the business. The formula is:

$$\frac{\text{profit before interest and tax}}{\text{capital employed}} \times 100$$

or, alternatively:

$$\frac{\text{profit from operations or operating profit}}{\text{capital employed}} \times 100$$

Perhaps an easy way to remember it is:

$$\frac{\text{profit}}{\text{capital employed}} \times 100$$

Capital employed is the total of the ordinary shares + reserves + non-current liabilities.

TOP TIP

Debentures and other long-term loans are included in capital employed.

Lladnar Limited's return on capital employed is:

2016	2015
$\frac{216}{1059} \times 100 = 20.40\%$	$\frac{182}{838} \times 100 = 21.72\%$

The capital employed in each year is the total of the ordinary shares + general reserve + retained earnings + 10% debenture.

So for 2016, it is ($400 + 280 + 229 + 150) = $1 059

and for 2015, it is ($400 + 220 + 118 + 100) = $838.

TOP TIP

Always make sure you add a percentage sign if the ratio should be expressed as a percentage.

It is most likely that you will be asked not only to calculate the ratio, but also to comment on what it identifies. This is an important part of the question and often carries high marks. For each of the ratios calculated in this chapter, a comment on what it shows will be included. Note the wording used in each case, it is important and will be discussed in more depth later.

The comments for Lladnar's return on capital employed are set out below.

Comment In 2015, $21.72 of every $100 of revenue was left as profit from operating the business before payment of any finance costs or taxation. In 2016, the return has decreased by just over 1%, to 20.40%. Although only a small change, this contrasts with the preferred result which would have been to see an increase over the previous year.

Return on equity

An alternative to calculating the return on capital employed is to calculate the return on equity. This ratio identifies the return made by the business for the ordinary shareholders. The decision whether they should remain as ordinary shareholders in the company or look for a better return elsewhere can be based on this ratio. The formula is:

$$\frac{\text{profit after tax or profit for the year}}{\text{ordinary shares issues + reserves}} \times 100$$

In effect, we are dividing the profit for the year which belongs to the ordinary shareholders. (Profit after tax or profit for the year ÷ ordinary shares issued × 100.)

Lladnar Limited's return on equity is:

2016	2015
$\frac{201}{909} \times 100 = 22.11\%$	$\frac{172}{738} \times 100 = 23.31\%$

Comment In 2015, the company made a return of $0.23 on every $1 owned by the ordinary shareholders. In 2016, this decreased, or became slightly worse, to $0.22, or by $0.01. This is only a small change and although the ordinary shareholders would have hoped to see an increase, they should not be worried. They should, however, compare this with the return they could expect on a similar investment in a suitable alternative.

TOP TIP

Notice that the fact the ratio can be expressed as a percentage means that the final figure is also a dollar and cents amount.

Profit before interest and tax (profit from operations) as a percentage of revenue/sales (or profit from operations as a percentage of revenue/sales)

This ratio is a measure of how efficient the management is at generating profit from trading activities. Finance costs and tax charged are excluded.

For Lladnar, the profit before interest and tax calculated as a percentage of sales is:

2016	2015
$\frac{216}{1600} \times 100 = 13.50\%$	$\frac{182}{1200} \times 100 = 15.17\%$

Comment Profit before interest and tax has fallen by 1.67%. When the gross margin is calculated, that ratio will be seen to have fallen even more (by 4.33%). It is not surprising, therefore, to find that the profit before interest and tax has fallen, although it should not fall by the same amount, as most overheads are more or less fixed and do not vary with turnover.

Profit margin

This ratio shows how much profit for the year is generated from revenue. It can be calculated by the following formula:

$$\frac{\text{profit for the year (after interest)}}{\text{revenue}} \times 100$$

For Lladnar Limited this is:

2016	2015
$\frac{201}{1600} \times 100 = 12.56\%$	$\frac{172}{1200} \times 100 = 14.33\%$

Comment The percentage has fallen by 1.77% from 14.33% in 2015 to 12.56% in 2016, even though turnover has risen by 33 % from $1 200 000 to $1 600 000. This is quite significant, as with an increase in sales it would be expected that the company would earn more profit. Yet this is not the case. Initially, the causes for the change in the profit percentage may be analysed by examining gross margin and the overheads as a percentage of revenue.

This ratio can be calculated by using either the profit after interest and before tax or the profit for the year.

The most likely cause for a decrease in this margin is that the business has not been able to control its expenses as well as the previous year. Likewise an increase in the margin will be as a result of better control of expenses.

However, further investigation is needed.

Gross margin

Both gross margin and mark-up were discussed in relation to preparing accounts from incomplete records (see Chapter 16). However, they will be reviewed again here, starting with gross margin. This ratio shows how much gross profit each dollar of revenue generates. For many businesses, this ratio will be broadly constant until the business or the suppliers change their pricing. For example, a garage selling petrol might expect to earn a gross margin of about $0.05 for every $1 of petrol sold. A furniture retailer on the other hand, would be looking for about $0.25 for every $1 of revenue.

The formula for gross margin is

$$\frac{\text{gross profit}}{\text{revenue}} \times 100$$

For Lladnar Limited this is:

2016

$$\frac{480}{1600} \times 100 = 30\%$$

2015

$$\frac{412}{1200} \times 100 = 34.33\%$$

Comment Gross margin has decreased by 4.33% from 34.33% to 30.00%. In theory, the gross margin should match the margin the business expects to make on all its sales. In practice, it is not as simple as that because most businesses sell more than one kind of good and a different mark-up may be added to each kind. The gross margin is affected by changes in the mix of the different products making up the turnover.

The reduction in the gross margin may be explained by a number of factors:

- a rise in the price of goods purchased may not have been passed on to customers
- it may have been necessary to purchase the goods from a different supplier at a higher price
- the selling price of the product may have had to be cut:
  - to increase the volume of sales
  - to fight competition from other businesses
  - as an introductory offer for a new product
  - as a result of seasonal sales
  - to dispose of out-of-date or damaged inventory
  - to increase cash flow when the business is short of cash
- the cost of sales may have been increased by the theft of inventory.

TOP TIP

The important thing to remember is that it is a change in the selling price per unit or the purchase cost per unit which will increase or decrease the gross margin.

An increase in sales or reduction in purchases will not have any effect on the margin. The business can buy one bottle of water for $1 and sell it for $2. This will earn a gross margin of 50%. If it increases sales and purchases to two bottles which it bought for $1 and sold for $2 total sales and purchases have increased but the margin is still 50%.

Operating expenses to revenue

Having identified that the gross margin is partly to blame for the loss in profit, the next thing to determine is whether or not managers have been able to control the business expenses.

This is done by calculating the operating expenses to revenue ratio.

The formula for this is:

$$\frac{\text{operating expenses (administrative expenses + distribution cost + finance costs)}}{\text{revenue}} \times 100$$

For Lladnar Limited the operating expenses expressed as percentage of revenue is:

2016	**2015**
$\frac{279\ (184+80+15)}{1600} \times 100 = 17.44\%$	$\frac{240\ (160+70+10)}{1200} \times 100 = 20\%$

TOP TIP

The overhead percentage may be calculated more quickly by finding the difference between the gross margin and profit margin.

Comment Although sales have increased in 2016 by 33%, the ratio of overheads to sales has decreased from 20% to 17.44%. However, the decrease in overheads as a percentage of sales has not been enough to cover the decrease in gross margin. This, in turn, has led to a decrease in the profit margin.

Notice how this is a good example of how ratios are linked together and a decrease in one can lead to a decrease in others. Sometimes, overheads may increase as a percentage of sales, but the increase may not match the increase in gross margin. The reason is that most overheads, such as rent, do not vary as a result of an increase in sales. Other overheads may vary, but not in proportion to sales. Salespeople's remuneration, for example, may consist of a fixed salary plus a bonus based on sales.

It is possible to analyse overheads further by expressing the individual items as percentages of sales but this is usually of very limited value because of the absence, in many cases, of any direct link between the individual overheads and sales.

Mark-up

The final ratio to consider in this section is **mark-up**. This ratio measures by how much the business marks-up its cost of sales to arrive at the selling price. The formula for this ratio is:

$$\frac{\text{gross profit}}{\text{cost of sales}} \times 100$$

For Lladnar the calculations are:

2016	2015
$\frac{480}{1120} \times 100 = 42.86\%$	$\frac{412}{788} \times 100 = 52.28\%$

Comment This ratio has fallen quite significantly in 2016, which is bad for the company. This fall also goes a long way to identifying why the gross margin fell during 2016. The company may have had to reduce the mark-up because of more competition in the market place. Alternatively, it might have had to buy from more expensive suppliers and been unable to pass on the full increase in purchase price to its customers.

Overall, in terms of profitability, the ratios calculated for Lladnar, show a worrying fall in gross margin, which in turn has reduced the profit margin. Management needs to take action to try to reverse this trend in 2017.

TOP TIP

If you are asked to decide which ratios to calculate, don't calculate both gross margin and mark-up. They are identifying the same thing in different ways and may not be as useful as calculating, say, gross margin, profit margin and expenses to revenue ratios.

27.5 Ratios showing the utilisation of resources

The profitability of a business depends on how efficiently it uses its resources, and the next group of ratios is designed to test the **utilisation of resources** by the business.

KEY TERM

Utilisation of resources: A group of ratios which will help to assess the efficiency with which the resources of a business have been used over a period of time.

Revenue as a percentage of capital employed

Capital invested in a business must be utilised efficiently if it is to produce a good ROCE. Capital of $100, producing sales of $300, is being used more efficiently than the same capital producing sales of only $200. Sales are expressed as a percentage of capital employed. This is found by dividing the revenue by the capital employed.

For Lladnar Limited, this is:

2016	2015
$\frac{1600}{1059} \times 100 = 151.09\%$	$\frac{1200}{838} \times 100 = 143.20\%$

Comment In 2015, sales were only about 1½ times the amount of capital employed. This is may be low, but further comment would be unhelpful without knowing the kind of business being carried on by Lladnar Limited. A low percentage may be normal for some businesses. The percentage for 2016 has only improved slightly.

The ratio of profit before tax and interest percentage, and revenue as a percentage of capital employed, are known as **secondary ratios** because they help to explain the primary ratio (ROCE). If the two ratios are multiplied together, they give the primary ratio:

$$\frac{\text{profit for the year}}{\text{revenue}} \times \frac{\text{revenue}}{\text{capital employed}} = \frac{\text{profit for the year}}{\text{capital employed}}$$

(Sales in the denominator of the first fraction cancel out sales in the numerator of the second fraction to give the third fraction.) For Lladnar Limited:

2016	2015
$13.5\% \times 151.09\% = 20.40\%$	$15.17\% \times 143.20\% = 21.72\%$

Utilisation of total assets

It is important for managers of a business to determine how well the non-current assets are being used to generate revenue. The main reason for purchasing a non-current asset is for it to either generate revenue for the business or reduce cost, both of which will hopefully increase the profit. This is done by calculating the non-current asset turnover ratio, using the following formula:

$$\frac{\text{net revenue}}{\text{total net book value of non-current assets}}$$

This will give the number of times the non-current assets are turned over.

Non-current asset turnover

The non-current asset turnover ratios for Lladnar are:

2016	2015
$\frac{1600}{924} = 1.73$ times	$\frac{1200}{670} = 1.79$ times

TOP TIP

In this case, the ratio calculated is expressed as the number of 'times'. Always make sure you include this.

Comment There has not been a significant change in the ratio in 2016. During 2016, the company purchased new non-current assets. If those assets are not owned for a full year, they will not earn a full year's revenue and, unless information is given about the dates the assets were purchased, further comment is impossible.

Net working assets to revenue

This ratio measures how effective management has been in generating sales from its 'working' assets. Working assets means its inventory (which it bought to resell and make profit), trade receivables and trade payables.

The formula to calculate this ratio is:

$$\frac{\text{Net working assets (inventory + trade receivables − trade payables)}}{\text{revenue}} \times 100$$

For Lladnar, the calculations are:

2016	2015
$\frac{106\ (100 + 200 - 194)}{1600} \times 100 = 6.63\%$	$\frac{68\ (54 + 115 - 101)}{1200} \times 100 = 5.67\%$

Comment This ratio has improved in 2016, indicating that management has been more active and successful in generating sales from its working assets.

27.6 Financial ratios

It may seem strange to have a group of ratios known as financial ratios, when everything we have looked at so far has involved money! However, most textbooks will class the following ratios under the main heading of financial ratios.

The first two ratios in this section though are known as liquidity ratios. Liquidity is a measure of how well the company is able to pay its day-to-day running expenses. There are two main ratios to consider.

Current ratio

This shows the relationship between the current assets of the business and its current liabilities.

Current assets are the funds out of which a business should pay its current liabilities; it should never have to sell non-current assets to pay its trade suppliers. It follows that there should be a margin of safety between the current assets and the current liabilities. The current ratio expresses the margin in the form of a true ratio:

current assets : current liabilities

Lladnar Limited's current ratios are:

2016	2015
329 : 194 = 1.70 : 1	269 : 101 = 2.66 : 1

TOP TIP

The right-hand figure in the ratio should always be expressed as unity or :1.

Comment The ratios show that, in both years, although the current assets comfortably exceed the current liabilities, the safety margin has been reduced in 2016. Textbooks often state that the current ratio should be between 1.5 : 1 and 2 : 1 to take account of slow-moving inventory and slow-paying customers, but much depends upon the kind of business. While a low ratio could signal danger, a high ratio may indicate that a business has resources that are not being used efficiently. High levels of inventory, trade receivables and cash mean that capital is lying idle in the business instead of being used profitably.

The current ratio is sometimes described as an indication of liquidity but that is incorrect. The liquidity of a business depends upon the liquidity of its current assets. A **liquid asset** is one that is in the form of cash (cash and bank balances), or in a form that may become cash in the short term (trade receivables). Inventory is not a liquid asset – no buyer has yet been found for it! The current ratio calculation includes inventory, so is not a measure of liquidity. Liquidity is measured by the **liquid (acid test) ratio**.

Liquid (acid test) ratio

The liquid (acid test) ratio excludes inventory from the calculation and shows the proportion of liquid assets (trade receivables and cash) that is available to pay the current liabilities. The ratio is calculated as:

current assets − inventory : current liabilities

The liquidity ratios of Lladnar Limited are:

2016	**2015**
(329 – 100) : 194 = 229 : 194	(269 – 54) : 101 = 215 : 101
= 1.18 : 1	= 2.13 : 1

Comment The liquidity ratio has fallen in 2016. Textbooks often state that the liquidity ratio should not fall below 1 : 1, or perhaps 0.9 : 1. This is generally a good guide, but as we have seen, supermarkets' sales are on a cash basis while they enjoy a period of credit before they have to pay for their supplies. In the meantime, they have a constant inflow of cash from sales. Their liquidity ratio may not exceed 0.8 : 1. On the other hand, a motor car manufacturer will be looking for more current assets than current liabilities. Without knowing more about Lladnar Limited's business, further comment may not be helpful. However, it would not appear to be supermarket!

It is now necessary to look at the individual items within the current assets and current liabilities to see how they impact on the performance of the business. Trade receivables, inventory and trade payables may be examined first in a little more detail.

Trade receivables turnover (also known as average collection period)

A business should have set a limit on the amount of time it allows its customers to pay (credit period). Many customers take longer than the time allowed and the customers' ratio calculates the average time customers are taking to pay.

The formula is:

$$\frac{\text{trade receivables}}{\text{credit sales}} \times 365 \text{ days}$$

The trade receivable turnover for Lladnar Limited is:

2016

$$\frac{200}{1600} \times 365 = 45.63, \text{ or } 46 \text{ days}$$

2015

$$\frac{115}{1200} \times 365 = 34.98, \text{ or } 35 \text{ days}$$

TOP TIP

Only credit sales should be used in the formula. If you are given both cash and credit sales, or perhaps cash sales are a certain percentage of total sales, the cash sales must be excluded.

As there is no information about any of Lladnar Limited's sales being on a cash basis, it has been assumed that all sales were on credit. It is sensible to round all fractions of days up to the next day.

TOP TIP

Generally, the answer should always be rounded **up** to the nearest whole day. This is the case even if the answer comes out at, say 26.12. This should be rounded **up** to 27 days.

Comment The customers are taking 11 more days in 2016 to pay their bills. It is usual in many businesses to allow customers 30 days, or 1 month, to pay. The company seems to be losing control over its customers' payments and to have a deteriorating cash flow. Customers' payments may be affected by a deterioration in the national economy or in the business sector. A business may try to attract new customers by offering more favourable payment terms. When customers are slow to pay there is an increased risk of incurring irrecoverable debts.

Inventory turnover

Inventory turnover is the rate at which the inventory is turned over, or the time that elapses before inventory is sold. This ratio is important for the following reasons:

- The more quickly inventory is sold, the sooner the profit on it is realised and the more times the profit is earned in the financial year.
- A slow turnover may indicate that excessive inventory is held and the risk of obsolete or spoiled inventory increases. Large quantities of slow-moving inventory means that capital is locked up in the business and is not earning revenue.

However, different trades have their own expected rates of inventory turnover. Food shops will expect to have a fast inventory turnover if their food is not to deteriorate before it is sold. On the other hand, shops selling furniture, refrigerators, radios and television sets, etc. will have slower inventory turnovers, while manufacturers of large items of plant and shipbuilders will have a very long inventory turnover periods. Generally, fast-moving inventories have lower profit margins than slow-moving inventories. (Compare the profit margin to be expected on the sale of food with that expected on the sale of motor cars.)

The formula for calculating the rate of inventory turnover is:

$$\frac{\text{cost of sales}}{\text{average inventory}}$$

where average inventory = (opening inventory + closing inventory) ÷ 2.

It is important to take average inventory because closing inventory may not be representative of the normal inventory level. If opening inventory is not given, use closing inventory for the calculation. This calculation will give the number of **times a year** the inventory is turned over. It is also acceptable to express it as the average number of days or months inventory remains in the business before it is sold.

The rate of inventory turnover in times per year for Lladnar Limited is:

2016

$$\frac{1120}{(54+100)\div 2} = 14.55 \text{ times a year}$$

2015

$$\frac{788}{(42+54)\ |\ 2} = 16.42 \text{ times a year}$$

Inventory turnover can also be calculated as a number of days. This is done by dividing 365 (the days in the year) by the number of times inventory is turned over each year.

For Llandar Limited this is:

2016

$$\frac{365}{14.55} = 26 \text{ days}$$

2015

$$\frac{365}{16.42} = 23 \text{ days}$$

Notice that the number of days doesn't work out exactly. Your answer must always be **rounded up** to the next whole day.

Comment The rate of inventory turnover has slowed a little in 2016. Without more knowledge about the company's business, further comment would only be speculation.

> **TOP TIP**
> Always check whether the question is asking for the inventory turnover as the number of times or number of days.

The cash at bank

It is not necessary to make up a formula for a cash ratio; it is sufficient to refer to the balances and, in the case of Lladnar Limited, to draw attention to the fact that the bank balance has fallen from $100 000 to $29 000. When a balance at bank is converted into an overdraft, it may be appropriate to recognise the fact with a suitable comment. For example, the change here could be a result of the increase in the trade receivables turnover and a reduction in the number of times the inventory turns over. Both of these factors will cause cash to flow out of the business, resulting in a decrease in the bank balance over the two years.

Trade payables turnover (also known as the average payment period)

This is calculated by using the formula:

$$\frac{\text{trade payables}}{\text{purchases on credit}} \times 365$$

> **TOP TIP**
> As with trade receivables turnover, only credit purchases must be used in the calculation. Any cash purchases are excluded. If the question doesn't give any way of calculating credit purchases, the figure for purchases in the cost of sales is normally used.

Assuming that all Lladnar Limited's purchases were made on credit, the trade payables turnover periods are:

2016	2015
$\frac{194}{1166} \times 365 = 61$ days	$\frac{101}{800} \times 365 = 47$ days

Comment The company is taking 14 days longer to pay its creditors and this is beneficial to its cash flow. However, it may be dangerous if it is greatly exceeding the period of credit allowed by suppliers as they may withdraw their credit facilities and require Lladnar Limited to pay cash for orders in future.

> **TOP TIP**
> Again, always round **up** to the nearest whole day.

Overtrading

Overtrading may occur when a business increases its turnover rapidly with the result that its inventories, trade receivables and trade payables also increase, but to a level that threatens its liquidity. The business may become insolvent and unable to pay its creditors as they fall due. The result may be that the business is forced to close.

Lladnar Limited has increased turnover by 33% in 2016. Inventory has increased by $46 000. Trade receivables turnover has increased from 35 to 46 days (31%), suggesting poor credit control by the company. Inventory turnover has increased, but only slightly. Lladnar Limited may be overtrading.

The working capital cycle

The working capital cycle measures the time it takes for cash to circulate around the working capital system. It calculates the interval that occurs between the time a business has to pay its creditors (trade payables) and the time it receives cash from its customers. It is calculated using the following formula:

inventory turnover in days + trade receivables turnover in days − trade payables turnover in days

The working capital cycle for Lladnar Limited is found as follows:

	2016	**2015**
	days	**days**
Rate of inventory turnover	26	23
Trade receivables turnover	46	35
	72	58
Trade payables turnover	(61)	(47)
Cash operating cycle	11	11

In both years, the company received its money from sales, on average, 11 days after it had paid its suppliers. During this time, the company was financing its customers out of its own money!

27.7 Investment (stock exchange) ratios

Investment ratios are of particular interest to people who have invested, or are intending to invest, in a company. These people include shareholders and lenders such as debenture holders and banks.

Gearing ratio

Gearing is fixed-cost capital expressed as a percentage of total capital. Fixed-cost capital is the money that finances a company in return for a fixed return and includes debentures and preference share capital. Total capital includes the equity (ordinary share capital and reserves) plus the fixed-cost capital.

The formula is:

Fixed cost capital (non-current liabilities, such as debentures or long term loans + redeemable preference share capital)

÷ Total capital (ordinary share capital + all reserves + non-current liabilities + redeemable preference share capital)

The answer is then expressed as a percentage by multiplying by 100.

Lladnar Limited's gearing is:

2016

$$\frac{150\,000}{909\,000 + 150\,000} \times 100 = 14.16\%$$

2015

$$\frac{100\,000}{738\,000 + 100\,000} \times 100 = 11.93\%$$

A company is described as highly geared if the gearing is more than 50%. If it is less than 50%, it is low geared. 50% is neutral gearing. Lladnar Limited is low geared.

Comment The key word in understanding the importance of gearing is risk. Lenders of money to a company may be concerned if it is highly geared; this may indicate that a large slice of profit is applied in the payment of interest. Risk arises if profits fall and fail to cover the interest payments. Banks approached by a highly geared company will question why, when the company is already heavily dependent upon loans, the shareholders are unwilling to invest more of their own money in their company. Perhaps they lack confidence in the company's future.

The risk to ordinary shareholders is increased in a highly geared company as the following example shows.

		Low geared company		Highly geared company
Gearing		20%		80%
		$		$
Ordinary share capital		800 000		200 000
10% debentures		200 000		800 000
		1 000 000		1 000 000
Year 1				
Profit before interest		100 000		100 000
Debenture interest		(20 000)		(80 000)
Profit left for ordinary shareholders		80 000		20 000
Profit as a percentage of ordinary share capital	80 000 / 800 000	10%	20 000 / 200 000	10%
Year 2				
Profit before interest		150 000		150 000
Debenture interest		(20 000)		(80 000)
Profit left for ordinary shareholders		130 000		70 000
Profit as a percentage of ordinary share capital	130 000 / 800 000	16.25%	70 000 / 200 000	35%
Year 3				
Profit before interest		50 000		50 000
Debenture interest		(20 000)		(80 000)
Profit (loss) left for ordinary shareholders		30 000		(30 000)
Profit (loss) as a percentage of ordinary share capital	30 000 / 800 000	3.75%	(30 000) / 200 000	–15%

The above example shows that if profit varies by ±$50 000 (50%) in the low geared company, the profit left for the ordinary shareholders varies by ±6.25%. In the highly geared company, the variation is ±25%. The swings in the fortunes of ordinary shareholders are greater (more risky) in a highly geared company than in a low geared company.

Debt/equity ratio

The formula for the debt/equity ratio is:

$$\frac{\text{debentures + long-term loans + preference share capital}}{\text{ordinary share capital + reserves}} \times 100$$

Lladnar Limited's debt/equity ratio is:

2016

$$\frac{150\,000}{909\,000} \times 100 = 16.5\%$$

2015

$$\frac{100\,000}{738\,000} \times 100 = 13.55\%$$

Comment This ratio is often taught as an alternative method of calculating the gearing ratio, but it is arguable whether expressing fixed-cost capital as a percentage of total capital employed is useful. In contrast to the debt/equity ratio, the gearing ratio is consistent with the formula for return on capital employed.

If the debt/equity ratio is less than 100%, the company is low geared; if it exceeds 100% the company is highly geared; 100% is neutral gearing.

Interest cover

Debenture holders and other lenders to a company need to be sure that the profit before interest adequately covers the interest payments. Interest must be paid even if a company makes a loss, but it is reassuring if the profit before interest covers the interest payments several times; a good cover provides a safety margin against a fall in profits in the future. Shareholders are also concerned to see a good interest cover, as their dividends can only be paid if profit is left after charging the interest in the income statement.

The formula for calculating interest cover is:

$$\frac{\text{profit from operations}}{\text{interest payable}}$$

The interest cover for Llandar Limited is:

2016

$$\frac{216^{*}}{15} = 14.4 \text{ times}$$

*201 + 15

2015

$$\frac{182^{*}}{10} = 18.2 \text{ times}$$

*172 + 10

Comment Lladnar Limited's interest cover has decreased by 3.8 times in 2016, but is still very satisfactory.

Income gearing

Income gearing is the interest expressed as a percentage of the profit from operations. It shows to what extent a company can pay for its borrowings or what the interest is as a percentage of the profit from operations.

The formula is:

$$\frac{\text{interest expense}}{\text{profit from operations}} \times 100$$

For Lladnar Limited the calculation is:

2016

$$\frac{15}{216} \times 100 = 6.94\%$$

2015

$$\frac{10}{182} \times 100 = 5.49\%$$

The same answer could have been obtained by dividing 100 by the number of times for interest cover calculated above:

2016

$$\frac{100}{14.4} = 6.94\%$$

2015

$$\frac{100}{18.2} = 5.49\%$$

Comment In this case, in 2016, the interest which Lladnar Limited has to pay is a higher percentage of profit than 2015. However, it is not very high and unlikely to cause the company difficulty.

The results shown for both interest cover and income gearing are an indication of the low gearing of Lladnar Limited.

Earnings per share

Earnings are the profit left for the ordinary shareholders after interest, tax and preference dividends have been provided for in the income statement. Ordinary dividends are paid out of earnings, and any earnings not distributed increase the reserves and the statement of financial position value of the shares. Earnings per share are expressed in cents ($0.00) per share, and are calculated using the formula:

$$\frac{\text{profit for the year} - \text{any dividend paid to } \textbf{non-redeemable} \text{ preference shareholders}}{\text{the number of ordinary shares issued}}$$

Lladnar Limited's earnings per share are:

2016

$$\frac{201\,000^*}{400\,000} = \$0.50 \text{ per share}$$

2015

$$\frac{172\,000}{400\,000} = \$0.43 \text{ per share}$$

* In this case, only the profit for the year is used as Lladnar Limited has no non-redeemable preference shares.

Comment Earnings per share have increased by $0.07 in 2016 and resulted in an increase in the retained earnings for the year. This is a satisfactory result for the shareholders.

Price earnings (P/E) ratio

This ratio is a measure of how confident investors are in the future performance of a company. The higher the P/E ratio, the more confidence investors have in the company earning increasing profits in the future, and possibly paying ordinary shareholders an increasing dividend. The price earnings ratio calculates what multiple of the price being paid for the shares on the market is of the earnings per share; it is calculated using the formula:

$$\frac{\text{market price per share}}{\text{earnings per share}}$$

The market price of Lladnar Limited's ordinary shares at 31 December 2015 was $1.80, and at 31 December 2016 it was $2.10. The price earnings ratios (PERs) are:

2016	2015
$\frac{2.10}{0.50} = 4.20$	$\frac{1.80}{0.43} = 4.19$

Comment The price earnings ratio has remained steady over both years. Shareholders have been prepared to pay just over four times the earnings per share. This is a measure of confidence in the ability of Lladnar Limited to maintain its earnings in future. A PER of four is not particularly good for a long-term investment in a company. PER is an important ratio for investors as it gives a quick and easily understandable indicator of the market's assessment of a company's prospects.

Dividend per share

Companies usually declare dividends as a certain number of cents per share, representing a certain percentage return based on the nominal value of the share. For example, a dividend of $0.03 per share paid on a share with a nominal value of $0.50, is a dividend of 6% on the share. Shareholders who have paid the market price for their shares need to know the return based on the price they have paid.

The dividend per share is calculated using the following formula:

$$\frac{\text{total ordinary dividends paid}}{\text{total number of ordinary shares issued}}$$

The answer is expressed in dollars and cents.

This presents a slight problem with the way accounts are presented. The statement of changes in equity shows dividends **paid** during the year. We have seen that this figure may include dividends paid in respect of a previous accounting period. The calculation of the ratio must be based on dividends in respect of the year in question.

Assume that in the years in question, the dividends for Lladnar Limited were: 2016, total dividend paid $35 000; 2015, total dividend paid $27 000.

Notice that these are not the figures in the statement of changes in equity.

Lladnar Limited's declared rates of dividend per share are:

2016	2015
$\frac{35\,000}{400\,000}$ = $0.0875 per share	$\frac{27\,000}{400\,000}$ = $0.0675 per share

TOP TIP

This assumes that the shares have a nominal value of $1 each. Check the question to see if this is the case. If the nominal value of the shares was $0.50 each then the denominator would have been 800 000, the total number of shares issued.

Comment There is a slight increase in the amount of the dividend per share in 2016. This is positive for the shareholders, especially as the market price of the share has also increased.

Dividend cover

The formula for dividend cover is:

Profit available to pay ordinary dividend (profit for the year − non-redeemable preference share dividend) ÷ ordinary dividend paid

Dividend cover is the number of times the profit, out of which dividends may be paid, covers the dividend. If the cover is too low, a decline in profits may lead to the dividend being restricted or not paid at all. On the other hand, if the cover is high, shareholders may decide that the directors are adopting a mean dividend policy.

The calculation of dividend cover for Lladnar Limited is:

2016	**2015**
$\frac{201\,000}{35\,000} = 5.74$ times	$\frac{172\,000}{27\,000} = 6.37$ times

Comment In both years the level of cover is good. It may indicate that the company is retaining cash for future expansion rather than paying it out as dividend. This will be of benefit to shareholders in the longer term.

An alternative to the above formula is:

$$\frac{\text{earnings per share}}{\text{dividend per share}}$$

Using this formula, the calculations for Lladnar are:

2016	**2015**
$\frac{0.50}{0.0875} = 5.71$ times	$\frac{0.43}{0.0675} = 6.37$ times

The 2016 figure is slightly different as a result of rounding.

Dividend yield

This ratio shows the relationship between the dividend paid per share and the market price of the share. The answer can be compared with dividend yields of shares in other companies or, alternatively, the return on less risky investments such as bank deposit accounts.

It is calculated as:

$$\frac{\text{dividend per share}}{\text{market price of one ordinary share}} \times 100$$

It is usual to take the market price of an ordinary share at the end of the financial year. The market price of each share is $2.10 for 2016 and $1.80 for 2015.

The dividend yields are:

2016	**2015**
$\frac{0.0875}{2.10} \times 100 = 4.17\%$	$\frac{0.0675}{1.80} \times 100 = 3.75\%$

Comment The small increase in the dividend yield in 2016 is the result of the share price increasing fractionally less than the increase in the dividend. There may be a connection between the increase in the market price and the small increases in the earnings per share and the dividend cover.

27.8 Trend analysis and inter-firm comparison

Individual ratios are usually of very limited value. The ratios of a business for past years are necessary if trends in progress or deterioration of performance are to be seen. The examples of Lladnar Limited have given the results for 2015 and 2016, and some limited trends have been observed. Given the results for, say, four, five or six years, more reliable trends may be discerned.

Trends may signal to investors whether they should stay with their investment, or sell it and re-invest in a more promising venture.

Inter-firm comparison (IFC) is possible when information about the performance of other similar businesses is available. Trade associations collect information from their members and publish the statistics as averages for the trade or industry. It is thus possible to compare the results of one company with the averages for businesses of the same type. Comparisons, however, must be made with care. It is not realistic to compare the statistics of a small trader with results achieved by large companies. Comparison should always be on a like-for-like basis as far as possible.

Inter-firm comparison can inform shareholders whether they have invested their money in the most profitable and stable institutions.

27.9 The limitations of ratios

- To be useful and reliable, ratios must be reasonably accurate. They should be based on information in accounts and notes to the accounts. Some useful information may not be disclosed in the accounts and some account headings may not indicate the contents clearly.
- Information must be timely to be of use. It may not be available until some time after the end of a company's financial year.
- Ratios do not explain the cause of the changes in the results but may indicate areas of concern; further investigation is usually necessary to discover causes of the concern.
- Ratios usually do not recognise seasonal factors in business:
  - profit margins will be lower than normal during periods of seasonal sales
  - inventory and trade receivables are unlikely to remain at constant levels throughout the year
  - companies, even in the same trade, will have different policies for such matters as providing for depreciation, doubtful debts, profit recognition, transferring profits to reserves and dividend policy.

Such limitations should be borne in mind when making comparisons between businesses. The benefits of ratio analysis are the opposite of its limitations:

- It allows managers to make comparisons between different years and between different businesses in the same trading sector. However, the businesses should, ideally be of a similar size.
- It helps identify where improvements need to be made for the future.
- It allows a trend of performance to be built up over a number of years.

27.10 The critical appraisal of accounting reports

The basis of modern financial reporting and its limitations

The annual accounting reports of limited companies consist of an income statement, statement of financial position, statement of cash flows and the directors' report. These reports are prepared within an accounting framework made up of the requirements of Companies Acts and the various published accounting standards. These requirements are intended to ensure a degree of uniformity that will enable the users of the reports to interpret them in a generally accepted context. The framework has been considered in Chapter 22.

Limitations of interpreting financial reports may be summarised as follows:

- While the accounting framework is intended to ensure that financial reports provide the information necessary for an understanding of a company's performance, the rules do not require confidential information which might provide an unfair advantage to competitors to be disclosed. The undisclosed information might, however, contain important clues to the better understanding of the company's performance.
- Companies are required to supplement the income statement and the statement of financial position with additional notes to explain how the items in those financial statements are made up. However, companies differ in their classification of many items of income and expenditure, and the notes may not be in sufficient detail to identify the differences. This may cast doubt on the usefulness of some accounting ratios calculated from the financial statements.
- Where accounting standards do not fit a particular business, the directors may adapt them, or even ignore them, provided they have good reason for doing so.
- Companies have different policies for the treatment of expenditure on non-current assets; some will capitalise all such expenditure, while others will treat the expenditure as revenue expenditure if it is not material compared with the size of the amounts shown in its statement of financial position. For example, a multinational company may not capitalise any expenditure on a single item, say equipment, below $5 000. However, to a small sole trader, a new piece of equipment costing $5 000 would almost certainly be treated as a non-current asset in the financial statements.
- A company may own its extensive properties or it may operate solely from rented accommodation. One will pay no rent, while the other may be burdened with very high rental payments. One will show the item in the statement of financial position, whist the other will show it in their income statement. This may make the comparison between the two companies using some ratios to be of little relevance.
- There are limits to the extent to which companies of considerably different sizes can be compared. For example, it would hardly be helpful to compare the performance of a company with an issued capital of $50 000 with the performance of a company with an issued capital of $5 million. There may also be difficulty in making a sensible comparison between a company with nil gearing and one that is very highly geared.
- Companies in the same line of business are often not comparable. For example, some may simply retail their goods, while others manufacture and retail them. Some companies may act as manufacturers and wholesalers only.
- Financial reports may be too historical to be useful by the time they are published. There will be a time delay of several months between the end of the financial year and date on which the accounts are presented to shareholders at the annual general meeting.
- The interpretation of financial reports may be subject to external factors such as developments in the industry, general political and economic conditions at home and overseas, changes in fashion, market demand and so on.
- The financial accounts and reports of companies in countries where there is high inflation can be seriously misleading if the accounts have been based on historic costs.

Window dressing

Company directors naturally desire annual financial reports to present the company performance in as favourable a light as possible. Indeed their remuneration may well depend on the profit the company makes. This may lead to 'window dressing' which may take various forms, including:

- reducing trade payables in the statement of financial position by drawing cheques at the end of the financial period to pay the creditors, but not posting the cheques until the start of the next financial year, or even cancelling them on the first day of the next financial year
- reducing the trade receivables in the statement of financial position by pressing them to pay before the end of the financial period.

Other methods of window dressing, such as changing the bases of calculating depreciation of non-current assets and the provision for doubtful debts, of inventory valuation, etc., are not permissible and contravene accounting standards. They may even amount to fraud.

Income-smoothing techniques

Income should be recognised as soon as it is realised and not before. A company carrying out work under a contract which spans two or more financial periods is required to spread the anticipated profit on the contract over the financial periods concerned. The amount of profit to be credited in each year is calculated by a formula which apportions the profit according to the amount deemed to have been earned in each period, less a prudent provision for any future unanticipated losses. (A more detailed explanation of contract accounts is outside the scope of this text, as you are not required to have a knowledge of the topic.)

When the directors of a company anticipate that a good trading year will be followed by a poor one, they may decide to delay invoicing some customers in the good year until the following one for the sake of appearances. This contravenes the concept of realisation and, if the financial statements are subject to audit, should not be allowed to happen without being reported.

Similarly, if customers are allowed to pay by instalments for work done or services rendered, and some of the instalments are payable in a subsequent financial period, any attempt to smooth income by partly deferring it until the instalments are received would be a contravention of the realisation principle.

27.11 The nature of company forecasts

Directors' reports and future developments

Directors' reports are required to include an indication of likely future developments in the business of the company. These statements are usually quite brief and lack sufficient detail to enable shareholders and others to form an accurate assessment of the future funding requirements of the business.

Company budgets

Every company, except some very small private companies, prepares budgets. Budgets are based on forecasts and express in money terms the plans and policies the directors intend to implement to achieve a company's long-term objectives. The budgets usually cover periods of one, two, three, five, ten or, for large companies, even more years ahead. Separate budgets are prepared for each of the company's activities: sales, production, purchasing, inventory holding, and so on. Cash budgets are prepared from these budgets to show if and when the company is likely to need additional cash. Master budgets, which take the form of forecast income statements and statements of financial position, will indicate when additional long-term finance is required.

The budgets are for internal use within the company and are not published, but they are an essential management tool if the directors are to avoid the embarrassment, and possibly the catastrophe, of suddenly finding that the company has insufficient funds to continue in business. Banks, and others approached to provide additional capital, will require to see the budgets before deciding whether or not to lend to the business. Budgeting is covered in Chapter 32.

ACTIVITY 1

(Based on the accounts of a sole trader.)

Najim wants to analyse the results of his trading for the year ended 31 December 2016 and has prepared his financial statements. He compares these with the financial statements for the previous year.

Income statements for the years ended 31 December

	2016		2015	
	$	$	$	$
Revenue		187 500		172 308
Less: cost of sales				
Opening inventory	16 000		12 000	
Purchases	125 500		116 000	
	141 500		128 000	
Closing inventory	(14 000)	(127 500)	(16 000)	(112 000)
Gross profit		60 000		60 308
Less: expenses		(32 678)		(38 769)
Profit for the year		27 322		21 539

Statements of financial position for the years ended 31 December

	2016		2015	
	$	$	$	$
Non-current assets (net book values)		93 750		78 322
Current assets				
Inventory		14 000		16 000
Trade receivables		12 511		9 914
Cash and cash equivalents		7 185		4 851
		33 696		30 765
Total assets		127 446		109 087
Capital and liabilities				
Opening capital		95 103		81 176
Add: profit		27 322		21 539
		122 425		102 715
Deduct drawings		(12 171)		(7 612)
		110 254		95 103
Current liabilities				
Trade payables		17 192		13 984
Total capital and liabilities		127 446		109 087

Additional information

1 60% of Najim's sales are on credit.

2 Najim purchases all his inventory of goods on credit.

3 The only current assets are inventory, trade receivables and a bank balance.

Required

a Calculate the following ratios to two decimal places for each of the years ended 31 December 2015 and 2016:

- **i** gross margin
- **ii** profit margin
- **iii** non-current asset turnover
- **iv** inventory turnover
- **v** trade receivables turnover
- **vi** trade payables turnover
- **vii** current ratio
- **viii** liquid (acid test) ratio.

b Compare the performance of Najim's business in 2016 with its performance in 2015, using the ratios calculated in **a**, and comment on the comparison.

ACTIVITY 2

(Based on the accounts of limited companies.)

A financial consultant has been asked by his client for advice on the relative performance of two companies, Flora Limited and Fauna Limited. Extracts from the financial statements for the year ended 31 December 2016, and the statement of financial position at that date of the two companies are as follows:

Extract from financial statement for the year ended 31 December 2016

	Flora Limited	Fauna Limited
	$000	$000
Profit from operations	300	420
Finance costs (debenture interest)	(60)	(120)
	240	300
Transfer to general reserve	(100)	(50)
Ordinary dividend paid	(90)	(150)
Retained earnings	50	100

Statement of financial position extracts at 31 December 2016

Flora Limited	$000	Fauna Limited	$000
Non-current liabilities		Non-current liabilities	
10% debentures 2019/2020	600	12% debentures 2018/2019	1000
Ordinary shares of $1 each	300	Ordinary shares of $2 each	2250
General reserve	120	General reserve	200
Retained earnings	80	Retained earnings	350
	500		2800

The market values of the ordinary shares at 31 December 2016 were as follows: Flora Limited $2.70, Fauna Limited $3.60.

Statement of financial position at 31 December 2015		
		$
Step 19	Total assets	270 041
	Capital and liabilities	
Step 26	Capital at 1 Jan 2016 (balancing figure)	133 638
Step 25	Add: profit for the year (from income statement)	75 307
	82 031 is profit from operations	
Step 24	(156 945 + 52 000)	208 945
Step 23	Less: drawings (1 000 × 52)	(52 000)
Step 22	(270 041 − [45 856 + 67 240])	156 765
	Non-current liabilities	
Step 21	10% long term loan	67 240
	Current liabilities	
Step 15	Trade payables $(257\,500 \times \frac{65}{365})$	45 856
Step 20	Total capital and liabilities	270 041

TOP TIP

Remember to always show your workings, either against the figures or state where to find them.

The steps show the order in which the items should be tackled, but the step numbers do not form part of the answer and should not be shown in answers to questions. It is a good idea to start with an outline for the financial statements (leaving spaces to insert additional items if necessary), and to fill in the items as soon as the figures are known. For example, inventory in the statement of financial position can be inserted immediately after it has been entered in the income statement. Similarly, profit for the year can be inserted in the statement of financial position as soon as it has been calculated in the income statement.

ACTIVITY 3

Patience has mislaid her financial statements for the year ended 31 December 2016, but has found the report, which her accountant has prepared, based on those accounts. She has decided to reconstruct the accounts from the information contained in the report.

The accountant's report contained the following data:

1 At 31 December 2016: Inventory $54 000. (This was 20% more than the inventory at 1 January 2016.)

2 For the year ended 31 December 2016:

Inventory turnover	10 times
Gross margin	35%

Profit margin	22%
Non-current asset turnover	4 times
Trade receivables turnover	34 days (based on 365 days in the year)
Trade payables turnover	42 days (based on 365 days in the year)
Current ratio	2.5 : 1

3 The current assets consist of inventory, trade receivables and bank balance.

4 All sales and purchases were made on credit.

5 Patience drew $140 000 from the business during the year.

Required

a Prepare, in as much detail as possible, Patience's income statement for the year ended 31 December 2016 and the statement of financial position at that date. Make all calculations to the nearest $.

Virtue carries on a similar business to that of Patience and has the following data for the year ended 31 December 2016:

Inventory turnover	12 times
Gross margin	40%
Profit margin	20%
Non-current asset turnover	5 times
Trade receivables turnover	31 days
Trade payables turnover	36 days

Required

b Compare Virtue's performance with that of Patience's and indicate the ratios that show which business is the more efficient. You should write your answer in sentence form and include supporting figures.

This chapter is important and is often asked as either a complete question or as part of another question. Study the following points and work back through the chapter to make sure you are happy with all the calculations and what they are identifying.

- Learn the headings under which ratios are shown in the pyramid of ratios and which ratios are included under each heading.
- Remember how each ratio is calculated (the model).
- Take care to calculate ratios on the correct figures and check your arithmetic.
- Express every ratio in the correct terms; for example, as a percentage, a number of times or days, a true ratio, and so on.
- Make sure you understand what each ratio is intended to explain.
- Your comments on ratios should be based on the information you are given, and justified by the ratios you have calculated. Do not assume facts you are not given.
- Avoid making definite statements that cannot be supported by the information given. You may suggest reasons for the comments you make.
- Your comments should be concise and relevant; avoid repetition of the same point. Avoid long rambling answers that stray from the point.
- When commenting on the ratios you have calculated, the wording is very important. Statements such as 'the gross margin is higher this year than last year' are not sufficient. You must explain that this means the situation has **improved**, or the company's trading was **better** or **worse** this year. Bullet points in the answers are perfectly acceptable and will save you time.
- Always use the relevant sign or wording with the ratio. For example, a % sign after the calculation of gross margin, or the number of times for dividend cover.

Chapter summary

In this chapter you have learnt about the limitations of financial statements, and how to analyse and interpret them effectively. Interpretation of financial statements is an important part of accounting, but so too is being able to analyse and write about the results when you have calculated them. You have therefore learnt how to use financial statements to calculate ratios and also to explain and comment on them (including when analysing the performance of a business), and to make suggestions as to how ratios can be improved in the future.

TOP TIP

Work back through the chapter and attempt the following exercises, especially the written sections about explaining your results.

Practice exercises

1 On 1 October 2015, Lamar Goswami and his wife formed a limited company, Goswami Limited, to run a beautician's business. They put in inventory to the value of $31 500 and cash of $43 500 in exchange for share capital. The bank loaned the company a further $80 000 at 9% interest per annum.

At 30 September 2016, the business's financial statements were drawn up as follows:

Income statement for the year ended 30 September 2016		
	$	$
Revenue		350 000
Less: cost of sales		
Inventory at 1 October 2015	31 500	
Purchases	280 000	
Inventory at 30 September 2016	(66 500)	(245 000)
Gross profit		105 000
Less: expenses		
Rent and rates	(3 950)	
Advertising	(1 750)	
Wages	(29 000)	
Heat and light	(5 250)	
Interest due	(7 200)	
Depreciation	(12 000)	(59 150)
Profit for the year		45 850

Statement of financial position as at 30 September 2016			
	Cost	**Depreciation**	**NBV**
	$	**$**	**$**
Non-current assets			
Premises	124 000		124 000
Fixtures and fittings	48 000	(12 000)	36 000
	172 000	(12 000)	160 000
Current assets			
Inventory			66 500
Trade receivables			21 500
			88 000
Total assets			248 000
Equity and liabilities			
Ordinary shares of $1			75 000
Retained earnings			45 850
			120 850
Non-current liabilities			
Long-term loan			80 000
Current liabilities			
Trade payables			21 000
Interest due			7 200
Bank			18 950
			47 150
Total equity and liabilities			248 000

Industry average ratios and other relevant data concerning businesses similar to Goswami Limited were as follows:

i	Gross margin	30.00%
ii	Profit margin	18.07%
iii	Current ratio	2.21 : 1
iv	Liquid (acid test) ratio	1.02 : 1
v	Rate of inventory turnover ratio	8 times
vi	Trade receivables turnover	25 days
vii	Trade payables turnover	30 days

Required

a State **two** advantages and **two** disadvantages of ratio analysis. **[4 marks]**

b Calculate to **two** decimal places each of the above ratios for Goswami Limited. **[14 marks]**

c Evaluate the performance of Goswami Limited compared to the industry average in respect of:

- **i** profitability
- **ii** liquidity. **[7 marks]**

d Advise the directors of any changes they can make to improve the performance of the business in the future. **[5 marks]**

Total: 30

2 The following information summarises the latest set of financial statements of Techno Hub, a sole trader.

At 30 April 2016: Inventory $45 000. (This was 50% more than the inventory at 1 May 2015.)

For the year ended 30 April 2016:

Inventory turnover	12 times
Gross margin	40%
Profit margin	18%
Non-current asset turnover	3 times
Average time taken by customers to pay	36 days (based on a year of 365 days)
Average time taken to pay suppliers	40 days (based on a year of 365 days)

The current ratio is 3 : 1.

The only current assets of the firm consist of inventory, trade receivables and balance at bank.

All sales and purchases were on a credit basis.

Additional information

At 1 May 2015, Techno Hub's capital was $60 000.

During the year ended 30 April 2016 he took drawings of $55 000.

Required

a Prepare, in as much detail as possible, making all calculations to the nearest $000:

i the income statement of Techno Hub for the year ended 30 April 2016 **[7 marks]**

ii the statement of financial position at that date. **[9 marks]**

Additional information

The following financial information is available for Zenapod, a similar business, for the year ended 30 April 2016:

Inventory turnover	10 times
Gross margin	45%
Profit margin	20%
Non-current asset turnover	3½ times
Time taken by customers to pay	30 days (based on a year of 365 days)
Time taken to pay suppliers	28 days (based on a year of 365 days)

Required

b Evaluate the performance of Techno Hub with that of Zenapod, suggesting any areas where Techno Hub could make improvements for the future. **[12 marks]**

c **i** State one other profitability ratio Techno Hub could calculate. **[1 mark]**

ii Explain what that ratio measures. **[1 mark]**

Total: 30

3 The directors of Oitar plc provided the following financial information for the year ended 30 April 2016:

	$000	$000
Profit from operations		1 000
Debenture interest (12.5%)		(250)
		750

Ordinary dividend paid for the year	(470)
Transfer to general reserve	(200)
Retained earnings	80

Oitar plc's issued share capital and reserves at 30 April 2016 consisted of:

	$000
Ordinary shares of $10	5 500
Capital and revenue reserves	900

The market price of the ordinary shares at 30 April 2016 was $30.

Note: The information given is from the accounts prepared for internal use by the managers and is, therefore, different from the IAS format.

Required

a Calculate from the information provided the following ratios for Oitar plc:

i interest cover

ii dividend cover

iii earnings per share

iv price earnings ratio

v dividend yield

vi gearing. **[12 marks]**

b Discuss why each of the ratios in **a** are important for investors in ordinary shares in the company. **[9 marks]**

c State, with reasons, what other documents shareholders might wish to see to enable them to assess the likely future performance of Oitar plc. **[4 marks]**

Total: 25

4 The directors of Gemmaton Limited provide the following financial information at 31 December 2015:

	$000
Profit from operations	1 000
Finance costs	(300)
Taxation	(100)
Profit for the year	600

Extracts from the company's statement of financial position at 31 December 2015 are:

	$000
Equity	
Ordinary shares of $1 each	6 000
Capital and revenue reserves	1 000
Non-current liabilities	7 000
10% debentures (2020)	3 000

Additional information

During the year, the company paid an interim dividend to its shareholders of $0.02 per share. At the end of the year, the directors propose to set aside $300 000 from profits to pay a final dividend to its shareholders.

At 31 December 2015, the market price of one ordinary shares in Gemmaton Limited is $2.

Required

a Calculate to **two** decimal places the following ratios at 31 December 2015:

- **i** return on capital employed
- **ii** dividends per share for the year
- **iii** dividend cover
- **iv** dividend yield
- **v** earnings per share
- **vi** price/earnings ratio. **[10 marks]**

Required

b State **two** benefits and **two** limitations of ratio analysis.

[4 marks]

Total: 14

Exam practice questions

Multiple-choice questions

1 Information about a business is given in the following table.

	Year 1	Year 2
	$	$
Turnover	200 000	250 000
Cost of sales	(125 000)	(140 000)
	75 000	110 000
Operating expenses	(32 000)	(64 000)
Profit from operations	43 000	46 000
Non-current assets	140 000	120 000
Net current assets	60 000	80 000
Long-term loans	(80 000)	(40 000)

Which of the following is true in year 2?

	Gross margin	Return on capital employed
A	decreased	decreased
B	increased	decreased
C	decreased	increased
D	increased	increased

2 Extracts from the income statement for two years for a business are given in this table:

	Year 1	Year 2
	$	$
Revenue	100 000	200 000
Gross profit	30 000	70 000

What might explain the change in the gross margin in year 2?

A an increase in sales
B an increase in the sales price
C a reduction in inventory
D suppliers offering higher cash discounts

3 What is the effect on the current ratio and liquid (acid test) ratio of a business if it uses cash to buy inventory?

	Current ratio	Liquid (acid test) ratio
A	decrease	decrease
B	decrease	increase
C	no change	decrease
D	no change	increase

4 The liquid (acid test) ratio of a business has fallen. What is the reason for the fall?

A a decrease in trade payables
B a decrease in inventory
C an increase in cash
D an increase in the bank overdraft

5 The closing inventory of a business was $30 000 and the cost of sales was $600 000. Inventory turnover is based on the average value of the opening and closing inventories.
If the inventory turnover was 15 times, what was the opening inventory?

A $10 000
B $40 000
C $50 000
D $80 000

6 The following information is extracted from the financial statements of a business:

	$
Opening inventory	6 000
Purchases (all on credit)	220 000
Closing inventory	28 000
Trade payables at end of year	21 096

What is the period taken to pay the suppliers?

A 31 days
B 32 days
C 34 days
D 35 days

7 The following is an extract from the income statement of a company:

	$
Profit from operations	360 000
Debenture interest	24 000
Profit for the year	336 000
Preference dividend paid	(16 000)
Ordinary dividend paid	(200 000)
Retained earnings	120 000

The company's share capital is as follows:

Issued: 200 000 8% preference shares of $1

800 000 ordinary shares of $1

What is the company's earnings per share?

A $0.32
B $0.40
C $0.42
D $0.45

8 A company has share capital of $1 for each of 500 000 shares. The following is an extract from its income statement:

	$
Profit from operations	400 000
Debenture interest	(60 000)
Profit for the year	340 000
Transfer to general reserve	(100 000)
Ordinary dividend paid	(200 000)
Retained earnings	40 000

The current market price of the shares is $3.60. What is the price earnings ratio?

A 5.29
B 7.5
C 8
D 11.25

Total: 8 marks

Part III
Elements of cost and managerial accounting

Chapter 28
Costing for materials, labour and overheads

Learning objectives

In this chapter you will learn:

- the nature and purpose of cost accounting
- how to analyse costs into direct and indirect costs
- how to record and value direct and indirect materials
- how to record and value direct and indirect labour
- the method of calculating gross wages, including overtime and bonus payments
- the advantages and disadvantages of paying overtime and bonus payments
- how to distinguish between direct and indirect materials and labour
- how to allocate and apportion overheads
- how to calculate overhead absorption rates (OARs)
- the causes of over-/under-absorption of overheads
- how to calculate over-/under-absorption of overheads.

28.1 The purpose and nature of cost accounting

Cost accounting is one of the management tools included in a number of systems of accounting known as **management accounting**. Management accounting provides management with information which is not obtainable from the financial accounts of a business.

As a result, the way data is collected and, more specifically presented, in this section is completely different to the way it is collected and presented in financial accounting. Some larger businesses will have specific departments in the organisation dedicated to cost and management accounting. They provide a valuable addition to the organisation. So far in financial accounting we have been looking at a history book. The financial statements are prepared after the end of the financial year. There is nothing the organisation can do to change the results they disclose.

With cost and management accounting the organisation is looking forward. It is gathering and analysing information which will be used as a basis for making future decisions affecting the performance and profitability of the firm. Throughout this section, how the information analysed can be used as a basis for decision making in the organisation will be considered. There is also some overlap with financial accounting, as information collected, particularly in relation to the cost of part completed units of product, will allow it to accurately value inventory in the financial statements. Consider the following example:

KEY TERMS

Cost accounting: A method of accounting where all the costs associated with a particular activity or product are collected together, classified and recorded.

Management accounting: The process of preparing reports and accounts which can be used by managers as a basis for making decisions on the future performance of the business.

Make It Limited
Manufacturing account for the year ended 30 June 2016

	$000	$000
Direct materials		
Inventory at 1 July 2015	10	
Purchases	140	
Carriage inwards	24	
	174	
Less: Inventory at 30 June 2016	(18)	156
Direct labour		222
Direct expenses		46
Prime cost		424
Indirect materials	45	
Indirect labour	72	
Rent of factory	100	
Heating, lighting and power	45	
Depreciation:		
Factory	20	
Machinery	36	318
		742
Work in progress 1 July 2015	38	
Work in progress 30 June 2016	(20)	18
Factory cost of finished goods		760

This manufacturing account has been prepared as part of the company's financial accounting system. It provides us with information about prime cost, overheads and the cost of producing goods. If only one type of goods has been produced, the unit cost can easily be found by dividing the factory cost by the number of units produced. The selling price for the goods is fixed by adding the required amount of profit per unit. So far, so good, but it does not go far enough to help management make important decisions.

Assuming that Make It Limited manufactures only one type of product and that the output for the year was 1 000 units of that product, each unit has cost $760 to produce. If the managers want to find the cost of producing 1 001 units, the answer will not be:

$$\$760\,000 \times \frac{1\,001}{1\,000} = \$760\,760, \text{ that is } \$(760\,000 + 760)$$

The additional unit will not result in additional costs of $760 because not all costs (rent and depreciation, for example) will be affected by the addition of one unit of output; they are **fixed costs**, which do not vary with the number of units produced. The effect on costs of increasing numbers of units produced is covered in Chapter 30 on marginal costing.

The problem is even more complicated if Make It Limited manufactures more than one type of product, and each type requires different types and quantities of materials, different numbers of labour hours and different processes. Management must know how much it costs to make a single unit of each product if they are to fix selling prices. This problem is considered now.

28.2 Direct and indirect costs

In Section 20.2 we saw that a distinction is made in manufacturing accounts between direct costs and indirect costs.

Direct costs include direct materials (those materials from which goods are made, and carriage inwards paid on the materials), direct labour (the wages of workers who actually make goods) and direct expenses (royalties, licence fees, and so on).

Indirect costs on the other hand are indirect materials (purchased for the factory, e.g. cleaning materials, or lubricating oil for any machinery), indirect wages (the wages of all factory workers who do not actually make the finished goods (factory managers, supervisors, store staff, cleaners, and so on) and other overhead costs (rent, heating and lighting, depreciation, and so on). This distinction is very important in the following chapters. It is important that you are able to classify costs in this way.

28.3 The behaviour of costs

Direct costs are deemed to vary in proportion to the number of units produced. Thus, they may sometimes be called 'variable costs'. For example, if 1 kg of material is required for one unit of production, 2 kg will be required for two units produced, 10 kg for ten units, and so on. It will be true for royalties and other direct expenses; if a royalty (an amount which has to be paid to the person or company who designed the product, tables in this case) of $0.05 has to be paid for every unit produced, the royalties payable will always be equal to the number of units produced times (×) $0.05. At one time, it might have been common for direct workers to be paid according to the amount they produced, so that direct wages would be proportionate to output. Now, direct workers are usually paid a fixed or basic wage regardless of their output. This wage may or may not be supplemented by a productivity bonus (see later). In practice, therefore, wages paid to direct labour will not be in relation to output, but we still tend to treat them in a theoretical way as being proportionate to production, and thus direct or variable costs.

KEY TERMS

Fixed cost: A cost that remains unchanged within a certain level of activity or output.

Variable cost: A cost which varies in direct proportion to changes in the level of output.

Indirect expenses may be **fixed costs** or **variable costs**. They are fixed if they are not linked directly to the level of activity. Rent is an example; it is fixed by a rental agreement. Straight-line depreciation is another fixed expense. However, it is important to remember that even fixed expenses are only fixed within certain limits. For example, it may be possible to increase the number of units produced only if additional machines are purchased, and that will increase the total depreciation charge. If production is increased still further and more machines have to be purchased, it may be necessary to lease more factory space and the rent will increase. Fixed costs then become 'stepped costs' and may be represented by a chart as follows:

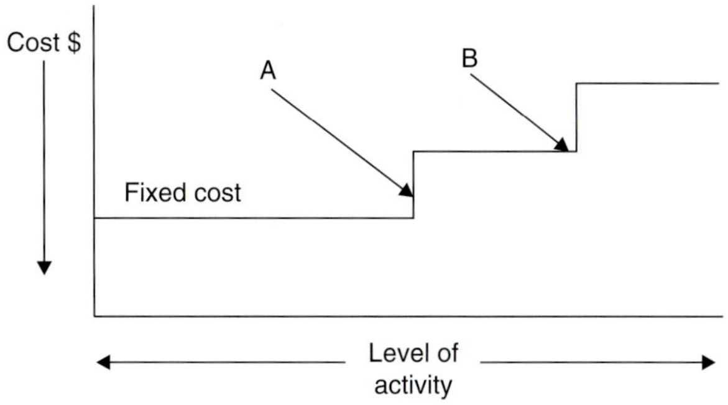

At A it has been necessary to buy an additional machine in order to increase production, and the depreciation of machinery charge has increased. At B, a further machine has been bought, and it has been necessary to rent additional factory space so that both the depreciation charge and the rent have increased. Looking at the fixed cost line, it moves upwards at both points A and B, making the whole line look like steps, hence stepped fixed costs.

28.4 Recording materials, labour and overheads

Cost accounting requires materials purchased to be classified as direct or indirect. The general rule is that if the materials are used as part of the finished product they are regarded as direct materials. For example, if the business manufactures computers, then the cost of the circuit boards and cases will be regarded as direct materials. Its cost can be traced directly to the product being produced, hence 'direct cost'. In cost accounting the name given to the unit produced, or unit of output is the **cost unit**. We would refer to the one circuit board which goes into a finished computer as having a direct materials cost per unit.

> **KEY TERM**
>
> **Cost unit:** The unit of output of a business to which costs can be charged.

If the business issues gloves to its workers to make sure no dust or fingerprints get onto the finished product, the cost of these materials will be regarded as indirect. They can be used a number of times during the manufacturing process. In this case, the cost of a pair of gloves is not taken as a direct materials cost per unit. The total cost of all the indirect materials are added together and they are then charged to each cost unit on a predetermined basis. This is covered in the next chapter.

Cost accounting requires both materials purchased and wages paid to be classified as direct or indirect. If expenditure has been incurred for particular departments within the business, it must be analysed by departments. Invoices for goods and services must be coded by the purchasing department to show the type of expenditure that has been incurred. The purchase journal must have additional columns so that the expenditure can be analysed according to the codes shown on the invoices.

Wages are analysed into different departments and then classified into direct and indirect wages on payroll summaries.

If the systems of analysis outlined above have been carried out, all expenses can be posted in the ledger to appropriate accounts to enable the allocation and apportionment of expenses to **cost centres** as described in Section 28.10.

28.5 Direct and indirect materials

Manufacturing businesses may hold a number of different items which are used in making the product. The cost of these items may vary, both over time and depending on which firm the business buys the items from. This causes a number of problems with the valuation of such inventory.

In Section 22.5, the valuation of inventory using IAS 2 was discussed. When considering a manufacturing company, IAS 2 allows **two** different methods to be used for valuing direct materials inventory. They are:

- First in, first out (FIFO). This assumes that the first items to be bought will be the first to be used, although this may not be the physical distribution of the goods. Thus, remaining inventory valuation will always be the value of the most recently purchased items.
- Average cost (AVCO). Under this method a new average value (usually the weighted average using the number of items bought) is calculated each time a new delivery of inventory is acquired.

In a very few cases, it may be possible to value goods at the price actually paid for them. For example, the owner of an art gallery may be able to say from whom she bought each of the pictures in her gallery, and how much she paid for them, because there would probably be a limited number of paintings and she would be able to recall how much she paid for them.

A manufacturer of computers, however, would not find it easy to say how much he paid for the parts he needed for the computers. Purchases of hard drives, for example, would be in bulk and made at different times and at different prices. It would be impossible to say at the year-end how much had been paid for any particular hard drive remaining at the year-end. The problem is solved by assuming that inventory movements occur in a particular pattern, even if that is not strictly so. This is often called a convention: something that is assumed to happen even if it is not strictly true, at least all the time.

Valuing material using FIFO

As we have seen, under this method goods are assumed to be used in the order in which they are received from the supplier.

Walkthrough

At 1 June, the inventory of a certain material consisted of 80 kg which had cost $0.60 per kg. The table below shows the receipts and issues of the material in June:

Date		Receipts [1] quantity	Price per kg [1]	Issues quantity [2]
		kg	$	kg
June 1	Inventory brought forward from May 31	80	0.60	
3		100	1.00	
7				70
16		200	1.20	
23				200
25		50	1.40	
30				80

[1] The receipt of goods from suppliers and the price paid per kg.

[2] The quantity in kg of goods issued from inventory to production.

The table below shows how issues and inventory are valued using FIFO.

Date	Receipts		Issues		Inventory	
	kg	Price per kg $	kg	Value $	kg	Value $
June 1					80	80×0.60 = 48
3 [1]	100	1.00			180 (80+100)	80×0.60 = 48 100×1.00 = 100 Total 148
7 [2]			70	70×0.60 = 42	110 (180−70)	10×0.60 = 6 100×1.00 = 100 Total 106
16	200	1.20			310 (110+200)	10×0.60 = 6 100×1.00 = 100 200×1.20 = 240 Total 346
23			200	10×0.60 = 6 100×1.00 = 100 90×1.20 = 108 Total 214	110 (310−200)	110×1.20 = 132
25	50	1.40			160 (110+50)	110×1.20 = 132 50×1.40 = 70 Total 202
30			80	80×1.20 = 96	80 (160−80)	30×1.20 = 36 50×1.40 = 70 Total 106

[1] The receipt on June 3 increased the total inventory to 180 kg. The costs of the two components are added together to arrive at an inventory value of $148.

[2] The issue on June 7 reduced the total inventory to 110 kg. The amount of 70 kg issued came from the first items in inventory, the 80 kg at 1 June. This left 10 kg of those items and 100 kg of the items received on June 3. These were valued at their respective purchase price per kg. This process can be followed through with each subsequent receipt and issue. In each case, the items issued are taken from the first items delivered which are still left in inventory. Thus, first in, first out (FIFO).

The same result for the value of closing inventory can be quickly calculated:

Units available (80+100+200+50)	430
Less: units issued (70+200+80)	(350)
Balance of units	80
Valuation:	
50 at latest price $1.40	$70
30 at previous price of $1.20	$36
	$106

ACTIVITY 1

At 30 September, Fiford Limited had an inventory of 100 kg of fifolium, which had cost $5 per kg. In October, it made the following purchases and sales of fifolium:

	Purchases		Issues
	kg	Price per kg $	kg
October 3			40
10	80	5.20	

	Purchases		Issues
12			75
14			50
15	50	5.24	
17			45
22	70	5.28	
29	100	5.32	
30			70

Required

Calculate the quantity and value of the inventory of fifolium at 31 October using the FIFO method.

Valuing inventory using AVCO

Unlike FIFO, no priority is given to the theoretical order in which goods are issued from inventory into production. When calculating the value of issues and inventory using AVCO, the weighted average cost of inventory is calculated **every time new goods are received**.

TOP TIP

This process is extremely important. The most common mistake is to try to value inventory after both receipt and issue of items.

Walkthrough

The process of valuation using AVCO will now be demonstrated using the same data as for the previous walkthrough, FIFO.

Note: This method often leads to dollars and cents.

Date	Receipts		Issues		Inventory	
	kg	Price per kg $	kg	Value $	kg	Value $
June 1					80	48
3	100	1.00			180	148
[1]					(80+100)	(100+48)
						(148÷180) =
						0.822 per kg
7			70	58 [1]	110	90
[2]				(70×0.822)	(180−70)	(148−58)
16	200	1.20			310	330 [2]
					(110+200)	(240+90)÷310 =
						1.065 per kg
23			200	213	110	117
				(200×1.065)	(310−200)	110×1.065
25	50	1.40			160	187 [3]
					(110+50)	(117+70)÷160 =
						1.169 per kg
30			80	94	80	93
				(80×1.169)	(160−80)	(80×1.169)

[1] After the receipt of goods on 3 June, a weighted average cost of inventory is calculated. On that date there was 180 kg in inventory at a total cost of $148. Thus, the weighted average cost per kg was:

$\frac{\$148}{180} = \$0.822$ per kg

This value was then used to calculate the cost of the issue of inventory on June 7:
70 kg × $0.822 = $58 (rounded to the nearest dollar).

[2] A new average cost per kg was calculated after the receipt of goods on June 16. This was applied to the issue on June 23.

[3] Finally, a new weighted average cost was calculated after the receipt on June 25. This was applied to the issue on June 30 and the closing inventory on that date.

TOP TIP

Figures have been rounded in some cases above. You may be told in questions how to round the figures and how many decimal places to use.

ACTIVITY 2

A. V. Co. had an inventory of 200 digital hammers at 31 May. The hammers were valued at $5 each. Transactions in digital hammers in the month of June were as follows:

Date	Quantity received	Price per hammer ($)	Quantity sold
June 4	100	5.20	
10			75
13	100	5.35	
20			150
26	80	5.40	
30			90

Required

Calculate the closing inventory of digital hammers at 30 June, showing quantity and total value based on weighted average cost.

28.6 Perpetual and periodic inventories

An **inventory** is a record of goods received by, and used or sold by, a business. A **perpetual inventory** maintains a running balance of inventory-on-hand after each transaction. The examples given above for FIFO and AVCO are a typical perpetual inventory.

A **periodic inventory** shows the balance of inventory only at intervals (e.g. at the end of each month). The total of items used in the period is deducted from the total of items received to give the balance of items. The 'quick' method, shown above, of calculating the value of closing inventory on the FIFO basis, is an example of a periodic inventory.

28.7 The effect of method of inventory valuation on profits over the life of a business

The profit made over the whole life of a business is not affected by the choice of method of valuing inventory. This is demonstrated in the following example.

Quad Limited began business in year 1 and stopped trading at the end of year 4. The following information is given for each of the four years.

	Year 1	Year 2	Year 3	Year 4
	$	$	$	$
Sales	1000	1400	1600	800
Purchases	600	800	700	400
Closing inventory:				
Using FIFO	80	100	90	–
Using AVCO	70	90	80	–

Income statement (using FIFO for valuing inventory)

	Year 1		Year 2		Year 3		Year 4	
	$	$	$	$	$	$	$	$
Revenue		1000		1400		1600		800
Opening inventory	–		80		100		90	
Purchases	600		800		700		400	
Closing inventory (FIFO)	(80)	(520)	(100)	(780)	(90)	(710)	–	(490)
Gross profit		480		620		890		310
Total gross profit								2300

Income statement (AVCO)

	Year 1		Year 2		Year 3		Year 4	
	$	$	$	$	$	$	$	$
Revenue		1000		1400		1600		800
Opening inventory	–		70		90		80	
Purchases	600		800		700		400	
Closing inventory (AVCO)	(70)	(530)	(90)	(780)	(80)	(710)	–	(480)
Gross profit		470		620		890		320
Total gross profit								2300

28.8 FIFO and AVCO compared

It is important to compare the advantages and disadvantages of FIFO and AVCO in order to decide which method is the right one to use in particular circumstances.

FIFO

Advantages

a It is a relatively simple system to use.

b It is generally realistic. Materials are normally used in FIFO order, and goods will be sold in that order, especially if they are perishable.

c Prices used are those that have actually been paid for goods.

d Closing inventory is valued on current price levels.

e FIFO is an acceptable method of inventory valuation for the purposes of the Companies Act 2006 and accounting standards (IAS 2).

Disadvantages

a Manufacturing businesses usually prefer to charge materials to production at current purchase prices or selling prices, but use FIFO to value inventories for their financial accounts.

b Identical items of inventory from batches bought at different times may be used for similar jobs, with the result that job A may be charged for the item at a different price from job B. The customer for job B may be unfairly treated as a result. Quotations for jobs when materials are based on FIFO may be unreliable.

c In times of rising prices, the closing inventory in the financial accounts will be priced at the latest (high) prices. This results in lowering cost of sales and increasing gross profit. It may be considered that this is not consistent with the concept of prudence. However, as stated above, the method is acceptable under IAS 2.

AVCO

Advantages

a The use of average prices avoids the inequality of identical items being charged to different jobs at different prices.

b AVCO recognises that identical items purchased at different times and prices have identical values. Averaged prices are truer to this concept than actual prices used for FIFO.

c Averaging costs may smooth variations in production costs, and comparisons between the results of different periods may be more meaningful.

d Averaged prices used to value closing inventory may be fairly close to the latest prices.

e AVCO is acceptable for the purposes of the Companies Act 2006 and IAS 2.

Disadvantages

a The average price must be recalculated after every purchase of inventory.

b The average price does not represent any price actually paid for inventory.

Neither method is better than the other. Indeed, both methods are used extensively in industry. The only comment to make is that once the method is chosen it should not be changed, unless doing so gives a more realistic value of the business. This is in line both with IAS 2 and the concept of consistency.

Neither does either method of valuation apply only to direct materials. It is quite common in manufacturing companies to have inventories of indirect materials, such as drill bits or saw blades. Rather than value inventories such as this using the replacement method discussed in Chapter 11, a computerised accounting system easily allows inventory records to be maintained using either FIFO or AVCO.

28.9 Direct and indirect labour

Labour costs must also be classified as direct or indirect. The principle is exactly the same as materials. If the wages paid to employees can be traced directly to the cost unit then they are regarded as direct labour. For example, the wages of an employee who is assembling the various components of the computer into the finished product will be treated as direct labour. In order to work out how much of the, say, hourly rate is charged to each cost unit, the time the worker takes on each product will be calculated.

Walkthrough

A worker is paid $20 an hour. In that time he can assemble four complete computers.

The direct labour cost per cost unit will be $\$20 \div 4 = \$5$ per cost unit.

If there is a supervisor in the assembly room who is not directly involved in assembling the finished product, the wages paid to them will be treated as an indirect labour cost. Again, as with indirect materials, the total of the indirect wages is calculated and charged to each cost unit on a pre-determined basis. Indirect labour is charged to a cost centre and then included when calculating an overhead absorption rate (see Section 28.10).

The ways in which labour is paid

There are three ways in which workers can be paid:

a An **hourly rate**. This is quite a common method for paying direct workers. As with the example above, you may have to divide the hourly rate by the amount the worker can produce in an hour to work out the direct labour cost per unit.

b By how much the worker produces. This is known as **piece rate**, as it is calculated on the number of units of output – or pieces – the worker makes.

c By means of an **annual salary**. This is the usual method for paying office staff or managers. This would be regarded as an indirect labour cost.

In addition to the three methods above, the employee may receive an additional amount either as an **overtime payment** or a **bonus payment**.

KEY TERMS

Overtime payment: An amount paid to an employee for working longer than the time they are contracted to work.

Bonus payment: The additional amount paid to an employee for producing goods in a time less than that allowed.

Walkthrough

Samira stitches together woollen sweaters from parts provided by the manufacturer. For each complete sweater she is paid $3. The manufacturer sends her enough individual pieces to make 20 complete sweaters. When she returns them, provided the manufacturer is happy with the quality of her work, she will be paid a total of $60. This piece rate method of payment would also be regarded as direct wages.

It may include a bonus if she can complete them within a certain time. Alternatively, the manufacturer may pay her $3 for, say, the first 20 completed units and $4 for every unit over that number.

Unlike the hourly rate, there is no time limit on how long it takes Samira and she can complete the work at home. This may lead to work being rushed, meaning the quality of the finished article may be an issue. Alternatively, Samira may take longer than expected to complete the work, which may cause problems with a customer.

Although this method is quite widely used, it is up to management to keep a close eye on both the time taken and the quality of work produced by the worker.

Walkthrough

Jacqueline works from home. Her employer sends her 1 000 letters to put into envelopes ready to be posted. Her employer offers Jacqueline two methods of payment:

1. she will be paid \$0.50 for each completed envelope and a bonus of \$20 if she completes the work within two days
2. she will be paid \$0.30 for the first 700 completed and \$0.60 for the next 300.

Under option **1** she will receive a total of $(1\,000 \times \$0.50) + \$20 = \$520$.

Under option **2** she will receive $(700 \times \$0.30) + (300 \times \$0.60) = \$390$.

Provided she is confident she can complete the work in two days she should accept method **1**.

Walkthrough

Jaiwan works as a carpenter, making and assembling office desks. He normally works a 38-hour week from Monday to Friday.

For the week ended 30 June, he worked 40 hours from Monday to Friday, 4 hours on Saturday and 5 hours on Sunday.

The hourly rate of pay is \$12.

Overtime is paid at time and one-third for overtime between Monday and Friday, time and a half on Saturday and double time on Sunday.

Below is how Jaiwan's total pay for the week ended 30 June is calculated:

$$\text{Normal week} = 38 \text{ hours} \times \$12 = \$456$$

$$\text{Overtime Monday to Friday} = 2 \text{ hours } (40-38) \times \$16 \ (\$12 \times 1\tfrac{1}{3}) = \$32$$

$$\text{Payment for Saturday} = 4 \text{ hours} \times \$18 \ (\$12 \times 1\tfrac{1}{2}) = \$72$$

$$\text{Payment for Sunday} = 5 \text{ hours} \times \$24 \ (\$12 \times 2) = \$120$$

$$\text{Total for the week} = \$456 + \$32 + \$72 + \$120 = \$680$$

Notice the terms used here. Time and one-third means that for every hour at this rate Jaiwan is paid an extra third on top of his normal hourly rate of \$12. Similarly, for time and a half he receives an extra half of his hourly rate and for double time twice his hourly rate.

In total, Jaiwan worked a total of 49 hours $(38 + 2 + 4 + 5)$ for the week. At his normal rate this would earn him $\$49 \times \$12 = \$588$. The difference between the two figures, \$92 (\$680 – \$588), is called the **overtime premium**. Some businesses treat the premium as indirect labour.

KEY TERM

Overtime premium: The additional amount given to employees for overtime working. For example, if an employee is paid overtime at a rate of 50% above their normal hourly rate (or time and a half) the extra 50% is the overtime premium.

Walkthrough

Lee works for the same firm and is paid an hourly rate of \$15 and is expected to work a 40-hour week. In that time, his employer expects him to complete 20 desks. He is paid a bonus of \$20 for every hour he saves, provided his work is satisfactory. Workers may also be paid a bonus based on the output produced.

During the week ended 24 August, he worked 40 hours and produces 23 desks. The calculation of Lee's gross pay for the week ended 24 August is as follows:

$$\text{Normal wages} = 40 \text{ hours} \times \$15 = \$600$$

Bonus payment:

Each desk should take Lee 2 hours (40 hours ÷ 20). The 23 desks should have taken him 46 hours to make (23 ÷ 20 × 40), or 23 desks × 2 hours.

Lee has saved 6 hours so the bonus payment will be 6 hours × \$20 = \$120. Lee's gross pay for the week will be \$600 + \$120 = \$720.

ACTIVITY 3

Chan usually works a 40-hour week. He is paid \$18 per hour. If he works overtime he is paid time and a half for every overtime hour worked.

In a week, he is expected to produce 360 completed units. Provided the work is satisfactory, for every unit he produces in excess of 360 he receives \$5. He also receives a bonus of \$12 per hour for every hour he saves.

For the week ended 31 March, Chan worked 44 hours. In that time he made 414 acceptable units.

Required

Calculate the following:

a Chan's basic pay for the week

b the amount paid in overtime, clearly showing the overtime premium

c the amount paid for excess production

d the bonus payment in respect of time saved

e Chan's total gross pay for the week ended 31 March.

Advantages to a firm of offering bonus and overtime payments

- Provided the work is of the correct standard, it will increase productivity.
- It will give the firm a greater number of units to sell and overall may increase total profit.

Disadvantages to a firm of offering bonus and overtime payments

- It may cause workers to rush at the expense of quality. Therefore all work should be checked thoroughly before any payment is approved.
- If the extra production cannot be sold, the firm will incur increased inventory holding costs.
- The business may not be able to pass on the extra costs incurred to customers.

28.10 How to apportion overheads to cost centres

A **cost centre** is any location in a business to which costs may be attributed. A cost centre is usually a department or process, but may be an item of equipment (a machine) or even a person (e.g. a marketing manager):

- **Production cost centres** are directly involved in producing goods (e.g. moulding or shaping raw material, assembling components, painting).
- **Service cost centres** are not involved in the production of goods, but provide services for the production cost centres (e.g. stores, building and plant maintenance or a canteen).

Allocation and apportionment of costs to production cost centres

Direct expenses and some overhead expenses, such as indirect labour or materials, can be identified with specific cost centres and are **allocated directly** to them (**allocation of costs**).

Overheads which may be identified with, and allocated to, specific cost centres include:

- wood, metal, plastic, chemicals, components, and so on (production department)
- paint (paints shop)
- packing materials (packing department) (take care though as sometimes these may be regarded as direct materials; you will be told whether or not they are direct or indirect items)
- lubricating oil (the machine shop)
- maintenance of handling equipment (the stores or warehouse)
- food (the canteen).

Other overheads are incurred for the business generally and are **apportioned** to cost centres on suitable bases (**apportionment of costs**).

Overhead	Basis of apportionment
Heating and lighting (when not separately metered to the cost centres) rent, insurance of buildings	In proportion to the respective floor areas of the departments
Power (if metered separately to cost centres)	Actual consumption (this is allocation rather than apportionment)
Insurance of plant, machinery and other assets	On cost or replacement values of assets in each department
Depreciation of non-current assets	On the cost or book value of assets in each department

KEY TERMS

Cost centre: Any location, usually a department, in a business to which costs may be attributed.

Production cost centres: Locations which are directly involved in producing goods.

Service cost centres: Locations which are not involved in the production of goods, but provide services for the production cost centres (e.g. stores, building and plant maintenance, canteen etc.).

Allocation of costs: Charging costs directly to the cost centres which can be directly identified with them.

Apportionment of costs: The process of charging costs to cost centres using a suitable basis. Such costs cannot be directly identified with a single cost centre.

Walkthrough

Oar Manufacturers has four production cost centres: moulding, machining, painting and packaging.

The following information is available:

Cost centres	Moulding	Machining	Painting	Packaging
Floor area (square metres)	1000	700	500	300
Plant and machinery at cost ($000)	50	40	20	10

Details of forecast expenditure for the year ended 31 December 2016 are as follows:

	$
Direct materials:	
Moulding	50000
Machining	7000
Painting	9000
Packaging	6000
Direct labour:	
Moulding	96000
Machining	80000
Painting	40000
Packaging	18000
Indirect labour:	
Moulding	11000
Machining	9000
Painting	4000
Packaging	1000
Overheads:	
Factory rent	45000
Repairs and maintenance of factory	5000
Factory depreciation	6000
Insurance of factory	2500
Heating and lighting	5500
Depreciation of plant and machinery	12000
Maintenance of plant and machinery	18000
Insurance of plant	3000

Apportioning overheads will involve a lot of calculations and time. You may be given the basis on which to apportion overheads. Sometimes you may have to decide. If you have to decide it will mean matching the overhead cost with a suitable basis of apportionment. Check back to the table earlier to see typical methods.

The overhead apportionment will be as follows:

Expense	Basis	Total	Moulding	Machining	Painting	Packaging
		$	$	$	$	$
Indirect labour [1]	Allocation	25 000	11 000	9 000	4 000	1 000
Factory:						
Rent [2]	Floor area	45 000	18 000	12 600	9 000	5 400
Repairs and maintenance	Floor area	5 000	2 000	1 400	1 000	600
Depreciation	Floor area	6 000	2 400	1 680	1 200	720
Insurance	Floor area	2 500	1 000	700	500	300
Heating and lighting	Floor area	5 500	2 200	1 540	1 100	660
Plant and machinery:						
Depreciation [3]	Cost	12 000	5 000	4 000	2 000	1 000
Maintenance	Cost	18 000	7 500	6 000	3 000	1 500
Insurance	Cost	3 000	1 250	1 000	500	250
Total overhead [4]		122 000	50 350	37 920	22 300	11 430

[1] Note that direct expenses (materials and labour) are not entered in the overhead analysis. You may also be given other ways in which indirect costs may also be already apportioned to cost centres. If this is the case use them as they have been given. **Don't try to reallocate them**.

[2] Some of the overheads are split using floor area as the basis of apportionment. Rent is a good example of this. The total rent expense was $45 000. The total floor area of the four cost centres is 2 500 (1 000 + 700 + 500 + 300) square metres. The cost per square metre for rent is therefore:

$$\frac{\$45\,000}{2\,500} = \$18 \text{ per square metre}$$

Thus, the total cost to apportion to moulding will be the number of square metres it occupies: (1 000) × $18 = $18 000. This is the figure shown in the table above.

[3] Similarly, with the depreciation of plant and machinery, the total expense is $12 000. The total cost of the plant and machinery is $120 000 (50 000 + 40 000 + 20 000 + 10 000). Thus, the calculation for moulding in this case is:

$$\frac{\$12\,000 \times \$50\,000^*}{\$120\,000} = \$5\,000$$

*cost of plant and machinery in the moulding department

[4] Always spend a little time making sure that the totals across the bottom of any table always add up. For example, in the apportionment chart above $50 350 + $37 920 + $22 300 + $11 430 = $122 000. This is important, as a mistake at this stage will probably affect the rest of the calculation.

TOP TIP

When calculating the overheads apportioned to each department, the answer is unlikely to come out as a round figure in every case. Round the figures up or down, but always make sure the totals for each department add across to the overall total for the expense.

It is now possible to calculate the total cost per cost centre including direct expenditure:

Expense	Basis	Total	Moulding	Machining	Painting	Packaging
		$	$	$	$	$
Direct costs:						
Materials	Actual	72 000	50 000	7 000	9 000	6 000
Labour	Actual	234 000	96 000	80 000	40 000	18 000
Total direct cost		306 000	146 000	87 000	49 000	24 000
Apportionment of overhead	From table above	122 000	50 350	37 920	22 300	11 430
Total cost per cost centre		428 000	196 350	124 920	71 300	35 430

ACTIVITY 4

Teepops Limited manufactures a single product which passes through four stages of production: machining, painting, assembly and packing. The following expenditure has been incurred by the company in the year ended 31 March 2016:

	$000
Direct materials:	
Machining	80
Painting	20
Assembly	5
Packing	12
Direct labour:	
Machining	136
Painting	74
Assembly	68
Packing	45
Indirect labour:	
Machining	51
Painting	32
Assembly	28
Packing	14
Factory expenses:	
Rent	90
Heating and lighting	70
Maintenance	30
Insurance	20
Plant and machinery:	
Depreciation	80
Repairs	32
Insurance	16

Additional information

1 The floor areas of the departments are:

	Square metres
Machining	500
Painting	200
Assembly	200
Packing	100

2 Plant and machinery at cost is:

	$000
Machining	90
Painting	40
Assembly	10
Packing	20

Required

a Calculate the total overhead cost for each department.

b Calculate the total cost of production for each department.

Apportionment of service cost centre overheads to production cost centres

The total cost of goods produced includes all overhead expenditure, including the overheads of service departments; these must be apportioned to the production departments on suitable bases. The bases usually adopted are:

Service cost centre	Apportioned on
Stores	Number or value of stores requisitions raised by production cost centre
Canteen	Number of persons in each production cost centre
Building maintenance	Area occupied by each production cost centre*
Plant and machinery maintenance	Number or value of machines in each cost centre*

* However, records of actual maintenance costs may be kept and the costs allocated accordingly.

There are a number of ways of apportioning service cost centre overheads to production cost centres and they all usually produce very similar results. The simplest, and quickest, way is the elimination method.

Walkthrough

Eliminator Limited has three production and two service departments for which the following information is available:

	Foundry	Finishing	Assembly	Canteen	Stores
No. of stores requisitions	200	100	50	70	–
No. of staff	40	15	20	10	7
Overheads ($000) [1]	110	60	50	30	35

[1] In this case, the total overheads have already been apportioned to cost centres using suitable bases.

It is now necessary to apportion the overhead of one service department to the other cost centres. That service department cost centre is then eliminated from future apportionments. If, as in this case, there is more than one service cost centre, there will be more steps until the last service cost centre is apportioned over the production cost centres.

The table below shows how the costs of the two service department cost centres are apportioned to the other cost centres.

	Foundry	Finishing	Assembly	Canteen	Stores [1]
	$	$	$	$	$
Overheads	110 000	60 000	50 000	30 000	35 000
First apportionment*	16 667	8 333	4 167	5 833	(35 000)
Second apportionment**	19 110	7 167	9 556	(35 833)	–
	145 777	75 500	63 723	–	–

[1] The stores cost centre has been allocated first because it does work for the canteen, whereas the canteen does not do any work for the stores.

*Based on 420 requisitions.

Based on 75 staff (40 + 15 + 20, the number of staff in each **production cost centre).

The calculation is identical to those earlier. The total costs allocated to the stores department is \$35 000. The total requisitions is (200 + 100 + 50 + 70) = 420. Thus, the costs to apportion to the foundry department is:

$$\frac{\$35\,000}{420} \times 200 = \$16\,667$$

As the canteen does some work for the stores (provides food for the workers of that department), some of the overheads of the stores department is apportioned to the canteen. As a result, the total costs of the canteen now increases from \$30 000 to \$35 833. It is important to remember to add this before apportioning the costs of the canteen.

Similarly, the costs of the canteen can now be apportioned. This is based on the number of staff.

The canteen costs apportioned to the foundry department is:

$$\frac{\$35\,833 \times 40}{75} = \$19\,111$$

(Note that figures have been rounded.)

ACTIVITY 5

Healthy Foods has three production departments: mixing, bakery and packaging. It also has two service departments: stores and canteen. The following information is provided.

	Mixing	Bakery	Packaging	Canteen	Stores
Overheads (\$000)	165	124	87	90	80
No. of staff	60	80	40	18	15
No. of stores requisitions	300	80	20	40	-

Required

Apportion the service department overheads to the production departments on appropriate bases.

28.11 How to calculate overhead absorption rates

KEY TERM

Overhead absorption rate (OAR): The rate at which costs apportioned to a cost centre are charged to the cost unit passing through it.

Once overheads have been apportioned to cost centres, the next step is to calculate **overhead absorption rates (OARs)**. The OARs are then used to calculate the amount of overhead to be attributed to each cost unit as it passes through each cost centre.

Cost units are units of production. For example:

- a computer (computer manufacturer)
- a garment (dress maker)
- a thousand electric lamps (manufacturer of electric lamps)
- a barrel of oil (oil well)
- passenger-mile (freight transport)
- a kilowatt-hour (electricity generation).

Overhead absorption rates are calculated for future periods because the cost of production must be known in advance to enable selling prices to be fixed. Calculations are based on planned volumes of output and budgeted, or forecast, overhead expenditure.

The amount of overhead absorbed by a cost unit is usually calculated by reference to the time taken to produce it. There are other methods but they are generally considered to be less satisfactory for reasons that will be discussed later. The two methods about to be described assume that a unit of production absorbs overheads (rent, heat and lighting, for example) proportionately to the time spent on processing it in the cost centres. This time is measured either in direct labour hours or machine hours.

Direct labour overhead absorption rate

A process is labour intensive when it requires the use of labour rather than machines, and the labour cost is greater than the cost of using machinery. The time is measured in direct labour hours.

Walkthrough

Working Limited makes two products, P and Q. The output for September is budgeted as follows:

Product P	10 000 units
Product Q	8 000 units

Each unit of P requires 1½ direct labour hours to make, and each unit of Q requires ¾ direct labour hour.

The total number of direct labour hours required to produce 10 000 units of P and 8 000 units of Q is:

$$(10\,000 \times 1\tfrac{1}{2}) + (8\,000 \times \tfrac{3}{4}) = 21\,000$$

If Working Limited's overheads for September are $131 250, the overhead absorption rate is:

$$\frac{\$131\,250}{21\,000} = \$6.25 \text{ per direct labour hour}$$

TOP TIP

The formula is the total cost divided by the basis of absorption. Often students get this the wrong way round. Always put the suffix of direct labour hours (or machine hours).

Therefore, the amount of overhead absorbed by each unit of P is $6.25 × 1½ = $9.375 and the amount absorbed by Q is ¾ × $6.25 = $4.6875. The total overhead is therefore fully absorbed as follows:

	$
Product P: 10 000 × $9.375	93 750
Product Q: 8 000 × $4.6875	37 500
Total overhead absorbed	131 250

ACTIVITY 6

Challenge Limited manufactures two products, firsts and seconds. The number of direct labour hours required for each unit is: firsts 1.3; seconds 0.7.

In July, the company plans to produce 5 000 firsts and 7 000 seconds. Challenge Limited's estimated overhead expenditure for July is $129 276.

Required

a Calculate the direct labour overhead absorption rate per unit of:

i first

ii second.

b Show how the overhead for July is absorbed by the planned production for the month.

Machine hour overhead absorption rate

A cost centre is capital intensive when the operations carried out in the centre are mechanised and the machinery running cost is greater than the direct labour cost. Overhead should then be absorbed on a machine hour rate (machine hour OAR).

Walkthrough

Jigsaw Limited has six machines which are used nine hours each day in a five-day working week. Therefore, the number of machine hours in a six-month period is (6×9×5×26) or 7 020 machine hours.

If Jigsaw Limited's overheads for the six months are $114 075, the machine hour absorption rate is:

$$\frac{\$114\,075}{7\,020} = \$16.25 \text{ per machine hour}$$

TOP TIP

Always make sure you choose the correct basis on which to calculate the overhead absorption rate.

Often both direct labour and machine hours are given for one cost centre. Always choose the greatest. For example, for a particular cost centre, direct labour hours are forecast to be 10 000 and machine hours to be 90 000. In this case choose machine hours.

Never add the two sets of hours together.

ACTIVITY 7

Robot Limited uses ten machines to produce its goods. The machines are used seven hours a day for six days per week. In a period of 13 weeks, it is planned to produce 1 200 units, and the overheads are estimated to amount to $141 960.

Required

a Calculate the machine hour overhead absorption rate.

b Calculate the amount of overhead absorbed by each unit of production.

The following is a comprehensive example which covers everything on absorption of overheads. Work through carefully, as this is an important topic.

Walkthrough

Jenx Limited manufactures two products, L and P, each of which requires processing in the company's three production departments, I, II and III.

The following information is available from the company's budget for the next six months:

Production departments	I	II	III
Budgeted overheads	$95 920	$86 250	$96 000
Budgeted machine hours	22 000	9 000	23 000
Budgeted direct labour hours	14 000	23 000	32 000

From this information it is possible to calculate a suitable overhead rate for each production department. This is shown below.

Department I is machine intensive and departments II and III are labour intensive. Thus, the overhead absorption rates (OARs) are:

Dept I machine hour $\frac{\$95\,920}{22\,000} = \$4.36$ per machine hour

Dept II direct labour hours $\frac{\$86\,250}{23\,000} = \$3.75$ per direct labour hour

Dept III direct labour hours $\frac{\$96\,000}{32\,000} = \$3.00$ per direct labour

Having calculated the overhead absorption rate for each production department, it is now possible to calculate the overheads absorbed by each cost unit. The accountant has identified the following budgeted data:

	Product L	Product P
Machine hours per unit:		
Dept I	3	2
Dept II	1	1
Dept III	2	3
Direct labour hours per unit:		
Dept I	1	2
Dept II	2	3
Dept III	3	4

Using the appropriate overhead absorption rate for each department, the overheads absorbed by each product can be calculated. This is shown below.

OAR per unit		Dept I		Dept II		Dept III	Total
Product L [1]	($4.36×3)	$13.08	($3.75×2)	$7.50	($3×3)	$9.00	$29.58
Product P	($4.36×2)	$8.72	($3.75×3)	$11.25	($3×4)	$12.00	$31.97

[1] Product L requires three machine hours in department I. Thus, the total overheads which will be charged to each unit of L as it passes through that department is three machine hours × $4.36 per machine hour = $13.08.

Similarly, product P requires four direct labour hours when it is being worked on in department III.

The overhead which will be charged to each unit of P as it is worked on in that department is:

4 direct labour hours × $3 per hour = $12.00

Adding across the **total** overhead charged or absorbed by each product as it passes through the three departments is:

Product L $13.08 + $7.50 + $9.00 = $29.58

Product P $8.72 + $11.25 + $12.00 = $31.97

When talking about production and overheads the term 'recovery' is often heard. Ideally a business will want to make sure that all the overheads it incurs are charged to production. As we have seen, each unit produced will be charged with an amount of overheads. Another way of expressing this is to say that each unit produced **recovers** some of the total overheads. Think of the total overheads as a 'well of costs'. Each unit produced is like a bucket placed in that well and drawing out, or recovering, some of the overheads.

It is now possible to see whether the total budgeted production will recover the total budgeted overhead.

Walkthrough

Jenx Limited is budgeting to sell 4 000 units of product L and 5 000 units of product P in the next six months. Will that recover all the budgeted overheads for that period? The following table will show whether or not this is the case.

Total overhead recovery		Dept I		Dept II		Dept III	Total
		$		$		$	$
Product L [1]	(4 000 × $13.08)	52 320	(4 000 × $7.50)	30 000	(4 000 × $9)	36 000	118 320
Product P [2]	(5 000 × $8.72)	43 600	(5 000 × $11.25)	56 250	(5 000 × $12)	60 000	159 850
		95 920		86 250		96 000	278 170

[1] Product L will recover a total of $53 320 overheads incurred in department I (4 000 units × $13.08).

[2] Adding the totals across the bottom, it can be seen that the budgeted production will indeed recover the budgeted overheads in the six months. This does though assume that everything goes according to plan!

Having calculated the overhead charged to each product, the next stage is to use it, together with other information, to calculate the factory cost of each unit. This is done by adding the overhead cost of each product with its direct materials and labour costs.

The accountant of Jenx Limited has provided the following information to help do this.

	Product L	Product P
Cost of direct materials per unit	$17	$16
Direct wages per unit	$10	$8

The total factory cost of each product is, therefore:

Total cost per unit	Product L	Product P
	$	$
Direct materials	17.00	16.00
Direct labour	10.00	8.00
Overhead	29.58	31.97
Total cost	56.58	55.97

The figure calculated is the factory cost as nothing has been added to cover other overheads, such as selling and distribution, administrative or finance costs. Some businesses will also add a percentage to the factory cost to contribute towards covering these other overheads.

You will also notice that we have referred to factory costs, selling and distribution, administrative and finance costs. This is known as classifying costs by **function**. The selling and distribution aspect, for example, is a function required to run a business.

Now that the factory cost has been calculated, it is possible to add an element of profit to it to arrive at a possible selling price of each product. The addition of something for profit is designed to cover all other overheads incurred by the business **and** leave some profit for the business.

Suppose that in this case the directors of Jenx Limited always want to earn a 40% mark-up on the cost of each unit sold. The budgeted selling price for each unit is, therefore:

	Product L	Product P
	$	$
Direct materials	17.00	16.00
Direct labour	10.00	8.00
Overhead	29.58	31.97
Total factory cost	56.58	55.97
Add: required profit at 40%	22.63	22.39
Budgeted selling price	79.21	78.36

The directors will be hoping that this selling price will cover all the other overheads and leave some profit.

Walkthrough

Anton produces a single product. The factory cost of each unit has been calculated as $120. Anton always aims to earn a profit margin of 40% on each unit.

The selling price in this case is calculated as follows. Looking back at what was covered in Section 16.7, we know that if the profit margin is 40% of the selling price of a unit, the cost must be 60% of the selling price. Therefore, to calculate the selling price in this case, use the calculation:

$$\frac{\$120}{60\%} = \$200$$

Anton will quote a selling price of $200 per unit to earn a 40% margin.

Walkthrough

A company calculated its overhead absorption rates for the six months to 30 June and the next six months to 31 December as follows:

	Six months to 30 June	Six months to 31 December
Budgeted overhead expenditure	$200 000	$240 000
Budgeted direct labour hours	80 000	100 000
Actual expenditure	$215 000	$230 000
Actual direct labour hours	76 000	106 000
Budgeted OAR	$\frac{200\,000}{80\,000}$ = $2.50 per direct labour hour	$\frac{240\,000}{100\,000}$ = $2.40 per direct labour hour
Overhead recovered [1]	76 000 × $2.50 = $190 000	106 000 × $2.40 = $254 400
(Under-)/over-absorption [2]	$(215 000 − 190 000) = ($25 000)	$(230 000 − 254 400) = $24 400

[1] T[he calculation of overhead recovered is the **actual** direct labour hours × **budgeted** overhead absorption rate. The most common mistake is to calculate an actual overhead absorption rate and use that to work out over- or under-absorption.

[2] The overhead recovered is then **deducted** from the **actual** overhead.

In the first six months, actual overhead is more than the recovered overhead, so overheads are under-absorbed. This is usually shown in brackets. This means that not enough overheads have been charged to production.

In the next six months, the reverse is the situation. Over- or under-recovery will impact on the profit of a business. In this case, one period virtually cancels out the other so the impact should be minimal.

TOP TIP

It is important to clearly identify over- or under-absorption.

ACTIVITY 9

Upandown Limited has provided the following information about its overhead expenditure for four quarterly periods ended 31 December:

	Three months to 31 March	Three months to 30 June	Three months to 30 September	Three months to 31 December
Budgeted overhead	$124 000	$128 000	$130 000	$131 000
Budgeted machine hours	1 000	1 000	1 000	1 000
Actual overhead	$128 000	$125 000	$129 500	$132 800
Actual machine hours	900	1 050	1 100	980

Required

Calculate the under-absorption or over-absorption of overhead in each of the four quarterly periods. State clearly in each case whether the overhead was under-or over-absorbed.

Key learning points

- Learn the definitions of **cost centre** and **cost unit**.
- Be prepared to apportion overheads to cost centres and to reapportion service cost centre overheads to production cost centres.
- Practise calculating overhead absorption rates.
- Be prepared to state when direct labour OARs and machine hour OARs should be used and to explain why other methods of calculating OARs are normally unsuitable.
- Learn how to calculate under-absorption and over-absorption of overheads.
- Check all calculations carefully.
- Make sure you understand the causes of under-absorption and over-absorption.

Chapter summary

This is an important chapter as it links aspects of financial accounting (margin, mark-up, manufacturing accounts) with the next six chapters. You have been introduced to the basics of cost accounting (what it is and what it is used for), including how to analyse costs, record and value materials and labour (including the method of calculating gross wages, taking into account both overtime and bonus payments, and the advantages and disadvantages of these payments for a business). When analysing, recording and valuing costs, you should also be able to tell the difference between direct and indirect materials, labour, and costs.

The final topic you have learnt about in this chapter is overheads, and you should now be familiar with how to allocate and apportion overheads, how to calculate overhead absorption rates (OARs), the causes of over-/under-absorption of overheads, and how to calculate this.

TOP TIP

Many of the terms used in this chapter will be used in the next chapters on cost and management accounting. Similarly, many of the techniques demonstrated will be used again. Take some time to work through everything covered here. Only move on to the next chapters when you are happy you understand everything.

Practice exercises

1 **a** Define the term 'overhead expenses'.

b Explain the meaning of the following terms as they relate to overhead expenditure:
i allocation
ii apportionment.

c Explain the meaning of the terms:
i overhead absorption
ii overhead under-absorption
iii overhead over-absorption.

d State reasons why a company might recover more in overheads than the amount spent on overheads in the period.

e Explain why estimated figures are used to calculate overhead absorption rates.

2 State **three** ways in which labour can be remunerated. Distinguish clearly which is treated as direct labour and which as indirect labour.

3 State **two** ways an employee can earn a bonus payment for work carried out.

4 Arthur works a standard 40-hour week. He is paid $20 per hour. If he works overtime he is paid time and a half for every overtime hour worked between Monday and Friday and double time for any hours worked on Saturday.

In a week he is expected to produce 480 completed units. Provided the work is satisfactory, for every unit he produces in excess of 480 he receives $3. He also receives a bonus of $10 per hour for every hour he saves.

For the week ended 19 November, Arthur worked 44 hours between Monday and Friday. He also worked four hours on Saturday. In that time he made 600 acceptable units.

Required
Calculate the following:

a Arthur's basic pay for the week

b the amount paid in overtime, clearly showing the overtime premium

c the amount paid for excess production

d the bonus payment in respect of time saved

e Arthur's total gross pay for the week ended 19 November.

Exam practice questions

Multiple-choice questions

1 A company bought and sold goods as follows:

	Bought		Sold
	Units	Unit price ($)	Units
March 1	20	2.00	
3	10	2.50	
4			12
5	20	3.00	
6			16

What is the value of the inventory at 6 March based on FIFO?

A $44 **B** $45
C $65 **D** $66

2 A company had the following inventory transactions in June:

June 1 Purchased 50 units at $3 per unit.
14 Purchased 100 units at $4.50 per unit.
23 Sold 70 units.
30 Purchased 62 units at $5 per unit.

What is the value of inventory at 30 June based on AVCO?

A $4.292 **B** $4.437
C $4.50 **D** $5.00

3 A company provides the following information:

Actual direct labour hours worked	13 000
Actual overhead expenditure	$520 000
Budgeted direct labour hours	14 000
Budgeted overhead expenditure	$532 000

What is the overhead absorption rate based on direct labour hours?

A $37.14 **B** $38
C $40 **D** $40.42

4 Which of the following could cause an under-absorption of overhead expenditure?

i absorption rate calculated on actual production and actual number of units produced
ii units produced exceeding the budgeted production
iii units produced being less than the planned production
iv overhead expenditure exceeding budget

A i and ii **B** i and iii
C ii and iv **D** iii and iv

5 The following information is provided by a company:

Actual direct labour hours	12 400
Actual overhead expenditure	$198 400
Budgeted direct labour hours	11 000
Budgeted overhead expenditure	$170 500

Which of the following correctly describes the overhead absorbed?

	Under-absorbed	Over-absorbed
A	$6 200	
B		$6 200
C	$21 700	
D		$21 700

6 Joe works a basic 40-hour week. In this time he is expected to produce 200 units. He is paid $12 per hour and overtime at the rate of time and a half for every hour of overtime worked. He is also paid a bonus of $5 for every unit produced in excess of 200. Last week Joe worked 44 hours and produced 210 units. What was Joe's gross pay for the week?

A $528 **B** $552
C $578 **D** $602

7 A company makes a single product. The following information is available:

Per unit	$
Direct materials	22
Direct labour 2 hours	8

Factory overheads are absorbed at $5 per direct labour hour. The company requires a selling price per unit to achieve a 50% margin.

What is the selling price per unit?

A $49 **B** $60
C $70 **D** $80

Total: 7 marks

Structured questions

1 Cleary Limited manufactures toy soldiers. The company has three production departments (moulding, sanding and painting) and two service departments (canteen and maintenance).

Required

a Explain the following terms:

i cost centre **[2 marks]**

ii cost unit. **[1 marks]**

Additional information

Estimated indirect overheads for the year ended 30 April 2016 are as follows:

Overhead	Cost ($)
Administration	104 000
Electricity	70 000
Depreciation	50 000
Indirect wages	78 565
Rent	80 500

Relevant information on the five departments is as follows:

	Moulding	Sanding	Painting	Maintenance	Canteen
No. of employees	40	50	40	40	38
Power (kW hours)	1400	1600	150	190	160
Cost of non-current asset	$162 000	$175 000	$40 000	$80 000	$43 000
Floor area (square metres)	625	475	500	400	300
Indirect wages	$6000	$11 250	$6375	$36 190	$18 750

Canteen costs are shared among all the other departments on the basis of number of employees. Maintenance costs are shared among the three production departments on the basis of floor area.

Required

b Complete the following table to show the **total** overheads apportioned to each production department.

	Overhead cost	Moulding	Sanding	Painting	Maintenance	Canteen
	$	$	$	$	$	$
Administration	104 000					
Electricity	70 000					
Depreciation	50 000					
Indirect wages	78 565					
Rent	80 500					
Total						
Reapportionment of canteen costs						
Reallocation of maintenance costs						
Total costs of production cost centres						

[10 marks]

Additional information

The following table shows the budgeted hours for each production cost centre for the year ended 30 April 2016:

	Moulding	Sanding	Painting
Direct labour hours	8000	5800	7500
Machine hours	5750	8650	1250

Required

c Calculate to **two** decimal places a suitable overhead absorption rate for each of the three production departments for the year ending 30 April 2016. **[6 marks]**

Additional information

To make one toy soldier requires direct material of $50. This table shows the following times and direct costs also required:

Department	Hours	Hourly rate
Moulding:		
Direct labour	1.00	$8
Machine hours	0.5	
Sanding:		
Direct labour	1.5	$6
Machine hours	2.00	
Painting:		
Direct labour	2.5	$10
Machine hours	0.20	

The company budgets to make a margin of 40% on each toy soldier.

Required

d Calculate the budgeted selling price of **one** toy soldier. **[6 marks]**

Additional information

The directors are considering changing to a single overhead absorption rate for use in the factory.

Required

e Advise the directors whether or not they should change to a single overhead absorption rate for the factory. Justify your answer.

[5 marks]

Total: 30

2 Auckland (Manufacturers) Limited has two manufacturing departments:

i machining

ii assembly.

It also has two service departments:

i maintenance

ii power house.

The budgeted information in the table below is available for the coming year:

	Machining	Assembly	Maintenance	Power house	Total
	$000	**$000**	**$000**	**$000**	**$000**
Indirect materials	298	482	132	152	1064
Indirect labour	706	918	282	672	2578
Rent and local taxes					1426
Supervision					660
Plant depreciation					1650
					7378

Further information is also available as follows:

	Machining	Assembly	Maintenance	Power house
No. of employees	40	80	20	10
Area (square metres)	3000	5000	1000	200
Plant valuation ($000s)	13000	5000	2400	1600
Direct labour hours	3200	4800		
Machine hours	11080	2320		
Maintenance hours	1800	600		
Units of power used	4200	1200	600	

Required

a Complete the following table to analyse the above indirect costs between the four departments showing the bases of apportionment you have used.

Expense	Basis of apportionment	Total	Machining	Assembly	Maintenance	Power house
		$000	**$000**	**$000**	**$000**	**$000**
Indirect materials						
Indirect labour						
Rent and taxes						
Supervision						
Plant depreciation						
Total allocated						

[5 marks]

b Complete the following table to reapportion the costs of the service departments over the two production departments using appropriate bases.

	Basis of apportionment	Machining	Assembly	Maintenance	Power house
		$000	**$000**	**$000**	**$000**
Reallocation of power house					
Reallocation of maintenance					
Final total for production areas					

[3 marks]

c Calculate to **two** decimal places a suitable overhead absorption rate for each production department. **[4 marks]**

d Explain the difference between overhead allocation and overhead apportionment. **[4 marks]**

Additional information

The actual data for Auckland (Manufacturers) Limited for the year was:

	Actual hours	Actual overheads
		$
Machining	12000	4100000
Assembly	4600	3300000

Required

e Explain what is meant by over-absorption of overheads? **[3 marks]**

f Calculate the over- or under-absorption of overheads for each department. **[4 marks]**

Additional information

The company manufactures a single product in batches of 100. The cost of manufacturing a batch has been calculated at $9500. The directors normally mark-up the cost by 30% to arrive at a selling price.

Required

g Calculate the budgeted selling price of a single unit of product. **[2 marks]**

Additional information

A customer is willing to place an order for 300 units. However, they want a discount of 20% on the usual selling price. The company has capacity to manufacture the order, but the directors are unhappy about giving a discount.

Required

h Advise the directors whether or not they should accept the order and allow the discount. Justify your answer. **[5 marks]**

Total: 30

Chapter 29
Unit, job and batch costing

Learning objectives

In this chapter you will learn:

- the difference between continuous and specific order operations
- what unit costing is
- what job costing is
- what batch costing is
- how to prepare a quotation for a job.

The overheads are an indirect cost. It probably relates to the cost of, say, running vans which the engineers work from, there may be some loose tools or perhaps they relate to office costs. These costs will be incurred whether or not Jobbings Limited had accepted this order or not.

If the quotation is accepted, the costs will be recorded on a job card as they are incurred by Jobbings Limited.

Job no. 107
Installation of central heating at XXXXXX

	Estimated	Actual
	$	$
Materials*	3000	2740
Labour*	1700	1920
Overhead (200% of labour)	3400	3840
Total cost [1]	8100	8500
Add: profit (25% of cost) [2]	2025	1625
Amount of quotation	10125	10125

[1] When the job had been completed, the actual costs entered on the job card show that actual cost exceeded the estimated cost by $400.

[2] The profit made is only $1625 instead of $2025.

*All the materials and labour are direct costs of the job.

The job card will provide useful information the next time Jobbings Limited quotes for a similar job. Not only that, but the directors are able to identify which areas have caused the overspend on the job: labour and overheads. They are now in a position to investigate the causes of this and take corrective action for future jobs.

This is one of the crucial advantages of cost accounting over financial accounting. As the costs have been classified for the job, the directors can focus on specific areas. In the financial accounts, these costs will be lost in amongst all the other labour, materials and overhead costs, giving the directors limited opportunities to analyse the cause of any differences or plan for the future.

ACTIVITY 2

State **two** actions the directors of Jobbings Limited can take to improve the profit earned on future jobs as a result of the above analysis.

ACTIVITY 3

Geoffrey Pannell is a professional researcher. He has been asked by the government to conduct research into allegations that mobile phones are bad for public health. Geoffrey estimates that the project will require 200 hours of his time, which he charges at $100 per hour. He will also require the services of Susan, his research assistant, for 100 hours at $60 per hour. Overheads are recovered at the rate of $40 per labour hour.

Required

a Prepare a statement to show the amount Geoffrey will charge for carrying out this research.

Additional information

An official of the government has looked at Geoffrey's quote. He has offered Geoffrey a fee of $30 000 for the work.

Required

b Advise Geoffrey whether or not he should accept the work. Justify your answer.

Batch costing

Batch costing is very similar to job costing and is applied when an order from a customer involves the production of a number of identical items. All the costs incurred are charged to the batch and the cost per unit is found by dividing the cost of the batch by the number of units in the batch.

KEY TERM

Batch costing: The costing procedure to find the cost of a batch of items produced.

Walkthrough

Evocation Limited sells reproductions of antique furniture. It places an order with Company Limited for 500 dining chairs at an agreed price of $30 000 for the batch of 500.

Company Limited has four production departments for which the following information is given:

Machining:	OAR $35 per machine hour
Finishing:	OAR $20 per direct labour hour
French polishing:	OAR $10 per direct labour hour
Assembly:	OAR $15 per direct labour hour

The costs incurred in the production of 500 dining chairs were:

Direct materials	$5 000
Direct labour:	
Machining	125 hours at $10 per hour
Finishing	180 hours at $9 per hour
French polishing	220 hours at $12 per hour
Assembly	100 hours at $8 per hour

160 machine hours were booked against the batch of chairs in the machining department.

Company Limited charges its administration expenses at 15% on the total cost of production.

The process of calculating the cost of the job is identical to the approach taken in Section 28.11. The batch cost, cost per chair and profit per chair are calculated as follows:

Costs for batch of 500 chairs		
	$	**$**
Direct materials		5 000
Direct labour:		
Machining (125 × $10)	1 250	
Finishing (180 × $9)	1 620	
French polishing (220 × $12)	2 640	
Assembly (100 × $8)	800	6 310

	$	$
Prime cost		11 310
Production overhead recovered [1]		
Machining (160 × $35)	5 600	
Finishing (180 × $20)	3 600	
French polishing (220 × $10)	2 200	
Assembly (100 × $15)	1 500	12 900
Cost of production		24 210
Add: administration costs		
($24 210 × 15%) [2]		3 632
Total cost of batch of 500 chairs		27 842
Profit		2 158
Price [3]		30 000

[1] The charge for production overheads is based on the number of hours multiplied by the overhead absorption rate. This is identical to the illustration of Jenx Limited in Section 28.11.

[2] This is an illustration of a business adding something to the factory cost of production to cover other overheads incurred.

[3] In this case, the price has been agreed at the outset as $30 000. Having analysed the job costs, the directors can see that they will expect to make a profit of $2 158 if everything goes to plan. Whether or not this is enough profit for them is not known. However, analysing in advance in this way will give them scope to think about asking for an increase in the price they will get, or where they can cut back on costs to increase the profit.

Once again we are seeing costing as something which allows a business to **plan** its future activities.

TOP TIP

You must be able to calculate a price to quote for a specific order. This was covered in Section 28.11 and is covered again here.

ACTIVITY 4

Clean Limited has received an order for 1 000 packs of paper towels. Each pack contains six rolls of towels. The following information is given:

	$
Raw materials per roll of towels	0.08
Labour hourly rate	6.00
Cost of setting up machinery	30.00
Overhead absorption rate per labour hour	9.35

100 packs of towels are manufactured per hour.

Required

a Calculate the cost of manufacturing the batch of 1 000 packs of paper towels.

b Calculate the cost of one roll of paper towels.

Chapter summary

This is a short chapter, but nonetheless a very important one. You should be familiar with the different types of costing, including definitions of unit, job and batch costing, and you should understand the difference between continuous and specific order operations. Finally, you should be able to apply your understanding of these topics to prepare a quotation for a job.

TOP TIP

Look back at Section 28.11 and this chapter to make sure you are able to work out something asked in a question. As always, with questions on costing there is no set format to set out your answer, unlike financial accounting. There are some formats presented which may help. However you set out your answer, make sure it is **clearly labelled** and that **all** your **workings** are shown.

Practice exercises

1 Burling Limited makes a number of products, one of which is Super Burling, which passes through three production departments, A, B and C. The following details are relevant to the production of Super Burling.

Monthly production		4000 units
Direct materials per unit		$8
Direct labour per unit:		
Dept A	1½ hours	
Dept B	1 hour	
Dept C	½ hour	

Other information is as follows:

Direct labour rate (all depts.)		$8.75
Departmental overhead:		
Dept A	$36000	
Dept B	$26000	
Dept C	$24000	
Total direct labour hours:		
Dept A	24000	
Dept B	20000	
Dept C	8000	

Departmental overhead absorption is based on direct labour hours.

Required

a Calculate the overhead absorption rate for each department.

b Calculate the cost of one month's production of Super Burling.

2 Successful Promotions Limited has two departments:

- printing
- marketing and promotion.

The following information is available for the next six months:

	Printing	Marketing and promotion
Direct wage rate per hour	$8	$12
Budgeted overheads	$127 400	$267 540
Budgeted labour hours	3 640	6 370

Departmental overhead is recovered on the basis of the number of direct labour hours.

Required

a Explain what is meant by the term 'overhead recovery'. **[4 marks]**

b Calculate the overhead absorption rate for each department. **[4 marks]**

Additional information

The company has been asked to promote a new product under the brand name 'Port Louis Chox'. The cost of the job is based on the following estimates by the directors of Successful Promotions Limited.

	Printing	Marketing and promotion
Materials	$1 300	$1 600
Direct labour	120 hours	300 hours

Successful Promotions Limited's charges to clients are based on cost plus 40%.

Required

c Prepare a statement to show the amount which Successful Promotions Limited will charge its client for the promotion of Port Louis Chox. **[10 marks]**

Additional information

When they received the quote from the directors of Successful Promotions Limited, the client was unhappy with the figure. They have offered to pay $25 000 for the work.

Required

d Advise the directors whether or not they should accept a price of $25 000 for the work. Justify your answer by discussing the advantages and disadvantages of accepting or rejecting the order. Also identify areas where the company can make cost savings to reach the price of $25 000. **[7 marks]**

Additional information

At the end of the six-month period, the accountant has calculated the following information for the printing department:

Actual overheads	$130 000
Actual labour hours	3 750

Required

e Calculate the under- or over-recovery of overheads for the printing department for the six-month period. **[3 marks]**

f Explain whether this would have an adverse or favourable effect on the company's profit. **[2 marks]**

Total: 30

3 A boot-making company has received a contract to manufacture 2 000 pairs of children's boots. The boots pass through three departments: moulding, lining and finishing. The following information is given:

	Moulding	Lining	Finishing
Direct materials per pair of boots	$2	$3	–
Direct labour rate per hour	$7	$6	$6
Budgeted overhead expenditure	$21 840	$11 375	$4 368
Budgeted machine hours	7 280	–	–
Budgeted direct labour hours	–	4 550	1 820
Direct labour hours per pair of boots	0.25	0.5	0.25
Machine hours per pair of boots	0.5	–	–

Required

a Explain the difference between a production cost centre and a service cost centre. **[4 marks]**

b Explain why it is necessary to reapportion the service cost centre costs to production before calculating an overhead absorption rate. **[3 marks]**

c Calculate suitable overhead absorption rates for each department. **[6 marks]**

d Calculate the **total** cost of producing the batch of 2 000 pairs of children's boots. **[10 marks]**

e Calculate the cost of **one** pair of boots. **[2 marks]**

Additional information

One of the owners of the boot-making company doesn't understand why there are different overhead absorption rates for each department. He is considering changing to a single overhead rate for the whole factory.

Required

f Discuss whether or not the factory should use a single overhead absorption rate. **[5 marks]**

Total: 30

Exam practice questions

Multiple-choice questions

1 Which of the following operations would involve a system of continuous costing?

A painting walls of houses
B generating electricity
C hiring out boats in a fun park
D publishing newspapers

2 Retep Limited hired a drilling machine for use on job 160. The machine was not used on any other job. Which of the following statements is true?

A Rent of the machine will be charged as a direct expense to job 160.
B Rent of the machine will be charged as an indirect expense to job 160.
C Rent and depreciation of the machine will be charged as a direct expense to job 160.
D Rent and depreciation of the machine will be charged as an indirect expense to job 160.

Total: 2 marks

Chapter 30
Marginal costing

Learning objectives

In this chapter you will learn:

- what marginal cost is and how it is used
- the importance of contribution and the contribution to sales (C/S) ratio
- what break-even is and how to calculate break-even point
- how to prepare a break-even chart
- how marginal costs are used to decide on a pricing policy
- when orders from customers may be accepted below normal selling price
- the use of marginal costs for make or buy decisions
- how to make the most profitable use of scarce resources
- the valuation of inventory using marginal and absorption costing
- the use and calculation of sensitivity analysis.

30.1 Marginal cost

In Chapter 29, we saw how total costing can be used to determine price and profit but, beyond that, its uses can be limited. In Chapter 28, we identified classification of costs as fixed or variable. In this chapter, the distinction between them is important. The distinction is that variable costs increase in direct proportion to changes in the level of output. Within a certain range, fixed costs remain unchanged as output increases or decreases. For many management decisions it is necessary to know the **marginal cost** of a unit of production. Marginal cost can be described as the cost of making one extra unit of an item. It is based on the principle that an additional unit of production will only result in an increase in the **variable** costs and that the fixed costs will not be affected. **Marginal cost of production** is, therefore, the total of the variable costs of production.

KEY TERMS

Marginal cost: The cost of making an extra unit of output.

Contribution: The difference between the selling price and variable cost of a unit of output. In total, it is also the difference between the total revenue and total variable costs.

TOP TIP

Remember that both terms relate to the same thing.

Walkthrough

The costs of producing 1 000 units of a product are shown in the table below, with the unit cost shown in the second column.

	Cost of 1000 units	Cost per unit
	$	$
Variable costs		
Direct materials	30 000	30
Direct labour	100 000	100
Direct expenses	5 000	5
Prime cost	135 000	135
Variable overheads	15 000	15
Marginal cost of production [1]	150 000	150
Fixed overheads	50 000	
Total cost of production	200 000	
Profit (20% of total cost)	40 000	
Contribution		90
Selling price	240 000	240

[1] The marginal cost of production for 1 000 units is $150 000 (or $150 for a single unit).

The difference between the total cost of production of $200 000 (i.e. including fixed overheads) and the total selling price of $240 000 gives the profit of $40 000, or $40 per unit ($400 000 ÷ 1 000 units).

Fixed overheads ($50 000) + profit ($40 000) = $90 000, or $90 per unit. This is called the **contribution** because it is the contribution that each unit of production makes towards covering the overheads and providing a profit.

The **contribution per unit** is calculated as follows:

selling price per unit (SP) less the total of the variable costs per unit (VC) or SP – VC (per unit).

In this case \$240 – \$150 = \$90.

TOP TIP

The calculation of contribution either in total or per unit is an important aspect of marginal costing. Ensure that you are fully aware of what it is.

The cost of making 1001 units will be \$(200 000 + 150) = \$200 150, not \$(200 000 ÷ 1 000) × 1001 = \$200 200 as it might seem if we only had a total cost statement. This is because as we increase production by one extra unit, only the variable costs of \$150 per unit will increase. The fixed costs will remain unchanged.

Contribution to sales ratio (C/S ratio)

The ratio of the contribution to the selling price is known as the **contribution to sales ratio (C/S ratio)**. In this example the C/S ratio is:

$$\frac{\$90}{\$240} \times 100 = 37.5\%$$

TOP TIP

This is a very useful ratio that can be used to calculate the answers to many problems. The use of the C/S ratio avoids the need to spend valuable time calculating marginal cost.

For example, if in the example the sales increase to \$300 000, then the total contribution will be \$112 500 (300 000 × 37.5%). Assuming fixed costs remain the same at this level of output, the profit will be \$62 500 (\$112 500 – \$50 000).

Walkthrough

The following is a summarised statement of producing 2 000 units of product X:

	Total	Per unit
	\$	\$
Revenue	126 000	63.00
Variable or marginal costs	(81 900)	(40.95)
Contribution	44 100	22.05
Fixed costs	26 000	

Profit = contribution – fixed costs: \$(44 100 – 26 000) = \$18 100

From this information it will be possible to calculate the profit or loss at different levels of output:

1 If sales increased to 2 400 units:

The contribution from 2 400 units is 2 400 × \$22.05 = \$52 920.

Profit = contribution – fixed costs = \$(52 920 – 26 000) = \$26 920.

2 If sales reduced to 1 800 units:

The contribution from 1 800 units will be 1 800 × \$22.05 = \$39 690.

Profit = \$(39 690 – 26 000) = \$13 690.

3 If sales reduced to 1 100 units:

the contribution from 1 100 units will be 1 100 × \$22.05 = \$24 255.

Loss = \$(26 000 − 24 255) = \$1 745.

ACTIVITY 1

The following is the marginal cost statement for the production of 3000 units of product Q:

	$
Revenue	325 000
Variable or marginal cost	178 750
Contribution	146 250

Fixed costs amount to \$82 000.

Required

Calculate the profit or loss from the sale of:

a 3 000 units

b 4 000 units

c 1 200 units of product Q.

30.2 The break-even point

The point at which a business or a product makes neither a profit nor a loss is the **break-even point**. Managers need to know the break-even point of a product when making decisions about pricing, production levels and other matters.

Break-even occurs when total contribution equals total fixed costs, or, alternatively, when total revenue – total variable or marginal costs equals fixed costs.

It is found by dividing the total fixed costs by the contribution per unit. The calculation gives the number of units that have to be produced and sold before the fixed costs are covered.

KEY TERM

Break-even point: The point at which a business makes neither profit nor loss. It is the point at which total contribution is exactly equal to total fixed costs.

Walkthrough

The following information relates to the production of product Y:

	$
Selling price per litre	50
Marginal cost per litre	26
Total of fixed costs	72 000

Step 1

Calculate the contribution per unit, in this case per litre:

The contribution per litre is \$(50 – 26) = \$24.

Step 2

Divide the total fixed costs by the contribution per litre to find the break-even point:

Break-even point = $\frac{\$72\,000}{24}$ = 3 000 litres.

This will give an answer in units of output (litres). You may also be asked for the answer in revenue.

Step 3

The revenue at which the product will break-even is 3 000 litres × $50 (selling price per unit) = $150 000.

This may also be found by using the contribution to sales ratio as shown in step 4.

Step 4

The contribution to sales ratio is:

Contribution per $ of selling price = $24 ÷ 50 = 48%.

This is used to calculate the break-even point in revenue, as follows:

$$\frac{\text{total fixed costs of \$72 000}}{\text{contribution per \$ of selling price 48\% or 0.48}} = \$150\,000$$

When the calculation of break-even point results in a fraction of a unit of production, the answer should **always** be rounded up to the next complete unit, for example:

Contribution per unit of product $23; total fixed costs $32 000.

$$\text{Break-even} = \frac{\$32\,000}{\$23} = 1\,391.304, \text{ shown as } 1\,392 \text{ units.}$$

TOP TIP

Always indicate whether the break-even figure you have calculated is in units or dollars.

The formula of selling price – variable costs can also be extended to calculate how many units need to be sold to earn a required level of profit.

Walkthrough

The break-even point is 3 000 litres. However, how many litres need to be sold to earn a profit of $12 000?

This is done by adding the required profit to the fixed costs and dividing the answer by the contribution per unit, as in the following illustration:

Total fixed costs of product Y are $72 000 + required profit $12 000 = $84 000.

$84 000 ÷ $24 = 3 500 litres

This can be proved as follows:

	$
Revenue (3 500 × $50)	175 000
Less: marginal costs (3 500 × $26)	(91 000)
Total contribution	84 000
Less: fixed costs	(72 000)
Profit	12 000

Again, the C/S ratio can also be used to calculate the revenue required to earn a target profit. In this case it will be $84 000 ÷ 48% = $175 000 (3 500 units × $50 each).

30.3 Break-even charts

A **break-even chart** is a diagrammatic representation of the profit or loss to be expected from the sale of a product at various levels of activity. The chart is prepared by plotting the revenue from the sale of various volumes of a product against the total cost of production. The break-even point occurs where the sales line cuts the total cost line and there is neither profit nor loss.

> **KEY TERM**
>
> **Break-even chart:** A diagrammatic representation of the profit or loss to be expected from the sale of a product at various levels of activity.

Walkthrough

Suppose the marginal cost of product X is $10 per litre. It is sold for $22.50 per litre. Fixed costs are $50 000.

This can be shown using a break-even chart as follows:

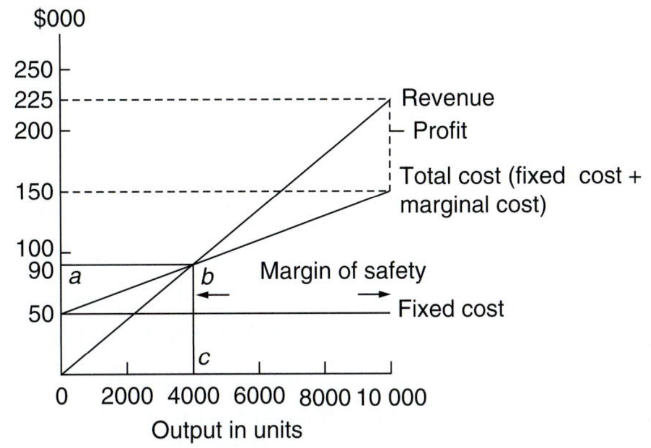

Break-even chart for product X

The break-even point is where the revenue and total costs lines intersect.

The line ***ab*** shows the revenue at break-even point ($90 000). The line ***bc*** shows the output in units at break-even point (4 000). At 10 000 units, the revenue is $225 000 and total cost is $150 000. The distance between those two lines shows the profit of $75 000.

The difference between the revenue line and the total cost line **before** the break-even point represents the loss that will be made if the output falls below 4000 units. The area **beyond** the break-even point represents profitable levels of sales.

The difference between the break-even point and 10 000 units is the **margin of safety**, or the amount by which output can fall short of 10 000 units before the business risks making a loss on product X. It may be expressed as a number of units, 6 000, or as a percentage, 60%.

> **TOP TIP**
>
> Always make sure that break-even charts are fully labelled.

The break-even charts of two products, A and B, will now be compared. Both products have similar total costs and revenues, but product A has high fixed costs while product B has low fixed costs.

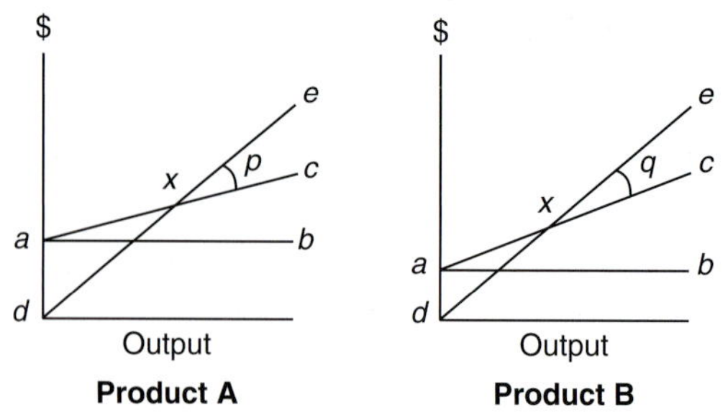

In each case, line ***ab*** represents fixed costs, line ***ac*** represents total cost, and line ***de*** represents revenue. The break-even point ***x*** for product A occurs further to the right of the chart (i.e. later) than that for product B. This shows that high fixed costs tend to result in high break-even points.

Product B with a low fixed cost has a lower break-even point even though the marginal cost is greater.

The angle ***p*** at which the revenue line ***de*** intersects the total cost line ***ac*** for product A is greater than the angle ***q*** for product B. The size of the angle of intersection is an indication of the **sensitivity** of the profitability of a product to variations in the level of activity. It can be seen that, as output increases for the two products, the profitability of product A increases at a faster rate than the profitability of product B. On the other hand, if output decreases for both products, the profitability of A decreases at a faster rate than for B. Product A is more sensitive to changes in output than product B. When the proportion of fixed cost to total cost is high, the risk to profitability is also high. Profit and break-even points are said to be sensitive to changes in prices and cost. This aspect will be considered later in Section 30.10.

ACTIVITY 2

Production of 5000 units of product Q is planned. The following information is given:

	$
Selling price per unit	95
Variable cost per unit	65
Total of fixed costs	75 000

Required

a Calculate:

i the break-even point of product Q in terms of units and revenue

ii the margin of safety.

b Draw a break-even chart for product Q.

KEY TERM

Profit/volume chart: A type of break-even chart which only shows the profit or loss at each level of output.

Profit/volume charts

Break-even charts may also be drawn to show only the profit or loss at each level of output. The cost and revenue lines are omitted. The break-even chart for product X given in the example above could be drawn as a **profit/volume chart**:

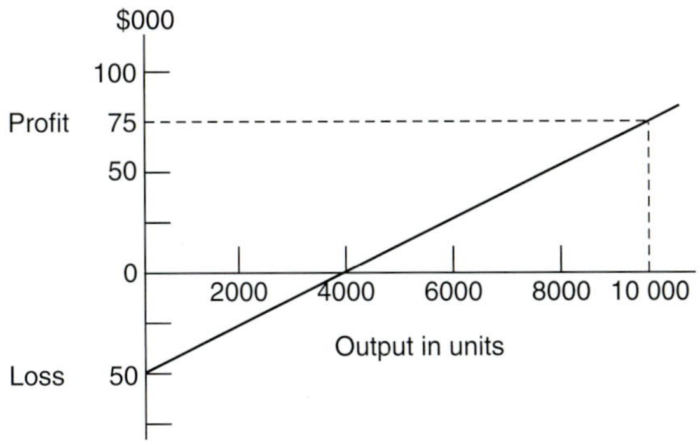

Profit/volume chart for product X

At zero output, the loss equals the total of the fixed costs, $50 000. At 10 000 units, the profit is equal to $75 000. A straight line joining the two points intersects the output line at the break-even point.

TOP TIP

Make sure that if you are asked to prepare a break-even chart you don't prepare a profit/volume chart, or vice versa.

30.4 The limitations of break-even charts

Break-even charts are useful visual aids for the study of the effect of changes in output, costs and revenues on the break-even point, especially for managers with little accounting knowledge. The charts, however, have their limitations:

TOP TIP

It is important that you know the limitations of a break-even chart. Try to learn them thoroughly.

- If revenue and costs are represented by straight lines they may be misleading. Maximum revenue may only be achieved if customers are given attractive discounts, while variable costs may be affected by quantity discounts when output is increased. These factors would be more accurately represented on charts by curves rather than straight lines.
- Some costs may be semi-variable. In other words, there is both an element of fixed cost and an element of variable cost included in the total. An example of this is a telephone. The fixed element may be the line rental, which must be paid whether any calls are made or not. The variable element would be the call charges which will increase each time a call is made. In order for break-even to work, the fixed and variable element must be calculated and added in with the appropriate figures.
- The charts may mislead people whose accounting knowledge is limited, but trained accountants will know when to make allowances for the charts' limitations.
- Many fixed costs are fixed only within certain limits and may increase with the level of activity; they are 'stepped' costs (see Section 28.3) or **semi-variable costs**. In order to prepare a break-even chart or work out the break-even point, it is essential to use only fixed and variable costs.

KEY TERM

Semi-variable cost: A cost which contains both an element of a variable and fixed cost within it.

Walkthrough

Ken has collected the following data in relation to his output and costs and revenue:

	Output 6 000 units		Output 8 000 units	
	Total	Per unit	Total	Per unit
	$	$	$	$
Revenue	126 000	21	168 000	21
Direct materials	30 000	5	40 000	5
Direct labour	18 000	3	24 000	3
Other overheads	48 000		60 000	
Fixed costs	37 000		37 000	

At both levels of output, the cost per unit for direct materials and direct labour are the same ($5 and $3 respectively). This means that they are wholly **variable** costs.

However, the cost per unit for other overheads is different at the two levels of output. For 6 000 units of output the other overheads are $8 per unit ($48 000 ÷ 6 000 units). When 8 000 units are produced the cost per unit is $7.50 ($60 000 ÷ 8 000 units). This means that these costs are not variable costs. Neither are they fixed costs, as the total amount would be the same at both levels of output, either $48 000 or $60 000. This means that the other overheads are semi-variable costs.

Before the break-even point can be calculated, the amount of variable and fixed costs included in each must be calculated.

This is done by looking at the change in costs and the change in output.

	Output (units)	Costs ($)
	8 000	60 000
	(6 000)	(48 000)
Change	2 000	12 000

An increase in output by 2 000 units has caused the costs to change by $12 000. The only type of cost which could cause this change is a variable cost. So the variable element of the costs = $12 000 ÷ 2 000 = $6 per unit.

For an output of 6000 units, this means that the total variable costs are $36 000 (6 000 × $6). The fixed element must be $12 000 ($48 000 – $36 000).

This can be proved by carrying out the same procedure for an output of 8000 units:

Variable costs = 8 000 × $6 = $48 000. Fixed costs are $60 000 – $48 000 = $12 000.

Having identified all costs as either fixed or variable, Ken can now work out his break-even point.

	$	$
Selling price per unit		21
Direct materials per unit	(5)	
Direct labour	(3)	
Other variable costs per unit (from the calculations above)	(6)	(14)
Contribution per unit		7

Break-even point = fixed costs (\$37 000 + \$12 000) ÷ \$7 = 7 000 units.

Unless Ken had split out his other overheads into their fixed and variable element, he would have been unable to calculate the break-even point.

TOP TIP

Sometimes you may not be specifically told that certain costs are semi-variable. Look for something like the illustration above, where for two different levels of output, the other costs have two different values in total and per unit.

30.5 Marginal costing and pricing

The price at which a good may be sold is usually decided by a number of factors:

- the need to make a profit
- market demand
- a requirement to increase market share for a product
- maximum utilisation of resources
- competition from other firms
- economic conditions
- political factors (price regulation, and so on).

Marginal costing can help management to decide on pricing policy, but first it is necessary to understand that some expenses, such as selling expenses, may be variable. An example is salespeople's commission based on the number of units sold. When variable selling expenses are included in marginal cost, the result is the **marginal cost of sales**:

	\$000
Direct materials	100
Direct wages	80
Direct expenses	30
Marginal cost of production	210
Variable selling expenses	15
Marginal cost of sales [1]	225
Other fixed expenses	175
Total cost	400

[1] Although the selling expenses will only be incurred when the goods are sold, they should be regarded as part of the marginal cost of sales as shown above.

It is important to use the correct marginal cost when using marginal costing for decision making.

Walkthrough

(Increasing market share.)

The Gamebusters Company produces and sells a computer game that sells at \$30 per game. Each year 6000 units of the games are sold.

a The marketing director suggests that if the price is reduced to \$28, sales will increase to 8 000 games.

b The sales manager thinks that sales will increase to 11 000 games if the price is reduced to \$25.

The following information is available for 6000 computer games:

	Total	Per unit
	$	$
Direct materials	48000	8.00
Direct labour	66000	11.00
Variable selling expenses (commission)	12000	2.00
Fixed expenses	48000	

There are three options to consider here:

1 keep things as they are
2 implement proposal **a**
3 implement proposal **b**.

It is therefore necessary to calculate the profit or loss from the sale of 6000, 8000, and 11000 units **and** recommend which option should be adopted.

Every unit sold incurs a variable selling expense (commission) and the marginal cost of sales is used.

	Option 1	Option 2	Option 3
Per unit:	$	$	$
Selling price	30	28 [1]	25 [2]
Direct materials	8		
Direct labour	11		
Variable selling expense	2		
Marginal cost of sales [3]	21	21	21
Contribution per unit [4]	9	7	4
Total contribution [5]	54000	56000	44000
Fixed expenses [6]	(48000)	(48000)	(48000)
Profit/(loss) [7]	6000	8000	(4000)

[3] The marginal cost of sales per unit remains unchanged for any option.

[4] Therefore, when faced with this type of question, calculate a revised contribution per unit.

[7] Thus, taking them away from the total contribution, the profit or loss of each option can be calculated.

[6] Fixed expenses will be the same under any option.

[5] This can then be multiplied by the current and forecast level of sales to arrive a total contribution under each option.

[1] Under option **1** the selling price per unit decreases to $28.

[2] Under option **2** the selling price per unit decreases to $25 per unit.

Therefore, the Gamebusters Company should reduce the price of the game to $28. If the forecast increase in sales happens as a result of reducing the selling price to $28 per unit, this option will give the highest profit of the three.

ACTIVITY 3

Ardson Limited makes and sells mobile phones. The following information is given.

Per phone:	$
Selling price	50
Direct materials	18
Direct labour	20
Variable selling expenses	3

Fixed overheads amount to $70 000.

Required

Calculate the profit or loss from the sale of:

a 10 000 phones at $50 each

b 15 000 phones at $48 each

c 20 000 phones at $42 each.

30.6 Acceptance of orders below normal selling price

There are occasions when orders may be accepted below the normal selling price. These may be considered when there is spare manufacturing capacity and in the following circumstances:

- when the order will result in further contribution to cover fixed expenses and add to profit
- to maintain production and avoid laying off a skilled workforce during a period of poor trading
- to promote a new product
- to dispose of slow-moving or redundant inventory.

The rule is that the selling price **must** always exceed the marginal cost of production. If it doesn't then each unit will be sold at a loss before taking fixed costs into account.

Walkthrough

K2 Altimeters Limited makes altimeters that it sells at $80 each. It has received orders for:

a 1 000 altimeters for which the buyer is prepared to pay $60 per altimeter

b 2 000 altimeters at $48 each.

The following information is available:

	$
Direct material per altimeter	21
Direct labour per altimeter	32

Fixed expenses will not be affected by the additional production.

TOP TIP

If you are told that fixed costs will also change, remember to take this into account in your calculation. The question here is whether K2 Altimeters Limited should accept either of the orders.

Again, work out the impact of each option:

a Order for 1 000 altimeters at $60 each:

- contribution per altimeter $(60 – 53) = $7
- additional contribution from order: $7 000 (1 000 units × $7 per unit).

b Order for 2 000 altimeters at $48 each:

- contribution per altimeter $(48 – 53) = ($5 loss).

K2 Altimeters Limited should **not** accept the order for 2 000 altimeters at $48 each.

The company would make a loss of $10 000 (2 000 units × $5 loss per unit) on the order so should not accept it. In this case the marginal cost of sales is greater than the selling price.

ACTIVITY 4

Peach Limited sells canned fruit for which the following information is given:

	$
Per 1 000 cans of fruit:	
Direct materials	5 500
Direct labour	8 750

The company has received orders for:

a 5 000 cans of fruit at $16 000 per 1 000 cans

b 3 000 cans of fruit at $14 100 per 1 000 cans.

The additional production will not require any additional fixed expenses.

Required

State which of the two orders, if any, Peach Limited should accept.

30.7 Make or buy decisions

We have already seen in Chapter 20 that a manufacturing account may suggest that it would be more profitable for a business to buy goods from another supplier than make the goods itself. This involves a '**make or buy**' **decision**. It may be relevant for goods that are already being produced, or to the introduction of a new product.

The decision will be based primarily on whether the cost of buying the goods from another supplier is more or less than the **marginal cost of production**. Notice that the marginal cost of sales is not relevant to this type of decision, as any variable selling costs will have to be incurred whether the goods are manufactured or purchased.

Walkthrough

Big Boxes Limited makes and sells boxes for which the following information is available:

	$ per box
Selling price	25
Direct materials	9
Direct labour	6
Variable selling expenses	7

Big Boxes Limited's fixed overheads amount to $60 300.

The variable selling expenses are ignored as they will have to be incurred anyway. The marginal cost of production is $(9 + 6) = $15. The contribution per unit is $(25 – 22) = $3. The current break-even point is:

$$\frac{\$60\,300}{\$3} = 20\,100 \text{ boxes}$$

Boxes may be bought from either Yes Boxes Limited for $16 per box or No Boxes Limited for $13 per box. Once more, evaluate each option:

- Purchase of the boxes from Yes Boxes Limited. In this case the marginal cost of production ($15 per unit) is lower than the purchase price ($16 per unit). This will have the effect of reducing the contribution by $1 per unit.
- If the boxes are bought from No Boxes Limited at $13 per unit, the marginal cost per unit is greater than the purchase price per unit and the contribution will increase by $2 per unit. Total profit will be increased and the break-even point will reduce to 12 060 boxes:

  $$\frac{\$60\,300}{\$(3+2)} = 12\,060 \text{ boxes}$$

This appears to be a good option. The principle in this situation is that **if the marginal cost of production is below the price quoted by the supplier then the offer should be rejected**.

There are however other matters which Big Boxes Limited should consider before finally deciding to buy the boxes from another supplier:

- How certain is it that No Boxes Limited will not increase the price above $13? If the price is increased to more than $15, it may not be easy for Big Boxes Limited to recommence manufacturing the boxes if it has rid itself of its workers and other resources.
- Will No Boxes Limited supply boxes of the proper quality?
- Will No Boxes Limited deliver the boxes promptly? Big Boxes Limited cannot afford to keep its customers waiting because it is out of boxes.
- Has Big Boxes Limited an alternative use for the resources which will become free when it ceases to make the boxes? Unless it can utilise the resources profitably to make another product, it will either have to shed the resources (labour, machines, etc.) or increase its unproductive costs.
- Can Big Boxes Limited afford to lose the services of a skilled and loyal workforce which may be difficult to replace at a later date when the need arises?

As we shall see again in Chapter 34 on capital investment appraisal, managers often need to take non-financial factors into account before deciding which course of action to take.

TOP TIP

Ensure that you remember the principle on which the decision should be accepted or rejected.

ACTIVITY 5

Canterbury Planes Limited supplies the following information for the production of 15 000 tools:

	$
Direct materials	45 000
Direct labour	37 500
Other direct expenses	15 000
Variable selling expenses	30 000

Fixed expenses total $74 000. The tools sell for $16 each.

Canterbury Planes Limited has received the following quotations for the supply of the tools:

North Island Tool Co.	$6 000 per 1 000 tools
South Island Tool Co.	$6 800 per 1 000 tools

Required

a Calculate the effect on profit and the break-even point of the quotations of:

i North Island Tool Co.

ii South Island Tool Co.

if either was awarded the contract to supply the tools to Canterbury Planes Limited.

b State whether Canterbury Planes Limited should continue to produce the tools or whether it should buy them, and if so, from whom. Support your answer with figures.

30.8 Making the most profitable use of limited resources

Anything which limits the quantity of goods that a business may produce is known as a **limiting factor**. Limiting factors include:

- shortage of materials
- shortage of labour
- shortage of demand for a particular product.

When faced with limited resources, a company making several different products should use the limited resources in a way that produces the most profit. In the previous decisions, the contribution per unit has been the important factor in making the decision. However, when making the best use of limited resources, the products must be ranked according to the amount of **contribution they make from each unit of the scarce resource**. Production will then be planned to ensure that the scarce resource is concentrated on the highest-ranking products.

Walkthrough

(Shortage of material.)

Development Limited makes three products: One, Two and Three. All three products are made from the same material called Four. The following information is given for the products and costs:

	One	Two	Three
Planned production – units	2 000	3 000	4 000
Selling price per unit	$54	$50	$105
Direct materials per unit	2 kg	4 kg	5 kg
Direct labour hours per unit	3	2	6

Direct materials cost $6 per kg. Direct labour is paid at $10 per hour.

Fixed costs are $72 000.

TOP TIP

You may be asked to calculate the profit if there is no shortage of material and then the revised profit taking into account the shortage of material.

Step 1

The first thing to do is set out a table which will show the contribution per unit. This is shown below:

	One	Two	Three
	$	$	$
Selling price per unit	54	50	105
Direct materials per unit	12	24	30
Direct labour per unit	30	20	60
Marginal cost per unit	42	44	90
Contribution per unit [1]	12	6	15
Ranking	2	3	1

[1] Notice that if the products were ranked on the contribution per unit, the order would be Three, One and Two. Thus, if there was no restriction on material, the company would make the products in this order.

Step 2

It is now possible to calculate the total profit the company will make from producing all the products. This is calculated below:

Product	Contribution per unit	Number of units produced and sold	Total
	$		$
One	12	2 000	24 000
Two	6	3 000	18 000
Three	15	4 000	60 000
Total contribution			102 000
Less: fixed costs			(72 000)
Expected profit			30 000

Step 3

Development Limited has discovered that the material Four is in short supply and only 30 000 kg can be obtained.

It is now necessary to work out the contribution per kg of material. This is shown below.

	One	Two	Three
Kg per unit	2	4	5
Contribution per unit	$12	$6.00	$15
Contribution per kg [1]	$6	$1.50	$3
Ranking [2]	1	3	2

[1] The contribution per kg has been calculated by dividing the contribution per unit by the kg per unit. So for One this is $12 ÷ 2 = $6.

[2] The ranking for producing the products is now One, Three and Two.

Step 4

Prepare a revised production plan, taking into account the shortage of raw materials.

To make the planned production, Development Limited will require (2 000 × 2 kg) + (3 000 × 4 kg) × (4 000 × 5 kg) = 36 000 kg of material, if all the planned production was made. However, as only 30 000 kg of material is available, a new production schedule needs to be prepared. The products will now be produced in the order of contribution per kg of raw material.

Revised plan of production:

	Units	Direct materials kg	Contribution per unit [3]	Total contribution and profit
			$	$
One	2 000	4 000	12	24 000
Three	4 000	20 000	6	60 000
Two [1]	1 500	6 000	15	9 000
		30 000		93 000
Less: fixed costs				(72 000)
Revised profit [2]				21 000

[1] There will be enough material to produce all the required One and Three. This will use 24 000 of the 30 000 kg available. This will only leave 6 000 kg. Each unit of Two takes 4 kg. Thus, only 1 500 (6 000 ÷ 4) of Two can be made.

[2] The effect of this is to reduce the expected profit from $30 000 to $21 000.

[3] Notice that the number of units produced is multiplied by the contribution per unit, **not** the contribution per kg.

Walkthrough

(Shortage of direct labour hours.)

The data for the manufacture of One, Two and Three is as given for the previous walkthrough but the number of direct labour hours available is limited to 33 000. There is no shortage of material. The procedure is identical to the shortage of materials, with the exception that this time the contribution per direct labour hour is calculated. This is shown below.

Calculation of contributions per direct labour hour:

	One	Two	Three
	$	$	$
Contribution per unit (as above)	12	6	15
Direct labour hours per unit	3	2	6
Contribution per direct labour hour	4	3	2.5
Ranking	1	2	3

The revised production plan is now calculated based on the total labour hours each product requires. This is shown below.

Revised plan of production:

	Units	Direct labour hours per unit	Total direct labour hours	Contribution
				$
One	2000	3	6000	24000
Two	3000	2	6000	18000
Three	3500	6	21000	52500
			33000	94500
Deduct fixed costs				(72000)
Profit				22500

TOP TIP

It is important you remember the rule in determining the order of production in the case of a limited resource.

ACTIVITY 6

Castries Limited makes three products: Gimie, Gros and Petit. The maximum production of each product and the budgeted production information for three months is as follows:

	Gimie	Gros	Petit
No. of units	1000	2000	800
Selling price per unit	$14	$25	$20
Direct materials per unit (litres)	2.5	3.25	4
Direct labour per unit (hours)	0.5	1.4	0.6

- direct materials cost $2 per litre
- direct labour is paid at $10 per hour
- fixed expenses are $10000.

Castries Limited has been informed that only 10575 litres of material is available.

Required

Prepare a revised production budget that will produce the most profit from the available materials.

ACTIVITY 7

Castries Limited has been informed that supplies of material are not limited, but only 3395 direct labour hours are available. All the other information is as in the previous activity.

Required

Prepare a revised production budget that will produce the most profit from the available direct labour hours.

ACTIVITY 8

Market Limited makes three products: A, B and C. All three products are made from the same material. The maximum production and budget for June is as follows:

	A	B	C
Budgeted production (units)	1000	2000	4000
Materials per unit (kg)	2	4	5
Direct labour per unit (hours)	3	5	6
Selling price per unit	$80	$130	$150

- material cost: $10 per kg
- labour rate of pay: $12 per hour
- total fixed costs for June: $115000.

Required

a Calculate the budgeted profit for June. Show your workings.

Additional information

After the budget for June was prepared, Market Limited learnt that there was a shortage of the material and that it would not be able to obtain more than 28000 kg in June.

Required

b Prepare a revised production budget which will ensure that Market Limited obtains the maximum profit from the available material.

c Prepare a calculation to explain the difference between the original budgeted profit you have calculated in **a** and the revised profit you have calculated in **b**.

30.9 Ceasing the manufacture of a product

Another important topic, and one in which marginal costing is important, is the decision whether or not to cease producing a product.

Walkthrough

Hutton Limited makes three products. The following data is available:

	Product X	**Product Y**	**Product Z**
Per unit:	**$**	**$**	**$**
Selling price	20	25	18
Direct materials	5	8	9
Direct labour	12	10	8
Fixed costs	2	1	2

Fixed costs are absorbed on the basis of direct labour hours.

For the next year, Hutton Limited is forecasting the following sales units:

Product X	5000
Product Y	4000
Product Z	3000
Total fixed costs	$20000

The directors are concerned that product Z is not profitable and are considering whether or not to stop producing it. The accountant has prepared the following analysis:

	Product X	Product Y	Product Z
Per unit:	$	$	$
Selling price	20	25	18
Direct materials	5	8	9
Direct labour	12	10	8
Contribution	3	7	1
Fixed costs	2	1	2
Profit	1	6	(1)

From this analysis, it appears that product Z should no longer be made as it is making a unit loss.

The accountant has also calculated the following forecasted profit statement for next year:

	Units	Contribution per unit	Total contribution and profit
		$	$
Product X	5000	3	15000
Product Y	4000	7	28000
Product Z	3000	1	3000
			46000
Less: fixed costs [1]			(20000)
Expected profit			26000

[1] Fixed costs are calculated by multiplying the fixed cost per unit by the number of units:

		$
Product X	$2×5000 =	10000
Product Y	$1×4000 =	4000
Product Z	$2×3000 =	6000
		20000

The accountant has argued that despite making a loss per unit, if the company ceased producing product Z they would actually make less profit. He has produced the following statement to prove this:

	Units	Contribution per unit	Total contribution and profit
		$	$
Product X	5000	3	15000
Product Y	4000	7	28000
			43000
Less: fixed costs			(20000)
Expected profit			23000

The accountant is correct. If Hutton Limited stop the production of product Z they will make less profit. The reason for this is that the two remaining products have to cover all the fixed costs. Product Z is making a positive contribution. It should therefore continue to be made. It may also be that people who buy product Z also buy other products, and if it was no longer produced, sales of those may suffer as well, reducing the profit even further.

If the directors could save at least $3 000 of fixed costs by ceasing the production of product Z then it will be worth considering. Once again, marginal costing has been used to make a managerial decision.

The situation would be the same if, rather than a product, a company had produced an analysis of three departments and found that one was making a positive contribution but a loss after taking into account fixed costs.

Walkthrough

Angelicus Limited manufactures three different qualities of lock, domestic, commercial and industrial. The company's results for the year ended 31 March 2016 were as follows:

	Domestic	Commercial	Industrial	Total
	$000	$000	$000	$000
Revenue	240	180	450	870
Total costs				
Direct materials	(108)	(66)	(84)	(258)
Direct labour	(60)	(30)	(150)	(240)
Variable overheads	(24)	(54)	(120)	(198)
Fixed overheads	(54)	(28)	(42)	(124)
	(246)	(178)	(396)	(820)
Profit / (loss)	(6)	2	54	50

Fixed overheads are absorbed on the basis of 50% of direct materials.

The directors are considering closing the department making the domestic locks as it makes a loss. However, the department should not be closed because it is making a positive contribution of $48 000, $(240 000 – [108 000 + 60 000 + 24 000]).

30.10 Sensitivity analysis

In Section 30.3, the sensitivity of contribution, profit and break-even points to changes in costs and revenue was mentioned. This topic will now be covered in more detail as errors in estimates of revenue and costs will affect profit. By definition, estimates are rarely likely to be accurate, and allowances should be made in budgets for possible differences between estimates and actual costs and revenue. The point will be illustrated by taking the example of a high-risk situation.

Walkthrough

The following information relates to the budget for a certain product:

No. of units produced and sold: 10 000

	Total	Per unit
	$	$
Revenue	180 000	18
Variable costs	(50 000)	(5)
Contribution	130 000	13
Fixed costs	(100 000)	
Profit	30 000	

Break-even occurs at $\frac{\$100\,000}{\$13} = 7\,693$ units.

If any of the following occurs then it will impact on the break-even point:

a If fixed costs rise by 10% to $110 000 and the increase is not passed on to customers, profit will be reduced by $10 000 to $20 000. Break-even will be increased to:

$$\frac{110\,000}{\$13} = 8\,462 \text{ units}$$

b If fixed costs do not increase, but variable costs rise by 10% to $55 000, or $5.50 per unit, and the increase is not passed on to customers, the profit will be reduced by $5 000 to $25 000, and the break-even point will be increased to:

$$\frac{\$100\,000}{\$12.50\ \$(18.00 - 5.50)} = 8\,000 \text{ units}$$

c If costs do not increase but the selling price per unit is only 90% of expectation, revenue will only be $162 000, profit will be reduced by $18 000 ($180 000 – 162 000) to $12 000. The contribution per unit will also fall to $11.20 ($16.20 – 5.00), and break-even will be increased to:

$$\frac{\$100\,000}{\$11.20} = 8\,929 \text{ units}$$

d If fixed costs increase by 10% and are not passed on to customers, **and** the selling price per unit is only 90% of expectation, profit will be reduced by $(10 000 + 18 000) to $2 000. The contribution will be $11.20, and break-even will be increased to:

$$\frac{\$110\,000}{\$11.20} = 9\,822 \text{ units}$$

e If **all** costs increase by 10% and are not passed on to customers, **and** the selling price per unit is only 90% of expectation, a loss of $3 000 ($30 000 – $15 000 – $18 000) will be incurred.

This is more complex than the others and the table below shows all the figures.

No. of units produced and sold: 10 000

	Total	**Per unit**
	$	**$**
Revenue ($180 000 × 90%)	162 000	16.20
Variable costs ($50 000 + 10%)	(55 000)	(5.50)
Contribution	107 000	10.70
Fixed costs ($100 000 × 10%)	(110 000)	
Loss	(3 000)	

Then break-even will be increased beyond the budgeted production:

$$\frac{110\,000}{\$10.70} = 10\,281 \text{ units}$$

ACTIVITY 9

The following budget has been prepared for the production and sales of 20 000 units of a product:

	$
Revenue	175 000
Variable costs	60 000
Fixed costs	80 000
Total costs	140 000
Profit	35 000

Break-even occurs at $\frac{\$80\,000}{\$5.75} = 13\,914$ units.

Required

Calculate the profit and the break-even point if:

a fixed costs increase by 15% and are not passed on to customers

b variable costs increase by 15% and are not passed on to customers (there is no increase in fixed costs)

c fixed and variable costs increase by 15% and the increases are passed on to customers.

30.11 Marginal costing vs absorption costing and inventory valuation

When we looked at FIFO and average cost, we saw that any difference in valuing closing inventory will produce different profit figures. The two methods of costing, marginal and absorption, will also produce totally different profits, as the closing inventory will be valued in two different ways.

Walkthrough

A company produces a single product. The results for the last month are as follows:

Quantity produced	400
Quantity sold	360
Selling price per unit	$100
Variable costs per unit	$60
Fixed overheads for the period	$2 000

Set out below is the calculation of profit using each method of inventory valuation.

Details	Marginal costing		Absorption costing	
	$	$	$	$
Revenue		36 000		36 000
Variable costs	24 000		24 000	
Less: closing inventory	(2 400) [1]			
	21 600			
Fixed overheads	2 000		2 000	

[1] When valuing inventory using marginal costing, fixed overheads are treated as period costs and written off in full in the month. No part of them is included in the closing inventory figure. Under this method, the closing inventory is valued at $60, the variable cost per unit, to give a value of 40 × $60 = $2 400.

Details	Marginal costing		Absorption costing	
	$	$	$	$
			26 000	
Cost of sales		(23 600)		
Less: closing inventory			(2 600) [2]	
Cost of sales				(23 400)
Gross profit		12 400		12 600

[2] However, with absorption costing some of the fixed overheads are included in the closing inventory. Under this method, total production cost of $26 000 is divided by the total production of 400 units to arrive at an inventory value per unit of $65 per unit. The closing inventory is, therefore, valued at 40 × $65 = $2 600.

The difference in gross profit is $200. The reason for this difference is purely due to the way in which fixed overheads are treated.

ACTIVITY 10

A company produces a single product, the Jonty. Details of its costs are as follows:

	$
Unit selling price	50
Unit variable costs	30
Fixed costs per month	15 000

Projected sales are 1 000 units for month 1 and 1 300 units for month 2. The company will produce 1500 units each month.

Required

a Calculate the profit each month if the closing inventory is valued using marginal costing.

b Calculate the profit each month if the closing inventory is valued using full absorption costing.

c Prepare a statement reconciling the profit in each case.

30.12 Advantages and disadvantages of marginal costing

Using marginal costing has both advantages and disadvantages. These are set out below:

Advantages of marginal costing

a The technique is easily understood. The reason is that the fixed costs are not included in the cost of production and there is no arbitrary apportionment of fixed costs.

b Contribution provides a reliable measure for short-term decision making.

c Marginal costing shows clearly the impact on profit of fluctuations in the volume of sales.

d Under-absorption and over-absorption of overheads are not a problem as there is no need to calculate an overhead absorption rate.

e The marginal costing technique can be used with standard costing (see Chapter 33).

f The technique shows the relative contributions to profit that are made by each product and shows where the sales effort should be contracted.

Disadvantages of marginal costing

The disadvantages of marginal costing are:

a Perhaps the biggest disadvantage of marginal costing is that it only useful for short-term decision making.

b Not all costs can easily be split into fixed costs and variable costs.

c Under marginal costing, the fixed costs remain constant and variable costs vary according to the level of output. In reality, the fixed costs do not remain constant and the variable costs do not vary according to the level of output. In the long run all costs are variable.

d In the case of loss by fire, if inventory is valued using marginal costing, the full amount of loss cannot be recovered from the insurance company since no element of factory fixed overheads is included.

e The management should not base decisions using contribution alone. The contribution may vary if new techniques are followed in the production process.

f Leading on from this, the technique assumes that production methods will remain constant. In practice this is not the case. Investment in new machinery at the expense of reducing labour will change the cost structure completely.

g It is really only useful for a business which makes a single product. A company making several products will have difficulty allocating fixed costs to each product with any degree of accuracy. This will make it difficult to calculate the break-even point for either a single product or the business as a whole.

On balance it may seem that the disadvantages of marginal costing are greater than the advantages. As we have seen though, marginal costing is widely used for short term decision making.

Chapter summary

This chapter has covered the basics of marginal costing, including what marginal cost is, how it is used, including how to decide on pricing policy, for make or buy decisions and to determine how to make the most profitable use of scarce resources.

The concept of break-even is an important one for businesses, and in this chapter you have learnt not only what it is, but how to calculate it and how to prepare a break-even chart. You have also learnt about the importance of contribution and the contribution to sales (C/S) ratio, the use and calculation of sensitivity analysis and how to value inventory using marginal and absorption costing. You have also learnt what happens when orders from customers may be accepted below the normal selling price.

TOP TIPS

- Once again, there is no set layout when answering questions on this topic. Try to use tables for the answers, setting things out in the ways used in this chapter. Always make sure you fully label everything and show all your workings.
- This is an important topic area so pay careful attention to it, and work logically through practice questions.

Practice exercises

1 Breathe Limited manufactures specialised containers for use under water. The business uses two machines. These machines have different levels of efficiency. The following information applies to production and costs:

	Machine X	Machine Y
Hourly rate of production	160	250
Material cost per unit	$5	$4.60
Hourly labour rate	$10	$10
Number of operatives	4	5
Fixed costs per order	$200	$500
Variable costs per order	$2.40	$2.60

Different orders have been received from different customers.

Required

a Which machine should be used for each order, in order to minimise cost? Orders may not be split between machines, but the same machine may be used for more than one order:

i Order 123/P for 800 containers.

ii Order 382/Q for 1 000 containers.

b Calculate the contribution to be made for order 123/P to make a profit of 25% on total cost, using each machine.

Additional information

Breathe Limited requires more funds to purchase an additional machine to complete further orders. Three methods of doing so have been discussed:

- rights issue
- an issue of shares to the public
- an issue of debentures.

Required

c Give one advantage and one disadvantage of each method.

2 The Country Limited has a maximum production capacity of 20 000 units. Each unit sells for $25. The following are the costs for a single unit of production:

Direct materials	4 kg at $4.10 per kg
Direct labour	$12 per hour; 3 units are produced in one hour
Variable expenses	$1.80 per unit for the first 16 000 units
	$1.70 per unit for all units in excess of 16 000 units
Fixed costs	$1.50 per unit at full production

Required

a Using marginal costing, calculate the profit if:

i 15 000 units are produced and sold

ii 18 000 units are produced and sold.

b Calculate the number of units required to break-even.

c Calculate the profit at full production capacity if all production is sold at the reduced price of $24 per unit.

d Advise the directors whether or not they should reduce the selling price to $24 per unit. Justify your answer.

e State **three** assumptions which are made in the preparation of break-even charts.

Exam practice questions

Multiple-choice questions

1 Information about a product is given:

	Per unit
	$
Selling price	110
Direct materials	50
Direct labour	40

Fixed costs total $50 000 and planned production is 2 000 units. Which action is necessary to break-even? Decrease cost of:

A direct labour by 20%
B direct labour by 25%
C direct materials by 10%
D direct materials by 20%

2 The annual results of a company with three departments are as follows:

	Department		
	X	Y	Z
	$	$	$
Revenue	210 000	100 000	140 000
Less: variable costs	(100 000)	(80 000)	(90 000)
Head office fixed costs	(75 000)	(35 000)	(50 000)
Profit (loss)	35 000	(15 000)	0

Head office fixed costs have been apportioned on the basis of the respective sales of the departments and will not be reduced if any department is closed. Which action should the company take, based on these results?

A close department Y
B close departments Y and Z
C close department Z
D keep all the departments open

3 A company makes three products, X, Y and Z, all of which require the use of the same material. Information about the products is as follows:

	Product X	Product Y	Product Z
	$	$	$
Per unit:			
Selling price	260	200	240
Direct materials	(96)	(80)	(90)
Direct labour	(50)	(40)	(50)
Variable overhead	(40)	(30)	(36)
Fixed overhead	(54)	(36)	(36)
Profit	20	14	28

The material is in short supply. Which order of priority should the company give to the products to maximise profit?

	Order of priority		
	1	2	3
A	Y	X	Z
B	Y	Z	X
C	X	Y	Z
D	X	Z	Y

4 The following information relates to product Q:

	$
Revenue at break-even point	72 000
Unit sales price	24
Fixed costs	18 000

What is the marginal cost of each unit of product Q?

A $4.00 **B** $6.00

C $10.00 **D** $18.00

Total: 4 marks

Structured questions

1 Marcos Limited makes a single product. The following budgeted information relating to it for the next year is available:

Output in units	4 000	6 000
	$	$
Revenue	80 000	120 000
Direct materials	(32 000)	(48 000)
Direct labour	(12 000)	(18 000)
Semi-variable costs	(14 000)	(18 000)
Fixed overheads	(10 000)	(10 000)
Profit for the year	12 000	26 000

Required

a Explain the following terms:

i variable cost **[2 marks]**

ii fixed cost **[2 marks]**

iii semi-variable cost. **[2 marks]**

b Calculate the break-even point in units **and** value. **[7 marks]**

c Calculate the margin of safety **in units** if the company sells 6 000 units. **[2 marks]**

Additional information

The company currently has spare capacity.

Required

d Calculate how many units must be produced and sold to make a profit of $40 000. **[3 marks]**

e Discuss the factors which the directors must consider before increasing the production and sales of the product. **[5 marks]**

Additional information

In order to increase sales the directors are considering two options:

- Increasing advertising by $9 800. They estimate that this will increase sales to 7 200 units in the next year.
- Reducing the selling price per unit by $2 per unit. They estimate this will increase the number of units sold to 8 750 in the next year.

Required

f Advise the directors which course of action they should take. Justify your answer by evaluating the effect of each proposal on the profit for the year. **[7 marks]**

Total: 30

2 XYZ Limited produces three different products. The following budgeted information is available for the next six months:

	Product Exe	Product Wye	Product Zed
Total sales units	5 000	4 000	2 000
Per unit:	$	$	$
Selling price	40	50	60
Direct materials at $6 per kg	(12)	(18)	(24)
Direct labour	(15)	(20)	(22)
Contribution	13	12	14

Total fixed costs are budgeted to be $82 000.

Required

a Explain what is meant by the term 'limiting factor'. **[3 marks]**

b Calculate the total budgeted material required to meet the sales. **[4 marks]**

c Calculate the total budgeted profit for the next six months. **[6 marks]**

Additional information

The directors have been advised that only 24 000 kg of material will be available in the next six months. However, they have existing orders for their products which they feel they should meet. They are considering two options:

- produce a minimum of 2 000 units of each product in order to meet sales demand
- not making 2 000 units of each product.

Required

d Calculate the maximum budgeted profit the company will make:

i if a minimum of 2 000 units of each product is made **[8 marks]**

ii if no minimum production requirement of any product is put in place. **[4 marks]**

e Advise the directors which course of action they should choose. Justify your answer. **[5 marks]**

Total: 30

Chapter 31
Activity-based costing (ABC)

Learning objectives

By the end of this chapter you will learn:

- how to apportion overheads using ABC costing
- how to calculate the cost of a cost unit
- how to calculate the value of inventory
- how to demonstrate the effect of different methods of overhead absorption on profit
- how to use ABC costing techniques to make business decisions
- the advantages and disadvantages of ABC.

31.1 What is activity-based costing?

In Section 28.11, we looked at absorption costing as a method of charging overheads to products. This was done by calculating an overhead absorption rate and then charging that rate to products on the basis of, usually, direct labour hours or machine hours. However, this method may lead to inaccurate results, because indirect overheads are not caused equally by all products.

Take for example a clothing manufacturer who makes shirts for men and blouses for women. To make a shirt for a man may take longer on a machine than a blouse for a woman, yet both take the same number of direct labour hours and direct materials. In this case the additional cost of using the machine is not being charged to the shirt. So for a business with a number of different products all sharing common costs, there is a danger of one product subsidising another.

Instead of using a single overhead absorption rate for every product, activity-based costing (ABC) tries to identify which specific costs should be charged directly to a product, by looking at the way each product uses an **activity**, and charging the product with overheads based on this usage. The technique can often identify products and areas of high overhead cost and can direct management to find ways of reducing the costs, stop producing products which do not earn sufficient profit, or charge more for more costly products to earn a higher profit.

31.2 Comparing ABC and absorption costing

Absorption costing

In Section 28.11, we identified that the basis of absorption costing is carried out in the following way:

1. Direct costs (direct materials and direct labour) associated with the cost units are identified and charged directly to them.
2. The overhead costs associated with the production process are then identified.
3. The overhead costs are then apportioned to cost centres using a logical basis (floor space or power usage).
4. A suitable overhead absorption rate is then calculated, usually on the basis of direct labour hours or machine hours.
5. Overheads are then charged to each product that passes through the cost centre using that overhead absorption rate.

KEY TERMS

Cost pool: The total of all the costs associated with a particular activity.

Cost driver: The activity which directly results in a specific cost being incurred.

Activity-based costing

ABC, on the other hand, aims to refine this process by looking at the individual costs incurred by each product. These individual costs are grouped together in a **cost pool**.

A cost allocation basis is then identified for each cost pool which reflects how much of the cost a particular product uses. In ABC this is called a **cost driver**.

Walkthrough

Jayaitch Limited manufactures two types of shirt, children's and adults'. When the raw materials arrive they are unloaded by a forklift truck.

The total costs of running the forklift trucks has been budgeted as follows:

	$
Drivers' wages	60 000
Maintenance costs	20 000
Power and fuel	12 000
Depreciation	8 000
Total forklift truck costs	100 000
Other factory overheads	400 000
	500 000

In this case, the total forklift truck costs of $100 000 represent the **cost pool** figure.

The budgeted production data for next year is:

	Children's shirts	Adults' shirts	Total
Units of production	40 000	30 000	70 000
Direct labour hours	6 000	14 000	20 000
Rolls of cloth	800	4 200	5 000

Using traditional absorption costing, a total overhead absorption rate based on direct labour hours would be calculated as:

$$\frac{\$500\,000}{20\,000} = \$25 \text{ per direct labour hour}$$

The overheads charged to each product will be:

	Children's shirts	Adults' shirts
Direct labour hours × $25	$150 000	$350 000

Included in this overhead absorption rate would be an amount for using the forklift trucks. It is possible to calculate this as follows:

An overhead absorption rate for using the forklift trucks will be:

$$\frac{\$100\,000}{20\,000} = \$5 \text{ per direct labour hour}$$

The forklift truck costs used by each product will be:

	Children's shirts	Adults' shirts
Direct labour hours × $5	$30 000	$70 000

However, the adult shirt takes far more cloth than the children's shirt and is therefore likely to use the forklift truck more. In this case, the amount each shirt uses the forklift truck is the **cost driver**. A more realistic way to split the forklift truck costs will be to charge each product with the amount it uses the forklift truck, based on the rolls of fabric carried. This can be done as shown below.

Step 1

Calculate an overhead absorption rate for the forklift truck using the rolls of cloth used by each shirt:

$$\frac{\$100\,000}{5\,000} = \$20$$

Step 2

Overheads charged to each type of shirt on this basis is:

	Children's shirts	Adults' shirts
Rolls of cloth × $20	$16000	$84000

From this it can be seen that the adults' shirts are more expensive in terms of forklift truck costs and are being subsidised by the children's shirts.

As a result of this information, management could increase the selling price of the adult shirt or look at how much cloth it uses in general. This would not have been picked up by traditional absorption costing.

ACTIVITY 1

Ann manufactures two types of dresses, children's and adults'. She currently uses absorption costing, based on direct labour hours and provides you with the following budgeted information:

	Children's	Adults'
Production in units	20000	5000
Direct labour hours	10000	15000
Rolls of cloth	1000	4000

Total storage costs for rolls of cloth are $60000.

Required

a Calculate the budgeted overhead absorption rate for storage costs using direct labour hours.

b Calculate the amount of storage cost charged to each product using absorption costing.

c Calculate the storage costs charged to each product if the cost is charged using ABC.

The use of ABC is identifying that low volume products tend to be under costed (cheaper) using traditional absorption costing.

31.3 Advantages and disadvantages of ABC

We have seen some **advantages** of using ABC. These are:

a Product costing may be more accurate, reliable and fairer because the technique focuses on the reason why a product incurs a cost.

b The products' selling price may be more accurate and fairer because costs are allocated to products on the basis of cost drivers rather than a simple overall overhead absorption rate.

c Cost control, product pricing and savings can be achieved more easily as expensive and high cost items can be identified. This should result in a higher profit for the business.

However, there a number of **disadvantages** with using the technique:

a It is very time-consuming to try to work out which specific costs a product incurs and why.

b It is very difficult to say with certainty which costs are cost drivers for a particular product.

c It requires a greater degree of analysis of costs than absorption costing. It may not, therefore, be suitable for small businesses where managers often lack the time and expertise to try to establish cost pools and cost drivers.

d Both absorption costing and ABC are ways of charging overheads incurred to the product produced. If all production made is sold, then, whichever method is used, all indirect costs incurred will be charged to each product. The question then becomes, is ABC worth all the effort?

The advantages and disadvantages seem to balance out. It is, therefore, mostly down to management preference, expertise and time available as to which method of absorption costing a firm uses. As with everything in accounting, which ever method is chosen, the company should not change it unless there is a valid reason for doing so. Remember that inventory valuation can include an element of overheads. Thus, to change the method of absorption arbitrarily is going against the accounting concept of consistency and IAS 2.

The following comprehensive example will highlight some of these advantages and disadvantages. It will also show a step-by-step approach to using ABC.

Walkthrough

Lenny Limited produces two products for use with IT in the home. The first is the Home Hub (HH) to use with wireless technology for home computing. The second is a satellite dish (SD) which can be used with home televisions. The following budgeted details are available:

	SD	HH
Units of production and sales	5000	20000
Selling price per unit	\$400	\$200
Direct materials and labour per unit	\$180	\$85
Total budgeted direct labour hours	30000	70000
Direct labour hours per unit	6	3.5

The total budgeted factory overheads for the year are \$1000000.

Step 1 Traditional absorption costing

The total budgeted direct labour hours are therefore:

SD	5000 units × 6 =	30000
HH	20000 units × 3.5 =	70000
		100000

Using traditional absorption costing the budgeted overhead absorption rate would be:

$$\frac{\$1\,000\,000}{100\,000} = \$10 \text{ per direct labour hour}$$

The budgeted profit per unit would therefore be:

	SD	HH
	\$	\$
Selling price per unit	400	200
Direct materials and labour	(180)	(85)
Factory overheads [1]	(60)	(35)
Budgeted profit per unit	160	80

[1] The factory overhead per unit is calculated by multiplying the hours per unit by the overhead absorption rate.

ACTIVITY 2

Joe Limited manufactures two furniture products, tables and chairs. The following budgeted information is available for each product:

	Tables	Chairs
Units of production and sales	3000	12000
Selling price per unit	$200	$80
Direct materials and labour per unit	$80	$30
Total budgeted direct labour hours	12000	24000
Direct labour hours per unit	4	2

Budgeted factory overheads are $216000.

Required

a Calculate the budgeted overhead absorption rate using direct labour hours.

b Calculate the budgeted profit per unit.

Step 2 Identification of cost pools and cost drivers

The company accountant has analysed the indirect overheads and discovered that the total factory overhead costs are made up of four cost pools. He has also identified the cost driver for each of the cost pools.

[1] The four figures are the cost pools for each cost driver.

Procedure	Budgeted cost [1]	Cost driver
	$	
Engineering	60000	Engineering hours
Machine set-up	100000	Number of times machine set up
Machine running time	750000	Machine hours
Packing costs	90000	Number of orders packed

Step 3

The accountant then went on to identify how much of each cost pool each product uses and produced the following analysis:

Cost driver	SD	HH	Total
Engineering hours	10000	5000	15000
Number of machine set-ups	150	350	500
Machine hours	75000	25000	100000
Number of orders packed	5000	20000	25000

TOP TIP

It is already possible to see one of the main disadvantages of ABC. There is a need to collect as much data as possible about the way in which a product is produced. This is time consuming. It is also a totally different approach to the way in which businesses traditionally collect costing data.

However, it also illustrates one of the main advantages of ABC. All the data collected relates specifically to the product, and the way in which it is produced directly causes a cost to be incurred.

Step 4

It is now possible to calculate an overhead absorption rate for each cost driver, based on the data collected:

Activity consumption cost driver	Cost	Total activity consumption	Overhead absorption rate using ABC (total cost ÷ total activity consumption)
	$		$
Engineering hours	60 000	15 000	4.00
Number of machine set-ups	100 000	500	200.00
Machine hours	750 000	100 000	7.50
Packing costs	90 000	25 000	3.60
	1 000 000		

TOP TIP

This procedure is similar to the way an overhead absorption rate is calculated when using absorption costing in Section 28.11. However, rather than a rate for each department, a rate for each **activity** has been calculated.

Step 5

It is now possible to calculate how much of the factory overhead can be charged to each product using ABC.

Allocation of indirect costs to products based on the activity rate:

a Satellite dishes (SD)

Number of units produced: 5 000 units.

Activity consumption cost driver	Activity overhead absorption rate	Number of activities used	Total factory overheads allocated [1]	Overhead rate per unit [2]
	$		$	$
Engineering hours	4.00	10 000	40 000	8.00
Number of machine set-ups	200.00	150	30 000	6.00
Machine hours	7.50	75 000	562 500	112.50
Packing costs	3.60	5 000	18 000	6.60
			650 500	133.10

[1] The activity rate is multiplied by the number of activities used to arrive at the total factory overhead allocated.

[2] This figure is then divided by the number of units produced and packed to arrive at the overhead cost per unit.

It is now necessary to carry out the exact same procedure for the Home Hubs (HH).

b Home Hubs (HH)

Number of units produced: 20 000 units.

Activity consumption cost driver	Activity overhead absorption rate	Number of activities used	Total factory overheads allocated	Overhead rate per unit
	$		$	$
Engineering hours	4.00	5 000	20 000	1.00
Number of machine set-ups	200.00	350	70 000	3.50
Machine hours	7.50	25 000	187 500	9.38
Packing costs	3.60	20 000	72 000	3.60
			349 500	17.80

The results of each of the above will give the following table:

Activity consumption cost driver	SD	HH
	$	$
Engineering hours	40 000	20 000
Number of machine set-ups	30 000	70 000
Machine hours	562 500	187 500
Packing costs	18 000	72 000
	650 500	349 500

TOP TIP

When tackling a calculation like this, always check that your total overheads allocated to each product adds back to the overall total overheads. In this case, SD has been allocated with a total of $650 500 of factory costs and HH $349 500 which together make the total of $1 000 000.

ACTIVITY 3

The accountant of Joe Limited has identified the cost pools and cost drivers for the company. He provides the following analysis:

Activity	Production overhead	Tables	Chairs
	$		
Machine maintenance	108 000	3 500 maintenance hours	5 500 maintenance hours
Materials handling	72 000	500 deliveries	700 deliveries
Packing	36 000	700 orders	1 100 orders

Required

a Calculate the absorption rate for each cost driver.

b Complete the following table to show the allocation of the **total** production overheads between tables and chairs using ABC.

Activity	Tables	Chairs
	$	$
Machine maintenance		
Materials handling		
Packing		
Total cost		
Cost per unit (to **two** decimal places)		

Step 6

It is now possible to calculate the product profitability using ABC:

	SD	HH
	$	$
Selling price per unit	400.00	200.00
Direct materials and labour	(180.00)	(85.00)
Factory overheads [1]	(133.10)	(17.48)
Budgeted profit per unit	86.90	97.52

[1] The figure for factory overhead per unit has been taken from the end column of the tables in step 5.

ACTIVITY 4

The accountant of Joe Limited has now been asked to use the information calculated in Activity 3 to work out the product profitability using ABC.

Required

Calculate using ABC, the profitability of:

a tables

b chairs.

Step 7 Comparison of the two methods

a Comparison of the overhead absorption rates using both methods of overhead absorption:

	SD	HH
Budgeted unit overhead cost	$	$
Rate using:		
Absorption costing	60.00	35.00
ABC	133.10	17.48
Difference	(73.10)	17.52

b Comparison of the budgeted unit profit margin:

	SD	HH
	$	$
Using absorption costing	160.00	80.00
Using ABC	86.90	97.53
Difference	73.10	(17.53)

Step 8 Analysing the results

The two methods have resulted in significantly different unit costs and, therefore, unit profits. One limitation of traditional absorption costing is that it will tend to under-price low volume, highly technical products. In this case, the satellite dish has low volume and, from the machine hours used on it, is technically more complicated to make than the home hub.

On the basis of this information, management of Lenny Limited can look at some options:

a try to increase the volume of satellite dishes produced

b try to reduce the number of machine hours spent on producing the dishes

c look at the machine hour costs to see if it is possible to reduce it

d increase the selling price of the satellite dishes if the market conditions allow.

This example also highlights some of the other disadvantages mentioned, which are that the calculations can be long and complex and the amount of analysis of the costs and how much each product uses likewise.

31.4 Valuing inventory using ABC

There is no reason why ABC can't be used to value inventory. However, as with any valuation of inventory method chosen, it must be used consistently. Similarly, as with the valuation of inventory using absorption or marginal costing (see Chapters 28 and 30), the stage of completion of any work in progress must be taken into account.

Using the information from Lenny Limited, we identified the budgeted unit overhead cost using ABC. This question assumed that all production was sold, which in reality may or may not be the case. Also, in practice, it would be usual to value inventory on an actual cost basis rather than a budgeted cost basis.

Walkthrough

Petra runs a manufacturing business making two products, shirts and trousers, and values inventory in line with IAS 2. For month 1 the following costs were incurred:

	Shirts	Trousers
	$	$
Direct materials and labour	3866	11602
Total allocated factory overheads using ABC	1104	3308
Total [1]	4970	14910

[1] The figure for total allocated factory overheads would have been found at step 5 in the example of Lenny Limited above.

During the month the company production was as follows:

	Shirts	Trousers
Fully completed units sold	472	2385
Fully completed units at end of month as inventory	20	50
Work in progress units	10	100

There was no opening inventory. The work in progress was 50% complete in respect of direct costs and factory overheads.

The accountant has been asked to calculate the valuation of inventory to include in the statement of financial position at the end of month 1.

The first thing she needs to do is calculate the equivalent units of production. She does this as follows:

	Shirts	Trousers
Fully completed units made and sold	472	2385
Fully completed units at end of month as inventory	20	50
Work in progress units equivalent units (50% complete)	5	50
Equivalent units produced	497	2485

From this information she can then calculate the cost per unit for each product like this:

	Shirts	Trousers
Total costs	$4970	$14910
Equivalent units	497	2485
Cost per unit	$10	$6

Finally, she can then work out the total value of inventory by multiplying the cost per unit with the number of equivalent units at the end of the month, as follows:

	Shirts	Trousers
Equivalent units × cost per unit [1]	$250 (25 × $10)	$600 (100 × $6)

[1] Notice that for the work in progress, it is the **equivalent** units of 5 and 50 which are used for shirts and trousers respectively, not the **actual** number of units.

Chapter summary

In this chapter, you have learnt the basics of activity-based costing (ABC), and the advantages and disadvantages of this method (as compared to traditional costing methods). Using the ABC method, you should now know how to apportion overheads, calculate cost units and inventory value, and demonstrate the effect of different methods of overhead absorption on profit. Finally, you should be able to apply these techniques to make business decisions.

TOP TIPS

- This chapter is a completely new topic for the Cambridge syllabus. All the relevant data will be there to allow you to work through the question. It is a topic which requires lots of calculations. Work methodically through the question.
- When answering questions, be prepared not only to calculate, but also to discuss the advantages and disadvantages of ABC. You may be expected to discuss the difference between ABC and the traditional costing methods. With this in mind, check back to Chapters 22, 28 and 30, where different methods of inventory valuation and costing are covered.

Practice exercises

1 Khalid runs a small manufacturing business making two products, the Pin and the Qua. He currently uses absorption costing to calculate an overhead absorption rate based on direct labour hours. This is then charged to each of the products.

Details of his budget for the month of April are as follows:

	Pin	Qua
Budgeted production and sales (units)	2800	9000
Budgeted selling price per unit	$500	$300
Direct materials and labour per unit	$200	$80
Direct labour hours per unit	5	1.5

Total budgeted factory overheads for April are $110 000.

Required

a Calculate the budgeted factory overhead absorption rate using absorption costing. **[4 marks]**

b Calculate the budgeted profit per unit for the month using absorption costing. **[2 marks]**

Additional information

Khalid's accountant has suggested that the company change to using activity-based costing to calculate the unit cost and profit of each product. He has analysed the data and identified the following information:

Total factory overheads	
	$
Machine set-up costs	20000
Maintenance costs	40000
Forklift truck costs	50000
	110000

The cost driver for each product is as follows:

Cost driver	Pin	Qua
Number of set-ups	300	100
Maintenance hours	8000	2000
Material carried by forklift trucks (tonnes)	350	150

Required

c State **two** advantages and **two** disadvantages of using activity-based costing. **[4 marks]**

d Calculate the overheads allocated to each product using activity-based costing. **[4 marks]**

e Calculate the cost per unit and profit per unit using activity-based costing. **[4 marks]**

f Reconcile the difference between the budgeted unit overhead cost and budgeted unit profit using absorption costing and activity-based costing. **[2 marks]**

Additional information

Kahlid is considering changing his method of overhead absorption to activity-based costing.

Required

g Advise Kahlid whether or not he should make this change. Justify your answer. **[5 marks]**

Total: 25

2 LW Limited produces two types of dresses, Straight and Flared. The following budgeted information is available:

	Straight	Flared
Production and sales units	8000	12000
Machine hours	4000	8000
Direct materials per unit	$13	$15
Direct labour per unit	$3	$3

Total production overheads for the next six months are budgeted to be $360 000 and are absorbed on the basis of machine hours.

The company adds 50% to the total production cost to set the selling price of each product.

Required

a Calculate the budgeted unit selling price for each product. **[6 marks]**

Additional information

Liz, the managing director of the company, has heard about activity-based costing and has asked the company accountant to investigate whether or not she should use it.

Required

b Explain the difference between activity-based costing and absorption costing. **[4 marks]**

Additional information

The company accountant has identified that production comprises four activities. She has also calculated the cost of each activity. This information is shown below:

Activity	Production overheads	Straight	Flared
	$		
Machine set-up	96 000	50 times	70 times
Machine maintenance	200 000	550 hours	950 hours
Inspection	64 000	800 times	1 200 times

Required

c Calculate the following if Liz decides to use activity-based costing:

i the budgeted unit cost **[4 marks]**

ii the budged unit selling price. **[4 marks]**

d Advise Liz whether or not she should change to activity-based costing. Justify your answer by discussing the advantages and disadvantages of changing. **[7 marks]**

Total: 25

Chapter 32
Budgeting and budgetary control

Learning objectives

In this chapter you will learn:

- how budgets differ from forecasts
- how budgets help management to plan and control
- factors to be considered in the preparation of budgets
- how to prepare sales, production, purchasing, expense and cash budgets
- how to prepare master budgets
- what flexible budgets are
- the advantages and disadvantages of budgeting and budgetary control.

accounts compare actual performance with budget and must be prepared promptly after the end of each period if they are to be useful. If actual revenue and expenditure are better than budget, the differences (or variances) are described as **favourable** because they increase profit. On the other hand, if 'actual' is worse than budget, the variance is described as **adverse**.

TOP TIP

When comparing actual and budgeted data, remember to use the terms favourable or adverse.

Departmental management accounts usually contain many items of revenue and expenditure with a mixture of favourable and adverse variances. Managers should concentrate their attention on items with adverse variances and, to help managers focus their attention on these, management accounts may report only the items with adverse variances. This is known as **management by exception** or **exception reporting**.

KEY TERMS

Fixed budget: A budget which is not changed when sales, or some other activity, increases or decreases.

Flexed budget: A budget which is changed to reflect changes in activity levels.

Fixed and flexible budgets

Experience shows that sales and costs rarely conform to the patterns anticipated by management when they prepare a **fixed budget**, that is, one that does not allow for different levels of activity and changing conditions. Fixed budgets may lose their usefulness as management tools as a result. If budgeted output is different from actual output we are not comparing like with like. Invariably, the number of units produced and sold is more or less than the number in a fixed budget. We saw in Section 30.4 that when activity levels change, variable and semi-variable cost also change. If output increases dramatically, fixed costs may also change. Thus, to compare actual results with a fixed budget in these circumstances is useless.

To overcome this, budgets may be 'flexed' to reflect various levels of activity and costs. Flexing budgets make use of marginal costing and is an important process when standard costing techniques are employed. **Flexed budgets** are described in Section 33.4.

TOP TIP

Make sure you understand the term 'flexing the budget' as it is commonly used.

32.3 Limiting (or principal budget) factors

This topic was discussed in Section 30.8. There, how to make the most profitable use of limited resources was covered. It is as a direct result of preparing a budget that limiting factors are identified.

Limiting factors, sometimes called **principal budget factors**, are circumstances which restrict the activities of a business. Examples are:

- limited demand for a product
- shortage of materials, which limits production
- shortage of labour, which also limits production
- shortage of space in which to produce the budgeted amount
- shortage of cash.

Limiting factors **must** be identified in order to decide the order in which the departmental budgets are prepared. If the limiting factor is one of demand for the product, a sales budget will be prepared first. The other budgets will then be prepared to fit in with the sales budget. If the limiting factor is the availability of materials or labour, the production budget will be prepared first and the sales budget will then be based on the production budget.

The starting point for the preparation of the budget must be the identification of the limiting factor. Once this has been determined the budgets are prepared starting from this point.

32.4 How to prepare a sales budget

In most cases, the starting point for the preparation of the budgets will be the sales. Sales budgets are based on the budgeted volume of sales **units**. The number of units is then multiplied by the selling price per unit of production to produce the revenue. For the sake of simplicity, the examples which follow assume that only one type of product is being sold.

What follows will be the preparation of the various budgets required by a business, in this case Xsel Limited. It will start with the first stage, the preparation of the sales budget.

Step 1 The sales budget

Walkthrough

Xsel Limited's sales for the six months from January to June are budgeted in units as follows:

January 1 000; February 800; March 1 100; April 1 300; May 1 500; June 1 400.

The current price per unit is $15 but the company plans to increase the price by 5% on 1 May. The sales budget was prepared by the company's accountant and is shown below.

Xsel Limited's sales budget for six months ending 30 June

	January	February	March	April	May	June	Total
Units	1 000	800	1 100	1 300	1 500	1 400	7 100
Price	$15	$15	$15	$15	$15.75 [2]	$15.75	
Sales [1]	$15 000	$12 000	$16 500	$19 500	$23 625	$22 050	$108 675

[1] The information given only provided the number of units sold and the selling price of each unit. The sales value is the result of these two figures being multiplied together.

[2] The information tells us that the price will increase by 5% on 1 May. This means that for May and June it will be $15.75 per unit ($15 + 5%).

ACTIVITY 1

Martha and Florence Limited's sales budget in units for six months ending 30 June is as follows:

January 1 000; February 1 200; March 1 300; April 1 500; May 1 700; June 1 800.

The price per unit will be $20 for the three months to 31 March, but will be increased to $22 from 1 April.

Required

Prepare Martha and Florence Limited's sales budget for the new product for the six months ending 30 June. (Keep your answer; it will be needed later.)

32.5 How to prepare a production budget

Manufacturing companies require production budgets to show the volume of production required monthly to meet the demand for sales. It is important to check that production is allocated to the correct months.

TOP TIP

It is likely you will be required to prepare budgets for a manufacturing business. The production budget will be the second budget to be prepared.

Step 2 The production budget

Walkthrough

Xsel Limited (see the example in Section 32.4) manufactures its goods one month before they are sold. Monthly production is 105% of the following month's sales to provide goods for inventory and for free samples to be given away to promote sales. Budgeted sales for July are for 1 800 units.

TOP TIP

There will often be an indication of the level of inventory required at the end of each month, usually based on the sales for the next month. Sometimes there may also be units damaged in the production process which have to be scrapped. These need to be accounted for in the budget.

The accountant prepared the following production budget from this information. Notice that at this point it is only in units.

	December	January	February	March	April	May	June
Production for sales (units) [1]	1 000	800	1 100	1 300	1 500	1 400	1 800
Add: 5% for inventory and samples	50	40	55	65	75	70	90
Monthly production [2]	1 050	840	1 155	1 365	1 575	1 470	1 890

[2] This includes the addition of 5% for samples.

[1] The budgeted sales units have been moved back by one month, as we are told the company will make them one month before they are sold. Thus, January's budgeted sales of 1 000 units are moved back to December, February's budgeted sales of 800 units to January, and so on. As the budgeted sales for July are 1 800 units these will need to be made in June.

ACTIVITY 2

Martha and Florence Limited (see Activity 1, Section 32.4) manufactures their goods one month before the goods are sold. Monthly production is 110% of the following month's sales. Budgeted sales for July are 2000 units.

Required

Prepare Martha and Florence Limited's production budget. (Keep your answer; it will be needed later.)

If there is some loss in the production process, it is important that this is built into the production budget at this time, as it will affect how much material needs to be purchased.

Walkthrough

Garden Ornaments Limited manufactures clay animals. Its budgeted sales for next month are 900 units. There is an opening inventory of 100 units and the company requires a closing inventory of 150 units. Without any loss in production the production budget would be:

Budgeted sales units	900
Opening inventory	(100)
Closing inventory	150
Production required	950

Notice that the opening inventory of units is deducted from the budgeted sales. There is no need to make them. The closing inventory is added. This is the opposite way round to how opening and closing inventory is shown in the income statement.

However, 5% of the production is lost due to damage in the production process. This loss will mean that more units have to be produced to cover the loss.

Production from above	950
Production to cover loss (950/95%)	1000

The budget would then look like this:

Budgeted sales units	900
Opening inventory	(100)
Closing inventory	150
Add: Loss in production	50
Production required	1000

TOP TIP

Notice that production is grossed up to achieve the required production. If 5% of 950 was taken as the amount of extra production, the loss in process would not have been covered.

32.6 How to prepare a labour budget

After the preparation of the production budget it may be necessary to prepare a labour budget. This will cover the wages payable to workers involved in the production.

For example, Xsel Limited requires 840 units to be produced in December. If each unit takes two hours of direct labour to produce and each worker is paid $10 per hour, then the budgeted wages for January would be:

840 x 2 x $10 = $16 800

Walkthrough

JP Limited has calculated its budgeted production to meet sales for the next four months. Details are shown below.

Month	Production units
1	1000
2	1200
3	1300
4	1400

Each unit requires three hours of direct labour. Workers are paid $15 per hour.

The labour budget in hours and value for the four-month period would look like this:

	Month 1	Month 2	Month 3	Month 4
Production units	1000	1200	1300	1400
Budgeted labour hours required (units x 3)	3000	3600	3900	4200
Budgeted labour cost (budgeted hours x $15) in $	45000	54000	58500	63000

The budgeted labour cost would then be entered as a payment in the cash budget. It will be clear how the payment is to be accounted for in the cash budget. Be sure to adjust for this when preparing the cash budget.

ACTIVITY 3

J Limited has prepared its production budget in units. This is shown in the following table:

Production budget in units			
December	January	February	March
2000	2200	2400	2600

- Each unit takes two hours of direct labour.
- Labour is paid at the rate of $10 per hour.
- 80% of the direct labour is paid in the month, with the remaining 20% paid in the following month.

Required

For each of the months January, February and March:

a Prepare the direct labour budget in hours.

b Prepare the direct labour budget in dollars in order to show the amount of direct labour to be included in the cash budget for each of those months.

32.7 How to prepare a purchases budget

Having worked out how many units need to be produced to make the goods to be sold, the company now has to buy the raw materials to produce them. This is done using a purchases budget.

A purchases budget may be prepared for either:

a raw materials purchased by a manufacturer (the most likely scenario)

b goods purchased by a trader.

A manufacturing company's purchases budget is prepared from the production budget, while a trader's purchases budget is prepared from the sales budget. The purchases budget is calculated as follows:

> Units produced per production budget × quantity of material per unit produced × price per unit of material

Take care to ensure that the purchases are made in the correct month.

Step 3 The purchases budget

Walkthrough

Xsel Limited (see the example in Section 32.5) purchases its raw materials one month before production. Each unit of production requires 3 kg of material, which costs $2 per kg.

The accountant has prepared the following purchases budget:

	November	December	January	February	March	April	May
No. of units [1]	1050	840	1155	1365	1575	1470	1890
Material required [2] (kg)	3150	2520	3465	4095	4725	4410	5670
Purchases ($ per kg) [3]	6300	5040	6930	8190	9450	8820	11340

[1] As the goods are required one month before they are required in production, the production budget prepared in Section 32.5 has been moved back another month. So the 1050 units to be made in December has been moved backwards by one month to November, the month when the goods are bought.

[3] Each kg costs $2, so the number of kg required is multiplied by $2 to find the cost.

[2] Each unit requires 3 kg of material. Therefore the number of units are multiplied by 3 to give the number of kg purchased.

ACTIVITY 4

Martha and Florence Limited (see Activity 2, Section 32.5) uses 2.5 litres of material in each unit of their product. The price of the material is currently $4.10 per litre, but the company has learnt that the price will be increased to $4.25 in March. The raw materials are purchased one month before production; 2100 units are budgeted to be produced in July.

Required

Prepare Martha and Florence Limited's purchases budget based on its production budget for the seven months from December to June. (Make all calculations to the nearest $.)

TOP TIP

Sometimes the figures have to be rounded up when preparing this type of budget.

Recap Up to this point the accountant of Xsel Limited has prepared the following budgets:

- sales in both units and value
- production in units
- purchases in both units and value.

It is important you know how to prepare these budgets. Work back through them to make sure you are familiar with how they are prepared, in particular the way things move back by one month.

32.8 How to prepare an expenditure budget

An expenditure budget shows the payments for purchased materials (from the purchases budget) plus all other expenditure in the period covered by the budget. Take care to ensure that:

- purchased materials are paid for in the correct month
- all other expenses are included in the budget in accordance with the given information.

Step 4 The payments for expenditure budget

Walkthrough

Xsel Limited pays for its raw materials two months after the month of purchase. Its other expenses are as follows:

a Monthly wages of $4 000 are paid in the month in which they are due.

b The staff are paid a commission of 5% on all monthly sales exceeding $15 000. The commission is paid in the month following that in which it is earned (see Section 32.4).

c General expenses are paid in the month in which they are incurred and are to be budgeted as follows: January $6 600; February $7 100; March $6 900; April $7 000; May $7 300; June $7 500.

d Xsel Limited pays interest of 8% on a loan of $20 000 in four annual instalments on 31 March, 30 June, 30 September and 31 December.

e A final dividend of $2 000 for the year ended 31 December is payable in March.

The accountant has prepared the following expenditure budget based on this information.

TOP TIP

The key here is to ensure that you put the payment for the expenditure in the correct month.

	January	February	March	April	May	June
	$	$	$	$	$	$
Purchases [1]	6 300	5 040	6 930	8 190	9 450	8 820
Wages	4 000	4 000	4 000	4 000	4 000	4 000
Commission	–	–	–	75	225	431
General expenses	6 600	7 100	6 900	7 000	7 300	7 500
Loan interest	–	–	400	–	–	400
Dividend	–	–	2 000	–	–	–
Total expenditure	16 900	16 140	20 230	19 265	20 975	21 151

[1] The information indicates that payments for raw materials are made two months **after** the goods are purchased. This means the goods purchased in November will be paid for in January. Those purchased in December will be paid for in February, and so on.

ACTIVITY 5

Martha and Florence Limited's overheads and other expenses for six months to 30 June are budgeted as follows:

1 Purchases are paid for in the following month.
2 Wages of $4 000 per month are paid in the same month as they are earned.
3 Staff are paid a bonus equal to 4% of the amount by which monthly sales exceed $20 000. The bonus is paid in the month following that in which it is earned.
4 Electricity bills are expected to be received in January, for $2 400, and in April for $1 800. The bills will be paid in the month following their receipt.
5 Other expenses are expected to amount to $6 000 per month. From April, they are expected to increase by 10%. They are paid in the month they are incurred.
6 Martha and Florence Limited has a loan of $20 000 on which interest at 10% is payable in four quarterly instalments on 31 March, 30 June, 30 September and 31 December.
7 The company will purchase a machine in May for $15 000.
8 A final dividend of $4 000 for the year ended 31 December will be paid in April.

Required

Prepare Martha and Florence Limited's expenditure budget for the six months ending 30 June. (Keep your answer; it will be needed later.)

32.9 How to prepare a trade receivables budget

The trade receivables budget has to be prepared before the cash budget and the master budget. This is in order to calculate the amount of cash that will be received from credit customers each month. This amount will be included in the cash budget. The final balance on the trade receivables budget will appear as the trade receivables figure under current assets in the master budget.

The preparation of the trade receivables budget for Xsel limited is quite complicated. It will serve as a good example for anything you might come across in future.

Walkthrough

Xsel Limited's sales in November were $18 000 and in December were $17 600.

Of the total sales, 40% are on a cash basis. Of the remainder, 50% are to credit customers who pay within one month and receive a cash discount of 2%. The remaining 10% of credit customers pay within two months.

The starting point is to calculate the opening trade receivables at the beginning of January. The figure is $12 360. This is made up of the November credit sales of the total credit sales for December $10 560 plus 10% of the total sales for November ($18 000 × 10% = $1 800). This makes a total of $12 360.

Set out below are the workings required to prepare the trade receivables budget for the period from January to June. Notice that the workings start at the previous November. This is because as we have seen some of the money from November's sales isn't received until January.

Workings								
	November	December	January	February	March	April	May	June
	$	$	$	$	$	$	$	$
Sales for the month	18 000	17 600	15 000	12 000	16 500	19 500	23 625	22 050
Cash sales	7 200	7 040	6 000	4 800	6 600	7 800	9 450	8 820
Credit sales	10 800	10 560	9 000	7 200	9 900	11 700	14 175	13 230
Cash received one month after sale [1]		8 820	8 624	7 350	5 880	8 085	9 555	11 576
Discount [2]		180	176	150	120	165	195	236
Balance of cash two months after sale [3]			1 800	1 760	1 500	1 200	1 650	1 950

[1] In January we receive cash from credit customers of December's sales ($17 600 × 50% × 98%) = $8624, plus 10% of the total sales in November = $18 000 × 10% = $1 800. This gives the total receipts for the month of January from credit customers of $10 424. These figures are shown as separate lines in the cash budget in Section 32.11.

[3] The balance of cash received after two months is 10% of the total sales made two months before. Thus, in January Xsel Limited will receive 10% of November's sales of $18 000 = £1 800.

[2] The discount figure is 2% of 50% of the sales for the previous month. Thus in January the discount = $17 600 × 50% × 2% = $176.

Trade receivables budget for the period January to June						
	January	February	March	April	May	June
	$	$	$	$	$	$
Opening trade receivables	12 360	10 760	8 700	11 100	13 350	16 125
Credit sales for the month	9 000	7 200	9 900	11 700	14 175	13 320
Less: cash received	10 424	9 110	7 380	9 285	11 205	13 526
Less: discounts allowed	176	150	120	165	195	236
Closing trade receivables	10 760	8 700	11 100	13 350	16 125	15 683

The layout of the trade receivables budget starts with the opening balance of trade receivables at the start of the month. The total credit sales for the month are added on to that figure. The cash received in the month and the discount allowed in that month are then deducted. The result is the closing figure for trade receivables. This is carried forward and forms the opening balance at the start of the next month.

The trade receivables budget can be quite complicated, as the one for Xsel Limited illustrates. However, by working logically through the data and setting it out with workings as shown above, with practice it should become straightforward.

32.10 How to prepare a trade payables budget

The preparation of the trade payables budget is the same as that used when preparing the trade receivables budget. The starting point of the calculation is the opening trade payables. On to this is added the credit purchases for the month. The cash paid and any discount received is deducted to leave the closing trade payables, which is carried forward to the start of the next month.

Walkthrough

Set out below is the trade payables budget for Xsel Limited for the months from January to May. Only this period is covered as the purchases needed beyond there have not been given in the earlier data.

Trade payables budget for the period from January to May

	November	December	January	February	March	April	May
	$	$	$	$	$	$	$
Opening trade payables [1]			11340	11970	15120	17640	18270
Credit purchases for month	6300	5040	6930	8190	9450	8820	11340
Cash paid			6300	5040	6930	8190	9450
Closing trade payables			11970	15120	17640	18270	20160

[1] As we saw in Section 32.8 Xsel Limited pays for its goods two months after they have been purchased. This means that at the beginning of January, Xsel Limited will owe its trade payables for goods bought in November ($6300) and December ($5 040) giving the total of $11 340. The workings can be expanded to include discount received in the same way as that shown for trade receivables.

32.11 How to prepare a cash budget

Usually, although it is called a cash budget, it really relates to the business bank account. Work through it to make sure you are fully familiar with where the information for it has come from and how it is constructed. The budget deals only with money received and paid and the months in which that takes place. **Non-cash** items such as depreciation or discounts (see below) must **never** be included.

Cash budgets are prepared from the sales and expenses budgets.

TOP TIP

Special care must be taken with respect to the following:

- Revenue must be allocated to the correct months. Receipts from credit customers who are allowed cash discounts must be shown at the amounts after deduction of the discounts. The discounts allowed to customers should **not** be shown separately as an expense.
- Payments to suppliers (purchases) must be shown in the correct months; check this carefully. The discounts received from suppliers should **not** be shown separately as an income.
- The reason for this is that no money changes hands in respect of discounts allowed and received. Thus, they must not be entered in the cash budget.

Step 5 Preparation of the cash budget

Walkthrough

1 Xsel Limited's credit sales in November were $18000, and in December were $17600.

2 Of total sales, 40% are on a cash basis; 50% are to credit customers who pay within one month and receive a cash discount of 2%. The remaining 10% of customers pay within two months.

3 $10000 was received from the sale of a non-current asset in March.

4 The balance at bank on 31 December was $12400.

TOP TIPS

Build up the cash budget in three stages:

- total receipts from **all** sources, not just revenue
- total expenditure (payments)
- calculate the opening and closing cash balances at the end of each month.

Set out below is the cash budget prepared by the accountant of Xsel Limited:

	January	February	March	April	May	June
	$	$	$	$	$	$
Receipts						
Cash sales [1]	6000	4800	6600	7800	9450	8820
Credit customers – one month [2]	8624	7350	5880	8085	9555	11576
Credit customers – two months [3]	1800	1760	1500	1200	1650	1950
Sale of non-current asset	–	–	10000	–	–	–
Total revenue	16424	13910	23980	17085	20655	22346
Expenditure [4]						
Purchases	6300	5040	6930	8190	9450	8820
Wages	4000	4000	4000	4000	4000	4000
Commission	–	–	–	75	225	431
General expenses	6600	7100	6900	7000	7300	7500
Loan interest	–	–	400	–	–	400
Dividend	–	–	2000	–	–	–
Total payments	16900	16140	20230	19265	20975	21151
Calculation of opening and closing bank balances						
Net receipts (payments) (total receipts minus total payments)	(476)	(2230)	3750	(2180)	(320)	1195
Bank balance brought forward	12400	11924	9694	13444	11264	10944
Bank balance carried forward	11924	9694	13444	11264	10944	12139

[2] Now for the tricky bit!

Credit sales in December were $17 600. Cash received from credit customers after one month = sales for previous month $17 600 × 50% = $8 800 × 98% = 8 624.

[4] The expenditure was calculated in step 4.

[1] Cash sales = 40% of sales for month. January's sales were budgeted to be $15 000 (see step 1). The cash sales were therefore $15 000 × 40% = $6 000. For February it would be $12 000 × 40% = $4 800, and so on.

[3] Credit sales in November (two months before January) were $18 000. Cash received from credit customers after two months = 10% of sales for two months previously $18 000 = $1 800.

TOP TIP

Prepare workings to cover all these and only show the final answer in the cash budget. Most importantly though, show your workings.

Note: At 30 June:

Trade receivables for sales	
	$
10% of May sales ($23 625 × 10%)	2 363*
50% of June sales ($22 050 × 50%)	11 025
10% of June sales ($22 050 × 10%)	2 205
	15 593

*Rounded

Trade payables for supplies: May purchases (paid for in July) = $11 340 + June purchases for production in July.

Accrued expenses: staff commission, 4% of $2 050 = $82.

Inventory: if information for July and August had been available the following would be known:

- raw materials purchased in June
- finished goods made in June.

ACTIVITY 6

1 Martha and Florence Limited's sales in November were $18 000 and in December were $17 600. Of total revenue, 50% is on a cash basis, 40% is received one month after sale. Cash discount of 2½% is allowed to customers who pay within one month. 10% of revenue is received two months after sale.

2 The company intends to sell plant and equipment for $12 000 in February.

3 The balance at bank on 31 December was $31 750.

Required

a Prepare Martha and Florence Limited's trade receivables budget for the six months ending June. Make all calculations to the nearest $.

b Prepare Martha and Florence Limited's trade payables budget for the five months ending May. Make all calculations to the nearest $.

32.12 How to prepare a master budget

A **master budget** is a budgeted income statement and statement of financial position prepared from sales, purchases, expense and cash budgets. The purpose of the master budget is to reveal to management the profit or loss to be expected if management's plans for the business are implemented, and the state of the business at the end of the budget period.

It is important to remember that the income statement must be prepared on a matching basis, and the information in the other budgets must be adjusted for accruals and prepayments; it is advisable to identify these when preparing the cash budget. Much information additional to that

KEY TERM

Master budget: The budgeted income statement and statement of financial position.

required for the functional budgets mentioned above will usually be given. Details of non-current assets which are to be sold or purchased will often be supplied; this information will usually be included in a **capital budget**.

Walkthrough

Meadowlands Limited
Statement of financial position at 31 December 2016

	Cost	Accumulated depreciation	Net book value
	$	$	$
Non-current assets			
Equipment	13 000	6 000	7 000
Motor vehicles	11 000	7 000	4 000
	24 000	13 000	11 000
Current assets			
Inventory			9 600
Trade receivables			33 600
Cash and cash equivalents			15 000
			58 200
Total assets			69 200
Equity and liabilities			
Share capital and reserves			
Ordinary shares of $1			40 000
Retained earnings			23 000
			63 000
Current liabilities			
Trade payables			6 200
Total equity and liabilities			69 200

Additional information

1 Goods are purchased one month before the month of sale.

2 Budgeted purchases and sales for the year ending 31 December 2017 are as follows:

	Purchases	Sales
	$	$
January–March	72 000	132 000
April–June	96 000	156 000
July–September	84 000	168 000
October–December	96 000	144 000

Sales and purchases accrue evenly over each quarter.

3 Meadowlands Limited receives one month's credit on all purchases and allows one month's credit on all sales.

4 The following expenses will be incurred in the year ending 31 December 2017:

- **i** rent of $1600 per quarter, paid in advance on 1 January, 1 April, 1 July, and 1 October
- **ii** wages of $7200, payable each month
- **iii** an insurance premium of $3000 for 15 months to 31 March 2018, paid on 1 January 2017
- **iv** other expenses of $20 000, paid quarterly.

5 The company will purchase additional equipment costing $15 000 on 1 April 2017.

6 A new motor vehicle will be purchased on 1 April 2017 for $12 000.

7 A motor vehicle which cost $6000, and has a written down value of $3000 at 31 December 2016, will be sold for $2000 on 1 July 2017.

8 The company depreciates equipment at 10% per annum on cost at the end of the year. It depreciates motor vehicles at 12½% per annum on cost at the end of the year.

9 The company's inventory at 31 December 2017 will be valued at $32 000.

Before preparing the master budget, the company accountant prepared a cash budget from the information provided. This is set out below:

Meadowlands Limited
Cash budget for the year ended 31 December 2017

	Jan/Mar	Apr/Jun	Jul/Sep	Oct/Dec
	$	$	$	$
Receipts				
Sales	121 600 [1]	148 000 [2]	164 000	152 000
Proceeds from sale of van	–	–	2 000	–
	121 600	148 000	166 000	152 000
Payments				
Purchases	54 200 [3]	88 000 [4]	88 000	92 000
Rent	1 600	1 600	1 600	1 600
Wages	21 600	21 600	21 600	21 600
Insurance	3 000	–	–	–
Other expenses	20 000	20 000	20 000	20 000
Purchase of equipment	–	15 000	–	–
Purchase of motor vehicle	–	12 000	–	–
	100 400	158 200	131 200	135 200
Net receipts/(payments)	21 200	(10 200)	34 800	16 800
Balance brought forward	15 000	36 200	26 000	60 800
Balance carried forward	36 200	26 000	60 800	77 600

[1] Trade receivables at 31 December 2016: ($33 600) + 2/3 of sales for January/March. ($132 000 × 2/3 = $88 000)

[2] 1/3 of previous quarter's sales + 2/3 of current quarter's sales.

[3] Trade payables at 31 December 2016: ($6200) + 2/3 of purchases for January/March.

[4] 1/3 of previous quarter's purchases + 2/3 of current quarter's purchases.

The accountant then prepared the following budgeted income statement:

Meadowlands Limited Budgeted income statement for the year ending 31 December 2017			
	$	$	$
Revenue [1]			600 000
Less: cost of sales:			
Opening inventory		9 600	
Purchases [2]		348 000	
		357 600	
Closing inventory [3]		(32 000)	(325 600)
Gross profit			274 400
Less: expenditure			
Wages		(86 400)	
Rent		(6 400)	
Insurance (12/15 × $3000)		(2 400)	
Other expenses		(80 000)	
Loss on sale of motor vehicle		(1 000)	
Depreciation:			
Equipment	(2 800)		
Motor vehicles	(2 125)	(4 925)	(181 125)
Profit for the year			(93 275)

[3] See note 9 in the additional information above.

[1] The revenue is the total of the sales made in the year $(132 000 + 156 000 + 168 000 + 144 000).

[2] Similarly, the purchases figure is the total of the purchases made in the year $(72 000 + 96 000 + 84 000 + 96 000). With both the sales and purchases, they are included when they are made, not when money is received or paid in respect of them.

As part of the workings, the accountant prepared a budgeted statement of non-current assets for the year ended 31 December 2017. (This is covered in Section 22.8)

	Equipment	Motor vehicles	Total
	$	$	$
Cost at 31 December 2016	13 000	11 000	24 000
Additions	15 000	12 000	27 000
Disposals		(6 000)	(6 000)
Cost at 31 December 2017	28 000	17 000	45 000
Accumulated depreciation at 31 December 2016	6 000	7 000	13 000
Additions	2 800	2 125	4 925
Disposals		(3 000)	(3 000)
Accumulated depreciation at 31 December 2017	8 800	6 125	14 925

This provided the information to include in both the budgeted income statement for the depreciation charge for the year, and the budgeted statement of financial position at 31 December 2017.

It was then possible for the accountant to prepare the following budgeted statement of financial position.

Meadowlands Limited
Budgeted statement of financial position at 31 December 2017

	Cost	Accumulated depreciation	Net book value
	$	$	$
Non-current assets			
Equipment	28 000	(8 800)	19 200
Motor vehicles	17 000	(6 125)	10 875
	45 000	(14 925)	30 075
Current assets			
Inventory			32 000
Trade receivables *			48 000
Prepaid insurance			
(other receivables)			600
Cash and cash equivalents			77 600
			158 200
Total assets			188 275
Equity and liabilities			
Share capital and reserves			
Ordinary shares of $1			40 000
Retained earnings			
(23 000 + 93 275)			116 275
			156 275
Current liabilities			
Trade payables **			32 000
Total equity and liabilities			188 275

* December sales ($144 000 × 1/3)

** December purchases ($96 000 × 1/3)

Note: As the master budget is prepared for management, there is no need to present it in line with IAS 1.

ACTIVITY 7

The directors of Greenfields Limited have prepared functional budgets for the four months ending 30 April 2017. To discover the effect that the budgets will have on the company at the end of the four months, they require the accountant to prepare master budgets. The accountant is provided with the following data:

Greenfields Limited
Statement of financial position at 31 December 2016

	Cost	Accumulated depreciation	Net book value
	$	$	$
Non-current assets			
Freehold premises	50 000	10 000	40 000
Plant and machinery	37 500	22 500	15 000
	87 500	32 500	55 000
Current assets			
Inventory			30 000
Trade receivables			42 500
Cash and cash equivalents			20 750
			93 250
Total assets			148 250
Equity and liabilities			
Equity			
Ordinary shares of $1			65 000
General reserve			30 000
Retained earnings			5 750
			100 750
Non-current liability			
12% debentures 2019/2020			25 000
Current liabilities			
Trade payables			22 500
Total equity and liabilities			148 250

Additional information

1 Sales and purchases for the four months from January to April 2017 are budgeted to be:

	Sales	Purchases
	$	$
January	62 500	25 000
February	70 000	20 000
March	75 000	30 000
April	82 500	37 500

Sales and purchases accrue evenly over each quarter.

2 40% of sales are to cash customers; one month's credit is allowed on the remainder.

3 The company pays for its purchases in the month following purchase.

4 Selling and distribution expenses amount to 10% of sales and are paid in the month in which they are incurred.

5 Administration expenses amount to $20 000 per month and are paid in the month in which they are incurred.

6 Inventory at 30 April 2017 is estimated to be valued at $22 500.

7 Additional plant and machinery costing $60 000 will be purchased on 1 March 2017.

8 Annual depreciation of non-current assets is based on cost as follows: freehold premises 3%; plant and machinery 20%. 50% of all depreciation is to be charged to selling and distribution expenses, and the balance to administration expenses.

9 Debenture interest is payable half-yearly on 30 June and 31 December.

10 A dividend of $0.10 per share will be paid on the ordinary shares on 30 April 2017.

11 $25 000 will be transferred to the general reserve on 30 April 2017.

Required

a Prepare a cash budget for each of the four months from January 2017 to 30 April 2017.

b Prepare a budgeted income statement for the four months ending 30 April 2017 in as much detail as possible.

c Prepare a budgeted statement of financial position as at 30 April 2017 in as much detail as possible.

TOP TIP

Students often try to prepare a budgeted income statement for each month. The question only requires a single budgeted income statement covering the whole four-month period.

32.13 The advantages and disadvantages of budgeting and budgetary control

Every business of any size should prepare budgets for the next year at least. Quite often, banks will require a cash flow forecast, which is another name for a cash budget, before granting further finance to a business, or simply to see that their investment is safe.

There are a number of advantages which budgeting and budgetary control can bring to a business:

- It forces managers to think about the future and the direction in which the business is heading.
- It helps identify areas where improvements are required or can be made before the start of a trading period.
- It is motivational. If managers play a part in preparing the budget then they will be motivated to achieve it. This is especially true if their performance is measured against the budget and they are paid a bonus for beating the budget.
- Often banks and lenders require budget information from the business. Thus, it may help in securing finance for the firm.

There are also some drawbacks associated with budgeting:

- It is time consuming to prepare.
- Often the budget process is started some months before the end of the current year. A number of things can happen between that time and the end of the year which will affect the future.
- It often requires specialist knowledge to prepare, especially the cash and master budgets. This can add to the expenses of the business, particularly for sole traders and partnerships who do not have the necessary expertise.
- If managers are paid on their performance against the budget, they may build in some extra costs or reduce the expected revenue to ensure they always beat it. This is known as 'budgetary slack'.

Whilst there are drawbacks with preparing budgets, they are vital to enable managers to do their jobs. There should be no excuse for not preparing them even for sole traders. Indeed, banks often require them as the basis for future lending.

TOP TIP

Preparation of budgets is often an exercise in arithmetic, so be accurate; but note the degree of accuracy required (e.g. to nearest $ or nearest $000).

Chapter summary

In this chapter you have learnt all about budgeting and budgetary control. When answering questions on this topic, you should know how to calculate the budgets and explain what they mean, including:

- how budgets differ from forecasts
- how budgets help management to plan and control
- factors to be considered in the preparation of budgets
- how to prepare sales, production, purchasing, expenditure, cash and master budgets
- the meaning of 'flexible' budgets.

In the case of the cash budget, you should also be able to explain ways in which, say, a bank overdraft can be improved or eliminated by taking actions to increase the cash received or reduce the cash paid.

Having mastered these topics, you should also be able to weigh up the advantages and disadvantages of budgeting and budgetary control.

TOP TIP

Work through the preparation of each budget covered and make sure you can prepare them. Also be prepared to discuss topics such as the benefits and drawbacks of preparing them.

Practice exercises

1 Banner Limited's budget for the four months from January to April includes the following data:

Month	Sales	Materials	Wages	Overheads
	$000	$000	$000	$000
January	615	114.4	30	360
February	636	118.8	33	390
March	690	132.0	36	412
April	684	128.0	39	420

Additional information

1 One-third of revenue is received one month after sale and the remainder is received two months after sale. The sales in the previous two months were: November $600 000; December $540 000.

2 One quarter of purchases of materials are paid for in the month of purchase. The remainder are paid for two months later. Purchases in the previous two months were: November $108 000; December $106 000.

3 Two-thirds of the wages are paid in the month in which they are earned, and the balance is paid in the following month. The wages for the previous December amounted to $30 000.

4 One half of the overhead expenditure is paid in the month in which it is incurred, and the balance is paid in the following month. The overheads for the previous December were $380 000.

5 Old machinery will be sold for $4 000 in April. New machinery will be purchased in March for $90 000 but only one half of the price will be paid in that month. The balance will be paid in August.

6 Banner Limited has an overdraft of $63 000 at the bank at 31 December.

Required

a Prepare Banner Limited's cash budget for each of the four months from January to April. The budget should be prepared in columnar form.

b Prepare a statement to show the accruals in part **a** which would appear in a statement of financial position at 30 April.

2 The sales budget for Roh Limited for the six months to 30 November 2017 is as follows:

	Units
June	600
July	800
August	1 000
September	900
October	980
November	1 020

Additional information

1 All units are sold for $60. Customers are allowed one month's credit.

2 Monthly production of the units is equal to the following month's sales plus 10% for inventory.

3 Costs per unit are as follows:

Material	3	kg
Cost of material	$4.00	per kg
Labour	2	hours
Labour rate of pay	$8.00	per hour
Absorption rates:		
Variable overhead	$14.00	
Fixed overhead	$3.50	

4 Materials are purchased one month before they are needed for production and are paid for two months after purchase.

5 Wages and variable overheads are paid in the current month.

6 Fixed overheads are paid in the following month.

7 The following information is to be taken into account: cash book balance at 30 June 2017 is $16 000.

Required

a Prepare the following budgets for the month of August 2017 **only**:
  i production budget (in units only) **[4 marks]**
  ii purchases budget in dollars. **[4 marks]**
  iii a cash budget. **[9 marks]**

b Explain how principal budget factors affect the preparation of budgets. **[3 marks]**

Additional information

The directors of Roh Limited are unsure of the benefits of preparing budgets. They argue that the accountant seems to spend a lot of time working on them and that he should no longer prepare them.

Required

c Advise the directors whether or not the company accountant should continue to prepare budgets for the business. Justify your answer. **[5 marks]**

Total: 25

3 Alan has been asked by his bank manager to produce a cash budget, budgeted income statement and budgeted statement of financial position for his next three months trading ending 30 June 2017.

His statement of financial position at 1 April 2017 is as follows:

	$000
Non-current assets	36
Current assets	
Inventory	4
Trade receivables	12
	16
Total assets	52
	$000

Capital and liabilities	
Capital account balance	25
Non-current liability	
10% bank loan	15
Current liabilities	
Trade payables	10
Bank overdraft	2
	12
Total capital and liabilities	52

Additional information

Alan has prepared the following budgeted data for the next three months ending 30 June 2017:

1 Budgeted sales and purchases for the next three months are as follows:

Month	Budgeted sales	Budgeted purchases
	$	$
April	11 000	8 000
May	14 000	9 000
June	15 000	9 500

2 Customers will pay 80% of the money in the month following the sale and the other 20% in the second month after the sale. However at 31 March, only March receivables were outstanding.

3 Suppliers for purchases will be paid in full in the month following purchase.

4 Monthly overheads are $4 000 and will be paid in full in the month.

5 Alan takes monthly drawings of $2 000.

6 In June, Alan intends to purchase a new delivery vehicle. This will cost $8 000. A 50% deposit will be paid in June. The balance will be added to the outstanding bank loan. No depreciation will charged on the vehicle in June.

7 Non-current assets are depreciated on a month-by-month basis at 10% per annum using the straight-line method.

8 Interest on the bank loan will be paid in July 2017.

9 At 30 June 2017, inventory is expected to be $5 000.

Required

a Prepare Alan's cash budget for the three months ending 30 June 2017. **[8 marks]**

b Prepare a budgeted income statement for the three months ending 30 June 2017. **[6 marks]**

c State **two** advantages and **two** disadvantages of a business preparing budgets. **[4 marks]**

d Evaluate Alan's cash budget and budgeted income statement for the three months ending 30 June 2017. Advise Alan of any actions you think he should take in respect of them. **[7 marks]**

Total: 25

Exam practice questions

Multiple-choice questions

1 A table is made from 4 kg of raw material. Production for six months is based on the following data.

Budgeted sales	5000 tables
Budgeted decrease in inventory of raw material	1200 kg
Budgeted increase in inventory of tables	800 tables

How many kg of raw material will be purchased for the six months?

A 18000
B 18800
C 22000
D 23200

2 Trade receivables at the year-end are $40000. It is planned to double turnover in the next year and to reduce the trade receivables' turnover from 45 days to 30 days. What will the trade receivables be at the end of the next year?

A $26667
B $53334
C $60000
D $80000

3 The sales budget for four months from January to April is as follows:

January	$80000
February	$100000
March	$110000
April	$130000

The cost of the raw material used in the goods is 40% of sales. The material is purchased one month before the goods are made, and manufacture takes place one month before sale. 50% of the material is paid for one month after purchase and the balance is paid for two months after purchase. How much will be paid for raw materials in March?

A $40000
B $42000
C $46000
D $48000

4 A company plans to purchase a new machine costing $40000. It will part exchange one of its existing machines for the new one. The existing machine has a net book value of $4000 and the part exchange will result in a loss on disposal of the machine of $1000. The company will pay the balance due on the new machine by cheque. How will the transaction be recorded in the cash budget?

A payment for new machine $37000
B payment for new machine $40000
C payment for new machine $40000; cash received for old machine $3000
D payment for new machine $40000; cash received for old machine $4000

Total: 4 marks

Chapter 33
Standard costing

Learning objectives

In this chapter you will learn:

- what standard costing is and how standards are set
- how to flex budgets
- how to calculate sales, materials, labour and fixed overhead variances
- how to reconcile the actual and budgeted profits
- how to recognise the possible causes of variances
- how standard costing can be used as an aid to improve the performance of a business
- the advantages and disadvantages of using a standard costing system.

KEY TERMS

Standard cost: The estimated, or budgeted, cost of a unit of output or activity. It can be compared with the actual cost of the unit of output or activity in order to take corrective action.

Variance: A difference between the standard cost and actual cost.

33.1 What is standard costing?

Standard costing is an accounting system that records the cost of operations at pre-determined standards. If the standards are realistic, the system informs managers of the material, labour and overhead costs that should be incurred if the business is managed efficiently. **Standard costs** are an essential tool for realistic budgeting. However, the costs actually incurred may differ from the standards for a variety of reasons:

- the quantity of goods produced may be more or less than budget
- the quantity of material used in each unit of production may be more or less than budget
- the cost of material many be more or less than budget because the price paid may have increased or decreased since the budget was prepared, or the material may have been obtained from alternative suppliers
- workers may have been more or less efficient than expected in the budget
- the rates of pay for workers may be more or less than those on which the budget was based.

In respect of fixed overheads, variances may arise because:

- more or less has been spent on fixed overheads than was budgeted for
- actual production may be more or less than was budgeted for.

Standards can also be set for revenue, and causes for differences between actual revenue and the standard may be:

- more or fewer units were sold than budgeted to be sold
- the selling price of the product may be higher or lower than the standard price set.

The link between the profit calculated on standard cost and the profit shown in a traditional income statement is provided by the preparation of a reconciliation statement between the standard profit or loss and the actual profit or loss.

The differences between actual and budgeted data are known as **variances**.

33.2 The advantages and disadvantages of standard costing

Standard costing is an important management tool. It provides a benchmark against which actual performance can be measured. There are a number of advantages of standard costing which are:

- The preparation of budgets is made easier if they are based on standard costs, and the budgets are likely to be more realistic. The standards are the building blocks of the budget. Quite often in practice, the terms 'budgeted' and 'standard' are used to mean the same thing.
- Differences between actual and budgeted results (variances) are easier to identify if standard costs are used.
- The activities that are responsible for variances are highlighted.
- Because it highlights activities that give rise to variances, standard costing is an essential part of responsibility accounting (see Section 32.2).
- Calculated standards facilitate the preparation of estimates for the costs of new products and quotations for orders.
- Although standard costing is usually associated in people's minds with manufacturing industries, it is of equal use in all kinds of businesses, including service industries such as hotels and hospitals.

However, standard costing does have some disadvantages:

- It takes time to collect all the data necessary to prepare the standard cost of a product.
- The standards need to be continually monitored and updated. There is little point in keeping direct labour times for production if new machinery has been purchased to replace labour.
- Although an advantage is the identification of variances, it does not in itself explain the cause of the variances. Further investigation is required if suitable changes are to be made.
- There may be factors outside the control of the business which cause the variance. For example, the business may anticipate prices of raw materials increasing by 5%. World prices may be higher or lower than this.

If it is used properly then the advantages of standard costing will outweigh the disadvantages and improve the future performance of the business.

33.3 Setting standards

Standards must be realistic if they are to be useful and not misleading. Unrealistic standards result in the loss of the advantages listed in the previous section. The various types of standards may be described, as follows:

- **Ideal standards** are standards that can only be met under ideal conditions. Since the conditions under which businesses work are very rarely ideal, these standards are unrealistic and are never likely to be attained. As a result, they may actually demotivate managers and cause them to perform less, rather than more, efficiently. Ideal standards should not be used.
- **Current standards** are based on present levels of performance, which may be quite inappropriate for the future. They do not offer management or workers any incentive to perform more efficiently. Current standards should only be used when present conditions are too uncertain to enable more appropriate standards to be set.
- **Attainable standards** recognise that there is normally some wastage of materials and not all the hours worked are productive. Time spent unproductively by workers is called **idle time** and may occur when machinery breaks down or the machinery has to be 'set up' for a production run. The standards should take reasonable account of these factors and give the workers an incentive to use their time and materials efficiently. The standards set should, therefore, be attainable ones.

Standard hours of production are measures of quantity of work and should not be confused with a period of time. If, under normal, or standard, working conditions, 20 units of output can be produced in one hour, the standard hour is 20 units. This concept of standard hours is useful when budgets are being prepared for departments that produce two or more different products.

Walkthrough

For example, in one month, a department of QF Limited's output consists of:

	Total standard hours
200 tables which take 1 hour each to make	200
400 wardrobes which take 1½ hours each to make	600
300 chairs which take 30 minutes each to make	150
Total standard hours of production	950

The output of the department can conveniently be expressed as 950 standard hours for budgeting purposes. Similarly, standard minutes are a quantity of work that can be done in a stated number of standard minutes.

A standard wage rate paid to direct workers will also be set. QF Limited's standard wage rate is $12 per hour. This means that the standard direct labour cost to make the products above will be:

[1] The total for each product is the total time taken × $12.

	Total standard hours	**Total standard wage cost [1]**
	$	**$**
200 tables which take 1 hour each to make	200	2 400
400 wardrobes which take 1½ hours each to make	600	7 200
300 chairs which take 30 minutes each to make	150	1 800
Total standard hours and wages cost of production	950	11 400

As with direct materials, the standard quantity of material required to make a single unit of output is calculated. A standard price for the material will also be set. To make the furniture will require an amount of wood. The standard set for the price of the wood is $20 per metre. It is now possible to construct a table showing the standard material cost of production:

[1] The total amount of metres required is multiplied by $20 per metre.

	Total standard material in metres	**Total standard material cost [1]**
	$	**$**
200 tables which each take 4 metres of wood to make	800	16 000
400 wardrobes which each take 8 metres of wood to make	3 200	64 000
300 chairs which each take 2 metres of wood to make	600	12 000
Total standard quantity and cost of material for production	4 600	92 000

Next, the standard amount of fixed overheads to be charged to the production is calculated. This will be based on the expected expenditure on fixed overheads such as rent, rates and so on. This was covered in Chapters 28 and 30. For example, QF Limited has set its budgeted fixed overheads at $38 000. If it is absorbed on the basis of direct labour hours, the standard overhead absorption rate is $40 ($38 000 ÷ 950 hours).

Finally, the standard selling price for each product is set. The standard selling prices per unit are:

Tables	$200
Wardrobes	$250
Chairs	$70

Using this information it will now be possible to set a budget for the department for the next month based on the information calculated.

QF Limited [1] Budgeted profit statement for month.....	Tables	Wardrobes	Chairs	Total
	$	$	$	$
Revenue	40 000	100 000	21 000	161 000
Direct materials	(16 000)	(64 000)	(12 000)	(92 000)
Direct labour	(2 400)	(7 200)	(1 800)	(11 400)
Fixed overhead at $40 per direct labour hour	(8 000)	(24 000)	(6 000)	(38 000)
Budgeted profit [2]	13 600	4 800	1 200	19 600

[1] Notice the heading. It is not a budgeted income statement as not all expenses have been included. It is also for management use and not for publication.

[2] As a result, it is a budgeted profit, and not a profit for the year. It would also be possible to label it budgeted gross profit.

The information to prepare the budgeted profit statement has been built up from the standard data prepared, hence the comment that standard costing is the foundation for budgeting and budgetary control.

ACTIVITY 1

Jumal runs a small manufacturing company which uses standard costing. The company manufactures two products, bicycles and tricycles. Both use the same materials and are made in the same workshop.

He is preparing his budget for the next six months and has prepared the following data:

Details	Bicycles	Tricycles
Total production and sales	4 000	2 500
Per unit information:		
Selling price	$600	$250
Direct materials	10 metres of steel tubing at $45 per metre	4 metres of steel tubing at $45 per metre
Direct labour	2 hours at $10 per hour	1 hour at $10 per hour

Total budgeted fixed overheads for the six-month period is $42 000.

Required

Prepare Jumal's budgeted profit statement for the next six-month period.

33.4 How to flex budgets

As was identified in Chapter 32 on budgeting, the actual volume of goods produced and sold is seldom the same as the volume on which a budget has been based. Sensible comparisons can only be made if 'like is compared with like', and the budget is based on the actual volume of output. This is done by **flexing** the budget. There are a number of reasons why it is important to flex the budget:

- It allows comparison of like with like. This means that if the actual data is different from the budgeted data, we are comparing costs and revenue at one level of output with those at a different level. Any differences identified will be of little use to managers in order to take corrective action.

- By flexing the budgets, therefore, any variances calculated will be more meaningful.
- Flexing the budget aids in management being better able to control the business.

When flexing the budget, therefore:

- budgeted sales volume must be adjusted to the actual sales volume
- the variable expenses in the budget must be adjusted to take account of the actual volume of goods produced
- any semi-variable expenses must be adjusted for the same reason.

Walkthrough

Many Marbles Limited produced the following budget for the production and sale of 10 000 marbles for the six months ending June.

Budget for 10 000 marbles, six months ending June	
	$
Revenue	500 000
Variable expenses:	
Direct materials	(50 000)
Direct labour	(100 000)
Variable production overheads	(40 000)
Variable selling and distribution	(8 000)
	(198 000)
Fixed expenses	(212 000)
Total cost	(410 000)
Budgeted profit	90 000

The output and sales for the six months ended 30 June was 12 000 marbles. Set out below is the flexed budget for the period. The budget is flexed by multiplying the revenue and variable expenses by $\frac{12\,000}{10\,000}$, that is by 1.2.

	$
Revenue	600 000
Variable expenses:	
Direct materials	(60 000)
Direct labour	(120 000)
Production overheads	(48 000)
Selling and distribution	(9 600)
	(237 600)
Fixed expenses	(212 000)
Total cost	(449 600)
Budgeted profit	150 400

Notice that it is the variable costs which change as a result of flexing the budget.

The fixed expenses have not changed.

TOP TIP

When calculating variances, the first thing you must do is to flex the budgeted (or standard) information provided.

ACTIVITY 2

Breakfast Limited's budget for the production of 100 000 packets of cereal in the year ending 31 December was as follows:

	$
Variable expenses:	
Direct materials	20 000
Direct labour	15 000
Production expenses	6 000
	41 000
Fixed expenses:	
Production expenses	13 000
Administration	29 000
	83 000

The actual output for the year ended 31 December was 110 000 packets of cereal.

Required

Prepare a flexed budget for the production of 110 000 packets of cereal.

Flexing budgets with semi-variable expenses

The way to split semi-variable costs into their fixed and variable elements was covered in Chapter 30. However, it is an important aspect when flexing the budget and is covered again here.

Budgets may not show a distinction between fixed and variable expenses. In these cases, the distinction must be found by inspection.

Walkthrough

Shield Limited has prepared flexed budgets for the production of 5 000 and 6 000 pairs of sunglasses.

	5 000 pairs of sunglasses	6 000 pairs of sunglasses
	$	$
Direct materials	10 000	12 000
Direct labour	15 000	18 000
Production overheads	16 000	18 000
Selling and distribution	19 000	22 000
Administration	12 000	12 000
	72 000	82 000

8 000 pairs of sunglasses were produced and a flexed budget for that output is required.

As we saw in Chapter 30, some expenses vary directly with output: direct materials are $2 per pair of sunglasses, and direct labour is $3 per pair at both levels of output. They must, therefore be **variable** costs. The cost of these items for 8 000 pairs of sunglasses will be: direct materials $16 000; direct labour $24 000.

Production overheads and selling and distribution expenses have not increased proportionately with the increased production. This can be proved by dividing the cost by the units produced at each level.

So for production overheads, when 5 000 pairs of sunglasses are produced the cost per unit is $3.20 ($16 000 ÷ 5 000 units) and for selling and distribution costs it is $3.80 per unit ($19 000 ÷ 5 000 units). When 6 000 pairs are produced the costs per unit are $3.00 and $3.67 respectively.

Each of these items contains a fixed element. To find the variable elements of these costs, deduct the costs for 5 000 units from the costs for 6 000 units to find the variable costs for 1 000 units, using the method described in Chapter 30.

The change in production overheads for 1 000 units = $(18 000 – 16 000) = $2 000, or $2 per unit. This represents the variable element per unit. For 5 000 units therefore, the total variable costs must be $2 × 5 000 = $10 000.

Fixed production costs are now found by deducting the variable cost for 5 000 units from the total production cost: $(16 000 – 10 000) = $6 000.

Production cost for 8 000 pairs of sunglasses is $6 000 + (8 000 × $2) = $22 000.

ACTIVITY 3

a Using the information above, calculate the total budgeted selling and distribution costs for 8 000 pairs of sunglasses.

b Prepared the flexed budgeted cost statement for 8 000 pairs of sunglasses.

ACTIVITY 4

Flexible Limited has prepared the following budgets for the production of padlocks:

	6 000 padlocks	8 000 padlocks
	$	$
Direct materials	15 000	20 000
Direct labour	36 000	48 000
Production overheads	25 000	31 000
Selling and distribution	24 000	28 000
Administration	80 000	80 000
	180 000	207 000

Required

Prepare a flexed budget for the production of 9 000 padlocks.

33.5 Variances

A variance is the difference between a standard cost and an actual cost or, in the case of revenue, between budgeted revenue and actual revenue. Variances may be calculated for:

- sales
- direct materials
- direct labour
- variable and fixed overheads.

Variances highlight activities that may need management intervention if the budgeted profit is to be achieved or, at least, to limit any adverse effect on profit. The variances may be further analysed into sub-variances to indicate the activities or operations that are performing adversely. An adverse variance decreases profit while a favourable variance increases profit.

Every variance must be described as either favourable (F) or adverse (A). Any variance not so described is meaningless and of no help to management.

Walkthrough

General Limited makes a product which it markets under the name of 'Capers'. The budget for **one month** is based on the following standard costs:

Number of Capers produced and sold:	18 000
Per Caper:	
Selling price per Caper	$32
Direct materials (kg)	1.25
Cost of material per kg	$4
Direct labour (minutes)	30
Labour rate per hour	$12
Budgeted fixed overheads for the month	$360 000

Step 1 Prepare the master budget

Master budget 18 000 Capers		
	$	$
Revenue (18 000 × $32)		576 000
Direct materials (18 000 × 1.25 × $4)	(90 000)	
Direct labour (18 000 × [30 mins ÷ 60] × $12)	(108 000)	(198 000)
Contribution		378 000
Fixed overheads		(360 000)
Budgeted profit		18 000

For the month, the actual number of Capers produced and sold was 20 000. It is therefore necessary to flex the budget to reflect the actual level of output and sales. This is, in effect, the new budgeted income statement for the month.

Step 2 Prepare the flexed budget for the 20 000 units produced and sold

	Flexed budget 20 000 Capers	
	$	$
Revenue (20 000 × $32)		640 000
Direct materials (20 000 × 1.25 kg × $4)	(100 000)	
Direct labour (20 000 × [30 mins ÷ 60] × $12)	(120 000)	(220 000)
Contribution		420 000
Fixed overheads		(360 000)
Flexed budgeted profit		60 000

Notice that, as before, only the variable costs are flexed to the actual level of output and sales.

The actual data for the month was:

	Actual
Selling price per unit	$30.60
Direct materials (kg) per unit	1.10
Cost of direct materials per kg	$4.15
Direct labour (minutes)	36
Direct labour rate per hour	$11
Fixed overheads	$370 000

It is therefore necessary to prepare an actual income statement for the month:

Step 3 Prepare a schedule of the actual results

	Actual results 20 000 Capers	
	$	$
Revenue (20 000×$30.60)		612 000
Direct materials (20 000 × 1.10 kg × $4.15)	(91 300)	
Direct labour (20 000 × [36 mins ÷ 60] × $11)	(132 000)	(223 300)
Contribution		388 700
Fixed overheads [1]		(370 000)
Actual profit		18 700

[1] It may seem odd that the fixed costs are higher than the budget. However, remember that these are the actual results and so the fixed costs for the budget may have been set at a different overhead absorption rate or perhaps General Limited received an unexpected invoice.

From the two sets of data it is now possible to prepare a flexed budget report for senior management.

Step 4 Prepare a flexed budget report

In practice, the accountant will prepare a statement which compares the budgeted and actual data and shows the difference (variance) between the two. This is shown below.

Preparation of the flexed budget statement for the month:

	Actual	Budget	Variance
Units ($)	20 000	20 000	
Revenue ($)	612 000	640 000	(28 000)
Direct materials ($)	(91 300)	(100 000)	8 700
Direct labour ($)	(132 000)	(120 000)	(12 000)
Contribution ($)	388 700	420 000	(31 300)
Fixed overheads ($)	(370 000)	(360 000)	(10 000)
Profit ($)	18 700	60 000	(41 300)

Understanding the data

The flexed budget report is an essential part of management control for the business. Notice that the report doesn't include the master budget data. Some companies may well show the fixed budget data as part of their report, but really the comparison between the actual results and the flexed budget is the most important thing.

The variances are shown either without brackets if they are favourable (direct labour), or in brackets if they are adverse. They give management an indication of where to look for the problems. In themselves though, they don't tell managers what has caused the variances; this requires further investigation. However, all the information is now available to enable the variances to be calculated.

TOP TIP

Always work through the data carefully. Remember to flex the budget before calculating the variances. The most common mistake is to calculate variance by comparing the actual data with the fixed budget.

ACTIVITY 5

Underpart Limited has prepared a budget based on standard costs. It is shown below together with the actual results:

	Budget	Actual
No. of units ($)	7 000	6 300
Revenue ($)	175 000	163 800
Direct materials ($)	23 800	20 890
Direct labour ($)	47 250	44 065
Variable overhead ($)	3 500	3 250
Fixed overhead ($)	62 000	62 000
Total costs ($)	136 550	130 205

Required

Prepare a flexed budget statement for 6 300 units, clearly showing the budgeted and actual profit, and all the relevant variances.

33.6 How to calculate sales variances

When a business sells more than one type of product, sales variances will occur when the mix of products sold differs from the budgeted mix and gives rise to a mix variance. However, it is only necessary in this text to consider situations involving a single product.

In the General Limited example above, two things could have happened to cause the sales variance of $36 000. Either General Limited sold more or less than the budget (this is a **sales volume variance**), or they may have sold the goods at a different price than was budgeted (this is a **sales price variance**). In this case both things have happened.

These variances are calculated as follows:

a **Sales volume variance**, which equals the difference between the total sales in the original budget and the total sales in the flexed budget.

General Limited's sales volume variance is $640 000 – $576 000 = $64 000 favourable.

This could also have been calculated as (20 000 units – 18 000 units) × $32 = $64 000 favourable. The variance is favourable because actual sales were more than the original amount budgeted.

b **Sales price variance**, which is the difference between the flexed budgeted sales and the actual sales.

General Limited's sales price variance is $612 000 – $640 000 = $28 000 adverse.

This could also have been calculated as 1.4 $(32 – 30.60) × 20 000 units = $28 000 adverse.

Here we are comparing the actual selling price per unit of the units sold with the standard selling price per unit.

TOP TIP

When calculating material and labour variances, always start with the standard and deduct the 'actual'. A positive remainder will indicate that the variance is favourable, and a negative remainder will indicate that the variance is adverse. Always describe variances as favourable (F) or adverse (A).

c **Total sales variance**, which allows you to check whether the variance has been calculated correctly.

This is done by using the formula:

Actual sales – budgeted sales = $(612 000 – 576 000) = $36 000 favourable.

Alternatively it can be shown as:

Sales volume variance – sales price variance = $(64 000 – 28 000) = $36 000 favourable.

TOP TIP

You may also be asked to calculate the total sales variance as well as the price and volume variance. If you have time, then calculate it as shown above. Otherwise just add together the sales price and sales volume variance you have calculated. Remember that if one is favourable and one adverse they must be netted off.

This is also true for all the other total variances calculated below.

Notice here that we are using the sales figures from the original or fixed budget. Calculating the variances has identified that although dropping the selling price has increased the volume sold, or amount General Limited sold, it has been at the expense of a loss of revenue.

ACTIVITY 6

For the month of January:

1 the budgeted sales of Polonius Limited is set at 10 000 units at $15 per unit

2 the actual results were 9 500 units at $15.50 per unit.

Required

Calculate for Polonius Limited for the month:

a the sales volume variance

b the sales price variance.

(Keep your answer; it will be needed later.)

33.7 How to calculate total direct materials and direct labour cost variances

The direct materials and direct labour cost variances may be summarised as follows:

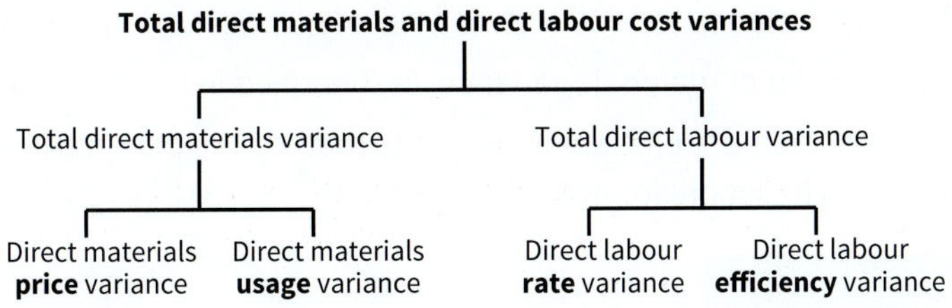

How to calculate direct materials cost variances

As with sales, the variance on the direct materials cost can be due to two things. General Limited may have used more or less material than was budgeted. This is called the **direct materials usage variance**.

It may also have purchased materials at a higher or lower price than was set in the budget. This is called the **direct materials price variance**.

This can be shown diagrammatically:

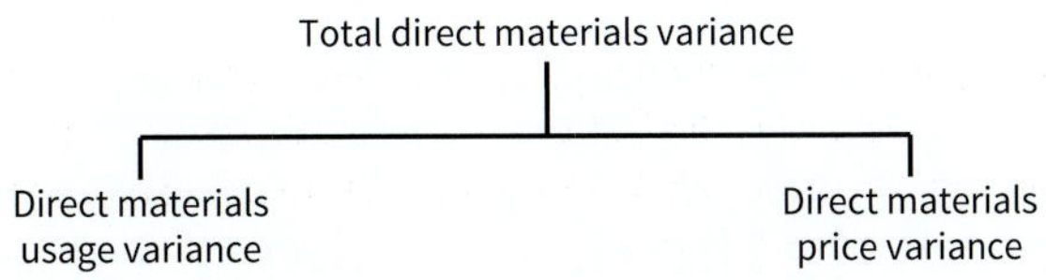

The variances are calculated as follows:

a **Total direct materials variance,** which is the difference between the **flexed** budget direct materials cost and the actual direct materials cost.

	$
Flexed budget direct materials cost	100 000
Actual direct materials cost	(91 300)
Favourable total direct materials variance	8 700

b **Direct materials usage variance**, which is the difference between the actual quantity of direct materials used and the quantity of direct materials which should have been used to produce the actual output. The difference between the two figures is multiplied by the standard cost per kg.

The actual quantity produced and sold was 20 000 units.

This should have used 20 000 × 1.25 kg = 25 000 kg.

The actual usage was 20 000 × 1.10 = 22 000 kg.

The standard cost per kg was $4.

The calculation is, therefore:

The difference of 3 000 kg × $4 = **$12 000 favourable direct materials usage variance**.

c **Direct materials price variance**, which is the difference between the actual price paid and the budgeted price for the actual quantity used.

The actual price per kg was $4.15.

The budgeted, or standard, price per kg was $4.

This difference of $0.15 $(4.00 – 4.15) × 22 000 kg = **$3 300 adverse material price variance**.

Check:

Direct materials usage variance $12 000 – direct materials price variance $3 300 =

$8 700 favourable total direct materials variance, as identified in the flexed budget.

General Limited has been more efficient in using the material, or perhaps it was of better quality, as it has had to pay more for it.

ACTIVITY 7

For the month of January:

- the budgeted direct materials required by Polonius Limited to produce one unit was one litre of material at $6 per litre
- Polonius Limited used 9 700 litres of materials at a total cost of $57 715.

Required

Calculate for Polonius Limited:

a the direct materials usage variance

b the direct materials price variance

c a statement reconciling the two variances with the total direct materials variance.

(Keep your answer; it will be needed later.)

33.8 How to calculate the direct labour variances

The calculation of the direct labour variances are identical to those required to calculate the direct materials variances. The only difference is in their names. For direct labour, a direct labour efficiency variance is the same thing as a direct materials usage variance. Both measure the efficiency with which the company used the resources.

Similarly, a direct labour rate variance measures the price the company paid for labour – the wage rate. This is the same as the direct materials price variance.

General Limited may have used more or less direct labour hours than were budgeted for to produce the output. This difference is the **direct labour efficiency variance**. It may also have paid a higher or lower wage rate than was budgeted for. This difference is the **direct labour rate variance**.

This can be shown diagrammatically:

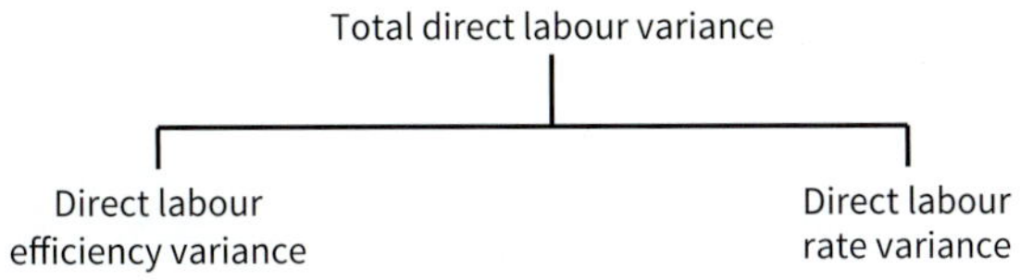

The variances are calculated as follows:

a **Total direct labour variance**, which is the difference between the flexed budget direct labour cost and the actual direct labour cost.

	$
Flexed budget direct labour cost	120 000
Actual direct labour cost	(132 000)
Adverse total direct labour variance	(12 000)

b **Direct labour efficiency variance**, which is the difference between the actual direct labour hours worked and the direct labour hours which **should** have been worked to produce the **actual** output. The difference between the two figures is multiplied by the standard cost per direct labour hour.

The actual quantity produced and sold was 20 000 units.

This should have used 20 000 × (30 ÷ 60) = 10 000 direct labour hours.

The actual usage was 20 000 × (36 ÷ 60) = 12 000 direct labour hours.

The difference of 2 000 direct labour hours × $12 = **$24 000 adverse direct labour efficiency variance**.

c **Direct labour rate variance**, which is the difference between the actual direct labour hour rate and the budgeted direct labour hour rate for the actual hours worked.

The actual direct labour hour rate was $11 per hour.

The budgeted, or standard direct labour hour rate was $12 per hour.

This difference of $1 ($12 – 11) × 12 000 = **$12 000 favourable direct labour rate variance.**

Check:

Direct labour efficiency variance $24 000 – direct labour rate variance $12 000 =

$12 000 adverse total direct labour variance, as identified in the flexed budget.

General Limited may have used cheaper labour but workers have not been as efficient as predicted.

621

ACTIVITY 8

For the month of January:

- the budgeted direct labour hours required by Polonius Limited to produce one unit was one hour at $4 per hour
- Polonius Limited used 9 450 direct labour hours at $3.98 per hour.

Required

Calculate for Polonius Limited for the month of January:

a the direct labour efficiency variance

b the direct labour rate variance

c a statement reconciling the two variances with the total direct labour variance.

(Keep your answer, you will need it later.)

ACTIVITY 9

Dandelion Limited has a standard direct labour cost for the production of one packet of Pickup based on one labour hour at $10 per hour. The production of 12 000 packets of Pickup required 1.25 hours each, paid at $8.50 per hour.

Required

Calculate the direct labour efficiency and rate variances for 12 000 packets of Pickup.

33.9 Calculation of fixed overhead variances

The objective of setting standard costs for fixed overheads is to absorb the amount of fixed overheads into the overall cost of output. Inevitably, actual costs and levels of production will vary from the standards or budgets set. Thus, there will be an under (shortfall) or over (surplus) absorption of overheads. This will be calculated by means of the following variances which can be shown diagrammatically:

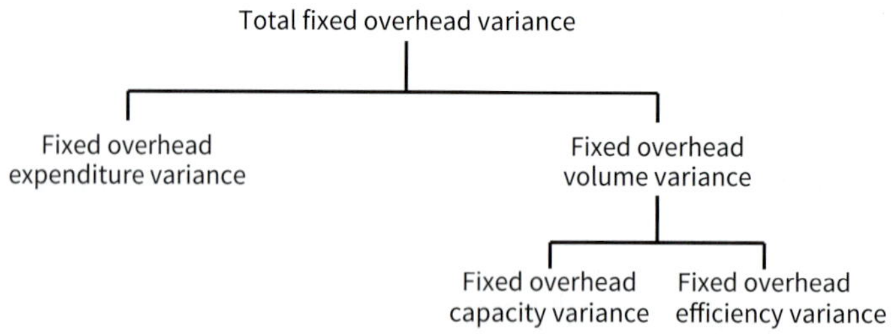

Notice here that the fixed overhead volume variance is made up of two other variances:

- the fixed overhead capacity variance
- the fixed overhead efficiency variance.

General Limited uses budgeted direct labour hours to absorb fixed overheads. The variances can be calculated as follows:

a **Fixed overhead expenditure variance**, which is the difference between the actual fixed overheads incurred and the budgeted fixed overheads.

The actual fixed overheads incurred were $370 000.

The budgeted fixed overheads were $360 000.

The **fixed overhead expenditure variance** was **$10 000 adverse**.

TOP TIP

This is the easiest overhead variance to calculate. Simply deduct the actual fixed overheads from the budgeted overheads.

b **Fixed overhead volume variance**, which is the difference between the standard hours for actual output and the budgeted hours. This difference in hours is then multiplied by the **budgeted** fixed overhead absorption rate.

TOP TIP

Only the budgeted fixed overhead absorption rate is used to calculate the following variances. Never calculate, or even bother with, the actual overhead absorption rate.

- Calculate the budgeted fixed overhead absorption rate.
- Budgeted fixed overhead absorption rate = $360 000 ÷ 9 000 hours = $40 per direct labour hour.
- Use this rate to calculate the variances:

i **Fixed overhead volume variance**

Actual output 20 000 units should have taken (20 000 × [30 ÷ 60]) = 10 000 direct labour hours.

Budgeted output 18 000 units should have taken (18 000 × [30 ÷ 60]) = 9 000 direct labour hours.

Difference = 1 000 direct labour hours.

Fixed overhead volume variance = 1 000 direct labour hours × $40 = **$40 000 favourable variance**.

It may seem strange that this is a favourable variance when the workforce of General Limited worked for 1 000 hours more than the budget. However, it is because they worked less than the budget that it is favourable.

ii **Fixed overhead capacity variance** is a sub-division of the volume variance, where actual direct labour hours for actual output differs from the budgeted direct labour hours. Again, this difference in hours is multiplied by the budgeted fixed overhead absorption rate.

Actual direct labour hours worked = 20 000 units × (36 ÷ 60) = 12 000 direct labour hours.

Budgeted direct labour hours = 9 000 direct labour hours.

Difference = 3 000 direct labour hours.

Fixed overhead capacity variance = 3 000 direct labour hours × $40 = **$120 000 favourable variance**.

iii **Fixed overhead efficiency variance**, again, is a sub-division of the volume variance, where the actual direct labour hours for the actual output differs from the standard direct labour hours for the actual output. This difference is multiplied by the budgeted fixed overhead absorption rate.

Actual direct labour hours worked = 12 000.

Standard direct labour hours for actual production = 10 000.

Difference = 2 000 direct labour hours.

Fixed overhead efficiency variance = 2 000 direct labour hours × $40 = **$80 000 adverse variance**.

It is now possible to prepare a summary of the fixed overhead expenditure variances from the calculations made:

	$
Expenditure variance	10 000 adverse
Volume variance*	40 000 favourable
Total fixed overhead expenditure variance	30 000 favourable

*The volume variance is sub-divided into:

	$
Capacity variance	120 000 favourable
Efficiency variance	80 000 adverse
Volume variance	40 000 favourable

The total fixed overhead variance is a positive situation for General Limited. Favourable here means that fixed overheads have been over-absorbed into production as a result of more units being produced and sold than was budgeted for.

The **total fixed overhead variance** is the difference between the fixed overheads absorbed into production (10 000 direct labour hours × $40 per hour) minus the fixed overheads actually paid. However, the situation is not altogether satisfactory as, despite higher production, the time it took to make the product was in excess of the budgeted time allowed. This has resulted in an adverse fixed overhead efficiency variance.

ACTIVITY 10

For the month of January:

- Polonius Limited's budgeted fixed overhead expenditure was $20 000
- the actual fixed overheads incurred were $19 800; fixed overheads are absorbed into production on the basis of direct labour hours.

Required

Calculate for Polonius Limited for the month of January:

a fixed overhead expenditure variance

b fixed overhead volume variance

c fixed overhead capacity variance

d fixed overhead efficiency variance

e prepare a statement reconciling the total fixed overhead variance with the fixed overhead expenditure and volume variances.

(Keep your answers, you will need them later.)

33.10 Reconciling standard cost and actual cost

Having calculated all the relevant variances, it is now possible prepare a statement reconciling the standard cost of the units produced with the actual cost of the units produced. In order to do this, it is first necessary to calculate the standard cost of production and sales.

Step 1

Calculate the standard (or budgeted) cost per unit of the product:

	$
Direct materials (1.25 kg per unit × $4)	5
Direct labour (30 min × $12 per hour)	6
Fixed overheads (30 min × $40 per hour)	20
Standard cost per unit	31

Step 2

Calculate the **total** standard cost of actual production and sales:

20 000 units × $31 per unit = $620 000.

Step 3

Prepare the statement reconciling the standard cost of actual production with the actual cost:

General Limited
Statement reconciling the standard cost of actual production with the actual cost

	Favourable variances	Adverse variances	Total
	$	$	$
Standard cost of actual production			620 000*
Direct materials usage variance	12 000		
Direct materials price variance		(3 300)	
Direct labour efficiency variance		(24 000)	
Direct labour rate variance	12 000		
Fixed overhead expenditure variance		(10 000)	
Fixed overhead volume variance	40 000***		
	64 000	(37 300)	(26 700)
Actual cost of production**			593 300

* The standard cost of actual production is greater than the figure in the flexed budget by $40 000 ($620 000 – $580 000 [direct materials $100 000 + direct labour $120 000 + fixed overheads $360 000]). This is due to the over-absorption of fixed overheads by the extra production and sales of 2 000 units × $20 per unit = $40 000.

** Actual cost of production is the direct materials cost ($91 300) + direct labour cost ($132 000) + actual fixed overheads ($370 000) = $593 300.

*** The statement could have shown the fixed overhead capacity variance of $120 000 favourable and the fixed overhead efficiency variance of $80 000 adverse, rather than the total volume variance of $40 000 favourable, but not all three variances. If the capacity variance is shown this is a true measure of fixed overheads over-absorbed.

ACTIVITY 11

Prepare a statement for the month of January reconciling the standard cost of actual production for Polonius Limited with the actual cost of production. (Keep your answer; you will need it later.)

33.11 Reconciling the actual profit with the flexed budget profit

It is now possible to prepare a statement reconciling the flexed budget profit for the year with the actual profit for the year.

General Limited
Statement reconciling the flexed budget profit for the year with the actual profit for the year

	Favourable variances	Adverse variances	Total
	$	$	$
Flexed budget profit for the year			60 000
Sales price variance		(28 000)	
Direct materials usage variance	12 000		
Direct materials price variance		(3 300)	
Direct labour efficiency variance		(24 000)	
Direct labour rate variance	12 000		
Fixed overhead expenditure variance		(10 000)	
	24 000	(65 300)	(41 300)
Actual profit for the year			18 700

Note: Only the variances which are reflected in the comparison between the flexed budget and the actual results are included in this statement.

TOP TIP

Never include the sales volume variance in your statement reconciling the actual profit with the budgeted profit.

ACTIVITY 12

Prepare a statement for the month of January reconciling the flexed budget profit for the year for Polonius Limited with the actual profit for the year.

ACTIVITY 13

Cantab Limited's standard costing records provide the following information for three months' production and sales:

	$
Master budget profit	98 970
Variances	
Quantity	17 009 (A)
Sales volume	6 210 (F)

	$
Sales price	3 730 (A)
Material usage	6 280 (A)
Material price	9 635 (F)
Labour efficiency	10 500 (F)
Labour rate	7 840 (A)
Overhead expenditure	5 760 (A)

Required

Prepare a statement to show the actual profit made by Cantab Limited in the three months covered by the given information.

It is possible to work backwards from the variances to arrive at the actual and standard costs.

Walkthrough

Winston Limited produces a single product. Details of the production and budget for month 5 are:

Actual output	10 000 units
Standard material cost 2 kg × $4	$80 000
Actual usage of material	18 000 kg
Total material variance	$6 200 favourable
Standard labour cost per unit 3 h × $10	$300 000
Actual labour rate	$9.95 per hour
Total labour variance	$18 400 adverse

From this data it will be possible to calculate the following variances:

- direct materials price and usage variances
- direct labour rate and efficiency variances.

It will also be possible to prepare a statement reconciling the actual direct materials and direct labour cost of producing 10 000 units with the standard cost.

a **Calculation of direct materials variances** Before the variances can be calculated, some base data must be prepared:

- actual cost of direct materials = $80 000 – $6 200 = $73 800
- actual cost per kg of direct materials = $73 800/18 000 = $4.10
- standard materials required to produce 10 000 units = 10 000 × 2 = 20 000 kg.

The direct materials price variance can now be calculated:

($4.00 – $4.10) × 18 000 = $1 800 A

The direct materials usage variance is (20 000 – 18 000) × $4 = $8 000 F.

b **Calculation of direct labour variances** Again, before the variances can be calculated some base data needs to be prepared:

- actual cost of direct labour = $300 000 + $18 400 = $318 400
- actual direct labour hours worked = $318 400/$9.95 = 32 000
- total standard direct labour hours for 10 000 units = 10 000 × 3 = 30 000 hours.

The direct labour rate variance can now be calculated:

($10.00 − $9.95) × 32 000 = $1 600 F

The direct labour efficiency variance is (30 000 − 32 000) × $10 = $20 000 A.

c Statement reconciling the actual direct materials and direct labour cost of producing 10 000 units with the standard cost:

	$	$
Actual direct materials and labour costs ($73 800 + $318 400)		392 200
Direct materials price variance	1 800 A	
Direct materials usage variance	8 000 F	
Direct labour rate variance	1 600 F	
Direct labour efficiency variance	20 000 A	(12 200) A
Standard direct materials and labour costs ($80 000 + $300 000)		380 000

33.12 How to comment generally on variances

You may be required to comment on variances you have calculated. This is not a difficult task if the following advice is heeded:

- Variances highlight operations that do not match standards. They do not explain the causes of differences but show management where further investigation is required if effective corrective action is to be taken.
- Without the further investigation mentioned above, it is not possible to do more than suggest possible reasons for variances. Some checks to support comments are suggested below.

Sales variances

A **favourable sales volume** variance may occur because:

- selling price has been reduced to increase volume
- seasonal sales have increased volume
- special discounts have been given to selected customers to increase orders
- local competition from other firms has disappeared.

An **adverse sales volume** variance may occur because:

- selling price has been increased to pass increased costs onto customers
- the goods have become unfashionable or obsolete
- customers have heard that new, improved products will be available soon and are waiting for those
- local competition from other firms may have increased.

A **favourable sales price** variance may occur because:

- increased costs have been passed onto customers in the selling price
- prices have been increased in line with inflation
- fewer discounts have been allowed to favoured customers
- improved products have allowed prices to be increased.

An **adverse sales price** variance may occur because:

- local competition has necessitated a price reduction
- selling prices have been reduced in seasonal sales
- some favoured customers have been given price concessions to increase volume of orders
- prices have been reduced generally to increase sales volume.

Direct materials variances

A **favourable material usage** variance may result from:

- use of material of a better quality than the standard – check for an adverse material price variance, or for a favourable labour efficiency variance (material easier to work with)
- the labour being of a higher skill than the standard skill, e.g. skilled labour used instead of semi-skilled – check for an adverse labour rate variance.

An **adverse material** variance may indicate:

- the use of substandard material – check for a favourable material price variance or for an adverse labour efficiency variance
- the employment of lower skilled labour – check for a favourable labour rate variance.

Direct labour variances

A **favourable labour rate** variance may result from the employment of a lower grade of labour than standard – check for an unfavourable labour efficiency variance or an adverse material usage variance.

An **unfavourable labour rate** variance may result from:

- employment of a higher skill of labour than standard – check for a favourable efficiency variance
- a wage increase (the standard should be revised).

A **favourable labour efficiency** variance will arise when the time taken by the workforce to produce the output took less than the standard time allowed. This is likely to be the case if better skilled workers were employed than was budgeted for. The use of a lower skilled labour will, therefore, result in an adverse labour efficiency variance.

Fixed overhead variances

- A **favourable fixed overhead expenditure** variance will arise from the actual fixed overhead spend being lower than the budgeted overhead spend, perhaps because of cost savings made after the budget was set.
- An **adverse fixed overhead expenditure** variance will arise when more has been paid for fixed overheads than was budgeted, perhaps because of an unexpected cost or a supplier increasing costs more than budgeted. A landlord, for instance, may increase the rent by a higher figure than was expected when the budget was set.
- A **favourable fixed overhead volume** variance will arise when the hours actually worked by direct labour is greater than the direct labour hours budgeted in the master budget. Perhaps a new order has been received which requires extra labour to be employed and therefore extra hours worked.
- An **adverse fixed overhead volume** variance will arise when the opposite occurs. Less direct labour hours were worked than were budgeted for in the master budget. It is worth noting here that in the case of General Limited, the fixed overheads were absorbed on the basis of direct labour hours. Sometimes they may be absorbed using machine hours. In that case the

comments above regarding the fixed overhead volume variance will apply to machine hours worked, rather than direct labour hours.

- A **favourable fixed overhead efficiency** variance will arise when the output produced by the direct workers took less time in actual hours than the standard hours set. This may be because higher skilled labour was used. The use of less skilled labour will lead to the opposite.

Whenever you are discussing the cause of the variances, make sure that your comments are consistent and do not contradict each other. For example, a comment such as:

> 'The direct labour efficiency variance was favourable because better skilled labour was employed. However, this has resulted in an adverse labour rate variance, but a favourable material usage variance.'

In this case, variances and their causes and effects are being correctly linked together. What would not be true is that more efficient labour will have an impact on the material price variance.

ACTIVITY 14

Larabee Limited prepared a budget for the production of 300 units in April as follows:

	$
Direct materials (4 kg per unit)	7 200
Direct labour ($11 per hour)	6 600

The production for the month was 400 units and the costs were as follows:

	$
Direct materials ($6.25 per kg)	9 000
Direct labour (2.25 hours per unit)	10 890

Required

a Calculate the following variances for April:

- **i** direct materials usage
- **ii** direct materials price
- **iii** direct labour efficiency
- **iv** direct labour rate.

b Comment on the variances in **a** and suggest possible causes.

Chapter summary

In this chapter you have learnt the basics of standard costing, including what it is, how standards are set, how standard costing can be used as an aid to improve the performance of a business, and the advantages and disadvantages of standard costing methods.

You have also learnt how to how to flex budgets, how to reconcile actual and budgeted profits, how to calculate sales, materials and labour variances, and how to recognise the possible causes of variances. There is some follow on from the previous chapter on budgeting, so refer back to this if you need extra help.

TOP TIP

This is an important chapter. Take some time to work through the example of General Limited and the other exercises.

Practice exercises

1 A company produces a single product. Details of the production for month 5 are as follows:

Actual output	10 000 units
Standard material cost 2 kg at $4 per kg	$80 000
Actual usage of material	18 000 kg
Total material variance	$6 200 favourable
Standard labour cost 3 hours at $10 per hour	$300 000
Actual labour rate	$9.95 per hour
Total labour variance	$18 400 adverse
Actual fixed overheads	$74 000
Budgeted fixed overheads	$77 550 for a budgeted production of 11 000 units

Overheads are absorbed on the basis of direct labour hours.

Required

a Explain why it is necessary for a business to prepare a flexed budget. **[3 marks]**

b Calculate the following variances:

i material price
ii material usage
iii labour rate
iv labour efficiency
v fixed overhead expenditure
vi fixed overhead volume. **[16 marks]**

c i Explain the possible causes of the material price variance and labour efficiency variances you have calculated in part **b**. **[4 marks]**

ii Suggest how the adverse labour variances could be improved. **[2 marks]**

Total: 25

2 The following information is available for Seaview Ferries Limited for the month of November:

	Budget	Actual
Number of sailings	6 500	5 900
Operating hours	7 800	7 200
Fuel	130 000 litres at $1.20 per litre	125 000 litres at a total cost of $175 000
Direct labour	9 750 hours at a total cost of $82 875	9 000 hours at $8.65 per hour
Total fixed overheads for November	$62 400	$58 000

Fixed overheads (only) are absorbed on the basis of operating hours.

Required

a Explain what is meant by variance analysis. **[4 marks]**

b Calculate the following variances:

i total material (fuel)

ii total labour

iii fixed overhead expenditure

iv fixed overhead capacity

v fixed overhead efficiency. **[10 marks]**

c Prepare a statement reconciling the actual cost of sailings with the standard cost of sailings. **[6 marks]**

Additional information

The ships used make sailings to three different locations at different prices. The journey time to each location is different. However, the directors believe that they could obtain more management information if the standard costing was expanded to include sales variances.

Required

d Advise the directors whether or not they should include sales variances in their analysis. Justify your answer. **[5 marks]**

Total: 25

3 Bertie Limited manufactures a single product. The budgeted information for the month of June was as follows:

Budgeted production and sales	5 000 units
Per unit:	
Direct materials	2 kg at $5 per kg
Direct labour	3 hours at $10 per hour

The selling price is calculated by adding 50% to the variable cost of production.

Required

a Calculate the budgeted selling price per unit. **[3 marks]**

Additional information

Actual production and sales	5 200 units at $58 per unit
Direct materials	10 920 kg at $4.80 per kg
Direct labour	16 640 h at $10.50 per hour

Required

b Prepare a statement to show the actual contribution made for the month of June. **[3 marks]**

c Calculate the following variances for the month of June:

i sales price
ii direct materials price
iii direct materials usage
iv direct labour rate
v direct labour efficiency. **[10 marks]**

d Prepare a statement reconciling the flexed budget profit with the actual profit for the month of June. **[4 marks]**

e Evaluate the performance of Bertie Limited for the month of June based on the information you have calculated. **[5 marks]**

Total: 25

Exam practice questions

Multiple-choice questions

1 A company manufactures a product which requires 2 hours of direct labour per unit. Normal output is 1 400 units and the standard labour rate is $6.50 per hour. In one month, the company manufactured 1 300 units of the product in 2 500 direct labour hours, costing $17 550. What is the direct labour efficiency variance?

A $650 (favourable)
B $675 (favourable)
C $1 300 (favourable)
D $1 350 (favourable)

2 A company makes a single product which requires two types of raw material: ionium and zetonium. The standard cost of materials to produce one unit of the product is shown:

Material	kg	Standard cost ($ per kg)
Ionium	30	2
Zetonium	45	3

100 units of the product have been made using 3 100 kg of ionium and 4 400 kg of zetonium. What is the total material usage variance?

A $100 (adverse)
B $100 (favourable)
C $500 (adverse)
D $500 (favourable)

3 The following information is available for the sales of a product:

Budgeted sales	40 000 units at $5 each
Actual sales	42 000 at a total revenue of $189 000

What is the sales volume variance?

A $10 000 favourable
B $11 000 favourable
C $11 000 adverse
D $21 000 adverse

4 The following information is available about a product:

Standard selling price per unit	$17
Budgeted sales (units)	45 000
Actual sales (units)	48 000
Total revenue	$744 000

What is the sales price variance?

A $51 000 (A) **B** $51 000 (F)
C $72 000 (A) **D** $72 000 (F)

5 Details of direct materials costs are as follows:

Budget	Actual
41 500 kg at $12 per kg	44 000 kg at $13.20 per kg

What is the direct materials price variance?

A $49 500 (A) **B** $49 500 (F)
C $52 800 (A) **D** $52 800 (F)

6 A company's cost of production is made up of the cost of direct materials and the cost of direct labour. The following variances have been calculated at the end of three months' production:

	$
Direct materials usage	1 600 adverse
Direct materials price	1 300 favourable
Direct labour efficiency	820 favourable
Direct labour rate	900 adverse

The actual cost of production was $23 440. What was the standard cost of production?

A $22 220 **B** $23 020
C $23 060 **D** $24 580

Total: 6 marks

Chapter 34
Investment appraisal

Learning objectives

In this chapter you will learn:

- what investment appraisal is
- how to calculate accounting rate of return (ARR)
- how to calculate payback period
- how to calculate net present value (NPV)
- how to calculate internal rate of return (IRR)
- how to calculate the sensitivity of an investment to errors in estimates.

KEY TERMS

Investment appraisal: The process of assessing whether it is worthwhile to invest funds into a particular project.

Time value of money: The principle that the same sum of money is worth more now than at some time in the future.

Accounting rate of return: The average profit from an investment expressed as a percentage of the average capital of the investment.

34.1 What is investment appraisal?

Investment appraisal is a process of assessing whether it is worthwhile to invest funds in a project. The project may be the replacement of an existing asset, acquiring an additional asset, introducing a new product, opening a new branch of a business, etc. Funds invested in a project may include additional working capital, as well as expenditure on non-current assets. These projects always involve making choices, including whether or not to proceed with the project, which assets to buy, which new products to introduce, and so on.

Accounting techniques are essential tools when these decisions have to be made. However, projects must sometimes be undertaken even when the accounting techniques appear to advise against them. For example, a business that is causing an environmental nuisance may face being closed down by health and safety inspectors unless it spends a considerable sum of money to abate the nuisance. It is well to remember that investment decisions should only be made after all relevant matters – economic, political, environmental, social, and so on – have been considered.

This chapter is concerned principally with the financial techniques of appraisal:

- accounting rate of return (ARR)
- payback period
- net present value (NPV)
- internal rate of return (IRR).

These techniques are designed to assess the quality of projects, benefits arising from them, and degrees of risk involved. **Only accounting rate of return is concerned with profitability; the others are based on cash flows**. The net present value and internal rate of return take the **time value of money** into account. They are all based on **additional** benefits and costs which will arise from a project. These are referred to as **incremental** profits and cash flows. Existing profit and cash flows are ignored as being irrelevant because they will continue whether the new project is undertaken or not. There are two new terms to learn:

- **Sunk costs** consist of expenditure that has been incurred before a new project has been considered. For example, a company plans to introduce a new product that will require the use of a machine it acquired some years ago and has been used in the production of an existing product. The cost of the machine is a sunk cost because it has already been incurred and is not **incremental**. Its cost is a historical fact and cannot have any bearing on future decisions.
- **Opportunity costs** are the values of benefits that will be sacrificed if resources are diverted from their present uses to other applications. For example, if a machine that has been earning annual net revenue of \$50 000 is to be used exclusively for another operation, it will cease to earn the \$50 000. The lost revenue is an opportunity cost. If the machine will earn net revenue of \$70 000 in its new capacity, the incremental net revenue will be \$20 000 (\$70 000 – \$50 000).

34.2 How to calculate the accounting rate of return (ARR)

The **accounting rate of return** expresses average **profit** from the investment as a percentage of the average of the capital investment:

$$\frac{\text{average profit}}{\text{average investment}} \times 100$$

Average profit is the average of the profit arising directly from the investment expected to be earned over the life of the project.

Walkthrough

Planter Limited is considering investing in a new item of plant which will increase the profit of the business. The equipment will cost $60 000 and have a life of five years. After that time, it will be scrapped at no value. The company policy is to depreciate the non-current assets by 20% using the straight-line method.

The accountant has prepared the following table of cash flows as a direct result of buying the new plant:

Year	Cash inflow	Cash outflow	Net cash flow	Annual depreciation	Expected annual profit
	$	$	$	$	$
1	68 000	27 000	41 000	12 000	29 000
2	74 000	29 000	45 000	12 000	33 000
3	78 000	30 000	48 000	12 000	36 000
4	80 000	31 000	49 000	12 000	37 000
5	82 000	32 000	50 000	12 000	38 000

The average profit for the purpose of calculating ARR is:

$$\$(29\,000 + 33\,000 + 36\,000 + 37\,000 + 38\,000) \div 5 \text{ (life of the project)} = \$34\,600$$

TOP TIP

In this case, the rate of depreciation has been given. If you do not have the rate of depreciation, it would be safe to write off the total cost of the non-current asset over the life of the project.

Unfortunately, there are different opinions as to how the average investment should be calculated. You need only be aware of the simplest method, which is:

$$\frac{\text{the cost of the asset(s) acquired}}{2} \times 100$$

Walkthrough

Walker Limited requires a new machine that will cost $160 000 and have a useful life of five years. The machine is expected to earn profits in those five years of $15 000, $18 000, $21 000, $21 000 and $20 000, a total of $95 000 over the life of the project. The average profit is $95 000 ÷ 5 = $19 000.

The average investment is $160 000 ÷ 2 = $80 000.

Average rate of return is:

$$\frac{\$19\,000}{\$80\,000} \times 100 = 23.75\%$$

Walker Limited is able to compare 23.75% with the rate of return that it expects to earn on capital to decide whether the project will be worthwhile. If it is currently earning a return on capital employed (ROCE) of less than 23.75%, the project should improve its overall profitability; if the present ROCE is more than 23.75%, the project will probably reduce its overall profitability.

TOP TIP

ARR is the only technique being considered that takes depreciation of the investment into account.

A project may require an increase in working capital because this may result in increased inventory and trade receivables. Any increase in working capital will be assumed to remain constant throughout the life of the project and no calculation is required to find the average increase. For example, if a project involves the purchase of a machine at a cost of $60 000, and an increase in working capital of $40 000, the average investment is:

$$\frac{\$60000 + \$40000}{2} = \$50000$$

Advantages of ARR

- The expected profitability of a project can be compared with the present profitability (ROCE) of the business.
- ARR is comparatively easy to calculate.

Disadvantages of ARR

- The average annual profit used to calculate ARR is unlikely to be the profit earned in any year of the life of the project.
- 'Profit' is a subjective concept. It depends upon a number of variable policies such as provisions for depreciation and doubtful debts, valuation of inventory, and other matters.
- The method does not take into account the timing of cash flows. The initial outlay on the project is at risk until the flow of cash into the business has covered the initial cost.
- ARR ignores the time value of money. Every dollar received now is more useful to a business than a dollar received at a later date.
- No account is taken of the life expectancy of a project. Questions will usually state that the item purchased will be disposed of at the end of the project. In practice, businesses keep plant and equipment or motor vehicles running for as long as possible, well beyond the scheduled life of the project. This isn't accounted for in the calculations.

ACTIVITY 1

Baseball Limited intends to introduce a new product that is expected to produce the following incremental profits over a period of six years:

	$		$
Year 1	23 000	Year 4	26 000
Year 2	24 000	Year 5	29 000
Year 3	25 000	Year 6	23 000

The project will require the use of a machine that was purchased some years ago at a cost of $16 000, and the use of a second machine that will have to be purchased for $120 000. It is estimated that inventory held will increase by $10 000, and trade receivables will increase by $15 000.

Required

Calculate the accounting rate of return that will be earned from the new product.

34.3 How to calculate payback period

Until the initial expenditure on a project has been covered by net cash receipts (cash inflow – cash outflow) from the venture, a business is at risk of being worse off than if it had not launched the project. Calculation of the **payback period** indicates the time over which the business is at risk. Short payback periods are preferred, especially in times of high inflation.

The **payback** method is concerned with cash flows, not with profitability, therefore depreciation **does not** enter into the calculations.

In order to carry out the evaluation, the net cash flows arising from the project must be calculated. This is the difference between the cash coming in from the project (this could be the revenue or savings) less the cash payments arising from the project. Profitability and depreciation do not enter into the calculations. It is important to consider when the cash comes in and goes out, not when sales or purchases are made. It may also be necessary to consider a build up of working capital. This needs to be shown at the start of the project as a cash outflow. At the end of the project it is brought back into the business as a cash inflow.

KEY TERM

Payback: The period of time it takes for the net receipts from a project to pay back, or equal, the total of the funds invested in the project.

Walkthrough

Dumbells Limited is proposing to market a new product which will involve the purchase of new plant costing $100 000.

Year	Cash receipts	Cash payments	Net cash receipts
	$	$	$
1	80 000	50 000	30 000
2	82 000	42 000	40 000
3	94 000	44 000	50 000
4	98 000	53 000	45 000

The payback period is calculated as follows:

Step 1

In the first two years, net receipts will amount to $70 000 ($30 000 + $40 000).

Step 2

The balance of $30 000 will be received in the third year:

$$\frac{[1]\ \$30\,000}{[2]\ \$50\,000} = 0.6 \times 12 \text{ months} = 7.2 \text{ months}$$

The payback period is, therefore, 2 years 8 months. (It would be unrealistic to be more precise than this.)

[1] $30 000 is the amount required so that the total cash inflows equal the total cost of the asset bought ($100 000 – 70 000).

[2] $50 000 is the total of the net cash flows in year 3. It is assumed that the cash flows accrue evenly over the year.

TOP TIP

Check to see if the payback period is to be to the nearest month. If so, always round up.

Advantages of payback

- It is relatively simple to calculate.
- Payback can compare the relative risks of different projects.
- Cash flow is less subjective than profitability.
- Payback highlights the timing and size of cash flows.
- Short payback periods result in increased liquidity and enable businesses to grow more quickly.

Disadvantages of payback

- The life expectancy of the project is ignored. Once the payback period has been evaluated, the net cash inflows after this time are ignored. This is a problem with this method of evaluation, as later in the life of the project, net cash flows may be negative.
- Projects with the same payback period may have different cash flows. For example:

	Project 1	Project 2
	$	$
Year 0 Initial cost [1]	(80 000)	(80 000)
Year 1 Net cash inflow	15 000	30 000
Year 2	25 000	40 000
Year 3	40 000	10 000

[1] The initial outlay is shown as made in year 0 because it is assumed, simply as a matter of convenience, that cash flows occur on the last day of the year. The initial outlay should be shown as occurring on the first day of year 1, and the last day of year 0 is the nearest we can get to the first day of year 1.

Both projects have a payback period of three years and similar amounts of cash inflows, but project 2 is more attractive as the cash flow is better in the early years.

The use of the term 'year' should not be confused with the accounting year start or end. It relates solely to the start of the project (year 0), the year at which the project starts. This will be at any point during the accounting period.

- The simple payback method ignores the time value of money, but it is possible to apply discounting techniques to it to overcome this failing.

ACTIVITY 2

Martinez Limited is planning to replace one of its machines. It has two choices of replacements: First and Last, each costing $90 000.

The following information is available for the machines:

	First		Last	
	Cash inflow	Cash outflow	Cash inflow	Cash outflow
	$	$	$	$
Year 0	–	90 000	–	90 000
Year 1	80 000	50 000	60 000	20 000
Year 2	90 000	54 000	68 000	28 000
Year 3	100 000	60 000	72 000	32 000

Required

a Calculate the payback periods for First and Last.

b State, with reasons, which machine Martinez Limited should purchase.

34.4 How to calculate net present value (NPV)

Net present value recognises the time value of money. $1 received now is more useful than $1 received some time in the future because it can be used now. If, for example, $100 is invested now at 10% compound interest it will be worth $\frac{\$110}{\$100}$, or $110, in one year's time, and in two years it will be worth $121. To put it another way, $90.91 invested at 10% compound interest now will be worth $\$90.91 \times \frac{\$110}{\$100} = \$100$, in one year's time, and $100 receivable in one year's time has a **present value** of $90.91 when discounted at 10%.

The time value of money is important when future cash flows are compared with present cash flows because 'like should be compared with like'. Future cash flows are discounted to present day values so that they can be compared with the initial outlay on a realistic basis.

In addition, the full life of the project is considered. This is a positive advantage of using net present value over payback.

Future cash flows are the estimated cash receipts less the estimated cash payments attributable to an investment, and will usually be known as **net receipts** or **net payments**. If assets purchased for the project are sold at the end of the venture, the proceeds of sale should be included in the net receipts in the last year.

The discounting rate taken for net present values is the cost of capital. For example, if money has to be borrowed at 8% interest per annum to finance the investment in a project, the cost of capital is 8% and the future cash flows will be discounted using the factors for that rate. A table of discounting factors can be found in Appendix 1.

Notes:

- It is widely thought that cash flows are discounted to net present value to allow for inflation, but that is not so. The rate used for discounting is the cost of capital, not the rate of inflation.
- The payback period is sometimes calculated using the net present values of the cash flows.

KEY TERMS

Net present value: The present value of future receipts from a project, less the present value of future payments in respect of the same project.

Present value: The present, or current, value of a future sum of money discounted at a given rate.

Walkthrough

Learning Limited is undertaking a project which involves an initial outlay of $100 000. The company accountant has estimated its net cash receipts from the project for the next five years to be as follows:

Year 1	$40 000
Year 2	$42 000
Year 3	$48 000
Year 4	$46 000
Year 5	$38 000

Learning Limited's cost of capital is 10%. The discounting factors for the present value of 10% are:

Year	Discount factor at 10%
0	1.00
1	0.909
2	0.826
3	0.751
4	0.683
5	0.621

The calculation of the net present value of the project is:

[1] The discounted cash flow is calculated by multiplying the net cash inflow for the year by the discount factor for the year. So for year 1 it is $40 000 × 0.909 = $36 360.

Year	Net cash inflow/(outflow)	Discount factor	Discounted cash flow [1]
	$		$
0	(100 000)	1.000 [2]	(100 000)
1	40 000	0.909	36 360
2	42 000	0.826	34 692
3	48 000	0.751	36 048
4	46 000	0.683	31 418
5	38 000	0.621	23 598
	Net present value [3]		62 116

[3] The net present value is the total of all the discounted cash flows for years zero to five.

[2] The discount factor in year zero is always 1.

TOP TIP

It is a good way to set out the calculation in a table like the one above. Always label the columns, especially the net present value.

The net present value is positive, showing that the project may be undertaken. A negative NPV would mean that the net receipts in present day terms would not cover the initial outlay and the project should not be undertaken. The higher the net present value, the better the project. If two or more projects are being considered, the one with the highest NPV would be preferred to the other(s).

ACTIVITY 3

Nomen Limited is considering buying a machine and has three options, machine A, B or C, only one of which it will buy. Each machine costs $135 000 and will have a five-year life with no residual value at the end of that time.

The net receipts for each machine over the five-year period are as follows:

	Machine A	Machine B	Machine C
	$	$	$
Year 1	50 000	38 000	26 000
Year 2	50 000	38 000	26 000
Year 3	38 000	38 000	38 000
Year 4	26 000	38 000	50 000
Year 5	26 000	38 000	50 000

Nomen Limited's cost of capital is 12%.

The discounting factors at 12% are:

Year	Discount factor at 12%
0	1.000
1	0.893
2	0.797
3	0.712
4	0.636
5	0.567

Required

Calculate the net present value of each option and state which machine Nomen Limited should choose.

34.5 How to calculate internal rate of return (IRR)

KEY TERM

Internal rate of return: The interest, or discount, rate at which the net present value of all the cash flows from a project (both positive and negative) equal zero.

Net present value compares future cash inflows with present cash outflow when the future cash flows are discounted to present day values, but it does not give the **rate of return** on investment based on discounted values. The **internal rate of return** enables managers to calculate the return on an intended investment and to compare it with the company's present return on capital.

The internal rate of return is the percentage required to discount cash flows to give a nil net present value. The percentage is found by selecting two discounting rates sufficiently wide apart to give positive and negative net present values. The results are then **interpolated** to find the percentage that will give a nil net present value. (Interpolation means finding an intermediate value between the two discounting rates.) Interpolation involves using the formula:

$$P + \left[(N - P) \times \frac{p}{p + n}\right] = \text{IRR}$$

where P is the rate giving a positive net present value
N is the rate giving a negative net present value
p is the positive net present value
n is the negative net present value.

For example, if NPV at 10% is \$14 000 and at 18% is \$(6000), then:

$$\text{IRR} = 10\% + \left(8\% \times \frac{14\,000}{14\,000 + 6\,000}\right) = 10\% + 5.6\% = 15.6\%$$

Therefore, discounted at 15.6%, the investment would have nil net present value.

Walkthrough

Learning Limited (see Section 34.4) has a net present value of $62 116 when discounted at 10%. To obtain a negative net present value it may be discounted at 40% as follows:

Year	$	at 40%	$
0	(100 000)	1.000	(100 000)
1	40 000	0.714	28 560
2	42 000	0.510	21 420
3	48 000	0.364	17 472
4	46 000	0.260	11 960
5	38 000	0.186	7 068
	Net present value		(13 520)

$$IRR = 10\% + \left(30\% \cdot \frac{62\,116}{62\,116 + 13\,520}\right) = 34.6\%$$

ACTIVITY 4

The information is given as for Nomen Limited in Activity 3 in Section 34.4. Discounting factors for 20% are:

Year	Discount factor at 20%
0	1.000
1	0.833
2	0.694
3	0.579
4	0.482
5	0.402

Required

Calculate the internal rate of return for machines A and B.

Note: IRR can be calculated from two positive net present values but will be less accurate. The denominator of the fraction in the formula must be amended as follows:

$$P + \left[(N - P) \times \frac{p}{p - n}\right]$$

Note also that N and n refer to the higher discount rate and the resulting NPV; n will be less than p but not negative.

TOP TIPS

- If the discounting factors in a question produce only positive net present values, do **not** try to find another discounting rate.
- When the receipts are constant for a number of consecutive years, the net present value of those receipts may be calculated quickly if the annual amount is multiplied by the sum of the factors for the years concerned. For example, if net receipts are $25 000 in each of the first five years and the cost of capital is 10%, the NPV for the five years is $25 000 × (0.909 + 0.826 + 0.751 + 0.683 + 0.621) = $25 000 × 3.790 = $94 750.

ACTIVITY 5

Flags Limited requires a new machine to use in the manufacture of a new product. Two machines are available: 1A and 1B. Flags Limited depreciates machinery using the straight-line method. Flags Limited will obtain a bank loan at interest of 10% per annum to buy the machine.

Additional information

		1A	1B
Cost of machine		$140 000	$180 000
		$	**$**
Additional receipts			
Year	1	98 000	101 000
	2	112 000	118 000
	3	126 000	126 000
	4	126 000	140 000
	5	100 000	110 000

Additional costs (including depreciation):

		$	**$**
Year	1	70 000	84 000
	2	84 000	98 000
	3	91 000	105 000
	4	98 000	112 000
	5	95 000	100 000
Useful life of machine		5 years	5 years
Present value of $1		10%	40%
Year	1	0.909	0.714
	2	0.826	0.510
	3	0.751	0.364
	4	0.683	0.260
	5	0.621	0.186

Required

a Calculate for each machine:

- **i** the accounting rate of return (ARR) (ignore the sale proceeds of the machine)
- **ii** the payback period
- **iii** the net present value
- **iv** the internal rate of return (IRR).

b State, with reasons, which machine Flags Limited should purchase.

34.6 Sensitivity analysis

Appraisal of future capital expenditure is based on estimated future profitability and cash flows. Inaccuracies in the estimates may be very misleading, and acceptable margins of error must be recognised. **Sensitivity analysis** indicates the maximum acceptable margin of error; a greater margin might produce disastrous results, especially as very large sums of money are involved.

The percentages of error that could produce unacceptable results must be determined and compared with the likely margins of error as shown by past forecasting experience.

Walkthrough

A project needs \$100 000 to buy a machine. Net receipts in each of the four years of the project are expected to be \$35 000. The cost of capital is 10%.

The net present value = \$100 000 − \$(35 000 × 3.169) = \$10 915. The net present value will be negative if:

- the cost of the machine exceeds \$110 915, that is an increase of 11% (\$100 000 × 11% = \$110 000); or
- the annual net receipts are less than \$100 000 ÷ 3.169 = \$31 555, that is a decrease of:

$$\frac{\$(35000 - 31555) \times 100}{\$35000} = 9.8\%$$

The company should compare its past degrees of accuracy in estimating capital expenditure and forecasts of revenue with the percentages calculated above.

ACTIVITY 6

A company proposes to replace an existing machine with a new one costing \$150 000. It is estimated that the use of the new machine will result in net savings over the next four years of \$50 000 per annum. The company will borrow \$150 000 at an interest rate of 10% per annum to pay for the machine.

Required

Calculate the degrees of sensitivity as regards the cost of the machine and the annual operational savings.

TOP TIP

This is a tricky topic. Work through the example, attempt the activity and check you answers to make sure you understand it.

34.7 Capital rationing

In some cases a company may evaluate a number of projects. However, because of the amount of capital it has, the company cannot invest in all the projects at the same time. It must ration its capital in such a way that the projects it invests in maximise the net present value of the company over a period of time.

Walkthrough

Gemma has evaluated four projects with the following results.

Project	Capital cost	Net present value
	\$	\$
A	300 000	80 000
B	500 000	250 000
C	200 000	180 000
D	300 000	100 000

However, she only has a maximum of \$500 000 to spend. Gemma needs to decide which projects she should invest in to maximise the net present value.

Initially calculate the profitability ratio for each project. This is done quite simply by dividing the net present value by the capital cost:

Project	Capital cost	Net present value	Profitability index
	$	$	
A	300 000	80 000	0.27
B	500 000	250 000	0.50
C	200 000	180 000	0.90
D	300 000	100 000	0.33

Project C has the greatest profitability index. This would use up $200 000 of her $500 000 available. The remaining $300 000 should be invested in project D. She doesn't have sufficient funds to invest in the next best project, B. Simply investing in B alone will only generate a net present value of $250 000, less than buying C and D.

Therefore, she should invest in projects C and D, as these will yield a total net present value of $280 000. Any other combination will not achieve this amount.

ACTIVITY 7

A Co Limited is operating under capital rationing. It can only invest in any one of the following three projects at one time. Details of the projects are set out below:

Project	Capital cost	Net present value
	$	$
A	400 000	70 000
B	500 000	60 000
C	600 000	120 000

Which order should the company invest in the projects to maximise the overall net present value?

TOP TIP

Be prepared to describe, explain or discuss the advantages and disadvantages of the various methods of investment appraisal, and which project to select based on your calculations.

Chapter summary

In this chapter you have learnt about the various investment appraisal techniques a business may use when buying new capital equipment or investing in new capital projects. In particular, you should know how to calculate:

- accounting rate of return (ARR)
- payback period
- net present value (NPV)
- internal rate of return (IRR)
- sensitivity investment to errors in estimates.

TOP TIP

Investment appraisal techniques are important topics, so a thorough understanding of them is essential. Work through the questions. Once you have grasped the principles this is a relatively straightforward topic.

Practice exercises

1 The directors of Station Limited intend to purchase an additional machine to manufacture one of their new products. Two machines are being considered: Red and Green. The company depreciates its machinery at 25% per annum using the straight-line method. Station Limited's cost of capital is 10%.

Estimates for the machines are as follows:

		Red	Green
		$	$
Cost of machine		100000	130000
Additional receipts:			
Year	1	70000	72000
	2	80000	84000
	3	90000	90000
	4	90000	100000
Additional costs (see note):			
Year	1	50000	60000
	2	60000	70000
	3	65000	75000
	4	70000	80000

Note: These costs include the charges for depreciation.

Useful life of the machine		4 years	4 years
Value at end of useful life		nil	nil
Present value of $1		10%	20%
Year	1	0.909	0.833
	2	0.826	0.694
	3	0.751	0.579
	4	0.683	0.482

Required

a Explain the difference between payback and accounting rate of return when used for investment appraisal. **[4 marks]**

b Calculate the net present value of **each** machine (round any figures to the nearest dollar). **[10 marks]**

c Advise the directors of Station Limited which machine they should purchase. Justify your answer. **[5 marks]**

Additional information

The directors require the machine to produce a return on outlay of not less than 25%.

Required

d Calculate the internal rate of return on the machine you have selected in **c** to see if it meets the required return on outlay. **[6 marks]**

Total: 25

2 A company has carried out successful trials of a new product. In order to make it, the company will have to purchase a machine costing $100 000. This will last for four years, after which it will be scrapped.

The following information has been provided by the company's accountant:

1 The expected sales units will be 10 000 units in year 1. This will increase by 1 000 units per annum.

2 The selling price, unit and other costs are:

	$	
Selling price per unit	20	this will increase by $1 per annum over the life of the project
Direct costs per unit	15	these will increase by $1 per annum over the life of the project
Annual fixed overheads	15 000	these will increase by $1 000 per annum over the life of the project

3 The company uses a 12% discount factor when evaluating any project. The relevant factors are:

Year	Discount factor at 12%	Discount factor at 25%
1	0.893	0.800
2	0.797	0.640
3	0.712	0.512
4	0.636	0.410

Required

a State **two** advantages the payback method of investment appraisal has over the net present value method of investment appraisal. **[4 marks]**

b Calculate the following for the project:

i payback **[8 marks]**

ii accounting rate of return. **[4 marks]**

Additional information

The company accountant has also produced the following data for an alternative machine which could be used for the project. This is as follows:

Capital cost	$150 000
Payback	3 years
Net present value	$15 000
Accounting rate of return	25%

The directors can only invest in one project.

Required

c Advise the directors on which machine they should buy. Justify your answer by using both financial and non-financial factors. **[9 marks]**

Total: 25

Exam practice questions

Multiple-choice questions

1 The net present value of a project has been calculated as follows:

	NPV ($)
at 10%	30 000
at 20%	(8 000)

What is the internal rate of return on the project?

A 10%
B 12.1%
C 17.9%
D 20%

2 Why are cash flows discounted for investment appraisal?

A $1 now is more useful that $1 receivable at a future time
B it is prudent to state future cash flows at a realistic value
C money loses its value because of inflation
D the risk of not receiving money increases with time

3 Which method of investment appraisal may be based on either actual cash flows or discounted cash flows?

A accounting rate of return
B internal rate of return
C net present value
D payback

4 A company has $4 million to invest. Its investment opportunities are as follows:

Opportunity	Amount of investment for a period of 5 years	NPV ($)
1	$3 million	600 000
2	$2.5 million	350 000
3	$1.5 million	280 000
4	$1 million	50 000

In which opportunities should the company invest?

A 1 and 3
B 1 and 4
C 2 and 3
D 2 and 4

Total: 4 marks

Structured question

1 JP Limited proposes to purchase a new machine costing $120 000. The company depreciates machinery at 25% per annum using the straight-line method.

The machine will earn revenue of $80 000 per annum and involve additional expenditure of $46 000 each year. The company's cost of capital is 10%.

The present value of $1 is as follows:

Year	10%	15%
1	0.909	0.870
2	0.826	0.756
3	0.751	0.658
4	0.683	0.572

Required

Calculate:

a the accounting rate of return **[5 marks]**
b the net present value **[3 marks]**
c the internal rate of return. **[4 marks]**

Appendix 1: Table showing net present value of $1

Present value of $1													
Years	5%	6%	7%	8%	9%	10%	11%	12%	13%	14%	15%	16%	17%
1	0.952	0.943	0.935	0.926	0.917	0.909	0.901	0.893	0.885	0.877	0.870	0.862	0.855
2	0.907	0.890	0.873	0.857	0.842	0.826	0.812	0.797	0.783	0.769	0.756	0.743	0.731
3	0.864	0.840	0.816	0.794	0.772	0.751	0.731	0.712	0.693	0.675	0.658	0.641	0.624
4	0.823	0.792	0.763	0.735	0.708	0.683	0.659	0.636	0.613	0.592	0.572	0.552	0.534
5	0.784	0.747	0.713	0.681	0.650	0.621	0.593	0.567	0.543	0.519	0.497	0.476	0.456
6	0.746	0.705	0.666	0.630	0.596	0.564	0.535	0.507	0.480	0.456	0.432	0.410	0.390
7	0.711	0.665	0.623	0.583	0.547	0.513	0.482	0.452	0.425	0.400	0.376	0.354	0.333
8	0.677	0.627	0.582	0.540	0.502	0.467	0.434	0.404	0.376	0.351	0.327	0.305	0.285
9	0.645	0.592	0.544	0.500	0.460	0.424	0.391	0.361	0.333	0.308	0.284	0.263	0.243
10	0.614	0.558	0.508	0.463	0.422	0.386	0.352	0.322	0.295	0.270	0.247	0.227	0.208
	18%	19%	20%	21%	22%	23%	24%	25%					
1	0.847	0.840	0.833	0.826	0.820	0.813	0.806	0.800					
2	0.718	0.706	0.694	0.683	0.672	0.661	0.650	0.640					
3	0.609	0.593	0.579	0.564	0.551	0.537	0.524	0.512					
4	0.516	0.499	0.482	0.467	0.451	0.437	0.423	0.410					
5	0.437	0.419	0.402	0.386	0.370	0.355	0.341	0.328					
6	0.370	0.352	0.335	0.319	0.303	0.289	0.275	0.262					
7	0.314	0.296	0.279	0.263	0.249	0.235	0.222	0.210					
8	0.266	0.249	0.233	0.218	0.204	0.191	0.179	0.168					
9	0.225	0.209	0.194	0.180	0.167	0.155	0.144	0.134					
10	0.191	0.176	0.162	0.149	0.137	0.126	0.116	0.107					

Glossary

TERM	MEANING
Accounting equation	Assets – liabilities = capital.
Accounting principles	Basic rules that are applied in recording transactions and preparing financial statements. They are also known as concepts.
Accounting rate of return	The average profit from an investment expressed as a percentage of the average capital of the investment.
Accounting system	A system of collecting, storing and processing financial information and accounting data used by managers.
Accrual	An expense which is due within the accounting period but which has not yet been paid. An example would be an unpaid electricity invoice. When preparing the statement of financial position these are collectively known as other payables.
Accumulated fund	The equivalent of the capital for a non-profit-making organisation.
Allocation of costs	Charging costs directly to the cost centres which can be directly identified with them.
Annual general meeting (AGM)	A meeting held after the end of the financial year. All ordinary shareholders are entitled to attend. At the meeting, the proposals made by the directors are voted on by the ordinary shareholders.
Apportionment of costs	The process of charging costs to cost centres using a suitable basis. Such costs cannot be directly identified with a single cost centre.
Appropriation account	An account prepared after the income statement. It is used to show how the profit for the year is divided between each partner.
Asset	Something which is owned by or owed to a business.
Auditor's report	A report prepared by the auditors of a limited company. It provides a statement to the shareholders as to whether or not the annual financial statements provide a true and fair view of the company's activities.
Balancing an account	The process of finding which side of a ledger account is the greater.
Bank reconciliation statement	A statement prepared periodically to ensure that the bank account in the business cash book matches the business bank account shown on the bank statement.
Batch costing	The costing procedure to find the cost of a batch of items produced.
Bonus payment	The additional amount paid to an employee for producing goods in a time less than that allowed.
Bonus share issue	An issue of free shares to existing shareholders from the accumulated reserves of the company. The issue is usually in proportion to the existing ordinary shares (e.g. one bonus share for every four held).
Book of prime entry	A book used to list all transactions of a similar nature before they are posted to the ledger.
Break-even chart	A diagrammatic representation of the profit or loss to be expected from the sale of a product at various levels of activity.
Break-even point	The point at which a business makes neither profit nor loss. It is the point at which total contribution is exactly equal to total fixed costs.

TERM	MEANING
Budget	A plan of a future activity, usually expressed in financial terms.
Capital	Initially the amount of money invested in the business by the owner. After the business has been trading for a period, it is adjusted by the profit for the year made by the business less any drawings made by the owner. It is the net amount which the business owes to the owner.
Capital account	An account to record the sum of money which a partner introduces into the partnership. It is only adjusted for any further capital introduced, any capital withdrawn, any share of goodwill or any profit on the revaluation of partnership assets.
Capital expenditure	Money spent on acquiring non-current assets.
Capital reserves	Gains which (usually) arise from non-trading activities, such as the revaluation of a company's non-current assets.
Carriage inwards	The additional delivery cost paid by a business in excess of the purchase price of the goods purchased for resale. It is added to the cost of goods by the supplier.
Carriage outwards	The additional cost charged by the seller to deliver goods sold.
Carrying amount	The net book value of the non-current asset. It is calculated by deducting the accumulated depreciation from the cost of the non-current asset.
Cash	Includes cash in hand and bank deposits repayable on demand, less any overdrafts repayable on demand. 'On demand' is generally taken to mean within 24 hours.
Cash book	A book of prime entry for all bank, cash and cash discount transactions.
Cash (or settlement) discount	An allowance given by a seller to a customer to encourage the customer to pay an invoice before its due date for payment.
Computerised accounting system	A set of programs which allow the accounts to be prepared using a computer. An alternative to manual bookkeeping.
Consignee	The party which receives the goods for sale.
Consignor	The party which transfers the goods for sale to the consignee.
Consistency	Transactions of a similar nature should be recorded in the same way (that is, consistently) in the same accounting period and in all future accounting periods.
Contra entry	The completing of the double entry within the bank or cash account.
Contribution	The difference between the selling price and variable cost of a unit of output. In total, it is also the difference between the total revenue and total variable costs.
Control account	Contains the totals of all postings made to the accounts in a particular ledger.
Cost accounting	A method of accounting where all the costs associated with a particular activity or product are collected together, classified and recorded.
Cost centre	Any location, usually a department, in a business to which costs may be attributed.
Cost driver	The activity which directly results in a specific cost being incurred.
Cost of sales	The net cost of the goods sold to customers.
Cost pool	The total of all the costs associated with a particular activity.
Cost unit	The unit of output of a business to which costs can be charged.
Credit balance	The amount by which the credit side of an account is greater than the debit side.
Credit note	A receipt given to a customer who has returned goods, which can be offset against future purchases.
Credit side	Right-hand side of an account.

TERM	MEANING
Credit transaction	A business transaction where no money changes hands at the time of the transaction.
Creditor	Suppliers (or other parties) to whom the business owes money.
Current account (partnership)	An account which records a partner's share of profits and any drawings made by them.
Current asset	Cash and other assets, typically inventory and trade receivables, that are expected to give rise to cash in the course of trading within 12 months.
Current liability	Those items which the business is due to pay less than 12 months after the date of the statement of financial position.
Debenture	A loan of a fixed amount given to a company. The loan is repayable at a fixed date in the future and carries interest at a fixed rate.
Debit balance	The amount by which the debit side of an account is greater than the credit side.
Debit side	Left-hand side of an account.
Debtor	A customer (or other party) that owes the business money.
Depreciation	The part of the cost of a non-current asset that is consumed during the period it is used by a business. For example, a motor purchased for $10 000 may be worth only $8000 one year later because it has been used by the business for a year.
Directors' report	A report prepared by the directors of a plc at the end of the financial year. The Companies Act specifies which items must be included in such a report.
Discount allowed	Cash discount allowed by the seller to the purchaser of goods.
Discount received	Cash discount received by the purchaser from the seller of goods.
Dissolution of a partnership	The process by which all the assets of the partnership are sold, and liabilities paid, when the partnership ceases trading.
Donations	Money given freely to an organisation. Sometimes donors may stipulate the use of the money (e.g. to purchase new catering equipment or to purchase trophies as prizes).
Double-entry bookkeeping	A system of recording accounting transactions that recognises that there are two sides (or aspects) to every transaction.
Doubtful debt	A debt due from a customer where it is uncertain whether or not it will be repaid by them.
Drawings	The money (or goods) taken from the business by the owner.
Duality	This recognises that there are two aspects for each transaction – represented by debit and credit entries in accounts.
Factory cost of production	The total of the prime cost, factory overheads and the net movement of work in progress.
Factory overheads / indirect costs	Costs incurred from the running of the factory. This would include such things as indirect factory wages and depreciation of factory machinery.
Factory profit	The amount added to the factory cost of production to arrive at the transfer price.
Final dividend	The dividend the directors recommend should be paid to shareholders after the end of the year. The directors can only propose the dividend. It must be approved by the shareholders at the annual general meeting.
Financing activities	Receipts from the issue of new shares or long-term loans. Payments made to redeem shares or to repay long-term loans.
Fixed budget	A budget which is not changed when sales, or some other activity, increases or decreases.
Fixed cost	A cost that remains unchanged within a certain level of activity or output.

TERM	MEANING
Flexed budget	A budget which is changed to reflect changes in activity levels.
Going concern	When there is no intention to discontinue a business in the foreseeable future. Unless stated to the contrary, it is assumed that the accounts of a business are prepared on a going concern basis.
Golden rule	For every debit entry in a ledger account there must be an equal credit entry in another ledger account.
Goods on sale or return	This is not a principle or concept but a very important point in relation to ownership of goods relating to a transaction. When a trader sends goods on sale or return to a customer, no sale takes place until the customer informs the seller that he has decided to buy them.
Goodwill	The amount by which the value of the partnership as a going concern exceeds the net value of its assets if they were sold separately.
Gross profit	The profit calculated by deducting the cost of sales from the revenue in the income statement.
Historic cost	Transactions are recorded at their cost to the business.
Impersonal account	Any account other than a personal account.
Income and expenditure account	The account prepared to determine if the non-profit-making organisation has made a surplus or deficit. The equivalent of the income statement.
Income statement	An account prepared periodically to find the profit or loss made by a business.
Incomplete records	Any method of recording transactions that is not based on the double-entry model.
Inherent goodwill	Goodwill which has not been paid for. It has been built up within the business by the owners. The amount is subjective.
Interest on capital	A share of the profit for the year (usually) based on a percentage of the amount of fixed capital each partner has contributed to the partnership.
Interest on drawings	A charge made on the annual drawings made by each partner, usually calculated as a percentage of the drawings made.
Interim dividend	A dividend paid to existing shareholders during the year provided the directors are satisfied that sufficient profits have been earned and the cash is available to pay the dividend.
Internal rate of return	The interest, or discount, rate at which the net present value of all the cash flows from a project (both positive and negative) equals zero.
International Accounting Standards (IASs)	Standards created by the International Accounting Standards Board stating how particular types of transactions or other events should be reflected in the financial statements of a business entity. Most commonly adopted by companies listed on a stock exchange.
Inventory	The unsold goods of a trading business at a point in time.
Investing activities	The acquisition and disposal of non-current and other long-term assets.
Investment appraisal	The process of assessing whether it is worthwhile to invest funds into a particular project.
Invoice	A document that a business issues to its customers, asking the customers to pay for the goods or services that the business has supplied to them.
Irrecoverable debt	A debt due from a customer which it is expected will never be paid by them.
Job costing	A costing method that calculates the cost of meeting a specific customer order or job.

TERM	MEANING
Joint venture	A business arrangement between two or more parties who agree to combine their skills and resources for the purpose of completing a specific task.
Journal (or general journal)	A book of prime entry for recording transactions and events for which there is no other book of prime entry.
Ledger	Book containing accounts.
Ledger account	A history of all transactions of a similar nature.
Life membership	The amount paid by a member of a club which entitles them to be members of the club for their lifetime.
Limited company	A separate legal entity whose existence is separate from its owners; the liabilities of the members are limited to the amounts paid (or to be paid) on shares issued to them.
Management accounting	The process of preparing reports and accounts which can be used by managers as a basis for making decisions on the future performance of the business.
Margin	The gross profit expressed as a percentage or fraction of selling price.
Marginal cost	The cost of making an extra unit of output.
Marginal costing	A method of costing which calculates the change in either unit or total costs as a direct result from increasing or decreasing output.
Mark-up	The gross profit expressed as a percentage or fraction of cost of sales.
Master budget	The budgeted income statement and statement of financial position.
Merger	Where two or more independent businesses combine their assets and form a completely new business.
Narrative	Something recorded under a journal entry to explain why the journal entry is to be made.
Net book value / written-down value	The cost of a non-current asset minus the accumulated depreciation.
Net present value	The present value of future receipts from a project, less the present value of future payments in respect of the same project.
Nominal (or par) value	The face value of a share.
Nominal account	An account used to record the revenue and expenses of a business. It also relates to an account or accounts which record the revenue of the business from sales.
Non-current asset	Items bought by a business which are not for resale. Examples are land and buildings, plant and machinery or motor vehicles.
Non-current liability	An amount owed by a business which is repayable more than 12 months after the date of the statement of financial position.
Operating activities	The main revenue generating activities of the company.
Ordinary share	A share which represents equity ownership in a limited company. It entitles the holder to vote in matters put before them by the directors. It also entitles the holder to a dividend at a varying amount, depending on the profits made by the company and after all other liabilities have been satisfied.
Overhead absorption rate (OAR)	The rate at which costs apportioned to a cost centre are charged to the cost unit passing through it.
Overtime payment	An amount paid to an employee for working longer than the time they are contracted to work.
Overtime premium	The additional amount given to employees for overtime working. For example, if an employee is paid overtime at a rate of 50% above their normal hourly rate (or time and a half) the extra 50% is the overtime premium.

TERM	MEANING
Partners' salary	A share of the partnership profit for the year paid to one (or more) of the partners in addition to their normal share of the profit for the year. Usually done to reward them for extra skill or work undertaken.
Partnership	Two or more people carrying on a business together with a view to making a profit.
Partnership Act 1890	The rules which govern a partnership in the absence of a formal partnership agreement.
Partnership agreement	An agreement, usually in writing, setting out the terms of the partnership.
Payback	The period of time it takes for the net receipts from a project to pay back, or equal, the total of the funds invested in the project.
Personal account	An account relating to a person.
Posting	The process of recording financial transactions in ledger accounts.
Preference share	A share which does not give the owner any ownership rights in the company. The holder will receive (usually) dividends at a fixed rate, payable before (in preference to) the ordinary shareholder.
Prepayment	Payments made by a business in advance of the benefits to be derived from them. An example would be rent of premises paid in advance. When preparing the statement of financial position these are collectively known as other receivables.
Present value	The present, or current, value of a future sum of money discounted at a given rate.
Prime cost / direct cost	The total of direct materials, direct labour and direct expenses.
Private limited company	A company whose shares are not freely traded on a recognised stock exchange. The shares of such a company are generally owned by a small number of shareholders, say a family, and can only be transferred to existing shareholders.
Production cost centres	Locations which are directly involved in producing goods.
Profit for the year	The profit calculated by adding other income to the gross profit and deducting the business expenses. Sometimes called 'the bottom line'.
Profit/volume chart	A type of break-even chart which only shows the profit or loss at each level of output.
Profitability ratios	A group of ratios which will help to assess the profitability over a period of time.
Prudence	This principle is sometimes known as the concept of conservation. The correct procedure is that profits should not be overstated and losses should be provided for as soon as they are recognised.
Public limited company (plc)	A company whose shares are freely traded on a recognised stock exchange.
Purchase ledger	The ledger which contains the individual accounts of all the business's credit suppliers.
Purchased goodwill	Goodwill which has been paid for by the purchasing business.
Real account	An account which contains the transactions relating to non-current assets.
Realisation	Revenue is recognised or accounted for by the seller when it is earned whether cash has been received from the transaction or not.
Realisation account	An account prepared when a partnership is ceasing to trade, to record the book value of the assets and liabilities and how much is received for them if sold, or paid out in respect of liabilities. The result will be a profit or loss on realisation.
Receipts and payments account	The bank account of the non-profit-making organisation.

TERM	MEANING
Reducing-balance depreciation	Depreciation calculated as a fixed percentage of the written-down (or net book) value of the asset each year.
Revaluation method of depreciation	Used to calculate the cost of consumption in the accounting period of small non-current assets such as power tools. It is calculated by opening valuation + purchases made during the period – closing valuation = depreciation charge for the period.
Revaluation of assets	Adjustments made to the value of the partnership assets to reflect their market value. It may result in some assets increasing in value, such as land, whilst others decrease, such as machinery.
Revenue expenditure (expense)	The day-to-day expenditure incurred in the day-to-day running of a business.
Revenue / turnover	The sales of goods or services made by a business.
Revenue reserves	The profits made by a company which have not been distributed to shareholders.
Rights issue of shares	An issue of shares made for cash. The shares are offered first to existing shareholders, usually in proportion to the shares held by them.
Sales ledger	The ledger which contains the individual accounts of all the business's credit customers.
Semi-variable cost	A cost which contains both an element of a variable and fixed cost within it.
Service cost centres	Locations which are not involved in the production of goods, but provide services for the production cost centres (e.g. stores, building and plant maintenance, canteen etc.).
Share	The smallest division of the total share capital of the company which can be sold in order to raise funds for the company.
Share capital	The capital raised by a business by the issue of shares (usually) for cash, but may also be for consideration for other than cash, such as non-current or current assets.
Share premium	The excess over the nominal or par value of a share when it is issued.
Single-entry bookkeeping	Only one aspect of each transaction is recorded.
Sole trader	The owner of a business who runs the business on their own.
Standard cost	The estimated, or budgeted, cost of a unit of output or activity. It can be compared with the actual cost of the unit of output or activity in order to take corrective action.
Statement of affairs	A list of the business assets and liabilities at a point in time, usually prepared to calculate the capital of the business at that point in time.
Statement of changes in equity	A statement prepared to show the changes in a company's share capital, reserves and retained earnings over a reporting period.
Statement of financial position	A list of the assets, liabilities, capital and reserves of a business at a particular point in time.
Straight-line depreciation	When the total depreciation is spread evenly over the useful life of the non-current asset.
Subscriptions	The amount paid by members to be part of the club or society. It is the main source of income for non-profit-making concerns and is the equivalent of sales for a profit-making organisation.
Substance over form	When deciding how or whether a transaction is recorded, this principle or concept states that the economic substance of the transaction must be recorded in the financial statements rather than its legal form. This is done to present a true and fair view of the affairs of the business.

TERM	MEANING
Surplus of income over expenditure	The equivalent of the profit for the year. The opposite would be a deficit of income over expenditure.
Suspense account	An account opened to record a difference between the debit and credit totals of the trial balance.
Time value of money	The principle that a sum of money is worth more now than at some time in the future.
Timing difference	The delay between items recorded in the cash book and their appearance on the bank statement.
Trade discount	A reduction in the selling price of goods made by one trader to another.
Transfer price	The cost at which goods are transferred from the factory to finished goods.
Trial balance	A list of the balances on each account extracted from the ledgers at a particular date. Its purpose is to check that the total of the debit balances equals the total of the credit balances.
Unit costing	The costing procedure to find the cost of a single unit of output (cost unit).
Unpresented cheques	Cheque payments recorded in the cash book but not yet appearing on the bank statement.
Utilisation of resources	A group of ratios which will help to assess the efficiency with which the resources of a business have been used over a period of time.
Variable cost	A cost which varies in direct proportion to changes in the level of output.
Variance	A difference between the standard cost and actual cost.
Work in progress	Inventory of partly finished goods in the factory at any point in time.

Index

Acknowledgements

The authors and publishers acknowledge the following sources of photographs:

Cover OJO Images/OJO Images/Superstock; Chapter opener images inside in order of appearance Glow Images, Inc/Getty Images, John Kuczala/Getty Images, Tim Macpherson/Getty Images, Getty Images, Getty Images, Joseph Clark/Getty Images, morrbyte/Getty Images, Carolyn Hebbard/Getty Images, Nicholas Rigg/Getty Images, studiocasper/Getty Images, dtv2/Getty Images, Getty Images, KatarinaGondova/Getty Images, monstArrr_/Getty Images, kirilova/Getty Images, John Smith/Fuse/Getty Images, Medioimages/Photodisc/Getty Images, Kristin Lee/Getty Images, Jeffrey Coolidge/Getty Images, seraficus/Getty Images, National Geographic Creative/Alamy Stock Photo, Ian Maxwell/EyeEm/Getty Images, Ian McKinnell/Getty Images, Dimitri Otis/Getty Images, Sudarshan v/Getty Images, loveguli/Getty Images, Lee Woodgate/Getty Images, MarianVejcik/Getty Images, RomoloTavani/Getty Images, Nicolas Vega/EyeEm/Getty Images, Peter Cade/Getty Images, Comstock/Getty Images, Wendy Wee/EyeEm/Getty Images, Jeffrey Coolidge/Getty Images